Relational Database Writings 1994–1997

C. J. Date

with special contributions by
Hugh Darwen and David McGoveran

⩕ Addison-Wesley

Harlow, England • Reading, Massachusetts • Menlo Park, California • New York
Don Mills, Ontario • Amsterdam • Bonn • Sydney • Singapore • Tokyo • Madrid
San Juan • Milan • Mexico City • Seoul • Taipei

© Addison Wesley Longman Limited 1998
Addison Wesley Longman Limited
Edinburgh Gate
Harlow
Essex CM20 2JE
England
and Associated Companies throughout the World.

The programs in this book have been included for their instructional value. They
have been tested with care but are not guaranteed for any particular purpose. The
publisher does not offer any warranties or representations nor does it accept any
liabilities with respect to the programs.

Many of the designations used by manufacturers and sellers to distinguish their
products are claimed as trademarks. Where those designations appear in this
book, and Addison Wesley Longman Limited was aware of a trademark claim,
the designations have been printed in caps or initial caps.

Produced by Addison Wesley Longman Singapore (Pte) Ltd.,
Printed in Singapore
First printed 1998
ISBN 0-201-398141

British Library Cataloguing-in-Publication Data

Date, C. J.
    Relational database writings, 1994–1997 / by C. J. Date: with
special contributions by Hugh Darwen and David McGoveran.
        p.   cm.
    Includes index.
    ISBN 0-201-39814-1 (alk. paper)
    1. Relational databases.   I. Darwen, Hugh.   II. McGoveran, D.
III. Title.
QA76.9.D3D3727   1998
005.75'6—dc21   98-17056
                                                           CIP

A catalogue record for this book is available from the British Library

This book is dedicated
to the redwood forests of California
and those doing their best to save
what little is left of them

About the Authors

C. J. Date is an independent author, lecturer, researcher, and consultant, specializing in relational database systems. He was one of the first people anywhere to recognize the fundamental importance of Codd's pioneering work on the relational model. He was also involved in technical planning for the IBM database products SQL/DS and DB2 at the IBM Santa Teresa Laboratory in San Jose, California. He is best known for his books, in particular the *Relational Database Writings* series (of which the present book is the fifth); *An Introduction to Database Systems* (sixth edition, Addison-Wesley, 1995), which is the standard text in the field and has sold well over half a million copies worldwide; and *Foundation for Object/ Relational Databases: The Third Manifesto*, a recent collaboration with Hugh Darwen (Addison-Wesley, 1998). Mr. Date enjoys a reputation that is second to none for his ability to explain complex technical material in a clear and understandable fashion.

Hugh Darwen has been involved in software development since 1967 as an employee of IBM United Kingdom Ltd. He has been active in the relational database arena since 1978, and he was one of the chief architects and developers of an IBM relational product called Business System 12, a product that faithfully embraced the principles of the relational model. His writings to date include his notable contributions to C. J. Date's *Relational Database Writings* series (Addison-Wesley 1990, 1992, and now the present book) and *A Guide to the SQL Standard* (4th edition, Addison-Wesley 1997). He has been an active participant in the development of SQL international standards since 1988. In his spare time he is a tutor and consultant in connection with the Open University's database courses in the UK.

David McGoveran has been president of Alternative Technologies (Boulder Creek, California), a relational database consulting firm, since its foundation in 1976. He has written numerous technical articles and is the publisher of the *Database Product Evaluation Report Series*. He is also the author (with C. J. Date) of the book *A Guide to SYBASE and SQL Server* (Addison-Wesley, 1992). He consults for RDBMS end users and vendors, covering needs such as database design, development methodology, design audits, application architecture, performance tuning, DBMS evaluation and selection and deployment, and migration and integration (e.g., with object-oriented programming—he was the main architect of one of the first uses of object-oriented programming with an RDBMS). He has consulted for virtually every major DBMS vendor. He is best known for his ability to blend practical solutions with a technical understanding, resulting in robust and flexible systems.

Contents

PART II   RELATIONAL DATABASE MANAGEMENT

CHAPTER 3
The Third Manifesto:
Foundation for Object/Relational Databases   **305**

CHAPTER 4
Some Remarks on Types, Units, and Type Design   **321**

PART III   THE PROBLEM OF MISSING INFORMATION

CHAPTER 8
Nothing from Nothing (Part 4 of 4): It's in the Way That You Use It

CHAPTER 9
Nothing to Do with the Case

Preface

This book is the fifth in a series. Its predecessors were published by Addison-Wesley in 1986, 1990, 1992, and 1995, respectively. Like those predecessors, the current book consists of a collection of papers, mostly by myself, on the general topic of relational database technology—basically all those of my papers from the period 1994 to the present that seem to me to be worth preserving in some more permanent form. There are also two papers by David McGoveran (one of them in four parts) and one paper by Hugh Darwen, plus three collaborative efforts—one involving Hugh and myself and two more involving all three of us.

The book is arranged into the same four parts as its predecessor:

I. Theory Is Practical!
II. Relational Database Management
III. The Problem of Missing Information
IV. Relational *vs.* Nonrelational Systems

Each part has its own introduction, and I will leave further details of the papers to those introductions. There is also an appendix, containing the script for a live presentation entitled "Database Graffiti," which I've given at a number of professional conferences recently.

A brief note on the book's structure: As with the earlier books in this series, each of the chapters was originally intended to stand alone; as a result, each typically contains figures, references, examples, etc., whose numbering is unique only within the chapter in question. To a very large degree, I have preserved the independence of individual chapters; therefore, all references within a given chapter to, say, Fig. 2 or Example 3 are to be taken as references to the indicated figure or example within the chapter in question. *Note:* There is, I fear, a certain amount of overlap among some of the chapters; I apologize for this fact, but felt it was better (as already indicated) to preserve the independence of each individual chapter as much as possible.

ACKNOWLEDGMENTS

Most of all, I would like to thank Hugh Darwen and David McGoveran for their major contributions to this book. I would also like to acknowledge the helpful suggestions and comments received on earlier drafts of some of the chapters from various friends and colleagues: Don Chamberlin, Hugh Darwen (again), Herb Edelstein, Adrian Larner, Nelson Mattos, David McGoveran (again), Mike Newton, Jim Panttaja, Fabian Pascal, Ron Ross, and Colin White. A special vote of thanks goes to David Stodder, Mo Marshall, and Diane Cheshire of *Database Programming & Design* magazine for their assistance and encouragement in connection with the material appearing in Part I. I would also like to thank my wife Lindy for her support throughout the production of this book and all of its predecessors.

As for my editor, Elydia Davis, and the staff at Addison-Wesley, the best I can do is repeat what I have said in the preface to earlier books in this series: Their assistance has been as friendly, obliging, and professional as it always is, and as I have come to expect. It is a pleasure to work with them.

Healdsburg, California   C. J. Date
1998

Publishing History

According to Date Installments 26–62
Originally published in *Database Programming & Design 7*, Nos. 10–12; *8*, Nos. 1–12; *9*, Nos. 1–12; and *10*, Nos. 1–10 (October 1994 through October 1997).

What A Database Really *Is: Predicates and Propositions*
Originally published in *Database Programming & Design 11*, No. 7 (July 1998).

The Relational Model Turns 25
Originally published in *DBMS Magazine 7*, No. 11 (October 1994).

The Third Manifesto: Foundation for Object/Relational Databases
Originally published (in somewhat different form) in C. J. Date and Hugh Darwen: *Foundation for Object/Relational Databases: The Third Manifesto* (Addison-Wesley, 1998). A version of this paper can also be found on the World Wide Web at *http://www.alternativetech.com*. An earlier version entitled *Introducing . . . The Third Manifesto* appeared in *Database Programming and Design 8*, No. 1 (January 1995).

Nothing from Nothing
Originally published in *Database Programming and Design 6*, No. 12 (December 1993) and *7*, Nos. 1–3 (January–March 1994).

Nothing to Do with the Case
Originally published in *Database Programming and Design 8*, No. 9 (September 1995).

Up to a Point, Lord Copper
   Originally published on the *Database Programming & Design* website
   http://www.dbpd.com (November 1996).

Why "The Object Model" Is Not a Data Model
   Originally published in *InfoDB 10,* No. 4 (August 1996).

Objects and Relations: Forty-Seven Points of Light
   Originally published in *Data Base Newsletter 23,* No. 5 (September/October 1995).

Don't Mix Pointers and Relations!
   Originally published in *InfoDB 10,* No. 6 (April 1997).

PART I

THEORY IS PRACTICAL!

INTRODUCTION

Note: The text that follows is a lightly edited version of the introduction to Part I that appeared in this book's predecessor.

This part of the book contains the text—slightly revised here and there—of Installments 26–62 of a regular series of columns by myself that have been appearing in the magazine *Database Programming & Design* every month since September 1992. *Note:* Installments 1–25 were included in this book's predecessor. A list of those first 25 installments is given at the end of this introduction (see Fig. 1).

Basically, what I have been, and still am, trying to do in that series of columns is to home in on a variety of theoretical aspects of relational database technology, with the aim of explaining in lay terms just why those aspects are important and why they should be of interest to the database practitioner. Given that objective, the reader will appreciate that the individual columns mostly do not cover much in the way of really new ground compared with various other publications of mine. Rather, the intent was to take issues that I had already considered more formally elsewhere and present them in a way that

1

was deliberately less academic—more chatty, perhaps—than my usual style. In particular, I wanted the series to be a little easier to read than some of my other publications in this field, though whether I succeeded in that aim I must leave for the reader to judge.

I should add that I found the exercise of having to condense my thoughts on any particular subject into a column of some 2,000 or so words a very

1. Theory Is Practical!
2. The Importance of Closure
3. What's in a Name?
4. Why Three-Valued Logic Is a Mistake
5. Nothing in Excess
6. Answers to Puzzle Corner Problems (Installments 1–5)
7. Tables with No Columns
8. Empty Bags and Identity Crises
9. The Power of the Keys
10. Expression Transformation (Part 1 of 2)
11. Expression Transformation (Part 2 of 2)
12. Answers to Puzzle Corner Problems (Installments 7–11)
13. How We Missed the Relational Boat
14. A Matter of Integrity (Part 1 of 3)
15. A Matter of Integrity (Part 2 of 3)
16. A Matter of Integrity (Part 3 of 3)
17. Toil and Trouble
18. Answers to Puzzle Corner Problems (Installments 13–17)
19. More on DEE and DUM
20. Divide—and Conquer?
21. Relational Comparisons
22. Domains, Relations, and Data Types (Part 1 of 2)
23. Domains, Relations, and Data Types (Part 2 of 2)
24. Answers to Puzzle Corner Problems (Installments 19–23)
25. Many Happy Returns!

Fig. 1   The first 25 installments

valuable discipline, albeit one that was a little frustrating on occasion. For example, sometimes I could not develop themes as fully as I felt they really deserved (though when that happened, I usually cheated and split the material into a miniseries of two or more separate installments). And in a few places—I hope not too many—I might be accused of some slight oversimplification, again in the interests of space. But overall I think the discipline was good for me: It forced me to rein myself back, instead of indulging my usual tendency to try to spell out every last detail of every ramification of every topic. I hope the reader finds the resulting informal discussions useful and worthwhile.

Let me close this introduction by acknowledging the support I have received with this series of columns from the editorial staff at *Database Programming & Design*—especially Editor-in-Chief David Stodder, whose idea the series originally was, and my series editors Mo Marshall and Diane Cheshire. I would also like to thank those readers who took the trouble to write in with comments and questions.

For purposes of reference, the titles of the first 25 installments (republished in this book's predecessor) are listed in Fig. 1.

All footnotes in this part of the book are new.

Oh Oh Relational . . .

*Notes toward an object/relational
rapprochement*

I find myself in something of a quandary this month. What I want to do is discuss the possibility of a *rapprochement* between object-oriented (OO) and relational technology; indeed, I promised in an earlier installment [3] that such a discussion would soon be forthcoming. As I said in that installment:

> A *domain* in the relational database world is (in general) a data type, possibly user-defined, of arbitrary complexity; an *object class* in the OO world is (in general) a data type, possibly user-defined, of arbitrary complexity . . . In other words, domains and object classes are **the same thing!** And so we have here the key to marrying the two technologies together. This is very obviously [a] topic that I need to discuss in detail some other time.

The problem is that the topic in question, though clearly of major practical significance, is really too big and too complex to do it justice in a limited forum like this column—and in any case, I've already discussed it in some detail elsewhere [4]. On the other hand, I would certainly like to air the issues again here (even though to do so is to repeat myself somewhat), simply in order to expose those issues to as wide a readership as possible.

I've therefore decided to compromise . . . Specifically, I'll content myself with making a series of statements—position statements, if you like—without

Originally published in *Database Programming & Design 7,* No. 10, October 1994.
Reprinted by permission of Miller Freeman Inc.

attempting, for the most part, to provide much in the way of justification for those positions. (In particular, I'll assume that you do at least have some basic understanding of OO concepts, and won't make any attempt to provide a tutorial on those concepts here.) In this way, you will at least be able to see what my position—and that of many other workers in this field, I hasten to add—on this important topic actually is. If you want to study the supporting arguments in detail, I'll point you to reference [4].

OVERVIEW

My overall position can be summed up very simply:

1. A marriage between relational technology and OO technology—at least, the good parts of OO technology—is both feasible and desirable.
2. There are two apparent ways to achieve this goal, a right way and a wrong way.
3. The right way builds on the equation "domain = object class." The wrong way builds on the equation "relation = object class."*
4. Most papers, prototypes, and products are going the wrong way!

No. 4 here is, of course, the reason I'm anxious to air the issues before as wide an audience as possible.

WHAT IS GOOD ABOUT OO?

Now let me begin my series of position statements.

- Today's relational products are inadequate in a variety of ways. "If you stray far from . . . suppliers-and-parts or employees-and-departments, relational systems tend to run into trouble very quickly" (slight paraphrase of a remark from reference [5]).
- Some people—not this writer!—would argue that the relational model is inadequate too.
- Some of the new features that seem to be needed in DBMSs have existed for many years in OO programming languages. The idea of incorporating those features into database systems is thus a natural one to investigate.

---

*"Relation" here should really be "relation *variable*"—see Installment 35, later in this book. A similar remark applies at many points throughout the installments prior to that one and elsewhere; for brevity, I won't bother to make it at every such point but will let this footnote do for all of them.

- Note, however, that it does *not* follow that "OO database systems" can or will replace relational ones. On the contrary, we should be looking for a *rapprochement* between the two technologies—that is, a way of marrying the two technologies together, so as to get the best of both worlds.

- Many OO concepts—or the published definitions of those concepts, at any rate—are unfortunately quite imprecise, and there's very little true consensus and much disagreement, even at the most basic level. In particular, there is *no* abstract, universally accepted, formally defined "OO data model," nor is there even consensus on an *in*formal model (which is why I usually place phrases such as "the OO model" in quotes).

- Any assessment of "the OO model" is therefore necessarily somewhat subjective. However, it's my belief that a careful study of "the OO model" will show that it contains **precisely two good ideas**—*user-defined data types* (which includes user-defined operators), and *type inheritance* (at least single inheritance). *Note:* Data types are usually called *object classes* in the OO world, and operators are usually called *methods*.

- Some might argue that (a) *polymorphism* and *substitutability* and (b) *multiple inheritance* are also good OO ideas. Here let me just say that (a) polymorphism and substitutability *are* good ideas, but they're an intrinsic part of inheritance and so are included *a fortiori;* (b) multiple inheritance is likely to prove important too, but there are significant conceptual and definitional issues to be resolved before such a feature can be included in a well-defined abstract "OO model" with any degree of confidence (more study is required).*

- By contrast, the following, which are usually regarded as features of "the OO model," are *not* good ideas (in the sense that they should *not* be exposed to the user; whether they should exist as part of the implementation is another matter entirely).

object IDs (OIDs)

instance variables

containment hierarchies

Note: The term "containment hierarchy" refers to the structure that results if objects are allowed to contain other objects (and so on, recursively).

---

*This was written in 1994; I now feel much more optimistic regarding this issue. See the book *Foundation for Object/Relational Databases: The Third Manifesto* [4] for a detailed inheritance proposal that includes multiple inheritance support.

- Certain other features, often regarded as part of "the OO model" but actually quite independent of whether the system is OO or not, are "nice to have" but not essential. Examples of such features include:

  database/programming language integration

  versions and configurations

  long and nested transactions

  (transparent) schema evolution

- There are also certain features, such as views and integrity constraints (further specifics beyond the scope of this discussion), that "the OO model" typically does *not* include and yet are essential for any true general-purpose DBMS [4].

ENCAPSULATION

Objects are supposed to be *encapsulated**—that is, they are meant to be accessible *only* via appropriate access operators (there should be no "public instance variables" at all). The advantage of encapsulation is basically that it provides *data independence.*

- It's important to understand, however, that (at least in principle) OO systems cannot provide any more data independence than relational systems can. For example, there's absolutely no reason (at least in principle) why a base relation called POINTS, with Cartesian coordinate columns X and Y, should not map to a stored relation that represents points by their polar coordinates R and Θ instead. (It's unfortunately the case, however, that—as we saw in an earlier installment [2]—today's relational products do not provide nearly as much data independence as we would really like, or as much as relational systems are theoretically capable of.)

- It's also important to understand that *it's possible to take the encapsulation idea too far.* There will always be a need to access the data in ways that weren't foreseen when the database was originally created, and the notion of having to write new procedural code every time a new data access requirement arises is simply not acceptable. Indeed, such was exactly the state of affairs with prerelational systems, and it was a major contributor to their downfall.

---

*The remarks in this installment regarding encapsulation are just a little off base, though not seriously so. See the two footnotes in Installment 37, later in this book, for more specifics on this point.

■ Therefore, the system should also support "objects" (I don't mean objects in the OO sense) that are *not* encapsulated but expose their "instance variables" for all the world to see. And those nonencapsulated "objects" are, precisely, *rows* in *relations.* As just explained, nonencapsulated relations can provide just as much data independence as encapsulated objects can; and, of course, relations can be accessed by the well-known, builtin, generic operators of the relational algebra (instead of just by methods that are specific to the particular relation in question), thus satisfying—at least in part—the "unforeseen requirements" objective mentioned in the previous paragraph.

DOMAINS *vs.* OBJECTS

■ As indicated in the introductory remarks to this installment, a domain and an object class are indeed the same thing. Thus, a relational system that implemented domains properly would be able to do all the things that— it's often claimed—OO systems can and relational systems can't.

■ In other words, domains (and therefore relational columns) can contain absolutely anything—arrays, lists, stacks, documents, photographs, maps, blueprints, etc., etc. Another (loose) way of saying this is: **Domains encapsulate, relations don't.**

■ So the system should support *relations,* with the "extension" (actually not an extension at all) that *domains* are properly supported and can be user-defined data types of arbitrary complexity. And you can call the elements of such domains *objects* if you like (though I'd rather not); note, however, that at the relational level *there's no need for OIDs*—the relational model requires relations to contain *actual objects* (at least conceptually), not pointers to objects.

RELATIONS *vs.* OBJECTS

■ Above, I equated object classes and domains. Many products and prototypes, however, are equating object classes and *relations* instead. I'll use the abbreviation "OCR" to refer to this latter equation or to a system based on it. Reference [4] gives a detailed OCR example and presents arguments in support of the contention that the OCR equation is **a serious mistake.** Here I'll just repeat some—not all—of the points raised in reference [4], with little further commentary.

- OCR "objects" are *rows* and OCR "instance variables" are *columns* (which are "public" by definition). OCR relations don't necessarily have any methods. In other words, whereas a pure OO class has methods and no public instance variables, an OCR "class" has public instance variables and quite possibly no methods. The OCR equation thus looks a little suspect right away.

- Columns in OCR relations are allowed—at least conceptually—to contain rows from other OCR relations as well as simple scalars, thereby providing support for the containment hierarchy concept. In fact, however, such columns really contain *pointers* (OIDs), and users must understand this point clearly. In particular, numerous questions arise in connection with update operations. For example, if EMPs "contain" the corresponding DEPT object, what happens if I update one particular EMP, changing (say) the name of the "contained" DEPT object? (*Answer:* There are side effects, which must be explained to the user.) Can I insert a new EMP and specify a value for the contained DEPT that doesn't currently exist in the DEPT relation? ("Yes" and "No" both lead to subsidiary questions.) Does deleting an EMP delete the corresponding DEPT? ("Yes" and "No" both lead to subsidiary questions.) What about an "ON DELETE RESTRICT" or "ON DELETE CASCADE" rule for DEPT? Etc., etc., etc.

- It follows from all of the above that we aren't really talking about the relational model any more. The fundamental data object isn't a relation containing values, it's a "relation" (?) containing values *and pointers*. As a consequence, operators such as projection and join require careful and subtle reinterpretation (a highly nontrivial matter!).

  Example: Suppose I project the EMP "object class," with its contained DEPT objects, over ENAME (employee name) and DNAME (department name). What does the result look like—is it of the form (ENAME, DNAME) or the form (ENAME,(DNAME))? If it's the latter (which is more logically correct), what's the name of the column that contains the nested DNAME values? Either way, what kind of "object class" is the result? What methods apply to it? (*Answer:* Probably none.) Can I join that result to some other "object class" over DNAME? Etc., etc., etc.

- In fact, it seems that when people equate relations and object classes, it's specifically *base* relations they're referring to; as soon as a derived relation is created (through a projection or a join, for instance), the OCR equation breaks down. In other words, the fundamental *closure* property applies to relations *per se* but not to object classes.

There's much, much more that could be said on why the OCR equation is flawed, but the foregoing should be enough to give the general idea.

BENEFITS OF TRUE *RAPPROCHEMENT*

In this section I briefly summarize the benefits of true *rapprochement* (that is, a *rapprochement* that exploits the relational concept of domains properly, not one that builds on the mistaken OCR equation).

First of all, the system is still a relational system, so all of the usual relational benefits apply [1]. In particular, the advantage of *familiarity* applies—the OO capabilities represent a very natural "extension" (actually not an extension at all) to the relational model.

Second, the system is also an OO system, which implies the following additional benefits:

- Open architecture (extendability)
- User-defined data types and operators, with (behavioral) inheritance
- Strong typing
- Improved productivity
- Object-level recovery, concurrency, and security

Furthermore, most of the criticisms usually leveled at OO systems no longer apply. To be specific, the following items, all usually regarded as problems for OO systems, can now be supported without any undue difficulty:

- *Ad hoc* query
- Dual-mode access
- Relationships of degree greater than two
- Methods that span classes
- Symmetric exploitation
- Declarative integrity constraints
- Integrity constraints that span classes
- Foreign key rules (ON DELETE CASCADE, etc.)
- Semantic optimization

In addition:

- OIDs and pointer chasing are now totally under the covers and hidden from the user
- "Difficult" OO questions (for instance, what does it mean to join two objects?) go away
- The benefits of encapsulation still apply (to values within relations, not to relations themselves)

- Relational systems can now handle "complex" application areas such as CAD/CAM, software engineering, document processing, etc.

And the approach is conceptually clean.

CONCLUDING REMARKS

Relational systems need to be enhanced to incorporate the good ideas of OO (but not the bad ones!), and I've argued that domains are the key to achieving this goal. Specifically, I've argued that the equation "domain = object class" is correct, and the equation "relation = object class" is incorrect. Relational vendors should accordingly be doing all in their power to extend their systems to include proper domain support. Indeed, an argument can be made that the whole reason OO systems look attractive is precisely that relational vendors have failed to support the relational model adequately. But this fact should not be seen as an argument for abandoning relational systems entirely (or at all!).

I'll close with this month's puzzle corner. The extended *rapprochement* discussion in reference [4] includes an example involving a database containing rectangles; part of the discussion shows what the user has to do if proper domain support is not provided, and the following problem is taken from that discussion.

We're given a database of rectangles, all "square on" to the X and Y axes—that is, all sides are either vertical or horizontal. Each rectangle can thus be uniquely represented by the coordinates $(x1,y1)$ and $(x2,y2)$, respectively, of its bottom left and top right corners (see Fig. 1). In SQL:

```
CREATE TABLE RECTANGLES
    ( X1 ..., X2 ..., Y1 ..., Y2 ..., ... ) ;
```

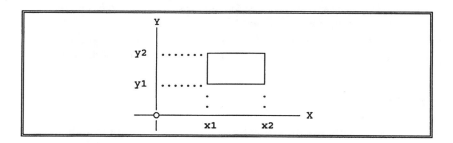

Fig. 1   The rectangle $(x1,x2,y1,y2)$

Now consider the query: "Find all rectangles that overlap the unit square (0,1,0,1)." The "obvious" (!) SQL representation of this query is as follows:

```
SELECT  *
FROM    RECTANGLES
WHERE   ( X1 >= 0 AND X1 <= 1 AND Y1 >= 0 AND Y1 <= 1 )
OR      ( X2 >= 0 AND X2 <= 1 AND Y2 >= 0 AND Y2 <= 1 )
OR      ( X1 >= 0 AND X1 <= 1 AND Y2 >= 0 AND Y2 <= 1 )
OR      ( X2 >= 0 AND X2 <= 1 AND Y1 >= 0 AND Y1 <= 1 )
OR      ( X1 <= 0 AND X2 >= 1 AND Y1 <= 0 AND Y2 >= 1 )
OR      ( X1 <= 0 AND X2 >= 1 AND Y1 >= 0 AND Y1 <= 1 )
OR      ( X1 >= 0 AND X1 <= 1 AND Y1 <= 0 AND Y2 >= 1 )
OR      ( X2 >= 0 AND X2 <= 1 AND Y1 <= 0 AND Y2 >= 1 )
OR      ( X1 <= 0 AND X2 >= 1 AND Y2 >= 0 AND Y2 <= 1 ) ;
```

However, the query can be expressed much more simply as:

```
SELECT  *
FROM    RECTANGLES
WHERE   ( X1 <= 1 AND Y1 <= 1 AND X2 >= 0 AND Y2 >= 0 ) ;
```

The problem is to prove that the two versions of the query are indeed equivalent.

REFERENCES

1. C. J. Date: "Why Relational?", in *Relational Database Writings 1985–1989.* Reading, Mass.: Addison-Wesley (1990).

2. C. J. Date: "The Importance of Closure," *Database Programming & Design 5,* No. 10 (October 1992). Republished in *Relational Database Writings 1991–1994.* Reading, Mass.: Addison-Wesley (1995).

3. C. J. Date: "Domains, Relations, and Data Types (Part 2 of 2)," *Database Programming & Design 7,* No. 7 (July 1994). Republished in *Relational Database Writings 1991–1994.* Reading, Mass.: Addison-Wesley (1995).

4. C. J. Date: "Object-Oriented Systems," Part VI of *An Introduction to Database Systems* (6th edition). Reading, Mass.: Addison-Wesley (1994). See also C. J. Date and Hugh Darwen: *Foundation for Object/Relational Databases: The Third Manifesto.* Reading, Mass.: Addison-Wesley (1998).

5. Michael Stonebraker: *Introduction to* "Extendibility," in M. Stonebraker (ed.): *Readings in Database Systems.* San Mateo, Calif.: Morgan Kaufmann (1988).

AFTERWORD

Although presumably not as a direct result of the foregoing installment *per se,* an article on the same general subject entitled "Domains, Relations and Religious Wars," by R. Camps, subsequently appeared in *ACM SIGMOD Record 25,* No. 3, September 1996. I responded to that letter in a later issue of that same publication (*ACM SIGMOD Record 25,* No. 4, December 1996). Since it's relevant to the topic at hand, I thought it worthwhile to reproduce that response here.

(Begin quote)

Since it quotes extensively from writings of my own, I feel obliged to respond to the article "Domains, Relations and Religious Wars," by R. Camps . . . In that article, Camps is clearly suggesting (among other things) that my definition of the term "domain" has changed over the years. I agree, it has! But Camps goes on to say:

> . . . considering that [Date's book *An Introduction to Database Systems*] was the *bible* where most university graduates all over the world learnt, I believe that Date can be held partly responsible for the lack of implementation of domains [in today's SQL DBMSs].

I reject this accusation, strongly; in fact, I object to it on several levels at once.

- First of all, the lack of domain support in today's SQL DBMSs is surely due, first and foremost, to the lack of domain support in SQL itself—and I can say with some assurance (and some feeling) that my influence on the design of SQL has never been more than minimal.

- Second, the question of which books happen to be selected by universities as "bibles" is quite beyond my control (I might wish it otherwise, but it isn't).

- Third, while it's true that I've made some changes to my definition of "domain" over the years, I would argue that those changes reflect merely improvements in my own understanding, not a rejection of what I once believed. In other words, the changes have, I think, always been "backward compatible"; a DBMS that implemented domains as I first described them would in no way be precluded from supporting domains as I now see them (i.e., as data types, in the full sense of that term).

- Fourth (as Camps does admit in his article, but too late), those definitional changes have all been made very much in the spirit of Bertrand Russell when he wrote:

> *I am not myself in any way ashamed of [having changed my opinions] . . . The kind of philosophy that I value and have endeavoured to pursue is scientific, in the sense that there is some definite knowledge to be obtained and that new discoveries can make the admission of former error inevitable to any candid mind. For what I have said . . . I do not claim the kind of truth which theologians claim for*

their creeds. I claim only, at best, that the opinion expressed was a sensible one to hold at the time . . . I should be much surprised if subsequent research did not show that it needed to be modified.

As I said when I first quoted these remarks (in the 6th edition of my book *An Introduction to Database Systems*): "Readers . . . will find that I too have changed my opinions on many matters (and will no doubt continue to do so).* I hope they will accept the remarks quoted above as adequate justification for this state of affairs. I share Bertrand Russell's perception of what the field of scientific inquiry is all about, but he expresses that perception far more eloquently than I could hope to do."

- Fifth, I object strenuously to the suggestion—reflected not only in the extract from Camps's article quoted above but also in the title, in one of the two epigraphs,† and indeed throughout the article—that the debate over data models is a "religious" matter. (Though in fairness I have to say that Camps is not alone in characterizing the debate in such a way.) Ever since its inception, database management, like the rest of computing, has aspired to be a *scientific* discipline. In this connection, the relational model represents a great leap forward, being founded as it is on logic, not religion. Why then do database professionals (some of them, anyway) so often talk as if logic and science had nothing to do with the matter? Do they perhaps not *wish* their discipline to be seen as scientific? If not, why not? (In this connection, note Bertrand Russell's remarks, already quoted, on "the kind of truth which theologians claim for their creeds.")

In addition to the foregoing, there are some specific points in Camps's article that I feel need some further response:

- "[First] normal form . . . was one of the most surprising, and most difficult to accept, of the RM principles . . . [it was] viewed . . . as a strong restriction and a step backwards . . . [and] was a major battlefield in the confrontation between DBTG-CODASYL and RM supporters."

  Frankly, I don't remember much of a fight over this one. *Au contraire*, in fact: I can remember the then chair of DBTG, Tax Metaxides, saying at a conference that he thought first (and indeed third) normal form was a good idea. No, the big argument was over *manual* vs. *automatic navigation* ("automatic navigation will never perform," etc.).

---

*For an illustration, see the next installment (Installment 27) in the present book!
†The epigraph in question ran as follows: *Data models have much in common with religion* (M. Stonebraker, 1988).

- "[During the] bitter fight between the relational camp and the DBTG-CODASYL camp . . . [the] relational camp was mainly composed by IBM . . . Under the cover of technical and scientific arguments, relevant commercial interests were being disputed."

  It's possible that "the DBTG-CODASYL camp" might have had some commercial interests at heart (and at stake) during this "bitter fight," but it's nonsense to suggest that "the relational camp" (or IBM) did so. There weren't any relational products! (certainly not IBM products)—nor were there even any such products under development at the time. (The "Great Debate" between the two camps was held in 1974. IBM's first mainstream relational product, SQL/DS, was announced over seven years later, in 1981, and DB2 wasn't announced until 1983.)

- "Would it not be more reasonable to look for the cause [of lack of commercial domain support] in the RM's lack of a type system?"

  No, it wouldn't. The relational model very deliberately does not prescribe any specific data types. As Hugh Darwen and I wrote in a recent article, "Introducing . . . *The Third Manifesto*" (*Database Programming & Design 8*, No. 1, January 1995), **the question as to what data types are supported is orthogonal to the question of support for the relational model.** Or, more catchily, *types are orthogonal to tables.* Thus, the relational model does require support for domains, which means (by definition) that users should be able to define their own; it doesn't spell out exactly which ones they must define.

- "How can Date claim that [user-defined types are] not an extension to the RM?"

  But they're not! See the previous bullet item.

- "[Had] the religious war of the late Seventies between DBTG and relational camps been a rational debate, free of fanaticism and commercial interests, today's scenario would be quite different."

  It was not a "religious" war. And, speaking here as a member of "the relational camp," I would say that that camp, at least, did do its best to make the debate as "rational" and as "free of fanaticism and commercial interests" as possible.

In closing, let me just say this: What's really important, of course, is not **who's** right or wrong, it's **what's** right or wrong. I concur with Camps that "it is always profitable to review our old opinions and beliefs," but I think it's more important to agree on how best to move forward. The work of Hugh Darwen and myself on *The Third Manifesto* is, and continues to be, aimed at this goal.

(End quote)

Integrity Revisited

*An improved classification
scheme for integrity rules*

The following quote appealed to me so much when I first encountered it that
I incorporated it into the preface of my book *An Introduction to Database
Systems* [3]:*

> *I have been accused of a habit of changing my opinions . . . I am not
> myself in any degree ashamed of [that habit]. What physicist who
> was already active in 1900 would dream of boasting that [his or
> her] opinions had not changed during the last half century? . . . The
> kind of philosophy that I value and have endeavoured to pursue is
> scientific, in the sense that there is some definite knowledge to be
> obtained and that new discoveries can make the admission of former
> error inevitable to any candid mind. For what I have said, whether
> early or late, I do not claim the kind of truth which theologians
> claim for their creeds. I claim only, at best, that the opinion ex-
> pressed was a sensible one to hold at the time . . . I should be much
> surprised if subsequent research did not show that it needed to be
> modified. [Such opinions were not] intended as pontifical pro-
> nouncements, but only as the best I could do at the time towards the*

Originally published under the title "Integrity Rules Revisited" in *Database Programming
& Design* 7, No. 11, November 1994. Reprinted by permission of Miller Freeman Inc.

*Apologies for the immediate duplication here with respect to the previous installment.

*promotion of clear and accurate thinking. Clarity, above all, has
been my aim.*

The quote is an edited extract from Bertrand Russell's preface to *The Bertrand
Russell Dictionary of Mind, Matter and Morals* (ed., Lester E. Denonn), Citadel Press, 1993, and is reprinted here by permission.

Why I like this quote so much is that—as readers of this column and
other writings of mine will know—I too have a habit of changing my opinions . . . so I'm delighted to find myself in such exalted company. I certainly
share Bertrand Russell's perception of what the field of scientific inquiry is
all about, but he expresses that perception far more eloquently than I could
hope to do.

The reason I mention all this is that one of the things I've recently
changed my mind about is (I'm embarrassed to admit) something I discussed
in this column as little as a year ago—namely, *integrity rules*. In a series of
three installments last year [1], I proposed a classification scheme for such
rules. In my column this month, I want to describe, and justify, a refined and
much improved version of that previous scheme.

LAST YEAR'S SCHEME

Let me begin by quickly reviewing the earlier scheme. First of all, integrity
rules were divided into *domain vs. table* rules, *immediate vs. deferred* rules,
and *state vs. transition* rules (see Fig. 1). *Table* rules were further subdivided
into *single- vs. multi-row* rules (and single-row rules that involved just a single column of the relevant table were called—loosely—*single-column* rules).
In a nutshell:

	immediate state	immediate transition	deferred state	deferred transition
domain	Y	N	N	N
single-row	Y	Y	N	N
multi-row	Y	Y	Y	Y

Fig. 1   Last year's scheme summarized

- A *domain* rule specifies legal values for a given domain.

- A *single-row* rule specifies legal values for individual rows within a given base table. In other words, it's a rule that can be checked for any given row by examining just that row in isolation. For example:

```
CREATE INTEGRITY RULE ER7
    IF EMP.JOB = 'Pgmr'
    THEN EMP.SAL < 50000 ;
```

("programmers must earn less than $50,000").

And a *single-column* rule is a special case of a single-row rule, specifying legal values for an individual column position within individual rows within a given base table. For example:

```
CREATE INTEGRITY RULE ER4
    EMP.SAL > 0 ;
```

- A *multi-row* rule specifies legal values for *combinations* of rows from one or more base tables. For example:

```
CREATE INTEGRITY RULE DE20
    IF DEPT.BUDGET < 1000000
    AND DEPT.DEPT# = EMP.DEPT#
    THEN EMP.SAL ≤ 100000 ;
```

("no department with budget less than $1,000,000 can have an employee with salary greater than $100,000").

- An *immediate* rule is a rule that's checked "immediately" (that is, whenever an update is performed that might violate it); a *deferred* rule is a rule that's checked at some later time (typically commit time).

- A *state* rule is a rule that's concerned with correct states of the database; a *transition* rule is a rule that's concerned with correct transitions from one state to another.

Note: Integrity rules could also include an ON ATTEMPTED VIOLATION clause to specify the *violation response* (telling the system what to do if the rule is violated). The new scheme is identical to the old scheme in this respect, and I won't bother to discuss this aspect any further in the present column.

THIS YEAR'S SCHEME

Note: A sketch of the new scheme was previously given in references [4–6], and a more extensive description (somewhat more accurate at the detail level) can be found in C. J. Date and Hugh Darwen, *Foundation for Object/Relational Databases: The Third Manifesto* (Addison-Wesley, 1998).

One difference between the new scheme and the old one is that the new one is a little more structured, in that it explicitly recognizes that (a) databases are defined over tables, tables are defined over columns, and columns are defined over domains, and (b) integrity rules make sense at each of these levels. We thus begin by classifying integrity rules into four categories, *viz.* database, table, column, and domain rules. Briefly:

1. A *database* rule specifies legal values for a given database.
2. A *table* rule specifies legal values for a given table.
3. A *column* rule specifies legal values for a given column.
4. A *domain* rule specifies legal values for a given domain.

For pedagogic reasons, however, it's convenient to discuss the four cases in the opposite order.

DOMAIN RULES

Domain rules in the new scheme are essentially identical to domain rules in the old one: Effectively, they just enumerate the values in the domain in question. Thus, there's no need for a separate "CREATE DOMAIN INTEGRITY RULE" statement—instead, the integrity rule can be specified as a direct part of the relevant CREATE DOMAIN statement. For example:

```
CREATE DOMAIN QTY NUMERIC (4)
     ( QTY > 0 AND QTY ≤ 5000 ) ;
```

Domain rules are checked whenever anyone tries to specify a value that's supposed to be a value from the domain in question (typically during an attempt to place such a value into some column defined on that domain).

COLUMN RULES

The column integrity rule for a given column is, precisely, the specification of the domain from which that column draws its values. There is thus no need for a separate "CREATE COLUMN INTEGRITY RULE" statement; instead, the integrity rule is specified as a direct part of the applicable column definition. Here's an example:

```
ENAME DOMAIN ( NAME )
```

(part of the CREATE TABLE for the employees base table EMP).

Column rules are always checked immediately;* that is, any attempt (via an INSERT or UPDATE operation) to introduce a column value into the database that isn't a value from the relevant domain will immediately be rejected.

As you can see, we've already begun to touch on one of the biggest differences between the old and new schemes. In the old scheme, anything that wasn't a domain rule was a table rule. In the new scheme, we have a more careful breakdown of "nondomain rules" into column, table, and database rules. Note in particular, therefore, that a column rule in the new scheme is *not* the same as a "single-column" table rule in the old scheme; in fact, a column rule in the new scheme is basically just a column *data type* specification, as discussed in earlier installments in this series [2].

TABLE RULES

In the old scheme, we distinguished between single- and multi-*row* rules. In the new scheme, by contrast, we distinguish between single- and multi-*table* rules; we call the former table rules *per se,* and we call the latter *database* rules. Thus, an old-style single-row rule will necessarily be a new-style table rule, but an old-style multi-row rule can be either a new-style table rule or a new-style database rule, depending (loosely) on whether the "multiple rows" belong to a single table or multiple tables. *Note:* These aren't the only distinctions between the old and new schemes—others are yet to be discussed.

A table rule, then, is a rule that refers to the table in question *only*—not to any other table, nor to any domain. We have already seen one example of such a rule:

```
CREATE INTEGRITY RULE ER7
    IF EMP.JOB = 'Pgmr'
    THEN EMP.SAL < 50000 ;
```

This example would have been called a single-row rule under the old scheme. By contrast, the following example would have been called a multi-row rule under the old scheme but is nevertheless a table rule, not a database rule, under the new scheme:

```
CREATE INTEGRITY RULE ER3
    IF  EX.EMP# = EY.EMP#
    THEN EX.ENAME  = EY.ENAME
    AND  EX.DEPT#  = EY.DEPT#
    AND  EX.SALARY = EY.SALARY ;
```

---

*At least in principle, though in practice no such checking will be needed at all if *domain* rules are properly enforced.

Meaning: "If two rows of EMP, EX and EY say, agree on their EMP# value, they also agree on the value of everything else" (in other words, they are the same row). The rule thus effectively states that EMP# is a candidate key for EMP. *Note:* As in the old scheme, I would of course advocate special-case syntax for important special cases such as candidate (and foreign) key definitions. I omit further discussion of this aspect here for space reasons.

One more table rule example:

```
CREATE INTEGRITY RULE ER9
    COUNT ( EMP WHERE EMP.DEPT# = 'D1' ) > 1 ;
```

("there must exist at least two employees in department D1").

Table rules are always checked immediately; that is, every update operation (INSERT, UPDATE, or DELETE) on a given table conceptually includes as its final step the checking of all table rules that apply to that table. Note that this fact constitutes another departure from the old scheme; under the old scheme, single-row rules were always checked immediately, but multi-row rules could be deferred, even if they referred to just one table. This change is consistent with another recent change of opinion on my part!—one that has to do with the true nature of relational update operations. I plan to discuss this particular matter in a future installment.[*]

DATABASE RULES

A database rule is a rule that refers to—or, more precisely, *interrelates*—two or more distinct tables. Again, we've already seen an example:

```
CREATE INTEGRITY RULE DE20
    IF DEPT.BUDGET < 1000000
    AND DEPT.DEPT# = EMP.DEPT#
    THEN EMP.SAL ≤ 100000 ;
```

Here's another:

```
CREATE INTEGRITY RULE DE1
    FORALL EMP ( EXISTS DEPT
        ( DEPT.DEPT# = EMP.DEPT# ) ) ;
```

Meaning: "For every employee, there exists a corresponding department." The rule thus effectively states that there's a referential constraint from EMP to DEPT.

We now come to another important difference between the old and new schemes: *Database rules are always deferred.* That is, the checking isn't done

---

[*]Installment 29, as it turned out.

until commit time, at least conceptually. Why is this? The answer is that database rules span several distinct tables (by definition), and therefore several distinct update operations will typically be needed in order to update all of those tables in a consistent way. Now, it might well be the case with certain database rules—possibly even most such rules—that the checking can in fact be done immediately (as it is with column and table rules), but such early checking should be regarded as an optimization, *not* as an intrinsic aspect of the rule in question.

FURTHER POINTS

In the old scheme, the user was allowed to specify whether a given (multi-row) rule was immediate or deferred. In the new scheme, as we've seen, this decision is no longer made by the user. One consequence is that the integrity language is slightly simpler than before (the explicit option AT COMMIT is no longer required).

The old scheme also distinguished between state and transition rules. This distinction still applies in the new scheme (though only to table and database rules).

Another important difference between the old and new schemes is that the new scheme explicitly recognizes the fact that *integrity rules apply to derived data as well as to base data*. In the old scheme—at least as described in reference [1]—there was an implicit assumption that integrity rules applied only to base tables; this was because, of course, it's the base tables that are supposed to "reflect reality," and hence it's the base tables that must be constrained to contain correct, or at least plausible, values. In fact, however, derived tables are subject to integrity rules as well. For example, the rule that applies to base table EMP that says that employee numbers are unique also applies to every restriction of that table, obviously.

As the foregoing example suggests, derived tables will automatically *inherit* certain integrity rules from the tables from which they're derived. But it's possible that certain derived tables will be subject to certain additional integrity rules, over and above the ones they automatically inherit. Thus, it might well be desirable to be able to state integrity rules explicitly for certain derived tables. An example might be a candidate key definition for a view.

Analogous remarks apply at the database level also. Each user will interact with a "derived" database that consists of certain views and/or base tables that are derived from the "base" database (where the "base" database is the collection of all base tables). And each such derived database will be subject to certain inherited database integrity rules, and possibly to certain explicitly stated database integrity rules as well.

CONCLUDING REMARKS

During the 25 or so years since the relational model was first invented, various integrity rule classification schemes have been proposed, by myself as well as other writers. It seems to me, however, that the new scheme described in this month's column is superior to past proposals in several ways. In particular, the fact that the scheme explicitly mirrors the structure of the data itself—that is, the fact that it recognizes that databases are defined over tables, tables are defined over columns, and columns are defined over domains—does have an intuitive feeling of rightness about it.

For this month's puzzle corner, you are invited to meditate on the following two questions:

1. Give an example of a database rule that can be checked "early" (that is, immediately), instead of at commit time. What are the implications of such early checking?

2. If table *T* is in fact a view and is derived from two underlying tables *T1* and *T2*, are not the table integrity rules that are inherited for *T* actually *database* rules rather than table rules (since they refer, implicitly, to two tables)?

REFERENCES

1. C. J. Date: "A Matter of Integrity," *Database Programming & Design 6*, Nos. 10–12 (October–December 1993). Republished in *Relational Database Writings 1991–1994*. Reading, Mass.: Addison-Wesley (1995).

2. C. J. Date: "Domains, Relations, and Data Types," *Database Programming & Design 7*, Nos. 6–7 (June–July 1994). Republished in *Relational Database Writings 1991–1994*. Reading, Mass.: Addison-Wesley (1995).

3. C. J. Date: *An Introduction to Database Systems* (6th edition). Reading, Mass.: Addison-Wesley (1995).

4. C. J. Date and David McGoveran: "Updating Union, Intersection, and Difference Views," *Database Programming & Design 7*, No. 5 (May 1994). Republished in C. J. Date, *Relational Database Writings 1991–1994*. Reading, Mass.: Addison-Wesley (1995).

5. C. J. Date and David McGoveran: "Updating Joins and Other Views," *Database Programming & Design 7*, No. 7 (July 1994). Republished in C. J. Date, *Relational Database Writings 1991–1994*. Reading, Mass.: Addison-Wesley (1995).

6. David McGoveran and C. J. Date: "A New Database Design Principle," *Database Programming & Design 7*, No. 6 (June 1994). Republished in C. J. Date, *Relational Database Writings 1991–1994*. Reading, Mass.: Addison-Wesley (1995).

Relations and Their Interpretation

*A meaningful look at
the relational model*

This month and next, I want to talk about a number of more or less interconnected ideas that are actually very fundamental and yet don't seem to be as widely appreciated as they ought to be. I've touched on some of these ideas in earlier installments, but the time has come to try and draw them all together.

WHAT DO RELATIONS MEAN?

Note: The discussions of this section and the next are an edited version of material from reference [3]. I first mentioned the basic idea when I discussed TABLE_DEE and TABLE_DUM in my column in March last year [1].

Although I haven't stressed the point in previous installments, every relation—be it a base relation, a view, a query result, or whatever—certainly does have an associated meaning. And, of course, users must be aware of those meanings if they're to use the database effectively (and correctly). For example, the meaning of the base relation EMP { EMP#, ENAME, DEPT#, SALARY } shown in Fig. 1 is something like the following:

Originally published under the title "Relations and their Meaning" in *Database Programming & Design 7,* No. 12, December 1994. Reprinted by permission of Miller Freeman Inc.

EMP	EMP#	ENAME	DEPT#	SALARY
	E1	Lopez	D1	40K
	E2	Cheng	D1	42K
	E3	Finzi	D2	30K
	E4	Saito	D2	35K

Fig. 1   Relation EMP (sample values)

*The employee with the specified employee number (EMP#) has the
specified name (ENAME), works in the specified department (DEPT#),
and earns the specified salary (SALARY). Also, no two employees have
the same employee number.*

This statement isn't very precise, of course, but it'll serve for present purposes.

Formally, this statement is an example of what's called a *predicate,* or
truth-valued function—a function involving four parameters, in this particular
case. Substituting arguments for the parameters is equivalent to *invoking* the
function (or "instantiating" the predicate), thereby yielding an expression that
evaluates to either *true* or *false.* For example, the substitution

```
EMP# = 'E1'
ENAME = 'Lopez'
DEPT# = 'D1'
SALARY = 25K
```

yields the value *true.* By contrast, the substitution

```
EMP# = 'E1'
ENAME = 'Abbey'
DEPT# = 'D3'
SALARY = 45K
```

yields the value *false.* And at any given time, of course, the relation contains
exactly those rows that make the predicate evaluate to *true* at that time.

It follows from the foregoing that if (for example) a row is presented as
a candidate for insertion into some relation, the DBMS should accept that row
only if it doesn't cause the corresponding predicate to be violated. More generally, the predicate for a given relation represents the **criterion for update
acceptability** for that relation—that is, it constitutes the criterion for deciding whether or not some proposed update is in fact valid (or at least plausible) for the given relation.

In order for it to be able to decide whether or not a proposed update is acceptable for a given relation, therefore, the DBMS needs to be aware of the
predicate for that relation. Now, it's of course not possible for the DBMS to

know *exactly* what the predicate is for a given relation. In the case of relation EMP, for example, the DBMS has no way of knowing *a priori* that the predicate is such that the row (E1,Lopez,D1,25K) makes it *true* and the row (E1,Abbey,D3,45K) doesn't. It also has no way of knowing exactly what certain terms appearing in that predicate (such as "works in" or "earns") really mean. However, the DBMS certainly does know a reasonably close approximation to that predicate. To be specific, it knows that, if a given row is to be deemed acceptable, all of the following must be true:

- The EMP# value must be a value from the domain of employee numbers
- The ENAME value must be a value from the domain of names
- The DEPT# value must be a value from the domain of department numbers
- The SALARY value must be a value from the domain of US currency
- The EMP# value must be unique with respect to all such values in the relation

In other words, for a base relation such as EMP, the DBMS does at least know all of the integrity rules (column rules and relation rules) that have been declared for that base relation. *Note:* The term "relation rule" here refers to what I called a *table* rule last month [2].

Formally, therefore, we can *define* the (DBMS-understood) "meaning" of a given base relation to be the logical AND of all column and relation rules that apply to that base relation (and it's this meaning that the DBMS will check whenever an update is attempted on the base relation in question). For example, the formal meaning of base relation EMP is the following:[*]

```
      EX.EMP# IN EMP#_DOM AND
      EX.ENAME IN NAME_DOM AND
      EX.DEPT# IN DEPT#_DOM AND
      EX.SALARY IN US_CURRENCY_DOM AND
  ( IF EX.EMP# = EY.EMP# THEN
          EX.ENAME = EY.ENAME AND
          EX.DEPT# = EY.DEPT# AND
          EX.SALARY = EY.SALARY )
```

(where EX and EY represent rows of the relation and EMP#_DOM, NAME_DOM, etc., are the relevant domains). We will refer to this expression—let's call it PE—as **the relation predicate** for base relation EMP.

DERIVED RELATIONS

So much for base relations. But what about derived relations—in particular, what about views? What's the relation predicate for a derived relation? Clearly, what we need is a set of rules such that if the DBMS knows the relation

---

[*]In case any logicians are reading this column, I should say that this "formal" meaning is still not very formal! (nor indeed accurate)—but, of course, it can be made so.

predicate(s) for the input(s) to any relational operation, it can deduce the relation predicate for the output from that operation. Given such a set of rules, the DBMS will then know the relation predicate for all possible relations, and will thus be able to decide the acceptability or otherwise of an arbitrary update on an arbitrary relation (derived or base).

In fact, it's very easy to state such a set of rules—they follow immediately from the definitions of the relational operators. For example, if A and B are two relations of the same type (that is, they have the same heading), and their respective relation predicates are PA and PB, then the relation predicate PC for relation C, where C is defined as A INTERSECT B, is obviously (PA) AND (PB). In other words, a row r will appear in C if and only if it appears in both A and B—that is, if and only if $PA(r)$ and $PB(r)$ are both *true*. So if, for example, we define C as a view and try to insert r into that view, r must satisfy both the relation predicate for A and the relation predicate for B, or the INSERT will fail [3].

Here's another example: The relation predicate for the relation that results from the *restriction* operation

```
R WHERE condition
```

is (PR) AND $(condition)$, where PR is the relation predicate for R. For instance, the relation predicate for EMP WHERE DEPT# = 'D1' is

```
( PE ) AND ( DEPT# = 'D1' )
```

where PE is the relation predicate for EMP as defined earlier.

Stating the relation predicates corresponding to the other relational operators is left as an exercise for the reader.

Incidentally, don't confuse relation *rules* and relation *predicates*. Loosely speaking, a relation rule is an individual integrity constraint; a relation predicate is the logical AND of many such constraints, and is—to repeat—*what the relation (formally) means*.

RELATIONS WITH NULLS AREN'T RELATIONS

Take another look at the relation predicate PE for base relation EMP as shown earlier. As you can see, that predicate is basically of the form

```
(column C1 has a value from domain D1) AND
(column C2 has a value from domain D2) AND
.......                                AND
(column Cn has a value from domain Dn) AND x
```

where the expressions "column C1 has a value from domain D1" (and so on) are all of the applicable column rules and x is the logical AND of all of the applicable relation rules. *Relation predicates are—obviously enough—always of this basic form.*[*]

Now suppose that we have a "relation" R in which some column, say column C2, has NULLS ALLOWED ("relation" in quotes, because I'm about to show that such an object is in fact not a relation at all). Then the corresponding predicate has to look something like this:

```
(column C1 has a value from domain D1) AND
(column C2 has a value from domain D2  OR
 column C2 does not have a value      ) AND
 .......                                AND
(column Cn has a value from domain Dn) AND x
```

But this is nonsense! To say that column C2 either has a value (from some domain) or it doesn't is to say *nothing* [4]. Suppose, for example, that relation R is EMP and column C2 is SALARY. Then the corresponding predicate will effectively say that each employee either does or doesn't have a salary. So what? To repeat, this tells us *nothing*.

The point is this. For pedagogic reasons, let's assume that each relation represents some type of entity. Then the relation predicate for a given relation is supposed to specify the properties that entities of that type must have in order to *be* entities of that type. To say that certain properties might *not* be held by certain of those entities is thus a contradiction in terms—it's to say that those entities aren't of that type after all! Indeed, once we permit the possibility of a relation predicate that specifies that some property might *not* be held, the possibilities are endless. Why stop with salaries? Why not say that each employee either does or does not have a spouse? A nationality? A pet cat? An airplane? A head?

Conclusion: A "relation" that permits nulls doesn't have a proper relation predicate and isn't a proper relation.

PUZZLE CORNER

A little light relief this month. The *Very Large Data Base* (VLDB) conference is held annually at various locations around the world. *N* people attended the VLDB Conference this year. You aren't told the value of *N;* however, you are told that *M,* the number of attendees who shook hands with other attendees an odd number of times, is even. Should you believe this claim? (Based on a puzzle in Martin Gardner, *More Mathematical Puzzles and Diversions,* Penguin Books, 1966.)

---

[*]Modulo the remarks in the previous footnote.

REFERENCES

1. C. J. Date: "Tables with No Columns," *Database Programming & Design 6,* No. 3 (March 1993). Republished in *Relational Database Writings 1991–1994.* Reading, Mass.: Addison-Wesley (1995).

2. C. J. Date: "Integrity Revisited" (see Installment 27).

3. C. J. Date and David McGoveran: "Updating Union, Intersection, and Difference Views," *Database Programming & Design 7,* No. 5 (May 1994). Republished in C. J. Date, *Relational Database Writings 1991–1994.* Reading, Mass.: Addison-Wesley (1995).

4. David McGoveran: "Nothing from Nothing" (Chapters 5–8 of the present book).

It's All Relations!

*Some fundamental aspects
of relations that aren't as
widely appreciated as they
ought to be*

One of my **pet peeves** is the phrase—frequently encountered in SQL contexts—"tables and views" (sometimes "tables or views"). Such phrasing clearly suggests that a view, whatever else it might be, is not a table. Indeed, the SQL language itself lends strong support to this interpretation, inasmuch as the keyword TABLE is often—though not invariably!—used to mean, very specifically, a *base* table (think of CREATE TABLE, ALTER TABLE, etc.).

It's my opinion that people who employ such a manner of speaking are *not thinking relationally*. It's my further opinion that such people are likely to make a number of serious mistakes as a consequence of their lack of relational thinking. I might even be tempted to level this accusation at the designers of the SQL language itself . . .

In fact, of course, the *whole point* about a view, and more generally about any kind of derived relation, is precisely that it *is* a relation (I deliberately switch now from tables to relations as the basis for my terminology). The fact that a view is a relation is important in relational systems for much the same reasons that the fact that a subset is a set is important in mathematics: Because a subset is a set, we can perform the same kinds of operations on a subset as we can on any other kind of set; likewise, because a view

Originally published in *Database Programming & Design 8,* No. 1, January 1995. Reprinted by permission of Miller Freeman Inc.

is a relation, we can perform the same kinds of operations on a view as we can on any other kind of relation.

KINDS OF RELATIONS

The phrase "any other kind of relation" implies that several kinds of relations can be distinguished, and so indeed they can. Let's take a moment to examine some of the most important kinds (refer to Fig. 1).

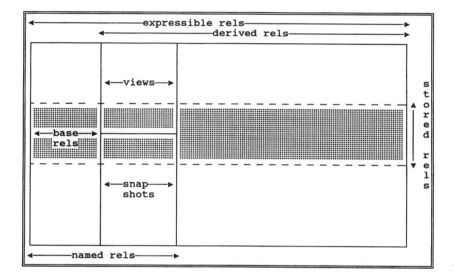

Fig. 1 Kinds of relations

Briefly:

1. A *named* relation is a relation that's been explicitly defined to the DBMS (for instance, via CREATE TABLE in SQL). Three important special cases are base relations, views, and snapshots (I discussed snapshots in an earlier installment [1]).

2. A *base* relation is a named relation that's not a derived relation.

3. A *derived* relation is a relation that's defined (by means of some relational expression) in terms of other, named relations—ultimately, in terms

of base relations. *Caveat:* Be warned, however, that some writers use "derived" to mean what I'm calling "expressible" (see the next paragraph).

4. An *expressible* relation is a relation that can be obtained from the set of named relations by means of some relational expression. Of course, every named relation is an expressible relation, but the converse is not true. Base relations, views, snapshots, and intermediate and final query results are all expressible relations. In other words, the set of all expressible relations is, precisely, the union (disjoint by definition) of the set of all base relations and the set of all derived relations.

5. A *view* is a named derived relation. Views are *virtual*—they're represented within the system solely by their definition in terms of other named relations.

6. A *snapshot* is also a named derived relation, like a view. Unlike a view, however, a snapshot is real, not virtual—i.e., it's represented not only by its definition in terms of other named relations, but also (at least conceptually) by its own separate data.

7. A *query result* is the unnamed derived relation that results from executing some specified query. Query results don't have persistent existence within the database (though they can, of course, be assigned to some named relation that does).

8. An *intermediate result* is an unnamed derived relation that results from the evaluation of some relational expression that's nested within some larger such expression.

9. Finally, a *stored* relation is an expressible relation—*not* necessarily a base relation, please note!—that's supported in physical storage in some "direct, efficient" manner (with appropriate definitions of "direct" and "efficient," of course—details beyond the scope of this discussion). *Note:* I discussed the fact that there isn't necessarily a 1:1 correspondence between stored and base relations in an earlier column [1]. Fig. 1 stresses the point by showing the band representing the set of stored relations at right angles to, and intersecting, all of the other bands.

I'll conclude this brief discussion by cautioning the reader once again *not* to fall into the common traps of (a) taking "relations" to mean, specifically, *base* relations only and (b) taking base and stored relations to be synonymous.

BASE RELATIONS *vs.* VIEWS

Following on from the foregoing discussion, there's another (important) point to be made—a point that's widely understood but only rarely appreciated. That point is the following:

For any given database, the choice as to which relations are to be base relations and which are to be views is to some extent arbitrary.

In the case of suppliers-and-parts, for example, we could make the familiar relation S a base relation and then define the two projections SNC (over S#, SNAME, and CITY) and ST (over S# and STATUS) as views; or we could define SNC and ST as base relations and then define S (the join of SNC and ST) as a view.

The foregoing situation is precisely analogous to the situation that obtains in logical systems in general (a database is just a special kind of logical system):

- In such a system, we start off with a set of *axioms* and we then follow certain procedures to obtain a set of derived *theorems*. Note that an axiom can be thought of as a theorem that's given, not derived.

- Likewise, in a database system we start off with a set of base relations and we then follow certain procedures to obtain a set of derived relations.

And, just as the choice of which theorems are to be taken as axioms in a logical system is often somewhat arbitrary, so the choice of which relations are to be taken as base relations in a database is often somewhat arbitrary too. The only requirement is that all choices must lead to the same set of *expressible* relations; in other words, the various choices must all be *information-equivalent*.

> *Aside:* Note in passing that database design disciplines, such as the discipline of further normalization or the discipline advocated in reference [5], can be seen as techniques for helping to decide which relations, out of the universe of expressible relations, should be chosen as base relations and which not. *End of aside.*

By the way, the work by David McGoveran and myself on updating views [2–3] is relevant here. The point is, of course, that the updatability of a given database shouldn't depend on the essentially arbitrary decision as to how we decide to represent that database—i.e., the decision as to which relations we decide to make base relations and which we decide to make views. In the suppliers-and-parts example quoted above, for instance, the updatability of relation S should not depend in any way on whether S is a base relation or a view.

RELATIONAL ISN'T ROW-AT-A-TIME

"Everyone knows" that the operators of the relational algebra are set-level—but (once again) the full implications of this fact have typically not been understood. More specifically, the implications for *retrieval* operations have usually been understood . . . but what about *update* operations? Recall from the last two installments that updates must be checked "immediately" against the relation predicate for the target relation. The implication is that certain multi-row updates *cannot* be simulated by a series of single-row updates (and this remark is true for both base relations and views, in general).

By way of an example, suppose relation S is subject to the constraint— part of the applicable relation predicate—that S2 and S3 must have the same city. Then the update

```
UPDATE S WHERE S# = 'S2' SET CITY = ... ;
```

must necessarily fail (unless it is a no-op).

As another example, consider the relation EMP { EMP#, SALARY, DEPT#, DEPTMGR# }, satisfying the functional dependency

```
DEPT# → DEPTMGR#
```

and consider an attempt to insert the row (E2,60K,D2,E9). This INSERT must necessarily fail if another row already exists with DEPT# equal to D2 and DEPTMGR# not equal to E9. (Note that EMP is not in third normal form, in- cidentally. One advantage of third normal form—3NF—is precisely that a 3NF relation will typically permit a wider range of "row-level" updates than a non3NF relation.) *Exercise for the reader:* Give an example in which a "row- level" DELETE must necessarily fail.

To pursue the point a moment longer: In fact there's no such thing as a "row-level" operation in the relational model—the operations are *always* set-level, at least conceptually. "Row-level" operations should be under- stood as shorthand for certain set-level operations in which the set happens to be of cardinality one. For example, the operation of "inserting a new row *r* into relation R" is logically equivalent to the following set-level assign- ment operation:

```
R := R UNION { r } ;
```

with the requirement that the cardinality of R after the assignment is one more than the cardinality of R before the assignment. Similarly for UPDATE and DELETE, of course.

One consequence of all of the foregoing is that SQL's cursor-based up- dates ("positioned UPDATE and DELETE"), which are row-level by defini- tion, are a very bad idea: Applications that work today might fail tomorrow, when proper integrity support is provided. (In this connection, it's interesting to note that IBM's DB2/MVS product already places certain restrictions on the updates that are allowed through cursors when referential integrity support is in effect [4].) Of course, cursor-based operations in general tend to be a bad idea anyway in today's distributed and client/server environments, because of their negative impact on performance.

PUZZLE CORNER

More light relief this month (some old chestnuts, in fact):

1. What is the missing entry x in this series?

    10 11 12 13 14 15 16 17 20 22 24 31 *x* 121 1000

2. What are the next two entries x and y in this series?

    1 18 4 13 6 10 15 2 *x* *y* ...

3. What are the missing entries x, y, and z in this series?

    1 2 3 *x* *y* *z* 5 6 7 8 9 10

REFERENCES

1. C. J. Date: "The Importance of Closure," *Database Programming & Design 5,* No. 10 (October 1992). Republished in *Relational Database Writings 1991–1994.* Reading, Mass.: Addison-Wesley (1995).

2. C. J. Date and David McGoveran: "Updating Union, Intersection, and Difference Views," *Database Programming & Design 7,* No. 5 (May 1994). Republished in C. J. Date, *Relational Database Writings 1991–1994.* Reading, Mass.: Addison-Wesley (1995).

3. C. J. Date and David McGoveran: "Updating Joins and Other Views," *Database Programming & Design 7,* No. 7 (July 1994). Republished in C. J. Date, *Relational Database Writings 1991–1994.* Reading, Mass.: Addison-Wesley (1995).

4. C. J. Date and Colin J. White: *A Guide to DB2* (4th edition). Reading, Mass.: Addison-Wesley (1993).

5. David McGoveran and C. J. Date: "A New Database Design Principle," *Database Programming & Design 7,* No. 6 (June 1994). Republished in C. J. Date, *Relational Database Writings 1991–1994.* Reading, Mass.: Addison-Wesley (1995).

Answers to Puzzle Corner Problems (Installments 26–29)

Time's up! How do your "puzzle corner" answers stack up?

My column this month is devoted to answering the various outstanding puzzle corner problems from the last few installments. Thanks as usual to those readers who wrote in with their own solutions.

THE RECTANGLES PROBLEM

Source: "Oh Oh Relational . . ." (see Installment 26).

Problem statement: We have a database of rectangles, all of which are "square on" to the X and Y axes—that is, all sides are either vertical or horizontal. Each rectangle can thus be uniquely represented by the coordinates $(x1,y1)$ and $(x2,y2)$, respectively, of its bottom left and top right corners. In SQL:

```
CREATE TABLE RECTANGLES
    ( X1 ..., X2 ..., Y1 ..., Y2 ..., ... ) ;
```

Now consider the query: "Find all rectangles that overlap the unit square $(0,1,0,1)$." The "obvious" SQL representation of this query is as follows:

Originally published under the title "Put Your Pencils Down!" in *Database Programming & Design 8,* No. 2, February 1995 (the subtitle was contributed by *DBP&D* too). Reprinted by permission of Miller Freeman Inc.

```
SELECT *
FROM     RECTANGLES
WHERE  ( X1 >= 0 AND X1 <= 1 AND Y1 >= 0 AND Y1 <= 1 )
OR     ( X2 >= 0 AND X2 <= 1 AND Y2 >= 0 AND Y2 <= 1 )
OR     ( X1 >= 0 AND X1 <= 1 AND Y2 >= 0 AND Y2 <= 1 )
OR     ( X2 >= 0 AND X2 <= 1 AND Y1 >= 0 AND Y1 <= 1 )
OR     ( X1 <= 0 AND X2 >= 1 AND Y1 <= 0 AND Y2 >= 1 )
OR     ( X1 <= 0 AND X2 >= 1 AND Y1 >= 0 AND Y1 <= 1 )
OR     ( X1 >= 0 AND X1 <= 1 AND Y1 <= 0 AND Y2 >= 1 )
OR     ( X2 >= 0 AND X2 <= 1 AND Y1 <= 0 AND Y2 >= 1 )
OR     ( X1 <= 0 AND X2 >= 1 AND Y2 >= 0 AND Y2 <= 1 ) ;
```

However, the query can be expressed much more simply as:

```
SELECT *
FROM     RECTANGLES
WHERE  ( X1 <= 1 AND Y1 <= 1 AND X2 >= 0 AND Y2 >= 0 ) ;
```

The problem is to prove that the two versions of the query are equivalent.

Solution: Of the various solutions I've seen to this problem, the most elegant was produced by a friend of mine, Bob White, from England.[*] His solution goes as follows.

First, we divide the X-Y plane into nine regions labeled 1 to 9 as indicated in Fig. 1, such that the unit square is region 5:

Any given rectangle will have its bottom left corner in exactly one of these nine regions and its top right corner in exactly one of these nine regions also. (If a corner actually lies on one or more of the boundary lines, we can consider that corner to be "in" either the lowest-numbered or the highest-numbered candidate region, depending on whether it's a bottom left or top right corner. We assume that all rectangles are "genuine rectangles"—that is, they don't degenerate to line segments or points.)

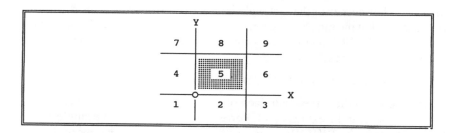

Fig. 1 The nine regions of the plane

---

[*]I subsequently discovered an even neater solution, but I don't want to rewrite history, so I'll let this installment stay as it originally was.

Now let *A* and *B* each be subsets of the set of nine regions. Denote by *A* X *B* the set of all rectangles with bottom left corner in some region of *A* and top right corner in some region of *B;* for example, {1} X {9} denotes the set of all rectangles that totally include the unit square, and {5} X {5} denotes the set of all rectangles that are totally included within the unit square. Then the set of rectangles that "obviously" overlap the unit square is the union of the following:

```
{ 5 } X { 5, 6, 9, 8 }
/* bottom left corner inside */

{ 1, 2, 5, 4 } X { 5 }
/* top right corner inside */

{ 2, 5 } X { 5, 6 }
/* top left corner inside */

{ 4, 5 } X { 5, 8 }
/* bottom right corner inside */

{ 1 } X { 9 }
/* rectangle totally includes */

{ 4 } X { 6, 9 }
/* bottom edge crosses */

{ 2 } X { 8, 9 }
/* left edge crosses */

{ 1, 2 } X { 8 }
/* right edge crosses */

{ 1, 4 } X { 6 }
/* top edge crosses */
```

The comments indicate exactly how the rectangle in question overlaps the unit square. For instance, the first comment ("bottom left corner inside") means the bottom left corner of the rectangle is contained somewhere inside the unit square. Note that the nine expressions correspond in sequence to the nine ORed terms in the WHERE clause in the original (long) version of the query.

The union of these nine sets is

```
U  =  { 1, 2, 4, 5 } X { 5, 6, 8, 9 }
```

because between them they pair each of {1}, {2}, {4}, {5} with each of {5}, {6}, {8}, {9}. But the expression U corresponds precisely to the single parenthesized term in the WHERE clause of the short version of the query. ∎

By the way, the question of proving the equivalence of the two forms of the query is not an idle one. The real question is whether a relational optimizer could transform the original long form into the corresponding short form. Reference [1] (which also includes an alternative—much longer!—equivalence proof) presents evidence to suggest that the answer to this question is almost certainly *no,* at least so far as today's commercial optimizers are concerned. By contrast, reference [2] shows how a relational system with proper domain support could provide a "good" solution to the rectangles problem (and problems like it).

INTEGRITY RULES

Source: "Integrity Revisited" (see Installment 27).

Problem statement: Actually there were two problems in this installment. The first was as follows:

1. Give an example of a database rule that can be checked "early" (that is, immediately, instead of at commit). What are the implications of such early checking?

Solution: Recall that a *database rule* is an integrity rule that refers to—or rather, interrelates—two or more distinct tables. One common example is provided by referential constraints (except for the special case where the referencing table and the referenced table happen to be one and the same, in which case the rule is a table rule rather than a database rule). For example:

```
CREATE INTEGRITY RULE DE1
    FORALL EMP ( EXISTS DEPT
        ( DEPT.DEPT# = EMP.DEPT# ) ) ;
```

("every employee has a corresponding department"). The following operations have the potential for violating this rule:

- INSERT on table EMP
- DELETE on table DEPT
- UPDATE on column EMP.DEPT#
- UPDATE on column DEPT.DEPT#

Since these are the *only* operations that can possibly violate the rule, it does seem reasonable—in the interests of efficiency—to suggest that the rule might be checked "early." But what about the following rule?

```
CREATE INTEGRITY RULE ED1
    FORALL DEPT ( EXISTS EMP
        ( EMP.DEPT# = DEPT.DEPT# ) ) ;
```

("every department must have at least one employee"; this too is a database rule, though not of course a *referential* rule as such). The operations that have the potential for violating this rule are as follows:

- INSERT on table DEPT
- DELETE on table EMP
- UPDATE on column EMP.DEPT#
- UPDATE on column DEPT.DEPT#

By exactly the same reasoning as before, we could argue that this rule too could be checked "early."

So what's going on? Clearly, if we start with tables DEPT and EMP both empty, the very first INSERT operation will necessarily violate either rule DE1 (if the INSERT is on EMP) or rule ED1 (if the INSERT is on DEPT), and hence one of the two checks must necessarily fail if done early. Indeed, there's nothing to stop us from replacing rules DE1 and ED1 by a single rule that is the logical AND of the two; could that single rule then logically be checked "early"?

In fact, the answer is yes. Note that—if update requests are issued in a "sensible" sequence, which they presumably will be most of the time—the rule will *not* be violated most of the time. But consideration of this issue brings us to the second part of the original question: What are the implications of doing checks early? The answer is as follows:

- If the check succeeds, there's no problem.
- If the check fails, an exception code is *not* returned to the user; instead, the DBMS simply has to remember to do the check again at commit time. If that commit-time check succeeds, there's no problem. If it fails, the appropriate violation response—probably rollback—must then be invoked.

Let me now turn to the second problem:

2. If table *T* is in fact a view and is derived from two underlying tables *T1* and *T2,* aren't the table integrity rules that are inherited for *T* actually *database* rules rather than table rules (since they refer, implicitly, to two tables)?

Solution: No, they're still table rules. It's true that any such inherited rule will refer to both *T1* and *T2,* but it will do so *in a separable way*—that is, it won't include any "join term" that interrelates the two tables. To see this is so, let's consider all possible cases:

```
• T = T1 UNION T2
• T = T1 MINUS T2
• T = T1 JOIN T2
```

Note that TIMES, INTERSECT, and DIVIDEBY aren't primitive operations and so needn't be considered (TIMES and INTERSECT are both special cases of JOIN; DIVIDEBY is left as a subsidiary exercise for the reader).

Let *t1* and *t2* be table rules for *T1* and *T2*, respectively. Then the corresponding inherited rules are as follows:

- UNION: `t1 OR t2`
- MINUS: `t1 AND NOT t2`
- JOIN: `t1 AND t2`

(In the case of JOIN, *t1* and *t2* are to be understood as applying to the *T1*-portion and the *T2*-portion, respectively, of (any given row of) table *T*.) It follows that if a given row is presented as a candidate for INSERTing into the view *T*, that row can be checked against the rules *t1* and *t2* independently. Similarly for UPDATE and DELETE.

HANDSHAKING

Source: "Relations and Their Interpretation" (see Installment 28).

Problem statement: The *Very Large Data Base* (VLDB) conference is held annually at various locations around the world. *N* people attended the VLDB Conference this year. You aren't told the value of *N;* however, you are told that *M,* the number of attendees who shook hands with other attendees an odd number of times, is even. Should you believe this claim?

Solution: The answer is yes. First, let's agree that if attendees *a* and *b* shake hands, that event constitutes *two* handshakes (one between *a* and *b* and one between *b* and *a*). Now suppose attendee *a* shakes hands *h* times, and let the total number of handshakes (that is, the sum of all such numbers *h,* taken over all attendees *a*) be *H*. Clearly *H* must be even. Next, let the total number of handshakes for attendees who shook hands an even number of times (that is, the sum of the numbers *h,* taken over all attendees *a* where *h* is even) be *He*. *He* is clearly even also, and so the difference $Ho = H - He$ is likewise even. But *Ho* is (by definition) the total number of handshakes for attendees who shook hands an odd number of times (that is, the sum of the numbers *h,* taken over all attendees *a* where *h* is odd). For a series of odd numbers to have an even sum, there must be an even number of numbers in the series. ∎

MISSING VALUES

Source: "It's All Relations!" (see Installment 29).

Problem statement: First of all, I asked in the body of the column for an example in which a "row-level" DELETE must necessarily fail. One possibility might be a relation EMP that's required to satisfy the constraint that a given DEPT# must appear in either no rows at all or at least three rows (that is, departments must either be empty or have at least three employees). For this relation, "row-level" INSERTs, UPDATEs, and DELETEs can all fail. In particular, a "row-level" DELETE will fail if it attempts to delete just one of exactly three rows that have a particular DEPT# value.

The puzzle corner problem in this installment was as follows:

1. What is the missing entry *x* in this series?

    10   11   12   13   14   15   16   17   20   22   24   31   *x*   121   1000

Solution: 100. The *i*th number in the series ($i = 1$ to 15) is the decimal number 16 expressed to base $17-i$.

2. What are the next two entries *x* and *y* in this series?

    1   18   4   13   6   10   15   2   *x*   *y*   ...

Solution: 17 and 3. The series represents the numbers on a dartboard, starting at 1 and proceeding clockwise.

3. What are the missing entries *x, y,* and *z* in this series?

    1   2   3   *x*   *y*   *z*   5   6   7   8   9   10

Solution: Lexington, Park, and Madison.

REFERENCES

1. C. J. Date: "An Optimization Problem," in C. J. Date and Hugh Darwen, *Relational Database Writings 1989–1991*. Reading, Mass.: Addison-Wesley (1992).
2. C. J. Date: "Object-Oriented Systems," Part VI of *An Introduction to Database Systems* (6th edition). Reading, Mass.: Addison-Wesley (1995).

Nested Relations (Part 1 of 2)

Nested relations—if done right—don't violate 1NF!

In my column some 18 months ago [1] I complained that values in SQL tables can't be SQL tables in turn (in other words, SQL tables can't be nested). And I went on to say that this was another topic we needed to discuss in detail some time soon. I'm sure many readers found my criticism of SQL surprising at the time; after all, doesn't the idea of "nested relations"—meaning relations that are nested inside other relations—violate one of the most fundamental requirements of the relational model, namely that all relations must be in (at least) first normal form?

Well, yes and no. It depends on how it's done. Recall that first normal form (1NF) requires every row-and-column slot to contain a single atomic value. So let's look at an example. Fig. 1 shows three versions of a simple shipments relation that indicates which suppliers (S#) supply which parts (P#).

Now, I'm sure we can all agree that relation R1 in the figure is 1NF. I'm equally sure we can all agree that relation R2 is *not* 1NF, because column P# in that relation is a "repeating group" column (different rows contain different numbers of values in that position). *But relation R3 is 1NF again!* By enclosing the "repeating group" values in set braces { } in the column P#_SET in R3,

Originally published under the title "Nested Relations, Part I" in *Database Programming & Design 8,* No. 3, March 1995. Reprinted by permission of Miller Freeman Inc.

R1			R2			R3	
S#	**P#**		**S#**	**P#**		**S#**	**P#_SET**
S2	P1		S2	P1,P2		S2	{P1,P2}
S2	P2		S4	P2,P4,P5		S4	{P2,P4,P5}
S4	P2						
S4	P4						
S4	P5						

Fig. 1   Three versions of the shipments relation

I've converted each repeating group value into *a single value*—a set value, to be sure, but a set is still (at a certain level of abstraction) a single object.

ATOMIC DATA VALUES

What we're really talking about here is *data value atomicity.* To repeat, 1NF requires every row-and-column slot to contain a single "atomic value." But what's an atomic value? The term is usually defined to mean a value that is "nondecomposable by the DBMS." So is (for instance) a string atomic? Are strings "decomposable by the DBMS"? Well, most DBMSs support operators such as SUBSTRING and LIKE, whose purpose is precisely to "decompose" strings; so it looks like strings aren't truly atomic after all. Yet we would surely all agree that relations must be allowed to contain strings.

A set like {P2,P4,P5} is no more and no less "decomposable by the DBMS" than a string is. Like strings, sets do have some internal structure, but (as with strings) it's convenient to ignore that internal structure for certain purposes. In other words, if strings are compatible with the requirements of 1NF, then sets must be too.

Note: In fact, of course, we've already seen in earlier installments [3] that values in domains, and hence in columns, can be as complex as we like—we can have domains of engineering drawings, domains of legal contracts, domains of geometric figures, and so on. Domains, and hence columns, that contain sets are just a special case of this more general situation.

To return to the shipments example *per se:* Probably you've already realized that the values in column P#_SET aren't just sets, they're very specifically *relations* (see Fig. 2). Thus, R3 is an example of a relation that contains other relations nested inside itself. And in general, of course, those other relations might contain still further relations nested inside them, and so on, recursively, to any number of levels.

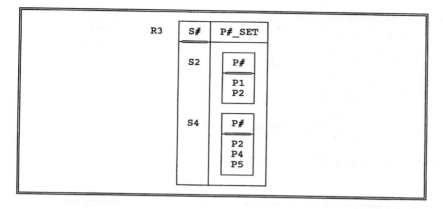

Fig. 2   A closer look at relation R3

"NF SQUARED" RELATIONS

There's one point I must make quite clear before going any further. Over the past few years, several researchers have proposed what they call "NF^2 relations," which certainly do violate the 1NF requirement (in fact, the name NF^2—short for NFNF—specifically stands for "non first normal form"). Columns in an NF^2 relation can be relation-valued, as in Fig. 2, but those values are quite definitely not "atomic." As a result, NF^2 relations are a considerably more complicated kind of object, mathematically speaking, than the usual 1NF relation, and they require significant additions and revisions to the relational algebra [4]. In particular they require new *NEST* and *UNNEST* operations for converting between nested and unnested forms of a relation. The approach I'm describing, by contrast, merely requires some comparatively minor extensions to the existing *EXTEND* operator (for both NEST- and UNNEST-like operations), as we'll see.

NESTED RELATIONS MAKE OUTER JOIN UNNECECESSARY

So far, I've shown (I hope) that nested relations are at least legal. But are they useful? Well, of course the answer is *yes*. First of all, it turns out that nested relations make outer join unnecessary! Second, they're in fact *required*, at least conceptually, to support the relational comparison operations I discussed in an earlier installment [2]. Third, there do seem to be cases where the best database design involves the use of nested *base* relations specifically.

For now, let me concentrate on just the first of these three points—namely, the fact that nested relations make outer join unnecessary. Here's an example, based on the usual suppliers-and-parts database. Consider the following assignment operation:

```
S_SP  :=  EXTEND S
          ADD ( MATCHING SP ) [ P#, QTY ]
          AS PQ ;
```

The result relation S_SP is shown in Fig. 3.

S#	SNAME	STATUS	CITY	PQ	
S1	Smith	20	London	**P#**	**QTY**
				P1	300
				P2	200
				..	...
				P6	100
S2	Jones	10	Paris	**P#**	**QTY**
				P1	300
				P2	400
..	.....	..	......	....	
S5	Adams	30	Athens	**P#**	**QTY**

Fig. 3   Relation S_SP

Explanation: For a given supplier in relation S, the expression (MATCHING SP)[P#,QTY] yields the set of shipments corresponding to that supplier, projected over P# and QTY. (I first discussed MATCHING in my column a few months ago [2].) Thus, for any given S# value, column PQ in relation S_SP shows the parts supplied by that supplier, together with the corresponding quantities. Notice the PQ value for supplier S5 in particular; given our usual sample data values, the set of shipments for supplier S5 is empty, and so the corresponding PQ value is an empty relation.

The example illustrates one of the extensions to the EXTEND operator that I referred to above. To be precise, the ADD operand has been specified as a *relational* expression instead of a scalar expression. (Please note, however, that this extended EXTEND format hasn't been checked for syntactic soundness.) Observe that (as is always the case with EXTEND):

- The degree of the result (here 5) is one more than the degree of the input.
- The cardinality of the result (also 5) is the same as the cardinality of the input.
- S# is a candidate key for the result, because it's a candidate key for the input.

I would now like to contrast the result S_SP with the relation that would result from computing the *left outer join* of relation S with relation SP (see Fig. 4; the dashes "--" and "---" in that figure are meant to represent nulls). Notice in particular that in Fig. 4 the empty set of parts supplied by supplier S5 is represented, not by an empty set as in Fig. 3, but rather by *nulls*—which (as every regular reader of this column will know) are, in my opinion, **very bad news!** To represent an empty set by an empty set, by contrast, seems to me like an obviously good idea. In fact, *there would be no need for the outer join operation at all* if nested relations were supported along the lines I'm suggesting here. Thus, one immediate advantage of nested relations is that they deal more elegantly with the problem that outer join is intended to solve than outer join does itself.

S#	SNAME	STATUS	CITY	P#	QTY
S1	Smith	20	London	P1	300
S1	Smith	20	London	P2	200
..	.....	..	......	..	...
S1	Smith	20	London	P6	100
S2	Jones	10	Paris	P1	300
S2	Jones	10	Paris	P2	400
..	.....	..	......	..	...
S5	Adams	30	Athens	--	---

Fig. 4   The left outer join of S with SP

NESTING AND UNNESTING

I have shown how to produce the nested relation S_SP from the unnested relations S and SP, using an extended form of EXTEND. Now let's consider the reverse process—producing S and SP from S_SP. Producing S is easy:

```
S  :=  S_SP [ S#, SNAME, STATUS, CITY ] ;
```

To produce SP, let me first define two new operators—EACHROW, which when applied to a relation *R* of *n* rows returns a set of *n* individual results (all distinct, by definition), each one being a row of *R;* and COMPONENT, which when applied to a row *r* returns the value of a specified component of *r*. Let me also extend the EXTEND operator (again), such that if the ADD operand evaluates to *n* distinct scalar values, then the EXTEND result contains *n* corresponding rows. Then:

```
T1 := S_SP ADD EACHROW ( PQ ) AS P_Q ;
T2 := ( EXTEND T1 ADD COMPONENT ( P_Q, P# ) AS P#,
                      COMPONENT ( P_Q, QTY ) AS QTY ) ;
SP := T2 [ S#, P#, QTY ] ;
```

Explanation: T1 has columns S#, SNAME, STATUS, CITY, PQ, and P_Q; the values in the P_Q position are *rows,* with two components, P# and QTY (T1 contains six rows for supplier S1, two for S2, one for S3, three for S4, and none at all for S5). T2 is identical to T1, except that it has two additional columns, P# and QTY, derived in an obvious way from the P# and QTY components of the P_Q column. Projecting T2 over S#, P#, and QTY yields the desired final result.

OPERATING ON NESTED RELATIONS

If relation *R* has a column *C* that contains numbers, I can apply operators such as "+", "−", "<", etc., to values from that column. It's important to understand, however, that—conceptually, at least—the DBMS doesn't know what it means, for example, to add two numbers together; what it does know is how to invoke a builtin function called "+" that can perform that operation on its behalf.

In exactly the same way, if relation *R* has a column *C* that contains relations, I can apply operators to values from that column, and the DBMS will simply invoke the appropriate builtin functions to perform the requested operations. But the operators that I want to apply to values in that column are (of course) things like *restrict, project,* and so on . . . In other words, "invoking the appropriate builtin functions" will effectively be just a recursive call on (certain portions of) the DBMS itself.

CONCLUDING REMARKS

Well, I've now introduced the basic idea of nested relations and shown how they can be used to avoid the need for outer join. Next month, I'll consider other applications of the nested relation idea. For now, let me leave you with this month's puzzle corner problem. I mentioned earlier that "NF^2 relations" require explicit *NEST* and *UNNEST* operations for converting between nested and unnested forms of a relation. In outline, those operators work as follows:

- Given a relation and a set of columns, NEST returns a corresponding nested relation. For example, nesting the usual suppliers relation "along" S#, SNAME, and STATUS yields a nested relation containing three rows, one for each of the three CITY values (London, Paris, and Athens); each of those rows contains the appropriate city name and a relation with heading { S#, SNAME, STATUS }, representing the suppliers in that city. *Note:* It might help to point out that if we partition the columns of relation *R* into two disjoint subsets *A* and *B,* then nesting *R* along *B* is equivalent to grouping *R* by *A.*

- UNNEST is the opposite of NEST, loosely speaking—though if we unnest *R* "along" some set of columns and then nest the result "along" those same columns again, we do not necessarily get back to *R!*

Give an example to show that—as just indicated—unnesting in the foregoing sense is not necessarily reversible. Can you find a set of conditions under which the unnesting *is* necessarily reversible?

REFERENCES

1. C. J. Date: "How We Missed the Relational Boat," *Database Programming & Design 6,* No. 9 (September 1993). Republished in *Relational Database Writings 1991–1994.* Reading, Mass.: Addison-Wesley (1995).

2. C. J. Date: "Relational Comparisons," *Database Programming & Design 7,* No. 5 (May 1994). Republished in *Relational Database Writings 1991–1994.* Reading, Mass.: Addison-Wesley (1995).

3. C. J. Date: "Domains, Relations, and Data Types," *Database Programming & Design 7,* Nos. 6–7 (June–July 1994). Republished in *Relational Database Writings 1991–1994.* Reading, Mass.: Addison-Wesley (1995).

4. Mark A. Roth, Henry F. Korth, and Abraham Silberschatz: "Extended Algebra and Calculus for Nested Relational Databases," *ACM TODS 13,* No. 4 (December 1988).

Nested Relations (Part 2 of 2)

Concluding our investigation into nested relations

Last month, I introduced the idea of nested relations and discussed some corresponding extensions to the EXTEND operator. I also pointed out that one advantage of nested relations was that they made the outer join operator logically unnecessary. This month I want to discuss some more applications of the nested relations idea.

NESTED RELATIONS *vs.* HIERARCHIES

One issue I need to get out of the way is the following. Recall the nested relation S_SP from last month (the structure of that relation is shown in Fig. 1, and some sample values are given in Fig. 2). Now, some people might argue that relation S_SP is really a *hierarchy* (*à la* IMS) with structure as shown in Fig. 3, and might further argue that it's therefore subject to all of the same criticisms that were leveled—by relational advocates!—at hierarchies 20 or more years ago.

Well, it's true that relation S_SP does look like a hierarchy—IF you look *inside* the PQ values at the same time as you look at the *outside* (only) of other values. But to do this is to mix levels! (in a sense)—it looks inside

---

Originally published under the title "Nested Relations, Part II" in *Database Programming & Design 8*, No. 4, April 1995. Reprinted by permission of Miller Freeman Inc.

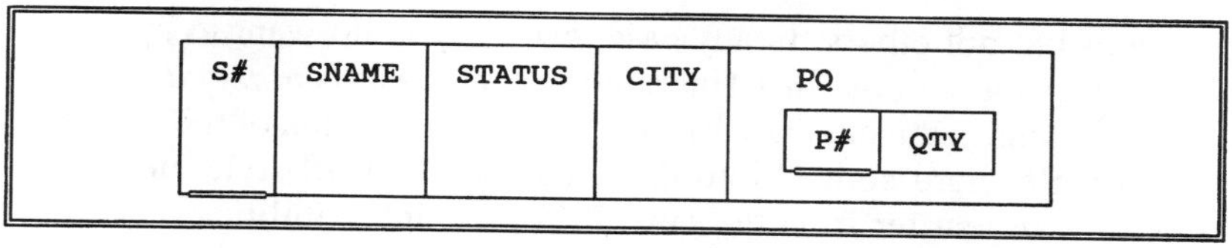

S#	SNAME	STATUS	CITY	PQ	
				P#	QTY

Fig. 1   Relation S_SP (structure)

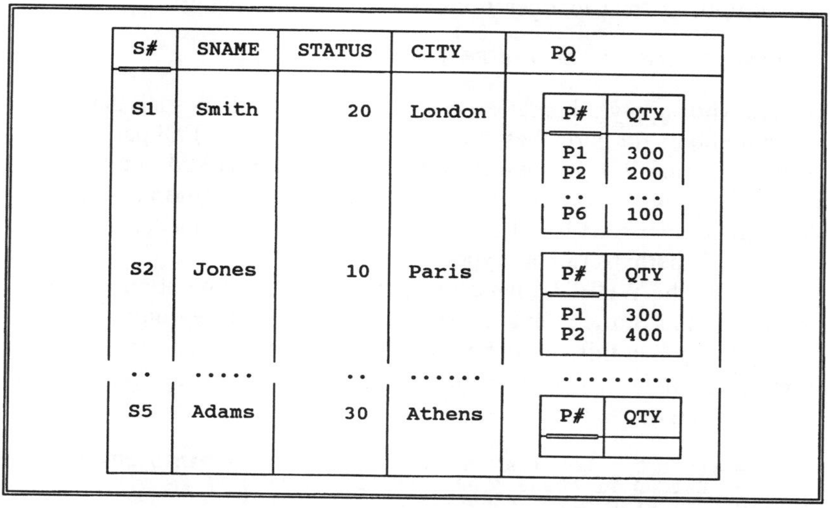

S#	SNAME	STATUS	CITY	PQ	
S1	Smith	20	London	P#	QTY
				P1	300
				P2	200
				..	...
				P6	100
S2	Jones	10	Paris	P#	QTY
				P1	300
				P2	400
..	.....	..	......	....	
S5	Adams	30	Athens	P#	QTY

Fig. 2   Relation S_SP (sample values)

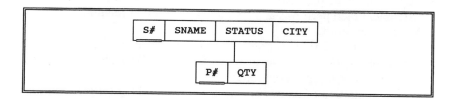

Fig. 3   S_SP as a hierarchy (?)

some values but not others. In any case, even if you do want to insist that S_SP is really a hierarchy, that "hierarchy" is at least *dynamically derived* from the relations in the database by means of an expression of the relational algebra; it isn't "hard coded" into the database like IMS-style hierarchies are, and it doesn't suffer from the same IMS-style inflexibilities.

RELATIONAL COMPARISONS REVISITED

In an earlier installment [2], I introduced the idea of relational comparisons, thereby permitting "restrict operations" such as the following:

```
S WHERE ( MATCHING SP ) [ P# ] = P [ P# ]
```

("suppliers who supply all parts"; more precisely, "suppliers such that the set of all part numbers for parts they supply is equal to the set of all part numbers in the parts relation P"). In passing, however, I also remarked in that installment that—to quote—"technically speaking, a restrict operation that includes [a relational comparison] is not a genuine restrict operation as such." Now I can explain this perhaps rather cryptic remark.

First of all, the WHERE clause in a genuine restrict operation is allowed to refer to columns of the relevant relation *only* [3]. The foregoing example is thus not "genuine" in this sense, because the two comparands certainly don't conform to this rather stringent requirement. But consider the following sequence of operations:

```
T1  :=  EXTEND S ADD ( MATCHING SP ) [ P# ] AS PARTS_SUPPLIED ;
T2  :=  EXTEND T1 ADD P [ P# ] AS ALL_PARTS ;
ANS :=  T2 WHERE PARTS_SUPPLIED = ALL_PARTS ;
```

Explanation: Relation T1 is identical to relation S except that each row additionally includes a PARTS_SUPPLIED value, representing the part numbers for all parts supplied by the applicable supplier. Relation T2 is identical to relation T1 except that each row additionally includes an ALL_PARTS value, representing the part numbers for all parts mentioned in relation P. The final assignment then performs a "genuine" restriction on relation T2 to produce the required result.

We can therefore define the original "nongenuine" restrict operation to be a shorthand for an appropriate sequence of two EXTENDs plus a "genuine" restriction, and everything is copacetic!

Note: As a matter of fact, we do exactly the same thing (at least conceptually) in the case of simpler "restrictions" such as this one:

```
S WHERE S# = 'S1'
```

Again this expression isn't a "genuine" restrict operation, because the literal operand "S1" isn't a reference to a column of relation S. This restrict operation is effectively defined to be shorthand for an EXTEND of the form

```
EXTEND S ADD 'S1' AS S1
```

followed by a "genuine" restriction in which the WHERE clause is of the form

```
... WHERE S# = S1
```

and again everything is now legitimate.

To revert to my major theme: The point is, the nested relation concept is actually *required* in order to make formal sense of the relational comparison idea previously introduced in that earlier installment [2]. And since I showed that one benefit of relational comparisons was that they solved certain "zero-case DIVIDE" problems, it follows that nested relation support is conceptually prerequisite to that solution too. (Furthermore, it turns out that relational comparisons also solve certain "zero-case SUMMARIZE" problems; I didn't discuss this issue in that earlier installment [2], but again it follows that nested relation support is prerequisite to that solution. See my book *An Introduction to Database Systems* [3] for further discussion.)

WHAT ABOUT NESTED *BASE* RELATIONS?

Given that nested *derived* relations are sometimes desirable, the obvious question is: What about nested *base* relations? Can we imagine a situation where we might want such a thing? Note that (of course) nested base relations must at least be *legal;* we certainly don't want any unnecessary formal distinctions between derived and base relations. Thus, the question is rather: Are nested base relations ever a good idea in practice? And the answer (of course!) is yes, sometimes they are.

Take another look at relation S_SP (Fig. 1). That relation is almost certainly a bad candidate for a base relation; in fact, all of the old arguments against hierarchies apply, despite the fact that (as we saw earlier) to think of S_SP as a hierarchy is a slightly confused thing to do.

> *Aside:* "The old arguments against hierarchies" can be summed up in one word: **asymmetry.** In the case of S_SP in particular, that asymmetry leads to problems over inserting a new shipment (a new operator is required), updating an existing shipment (a new operator is required), deleting an existing shipment (a new operator is required), deleting a part (a complex CASCADE is required), and other operations. And what criteria are there for choosing one hierarchy

over another?—for example, why not nest shipments inside parts instead of inside suppliers? To quote Polya [4] (writing in a different context): "Try to treat symmetrically what is symmetrical, and do not destroy wantonly any natural symmetry." *End of aside.*

However, the fact that nested relations do very often seem to make bad base relations should best be seen as a *guideline,* not as a hard and fast prohibition. Consider the following example. The requirement is to design a base relation to document the candidate keys for an arbitrary relation R (note that such a base relation might be needed, for example, inside a database design tool—or even inside the regular database itself, as part of the catalog). Recall that a candidate key for R is a *set* of columns of R. Hence the obvious design is

```
R_CKS { CK }
```

where the values in column CK are relations, representing sets of columns of R. For example, suppose R is the relation MARRIAGES, defined as follows:

```
MARRIAGES { WIFE    ... , HUSBAND ... , WEDDING_DATE ... }
          CANDIDATE KEY { WIFE, HUSBAND }
          CANDIDATE KEY { HUSBAND, WEDDING_DATE }
          CANDIDATE KEY { WEDDING_DATE, WIFE }
```

Then the corresponding relation MARRIAGES_CKS would look as shown in Fig. 4. Note that this relation consists of one column and three rows. Note too that it has a relation-valued column as its (sole) candidate key!—in other words, it satisfies the constraint

```
CANDIDATE KEY { CK }
```

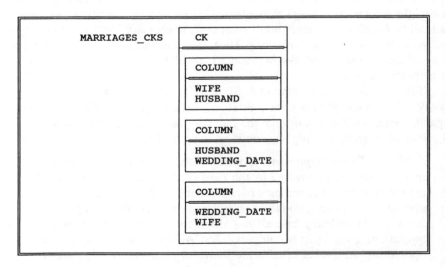

Fig. 4   Relation MARRIAGES_CKS (first version)

Now, it would certainly be possible to come up with an alternative design that does not involve a nested relation, by inventing a unique name for each candidate key (see Fig. 5). But it seems to me that this alternative design is awkward and unnatural. It's certainly more difficult to manage than the previous design. For example, consider what's involved in guaranteeing that no candidate key is represented twice. In the first version, the constraint CANDIDATE KEY (CK) suffices. In the second version, the constraint has to look—at its simplest!—something like this:

```
IF MY.CK ≠ MX.CK THEN
     EXISTS MZ ( MZ.CK = MX.CK
               AND NOT EXISTS MW
                  ( MW.CK = MY.CK AND
                    MW.COLUMN = MY.COLUMN ) )
```

Here MX, MY, MZ, and MW represent rows of relation MARRIAGES_CKS (Fig. 5 version). *Exercise for the reader:* What's involved in each of the two cases in guaranteeing that no "candidate key" contains any of the other candidate keys as a proper subset?—i.e., no "candidate key" violates the irreducibility requirement for candidate keys?

MARRIAGES_CKS	CK	COLUMN
	CK1	WIFE
	CK1	HUSBAND
	CK2	HUSBAND
	CK2	WEDDING_DATE
	CK3	WEDDING_DATE
	CK3	WIFE

Fig. 5   Relation MARRIAGES_CKS (second version)

Overall, therefore, it does seem that the nested relation design is more attractive. In this connection, the following quote from Codd's 1970 paper on the relational model is interesting: "The writer knows of no application that would require some candidate key to have a relation-valued component" (slightly paraphrased). The MARRIAGES example does seem to be a case where a relation-valued candidate key component is at least desirable, if not exactly 100 percent required.

CONCLUDING REMARKS

There's one final point I'd like to make, as follows: Permitting domains (and therefore columns) to contain relations involves comparatively little in the way of additional learning on the part of the user! To paraphrase Hugh Darwen [1], we need relations anyway "on the outside"; and if we need them on the outside, we have to understand them anyway, and we have to know how to perform relational algebra operations, and relational comparisons, and relational assignments (and so on) anyway. Thus, if we need any kind of collective data type at all on the "inside," then surely relations are the one requiring the minimum of extra learning. And the minimum amount of extra syntax in the query language. And the minimum number of extra pages in the documentation. And so on.

To close, here's this month's problem (acknowledgments to Hugh Darwen again for this one). I decided to throw a party, so I drew up a list of people I wanted to invite and made some preliminary soundings. The response was good, but several people made their acceptance conditional on the acceptance of certain other invitees. For example, Bob and Cal both said they would come if Amy came; Hal said he would come if either Don and Eve both came or Fay came; Guy said he would come anyway; Joe said he would come if Bob and Amy both came; and so on. Design a database to show whose acceptance is based on whose. Also (much harder!), write a query to determine who I need to persuade to attend in order to ensure that *every* invitee in fact attends.

REFERENCES

1. Hugh Darwen: "Relation-Valued Attributes," in C. J. Date and Hugh Darwen, *Relational Database Writings 1989–1991.* Reading, Mass.: Addison-Wesley (1992).

2. C. J. Date: "Relational Comparisons," *Database Programming & Design 7,* No. 5 (May 1994). Republished in *Relational Database Writings 1991–1994.* Reading, Mass.: Addison-Wesley (1995).

3. C. J. Date: *An Introduction to Database Systems* (6th edition). Reading, Mass.: Addison-Wesley (1995).

4. G. Polya: *How To Solve It* (2nd edition). Princeton: Princeton University Press (1971).

We Don't Need Composite Columns

Why language design is hard—a case study

Relations often have composite keys. And composite keys can lead to clumsy and awkward queries. For instance, consider the following education database:

```
COURSE { COURSE#, TITLE }
   PRIMARY KEY { COURSE# }

OFFERING { COURSE#, OFF#, LOC }
   PRIMARY KEY { COURSE#, OFF# }
   FOREIGN KEY { COURSE# }
         REFERENCES COURSE ...

ENROLLMENT { COURSE#, OFF#, EMP#, GRADE }
   PRIMARY KEY { COURSE#, OFF#, EMP# }
   FOREIGN KEY { COURSE#, OFF# }
         REFERENCES OFFERING ...
```

The SQL query to get course number and offering number for all New York offerings in which employee E1 is enrolled might look like this:

```
SELECT  E.COURSE#, E.OFF#
FROM    ENROLLMENT E, OFFERING O
WHERE   E.EMP# = 'E1'
AND     E.COURSE# = O.COURSE#
AND     E.OFF# = O.OFF#
AND     O.LOC = 'New York' ;
```

Notice that each of COURSE# and OFF# is mentioned three times in this query. Wouldn't it be nice if we could somehow regard the combination of

Originally published under the title "Say No to Composite Columns" in *Database Programming & Design 8,* No. 5, May 1995. Reprinted by permission of Miller Freeman Inc.

COURSE# and OFF# as a single thing, with a single name—CO#, say? Certainly we could save ourselves some writing:

```
SELECT  E.CO#
FROM    ENROLLMENT E, OFFERING O
WHERE   E.EMP# = 'E1'
AND     E.CO# = O.CO#
AND     O.LOC = 'New York' ;
```

It thus seems natural to consider the possibility of introducing single names for column combinations—in other words, supporting *composite columns*. *Note:* It's not just key columns that might benefit from such support, of course, but keys are probably the most important case.

ARE "COMPOSITE COLUMNS" COLUMNS?

Seems like a simple enough requirement and a simple enough thing to do, doesn't it? But sometimes "simple" things can turn out to be surprisingly complicated. Let's investigate.

First of all, let $R1\{A,B,C\}$ and $R2\{A,B,C\}$ be two relations of the same type. (Recall that two relations are of the same type if and only if they have the same heading, which means in particular that they have the same column names [1]. Of course, I'm assuming here that A, B, and C are good old *non*-composite columns.) Now, I can certainly agree that we might want to refer to the combination of A and B in $R1$ as, say, X and the combination of B and C in $R2$ as, say, Y. But I don't want the introduction of those names X and Y to have any effect on the "true" make-up of $R1$ and $R2$. In particular, I don't want to find that we now suddenly have two relations $R1\{X,C\}$ and $R2\{A,Y\}$ that are no longer of the same type! I conclude that X and Y, whatever else they might be, aren't column names in the usual sense—not even dynamically introduced column names—and hence that the "composite columns" they denote aren't really columns *per se* at all.

Another example: Given $R1\{A,B\}$ and $R2\{B,C\}$, I want $R1$ JOIN $R2$ to mean what it always did mean, namely the join of $R1$ and $R2$ on B, even if I choose to introduce the name X for the combination of A and B in $R1$ and that very same name X for the combination of B and C in $R2$. Again I conclude that the objects denoted by names like X in this example, whatever else they might be, aren't columns in the usual sense.

Now, given two relations $R1\{A,B\}$ and $R2\{A,C\}$ that are "almost" of the same type except for the B *vs.* C naming difference, we do already have a mechanism (column renaming—"RENAME *column* AS *column*") for making them fully of the same type. I don't want two different ways of doing the same thing if I can avoid it; thus, I don't want whatever mechanism we invent for composite columns to duplicate or overlap with the mechanism we already have for renaming individual columns. Once again I conclude that objects like X and Y in the examples above aren't just column names (especially as I think—see below—that the ability to rename columns in the RENAME sense is required, in general, in order even to be able to *define* things like X and Y).

Next, I can see that, given relation $R\{A,B,C\}$, we might want to refer to the combination of A and B in R as X and the combination of B and C in R as Z (so that X and Z "overlap" in R). Yet again I conclude that the things denoted by names like X and Z here, whatever else they might be, aren't columns in the usual sense (genuine columns don't overlap).

Furthermore, if a "composite column" is indeed a column, then presumably we would have to allow "composite column" components to be composite columns in turn (certainly it would be very artificial in the theory to prohibit such a thing). Now, I'll admit that I haven't thought this aspect through in detail, but it does seem likely on the face of it to lead to additional complexities—complexities that are primarily just an annoyance, too, because it also seems likely that such a feature wouldn't be used much in practice. Once again I conclude that "composite columns," whatever else they might be, aren't columns in the usual sense.

WHAT ABOUT COMPOSITE TYPES?

Earlier in this series [1] I explained that **"row"** is a type constructor in the relational model.* You might think, therefore, that in order to introduce the name X for the combination $\{A,B\}$ in $R\{A,B,C\}$, we could first introduce a new data type XT defined as ROW(A:AT,B:BT)—where AT and BT are the data types corresponding to A and B, respectively—and then redefine R to replace columns A and B by a single column X, where X is defined on XT. (We would also have to define access operators called A and B to provide access to the A and B components of X, for otherwise existing programs that refer to A and B will now fail!)

This approach works, but it does seem to be using a sledgehammer to crack a nut; indeed, the user-defined data type mechanism is much too cumbersome for the comparatively trivial requirement under consideration here.

---

*This statement is true, but only in the sense that **"row"** is effectively invoked by the type constructor **"relation"** (in particular, there are no row *variables* in the relational model. See Chapter 12.

ARE "COMPOSITE COLUMNS" JUST SHORTHANDS?

So let's try the following. First, let's agree, just for the duration of the present installment, to refer to "composite column names" as *shorthands*. Then we can introduce a new operation of the form

```
CREATE SHORTHAND shorthand
    FOR relation . { item-commalist } ;
```

where *relation* is a named relation (typically a base relation), each *item* is either a column of that relation or an expression of the form RENAME *column* AS *column,* and *shorthand* is a name that can be used as a shorthand for the specified set of column names, considered as a single object. It's an error if *shorthand* is identical to any existing column name or existing shorthand for the specified relation. No significance attaches to the sequence in which items are specified within the commalist. Here are some examples:

```
CREATE SHORTHAND CO#
    FOR OFFERING . { COURSE#, OFF# } ;

CREATE SHORTHAND CO#
    FOR ENROLLMENT . { COURSE#, OFF# } ;
```

For the sake of the next example, suppose that the course number column in OFFERING is called C# instead of COURSE#. Then the shorthand CO# for OFFERING might be defined as follows:

```
CREATE SHORTHAND CO#
    FOR OFFERING . { RENAME C# AS COURSE#, OFF# } ;
```

With this definition, the shorthand CO# for OFFERING will still match the shorthand CO# for ENROLLMENT, as is presumably required. (See the next section for an explanation of exactly how that "matching" process works.)

We also need:

```
DROP SHORTHAND shorthand FOR relation ;
```

(semantics left as an exercise for the reader). Note that operations such as DROP BASE RELATION, DROP VIEW, etc., will cause certain implicit DROP SHORTHANDs to be executed, in general.

"COMPOSITE COLUMN" OPERATORS

Now we need to consider what it means to *compare* two "composite columns." In keeping with our usual rules for such operations, I will first of all insist that the comparison "*S1* Θ *S2*" is legal only if the shorthands *S1* and *S2* are of the same type—meaning, specifically, that each of *S1* and *S2* has exactly the same set of column-name components, and columns with the same name are of the same type in turn.

Next, "=" and "≠" comparisons present no problem and can easily be supported. That is, if *S1* and *S2* are shorthands of the same type, each with components *A, B, . . . , Z*, then the expression "*S1* = *S2*" is defined to be shorthand for the expression

```
S1.A = S2.A AND
S1.B = S2.B AND
........ AND
S1.Z = S2.Z
```

where *S1.A* denotes the *A* component of *S1* and so on (see the second SQL query near the beginning of this installment for an illustration). Likewise, the expression "*S1* ≠ *S2*" is defined to be shorthand for the expression

```
S1.A ≠ S2.A OR
S1.B ≠ S2.B OR
........ OR
S1.Z ≠ S2.Z
```

(Neither of these "expansions" is intended to be valid syntax, of course; specifically, qualified names of the form *S1.A* (etc.) aren't meant to be legal.)

Note carefully, however, that no other comparison operators make sense. For example, the expression "*S1* < *S2*" makes sense only if the components of *S1* and *S2* are regarded as having a left to right sequence (why, exactly?), which by definition they don't. Indeed, such left to right sequencing is deliberately *not* part of the relational model (although it *is* part of SQL!). Note, therefore, that "composite columns" are of no help with ORDER BY clauses.

We also need to be able to write shorthand "literals," so that we can (for example) compare a value of CO# in the OFFERING relation with some literal value. An obvious syntax is as suggested in this example:

```
SELECT  ...
FROM    OFFERING
WHERE   CO# = ( COURSE#:'C1', OFF#:'O1' ) ;
```

(though SQL would probably rely on left to right component sequence instead of using explicit component names).

We also have to think about *assignments*. I don't think there are any significant new problems in this area. Here's an example:

```
UPDATE OFFERING
SET    CO# = ( COURSE#:'C9', OFF#:'O9' )
WHERE  CO# = ( COURSE#:'C1', OFF#:'O1' ) ;
```

EFFECT ON THE RELATIONAL ALGEBRA

I now consider the effect of shorthands as described above on the operators of the relational algebra. The only operators that refer explicitly to columns by name (in our dialect of the algebra) are *rename, restrict, project,* and *summarize.* For these operations, it seems reasonable to permit shorthands to appear wherever column names can appear. Hence:

- *Rename:* We might as well permit the renaming of a shorthand (though I can't immediately see why you would ever want to do this). Such renaming would *not* rename the components.

- *Restrict:* Shorthands can appear in the comparison portion of a restriction, as already discussed.

- *Project:* Shorthands can appear as elements within the set of things over which a projection is taken (though there are some nasty implications here, having to do with the avoidance of duplicate column names in the result, that I don't want to discuss in detail).

- *Summarize:* Shorthands can appear as elements within the BY clause— that is, the set of things over which the summarization is done—though again there are some nasty implications that I choose not to discuss here.

    Aside: As I suggested earlier (when I said that *R1* JOIN *R2* means what it always did mean, namely the join of *R1* and *R2* on common columns), other operations, which refer to columns only implicitly, are not affected by the presence of shorthands. But I should point out in passing that this fact could be a trap for the unwary, who might—not unreasonably—expect such operations to be performed on the basis of common *shorthands* instead of, or as well as, common columns. *End of aside.*

Next, we have to worry about *closure*—specifically, about *inheritance* of shorthands. For example, if I restrict ENROLLMENTs to just the ones for employee E1, I presumably still want the shorthand CO# to apply to the result; in fact, I was tacitly relying on this fact in my original example. Indeed, without such inheritance the whole exercise would be pretty pointless!

For *rename, restrict,* and *extend,* inheritance seems straightforward. For *project,* however, complications start to creep in. What if the projection is taken over all the columns of a given shorthand but not over the shorthand *per se?* Perhaps we can agree that the given shorthand does still apply to the result in such a case, though I would be the first to stress that this idea would need further investigation before we could be sure it was acceptable. Analogous remarks apply to *summarize.*

Turning to the operators that take two operands: First, *join* seems fairly straightforward, since all of the columns (and hence all of the shorthands) of both inputs appear in the output. But problems arise over *union* and *difference.* Do we have to say that a given shorthand must apply to both inputs in order to apply to the output? That would seem unduly restrictive. Do we then rather have to say that the output inherits *all* shorthands from both inputs? That would seem especially odd in the case of *difference,* if the second operand had a shorthand and the first didn't.

CONCLUDING REMARKS

What an awful lot of complication arises from such an apparently simple requirement! And how easy it would be to provide a "quick fix" solution to the problem that would lead to other complications further down the road! Language design is indeed difficult, if you want to make a good job of it.

Frankly, it's my considered opinion that the rather trivial piece of functionality we've been trying to provide is simply not worth all of the complexity it seems to engender. In fact, let me now point out what some of you will already have realized, namely that in many cases the conventional view mechanism can be used to provide the required functionality anyway (*without* cluttering up the language and the manual and the implementation and the poor user's brain with all kinds of additional complications). For example:

```
CREATE VIEW OV AS
     SELECT ( COURSE# || '    ' || OFF# ) AS CO#, LOC
     FROM    OFFERING ;

CREATE VIEW EV AS
     SELECT ( COURSE# || '    ' || OFF# ) AS CO#, EMP#, GRADE
     FROM    ENROLLMENT ;

SELECT EV.CO#
FROM   OV, EV
WHERE  EV.EMP# = 'E1'
AND    EV.CO# = OV.CO#
AND    OV.LOC = 'New York' ;
```

Furthermore, the derived column CO# (unlike the CO# shorthand discussed earlier) *can* be useful in an ORDER BY clause.

In closing, I remark that SQL/92 does in fact include some composite column support—it has something it calls a *row constructor,* which basically consists of a commalist of scalar expressions enclosed in parentheses:

```
( scalar-expression, scalar-expression, ... )
```

Row constructors can be used in various contexts, including in particular INSERT statements (though not UPDATE statements) and comparisons. Furthermore, the comparison operator is not limited to = and ≠ but can also be <, >, ≤, or ≥. For this month's puzzle corner, you're invited to give as precise a definition as you can of the semantics of such comparisons. Don't forget that some of the scalar-expression components might evaluate to null . . .

REFERENCES

1. C. J. Date: "Domains, Data Types, and Objects," *Database Programming & Design 7,* Nos. 6–7 (June–July 1994). Republished in *Relational Database Writings 1991–1994.* Reading, Mass.: Addison-Wesley (1995).

The Department of Redundancy Department

The arguments against duplicate rows revisited

In an earlier installment [1] I tried to explain why duplicate rows (hereinafter abbreviated to just *duplicates*) are prohibited in the relational model. A subsequent letter from a reader, Robert A. Alps, dated December 10th, 1993, raised questions about some of the arguments in that earlier installment. And it seemed to me that it might be worth airing some of the comments from Alps's letter, and my responses to them, before a wider audience; hence this month's column.

First of all, I should make it clear that Alps wasn't saying that duplicates were a good thing. To quote his letter:

> I am not arguing in favor of duplicates, rather against some of your arguments opposing [them]. I only want to be sure the arguments are sound before concluding "Out, damned duplicate."

THE PENNIES EXAMPLE

In my original column, I said that individual objects must be identifiable (that is, distinguishable from all other objects), because if an object isn't identifiable, it's impossible even to talk about it, let alone perform any kind

Originally published under the title "And Cauldron Bubble" in *Database Programming & Design 8,* No. 6, June 1995. Reprinted by permission of Miller Freeman Inc.

of operation upon it or use it for any sensible purpose. Alps countered with the following example:

> Imagine a bag of 100 newly minted pennies. You can reach into the bag and pull one out and while it is in your hand it has a special identity (of being the penny in your hand). But as soon as you place that penny back in the bag, it loses that special identity and becomes, once again, indistinguishable from the others. Is there some useful operation we can perform on indistinguishable objects? Certainly. To the extent that we have information regarding their number, we may perform mathematical operations using that information. If we know that one bag contains 100 pennies and another contains 200 pennies then we know that the combination of the two bags holds 300 pennies. This is a useful operation.

Now, obviously I agree that the individual pennies in a bag of 100 pennies can be regarded as indistinguishable from one another **at a certain level of discourse.** Surely, however, the point is that the entities under discussion here aren't individual pennies; rather, they're the *collective* entities "bags of pennies." Those collective entities in turn have a certain property (namely, cardinality), with values 100, 200, and so on. Furthermore, those collective entities have some **id**entity, because otherwise (as I said before) we can't even refer to them; at the very least, we have to say something like "This is *this* bag of pennies and that is *that* one."

But if we ask ourselves the question "How are values of the cardinality property determined?" then I contend that we have to descend to a lower level of discourse and consider individual pennies as entities. And at this level we must be able to distinguish them in order to be able to count them! As I put it in my earlier column:

> [A] common reaction to this argument is "But I really *don't* need to distinguish among the duplicates—all I want to do is to be able to count them." The point I'm trying to make is that you do need to distinguish them, even just to count them.* This point is crucial, of course, and I really don't know how to make it any more strongly than I already have.

I further contend that Alps's example of a "useful operation"—namely, the operation of combining the bag of 100 pennies and the bag of 200 pennies to obtain a bag of 300 pennies—is (self-evidently!) an operation on bags of pennies, not an operation on individual pennies *per se*.

---

*Otherwise, how do you know which ones you've already counted?

To revert to my original column, I went on to say that the way we distinguish duplicates in general is *by their relative position;* in a bag (*aka* multiset) containing two 6's, for example, we say something like "This 6 is **here** and that 6 is over **there**," or "This is the **first** 6 and that 6 is the **second**." Alps counters by claiming that ". . . the suggestion that we place a positional ordering on duplicates in all situations appears highly artificial and patently false." Well, perhaps I should turn the argument around at this point; specifically, if you're one of those people who think that duplicates "truly exist" in some sense, then please tell me exactly—exactly, please!—how you propose to count those 100 "duplicate" pennies. I do think that anyone who advocates the position that duplicates are a good idea needs to provide a good, convincing answer to this question.

BAG THEORY

Recall that (loosely speaking) a *bag* in mathematics is a set that permits duplicates. Duplicate advocates thus sometimes claim that their approach is just as respectable as the relational approach because it too is based on solid theory (bag theory instead of set theory). In my previous column, however, I claimed that mathematical "bag theory" treatments usually start by assuming that there is a way to count duplicates! I further claimed that that assumption effectively means that *bags* are defined in terms of *sets*.

Alps replied by constructing an outline bag theory that—he claimed—didn't start with such an assumption. But I think it does! One of the three primitives of his theory is an expression of the form "count xA" which (to quote) "is intended to denote the number of times the [object] x occurs in the bag A." Now, this quote might have been meant only as an informal, intuitive remark, not as part of the theory as such, but I'm still suspicious.

In any case, the question of whether such an assumption is necessary is perhaps a red herring (and I was perhaps wrong to raise it in my original column). The point rather is that bag theory:

- Is more complex than set theory;
- Includes set theory as a proper subset (perhaps I should say *subbag*);
- Is reducible to set theory.

Occam's Razor would thus clearly suggest that we stay with sets and not get into the unnecessary complexities of bags. (As so often in a database context, Occam's Razor is peculiarly apt here; one simple way of stating it is "Entities should not be multiplied beyond necessity." A simpler way still is just "No unnecessary entities.")

THE PERFORMANCE ISSUE

In my original column I recommended that users should always ensure that query results contain no duplicates—for instance, by specifying DISTINCT at appropriate points in the query—and thus simply forget about the whole problem. However, I also pointed out that SELECT DISTINCT takes longer to execute than SELECT ALL, in general, even if the DISTINCT is effectively a "no op." Alps commented that the [performance] problem doesn't go away if the system is (re)defined to eliminate duplicates automatically:

> Imagine an address table containing street, city, state, and zip data. If a query is performed selecting city from the table under a system that [eliminates duplicates automatically], the system is going to have to go through all the same checking for duplicates that would be required if [it didn't eliminate duplicates automatically but] the query asked for DISTINCT cities.

Here I think Alps missed my point slightly. What I meant was that, because it appears that always eliminating duplicates implies performance problems, there was a strong motivation for the SQL language designers to make *not* eliminating duplicates the default. (In fact, I very specifically pointed out in reference [1] that support for duplicates can actually have a *negative* impact on performance, and my reason for doing so was precisely to provide a counterbalance to this familiar argument.) But the full implications, psychological and otherwise, of this very bad language design decision weren't thought through at the time. It's my belief that the *occasional* overhead incurred (in a well-implemented system) in always eliminating duplicates would be vastly outweighed by the benefits—including performance benefits—that such a system would provide.

Of course I understand that checking for duplicates is required regardless of whether (a) the system prohibits them or (b) the system permits them but the user specifies DISTINCT. But note that if the language is *defined* always to eliminate duplicates (at least conceptually), then the system will sometimes be able *not* to eliminate them (for intermediate results, at least, though not of course for final results) as an optimization.

SOME MORE SQL PROBLEMS

At this juncture I'd like to digress for a moment and talk about a couple of problems that are caused by duplicates for the SQL standard specifically. The following discussions are based on material from Appendix D ("Some

Outstanding Issues") from the book by Hugh Darwen and myself on the SQL/92 standard [2].

The first problem concerns Cartesian product. Part of the standard's explanation of the SQL FROM clause reads as follows:

> . . . the result of the <from clause> is the . . . Cartesian product of the tables identified by [the] <table reference>s [in that <from clause>]. The . . . Cartesian product, *CP*, is the multiset of all rows *R* such that *R* is the concatenation of a row from each of the identified tables. . . .

Note, therefore, that *CP* is not well-defined!—the fact that the standard goes on to say that "The cardinality of *CP* is the product of the cardinalities of the identified tables" notwithstanding. Consider the tables T1 and T2 shown below:

T1	C1
	0
	0

T2	C2
	1
	2

Either of the following fits the above definition for "the" Cartesian product *CP* of T1 and T2 (that is, either one could be "the" multiset referred to):

CP1	C1	C2
	0	1
	0	1
	0	2
	0	2

CP2	C1	C2
	0	1
	0	2
	0	2
	0	2

For this month's puzzle corner, the reader is invited to try his or her hand at fixing up the wording of the standard appropriately (good luck!).

Here's the second problem. Consider the following cursor definition, which is based (as usual) on the suppliers-and-parts database:

```
DECLARE X CURSOR
    FOR SELECT SP.S#, SP.QTY
        FROM    SP
```

Note that (a) cursor X permits updates; (b) the table that is visible through cursor X permits duplicates; (c) the underlying table (table SP) does *not* permit duplicates. Now suppose a positioned UPDATE or DELETE operation is executed via cursor X (UPDATE or DELETE . . . WHERE CURRENT OF X). Then there's no way, in general, of saying precisely which row of table SP is being updated or deleted by that operation. How would you fix *this* problem?

(After you've given solutions to these two SQL problems, please write out one googol times "There's no such thing as a duplicate.")

CONCLUDING REMARKS

The letter from Alps concludes: "Whether or not to allow duplicates in SQL and relational databases seems to me to be more a practical question than a theoretical one." Well, regular readers of this series will know that I don't subscribe to the notion that "theoretical" and "practical" issues are at odds with one another. *Au contraire,* it's my strong position that theory—meaning relational theory specifically—is a highly practical matter. Thus, I want the system to be built on a solid, well-established theoretical foundation (for all the obvious good *practical* reasons), and I contend that bag theory, even if it can be made independent and respectable, simply doesn't enjoy the same long pedigree and high level of acceptance that set theory does. Thus, I want to build on set theory.

Finally—at the risk of beating a dead horse—let me add the following comments (they're based on some remarks made by Hugh Darwen in a private letter to myself, and effectively sum up my position on this whole business of duplicates):

1. We all agree that databases are made up of collections of "records"—or "rows," or "tuples," or whatever—of similar format, where each record has exactly one value for each item in the format (*aka* 1NF).

2. We all agree that different kinds of collections are useful for different purposes. Sometimes lists are wonderful, sometimes arrays, sometimes queues or stacks, sometimes sets, sometimes bags, etc.

3. Of these different kinds of collections, only one is *known* to provide, singlehanded, a basis for a complete model of data. And all of the others can be mapped, if need be, to this one.

4. To insist on supporting bags is equivalent to at least one of the following (probably more than one):

   ▪ To insist on using at least two kinds of collection in one's model of data;

   ▪ To fall back on one of those kinds of collection for which no complete model of data has yet been developed, and therefore to have to go to the trouble of developing that theory (if it is available to be developed);

   ▪ To be like SQL and attempt to apply the theory of relations to bags of tuples without fully checking its applicability, consequently making mistakes (like taking relational theorems to hold equally well for such bags, or misdefining UNION), failing to provide interpretations for operations whose relational interpretations don't hold for such bags (for example, Cartesian product is no longer just AND, and projection is no longer existential quantification), and delivering inferior products to the folks who are sensible and knowledgeable enough to stay with relations only.

We don't need to argue against the (occasional) utility of bags of tuples, any more than we need to argue against the occasional utility of lists of tuples (why, those are what SQL cursors deliver!), or even stacks of tuples, queues of tuples, and arrays of tuples for that matter. In fact, why do the duplicate advocates specifically single out *bags* of tuples (only) for inclusion in their model?

REFERENCES

1. C. J. Date: "Toil and Trouble," *Database Programming & Design 7*, No. 1 (January 1994). Republished in *Relational Database Writings 1991–1994*. Reading, Mass.: Addison-Wesley (1995).

2. C. J. Date and Hugh Darwen: *A Guide to the SQL Standard* (4th edition). Reading, Mass.: Addison-Wesley (1997).

A Note on Orthogonality

What orthogonality is and why it's
A Good Thing

I've mentioned the concept of orthogonality in several previous installments without really explaining what the term means (in particular, I complained in my September 1993 column [3] about the *lack* of orthogonality in the SQL standard prior to SQL/92). It's time to clarify matters.

WHAT IS ORTHOGONALITY?

Fundamentally, orthogonality means **independence.** The specific application of the term we're concerned with here originated in the programming languages world, most particularly in the design of the language ALGOL 68 [6]. We all know that some languages are hard to learn and use and others are easy; orthogonality is one of the things that makes the easy ones easy. We say that a language is **orthogonal** if it provides (a) a comparatively small set of primitive constructs, together with (b) a consistent set of rules for putting those constructs together, and (c) every possible combination of those constructs is both legal and meaningful (in other words, a deliberate attempt has been made to avoid arbitrary restrictions).

- A simple example is provided by numbers in PL/I. Numbers in PL/I are (of course) represented by numeric expressions, and numeric expressions

Originally published in *Database Programming & Design 8,* No. 7, July 1995. Reprinted by permission of Miller Freeman Inc.

of arbitrary complexity can be used throughout the language wherever a numeric value is required—for example, as an array subscript. In other words, the concepts of **numeric expression** and **array** are clearly independent; hence, there should be no special rules regarding the combination of the two, such as (say) a rule to the effect that a numeric expression that specifies a subscript value is allowed to use "+" and "–" but not " * " or "/".

- A counterexample is provided by numbers in the SQL standard prior to SQL/92. Numbers in SQL are (again) represented by numeric expressions, but there's at least one context, namely the VALUES clause on INSERT, in which numbers must be represented by literals instead of by general expressions.

Here's another counterexample, also from SQL. Clearly, the form of the expression that's used to refer to a given column should not depend on the context in which that reference appears; yet (for example) the SALARY column of relvar EMPS is referred to as EMPS.SALARY in some contexts, as SALARY (explicitly unqualified) in others, as SALARY FROM EMPS in others, and as EMPS(SALARY) in still others.

> *Aside:* The term **relvar**—short for *relation variable*—is taken from *The Third Manifesto* [1]. From now on I intend to talk in terms of relvars, rather than tables or relations, whenever "relvar" really is the more accurate term. *End of aside.*

WHY IS ORTHOGONALITY IMPORTANT?

Orthogonality is desirable because (as can be seen from the foregoing examples) the less orthogonal a language is, the more complicated it is and—paradoxically but simultaneously—the less powerful it is.

- The language is *more complicated* because of the additional rules needed to define and document all of the various exceptions and special cases. And those additional rules make the manuals thicker, the training courses longer, the language harder to teach and learn and describe and remember and use (and so on and so on). In other words, the language gets too big and becomes intellectually unmanageable.

- The language is *less powerful* because the purpose of those additional rules is precisely to prohibit certain combinations of constructs, and hence to reduce the language's functionality. In other words, there are too many exceptions, special cases, arbitrary restrictions, and surprises (usually of an unpleasant nature).

As reference [5] puts it: "A small number of primitive constructs and a consistent set of rules for combining them is much better than simply having a large number of primitives . . . [the user] can achieve the complexity required for a given problem solution after learning only a simple set of primitive constructs." Or to quote the ALGOL 68 specification [6]: "Orthogonal design maximizes expressive power while avoiding deleterious superfluities" (this is one of my favorite quotes).

Mind you, some people would argue that it's possible to go overboard with the notion of orthogonality. The following example is based on one given by Hoare in reference [4]. In a scientific language, at least, we would probably all agree that there should be support for (a) both integer and fractional numbers and (b) both real and complex numbers. So the principle of orthogonality would apparently dictate that there should be support for complex integers! As Hoare puts it:

> In the early days of hardware design, some very ingenious but arbitrary features turned up in [instruction sets] as a result of orthogonal combinations of the function bits of an instruction, on the grounds that some clever programmer would find a use for them—and some clever programmer always did. Hardware designers have now learned more sense; but language designers are clever programmers and have not.

Indiscriminate application of the orthogonality principle should always be tempered with a little common sense.

ORTHOGONALITY AND CLOSURE

The concept of orthogonality and the concept of **closure** are related, though they're not the same thing. Closure can be defined as follows. Suppose we have a set of objects called OBJS and a set of operators called OPS that apply to the objects in OBJS. Suppose too that each operator in OPS when applied to specific objects from OBJS always produces another object in OBJS. Then the objects in OBJS and the operators in OPS together form a *closed system*. For example, the relational model is closed in this sense, because the result of applying any relational algebra operation to any relation(s) is always another relation.

If the objects in OBJS and the operators in OPS form a closed system, orthogonality then dictates that any OBJ-valued expression should be allowed wherever an OBJ value is required—*including as an operand within another OBJ-valued expression*. And so we get **nestability** (that is, the ability to write nested expressions). In the relational model, for example, the (relational) operands to any relational algebra operation can be specified by means of arbitrary relational expressions, provided only that those expressions evaluate to relations of the right type for the operation in question.

SOME SQL EXAMPLES

It's time to try and make this whole discussion a little less abstract. Here's an example I got from a friend, Chris Hultén, a few years ago. Suppose we're given the usual suppliers relvar S { S#, SNAME, STATUS, CITY }, with sample values as shown in Fig. 1. Suppose, moreover, that the relvar satisfies the functional dependency CITY → STATUS (note that the sample values of Fig. 1 are consistent with this constraint). I remark in passing that the existence of this constraint means that relvar S isn't in third normal form.

S	S#	SNAME	STATUS	CITY
	S1	Smith	20	London
	S2	Jones	10	Paris
	S3	Blake	10	Paris
	S4	Clark	20	London
	S5	Adams	30	Athens

Fig. 1   The suppliers relvar: sample values

Now consider the query "Find the average status of cities" (given the sample data of Fig. 1, the expected answer is 20). I suggest you try to formulate this query in SQL before reading further.

Discussion: The first "obvious" formulation is

```
SELECT AVG ( STATUS ) AS AVGSTAT
FROM   S ;
```

Result (incorrect): 18.
    Next attempt:

```
SELECT CITY, AVG ( STATUS ) AS AVGSTAT
FROM   S
GROUP  BY CITY ;
```

Note that the SELECT clause *must* include the CITY column (because it's mentioned in the GROUP BY clause). The trouble now, of course, is that the result contains three rows—(London,20), (Paris,10), and (Athens,30). What we really want is the *average* of the three AVGSTAT values in this result. So let's try:

```
SELECT CITY, AVG ( AVG ( STATUS ) ) AS AVGSTAT
FROM    S
GROUP   BY CITY ;
```

Well, this doesn't work—in fact, it's syntactically invalid—because SQL doesn't allow aggregate operators like AVG to be nested in this fashion.

Here at last is a correct formulation:

```
SELECT AVG ( STATUS ) AS AVGSTAT
FROM ( SELECT DISTINCT CITY, STATUS
       FROM    S ) AS XYZ ;
```

Observe the use of a nested SELECT expression in the FROM clause. The overall statement is the SQL/92 analog of the following relational algebra expression [2]:

```
SUMMARIZE S [ CITY, STATUS ] BY CITY
      ADD AVG ( STATUS ) AS AVGSTAT
```

Note carefully, however, that the correct SQL formulation (a) was not legal in the SQL standard prior to SQL/92 and (b) is still not supported by most commercial SQL implementations.* Also, I should explain that SQL/92's syntax rules expressly require the introduction of a name—XYZ in the example—for the result of the inner SELECT expression, even though that name is never referenced anywhere else in the query!

> *An aside regarding denormalization:*   Denormalization—that is, the practice of having base relvars in less than fully normalized form—is widely regarded as being "good for retrieval but bad for update." Although denormalization is not the principal subject of this month's column, it's interesting to note in passing that (as the example illustrates) it can be bad for retrieval too, in that it makes certain queries harder to express. It's worth pointing out too that even in a retrieve-only database it's still necessary to state the integrity constraints (since they define the *meaning* of the database), and full normalization provides a very simple way of stating certain important constraints. To be specific, full normalization implies that the *only* functional, multivalued, and join dependencies that hold are those that are implied by candidate keys; hence it's sufficient just to declare those keys to state those dependencies.   *End of aside.*

---

*This sentence is still true today (1998).

Here's another example. We're given the following relvars:

```
EMPS     { EMP#, INCOME }
BONUSES  { EMP#, BONUS }
```

The problem is to increment each employee's income by the applicable bonus (we assume for simplicity that every employee in EMPS is also represented in BONUSES; what difference would it make if this were not the case?).

Prior to SQL/92, the only way to deal with this problem would be to write a program that runs a cursor through the rows of EMPS, using the EMP# value from each row in turn to retrieve the applicable BONUSES row and then updating the EMPS row appropriately through that cursor. In SQL/92, however, the entire update can be done with a single statement:

```
UPDATE EMPS
SET    INCOME = INCOME + ( SELECT BONUS
                          FROM    BONUSES
                          WHERE   EMP# = EMPS.EMP# ) ;
```

The point of the example is that in an arithmetic expression such as INCOME + x, the operand x should be allowed (by virtue of orthogonality) to be *any expression that evaluates to a numeric value*—including in particular an expression such as "(SELECT BONUS ...)" that retrieves a numeric value from the database.

Note: Strictly speaking, the expression "(SELECT BONUS ...)" evaluates not to a number but to a one-row, one-column relation that *contains* a number. The implications of this point—which are serious—are unfortunately beyond the scope of the present discussion.

PUZZLE CORNER

A nondatabase puzzle this month: You're given a set of 25 statements labeled S1 to S25. Statement Si (i = 1, 2, ... , 25) is of the form "Exactly i statements in this set are false." For which values of i (if any) is Statement Si true?

REFERENCES

1. Hugh Darwen and C. J. Date: "Introducing ... The Third Manifesto," *Database Programming & Design 8,* No. 1 (January 1995). See also (a) Chapter 3 in the present book; (b) the book *Foundation for Object/Relational Databases: The Third Manifesto.* Reading, Mass.: Addison-Wesley (1998).

2. C. J. Date: "What's in a Name?", *Database Programming & Design 5,* No. 11 (November 1992). Republished in *Relational Database Writings 1991–1994.* Reading, Mass.: Addison-Wesley (1995). *Note:* This installment introduced the SUMMARIZE operation but used the keyword GROUPBY in place of BY. In future installments I'll always use BY.

3. C. J. Date: "How We Missed the Relational Boat," *Database Programming & Design 6,* No. 9 (September 1993). Republished in *Relational Database Writings 1991–1994.* Reading, Mass.: Addison-Wesley (1995).

4. C. A. R. Hoare "Hints on Programming Language Design," in Proc. SIGACT/SIGPLAN Symposium on Principles of Programming Languages (October 1973).

5. Robert W. Sebesta: *Concepts of Programming Languages.* Redwood City, Calif.: Benjamin/Cummings (1989).

6. A. van Wijngaarden et al. (eds.): *Revised Report on the Algorithmic Language ALGOL 68.* New York, NY: Springer-Verlag (1976).

Answers to Puzzle Corner Problems (Installments 31–35)

You're not still puzzling over the "puzzle corner" problems, are you?

My column this month is devoted once again to answering the various outstanding "puzzle corner" problems from the last few installments. Thanks as usual to those readers who wrote in with their own solutions.

NESTING AND UNNESTING

Source: "Nested Relations (Part 1 of 2)" (see Installment 31).

Problem statement: "NF² relations" require explicit *NEST* and *UNNEST* operations for converting between nested and unnested forms of a relation. In outline, those operators work as follows:

- Given a relation and a set of columns, NEST returns a corresponding nested relation. For example, nesting the usual suppliers relation "along" S#, SNAME, and STATUS yields a nested relation containing three rows, one for each of the three CITY values (London, Paris, and Athens); each of those rows contains the appropriate city name and a relation with heading { S#, SNAME, STATUS }, representing the suppliers in that city.

Originally published under the title "End of the Summer Blues: Did You Do Your Homework?" in *Database Programming & Design 8,* No. 8, August 1995 (the subtitle was contributed by *DBP&D* too). Reprinted by permission of Miller Freeman Inc.

■ UNNEST is the opposite of NEST, loosely speaking—though if we unnest *R* "along" some set of columns and then nest the result "along" those same columns again, we don't necessarily get back to *R!*

Give an example to show that (as just indicated) unnesting in the foregoing sense is not necessarily reversible. Can you find a necessary set of conditions under which the unnesting *is* reversible?

Solution: The following example and discussion are based on material from the paper "Relation-Valued Attributes," by Hugh Darwen [2]. Refer to Fig. 1. If we unnest relation TWO along RVX, we obtain THREE. If we now nest THREE along X (and name the resulting relation-valued column RVX once again), we obtain not TWO but ONE.

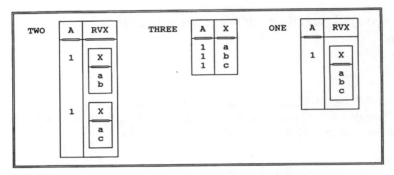

Fig. 1   Unnesting is not necessarily reversible

If we now unnest ONE along RVX, we return to THREE, and we've already seen that THREE can be nested to give ONE; thus, the NEST and UNNEST operations are indeed inverses of one another for the pair of relations THREE and ONE.

Note that in ONE, RVX is (necessarily) functionally dependent on A, which is thus a candidate key—and this fact gives us a clue to the problem of determining whether or not a given unnesting is reversible. In fact, if relation *R* has a relation-valued column *RVX*, then *R* is reversibly unnestable along *RVX* if and only if the following conditions are both satisfied:

■ No row of *R* has an empty relation as its *RVX* value (note that unnesting such a row produces no row at all in the result).

■ *RVX* is functionally dependent on the combination of all other columns of *R*. Another way of saying the same thing is that there must be some candidate key of *R* that doesn't include *RVX* as a component.

PARTY FAVORS

Source: "Nested Relations (Part 2 of 2)" (see Installment 32).

Problem statement: I decided to throw a party, so I drew up a list of people I wanted to invite and made some preliminary soundings. The response was good, but several people made their acceptance conditional on the acceptance of certain other invitees. For example, Bob and Cal both said they would come if Amy came; Hal said he would come if either Don and Eve both came or Fay came; Guy said he would come anyway; Joe said he would come if Bob and Amy both came; and so on. Design a database to show whose acceptance is based on whose. Also (much harder!), write a query to determine who I need to persuade to attend in order to ensure that *every* invitee in fact attends.

Solution: First, let me use the notation X → Y to mean that if everyone in the set of people X attends then everyone in the set of people Y will attend as well (this choice of notation is not arbitrary, of course!). For the moment, let me refer to expressions such as X → Y as *statements*.

The first and most obvious design thus consists of a single relation, IXAYWA ("if X attends, Y will attend"), containing a row for each of the given statements as shown in Fig. 2 (INV in that figure stands for invitee). Observe that columns X and Y are both relation-valued.

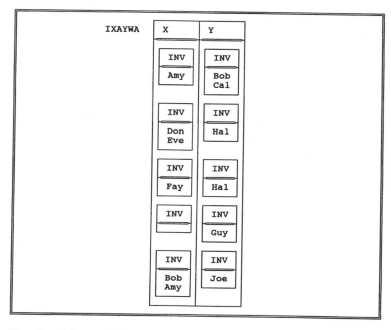

Fig. 2   Relation IXAYWA (first attempt)

However, we can do better than this. As already indicated, I chose the notation of functional dependencies (FDs) deliberately. Indeed, the statement "if X attends, Y will attend" is clearly isomorphic to the statement "the FD $X \to Y$ holds" (imagine a relation with a yes-or-no column for each of Amy, Bob, Cal, and so on, in which each row represents an attendance list that's consistent with the specified conditions). It follows that we can use the theory of FDs to reduce the amount of information we need to record explicitly in our database. In fact, we can use that theory to find what is sometimes called a *canonical cover* for the given set of statements—that is, a (usually small) set of statements that includes no redundant information and has the property that all of the original statements are implied by the statements in that set.

Detailed consideration of how to find such a cover is beyond the scope of the present discussion; indeed, this would be a suitable topic for a future installment* (however, a tutorial introduction to such matters can be found in my book *An Introduction to Database Systems* [3]). For now, let me just give a brief idea of what's involved. First, note that if the statement $X \to Y$ is true, then the statement $X' \to Y'$ is necessarily true for all supersets X' of X and all subsets Y' of Y (think about it!). We can therefore reduce the amount of information we need to record explicitly by ensuring that every statement $X \to Y$ we do record is such that the set X is as small as possible and the set Y is as large as possible—meaning, more precisely, that:

- Nobody can be removed from the set X without the resulting statement no longer being true;
- Nobody can be added to the set Y without the resulting statement no longer being true.

Note further that the statement $X \to Y$ is necessarily true for all sets Y such that Y is a subset of X (in particular, $X \to X$ is always true; for example, "if Amy attends, Amy will attend" is obviously true). We refer to such cases as *trivial* and need not bother to record them explicitly in the database.

Note too, incidentally, that if relation IXAYWA contains only those statements that constitute a canonical cover, then column X will be a candidate key for the relation.

Finally, the problem of determining who I need to persuade to attend in order to ensure that every invitee in fact attends is equivalent to the problem of determining the candidate keys for a relation given the FDs that hold for that relation. Detailed consideration of this latter problem is (again) beyond the scope of the present discussion; see the paper "Candidate Keys for Relations," by Lucchesi and Osborn, for a detailed treatment [5].

---

*See Installments 39–40.

ROW COMPARISONS

Source: "We Don't Need Composite Columns" (see Installment 33).

Problem statement: SQL/92 supports something it calls a *row constructor,* which basically consists of a commalist of scalar expressions enclosed in parentheses:

```
( scalar-expression, scalar-expression, ... )
```

Row constructors can be used in various contexts, including in particular INSERT statements (though not UPDATE statements) and comparisons. Furthermore, the comparison operator is not limited to = and ≠ but can also be <, >, ≤, or ≥. You're invited to give as precise a definition as you can of the semantics of such comparisons (don't forget that some of the scalar-expression components might evaluate to null).

Solution: It's worth noting that the SQL/92 committee got into considerable difficulty over this very issue!—several iterations were needed before they got it right. The following explanations are taken from the book *A Guide to the SQL Standard,* by Hugh Darwen and myself [4]. First, let the two row constructors evaluate to rows *Left* and *Right*, respectively. *Left* and *Right* must be of the same degree (that is, they must contain the same number, n say, of scalar values each). Let i range from 1 to n, and let the ith components of *Left* and *Right* be Li and Ri, respectively (note that the components are indeed ordered left to right in SQL, and thus the term "ith component" makes sense). The data types of Li and Ri must be compatible.[*] Then the result of the comparison condition is defined as follows. First we define the *true* cases:

- "*Left = Right*" is *true* if and only if for all i, "$Li = Ri$" is *true*
- "*Left ≠ Right*" is *true* if and only if there exists some j such that "$Lj \neq Rj$" is *true*
- "*Left < Right*" is *true* if and only if there exists some j such that "$Lj < Rj$" is *true* and for all $i < j$, "$Li = Ri$" is *true*
- "*Left > Right*" is *true* if and only if there exists some j such that "$Lj > Rj$" is *true* and for all $i < j$, "$Li = Ri$" is *true*
- "*Left ≤ Right*" is *true* if and only if "*Left < Right*" is *true* or "*Left = Right*" is *true*
- "*Left ≥ Right*" is *true* if and only if "*Left > Right*" is *true* or "*Left = Right*" is *true*

---

[*]According to the SQL definition of type compatibility, that is—see Installment 38.

Next the *false* cases:

- *"Left = Right"* is *false* if and only if *"Left ≠ Right"* is *true*
- *"Left ≠ Right"* is *false* if and only if *"Left = Right"* is *true*
- *"Left < Right"* is *false* if and only if *"Left ≥ Right"* is *true*
- *"Left > Right"* is *false* if and only if *"Left ≤ Right"* is *true*
- *"Left ≤ Right"* is *false* if and only if *"Left > Right"* is *true*
- *"Left ≥ Right"* is *false* if and only if *"Left < Right"* is *true*

Finally, let "$" stand for any of $=, ≠, <, ≤, >, ≥$. Then:

- *"Left $ Right"* is *unknown* if and only if it is not *true* and not *false*

There's quite a lot more that could be said on this topic, but I'm a little short on space. Without going into details, therefore, I'll just mention a couple of strange aspects of SQL's row comparisons, both of them having to do with nulls. First, the IS NULL and IS NOT NULL operators are extended to apply to rows as well as scalars—with the counterintuitive consequence that the expressions

```
r IS NOT NULL
```

and

```
NOT r IS NULL
```

are no longer interchangeable!

Second, some new comparison operators—IS [NOT] TRUE, IS [NOT] FALSE, and IS [NOT] UNKNOWN—are also added. Each of them applies to conditional expressions; for example, we might write

```
( X > Y ) IS UNKNOWN
```

This expression will return *true* if and only if at least one of X and Y evaluates to null (in other words, if and only if the comparison X > Y evaluates to *unknown*). And one counterintuitive aspect of these operators is that the expressions

```
p IS NOT TRUE
```

and

```
NOT p
```

are no longer interchangeable!

Again, refer to *A Guide to the SQL Standard* [4] for further discussion of both of these strange properties.

I might mention too that in his book [1], Codd also gets into some difficulty over this business of row comparisons. In this context, Codd's rows (like SQL's) have a left to right ordering to their components. To quote: " To explain the meaning of a comparator such as LESS THAN ... suppose that C, consisting of C1, then C2, then C3, is to be compared with D, consisting of D1, then D2, then D3. The condition C < D is equivalent to making the sequence of tests

```
C1 < D1, then C2 < D2, then C3 < D3
```

The first test that fails causes the whole comparison to fail." (Slightly paraphrased.) The implication is that the whole comparison succeeds—that is, evaluates to *true*—if and only if every component test succeeds (I ignore nulls, of course!). If this implication is correct, then the following comparisons evaluate as indicated:

```
( 1, 4 ) ≠ ( 1, 2 )  :  false
( 1, 7 ) < ( 2, 6 )  :  false
( 1, 7 ) ≥ ( 2, 6 )  :  false
```

Yet intuition would surely say that (a) the first should be *true,* and (b) of the second and third, exactly one should be *true* and exactly one *false*—though which should be which is highly debatable. (Perhaps I should remind you at this point that my own position is that row components should *not* have a left to right ordering, and hence that operators such as "<" actually make no sense at all.)

BAGS AND BAGGAGE

Source: "The Department of Redundancy Department" (see Installment 34).

Problem statement: Part of the SQL standard's explanation of the FROM clause reads as follows:

> [The] result of the <from clause> is the ... Cartesian product of the tables identified by [the] <table reference>s [in that <from clause>]. The ... Cartesian product, *CP,* is the multiset of all rows *r* such that *r* is the concatenation of a row from each of the identified tables.

Note, therefore, that *CP* is not well-defined!—the fact that the standard goes on to say that "the cardinality of *CP* is the product of the cardinalities of the identified tables" notwithstanding. Consider the tables T1 and T2 shown below:

T1	C1
	0
	0

T2	C2
	1
	2

Either of the following fits the above definition for "the" Cartesian product *CP* of T1 and T2 (that is, either one could be "the" multiset referred to):

CP1

C1	C2
0	1
0	1
0	2
0	2

CP2

C1	C2
0	1
0	2
0	2
0	2

The reader is invited to try his or her hand at improving the wording of the standard appropriately.

Solution: The solution, of course, involves defining a mapping from each of the (bag) argument tables to a proper *set*, and likewise defining a mapping of the (bag) result table—that is, the desired Cartesian product—to a proper *set*. The details are tedious but straightforward, and I omit them here. In my opinion, however, this exercise serves to point up the fact yet again that one of the most fundamental concepts in the entire SQL language (namely, the concept that tables should permit duplicate rows) is *fundamentally flawed*—and cannot be repaired without, in effect, dispensing with the concept altogether.

A LOGICAL PROBLEM

Source: "A Note on Orthogonality" (see Installment 35).

Problem statement: You're given a set of 25 statements labeled S1 to S25. Statement Si ($i = 1, 2, \ldots, 25$) is of the form "Exactly i statements in this set are false." For which values of i (if any) is Statement Si true?

Solution: Note first of all that every statement in the set contradicts all the rest; hence at most one can be true. If none of them is true, then statement S25 is true, which is a contradiction! So exactly one statement is true, implying that 24 statements are false, implying that statement S24 (only) is true.

Of course, there's nothing special about the value 25—a similar analysis will apply to a set of such statements of cardinality N for any N greater than one. (What happens if N is one?)

REFERENCES

1. E. F. Codd: *The Relational Model for Database Management Version 2.* Reading, Mass.: Addison-Wesley (1990).

2. Hugh Darwen: "Relation-Valued Attributes," in C. J. Date and Hugh Darwen, *Relational Database Writings 1989–1991.* Reading, Mass.: Addison-Wesley (1992).

3. C. J. Date: "Functional Dependencies," Chapter 9 of *An Introduction to Database Systems* (6th edition). Reading, Mass.: Addison-Wesley (1995).

4. C. J. Date and Hugh Darwen: *A Guide to the SQL Standard* (4th edition). Reading, Mass.: Addison-Wesley (1997).

5. Claudio L. Lucchesi and Sylvia L. Osborn: "Candidate Keys for Relations," *J. Comp. and Sys. Sciences 17,* No. 2 (1978).

Domains Aren't Relations!

Addressing a serious and all too common misconception

I have little new to say this month—little, that is, that I haven't said in previous articles [7] and/or installments of my regular column [3–6]. But the topic I want to address is such a crucial and fundamental one, and one that still seems to cause so many people so much confusion, that I felt I ought to try to clarify matters one more time. So here goes.

As my title indicates, the "crucial and fundamental" point at issue is this:

Domains aren't relations!

The contrary—I'm tempted to say heretical—view that domains *are* relations, or at least a special case thereof, does raise its head from time to time; an item by Douglas W. Hubbard in *DBMS* [8] provides a recent example. In what follows, I want to point out some of the many reasons why this contrary view is seriously in error.

HEADINGS AND BODIES

Note added on republication: It's probably only fair to warn the reader that the material of this section and the next is repeated at several points throughout this book (primarily in Installments 59 and 60 and Chapters 3 and 13). I apologize

Originally published in *Database Programming & Design 8,* No. 9, September 1995. Reprinted by permission of Miller Freeman Inc.

for the overlap, but it's a direct consequence of the material's importance, of course.

I begin by reminding you that every relation has two parts, a *heading* and a *body* [1]; the heading is a set of column-name/domain-name pairs, and the body is a set of rows that conform to that heading. An example (a bill-of-materials relation) is given in Fig. 1. In that example:

- The column names are MAJOR_P#, MINOR_P#, and QTY;

- The corresponding domain names are P#, P#, and QTY, respectively;

- Each row includes a MAJOR_P# value (drawn from the P# domain), a MINOR_P# value (also drawn from the P# domain), and a QTY value (drawn from the QTY domain).

Informally, of course, we often ignore the domain-name components of the heading, and say, for example, that the heading of the relation in Fig. 1 is just the set of column names { MAJOR_P#, MINOR_P#, QTY }. See also the PD/PV example in the section "A Superficial Similarity," later, for another illustration of this point.

MAJOR_P# : P#	MINOR_P# : P#	QTY : QTY
P1	P2	2
P1	P3	4
P2	P3	1
P2	P4	3
P3	P5	9
P4	P5	8
P5	P6	3

Fig. 1   A bill-of-materials relation (P# = part number)

You'll also recall that the heading represents a certain *predicate* (or truth-valued function), and each row in the body represents a certain *true proposition,* derived from that predicate by substituting certain domain values (arguments) for that predicate's parameters ("instantiating the predicate") [5]. In the case of the bill-of-materials relation, for example, the predicate is:

```
part MAJOR_P# contains QTY of part MINOR_P#
```

(the three parameters are MAJOR_P#, QTY, and MINOR_P#). And the corresponding true propositions are

```
part P1 contains 2 of part P2
```

(obtained by substituting the arguments P1, 2, and P2);

```
part P1 contains 4 of part P3
```

(obtained by substituting the arguments P1, 4, and P3); and so on. As the example illustrates, therefore:

- *Domains* **represent the things we can talk about;**
- *Relations* **represent the truths we utter about those things.**

One immediate consequence is that domains and relations are clearly different things!—and I would be within my rights to stop the discussion right here. However, there are several more points that need to be made regarding this overall question.

RELATIONS AND RELVARS

In this column a couple of months ago I mentioned that henceforth I would try always to use the term **relvar** (short for *relation variable*), instead of "table" or "relation," whenever "relvar" really was the more accurate term. The distinction between relvars and relations is particularly relevant to the subject of this month's column, so I'd like to digress for a moment to explain it one more time. (The explanation that follows is taken from an earlier article by Hugh Darwen and myself [7].)

Suppose we say (in some programming language):

```
DECLARE N INTEGER ...
```

N here isn't an integer *per se,* it's an integer *variable* whose *values* are integers *per se* (different integers at different times). Likewise, if we say (in SQL):

```
CREATE TABLE T ...
```

T here isn't a relation (or table) *per se,* it's a relation *variable* whose *values* are relations *per se* (different relations at different times).

In practice, we tend to use the term *relation* when we really mean *relation variable* (and I've followed this practice myself throughout most of this series, as you might have noticed). But the practice is unfortunate, and historically has led to much confusion—including the confusion that is the major topic of this month's column. As already stated, therefore, I'll try to be as clear as I can on this point for the rest of this month's column, and indeed throughout this series of columns from this installment forward. Specifically, I'll use the term *relvar* as a convenient shorthand for *relation variable,* and I'll take care to phrase my remarks in terms of relvars rather than relations when it's really relvars that I mean. (And I'd like to encourage you to do likewise!)

Having clarified this distinction, I now claim that when people say that domains are relations (of a kind), they usually mean that domains are *relvars* (of a kind). Let's take a closer look . . .

A SUPERFICIAL SIMILARITY

Consider Fig. 2, which shows a domain PD and (the current value of) a relvar PV, both containing part numbers. PD and PV certainly do look rather similar to one another, at least superficially. But their interpretations are very different! Domain PD contains the set of *all possible* part numbers (I assume for the sake of the example that there are exactly six such). Relvar PV, by contrast, contains the set of part numbers *currently represented in the database* (in other words, the set of part numbers currently of interest to the business for some reason).

PD	P#		PV	P#
	P1			P1
	P2			P3
	P3			P5
	P4			P6
	P5			
	P6			

Fig. 2   Domain PD and relvar PV (sample values)

Furthermore, of course, the value of relvar PV *changes over time:* We can perform INSERT, UPDATE, and DELETE operations that have the effect of changing PV's current value (from one relation to another). The value of domain PD, by contrast, does *not* change over time; to repeat, it's the set of *all possible* part numbers. I often sum up this state of affairs by saying:

- **Domains are static; relvars are dynamic.**

Another way of saying the same thing is to say that relvars are—by definition—*variables,* whereas domains are certainly not variables. See the section "Values Exist Forever" for further discussion of this point.

Now, I mentioned earlier that we often ignore the domain-name components of headings, as Fig. 2 illustrates. However, this fact too helps to obfuscate matters. A good question to ask anyone who still thinks that domain PD

in Fig. 2 is really just a relation is: *What domain is that relation's single column defined on?* And another: *What **true proposition** does the appearance of
the value P1 in domain PD represent?* (Subsidiary questions for the reader:
What domain is relvar PV's single column defined on? What true proposition
does the appearance of a row containing the value P1 in relvar PV represent?)

DOMAINS ARE DATA TYPES

Elsewhere [4,7] I've raised the question: What is it in the relational world that
is the analog of the *object class* in the object-oriented world? And I've said
that the answer to that question is the *domain;* that is, I've argued strongly that
"domain = object class" is a correct equation. I've also argued strongly that
"relation = object class" (more accurately, "relvar = object class") is an incorrect equation. Once again, it follows immediately that domains and relvars are
different things. Once again, however, there is more that can usefully be said.

   First of all, when I say that a domain and an object class are the same
thing, what I mean is that they're both *data types*—where I take the term "data
type" (*type* for short) to include all of the following:

1. Both system-defined and user-defined types
2. Part of the definition of any given type is a specification of the set of all
   possible values of that type
3. Such values can be of arbitrary complexity
4. The internal representation of such values is hidden from the user
5. Such values are manipulable solely by means of the operators defined for
   the type in question
6. Some types may be *subtypes* of other *supertypes*
7. If *B* is a subtype of *A,* then all operators that apply to values of type *A*
   apply to values of type *B* also (*inheritance*), but values of type *B* might
   have operators of their own that don't apply to values of type *A*

So a domain is a type. What about a relvar? Well, as I explained in an earlier
installment [3], relvars certainly do *have* a type; if I create a new relvar (perhaps via CREATE TABLE in SQL), I am in fact defining a *variable,* and that
variable does have a type—namely, the composite type "set of rows," where
the rows in turn are all of the particular *row* type specified by the heading of
the relvar in question. So here's another big distinction:

■ **Domains *are* types; relvars *have* types.**

Now, it's convenient to refer to the values in a domain generically as *scalar values,* or just *scalars* for short.* Thus, another point of difference between domains and relvars is this:

- **Domains contain scalars; relvars contain rows.**

I hinted at this distinction at the end of the previous section when I pointed out (in one of my "subsidiary questions") that relvar PV contained, not the scalar value P1 *per se,* but rather a row that contained that scalar value. By the way, I do hope it's obvious that even if a row *r* contains just a single scalar *s,* that row *r* is still not identical to that scalar *s*—there's all the difference in the world between the two concepts. To be specific (refer to Fig. 2 once again): Domain PD contains, among other things, the scalar value P1; relvar PV, by contrast, contains, among other things, the row (P#:P1).

(I suppose I should note in passing that since the values in a domain can be of arbitrary complexity, it would in fact be possible to define a domain in which the values were rows, not scalars. But just because some domains might contain rows, it doesn't follow that all domains do, and of course most don't.)

Here's yet another important distinction:†

- **Domains encapsulate; relvars don't.**

Domain values can be operated on *solely* by means of the operators that are defined for the domain in question (points 4 and 5 in the list above). Relvars, by contrast, expose their structure for all the world to see—that's what makes it possible to do *ad hoc* joins, projections, unions, and so forth. And note too that those relational operators apply to *every relation*—they're not specific to just specific relations, whereas domain operators certainly are specific to just specific domains.

---

*Actually, domains of nonscalar values are legal too, by virtue of point 3 above, but most of the domains encountered in practice do indeed contain scalars. See C. J. Date and Hugh Darwen, *Foundation for Object/Relational Systems: The Third Manifesto* (Addison-Wesley, 1998), for further discussion of this issue.

†The distinction is inaccurate as stated. To be specific, it's *domains that contain scalars* that encapsulate (but in practice most domains do indeed contain scalars). The point is, *scalars* are encapsulated, nonscalars aren't; in fact, the terms *scalar* and *encapsulated* really mean the same thing. For this reason, I've since come to believe the whole idea of encapsulation is something of a red herring!—the important point is simply to distinguish clearly between *type* and *representation* (regardless of whether the type is encapsulated or not). In this connection, see Installment 61, later in this part of the book.

VALUES EXIST FOREVER

Consider the integer (say) "4". Conceptually, this integer is a value that simply *exists;* we can use it whenever we need to—for example, to answer the question "How many symphonies did Brahms write?" What we certainly can't do is somehow "create" or "destroy" that value.

In exactly the same way, the set of values (say) "integers in the range 1 to 100" is something that simply exists, conceptually speaking, and there's no way we can somehow "create" or "destroy" it. Thus, suppose we're allowed to say (in some database language):

```
CREATE DOMAIN STATUS INTEGER
    ( STATUS ≥ 1 AND STATUS ≤ 100 ) ... ;
```

This statement doesn't actually *create* the set of values 1 to 100; rather, it simply indicates that until further notice we happen to be interested in that set, and we want to refer to it by the name STATUS. Likewise, the statement

```
DROP DOMAIN STATUS ;
```

simply indicates that we're now no longer interested in the set of values 1 to 100 that we happened to call STATUS. But that set of values 1 to 100 obviously continues to exist, conceptually; all the DROP statement does is drop the *name*.

Now suppose some business rule changes, so that status values are allowed to be in the range 1 to 200, instead of 1 to 100. Then what we have to do is:

1. DROP domain STATUS ("I'm no longer interested in this set of values"), and then

2. CREATE another domain with the same name STATUS that includes the additional values 101 to 200.

Of course, the system might provide some kind of ALTER DOMAIN shorthand for this sequence of operations, but that fact doesn't materially affect the true state of affairs.

At this point the reader might object that the domain called STATUS is therefore just as much a variable as any relvar is, because (for instance) the foregoing sequence of operations effectively "inserts" some new values into that domain. But note carefully that (as we've already agreed) when we CREATE a domain, we also have to define all of the operations that can be performed on values in that domain (see point 5 in the previous section). So "inserting a value into" a domain (or "deleting a value from" a domain) means that all such operations have to be redefined!

Aside: As a particularly nauseating example of the foregoing, consider what happens to the logical operations—NOT, AND, OR, and so on—if we "insert" the value *unknown* into the domain of truth values { *true, false* } (in other words, we switch from two- to three-valued logic). In this case, as I have shown in an earlier installment [2], even the *number* of such operations increases dramatically in this particular case, from 20 to well over 19,000. *End of aside.*

So: Even if we were to agree that STATUS is really a variable (of a kind), I think we'd also have to agree that it's much more of a sweat to update that variable than it is to update a relvar. Or to put it another way: STATUS is a very special kind of variable, precisely because it does have operations associated with it (ordinary variables don't have this property—*types* do).

SUMMARY

Domains really aren't relvars (and they're not relations either!). I've identified the following key differences between the two constructs:

- **Domains are static; relvars are dynamic.**
- **Domains *are* types; relvars *have* types.**
- **Domains contain scalars; relvars contain rows.**
- **Domains encapsulate; relvars don't.**

And the truly crucial—in fact, overriding—conceptual distinction is this:

- **Domains represent the things we can talk about; relations** (or relvar values) **represent the truths we utter about those things.**

So what's the significance of all this? Well, first, we should always strive for clarity and precision in our thinking; anything we can do to reduce confusion is by definition *A Good Thing.* More to the point, we can now see why the idea of taking the equation "object class = relvar" (in other words, "domain = relvar") as a basis on which to build systems—which is what certain of the so-called "object/relational" DBMS vendors are doing—is a huge mistake [4,7]. *Theory is practical!* Having such a truly colossal theoretical blunder at the very foundation of a system does not bode well for the future of that system in practice.

By way of conclusion, let me throw out the following challenge as this month's puzzle: Assuming that you now understand the *domain* concept, give definitions—as precise as you can—of the *relation* and *relvar* concepts.

REFERENCES

1. C. J. Date: "What's in a Name?", *Database Programming & Design 5*, No. 11 (November 1992). Republished in *Relational Database Writings 1991–1994*. Reading, Mass.: Addison-Wesley (1995).

2. C. J. Date: "Nothing In Excess," *Database Programming & Design 6*, No. 1 (January 1993). Republished in *Relational Database Writings 1991–1994*. Reading, Mass.: Addison-Wesley (1995).

3. C. J. Date: "Domains, Data Types, and Relations (Part 1 of 2)," *Database Programming & Design 7*, No. 6 (June 1994). Republished in *Relational Database Writings 1991–1994*. Reading, Mass.: Addison-Wesley (1995).

4. C. J. Date: "Oh Oh Relational . . ." (see Installment 26).

5. C. J. Date: "Relations and Their Interpretation" (see Installment 28).

6. C. J. Date: "It's All Relations!" (see Installment 29).

7. Hugh Darwen and C. J. Date: "Introducing . . . The Third Manifesto," *Database Programming & Design 8*, No. 1 (January 1995). See also (a) Chapter 3 in the present book; (b) the book *Foundation for Object/Relational Databases: The Third Manifesto*. Reading, Mass.: Addison-Wesley (1998).

8. Douglas W. Hubbard: Response to a letter to the editor, *DBMS 7*, No. 10 (September 1994).

SQL Domains Aren't Domains!

SQL "domains" aren't very well named,
to say the least

In my column last month, I showed that domains aren't relations (more accurately, domains aren't *relvars;* I revert for a moment to the more familiar term). However, if you happen to know the domain concept only as defined in the SQL standard [6,7]—as opposed to the relational model—you might have had some difficulty in following my arguments. The fact is, SQL's "domains" are unfortunately a long, long way from being true relational domains; the two concepts are so far apart, in fact, that I think it would have been better to use some other name for the SQL construct. This month, I want to explain some of the key differences between SQL domains and relational domains.

RELATIONAL DOMAINS

To repeat from last month, a domain in the relational model is nothing more nor less than a *data type*—where the term "data type" (*type* for short) is understood to include all of the following:

1. Both system-defined and user-defined types
2. Part of the definition of any given type is a specification of the set of all permissible values of that type
3. Such values can be of arbitrary complexity

Originally published in *Database Programming & Design 8,* No. 10, October 1995. Reprinted by permission of Miller Freeman Inc.

4. The internal representation of such values is hidden from the user

5. Such values are manipulable solely by means of the operators defined for the type in question

6. Some types may be *subtypes* of other *supertypes*

7. If *B* is a subtype of *A,* then all operators that apply to values of type *A* apply to values of type *B* also (*inheritance*), but values of type *B* might have operators of their own that don't apply to values of type *A*

Relational domains thus provide a basis for achieving what the programming languages community calls *strong typing.* Loosely speaking, strong typing just means that whenever the user writes an expression, the system checks that the operands of each operator in that expression are of the right type for that operator. Strong typing is a good idea, because it allows type errors to be caught at compilation time instead of run time ("static type checking").

Please note too that when I say *operator* here, I don't mean just comparison operators!—despite the emphasis on comparison operators in most of the database literature. For example, suppose we have the suppliers-and-parts database (as usual), with relvars S (suppliers), P (parts), and SP (shipments). Consider the following expressions:

```
P.WEIGHT + SP.QTY    /* part weight plus shipment quantity  */

P.WEIGHT * SP.QTY    /* part weight times shipment quantity */
```

The first of these presumably makes no sense, and the DBMS should reject it. The second, on the other hand, certainly does make sense—it represents the total weight for all parts involved in the shipment. So the operators defined for the combination of domains WEIGHT and QTY would presumably include "*" but not "+". In other words, relational domains are relevant to very much more than just comparisons; they are (to repeat) relevant to *all* operators.

SQL DOMAINS

In contrast to the foregoing, SQL domains really aren't data types at all. In fact, almost the only purpose of domains in SQL is to allow a primitive (builtin, system-defined) data type to be given a name that can be used as a shorthand by several columns in several base table definitions. Here's an example:

```
CREATE DOMAIN S#_DOM AS CHAR(5) ;
```

Now, instead of defining columns S.S# and SP.S# explicitly as CHAR(5), we can define them to be "based on" the S#_DOM domain:

```
CREATE TABLE S  ( S# S#_DOM, ... ) ;

CREATE TABLE SP ( S# S#_DOM, ... ) ;
```

The S#_DOM definition thus effectively serves as a shorthand, as previously suggested.

As the example illustrates, every SQL domain has a *name* (S#_DOM in the example) and an underlying *representation,* specified as one of the primitive, builtin, system-defined data types (CHAR(5) in the example). Optionally, an SQL domain can also have an associated *integrity constraint,* the purpose of which is to define the set of permissible values for the domain. For example:

```
CREATE DOMAIN CITY_DOM AS CHAR(15)
       CONSTRAINT VALID_CITIES
       CHECK ( VALUE IN ( '???', 'Athens', 'London',
                          'Madrid', 'New York', 'Oslo',
                          'Paris', 'Rome', 'Stockholm' ) ) ;
```

If no such constraint is specified, the domain is constrained only by the underlying representation (as character strings of length 15, in the example).

Before going any further, I should point out that the CHECK clause in the example doesn't quite mean what it says! It *seems* to say that the legal values are exactly the nine listed. What it *means,* however, is that the legal values are the nine listed *and NULL.* If we wanted to exclude this latter possibility, we would have to extend the constraint in the CHECK clause to include the specification

```
... AND VALUE IS NOT NULL
```

This oddity is just a quirk of SQL, of course.

Note: Optionally, an SQL domain can also have an associated *default value,* the purpose of which is basically to serve as the default value for every column based on the domain that has no explicit default value of its own. In the case of CITY_DOM, for example, we might decide to specify "???" as the applicable default value. The details of this option are surprisingly complex, however (especially in view of the apparently trivial functionality it provides), and for that reason I won't bother to discuss it further here. The specifics can be found in the book *A Guide to the SQL Standard,* by Hugh Darwen and myself [6], or in the SQL standard itself [7].

SQL DOMAINS *vs.* RELATIONAL DOMAINS

Now I can summarize some of the principal differences between true relational domains and the SQL construct of the same name. The discussion that follows is an elaboration of one previously given in my book *An Introduction to Database Systems* [2].

1. As already suggested, SQL domains are really just a syntactic shorthand. They're not really *data types* (as such) at all, and they're certainly not *user-defined* data types.

2. Values in SQL domains certainly can't be "of arbitrary complexity"; rather, they're limited to the complexity—what complexity there is— of the builtin, system-defined data types.

3. SQL domains don't even have to be used—columns in base tables can be defined directly in terms of the builtin, system-defined data types such as FLOAT or INTEGER.

4. There's no SQL support for "domains on domains": An SQL domain must be defined in terms of one of the builtin, system-defined data types, not another user-defined domain. Thus, for example, the following (possibly useful) sequence of definitions is *** *ILLEGAL* ***:

```
CREATE DOMAIN INT2 AS INTEGER
       CONSTRAINT TWO_BYTES
       CHECK ( VALUE >= -32768 AND VALUE <= +32767 ) ;

CREATE DOMAIN INT1 AS INT2
       CONSTRAINT ONE_BYTE
       CHECK ( VALUE >= -128 AND VALUE <= +127 ) ;
```

5. An SQL domain must be defined in terms of *exactly* one system-defined data type. Thus, for example, it isn't possible to define a domain called COMPLEX (complex numbers) with representation consisting of two FLOAT numbers (the real and imaginary components), or a domain called POINT (geometric points) with representation consisting likewise of two FLOAT numbers (the X and Y coordinates).

    Note, incidentally, that COMPLEX and POINT—if they *could* be defined—would be two different domains; the fact that they happened to have the same representation would be irrelevant. In other words, type and representation are different things!

6. Which brings us to the next point: SQL in fact doesn't make a clear distinction between type and representation. For example, suppose we define a domain DEPT# (department numbers) with representation INTEGER:

```
CREATE DOMAIN DEPT# AS INTEGER ;
```

    Then we'll be allowed to perform arithmetic operations such as add and subtract on department numbers, even though such operations probably make no sense.

7. SQL doesn't provide anything like strong typing. There's very little true type checking. In particular, SQL domains don't constrain comparisons—the only requirement on comparisons is that the comparands must be of the same *basic* type (both numeric or both character strings or both

dates or both times, or whatever). For example, suppose we have the following definitions:

```
CREATE DOMAIN S#_DOM AS CHAR(5) ;

CREATE DOMAIN P#_DOM AS CHAR(6) ;

CREATE TABLE  S  ( S# S#_DOM, ... ) ;

CREATE TABLE  SP ( S# S#_DOM, P# P#_DOM, ... ) ;
```

Then the following SELECT statement will *not* give rise to a type error on the comparison in the inner WHERE clause, though it logically should:

```
SELECT  S.*
FROM    S
WHERE   NOT EXISTS
      ( SELECT *
        FROM    SP
        WHERE   SP.P# = S.S# ) ;
```

Presumably, the user here is trying to find suppliers who supply no parts; by mistake, however—probably just a slip of the fingers—he or she has typed "SP.P#" instead of "SP.S#" in the inner WHERE clause. And it would be a friendly act on the part of the DBMS to interrupt the user and point out that the query doesn't seem to make sense. Unfortunately, SQL regards the query as perfectly legal.

Analogous remarks apply to numeric expressions, character string expressions, bit string expressions, and all the rest: In all cases, domains as such—*SQL* domains, that is—are essentially irrelevant.

Note: Another way to regard the foregoing is to say that SQL does support *exactly eight* true relational domains, namely the following eight "basic types":

numbers
character strings
bit strings
dates
times
timestamps
year-month intervals
day-time intervals

We could then say that type checking *is* performed, but only on the basis of these eight types. Thus, for example, an attempt to compare a number and a bit string is illegal, but an attempt to compare two numbers is legal, even if those numbers have different representations—one as INTEGER and one as FLOAT, say. (In the case of character strings there are some additional complications, having to do with such matters as character sets, collating sequences, and so forth, but I don't want to get into those complications here.)

8. SQL doesn't support the ability for users to define the operators that apply to a given domain. Instead, the operators that apply are, precisely, the predefined (system-defined) operators that apply to the *representation* of the domain. In particular, values can be converted—the SQL term is *cast*—from one type or domain to another precisely to the extent that such conversions are defined for the representations.

9. SQL has no concept of subtypes and supertypes, and hence no concept of operator inheritance.

10. Finally, SQL doesn't even support what is arguably the most fundamental domain of all, namely the domain of truth values! As I explained in an earlier installment [5], this is one reason why yes/no queries are so awkward in SQL; it's also the reason why there are no *true* and *false* literals, and why we can't write "SELECT EXISTS(. . .)" to test for the existence of something. In this connection I agree wholeheartedly with Hugh Darwen when he writes in reference [1] that he finds it "easier to imagine a . . . system that fails to support numbers than one that fails to support a truth-valued data type!"

To close this section, I can't resist pointing out that the next version of the SQL standard, code-named "SQL3," probably will include support for true relational domains (or something very like them)—but it won't be able to call them domains, because the term has already been usurped by the current standard.

DOMAIN CONSTRAINTS

I want to mention one final point. As we saw earlier, an SQL domain can have an associated integrity constraint, the purpose of which is to define the set of permissible values for the domain. Now, logically speaking, such constraints should be limited to a particularly simple form [3] that effectively just enumerates the values in the domain (the VALID_CITIES constraint in the CITY_DOM example provides an illustration). Unfortunately, however, SQL allows such a constraint to be arbitrarily complex. For example:

```
CREATE TABLE T ( C ... ) ;

CREATE DOMAIN D ...
        CHECK ( VALUE IN ( SELECT T.C FROM T ) ) ;
```

In this example, the legal values of domain D are defined to be the values currently appearing in column C of table T, and therefore *change with time!* The provision of such a capability in SQL reflects some of the exact same confusions I was talking about in my column last month (between relations and domains). As I wrote in an earlier installment [4], this unwarranted permissiveness on the part of SQL muddles and muddies some very fundamental concepts. I recommend very strongly that users not "take advantage" of this very strange SQL "feature."

PUZZLE CORNER

I close as usual with a puzzle corner problem (nothing to do with SQL or domains, however—it's another of those annoying ladder problems, in fact). Fig. 1 represents an alley with horizontal floor *BD* and vertical walls *BC* and *DA*. *AB* and *CD* are ladders, 41 feet 8 inches long and 31 feet 3 inches long respectively. They intersect at right angles. How high is that point of intersection above the ground?

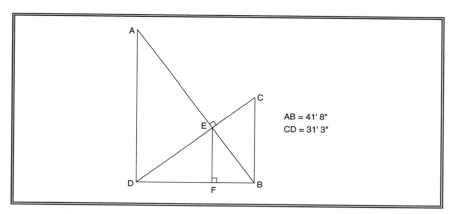

Fig. 1   The intersecting ladders

REFERENCES

1. Hugh Darwen: Introduction to Part III of C. J. Date and Hugh Darwen, *Relational Database Writings 1989–1991*. Reading, Mass.: Addison-Wesley (1992).

2. C. J. Date: *An Introduction to Database Systems* (6th edition). Reading, Mass.: Addison-Wesley (1995).

3. C. J. Date: "Integrity Revisited" (see Installment 27).

4. C. J. Date: "A Matter of Integrity Part III," *Database Programming & Design 6,* No. 12 (December 1993). Republished in *Relational Database Writings 1991–1994.* Reading, Mass.: Addison-Wesley (1995).

5. C. J. Date: "How We Missed the Relational Boat," *Database Programming & Design 6,* No. 9 (September 1993). Republished in *Relational Database Writings 1991–1994.* Reading, Mass.: Addison-Wesley (1995).

6. C. J. Date and Hugh Darwen: *A Guide to the SQL Standard* (4th edition). Reading, Mass.: Addison-Wesley (1997).

7. International Organization for Standardization (ISO): *Database Language SQL.* Document ISO/IEC 9075:1992. Also available as American National Standards Institute (ANSI) Document ANSI X3.135-1992.

Functional Dependencies Are Fun (Part 1 of 2)

An informal look at the formal world of FDs

This month and next, I want to introduce you to the formal world of *functional dependencies* (FDs). I'm sure you're familiar with the basic FD concept, at least informally, but let me begin by reviewing it briefly. Suppose *A* and *B* are sets of columns of some relation *R* (more accurately, some *relvar R* [5]). Then we say that the functional dependence $A \rightarrow B$ holds in *R* if and only if, whenever two rows of *R* have the same value for *A*, they also have the same value for *B*. For example, in the employees relvar

```
EMP { EMP#, SALARY, DEPT#, DEPTMGR }
```

the FD

```
{ DEPT# } → { DEPTMGR }
```

holds, because any two employees that have the same department number must—I presume!—also have the same department manager.

Note that (as the definition states) the left hand side and right hand side of an FD are both *sets* of columns. When such a set contains just one column, however, we usually drop the set brackets, as here:

```
DEPT# → DEPTMGR
```

Originally published under the title "Functional Dependencies Are Fun, Part I" in *Database Programming & Design 8,* No. 11, November 1995. Reprinted by permission of Miller Freeman Inc.

Now, I'm sure you understand the use of FDs in connection with such matters as third normal form and database design. But the applicability of the FD concept is much wider than just the area of normalized database design, as we'll see.

FDs are fundamentally just a special kind of *integrity constraint*. However, they've received much more attention in the research world than integrity constraints in general have. This is because FDs possess a rich set of interesting formal properties—properties that make it possible to use FDs as a basis for a scientific attack on a number of practical problems. I'll come back to this point in my closing remarks next month.

THE PARTY INVITATIONS EXAMPLE

As a motivating example for the discussions that follow, let me return to the party invitations problem from an earlier installment [3]. Here to repeat is the problem statement (with acknowledgments to Hugh Darwen):

- I decided to throw a party, so I drew up a list of people I wanted to invite and made some preliminary soundings. The response was good, but several people made their acceptance conditional on the acceptance of certain other invitees. For example, Bob and Cal both said they would come if Amy came; Hal said he would come if either Don and Eve both came or Fay came; Guy said he would come anyway; Joe said he would come if Bob and Amy both came; and so on. Design a database to show whose acceptance is based on whose.

And here is an edited version of the solution as presented in a subsequent installment [4]. Let me use the notation $X \rightarrow Y$ to mean that if everyone in the set of people X attends then everyone in the set of people Y will attend. It's easy to see [4] that statements such as $X \rightarrow Y$ are indeed FDs (hence my choice of notation, of course), so I'll refer to them as such. Thus, the first and most obvious design consists of a single relvar, IXAYWA ("if X attends, Y will attend"), containing a row for each of the given FDs. Refer to Fig. 1, and note that (a) INV in that figure stands for invitee; (b) columns X and Y are both relation-valued [2–3].

However, we can do better than this. First, note that if the FD $X \rightarrow Y$ holds, then the FD $X' \rightarrow Y'$ necessarily holds for all supersets X' of X and all subsets Y' of Y; for example, "if Amy attends, Bob and Cal will attend" certainly implies (among other things) that "if Amy and Don both attend, Bob will attend." We therefore reduce the amount of information we need to record explicitly by ensuring that every FD $X \rightarrow Y$ we do record is such that the set X is as small as possible and the set Y is as large as possible—meaning, more precisely, that:

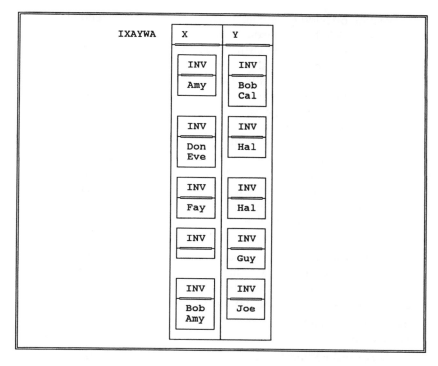

Fig. 1   Relvar IXAYWA (first attempt)

- Nobody can be removed from set X without the resulting FD no longer holding;
- Nobody can be added to set Y without the resulting FD no longer holding.

Note further that the FD X $\rightarrow$ Y necessarily holds for all sets Y such that Y is a subset of X (in particular, X $\rightarrow$ X always holds; for example, "if Amy attends, Amy will attend" obviously holds). We refer to such FDs as *trivial* and need not bother to record them explicitly in the database.

CANONICAL COVERS

Formally, the problem of reducing the amount of information we need to record explicitly in the party invitations example is equivalent to the problem of finding a *canonical cover* for the given set of FDs. A canonical cover, loosely speaking, is a set of FDs that includes no redundant information and has the property that all of the given FDs are implied by the FDs in that set.

The question of finding canonical covers is one of considerable practical interest. Why? Well, one reason is that (as already stated) FDs represent
integrity constraints, and so the DBMS needs to check them when updates
are performed. The trouble is, the set of FDs that hold in a given relvar
can be very large! By way of illustration, you're invited to write down
all the FDs—trivial as well as nontrivial—that hold in the familiar relvar
SP { S#, P#, QTY } from the suppliers-and-parts database (this is this
month's puzzle corner problem).

Given some set *S* of FDs that hold in some relvar, therefore, it would be
nice to find some other set *T* that is much smaller than *S* and has the property
that every FD in *S* is implied by the FDs in *T*. If such a set *T* can be found, it
is sufficient that the DBMS enforce the FDs in *T*, and the FDs in *S* will then
be enforced automatically.

In order to address this problem, let me first define some relevant concepts. Let *S* and *T* be sets of FDs that apply to some relvar *R*. Then:

1. The set of all FDs implied by the FDs in *S* is called the **closure** of *S*.
   (Don't confuse this notion with the notion of closure as it applies to the
   relational algebra [1]. The two concepts are somewhat similar, logically
   speaking, but they're certainly not the same thing.)

2. If every FD implied by the FDs in *S* is implied by the FDs in *T*, then *T* is
   a **cover** for *S*.

3. If *T* is a cover for *S* and *S* is a cover for *T* (in other words, if the closures
   of *S* and *T* are the same), then *S* and *T* are **equivalent.**

4. The set *S* is **irreducible** if and only if:

   a. The right hand side of every FD in *S* involves just one column, and

   b. The left hand side of every FD in *S* is such that no column can be dis-
      carded without changing the closure, and

   c. No FD can be discarded from *S* without changing the closure.

5. If *S* and *T* are equivalent and *T* is irreducible, then *T* is an **irreducible
   cover** for *S*.

So our problem can be restated: Given a set of FDs *S*, find an irreducible cover
T for *S*. Note that I say "an" irreducible cover; it's true that every set *S* does
possess at least one such cover *T*, but *T* isn't necessarily unique (as we'll see
next month). Anyway, the algorithm for computing such a *T* given *S* is conceptually straightforward (it follows immediately from the definition, in fact):

1. For each FD in *S* of the form *LHS* → *RHS*, replace that FD by a set of FDs
   of the form *LHS* → *Y*, one for each column *Y* in *RHS*.

2. For each FD in *S* of the form *LHS* → *RHS* and for each column *X* in *LHS*, if deleting *X* from *LHS* doesn't change the closure of *S*, then delete *X* from *LHS*.

3. For each FD *F* in *S*, if deleting *F* from *S* doesn't change the closure of *S*, then delete *F* from *S*.

The final version of *S* that results from this algorithm is an irreducible cover *T* for the original version of *S*. Thus, enforcing the FDs in that final version will have the effect of enforcing the FDs in the original version automatically. ∎

Now, I realize the foregoing is all pretty abstract! I'll give an example next month that should help to make it a little more concrete. I can't do it now, unfortunately, because I've very deliberately not yet explained a crucial concept; to be specific, I've not yet explained precisely what it means for a given FD to be *implied* by others. Note that this concept was used explicitly in the definitions of *closure* and *cover* above, and hence (implicitly) in all the other definitions too. Of course, you probably have a good intuitive understanding of the concept already—for example, you probably know that the two FDs *A* → *B* and *B* → *C* together imply the FD *A* → *C*—but, to repeat, I'll make the matter more precise next month.

To get back to the main thread of our discussion: I still haven't fulfilled my promise to explain what a *canonical* cover is. Let's go back to the party invitations example for a moment. An irreducible cover for the FDs in that example might include both of the following FDs:

```
Amy → Bob
Amy → Cal
```

(Recall from the definition that every FD in an irreducible cover has a single-column right hand side.) In order to minimize the number of rows we need to record in IXAYWA, however, we can combine these two FDs into a single FD looking like this:

```
Amy → { Bob, Cal }
```

A **canonical** cover is derived from an irreducible cover by exhaustively combining all sets of FDs with a common left hand side into single FDs, as in this example.

Incidentally (as I pointed out when I discussed this example before [4]), if IXAYWA contains only those statements that constitute a canonical cover, then column X will be a candidate key for IXAYWA—for it is certainly true that no two rows will have the same value for X.

REFERENCES

1. C. J. Date: "The Importance of Closure," *Database Programming & Design 5,* No. 10 (October 1992). Republished in *Relational Database Writings 1991–1994.* Reading, Mass.: Addison-Wesley (1995).

2. C. J. Date: "Nested Relations (Part 1 of 2)" (see Installment 31).

3. C. J. Date: "Nested Relations (Part 2 of 2)" (see Installment 32).

4. C. J. Date: "Answers to Puzzle Corner Problems (Installments 31–35)" (see Installment 36).

5. C. J. Date: "Domains Aren't Relations!" (see Installment 37).

Functional Dependencies Are Fun (Part 2 of 2)

Concluding our informal look at the formal world of FDs

In my column last month, I promised that this time I would explain exactly what it meant for a given functional dependency (FD for short) to be implied by others. I also said that you probably had a good intuitive understanding of this idea already; for example, you probably know that the two FDs $A \rightarrow B$ and $B \rightarrow C$ together imply the FD $A \rightarrow C$. Let's start by taking a closer look at this example. *Note:* Much of this month's column is based on material from my book *An Introduction to Database Systems* [5], where more details can be found.

FD TRANSITIVITY

When we say that $A \rightarrow B$ and $B \rightarrow C$ together imply $A \rightarrow C$, what we mean is the following:

1. A, B, and C are understood to be subsets of the columns of some relvar R, and

2. If $A \rightarrow B$ and $B \rightarrow C$ both hold in R, then $A \rightarrow C$ also holds in R (that is, whenever two rows of R agree on A, they also agree on C).

Originally published under the title "Functional Dependencies Are Fun, Part II" in *Database Programming & Design 8*, No. 12, December 1995. Reprinted by permission of Miller Freeman Inc.

This property is known as the **transitivity** rule for FDs. Let's see if we can prove it's valid. Well, assume it isn't; that is, assume that $A \rightarrow B$ and $B \rightarrow C$, but there exist two distinct rows $r1$ and $r2$ of R that agree on A but not on C. Then if $r1$ and $r2$ agree on B, we have a contradiction, because $B \rightarrow C$; if $r1$ and $r2$ don't agree on B, we have a contradiction, because $A \rightarrow B$. Either way, it follows that our original assumption must be wrong, and hence the transitivity rule must in fact be valid. ∎

FD INFERENCE RULES

As we saw last month, the set of all FDs implied by a given set S is called the **closure** of S. Clearly we need a way of computing such closures. The first attack on this problem appeared in a now famous paper by Armstrong [1], which gave a set of *rules of inference* (usually called *Armstrong's axioms*) by which new FDs can be inferred from given ones. Those rules can be stated in a variety of equivalent ways, one of the simplest of which is as follows. Let A, B, and C be arbitrary subsets—possibly even overlapping subsets—of the set of columns of relvar R. Let's agree to write (for example) AB to mean the union of A and B. Then:

1. If B is a subset of A, then $A \rightarrow B$ (the **reflexivity** rule).
2. If $A \rightarrow B$, then $AC \rightarrow BC$ (the **augmentation** rule)
3. If $A \rightarrow B$ and $B \rightarrow C$, then $A \rightarrow C$ (the **transitivity** rule).

Each of these three rules can be proved directly from the definition of functional dependence. (*Exercise:* I've already given you a proof for the transitivity rule; prove the other two for yourself. Note that the reflexivity rule is essentially just the definition of a *trivial* FD, as discussed last month.)

Armstrong's rules are **complete,** in the sense that, given a set S of FDs, all FDs implied by S can be derived from S using the rules. They're also **sound,** in the sense that no additional FDs (that is, FDs not implied by S) can be so derived. In other words, the rules can be used to compute precisely the closure of S.

Several further rules can be derived from the three given above, the following among them. These additional rules can be used to simplify the practical task of computing closures. *Note:* D here is another arbitrary subset of the set of columns of R. What follows isn't an exhaustive list, of course.

4. $A \rightarrow A$ (the **self determination** rule).
5. If $A \rightarrow BC$, then $A \rightarrow B$ and $A \rightarrow C$ (the **decomposition** rule).
6. If $A \rightarrow B$ and $A \rightarrow C$, then $A \rightarrow BC$ (the **union** rule).

7. If $A \rightarrow B$ and $C \rightarrow D$, then $AC \rightarrow BD$ (the **composition** rule).

8. If $A \rightarrow B$, then $AC \rightarrow B$ (the **left augmentation** rule).

By way of an example, here's a proof that the *decomposition* rule follows from Armstrong's three rules. (As another exercise, you might like to try proving the other rules for yourself.) Since B and C are both subsets of BC, we have $BC \rightarrow B$ and $BC \rightarrow C$ by reflexivity. Also, we're given that $A \rightarrow BC$; hence $A \rightarrow B$ and $A \rightarrow C$ by transitivity. ∎

Let's consider an example of the application of these rules. Suppose we have the following relvar:

```
EMP { EMP#, DEPT#, MGR#, PROJ#, DNAME, MGRTIME }
```

Here EMP#, DEPT#, and DNAME are meant to be self-explanatory, MGR# is the employee's manager's employee number, PROJ# is the project number for some project directed by that manager (unique within manager), and MGRTIME is the percentage of time spent by the specified manager on the specified project. Suppose too that the following FDs hold, among others:

```
EMP# → { DEPT#, MGR# }
DEPT# → DNAME
{ MGR#, PROJ# } → { DNAME, MGRTIME }
```

Now I want to consider the question: Is it true that the FD

```
{ EMP#, PROJ# } → MGRTIME
```

holds in EMP?—that is, is this latter FD implied by the given FDs? Equivalently, is it part of the closure of the given FDs? (By the way, I don't think the answer to this question is immediately obvious, though you might not agree.)

In trying to answer questions like this one from the inference rules, it's often a good idea to drop "meaningful" names like MGR#; such names tend to carry too much unwanted semantic baggage with them, thereby making arguments and examples unnecessarily confusing and error-prone. To make the formal manipulations easier to follow, therefore, let me rename relvar EMP as simply R, and let me rename the columns of EMP (in sequence as stated) as A, B, C, D, E, and F, respectively. Then the FDs become:

```
A → BC
B → E
CD → EF
```

Now we can apply the inference rules in a purely mechanical way, without paying any attention to the fact that (for example) column C is "really" MGR#. The question we want to address becomes: Is it true that the FD $AD \rightarrow F$ holds in R?

(Observe, incidentally, that I'm extending my notation slightly—but not incompatibly—by writing, for example, *AD* for the set consisting of columns *A* and *D*. Previously, *AD* would have meant the *union* of *A* and *D*, where *A* and *D* were *sets* of columns.)

In fact, the FD *AD* → *F* does hold in *R*, and so is a member of the closure of the given set of FDs. Proof:

```
1. A  → BC  (given)
2. A  → C   (1, decomposition)
3. AD → CD  (2, augmentation)
4. CD → EF  (given)
5. AD → EF  (3 and 4, transitivity)
6. AD → F   (5, decomposition)  ■
```

IRREDUCIBLE COVERS

Recall from last month that an irreducible cover for a set *S* of FDs is a set *T* of FDs that has the same closure as *S* and satisfies the following properties:

1. The right hand side of every FD in *T* involves just one column.

2. The left hand side of every FD in *T* is irreducible in turn—meaning that no column can be discarded without changing the closure.

3. No FD can be discarded from *T* without changing the closure.

Now, I promised last month that I'd give an example showing how to compute an irreducible cover for some given set of FDs—so here goes. Suppose we have a relvar *R* with columns *A*, *B*, *C*, *D*, and FDs

```
A  → BC
B  → C
A  → B
AB → C
AC → D
```

(As in the previous section, I prefer to work with abstract names like *A*, *B*, *C*, *D*. If you'd prefer a more concrete example, you might like to try coming up with a set of concrete names for columns that might intuitively be expected to satisfy the specified FDs.)

Let's now compute an irreducible set of FDs that is equivalent to this given set.

1. The first step is to rewrite the FDs such that each one has a single-column right hand side:

```
A  → B
A  → C
B  → C
A  → B
AB → C
AC → D
```

We can now see immediately that the FD $A \rightarrow B$ occurs twice, so one occurrence can be eliminated.

2. Next, column C can be eliminated from the left hand side of the FD $AC \rightarrow D$, because we have $A \rightarrow C$, so $A \rightarrow AC$ by augmentation, and we're given $AC \rightarrow D$, so $A \rightarrow D$ by transitivity; thus the C on the left hand side of $AC \rightarrow D$ is redundant.

3. Next, note that the FD $AB \rightarrow C$ can be eliminated, because again we have $A \rightarrow C$, so $AB \rightarrow CB$ by augmentation, so $AB \rightarrow C$ by decomposition.

4. Finally, the FD $A \rightarrow C$ is implied by the FDs $A \rightarrow B$ and $B \rightarrow C$, so it too can be eliminated. We're left with:

```
A → B
B → C
A → D
```

This set is obviously irreducible. ∎

Incidentally, if we replace the first and third of these FDs by the single FD $A \rightarrow BD$, we have a *canonical* cover for the original set. (Recall from last month that a canonical cover is derived from an irreducible cover by exhaustively combining all sets of FDs with a common left hand side into single FDs.)

CONCLUDING REMARKS

The detailed examples in the two preceding sections were both fairly trivial, of course; I'm sure you'll appreciate that real-life examples typically involve a huge amount of computation and quickly become very tedious. This kind of work is much better performed by machines! Which is precisely why the fact that FD theory is *formal* is so important: If we can *formalize* something, we can *mechanize* it, and so we can get the machine to do the work.

Given that the formalization of FDs is a good idea, a natural question to ask is: Can we similarly formalize other integrity constraints? (Recall from last month that an FD is essentially just a special kind of integrity constraint.) Well, it's certainly true in principle that many of the ideas we've been discussing do apply to constraints in general, not just to FDs. For example, all of the following remarks do apply to constraints in general:

1. Certain constraints are trivial (meaning they can't possibly be violated).

2. Certain constraints imply others.

3. The set of all constraints implied by a given set of constraints can be regarded as the closure of the given set.

4. The question of whether a specific constraint is in a certain closure—that is, whether the specific constraint is implied by certain given constraints—is an interesting practical problem,

5. The question of finding an irreducible (or canonical) cover for certain given constraints is an interesting practical problem.

What makes FDs in particular much more tractable than constraints in general is the existence of a sound and complete set of inference rules for FDs. It turns out that there are several other specific kinds of constraints for which such sets of inference rules also exist, including:

- multivalued dependencies (MVDs)
- join dependencies (JDs)
- inclusion dependencies (INDs)

In these cases, however, the inference rules are typically much more complex than those for FDs [2–3,8]. And the more general problem of finding inference rules for constraints of arbitrary complexity has not yet been solved (so far as I know).

I have one last piece of unfinished business to attend to. In an earlier installment [4], I pointed out that if we know the FDs that hold for an arbitrary relvar, we can deduce the candidate keys for that relvar. In fact, the candidate keys for *R* are precisely those subsets *K* of the columns of *R* that are irreducible and have the property that the FD *K* → *C* holds for all columns *C* of *R*. An algorithm for performing this task (of deducing candidate keys) is presented in a paper by Lucchesi and Osborn [7]. Space doesn't allow me to go into details on that algorithm here; as I pointed out in my answer to the party invitations problem [6], however, that algorithm is exactly what we need in order to answer the second part of the problem ("Who do I have to persuade to attend in order to ensure that *every* invitee in fact attends?").

PUZZLE CORNER

Two puzzle corner problems this month:

1. We're given relvar *R{A,B,C,D,E,F,G}* with FDs:

    ```
    A   → B
    BC  → DE
    AEF → G
    ```

    Is the FD *ACF* → *DG* implied by this set of FDs?

2. We're given relvar *R{A,B,C,D,E,F}* with FDs:

    ```
    AB  → C
    C   → A
    BC  → D
    ACD → B
    BE  → C
    CE  → FA
    CF  → BD
    D   → EF
    ```

    Find an irreducible cover for this set of FDs.

REFERENCES

1. W. W. Armstrong: "Dependency Structures of Data Base Relationships," Proc. IFIP Congress, Stockholm, Sweden (1974).

2. Catriel Beeri, Ronald Fagin, and John H. Howard: "A Complete Axiomatization for Functional and Multivalued Dependencies," Proc. 1977 ACM SIGMOD International Conference on Management of Data, Toronto, Canada (August 1977).

3. Marco A. Casanova, Ronald Fagin, and Christos H. Papadimitriou: "Inclusion Dependencies and Their Interaction with Functional Dependencies," Proc. 1st ACM SIGACT-SIGMOD Symposium on Principles of Database Systems, Los Angeles, Calif. (March 1982).

4. C. J. Date: "The Power of the Keys," *Database Programming & Design 6,* No. 5 (May 1993). Republished in *Relational Database Writings 1991–1994.* Reading, Mass.: Addison-Wesley (1995).

5. C. J. Date: *An Introduction to Database Systems* (6th edition). Reading, Mass.: Addison-Wesley (1995).

6. C. J. Date: "Answers to Puzzle Corner Problems (Installments 31–35)" (see Installment 36).

7. Claudio L. Lucchesi and Sylvia L. Osborn: "Candidate Keys for Relations," *J. Comp. and Sys. Sciences 17,* No. 2 (1978).

8. E. Sciore: "A Complete Axiomatization of Full Join Dependencies," *JACM 29,* No. 2 (April 1982).

The Saga of IEFBR14

*A fable of application development
and execution*

Some people probably found the last two installments of this column (which discussed functional dependencies) rather heavy going in places. Out of sympathy for my long-suffering readers, therefore, I offer some light relief this month. Though there is—as always—a serious point to be made, in fact more than one . . .

The tale that follows is well known in programming circles, but I haven't seen it documented anywhere in any reasonably permanent form, and it would be a shame to lose it for lack of such a permanent record. I must explain right up front too that it doesn't have anything directly to do with databases, but the moral is relevant to database people (among others, of course). Furthermore, as I've already indicated, the story—parable, rather—wasn't invented by me; indeed, I don't know who the original inventor was (I only wish I did). It originated, so far as I know, inside IBM in the "good old days" of IBM System/360 Assembler Language programming, and I'm grateful to those friends in IBM who first drew my attention to it. Since I'm plagiarizing *somebody,* therefore, as an act of good faith—and since it's holiday season, more or less—I hereby promise to donate my regular column fee this month to a registered charitable organization (of my choice!—the author's decision is final).

Originally published in *Database Programming & Design 9,* No. 1, January 1996. Reprinted by permission of Miller Freeman Inc.

THE REQUIREMENT

Once upon a time the need was discovered for a "no-op" application—in other words, an application that didn't do anything at all. The design aim was that the application would process no data, but simply cause certain data sets to be allocated and deallocated. (*Note:* In the days of Operating System/360, files were called data sets. It is not known why this is.) For reasons that need not concern us here, such a no-op application was deemed to be A Good Thing.

Obviously this application would be extremely simple to code, so no specifications were written; there wasn't even a test plan, nor a maintenance plan. "Even a *&Silly_Person* like *<supply your own favorite name here>* could code this in a morning!" said the Planning Manager. "Register 15 contains the entry address and register 14 the return address. What could be easier, just a simple one-line program. Why, I could even code it myself!"

THE CODE

The Planning Manager explained his idea to the Programming Manager, and she put a trainee to work on it. The trainee—let's call him Joe—quickly realized that it wasn't a one-line program after all but a two-line one. But everyone knows that estimates are always out by 100 percent, so this little discrepancy didn't matter very much.

Joe's code looked like this:

```
IEFBR15   CSECT
          BR    R15
```

He punched out two cards (this really was a long time ago) and put his program in for assembly. Gosh, imagine his surprise when it came back with not one but *two* errors!—to wit:

```
- R15 is an undefined symbol
- No END statement
```

Well, such things happen. So Joe corrected these two errors and got a nice clean assembly.

TESTING

As it was so simple, the System Test people decided not to bother to test Joe's program at all. During Integration Testing, however, it was noticed that the system light was on more or less permanently. A lot of time and effort were spent in tracing the error back to its source, whereupon it was carefully explained to trainee Joe in words of one syllable that register 15 holds the entry address and register 14 the return address and not the other way around. So eventually the application—now called IEFBR14, not IEFBR15!—was made to work, and the code was ready for distribution to customers.

MAINTENANCE

About a month later, an APAR was received. (*Note:* APAR—Authorized Program Analysis Report—is IBM jargon for a bug report.) Everyone fell over backwards. "Impossible," they said.

But you see, Joe had forgotten to clear register 15 to zero (to specify a "success" return code), and applications that invoked Joe's program were failing in unpredictable ways. So a fix was developed; and, remembering what happened last time, the System Test people actually tested it. It worked and they shipped it.

A year went by, and IEFBR14 won great customer acceptance. Much to everyone's dismay, however, another APAR was then received: "This program wasn't link-edited with the RENT attribute and it won't go in the MVS link pack area!" (*Note:* RENT = reentrant.)

"Ho hum, oh well, back to the drawing board—and send that *$Silly_ Person* Joe in here!" said the Maintenance Manager.

MORAL (I)

This sad little story just goes to show that even the simplest program can have bugs in it, all programs should always be tested, and all programs need maintenance.

FURTHER MISDAVENTURES

Not all run-time failures can be attributed to errors of commission or omission during the development cycle. The following harrowing story is based on a true-life situation. A senior manager at an important IBM customer site—let's call her Bonnie—submitted an IEFBR14 job for execution. The job failed with the diagnostic message "Data Set Not Found." Apparently Bonnie was supposed to allocate a data set on a disk volume in order to run the job. So she wrote some job control statements as follows and resubmitted the job.

```
//jobname    JOB    accounting info etc.
//stepname   EXEC   PGM=IEFRB14
//ddname     DD     DSNAME=BONNIES,
//                  VOL=SER=volser,
//                  DISP=(NEW,KEEP),
//                  SPACE=etc.
```

Note: System/360 Job Control Language (usually known as JCL) has been described, not without some justification, as the world's second worst computer language.

This time the job failed with an ABEND code of X06 ("Program Not Found"), and a lot of strange JCL error messages were produced.

Bonnie then asked a very junior programmer—I'll call him Clyde—why the job had failed. Clyde told Bonnie that the operating system (OS/360) could not locate the program named in the JCL EXEC statement because Bonnie had spelled that name incorrectly. So she changed the second JCL statement to read as follows—

```
//stepname   EXEC   PGM=IEFBR14
```

—and resubmitted the job. It failed, with a diagnostic message that read "Not Run - JCL Error."

Bonnie again consulted junior programmer Clyde, who explained that the failure was caused by an attempt to allocate a new data set with a data set name (DSNAME = BONNIES) identical to that of a data set that already existed on the volume. This explanation caused Bonnie much distress.

Clyde then further explained that the program IEFBR14 did not actually perform any function except to make the services of the OS/360 initiator/terminator component available to anyone who could code JCL. He referred Bonnie to the JCL and message listing from her attempt to execute the nonexistent program IEFRB14; that listing clearly showed that the data set had been allocated at initiate time, and retained at terminate time.

MORAL (II)

You can probably draw your own moral from the tale of Bonnie and Clyde. Actually I can see several such morals: One has to do with user-friendly language design; another has to do with reading the output in the event of a failure; and yet another has to do with managers . . . There's at least one nullological moral too [1]. I leave the specifics to you.

PUZZLE CORNER

Since I'm in a plagiarizing mood, and since I have little to say regarding databases this month anyway, I'll close with a plagiarized, nondatabase puzzle corner problem. It's taken from one of Martin Gardner's *Scientific American* columns [2]; Gardner himself says he doesn't know the origin of "this beautiful problem," which he actually refers to tongue in cheek as "impossible" because, as he says, it seems to lack sufficient information for a solution.*

Two positive integers *a* and *b,* not necessarily distinct, are chosen such that $1 < a,b \leq 20$. Mathematician *S* is told the sum $a + b$ (only). Mathematician *P* is told the product $a * b$ (only). *S* says to *P:* "I see no way you can determine my sum." Later, *P* says to *S:* "I know your sum." Later still, *S* says to *P:* "Now I know your product." What are the values of *a* and *b?*

REFERENCES

1. Hugh Darwen: "The Nullologist in Relationland," in C. J. Date and Hugh Darwen, *Relational Database Writings 1989–1991.* Reading, Mass.: Addison-Wesley (1992).

2. Martin Gardner: "Mathematical Games," *Scientific American* (December 1979).

Note added on republication: The problem as stated here unfortunately *is* impossible! See Installments 43 and 46 later in this part of the book.

Round and Round the Nullberry Bush

Hugh Darwen and Chris Date respond to Jim Melton

My column this month should by rights be devoted to answering the various outstanding "puzzle corner" problems from the last few installments. However, I've decided to hold those answers over till next month, giving the bulk of the space instead to a letter from my friend and colleague Hugh Darwen. Hugh's letter was originally intended as a regular letter to the editor of *Database Programming & Design;* however, it turned out to be too long for inclusion (without drastic cuts) in the usual letters section. I therefore offered him my regular column as an alternative forum, and he accepted.

BACKGROUND

The September 1995 issue of *Database Programming & Design* contained no fewer than three separate contributions to "The Great MVL Debate" (as Editor-in-Chief David Stodder referred to it in that same issue): a letter from Lee Fesperman [4], an article by Jim Melton [7],[*] and the response by Hugh Darwen, David McGoveran, and myself [3] to an earlier article by Tom Johnston [5]. And Tom Johnston's response to our response appeared two

---

Originally published in *Database Programming & Design 9,* No. 2, February 1996. Reprinted by permission of Miller Freeman Inc.

[*]Jim Melton was editor of the SQL standard at the time.

months later [6]. *Note for new readers:* "MVL" stands for multi- or many-valued logic; "The Great MVL Debate" concerns the suitability or otherwise of MVL as a basis for dealing with missing information in databases.

Now, I'm quite sure that by now many readers are bored to tears with this whole subject. But the sad truth is that the debate is *fundamentally important!* What's more, it isn't going to go away (indeed, nor should it), so long as the MVL advocates fail even to address—let alone answer—the many serious and well-founded objections to their position. We (Darwen, McGoveran, and myself) stand by our contention that MVL is not only not a good approach to the problem at hand, but has the potential to be a disastrously bad one. Over the next few months or so, therefore, readers can expect to see a series of further rebuttals to the publications by Fesperman, Melton, and Johnston (probably others besides). Hugh Darwen's letter, which follows immediately, can be regarded as the—deliberately not too deep—opening salvo in that series.

DARWEN'S LETTER

Subject: Oh no, not *that* again!

Dear Editor:

We're not sure how many laps there are still to go, in the Nulls Marathon, but we're far enough along for it to be annoying when somebody joins in at Lap 1, as Jim Melton did in his article "The Debate Rages On: Much Ado About 'Nullthing'" [7].

Melton's first two-and-a-bit pages (up to the section headed "BUT, WARDEN . . .") say nothing that hasn't already been said. They present certain well-known approaches to the problem of missing information that have been proposed (in particular, by E. F. Codd) or implemented (in particular, by SQL products). Melton tells his readers that Date, McGoveran, and I are among those who have raised objections to those approaches, but he neither describes nor addresses the most important points in those objections.

Furthermore, he doesn't really tell us where he stands on the issue. He mentions Codd's approach on the one hand and SQL's on the other, but he doesn't mention the fact that Codd's is radically different from SQL's, nor does he say which he prefers. He cites an ANSI report that lists "between 20 and 40 different meanings" for "the notion of 'nullness'", but he doesn't discuss how that variety might be addressed with just two different null markers and 4VL (Codd), or just one and 3VL plus a few bugs (SQL).

I won't give a blow-by-blow rebuttal of this part of Melton's article, because that job has already been done. I must, however, address his final section, if only to correct some impressions your readers might have acquired from certain egregious things he says about me. And here I do have to go into blow-by-blow mode, I'm afraid:

- "Darwen goes further than objections of the kind I've mentioned so far."
  This statement is absolutely true. I do go a lot further. But the apparent implication is that Date and McGoveran don't. I go exactly as far as Date and McGoveran go.
- "He has expressed concerns based on arguments related to mathematical correctness."
  I don't know what distinction Melton has in mind, between correctness that is mathematical and correctness that is not. Nor do I know what arguments based on mathematical correctness he rejects, or what arguments he propounds that are based on incorrectness. Whatever the answers to these questions might be, I certainly haven't expressed any concerns based on mathematical correctness that haven't also been expressed by Date and McGoveran.
- "Darwen is, I think, really a research scientist through and through."
  I don't care if Jim Melton thinks this, but I do care greatly if your readers think so too as a result of reading his article.
  First, my published *oeuvre* in the database field is very slender; it consists almost exclusively of contributions to two books in Chris Date's *Relational Database Writings* series [2].* (By the way, Melton demonstrates no familiarity with those contributions, in spite of his stated claim that he is more familiar with my work "in this area" than he is with Date's.) One chapter by me, entitled "The Askew Wall," in the 1989–1991 volume, is autobiographical. One reason for writing that chapter was to let readers know exactly where I was coming from, as they say: not at all from research science, but rather from the hotbed of industry-strength DBMS implementation over 15 years or more (covering the end of the prerelational era and the beginning of the relational one).
  Further, my main contribution on the missing values problem was a chapter in my *Adventures in Relationland* series entitled "Into The Unknown," in the 1985–1989 volume. The style of that chapter is a million miles from research science; what's more, the chapter makes no claim to novelty of thought or suggestion (though it does ask some of the still unanswered questions).
  I am not now and never have been a research scientist. I have made one or two minor observations of some novelty in the relational field, but

---

*Hugh is, of course, also coauthor on *A Guide to the SQL Standard* (4th edition, Addison-Wesley, 1997) and *Foundation for Object/Relational Databases: The Third Manifesto* (Addison-Wesley, 1998), as well as a contributor to the present book.

even the one that my friends tell me they have most enjoyed (concerning tables with no columns at all) was merely my own development of an observation put my way by Stephen Todd in 1979. I have never set out to write a paper in the academic or "research" style, and even when I once thought I had produced one willy-nilly, I was soon disabused of the thought when it (the paper) was resoundingly rejected by SIGMOD referees.

- "Darwen seems particularly offended by this situation . . ."

    This assertion is followed by a description of a situation that offends me hardly at all, compared with the major objections to the consequences of nulls that Melton has heard me voice more than once at international SQL standardization meetings. For example, I strongly object to the fact that comparison of nulls for the purposes of DISTINCT, GROUP BY, and UNION is not the same as that used for "equals" in a WHERE clause.

One final word, if I may, on the term "research scientist": I cannot help recalling that SQL itself, the butt of those diatribes by me and Date that upset Jim Melton so, was invented by a team of "research scientists through and through." And to that remark I must very quickly add what I've already said many times in public: namely, that the team of research scientists in question is one that has my highest admiration. I say this, despite my severe criticism of the world's acceptance of one particular aspect of their magnificent contribution—a contribution that started in the mid-seventies and continues to the present day.

(Signed)   Hugh Darwen

CLOSING REMARKS

This is Chris Date speaking again; I'd just like to add one comment of my own to those in Hugh's letter. Jim Melton claims that my own objections to "nulls in SQL" can be summarized as follows:

> Whenever data contains nulls, the SQL language required to deal with them properly is often counterintuitive and usually easy to get wrong.

And he goes on to discuss the case of the SQL EXISTS operator in particular:

> Why . . . should the definition of the English word "exists" be the only reasonable definition for the SQL keyword EXISTS? I often suggest to programmers who rely too much on intuition that they should look in their programming language's specifications rather than the unabridged dictionary when using a language construct.

He then examines the SQL definition of EXISTS in some detail.

In response to these claims on Melton's part, let me say first of all that his attempted summary of my objections to "nulls in SQL" is very far from complete! Counterintuitveness is only one of those objections, and a pretty minor one at that. Some of the more major ones are—serendipitously enough—listed on page 47 of the very same issue of *Database Programming & Design* that Melton's article appeared in, in the response to Johnston's article mentioned earlier [3].

That said, however, I do want to take Melton to task over the counterintuitiveness of the SQL EXISTS operator in particular. Obviously I agree that we can define some operator that behaves in the way that EXISTS in SQL actually does behave. But I seriously question the wisdom of calling that operator EXISTS. ("You can call black white if you wish—and furthermore I would defend your right to do so—but I would have to question your wisdom if you actually did such a thing.") The point is this:

- SQL is (of necessity) a *formal* language—one that's supposed to be, in part, an embodiment of the *formal* ideas of first-order predicate logic.
- In particular, SQL's *formal* EXISTS operator is supposed to be SQL's counterpart, not to "the English word 'exists,'" but to the *formal* EXISTS quantifier of that logic.

It seems to me, therefore, that it would have been a good idea if the semantics of the SQL operator were the same as those of the logic quantifier (as was in fact originally intended—I know this from first-hand involvement at the time—and was indeed the case before 3VL got into the act). In fact, however, SQL's EXISTS operator, whatever else it might be, is *not* an implementation of the EXISTS quantifier of 3VL. And that's the crux of my complaint.

Perhaps I should close by apologizing to readers for the title of this month's column. Silly titles seem to have become *de rigueur* in connection with The Great MVL Debate. Melton's own article [7] includes a section entitled "Nulls Aren't Nothing" (though personally I prefer Ed Boyno's variant on this one [1]), and I've used several silly titles myself in this area over the years. For this month's puzzle corner, you might try coming up with some silly titles of your own. I *might* award a small prize for the best suggestion submitted.

REFERENCES

1. Ed Boyno: "Nulls Ain't Nuthin'" (presentation at Ingres World 94, October 1994).

2. C. J. Date: *Relational Database: Selected Writings* (Addison-Wesley, 1986); *Relational Database Writings 1985–1989* (Addison-Wesley, 1990); *Relational*

Database Writings 1989–1991 (Addison-Wesley, 1992); *Relational Database Writings 1991–1994* (Addison-Wesley, 1995).

3. C. J. Date, Hugh Darwen, and David McGoveran: "Nothing to Do with the Case" (Chapter 9 of the present book).

4. Lee Fesperman: Letter to the editor, *Database Programming & Design 8*, No. 9 (September 1995).

5. Tom Johnston: "MVL: Case Open," *Database Programming & Design 8*, No. 2 (February 1995); "The Case for MVL," *Database Programming & Design 8*, No. 3 (March 1995).

6. Tom Johnston: "More to the Point," *Database Programming & Design 8*, No. 11 (November 1995).

7. Jim Melton: "The Debate Rages On: Much Ado About 'Nullthing'," *Database Programming & Design 8*, No. 9 (September 1995).

Answers to Puzzle Corner Problems (Installments 37–42)

Some answers for those who are still puzzling

My column this month is devoted once again to answering the various outstanding "puzzle corner" problems from previous installments. Thanks as usual to those readers who wrote in with their own solutions.

RELATIONS AND RELVARS

Source: "Domains Aren't Relations!" (see Installment 37).

Problem statement: Assuming you understand the *domain* concept, give definitions—as precise as you can—of the *relation* and *relvar* concepts.

Solution: The following definitions are based on those given in *The Third Manifesto*, by Hugh Darwen and myself [1]. We start by defining the term *tuple:*

- A **tuple** *t* is a set of ordered triples of the form $<A,T,v>$, where:
    a. *A* is the name of an **attribute** of *t*. No two distinct triples in *t* have the same attribute name.
    b. *T* is the name of the **type** (domain) of attribute *A* of *t*.

Originally published under the title "Solutions at Last!" in *Database Programming & Design 9*, No. 3, March 1996 (the subtitle was contributed by *DBP&D* too). Reprinted by permission of Miller Freeman Inc.

c. *v* is a value of type *T*, called the **attribute value** for attribute *A* of *t*.

The set of ordered pairs <*A,T*> that is obtained by eliminating the *v* (value) component from each triple in *t* is the **heading** of *t*.

Now we can define the term *relation:*

■ A **relation** *r* consists of a *heading* and a *body*. The **heading** of *r* is a tuple heading *H* as defined above. The **body** of *r* is a set *B* of tuples, all having that same heading *H*. The attributes and corresponding types (domains) identified in *H* are the **attributes** and corresponding **types** (domains) of *r*.

Finally, *relvar:*

■ A **relation variable—relvar** for short—**of type *H*** is a variable whose permitted values are relations with the specified relation heading *H*.

Observe that relvars as just defined can be either *base* or *derived*. A **derived relvar** is a relvar whose value at any given time is a relation that is defined by means of a specified relational expression. A **base relvar** is a relvar that is not derived. *Note:* Base and derived relvars are called *real* and *virtual* relvars, respectively, in *The Third Manifesto* [1]. They correspond to what are known in common parlance as "base relations" and (updatable) "views," respectively.

THE LADDER PROBLEM

Source: "SQL Domains Aren't Domains!" (see Installment 38).

Problem statement: Fig. 1 represents an alley with horizontal floor *BD* and vertical walls *BC* and *DA*. *AB* and *CD* are ladders, 41 feet 8 inches long and

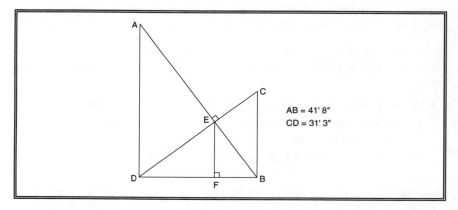

Fig. 1 The intersecting ladders

31 feet 3 inches long respectively. They intersect at right angles. How high is that point of intersection above the ground?

Solution: Let the ladders intersect at *E*, and let *F* be the point on the ground vertically below *E*. For a first attack on the problem, let's see if we can make an intelligent *guess* at the answer. Noting that $AB = 41'8'' = 500'' = 5 * 100''$ and $CD = 31'3'' = 375'' = 5 * 75''$, let's see what happens if the two right angle triangles *ADB* and *CBD* are in fact 3-4-5 triangles. For triangle *ADB*, we would have $AD = 400''$ and $BD = 300''$ (or the other way around); for triangle *CBD*, we would have $CB = 300''$ and $BD = 225''$ (or the other way around). The only consistent possibility is obviously $BD = 300''$, $AD = 400''$, $CB = 225''$.

Since triangle *EFB* is similar to triangle *ADB*, it would then follow that $EF/BF = AD/BD = 4/3$, whence $BF = (3/4) * EF$; since triangle *EFD* is similar to triangle *CBD*, it would also follow that $EF/FD = CB/BD = 3/4$, whence $FD = (4/3) * EF$. But $BF + FD = 300''$, so $EF = (12/25) * 300'' = 144'' = 12'$ (whence $BF = 9'$ and $FD = 16'$).

So our guess at an answer is 12 feet. The fact that $12 = 3 * 4$ is encouraging! But the question is, is this guess consistent with the stipulation that angle *BED* must be a right angle? Well, if $EF = 12'$, we have $BE = 15'$ (from the 3-4-5 triangle *EFB*) and $ED = 20'$ (from the 3-4-5 triangle *EFD*); but $BD = 25'$, so triangle *BED* is a 3-4-5 triangle, and angle *BED* is indeed a right angle. ∎

Here by contrast is a more traditional approach to a solution. In such approaches, it's usually a good idea to work with symbols for as long as possible. So, let:

```
AE = a,  EB = b,  a + b = m  (= 41'8");
CE = c,  ED = d,  c + d = n  (= 31'3");
BD = w  and  EF = h.
```

Then we have:

```
1. w² = b² + d²                          (triangle BED, Pythagoras)
2. w² = (a + b)² - AD²                   (triangle BDA, Pythagoras)
     = (a + b)² - (a² + d²)              (triangle AED, Pythagoras)
     = b² + 2ab - d²
3. d² = ab                               (from 1 and 2)
4. w² = (c + d)² - BC²                   (triangle DBC, Pythagoras)
     = (c + d)² - (b² + c²)              (triangle BEC, Pythagoras)
     = d² + 2cd - b²
5. b² = cd                               (from 1 and 4)
6. wh = bd                               (area triangle BED
                                            measured two ways)
7. ac = bd                               (similar triangles AED, BEC)
     = wh                                (from 6)
8. m² - n²
     = (a + b)² - (c + d)²
     = a² + 2ab + b² - c² - 2cd - d²
     = a² + 2ab + cd - c² - 2cd - ab     (from 3 and 5)
     = a² + ab - c² - cd
     = a(a + b) - c(c + d)
     = am - cn
```

```
 9. m² - n²
      = a² + 2ab + b² - c² - 2cd - d²        (repeat from 8)
      = a² + 2d² + b² - c² - 2b² - d²        (from 3 and 5)
      = a² - b² - c² + d²
      = (a - b)(a + b) - (c - d)(c + d)
      = (a - b)m - (c - d)n
      = (am - cn) - (bm - dn)
10. bm = dn                                  (from 8 and 9)
```

Now we can substitute back for *m* and *n*. Observing that *m* = 4*x* and *n* = 3*x* (where *x* = 10′5″ = 125″), we can simplify our calculations by simply setting *m* = 4 and *n* = 3. We have:

```
11.   d = 4b/3                         (from 10)
12.   a = d²/b                         (from 3)
        = 16b/9                        (from 11)
13.   c = b²/d                         (from 5)
        = 3b/4                         (from 11)
14.   7 = 16 - 9
        = m² - n²
        = am - cn                      (from 8)
        = 4a - 3c
        = 64b/9 - 9b/4                 (from 12 and 13)
15.   b = 36/25                        (from 14)
16.   a = 64/25                        (from 12)
17.   c = 27/25                        (from 13)
18.   d = 48/25                        (from 11)
19.   w²= (36² + 48²)/25²              (from 1)
20.   w = 60/25                        (from 19)
21.   h = (36 * 48)/(60 * 25)          (from 6)
        = 144/125
        = 144 inches                   (125" is the unit)
        = 12 feet.  ∎
```

THE FD CLOSURE PROBLEM

Source: "Functional Dependencies Are Fun (Part 1 of 2)" (see Installment 39).

Problem statement: Write down all of the FDs, trivial as well as nontrivial, that hold in the familiar suppliers relvar SP { S#, P#, QTY } from the suppliers-and-parts database.

Solution: The complete set of FDs—i.e., the *closure*—for relvar SP is as follows:

```
{ S#, P#, QTY } → { S#, P#, QTY }
{ S#, P#, QTY } → { S#, P# }
{ S#, P#, QTY } → { P#, QTY }
{ S#, P#, QTY } → { S#, QTY }
{ S#, P#, QTY } → { S# }
{ S#, P#, QTY } → { P# }
{ S#, P#, QTY } → { QTY }
{ S#, P#, QTY } → { }
```

```
{ S#, P# }        →  { S#, P#, QTY }
{ S#, P# }        →  { S#, P# }
{ S#, P# }        →  { P#, QTY }
{ S#, P# }        →  { S#, QTY }
{ S#, P# }        →  { S# }
{ S#, P# }        →  { P# }
{ S#, P# }        →  { QTY }
{ S#, P# }        →  { }

{ P#, QTY }       →  { P#, QTY }
{ P#, QTY }       →  { P# }
{ P#, QTY }       →  { QTY }
{ P#, QTY }       →  { }

{ S#, QTY }       →  { S#, QTY }
{ S#, QTY }       →  { S# }
{ S#, QTY }       →  { QTY }
{ S#, QTY }       →  { }

{ S# }            →  { S# }
{ S# }            →  { }

{ P# }            →  { P# }
{ P# }            →  { }

{ QTY }           →  { QTY }
{ QTY }           →  { }

{ }               →  { }
```

Subsidiary problem: Let *R* be of degree *n* (have *n* columns). What is the maximum number of FDs that can possibly hold in *R?*

Solution: An FD is a statement of the form $A \rightarrow B$ (where *A* and *B* are each subsets of the set of columns of *R*). Since a set of *n* elements has 2^n possible subsets, each of *A* and *B* has 2^n possible values, and hence an upper limit on the number of possible FDs is 2^{2n}. ∎

FD INFERENCES AND COVERS

Source: "Functional Dependencies Are Fun (Part 2 of 2)" (see Installment 40).

Problem statement: The first problem was as follows. We're given relvar $R\{A,B,C,D,E,F,G\}$ with FDs:

```
A    → B
BC   → DE
AEF  → G
```

Is the FD $ACF \rightarrow DG$ implied by this set of FDs?

Solution: The answer is yes, the FD $ACF \rightarrow DG$ does hold, and is thus a member of the closure of the given set of FDs. Proof:

```
 1. BC    → DE      (given)
 2. ABCF  → ADEF    (1, augmentation)
 3. AEF   → G       (given)
 4. ADEF  → DG      (3, augmentation)
 5. ABCF  → DG      (2 and 4, transitivity)
 6. A     → B       (given)
 7. ACF   → BCF     (6, augmentation)
 8. ACF   → B       (7, decomposition)
 9. ACF   → ACF     (self determination)
10. ACF   → ABCF    (8 and 9, union)
11. ACF   → DG      (10 and 5, transitivity)    ∎
```

The second problem was as follows. We're given relvar $R\{A,B,C,D,E,F\}$ with FDs:

```
AB   → C
C    → A
BC   → D
ACD  → B
BE   → C
CE   → FA
CF   → BD
D    → EF
```

Find an irreducible cover for this set of FDs.

Solution: The first step is to rewrite the given set such that every FD has a single-column right hand side:

```
 1. AB   → C
 2. C    → A
 3. BC   → D
 4. ACD  → B
 5. BE   → C
 6. CE   → A
 7. CE   → F
 8. CF   → B
 9. CF   → D
10. D    → E
11. D    → F
```

Now:

- 2 implies 6, so we can drop 6.
- 8 implies $CF \rightarrow BC$ (by augmentation), which with 3 implies $CF \rightarrow D$ (by transitivity), so we can drop 9.
- 8 implies $ACF \rightarrow AB$ (by augmentation), and 11 implies $ACD \rightarrow ACF$ (by augmentation), and so $ACD \rightarrow AB$ (by transitivity), and so $ACD \rightarrow B$ (by decomposition), so we can drop 4.

No further reductions are possible, and so we're left with the following irreducible set:

```
AB  →  C
C   →  A
BC  →  D
BE  →  C
CE  →  F
CF  →  B
D   →  E
D   →  F
```

Alternatively:

■ 2 implies $CD \rightarrow ACD$ (by composition), which with 4 implies $CD \rightarrow B$ (by transitivity), so we can replace 4 by $CD \rightarrow B$.

■ 2 implies 6, so we can drop 6 (as before).

■ 2 and 9 imply $CF \rightarrow AD$ (by composition), which implies $CF \rightarrow ADC$ (by augmentation), which with the original 4 implies $CF \rightarrow B$ (by transitivity), so we can drop 8.

No further reductions are possible, and so we're left with the following irreducible set:

```
AB  →  C
C   →  A
BC  →  D
CD  →  B
BE  →  C
CE  →  F
CF  →  D
D   →  E
D   →  F
```

Observe, therefore, that there are two distinct irreducible covers for the original set of FDs. *Note:* Corresponding *canonical* covers can be derived from these two irreducible covers by combining the last two FDs ($D \rightarrow E$ and $D \rightarrow F$) into a single FD $D \rightarrow EF$ in each case.

In the same installment, I also asked you to give proofs of the augmentation and reflexivity rules from first principles. Here are such proofs:

■ *Reflexivity:* Let B be a subset of A. Then, whenever two rows $r1$ and $r2$ agree on A, they must necessarily agree on B. Hence $A \rightarrow B$. ■

■ *Augmentation:* Let $A \rightarrow B$. Then, whenever two rows $r1$ and $r2$ agree on A, they also agree on B. Suppose $r1$ and $r2$ agree on AC but not on BC. Since $r1$ and $r2$ obviously agree on C, they must therefore disagree on B. But this is a contradiction, since $r1$ and $r2$ agree on AC and hence on A, and $A \rightarrow B$. Hence $AC \rightarrow BC$. ■

I also asked you to prove the self determination, union, composition, and left augmentation rules from Armstrong's original three rules. Here are such proofs:

■ *Self determination*: A is a subset of A. Hence $A \rightarrow A$ by reflexivity. ■

- *Union: $A \to B$* (given); hence $AA \to AB$ by augmentation, and so $A \to AB$. $A \to C$ (given); hence $AB \to BC$ by augmentation. Hence $A \to BC$ by transitivity. ∎

- *Composition: $A \to B$* (given); hence $AC \to BC$ by augmentation. $C \to D$ (given); hence $BC \to BD$ by augmentation. Hence $AC \to BD$ by transitivity. ∎

- *Left augmentation: $A \to B$* (given); hence $AC \to BC$ by augmentation; hence $AC \to B$ by decomposition. ∎

THE IMPOSSIBLE PROBLEM

Source: "The Saga of IEFBR14" (see Installment 41).

Problem statement: Two positive integers a and b, not necessarily distinct, are chosen such that $1 < a,b \leq 20$. Mathematician S is told the sum $a + b$ (only). Mathematician P is told the product $a * b$ (only). S says to P: "I see no way you can determine my sum." Subsequently, P says to S: "I know your sum." Later still, S says to P: "Now I know your product." What are the values of a and b? (Taken from one of Martin Gardner's *Scientific American* columns [2].)

Solution: I fear I have egg on my face over this one. When I set the problem, I hadn't studied Martin Gardner's solution very carefully. When it came time to prepare this month's column, I naturally tried to produce my own solution first—and in so doing, managed to convince myself that the problem was indeed (as stated) impossible! So I looked at Gardner's solution again, and found that it seemed to have bugs in it. Space prevents me from going into details here (I'll do that in a future column);* let me just say that Gardner claims that the numbers are 4 and 13, but it's immediately obvious that they can't be. (If P were given the product 52, he or she would immediately know that the only factors in range were 4 and 13 and would thus know S's sum, contrary to S's assertion that there is "no way" for P to know that sum.)

STUFF AND NONSENSE

Source: "Round and Round the Nullberry Bush" (see Installment 42).

Problem statement: Silly titles seem to have become *de rigueur* in connection with nulls and The Great MVL Debate. Readers are invited to try coming

---

*See Installment 46.

up with some silly titles of their own. I *might* award a small prize for the best suggestion submitted.

Solution: *Database Programming & Design* deadlines mean I'm writing this "solution" before the problem itself has appeared in print, so readers have had no chance to offer their own suggestions yet. Let me therefore now stipulate that entries must be received by me before the end of March this year (1996) in order to be considered for a prize. In the meantime, I'll simply mention a few titles that have already been used by one writer or another. Here first are some of my own:

NOT Is Not "Not"!

Nothing in Excess

Much Ado about Nothing

Oh No Not Nulls Again

Round and Round the Nullberry Bush

Null and Void

Nothing to Worry About

Stuff and Nonsense

David McGoveran has contributed:

Nothing from Nothing

Basic Logic: Nothing Compares 2 U

Can't Lose What You Never Had

Ed Boyno has given us:

Nulls Ain't Nuthin'

And Hugh Darwen has proposed:

The Null Before the Storm

REFERENCES

1. C. J. Date and Hugh Darwen: *Foundation for Object/Relational Databases: The Third Manifesto.* Reading, Mass.: Addison-Wesley (1998).
2. Martin Gardner: "Mathematical Games," *Scientific American* (December 1979).

Aggregate Operators

*An investigation into the true
nature of operators such as SUM*

An *aggregate operator* is an operator that takes an aggregate value argument—that is, a collection of zero or more scalar values—and produces a single scalar value as its result. In the world of SQL, the best known examples (and the only ones in the standard) are of course COUNT, SUM, AVG, MAX, and MIN. For these particular operators, the aggregate argument is the collection of scalars appearing in a specified column of a specified relation (or, in the case of COUNT(*) only, the collection of rows appearing in a specified relation), and the scalar result is computed from that collection in the obvious way. (Actually it's not as obvious in SQL as it might be, given the possibility that columns in SQL can include nulls. However, there's no such thing as a null in *my* relational model, so I choose to ignore this latter complication.)

Every reader of this column will be familiar with the basic idea of aggregate operators, and of course I've made liberal use of them in earlier installments. These facts notwithstanding, there's a little more to the concept than meets the eye, and so I thought it would be worth our while this month to take a slightly closer look at this topic.

Originally published under the title "Aggregate Functions" in *Database Programming & Design 9,* No. 4, April 1996. Reprinted by permission of Miller Freeman Inc.

BAGS NOT SETS

First, I want to stress the point that the aggregate argument is (in general) a bag, not a set. (A bag is a set that permits duplicates, loosely speaking.) For example, if employees Joe and Alice happen to make the same salary, say $50,000, we want to include the value $50,000 twice, not once, in computing the average employee salary. Thus, the argument to the AVG operator here is certainly not the projection of the employees relation over the salary column, since that projection would, by definition, eliminate one of those two $50,000 figures.

As a matter of fact, it would be doubly wrong to think of that AVG argument as a projection. First, a projection is a set, not a bag, as just explained. Second, it's not a set of scalars, it's a set of *rows* (and the AVG argument is certainly supposed to be scalars, not rows). As I pointed in an earlier installment [5], there's all the difference in the world between a scalar s and a row r that happens to contain just that scalar s.

For simplicity, however, let's ignore this latter refinement for the moment and get back to the main point, which is this: Since the aggregate argument isn't a set, it isn't a relation either, *a fortiori*. It follows that, syntactically, the aggregate argument must *not* be specified as a relational expression. On the other hand, we really don't want to clutter up the language—the relational algebra or whatever it is we're dealing with—with some new kind of "bag expression" construct, especially since "bag expressions" would probably look rather similar to relational expressions and thereby cause some confusion. So what's the best thing to do?

> *Aside:* In fact, it could be argued that the SQL language designers themselves fell into a trap here. Recognizing that in one context at least—namely, arguments to aggregate operator invocations—duplicate elimination was contraindicated, they decided to make duplicate elimination the exception instead of the norm, and so built the language around bag expressions instead of relational expressions. The basic data object in SQL thus became, not the relation, but the row-bag; in other words, duplicate rows were allowed. The rest, as they say, is history. *End of aside.*

The way out of this dilemma is to realize that, in general, aggregate operators take *two* arguments, not one. One of those arguments is indeed specified as a relational expression, and thereby defines a certain relation; the other is the name of a column of that relation, and defines the column over which the aggregation is to be done. Here are some examples (expressed in relational algebra, not SQL):

```
1. AVG ( EMP, SALARY )

2. AVG ( EMP [ SALARY ], SALARY )

3. AVG ( EMP WHERE DEPT# = 'D1', SALARY )
```

In each case, the relational expression argument (that is, the first argument) evaluates to a relation, from which duplicates are eliminated by definition. The column name argument (the second argument) then specifies the column of that relation over which the aggregation is to be performed, and duplicate values are *not* eliminated from that column before the aggregation is done. Note the difference between the first and second examples, therefore; the first gives the average of all employee salaries, the second gives the average of all *distinct* employee salaries. The third gives the average salary for employees in department D1.

SYNTAX

As the examples suggest, the relational algebra syntax for an aggregate operator reference looks like this:

```
agg-fun ( rel-exp [, column ] )
```

Here *agg-fun* is the name of the aggregate operator in question (COUNT, SUM, or whatever), and *rel-exp* and *column* have already been explained. *Note:* For COUNT, *column* is irrelevant and should be omitted; for SUM, AVG, MAX, and MIN, it can optionally be omitted if and only if *rel-exp* evaluates to a single-column relation (as in Example 2 at the end of the previous section), in which case that single column is assumed by default. (Note that, by definition, that single column won't include any duplicate values.)

I won't bother to spell out the semantics of the various operators here, since you already know them, but let me remind you what happens if the aggregate argument happens to be empty—to wit, COUNT and SUM both return zero, MAX and MIN return the smallest and largest value in the domain ("minus infinity" and "plus infinity"), respectively, and AVG is undefined [3]. (SQL, of course, incorrectly returns null in all of these cases, except for COUNT, where it does correctly return zero [3].)

Since an aggregate operator reference returns a scalar value, orthogonality [4] dictates that such a reference must be permitted wherever a scalar literal is permitted—for example, as an operand in a scalar expression (in other words, an aggregate operator reference is itself a new kind of scalar expression). Thus we might write a comparison such as

```
SUM ( EMP, SALARY ) * 2 > 1000000
```

(within a restriction operation, for example). The following, by contrast, is *not* legal (why not?):

```
SUM ( EMP, 2 * SALARY )  >  1000000
```

EXTEND *vs.* SUMMARIZE

Consider the following example (based on the usual suppliers-and-parts database): *For each supplier, get the supplier number and the total number of parts supplied.* A user familiar with the relational algebra would probably propose the following formulation of this query [1]:

```
SUMMARIZE SP BY ( S# ) ADD COUNT AS NPS
```

Given aggregate operator support as sketched in the previous sections, however, we could instead formulate the query as follows:

```
( EXTEND S ADD COUNT ( MATCHING SP ) AS NPS ) [ S#, NPS ]
```

(For a given S row, the relational expression MATCHING SP evaluates to that restriction of SP for which the supplier number is the same as the supplier number in that S row.) Points arising:

1. SUMMARIZE isn't a primitive operation! Any query that can be formulated in terms of SUMMARIZE can always be formulated in terms of EXTEND and aggregate operators instead. (I'm not suggesting that we give up our useful SUMMARIZE operator, of course, but it's interesting, and perhaps pedagogically useful, to note that it can be expressed in terms of other, simpler operations.)

2. Actually, there's at least one reason to prefer the EXTEND version, and that's the following: The EXTEND version (unlike the SUMMARIZE version) produces a result that includes a row for every supplier, even suppliers who currently supply no parts (the count for such a supplier will be zero).

3. To return to the SUMMARIZE version: Note that the expression "COUNT" in that formulation is *not* an aggregate operator reference, according to our definition of that term. Rather, it's just an operand to the SUMMARIZE operation. It has *no meaning* outside that context and cannot appear in other contexts.

Here's another example: *Get part cities that store (a) more than two red parts, (b) two red parts or less.* First, a SUMMARIZE solution to part (a):

```
( ( SUMMARIZE ( P WHERE COLOR = 'Red' )
            BY ( CITY ) ADD COUNT AS N ) WHERE N > 2 ) [ CITY ]
```

What about part (b)? Counterintuitively, just replacing "$>$" by "$\leq$" in the foregoing expression—

```
( ( SUMMARIZE ( P WHERE COLOR = 'Red' )
            BY ( CITY ) ADD COUNT AS N ) WHERE N ≤ 2 ) [ CITY ]
```

—does *not* produce the correct answer, because it fails to include part cities that store no red parts at all! (Note, incidentally, that analogous remarks also apply to the SQL counterparts to these SUMMARIZE expressions, using GROUP BY and HAVING.)

Here by contrast are EXTEND solutions. First, part (a):

```
( EXTEND P [ CITY ] ADD
  COUNT ( ( MATCHING P ) WHERE COLOR = 'Red' ) AS N )
  WHERE N > 2 ) [ CITY ]
```

Unlike its SUMMARIZE counterpart, this solution *can* be converted into a solution for part (b) by simply replacing "$>$" by "$\leq$"—another reason for preferring the EXTEND approach as a general strategy for dealing with aggregate queries.

One final example: *Get the total number of shipments.* The SUMMARIZE formulation—

```
SUMMARIZE SP BY ( ) ADD COUNT AS GRANDTOTAL
```

—fails to give the correct result (zero) if SP happens to contain no rows at all. (More precisely, the correct result is a relation of one column and one row, containing the value zero. The SUMMARIZE formulation, however, gives a relation of one column and *no* rows.) By contrast, the EXTEND formulation—

```
EXTEND TABLE_DEE ADD SUM ( SP, QTY ) AS GRANDTOTAL
```

—always gives the correct result, even if SP contains no rows at all. (Recall that TABLE_DEE is the relation that contains no columns and one row [2].)

SOME REMARKS ON SQL

I'd like to close by drawing your attention to some differences between aggregate operators in the relational algebra, as discussed in the foregoing sections, and their counterparts in SQL.

- By allowing aggregate operators to take two arguments, *rel-exp* and *column,* we stay within the pure framework of the relational model; we don't need "bag expressions," and we therefore also don't need to use SQL's *ad hoc* DISTINCT operator to eliminate duplicates (if required) before the aggregation is done.

- We also don't need SQL's *ad hoc* COUNT(*) operator to count rows instead of scalar values; our analog of COUNT(*) is merely a special case of our general COUNT operator.

- Because the collection of values over which the aggregation is to be done is completely specified (syntactically speaking) as part of the relevant aggregate operator reference, *orthogonality is preserved*. By contrast, consider the following SQL statement:

```
SELECT  SUM ( QTY ) AS SQ
FROM    SP
WHERE   QTY > 100 ;
```

The argument to SUM here is really QTY FROM SP WHERE QTY > 100, and a more syntactically orthodox language would enclose this whole expression in parentheses. But SQL doesn't. One immediate consequence is that an expression of the form AVG(SUM(QTY)) is illegal, because SQL can't figure out which parts of the rest of the statement belong to the AVG argument and which to the SUM argument! To put this another way: SQL effectively supports (a defective form of) our SUMMARIZE operation, but *doesn't* support aggregate operators as such. As a result, orthogonality is lost.

Note: An SQL advocate might argue that at least the SQL statement

```
SELECT  SUM ( QTY ) AS SQ, AVG ( QTY ) AS AQ
FROM    SP
WHERE   QTY > 100 ;
```

is preferable to our "equivalent" version:

```
( EXTEND TABLE_DEE
        ADD SUM ( SP WHERE QTY > 100, QTY ) AS SQ,
        ADD AVG ( SP WHERE QTY > 100, QTY ) AS AQ )
```

because the condition QTY > 100 is stated only once in the SQL version, thereby saving the user some writing (and implying too that the result might be computed in one pass over the rows of SP instead of two). For this month's puzzle corner, I invite you to produce a cogent counterargument to this position.

- My final remark concerns the existential quantifier EXISTS of predicate logic. SQL implements this quantifier (or, rather, an approximation to this quantifier) by, in effect, treating it as an aggregate operator that takes a row-bag argument—just as COUNT(*) does—and returns the scalar value *false* if that row-bag is empty and *true* otherwise. However, observe the following:

1. The aggregate argument for EXISTS is not expressed in the same unorthodox syntactic style as it is for the other SQL aggregate operators, but actually in a more logical style (namely, as a subquery). As

a consequence, EXISTS references, unlike other aggregate operator references, *can* be directly nested in SQL.

2. The data type of the result (*true* or *false*) is not one of the regular SQL data types. As a result, EXISTS operator references can't appear wherever a scalar literal is permitted (in fact, they can't even appear wherever an SQL aggregate operator reference is permitted)—a *major* loss of orthogonality, leading in turn to a major loss of functionality.

REFERENCES

1. C. J. Date: "What's in a Name?", *Database Programming & Design 5,* No. 11 (November 1992). Republished in *Relational Database Writings 1991–1994.* Reading, Mass.: Addison-Wesley (1995).

2. C. J. Date: "Tables with No Columns," *Database Programming & Design 6,* No. 3 (March 1993). Republished in *Relational Database Writings 1991–1994.* Reading, Mass.: Addison-Wesley (1995).

3. C. J. Date: "Empty Bags and Identity Crises," *Database Programming & Design 6,* No. 4 (April 1993). Republished in *Relational Database Writings 1991–1994.* Reading, Mass.: Addison-Wesley (1995).

4. C. J. Date: "A Note on Orthogonality" (see Installment 35).

5. C. J. Date: "Domains Aren't Relations!" (see Installment 37).

SUMMARIZE Revisited

A proposal for revising the relational
SUMMARIZE operator

I first described the SUMMARIZE operation (an operation of the relational algebra) in one of the earliest columns in this series [1]. SUMMARIZE is intended for "column-wise" computation; in other words, it performs much the same function as the combination of GROUP BY and aggregate operators (COUNT, SUM, and so forth) does in SQL. The syntax is as follows:

```
SUMMARIZE rel-exp BY ( cols ) ADD agg-exp AS col
```

For example, the expression

```
SUMMARIZE SP BY ( P# ) ADD SUM ( QTY ) AS TOTQTY
```

("for each part, get the total shipment quantity") yields a relation with heading { P#, TOTQTY }, in which there is one row for each distinct P# value in SP, containing that P# value and the corresponding total quantity. *Note:* As usual, I base my examples on the suppliers-and-parts database (see Fig. 1). The result produced by this particular SUMMARIZE example is shown in Fig. 2. An SQL analog of the example would look like this:

```
SELECT P#, SUM ( QTY ) AS TOTQTY
FROM   SP
GROUP  BY P# ;
```

Originally published in *Database Programming & Design 9,* No. 5, May 1996. Reprinted by permission of Miller Freeman Inc.

S	S#	SNAME	STATUS	CITY
	S1	Smith	20	London
	S2	Jones	10	Paris
	S3	Blake	30	Paris
	S4	Clark	20	London
	S5	Adams	30	Athens

P	P#	PNAME	COLOR	WEIGHT	CITY
	P1	Nut	Red	12	London
	P2	Bolt	Green	17	Paris
	P3	Screw	Blue	17	Rome
	P4	Screw	Red	14	London
	P5	Cam	Blue	12	Paris
	P6	Cog	Red	19	London

SP	S#	P#	QTY
	S1	P1	300
	S1	P2	200
	S1	P3	400
	S1	P4	200
	S1	P5	100
	S1	P6	100
	S2	P1	300
	S2	P2	400
	S3	P2	200
	S4	P2	200
	S4	P4	300
	S4	P5	400

Fig. 1   Suppliers and parts (sample values)

P#	TOTQTY
P1	600
P2	1000
P3	400
P4	500
P5	500
P6	100

Fig. 2   SUMMARIZE SP BY (P#) ADD SUM(QTY) AS TOTQTY

EMPTY-SET PROBLEMS

Unfortunately, as I showed in my column last month [2], SUMMARIZE runs into problems—at least, it behaves in ways that might reasonably be argued to be somewhat counterintuitive—when it has to deal with empty-set arguments. (Analogous criticisms apply to the use of GROUP BY with aggregate operators in SQL, of course.) For example, the expression

```
1. SUMMARIZE SP BY ( ) ADD COUNT AS GRANDTOTAL
```

(loosely, "get the total number of shipments") might be expected to give zero if SP happens to be empty, but it doesn't; instead, it gives an empty result.

(More precisely, it gives a relation of one column, called GRANDTOTAL, and no rows.)

In a similar manner, the expression

```
2. SUMMARIZE SP BY ( S# ) ADD COUNT AS NPS
```

(loosely, "for each supplier, get the total number of shipments") might be expected to give a result row with a count of zero for any supplier for whom the corresponding set of shipments happens to be empty, but it doesn't; instead, such suppliers simply aren't represented in the result relation at all.

As a third and final example, I showed last month that the expression

```
3. ( ( SUMMARIZE ( P WHERE COLOR = 'Red' )
       BY ( CITY ) ADD COUNT AS N ) WHERE N ≤ 2 ) [ CITY ]
```

(loosely, "get part cities that store two red parts or less") once again fails to produce the right answer, because it fails to include part cities that store no red parts at all.

Before going any further, I should point out that the foregoing problems aren't really problems with the SUMMARIZE operation as such; rather, they're problems caused by the fact that the *argument* to that operation already excludes certain important information. In the third example, for instance, that argument is defined to exclude parts that aren't red; thus, there's no way we can obtain part cities in the final result that store no red parts at all. This explanation doesn't make the overall behavior any less counterintuitive, however.

I went on to point out last month that we could always formulate queries such as those just discussed in terms of EXTEND instead of SUMMARIZE and thereby avoid the counterintuitive behavior. Here are EXTEND analogs of the three examples:

```
1. EXTEND TABLE_DEE ADD SUM ( SP, QTY ) AS GRANDTOTAL
```

(Recall that TABLE_DEE is the relation that contains no columns and one row.)

```
2. ( EXTEND S ADD COUNT ( MATCHING SP ) AS NPS ) [ S#, NPS ]
```

```
3. ( EXTEND P [ CITY ]
     ADD COUNT ( ( MATCHING P ) WHERE COLOR = 'Red' ) AS N )
     WHERE N ≤ 2 ) [ CITY ]
```

FIXING THE PROBLEMS

Despite the fact that we can fix the problems by using EXTEND instead, it would be a pity to give up on our user-friendly SUMMARIZE operator just because it happens to suffer from what many people would regard as a mere glitch. In this section, therefore, I want to present an improved version of SUMMARIZE, one that

a. doesn't suffer from that glitch, and yet

b. is otherwise functionally identical to the original version.

(In other words, I'm talking about a compatible extension!) *Note:* This improved version of SUMMARIZE is due to Hugh Darwen. I previously discussed it (briefly) in my book *An Introduction to Database Systems* [3].
The syntax is as follows:

```
SUMMARIZE rel-exp-1 BY rel-exp-2 ADD agg-exp AS col
```

Explanation:

- The two relational expressions *rel-exp-1* and *rel-exp-2* must evaluate to relations, *R1* and *R2* say, such that the heading of *R2* is some subset of the heading of *R1*. In other words, every column of *R2* must have the same name as some column of *R1* (also, columns with the same name must be of the same type); to put it yet another way, *R2* must be of the same type as some projection of *R1*.

- The result, *R3* say, is a relation with a heading consisting of the entire heading of *R2*, extended with the specified column name *col*. Each row of *R2* generates exactly one result row in *R3*. Each such row consists of the corresponding row of *R2*, extended with the specified aggregate (*agg-exp*) value; that aggregate value is computed over all rows of *R1* that match that *R2* row over all common columns (that is, over all columns of *R2*).

Let's see how the three examples from the previous section fare with this new version of SUMMARIZE. I'll skip Example 1 for a moment. Example 2 looks like this:

```
2. SUMMARIZE SP BY S [ S# ] ADD COUNT AS NPS
```

If you compare this expression with the previous version, you'll see that the only change is that the BY clause has changed from BY (S#) to BY S[S#]. (The expression S[S#], of course, denotes the projection of suppliers S over column S#.) And indeed this change is an intuitively reasonable one, because we want a result that includes one row for each supplier number in S, not each supplier number in SP (as the previous version SUMMARIZE SP BY . . . gave us). The new result has heading { S#, NPS } and consists of five rows, one for each of the five supplier numbers in the projection S[S#]. Each such row contains the applicable supplier number and the corresponding shipment count. In particular, of course, a supplier who supplies no parts (such as supplier S5 in Fig. 1) *is* represented in S[S#] and therefore appears in the result, with a count of zero.

Here's Example 3:

```
3. ( ( SUMMARIZE ( P WHERE COLOR = 'Red' )
      BY P [ CITY ] ADD COUNT AS N ) WHERE N ≤ 2 ) [ CITY ]
```

This one requires a little more explanation. Again, I've changed the BY clause, this time from BY (CITY) to BY P[CITY]; and, once again, the change is reasonable, because we want the SUMMARIZE to produce a result that includes a row for *every* part city, not just for every part city that happens to store at least one red part. Given the sample data of Fig. 1, the SUMMARIZE result thus looks as shown in Fig. 3. (For London, there are three matching rows in the restriction P WHERE COLOR = 'Red'; for Paris and Rome, there are no such matching rows at all.) The SUMMARIZE result is then restricted to just those rows for which N ≤ 2; finally, that restriction is projected over CITY to produce the desired overall result (consisting of just the cities Paris and Rome).

CITY	N
London	3
Paris	0
Rome	0

Fig. 3   SUMMARIZE (P WHERE COLOR = 'Red')
BY P [CITY] ADD COUNT AS N

Now let's return to Example 1 ("find the total number of shipments"):

```
1. SUMMARIZE SP BY TABLE_DEE ADD COUNT AS GRANDTOTAL
```

I've replaced the BY clause BY () by BY TABLE_DEE. Recall once again that TABLE_DEE is the relation that contains no columns and one row; in particular, observe that TABLE_DEE is of the same type as "some" projection of *every* relation (namely, the projection over no columns at all), so that summarizing by TABLE_DEE is always a legal operation! In the example, the overall expression evaluates to a relation with one column, called GRANDTOTAL, and one row; and, if there aren't any shipments, then that one row will contain the value zero, as desired.

A note on syntax: We might as well agree that TABLE_DEE is the default for *rel-exp-2* and thereby agree that a BY clause of the form BY TABLE_DEE can optionally be omitted. Example 1 would then become just

```
1. SUMMARIZE SP ADD COUNT AS GRANDTOTAL
```

which seems (to me, at least) a nice user-friendly formulation.

A COMPATIBLE EXTENSION

So far I've shown that the "new, improved" version of SUMMARIZE doesn't suffer from the empty-set glitch. What about our other requirement, that the "new, improved" version be a compatible extension of our original SUMMARIZE? Well, let's consider what happens if *rel-exp-2* doesn't just have the same heading as some projection of *rel-exp-1* but actually *is* such a projection. For example:

```
SUMMARIZE SP BY SP [ S# ] ADD COUNT AS NPS
```

The result will have heading { S#, NPS } and will have one row for each supplier number appearing in the projection SP[S#]—in other words, each supplier number in SP. And each such row will consist of the applicable supplier number, together with the corresponding shipment count. In other words, this overall expression is functionally identical to its original SUMMARIZE analog:

```
SUMMARIZE SP BY ( S# ) ADD COUNT AS NPS
```

It follows that (at least semantically) our new SUMMARIZE is indeed a compatible extension of the original version.

PUZZLE CORNER

Use the new version of SUMMARIZE described in this month's column to give relational algebra formulations of the following queries:

1. For each blue part, get the part number and the corresponding total quantity.
2. Get part numbers of parts supplied in a total quantity less than 300.
3. Get part numbers of parts supplied in an average quantity less than 300.

REFERENCES

1. C. J. Date: "What's in a Name?", *Database Programming & Design 5,* No. 11 (November 1992). Republished in *Relational Database Writings 1991–1994.* Reading, Mass.: Addison-Wesley (1995).

2. C. J. Date: "Aggregate Operators" (see Installment 44).

3. C. J. Date: *An Introduction to Database Systems* (6th edition). Reading, Mass.: Addison-Wesley (1995).

The Art of the Possible

A detailed look at the "impossible problem" from Installment 41

I set the following "impossible problem" in my January 1996 column. It was taken from Martin Gardner's December 1979 "Mathematical Games" column in *Scientific American*. Gardner himself described the problem as "impossible" because, as he put it, it seems to lack sufficient information for a solution.

- *Problem (first version):* Two positive integers a and b, not necessarily distinct, are chosen such that $1 < a,b \leq 20$. Mathematician S is told the sum $a + b$ (only). Mathematician P is told the product $a * b$ (only). S says to P: "I see no way you can determine my sum." Later, P says to S: "I know your sum." Later still, S says to P: "Now I know your product." What are the values of a and b?

By rights I should have given a solution to this problem in my March 1996 column, but I didn't. Instead, I said this:

- I fear I have egg on my face over this one. When I set the problem, I hadn't studied Martin Gardner's solution very carefully. When it came time to prepare this month's column, I naturally tried to produce my own solution first—and, in doing so, managed to convince myself that the problem was indeed (as stated) impossible! So I looked at Gardner's solution again, and found that it seemed to have bugs in it. Space prevents me from going into details here (I'll do that in a future column); let me

Originally published in *Database Programming & Design 9,* No. 6, June 1996. Reprinted by permission of Miller Freeman Inc.

just say that Gardner claims the numbers are 4 and 13, but it's immediately obvious that they can't be. (If *P* were given the product 52, he or she would immediately know that the only factors in range were 4 and 13 and would thus know *S*'s sum, contrary to *S*'s assertion that there is "no way" for *P* to know that sum.)

This is that promised future column.

WHY THE FIRST VERSION IS IMPOSSIBLE

I'll begin by showing just why the problem as I stated it in January is indeed impossible. First, note that *S*'s statement "I see no way you can determine my sum" implies immediately that *S*'s sum can't be the sum of two primes, *q* and *r* say. For if *a* and *b* actually were *q* and *r*, then *P*'s product would be $q * r$ and the only possible factors would be *q* and *r* themselves, whence *P* would know that *S*'s sum is $q + r$, contrary to *S*'s assertion that there's "no way" *P* could know that sum.

So *P* knows that *S*'s sum is not the sum of two primes. Now we appeal to *Goldbach's Conjecture,* which asserts that every even number greater than two *is* the sum of two primes. Goldbach's Conjecture has never been formally proved, but according to Gardner it has at least been verified for all even numbers up to 100 million (!). Thus, we know that *S*'s sum is none of the following: 4, 6, 8 . . . , 40 (40 is the upper limit, of course, since *a* and *b* are each less than or equal to 20).* And since 2 is a prime, we can also eliminate all odd sums (in the range) of the form $q + 2$, where *q* is a prime less than 20; this allows us to eliminate 5, 7, 9, 13, 15, 19, and 21. We're left with the following "initially plausible" sums:

    11   17   23   25   27   29   31   33   35   37   39

Suppose *S*'s sum were 11. Then a possible (a,b) pair would be (3,8). But if these are in fact the actual (a,b) values, *P*'s product would be 24, for which the only factors in range that add up to one of the plausible sums are 3 and 8 themselves. *P* would thus know that *S*'s sum was 11, contrary to *S*'s assertion "I see *no way* you can determine my sum" (emphasis added).

It turns out that all of the "initially plausible" sums can be eliminated in a similar manner! I omit the details here, but show a pair of candidate (a,b) values in each case that can serve as a basis for performing that elimination:

---

*We do have to assume that *S* and *P* are each aware of this fact (namely, that *a* and *b* are each less than 20), though actually the original problem statement did not say as much.

```
17:    4,13
23:   10,13
25:   12,13
27:   13,14
29:   13,16
31:   13,18
33:   13,20
35:   17,18
37:   17,20
39:   19,20
```

So there is no solution; that is, there are no values for a and b that satisfy the conditions of the problem as stated. More precisely, there are no numbers a and b such that:

1. $1 < a,b \leq 20$

2. The sum $a + b$ can be deduced from the assertion that it *cannot* be deduced.

Note too that:

1. The product $a * b$ is irrelevant to the problem.

2. The final assertion ("Now I know your product") is irrelevant to the problem.

3. If the sum *could* be deduced from the assertion that it couldn't, that assertion would be self-contradictory.

With hindsight, it's tempting to claim that this last fact alone should have been sufficient to show immediately, without detailed analysis, that the problem in fact has no solution.

REVISED PROBLEM STATEMENT

Gardner subsequently agreed that the problem as originally stated was impossible: "Because I gave an upper bound of 20 for the two selected numbers, [my] solution became totally inapplicable . . . [the] correct upper bound [should have been] 100" (from Gardner's March 1980 *Scientific American* column). He went on to say that the problem was due to David J. Sprows, who published it in *Mathematics Magazine 49*, No. 2 (March 1976); a solution appeared in the November 1977 issue (*Mathematics Magazine 50*, No. 5). And in his May 1980 column, Gardner stated that an earlier version of the problem, due to Hans Freudenthal, had appeared in the Dutch journal *Nieuw Archief Voor Wiskunde (Series 3) 17* (1969) and *18* (1970).

However, my own investigations into the origins of the problem turned up two apparently small, but important, additional errors in the way the first version had been stated:

1. The upper bound of 100 was supposed to apply to the *sum* of the two numbers $a + b$, not to the numbers a and b themselves.

2. S was not supposed to say to P "I see no way you can determine my sum," but rather just to agree with P that P doesn't know it. The self-contradiction inherent in the idea that the sum could be deduced from the assertion that it couldn't is thus avoided.

Here then is a revised statement of the problem that corrects these errors:

■ *Problem (second version):* Two positive integers a and b, not necessarily distinct, are chosen such that $a, b > 1$ and $a + b \leq 100$. Mathematician S is told the sum $a + b$ (only). Mathematician P is told the product $a * b$ (only). P says to S: "I don't know your sum." S says to P: "Yes, I knew that." Later, P says to S: "Now I know your sum." Later still, S says to P: "Now I know your product." What are the values of a and $b?$[*]

A SOLUTION TO THE REVISED PROBLEM

P says "I don't know your sum"; hence P's product (p, say) can't be the product of two primes. S says "Yes, I knew that"; hence, by the same argument we used earlier, S's sum (s, say) can't be the sum of two primes. Thus, the only initially plausible values for s are:

11			17	
	23		27	29
		35	37	
41			47	
51	53		57	59
		65	67	
71			77	79
	83		87	89
	93	95	97	

Let's agree to refer to this set of numbers as IPV.

Next, exactly one of a and b must be even (for if they were both even or both odd, their sum would be even and hence not in IPV). Consider the possibility that the even member of the pair is a power of two, 2^n say, and the odd member is a prime, q say. Then P's product would be $2^n * q$, and the only possible factors—under the requirement that one be even and the other odd—would in fact be those two numbers 2^n and q, whence P would indeed be able to say "Now I know your sum."

However, if that sum could be expressed as the sum of a power of two and an odd prime *in two different ways*, then S would still not be able to say "Now

---

[*]Again it is necessary to assume that S and P are aware of the constraints on a and b—namely, that they are both greater than one and their sum is not greater than 100.

I know your product." For example, the sum 11, a member of IPV, is equal to both $4 + 7$ and $8 + 3$, corresponding to products 28 and 24 respectively, for which the only possible factors—under the requirement that one be even and the other odd—are (4,7) and (3,8) respectively. So *P* would indeed be able to determine that *s* was 11, but *S* would not know whether *p* was 28 or 24.

These observations allow us to eliminate all of the numbers in IPV except the following as possible values for *s:*

17   29   41   53   59   65   89   97

Note carefully, however, that whereas *we* can eliminate (e.g.) the value 11 as a possible sum, *P cannot*—not yet, at any rate—because, at the time he or she says "Now I know your sum," *S* has not yet said "Now I know your product." At that time, in other words, *P* knows only that the values in IPV are still "plausible" values for *s*.

Suppose $s = 97$. Then:

- A possible (a,b) pair would be (8,89). But if these were in fact the actual (a,b) values, *P*'s product would be $8 * 89$, for which the only factors in range—under the requirement that one be even and the other odd—would in fact be 8 and 89 themselves (note that 8 is a power of two). *P* would thus know that *S*'s sum was 97.

- Another possible (a,b) pair would be (33,64) (note that 64 is a power of two); a similar analysis shows that, again, *P* would know that *S*'s sum was 97.

It follows that, if $s = 97$, then whereas *P* would know *s*, *S* could not know *p*—that is, *S* could not determine whether the (a,b) values were (8,89) or (33,64), and so could not determine *P*'s product. Thus, $s \neq 97$.

A similar analysis allows us to eliminate the following as possible values for *s* as well (note in each case that the value in question can be expressed as the sum of a power of two and an odd number—not necessarily an odd *prime*—in two different ways):

```
89  =  16 + 73  =  25 + 64
65  =   4 + 61  =  32 + 33
59  =  16 + 43  =  27 + 32
53  =  16 + 37  =  21 + 32
41  =   4 + 37  =  16 + 25
29  =   2 + 27  =  13 + 16
```

So *s* must be 17. Thus, there are seven possible (a,b) values: (2,15), (3,14), (4,13), (5,12), (6,11), (7,10), (8,9). Let's examine them one by one.

- (2,15): *P*'s product would be 30, which can be factored as $2 * 15$, $3 * 10$, or $5 * 6$. Since $2 + 15 = 17$ and $5 + 6 = 11$ are both in IPV, *P* would have no way of determining which of the two—17 or 11—*S*'s sum actually was and thus could not say "Now I know your sum." Hence $(a,b) \neq (2,15)$.

In a like manner we can eliminate:

- (3,14), which gives a product of $42 = 2 * 21 = 3 * 14$;
- (5,12), which gives a product of $60 = 3 * 20 = 5 * 12$;
- (6,11), which gives a product of $66 = 2 * 33 = 6 * 11$;
- (7,10), which gives a product of $70 = 2 * 35 = 7 * 10$; and
- (8,9), which gives a product of $72 = 3 * 24 = 8 * 9$.

Hence $(a,b) = (4,13)$. P, of course, already knows that the product is 52, for which the only plausible factors (one even, one odd) are 4 and 13; hence P can validly say "Now I know your sum." From this claim, S (who of course already knows that the sum is 17) is able to use exactly the same arguments as we just did to eliminate all pairs of numbers that add up to 17, except for the pair (4,13). Hence S can validly say "Now I know your product." ∎

So Martin Gardner's original answer was in fact the right one! It was the problem that was wrong.

BACK TO DATABASES

In order to give this month's column at least a tenuous connection to the real world (I mean the world of database management, of course), I'll close with a squib I composed recently. I make no claims of great artistic merit for this piece, but a serious message does lie not too far beneath the doggerel. I call it *Heed Relation Rules. Note:* "SQL" is meant to be pronounced "sequel" unless hyphenated (S-Q-L), when it is pronounced as spelled ("ess-cue-ell").

The tables in the database
Though fully normalized
Were still somewhat anomalous—
It couldn't be disguised.

The trouble was the schema
Had, sad enough to tell,
Been designed by someone who
Believed in S-Q-L.

As a result, the tables
Were filled with nulls—a state
Of affairs that S-Q-L
Allows, though one I hate.

(As an aside, I note that
To say a table might
"Contain a null" is nonsense!—
In fact the very height

Of auto-contradiction—
Since nulls "do not exist";
But suchlike solecisms
Always arise in this

Absurd and self-negating
Approach to this whole mess.
I could go on much longer—
However, I digress.)

What's more, the tables also
Had duplicates! I mean,
In table *t,* rows *a* and *b*—
No diff'rence to be seen—

Could be identical in all
Respects (it's true, it's true!)
And yet the users had to know
They were not one but two.

The set containing *a* and *b*
Has cardinality
Not two but one!—and here I speak
Completely logic'lly.

It follows that in S-Q-L
A table's not a set;
In fact a table is a *bag,*
That is, a *multiset.*

How *can* a crazy concept
Like this one possibly
Make sense to poor old users
Plain folks like you and me?

I haven't even mentioned yet
The way the silly notions
Discussed so far interreact
And lead us into oceans

Of complication and despond
And general distress.
Are two nulls equal (duplicates)?
I fear, both *no* and *yes*.

The moral of my poem is
(In case it isn't plain)
We should eschew those concepts that
Do not seem very sane.

The heresy of duplicates,
The heresy of nulls:
Both lead to awful problems;
The combination dulls

(Unless we're very careful)
The analytic sense,
The intellectual faculty,
And causes much intense

Frustration, pain, and frenzied
Attempts to extricate
Data from the database
And make the crooked straight.

And so I say it one more time:
Do what you know is cool;
Take my advice, as One Who Knows,
And **HEED RELATION RULES.**

Quota Queries
(Part 1 of 3)

*A common requirement
that's not widely understood*

The Third Manifesto [2], by Hugh Darwen and myself, includes the following
"very strong suggestion" (slightly paraphrased here):

- *The system should provide some convenient means of expressing **quota
  queries**.*

Examples of quota queries might be "get the three shortest employees" or "get
the two highest-budget departments" (in a personnel database). The term *quota
query* itself derives from Codd's 1971 paper on Data Sublanguage ALPHA
[1]; ALPHA was a hypothetical language, unfortunately never implemented,
that did include some quota query features.

Quota queries are needed quite often in practice, yet the SQL standard has
no direct support for them. Well, perhaps this criticism is a little unfair; as
we'll see later, the standard does include some support that might be characterized as "almost direct," or at least not too indirect. In addition, certain SQL
products do provide features that can be regarded as more directly supporting
the requirement, though of course those features are nonstandard and usually
of an *ad hoc* nature; details can be found in a paper by Fabian Pascal [4], which
also discusses various workaround approaches to the problem.

Originally published in *Database Programming & Design 9,* No. 7, July 1996. Reprinted
by permission of Miller Freeman Inc.

Be that as it may, a typical SQL formulation of (for example) the "three shortest employees" query will tend to look something like the following pseudocode:

```
DECLARE CURSOR TSE FOR
        SELECT EMP#
        FROM    EMP
        ORDER   BY HEIGHT ;

DECLARE I INTEGER ;
DECLARE TEMP# CHAR(5) ;
DECLARE RESULT(3) CHAR(5) ;

OPEN TSE ;
DO I = 1 TO 3 ;
   FETCH NEXT FROM TSE INTO TEMP# ;
   RESULT(I) :=  TEMP# ;
END ;
CLOSE TSE ;
```

But we wanted a *convenient* solution—and whatever else it might mean, "convenient" here surely has to mean *nonprocedural*. The code just shown is not nonprocedural. One consequence is that the DBMS has no way of knowing that the user is trying to find just three rows; in particular, the system optimizer doesn't have this information, and performance is thus likely to be poor. Other consequences include a loss of usability and a concomitant loss of productivity—not to mention the fact that such a procedural solution is not available to the (nonprogrammer) end user at all.

A PROPOSED SOLUTION

A colleague, Adrian Larner, reviewing an early draft of *The Third Manifesto,* commented on the quota queries suggestion as follows [3] (thanks to Adrian for permission to quote him here):

(Begin quote)

I don't quite understand this problem. Isn't "get the three shortest employees" given by:

```
SELECT EX.EMP#
FROM   EMP EX, EMP EY
WHERE  EX.HEIGHT ≥ EY.HEIGHT
GROUP  BY EX.EMP#
HAVING 3 ≤ COUNT (*) ;
```

(We could get more than three, if several employees are of equal height.) Or is all that is being requested a sort of shorthand for this kind of query—a convenient sugaring?

(End quote)

Well, let's think about these comments for a moment:

- First of all, can you understand right away how the proposed SQL solution works? I don't think it's very obvious; the intuitive meaning doesn't exactly leap off the page, in my opinion.

- Second, of course (as Adrian admits), that proposed solution might return more than three employees. It might also return less than three, if less than three exist in total. (I should note in passing that the procedural "solution" shown earlier suffers from related—though not identical—problems. For one thing, that procedural code as it currently stands will fail if there are less than three employees. For another, it might conceivably return different results on different occasions—even if the database remains unchanged in the interim! I'll return to these two points in my column next month.)

- Third, Adrian's proposed solution gives the wrong answer anyway! I'll leave it to you to verify that, given the sample data of Fig. 1, it actually returns all seven employees. (The correct answer is, of course, the set of employees E1, E4, and E6.)

EMP	EMP#	WEIGHT	HEIGHT
	E1	120	70
	E2	170	71
	E3	170	72
	E4	140	70
	E5	120	71
	E6	190	70
	E7	120	72

Fig. 1   A sample employees relation

First moral: It's easy to lose your way in SQL statements that involve a Θ-join (that is to say, a Cartesian product followed by a restriction) of a relation with itself, together with GROUP BYs and SELECTs that refer to one side of that join, HAVINGs that refer to the other, and "backward comparisons" such as $3 \leq \text{COUNT}(*)$ instead of $\text{COUNT}(*) \geq 3$. In other words, I would take the position that—quite apart from the fact that it's wrong!—a statement such as the one under consideration doesn't constitute a very "convenient" means of expressing the desired query.

CORRECTING THE FIRST ATTEMPT

Well, Adrian quickly followed up his first comment with another [3]:

(Begin quote)

Rats! . . . What I wanted to say was:

```
SELECT  EX.EMP#
FROM    EMP EX, EMP EY
WHERE   EX.HEIGHT > EY.HEIGHT
OR      EX.EMP# = EY.EMP#
GROUP   BY EX.EMP#
HAVING  3 ≥ COUNT (*) ;
```

(End quote)

Well, I'll leave it to you to verify that—again using the sample data of Fig. 1, which we might as well take as our running example—this second attempt actually yields no employees at all! *Second moral:* Same as the first.

To be fair, Adrian knew that his second proposed solution didn't produce the right answer: "Although this was what I *wanted* to say, SQL (in this case, not strictly SQL but the relational model) doesn't allow it—no empty groups" [3]. Personally, I don't think the fault here lies with either SQL or the relational model, but rather with an incorrect perception of how SQL and the relational model "ought" to work; I also think that "no empty groups" is inadequate as an explanation of why the second proposed solution fails. Anyway, Adrian then went on to give a correct formulation:

```
SELECT  EX.EMP#
FROM    EMP EX, EMP EY
WHERE   EX.HEIGHT > EY.HEIGHT
OR      EX.EMP# = EY.EMP#
GROUP   BY EX.EMP#
HAVING  3 ≥ COUNT (*) ;
```

I leave it to you to verify that this formulation is indeed correct and does yield the correct result. Well, more precisely, it *happens* to yield exactly the three employees E1, E4, and E6 in the example; but if (say) employee E7 also had height 70 inches instead of 72 inches, then it would yield employee E7 as well (in other words, it doesn't guarantee that exactly three employees are returned). Even if we ignore this latter point, however, do you think the formulation is "convenient"? I don't; in fact, I think it's very awkward—not least because it's far from obvious, at first glance, what it means.

AN IMPROVED SOLUTION

Can we do better than Adrian's GROUP BY and HAVING formulations of the query? Well, consider the following slightly more precise restatement of the original problem:

■ Get all employees *EX* such that the number of shorter employees *EY* is less than three.

(This restatement ignores the requirement—if requirement it truly is—that exactly three employees are wanted. I propose to ignore this particular detail for the remainder of this installment; I'll come back to it next month.) Given this restatement of the problem, a correct SQL formulation becomes obvious, surely:

```
SELECT  EX.EMP#
FROM    EMP EX
WHERE   (SELECT COUNT (*)
         FROM    EMP EY
         WHERE   EY.HEIGHT < EX.HEIGHT) < 3 ;
```

Not only is this formulation correct (at least for the simplified version of the problem), I would argue that it's much easier to understand and very much less error-prone than the GROUP BY and HAVING formulations we looked at earlier. In a word, I think this formulation is "convenient."

Note: This "convenient" SQL formulation (which I should point out in passing would have been invalid in SQL prior to SQL/92!) is in fact a fairly direct transliteration of its relational calculus counterpart:

```
EX.EMP# WHERE COUNT ( EY WHERE EY.HEIGHT < EX.HEIGHT ) < 3
```

(where EX and EY both represent EMP rows). For interest—and by way of contrast—here is a relational algebra equivalent:

```
T1  :=  EMP RENAME HEIGHT AS HX ;
T2  :=  EMP RENAME HEIGHT AS HY ;
T3  :=  EXTEND T1 ADD COUNT ( T2 WHERE HY < HX ) AS #_SHORTER ;
T4  :=  T3 WHERE #_SHORTER < 3 ;
T5  :=  T4 [ EMP# ] ;
```

Of course, this sequence of five steps can be compressed into a single expression:

```
( ( EXTEND ( EMP RENAME HEIGHT AS HX )
    ADD COUNT ( ( EMP RENAME HEIGHT AS HY ) WHERE HY < HX )
    AS #_SHORTER )
  WHERE #_SHORTER < 3 ) [ EMP# ]
```

CONCLUDING REMARKS

This concludes my introduction to what the quota queries problem is all about—though I haven't yet dealt properly with the cardinality issue (that is, the question as to how we might restrict the result to a specified number of rows, or even whether we truly want to impose such a restriction). Next month, I'll focus in on a more precise restatement of the problem and consider a more systematic method of addressing it.

I'll close as usual with a small puzzle (nothing to do with quota queries, however). Fig. 2 represents four cards displayed on a table. You're told that each card has either a blue or a yellow back, and either a square or a triangle on the front. What's the minimum number of cards you need to turn over in order to give a guaranteed correct answer to the question: *Does every card with a blue back have a square on the front?*

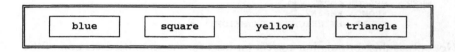

Fig. 2   The cards as displayed

REFERENCES

1. E. F. Codd: "A Data Base Sublanguage Founded on the Relational Calculus," Proc. 1971 ACM SIGFIDET Workshop on Data Description, Access and Control, San Diego, Calif. (November 1971).

2. Hugh Darwen and C. J. Date: "The Third Manifesto," *ACM SIGMOD Record 24,* No. 1 (March 1995). See also the book-length version *Foundation for Object/ Relational Databases: The Third Manifesto.* Reading, Mass.: Addison-Wesley (1998).

3. Adrian Larner: Private communications (July 13th–4th, 1994).

4. Fabian Pascal: "Will SQL Come to Order?" Part I, *SQL Forum 1,* No. 10 (July/August 1992); Part II, *SQL Forum 1,* No. 11 (September/October 1992).

Quota Queries
(Part 2 of 3)

*Refining the basic quota
query requirement*

Last month I introduced the basic idea of quota queries, using the example "get
the three shortest employees" (given the sample data of Fig. 1, the result of this
query consists of the employees E1, E4, and E6). I tried to show that, even if
we simplify matters somewhat by ignoring certain special cases—for instance,
what happens if the relation contains too few rows?—the quota query problem
is a little more complex than it might appear at first glance. This month, I want
to try and pin the problem down more precisely. Next month, I'll conclude this
three-part series by examining further applications and implications of the
overall quota query concept.

EMP	EMP#	WEIGHT	HEIGHT
	E1	120	70
	E2	170	71
	E3	170	72
	E4	140	70
	E5	120	71
	E6	190	70
	E7	120	72

Fig. 1 A sample employees relation

Originally published in *Database Programming & Design 9,* No. 8, August 1996. Reprinted
by permission of Miller Freeman Inc.

q-QUOTAS

As we did last month, let's take the query "get the the three shortest employees" as our running example, at least until further notice. Well, of course, the first point to make is that the phrase "the three shortest employees" is ambiguous. For one thing, the relation might be too small—that is, there might not even be three employees. For another, different employees might have the same height, with the result that there might be more than three who are shorter than everyone else (I'm speaking rather loosely here, of course). So let's try to make matters more precise.

Refer again to the EMP relation in Fig. 1. Let's continue to refer to individual rows of that relation by their EMP# value, and let's rank those rows by increasing HEIGHT value:

```
E1   1=   ("first equals")
E2   4=
E3   6=
E4   1=
E5   4=
E6   1=
E7   6=
```

Actually, as we'll see in a moment, it's more convenient to number the ranking positions from zero instead of one. So, rearranging the rows into their ranking order, listing them horizontally instead of vertically, and dropping the equals signs, we have the following pairings:

```
E1   E4   E6   E2   E5   E3   E7
0    0    0    3    3    5    5
```

It's also convenient to extend this set of pairings with one extra pair $<*,N>$, where N is the cardinality of the original relation:

```
E1   E4   E6   E2   E5   E3   E7   *
0    0    0    3    3    5    5    7
```

Let's refer to the second line here, the list of ranking positions, as the *ordinal list* for the original EMP rows (by increasing HEIGHT). From that list, we can see immediately that the three shortest employees are E1, E4, and E6; the five shortest are E1, E4, E6, E2, and E5; and so on. We can formalize these ideas as follows:

- Given an integer q that appears in the ordinal list, we define the *q-quota* to be exactly that set of rows whose ranking position is strictly less than q.

For example, the 3-quota is exactly the set of rows

```
{ E1, E4, E6 }
```

Here is the complete set of defined *q*-quotas for our sample data:

```
0-quota  :  { } -- the empty set
3-quota  :  { E1, E4, E6 }
5-quota  :  { E1, E4, E6, E2, E5 }
7-quota  :  { E1, E4, E6, E2, E5, E3, E7 }
```

Note that the 0-quota always exists, and is always empty; likewise, the N-quota, where N is the cardinality of the original relation, also always exists, and is always equal to the entire relation.

Given the sample data of Fig. 1, therefore, the query "get the three shortest employees" happens to be well defined—it's a request for the relevant 3-quota. But what about (say) the query "get the *four* shortest employees"? Each of the following is at least arguably an appropriate response to this query:

1. The 3-quota { E1, E4, E6 }—the maximal exact quota that contains no more than four employees.

2. The set { E1, E4, E6, E2 }—a set S of exactly four employees such that, for each employee in S, the number of shorter employees is less than four.

3. The set { E1, E4, E6, E5 }—another set S of exactly four employees such that, for each employee in S, the number of shorter employees is less than four.

4. Error!—because (a) the query is asking for a set S of exactly four employees such that, for each employee in S,

   - the number of shorter employees is less than four, and

   - every employee in S is shorter than all employees not in S,

   and (b) no such set S exists.

5. The 5-quota { E1, E4, E6, E2, E5 }—the minimal exact quota that contains no less than four employees.

Of these five options:

- Option 4 (raising an error) seems a little harsh, given that the system is obviously capable of returning *something* useful, even if it can't return quite what the user asked for.

- Options 2 and 3 do look superficially attractive; intuitively speaking, they're what we'd get if we ordered the rows of the original relation by increasing HEIGHT value ("ORDER BY HEIGHT" in SQL) and then skimmed off the first four rows according to that ordering. Indeed, this intuitive characterization is pretty much how the quota query requirement is usually—albeit informally—explained.

  The trouble is, there's no logical reason to prefer either Option 2 or Option 3 over the other. So—assuming we had a language that allowed us to formulate the "four shortest employees" query in the first place—we'd have to define that language in such a way that the result of the query could be, arbitrarily, *either* Option 2 *or* Option 3. And which result we actually obtained on any particular occasion would be unpredictable.

To see that such a state of affairs would be most undesirable in practice, observe that queries are normally assumed to be *functions*. That is, given a particular state *D* of the database and a particular query *Q*, it is normally assumed that executing *Q* against *D* will always return the same answer, no matter how many times we repeat the attempt. In other words, if we execute the following pseudocode:

```
A  :=  Q ( D ) ;
B  :=  Q ( D ) ;
```

we can guarantee that after the two assignments *A* and *B* will be equal. But if *Q* is allowed not to be a function—if it's allowed to return different results on different invocations, even if the state *D* of the database remains unchanged in the interim—then we can no longer make that guarantee. The implications for optimization (among other things) are quite serious.

Note: As a matter of fact, the language SQL already has the property that certain legal SQL queries are not functions and can indeed return different answers on different invocations against the same database state (the SQL standard refers to such queries as "possibly nondeterministic" [1]). But the existence of such queries is a serious flaw in SQL! It certainly doesn't constitute a good argument (or precedent) for introducing further unnecessary unpredictability, into SQL or any other language.

- Option 1, by contrast, at least does have the advantage that the query would be a function, implying that its behavior would be predictable. (As we'll see in the next section, the approach represented by this option has the additional advantage that it works no matter how many rows are requested and no matter how many rows there are in the original relation—though the result might sometimes be empty.) On the other hand, the user might be surprised to find in the case at hand that only three rows are returned; that is, the request for four rows has been taken to mean *at most* four rows, when it could equally well have been taken to mean *at least* four (see the next paragraph).

- Option 5 likewise means that the query would be a function. It also has the advantage that "the four shortest" employees—whatever that phrase is taken to mean—will certainly be returned, possibly along with some extra ones, which the user can presumably ignore if he or she desires.

Overall, Option 5 does seem the most reasonable, so let's agree to adopt it from this point forward. There's still a problem, though. Suppose the query had asked for the *ten* shortest employees (the point being that fewer than ten employees exist in total). The most reasonable response here is surely *not* to adopt the Option 5 approach of returning "the minimal exact quota that contains no less than ten employees"—no such exact quota exists!—but rather to return the maximal exact quota that does exist (namely, all seven employees). So matters still need a little further refinement.

q-UNDERQUOTAS AND q-OVERQUOTAS

At this point it's convenient to introduce a couple more concepts, the *underquota* and the *overquota*. Let's take another look at our sample data with its corresponding ordinal list and quotas:

```
E1    E4    E6    E2    E5    E3    E7    *
0     0     0     3     3     5     5     7

0-quota   :   { }
3-quota   :   { E1, E4, E6 }
5-quota   :   { E1, E4, E6, E2, E5 }
7-quota   :   { E1, E4, E6, E2, E5, E3, E7 }
```

Given a particular ordinal list, such as the one just shown, we now define the *q-underquota* to be that p-quota such that p is the greatest integer in the ordinal list that's less than or equal to q. (Intuitively, the q-underquota is the biggest quota containing q rows or less.) In terms of our running example, we have:

```
0-underquota  =  0-quota : { }
1-underquota  =  0-quota : { }
2-underquota  =  0-quota : { }
3-underquota  =  3-quota : { E1, E4, E6 }
4-underquota  =  3-quota : { E1, E4, E6 }
5-underquota  =  5-quota : { E1, E4, E6, E2, E5 }
6-underquota  =  5-quota : { E1, E4, E6, E2, E5 }
7-underquota  =  7-quota : { E1, E4, E6, E2, E5, E3, E7 }
```

If N is the cardinality of the original relation (N is 7 in our example), the q-underquota is the same as the N-quota for all q greater than N. *Note:* If we had adopted the Option 1 approach in the previous section, we would effectively have been saying that quota queries should be defined to return the corresponding underquota.

We also define the *q-overquota* (analogously) to be that r-quota such that r is the smallest integer in the ordinal list that's greater than or equal to q. (Intuitively, the q-overquota is the smallest quota containing q rows or more.) In terms of our example, we have:

```
0-overquota  =  0-quota : { }
1-overquota  =  3-quota : { E1, E4, E6 }
2-overquota  =  3-quota : { E1, E4, E6 }
3-overquota  =  3-quota : { E1, E4, E6 }
4-overquota  =  5-quota : { E1, E4, E6, E2, E5 }
5-overquota  =  5-quota : { E1, E4, E6, E2, E5 }
6-overquota  =  7-quota : { E1, E4, E6, E2, E5, E3, E7 }
7-overquota  =  7-quota : { E1, E4, E6, E2, E5, E3, E7 }
```

The q-overquota is not defined for q greater than N (where N is the cardinality of the original relation).

Now—at long last—we can give a precise meaning to the query "get the q shortest employees," where the exact q-quota may or may not exist. Specifically, we define that query to return a result as follows:

- If $q > N$ (the cardinality of the original relation), the result is the q-underquota, or in other words that entire relation;

- If $q \leq N$, the result is the q-overquota.

This definition accords with our discussions of the special cases $q = 4$ and $q = 10$ in the previous section. It also has the advantage of according with intuition if the exact q-quota does exist, as in the case $q = 3$ (the q-overquota being identical to the q-quota in such a case). Moreover, it is (of course) a *functional* definition, and it works regardless of the values of q and N. ∎

Finally, it's worth pointing out that—bonus!—this definition accords precisely with the semantics of what I claimed last month was a "convenient" SQL formulation of the query:

```
SELECT  EX.EMP#
FROM    EMP EX
WHERE (SELECT  COUNT (*)
       FROM    EMP EY
       WHERE   EY.HEIGHT < EX.HEIGHT) < q ;
```

CONCLUDING REMARKS

I'd like to thank Adrian Larner for his major contribution to this month's column. The definitions of the terms *ordinal list,* (exact) *quota, underquota,* and *overquota* are all due to Adrian; also, it was Adrian who made me appreciate the importance of ensuring that quota queries were functions, with predictable behavior (I'm embarrassed to admit that my first attempt at a solution to the quota queries problem involved operators that weren't functions at all!).

To close, here are a couple of puzzle corner problems to test your understanding of the concepts introduced in this column:

1. Given the parts relation P of Fig. 2:

    a. Rank the rows by decreasing WEIGHT value.

    b. Show all corresponding quotas, underquotas, and overquotas.

2. To refer once again to our running example, the following sequence of relational algebra operations computes the q-overquota of employees by increasing height:

```
T1   :=   EMP RENAME HEIGHT AS HX ;
T2   :=   EMP RENAME HEIGHT AS HY ;
T3   :=   EXTEND T1
          ADD COUNT ( T2 WHERE HY < HX )
          AS #_SHORTER ;
T4   :=   T3 WHERE #_SHORTER < q ;
```

(Assume for simplicity that q does not exceed the cardinality of the EMP relation.) Can you find an analogous sequence of algebraic operations for the corresponding q-underquota?

P	P#	PNAME	COLOR	WEIGHT	CITY
	P1	Nut	Red	12	London
	P2	Bolt	Green	17	Paris
	P3	Screw	Blue	17	Rome
	P4	Screw	Red	14	London
	P5	Cam	Blue	12	Paris
	P6	Cog	Red	19	London

Fig. 2   The parts relation

REFERENCES

1. C. J. Date and Hugh Darwen: *A Guide to the SQL Standard* (4th edition). Reading, Mass.: Addison-Wesley (1997).

2. Adrian Larner: Private communications (September 13th–16th, 1994).

Quota Queries
(Part 3 of 3)

Quota expressions and their uses

Last month I described the concepts *q-quota, q-underquota,* and *q-overquota,* and used them to give a precise interpretation of quota queries. For example, I defined the query "get the q shortest employees" (where the exact q-quota might or might not exist) to return a result as follows:

- If $q > N$ (the cardinality of the original relation), the result is the q-underquota, or in other words that entire relation;
- If $q \leq N$, the result is the q-overquota.

I also showed that quota queries, with semantics as just defined, can be formulated in the relational algebra. However, the formulation in question is (at least arguably) not very "convenient." This month, therefore, I wish to propose some useful shorthands, in order to make the formulation of quota queries (and other queries of a similar nature) a little more user-friendly.

QUOTA EXPRESSIONS

The first shorthand consists of a new kind of relational expression, a *quota expression,* which takes the following form:

```
rel-exp quota-spec
```

Originally published in *Database Programming & Design 9,* No. 9, September 1996. Reprinted by permission of Miller Freeman Inc.

(where *rel-exp* is an arbitrary relational expression). Here's an example:

```
EMP QUOTA ( 3, HEIGHT ASC )
```

(refer to the sample data in Fig. 1, a repeat of the example from the last two installments).

EMP	EMP#	WEIGHT	HEIGHT
	E1	120	70
	E2	170	71
	E3	170	72
	E4	140	70
	E5	120	71
	E6	190	70
	E7	120	72

Fig. 1 A sample employees relation

Explanation: The *rel-exp* here is just EMP. The specification HEIGHT ASC means "for the purposes of filling the quota, conceptually sequence the rows of EMP by ascending HEIGHT" (but note that there is no implication that the system has to implement the query by physically sorting the rows, of course). Thus, the *quota-spec* is asking for the three (?) rows of EMP that come first according to that sequencing. The overall expression evaluates to a relation with the same heading as EMP, containing either all EMP rows (if the cardinality of EMP is less than three) or the 3-overquota (otherwise), as required by our defined semantics for quota queries.

Here's another example:

```
EMP QUOTA ( 4, WEIGHT DESC )
```

Meaning: "Get the four heaviest employees." The result is the exact 4-quota (by descending weight) { E6, E2, E3, E4 }.

And one more example:

```
EMP QUOTA ( 4, HEIGHT ASC, WEIGHT ASC )
```

Meaning: "Get the first four (?) employees by (ascending) weight within (ascending) height." The result is the set { E1, E4, E6, E5 }. Incidentally, note the difference between the specifications HEIGHT ASC, WEIGHT ASC and WEIGHT ASC, HEIGHT ASC—the first means ascending weight within ascending height, the second ascending height within ascending weight.

Here then is the full syntax for *quota-spec:*

```
quota-spec
    ::=  QUOTA ( integer-exp, sequence )
```

The *integer-exp* is an arbitrary scalar expression that evaluates to a nonnegative integer.

```
sequence
    ::=  sequence-item [, sequence-item ] ...

sequence-item
    ::=  column direction

direction
    ::=  ASC | DESC
```

Each *column* must be a column of the relation represented by *rel-exp*. Furthermore, of course, that column must be "orderable"—that is, the operator "<" must be defined for the underlying domain.

Let me close this section by stressing the point (already mentioned in the introduction) that quota expressions are really just shorthand for combinations of other operations—they're certainly not a new kind of primitive. For example, the quota expression

```
EMP QUOTA ( q, HEIGHT ASC )
```

is shorthand for an expression that might look something like this:

```
( EXTEND ( EMP RENAME HEIGHT AS HX )
         ADD COUNT
               ( ( EMP RENAME HEIGHT AS HY ) WHERE HY < HX )
         AS #_SHORTER )
  WHERE #_SHORTER < q
```

To repeat, the advantage of introducing the quota expression construct is merely one of "convenience" or usability.

THE *n*TH LARGEST AND SMALLEST

The usefulness of quota expressions isn't restricted to the rather simple quota queries we've been examining in this series thus far. Consider the following example. Suppose we want to get all employees whose height is one of the two smallest (given the sample data of Fig. 1, the two smallest heights are 70 inches and 71 inches, and the required result consists of all of the employees except E3 and E7). Now, we do know how to get all employees whose height is *the* (single) smallest:

```
( ( EXTEND EMP ADD MIN ( EMP, HEIGHT ) AS MINH )
    WHERE HEIGHT = MINH ) [ EMP#, WEIGHT, HEIGHT ]
```

Or if you prefer SQL:

```
SELECT  EX.EMP#, EX.WEIGHT, EX.HEIGHT
FROM    EMP EX
WHERE   EX.HEIGHT =
      ( SELECT MIN ( EY.HEIGHT )
        FROM    EMP EY ) ;
```

However, a solution to "the *two* smallest heights" problem using MIN is quite awkward:

```
T1  :=  EXTEND EMP ADD MIN ( EMP, HEIGHT ) AS MINH ;
T2  :=  T1 WHERE HEIGHT = MINH ;
T3  :=  T2 [ EMP#, WEIGHT, HEIGHT ] ;
T4  :=  EMP MINUS T3 ;
T5  :=  EXTEND T4 ADD MIN ( EMP, HEIGHT ) AS MINH ;
T6  :=  T5 WHERE HEIGHT = MINH ;
T7  :=  T6 [ EMP#, WEIGHT, HEIGHT ] ;
```

(Try this in SQL!) What's more, extending this solution to "the n smallest heights" analog, where n is a parameter, is far from straightforward (another exercise for the reader).

By contrast, consider the following expression:

```
( ( EMP [ HEIGHT ] ) QUOTA ( 2, HEIGHT ASC ) ) JOIN EMP
```

The quota expression here (that is, the expression within the outermost parentheses) yields a relation of one column, called HEIGHT, that contains the two smallest heights from relation EMP. The join then yields a relation containing exactly those employees having one of those two heights. ∎

Note how easy it is to extend this solution to the n smallest heights case for arbitrary n. *Exercise for the reader:* What happens if relation EMP contains less than n distinct heights?

Here's another example of the usefulness of quota expressions. The query is "get all employees whose height is the nth smallest" (in terms of our usual example, if $n = 3$ then the result is E3 and E7; if $n = 4$ then nobody qualifies—that is, the result is an empty relation).

```
T1  :=  ( EMP [ HEIGHT ] ) QUOTA ( n, HEIGHT ASC ) ;
T2  :=  EXTEND T1 ADD COUNT ( T1 ) AS #_HEIGHTS ;
T3  :=  T2 WHERE #_HEIGHTS = n ;
T4  :=  EXTEND EMP ADD MAX ( T3, HEIGHT ) AS NTH_SMALLEST ;
T5  :=  T4 WHERE HEIGHT = NTH_SMALLEST ;
T6  :=  T5 [ EMP#, WEIGHT, HEIGHT ] ;
```

Space prohibits a detailed explanation of this sequence of operations, but note that T3 is *either* identical to T2 (if there are at least n distinct heights in EMP) *or* empty (otherwise), and in the latter case the MAX operator returns the smallest value ("minus infinity") in the HEIGHT domain [1]. Once again it's desirable to introduce a shorthand. In the case at hand (and taking n to be 3), such a shorthand might look like this:

```
EMP : IS_NTH_SMALLEST ( 3, HEIGHT )
```

The general syntax is

```
rel-exp : IS_NTH_SMALLEST ( integer-exp, column )
```

Such expressions (like quota expressions) constitute a new kind of relational expression. Let *r* be the relation denoted by *rel-exp* and let *n* be the value denoted by *integer-exp* (*n* must be a positive integer); *column,* of course, must denote a column of *r.* Then the overall value of the expression is defined to be a relation with the same heading as *r,* containing just those rows of *r* in which the value of *column* is the *n*th smallest currently appearing in that column within *r.*

Of course, we can also define the expression

```
rel-exp : IS_NTH_LARGEST ( integer-exp, column )
```

in an analogous fashion.

Note: There are syntactic reasons, beyond the scope of the present discussion, for using a colon (":") instead of the more obvious keyword WHERE to separate the IS_NTH_SMALLEST (or IS_NTH_LARGEST) reference from the *rel-exp* that precedes it.

AGGREGATION QUERIES

For a final example, consider the query "For each height, get the two heaviest employees." The result we're looking for here is as shown in Fig. 2; note that column EMPS in that result is relation-valued [2]. (Note too that it so happens that, given the sample data of Fig. 1, each height does have exactly two corresponding employees who are the heaviest for that height. In general, however, such might not be the case. For example, if employee E1 weighed 140 pounds instead of 120, then—in accordance with our agreed semantics for quota queries—the "two" heaviest employees for height 70 inches would be E1, E4, and E6.)

How can we produce such a result? Well, you might recall from an earlier installment [2] that in order to be able to construct derived relations with relation-valued columns, I extended the EXTEND operator, permitting the ADD operand to be a *relational* expression instead of a scalar expression. (I did point out, however, that I hadn't checked that extended EXTEND format for syntactic soundness.) Since quota expressions are just a new kind of relational expression, therefore, we can proceed as follows:

HEIGHT	EMPS	
70	EMP#	WEIGHT
	E4	140
	E6	190
71	EMP#	WEIGHT
	E2	170
	E5	120
72	EMP#	WEIGHT
	E3	170
	E7	120

Fig. 2   The two heaviest employees for each height

```
T1  :=  ( EMP RENAME EMP# AS EX, WEIGHT AS WX ) ;
T2  :=  EXTEND T1 ADD
          ( ( MATCHING EMP ) QUOTA ( 2, WEIGHT DESC ) )
                                        [ EMP#, WEIGHT ] )
                 AS EMPS ;
T3  :=  T2 [ HEIGHT, EMPS ] ;
```

(I explained the MATCHING construct in that same earlier installment [2].)
Once again it would probably be feasible to define a shorthand for queries like
this one. In the case at hand, such a shorthand might look as follows:

```
SUMMARIZE EMP BY ( HEIGHT )
          ADD ( QUOTA ( 2, WEIGHT DESC ) ) AS EMPS
```

Certainly such a shorthand would be preferable from a usability point of view,
though again I must stress that I haven't checked it for syntactic soundness.

PUZZLE CORNER

Given the usual suppliers-and-parts database, use the constructs introduced in
this month's column to formulate the following queries.

1. Get the two highest-status suppliers.

2. Get the first four parts by weight within city.

3. Get all parts whose weight is one of the three greatest.

4. Get all shipments whose quantity is the second lowest.

5. For each part, get the highest-quantity shipment.

You might like to try giving SQL solutions too (if you're a glutton for punishment).

REFERENCES

1. C. J. Date: "Empty Bags and Identity Crises," *Database Programming & Design 6,* No. 4 (April 1993). Republished in *Relational Database Writings 1991–1994.* Reading, Mass.: Addison-Wesley (1995).

2. C. J. Date: "Nested Relations (Part 1 of 2)" and "Nested Relations (Part 2 of 2)" (see Installments 31–32).

Answers to Puzzle Corner Problems (Installments 44–49)

Stop racking your brains—the answers are in!

My column this month is devoted once again to answering the various outstanding "puzzle corner" problems from previous installments. Thanks as usual to those readers who wrote in with their own solutions. *Note:* Installment 46 did not include a puzzle corner problem.

AGGREGATE OPERATORS

Source: "Aggregate Operators" (see Installment 44).

Problem statement: An SQL advocate might argue that the SQL statement

```
SELECT SUM ( QTY ) AS SQ, AVG ( QTY ) AS AQ
FROM    SP
WHERE   QTY > 100 ;
```

is preferable to the relational algebra version

```
( EXTEND TABLE_DEE
        ADD SUM ( SP WHERE QTY > 100, QTY ) AS SQ,
        ADD AVQ ( SP WHERE QTY > 100, QTY ) AS AQ )
```

Originally published under the title "Those Puzzle Corner Problems" in *Database Programming & Design 9*, No. 10, October 1996 (the subtitle was contributed by *DBP&D* too). Reprinted by permission of Miller Freeman Inc.

because the condition QTY > 100 is stated only once in the SQL version, thereby saving the user some writing (and implying too that the result might be computed in one pass over the rows of SP instead of two). You're invited to produce a cogent counterargument to this position. *Note:* I'm not concerned here—though perhaps I should be!—with the fact that the SQL version actually gives the wrong answer if no shipment row has QTY > 100.

Solution: By its nature, this problem doesn't have a unique "correct" solution; however, the following observations are pertinent.

1. There's no excuse for illogical language design. The slight inconvenience to the user of occasionally having to write out the same expression twice is a very minor matter compared with the vastly greater degree of orthogonality the clean design affords.

2. In any case, the user is required to write out the same expression twice only when he or she wants to apply two different aggregate operators to the same aggregate argument within a single query, and it could be argued that such queries are uncommon. (In fairness, however, I should mention that at least one reviewer felt that this point was "pretty weak"—"asking for the MIN and MAX simultaneously, or the SUM and AVG likewise, is not all that uncommon.")

3. Be that as it may, realizing that the result can be computed in one pass over the data instead of two is a matter of *optimization*. The question is simply: Can the optimizer recognize that the query involves a common subexpression? Much work has been done on common subexpression recognition in traditional programming language optimization, and there's no reason why the results of such research shouldn't carry over into database language optimization too. Sacrificing language orthogonality in the interest of performance in general, or making optimization easier in particular, is a dubious proposition at best.

4. In any case, it's a trivial matter to devise some syntax that would make the query in question a little more user-friendly (as well as making optimization easier!)—for example:

```
WITH ( SP WHERE QTY > 100 ) AS TEMP :
( EXTEND TABLE_DEE
         ADD SUM ( TEMP, QTY ) AS SQ ,
         ADD AVQ ( TEMP, QTY ) AS AQ )
```

Furthermore, the somewhat arcane idea of "extending TABLE_DEE" could also be buried in some nice syntactic sugar—for example:

```
WITH ( SP WHERE QTY > 100 ) AS TEMP :
MAKE_ONEROW_REL ( SUM ( TEMP, QTY ) AS SQ ,
                  AVQ ( TEMP, QTY ) AS AQ )
```

Here I'm assuming that MAKE_ONEROW_REL is an operator that constructs a relation containing just one row from a specified set of scalar-value/column-name pairs.

The overall point is, syntax isn't important (so long as it's logical); what's important is semantics.

SUMMARIZE

Source: "SUMMARIZE Revisited" (see Installment 45).

Problem statement: You were asked to use the new version of SUMMARIZE described in this month's column to give relational algebra formulations of certain queries. For readability, in what follows I'll interleave the queries and their SUMMARIZE formulations.

1. For each blue part, get the part number and the corresponding total quantity.

```
SUMMARIZE SP BY ( P WHERE COLOR = 'Blue' ) [ P# ]
          ADD SUM ( QTY ) AS TQ
```

By the way, what happens here if there are no blue parts? (*Answer:* The result relation is empty.)

2. Get part numbers of parts supplied in a total quantity less than 300.

```
( ( SUMMARIZE SP BY P [ P# ] ADD SUM ( QTY ) AS TQ )
    WHERE TQ < 300 ) [ P# ]
```

3. Get part numbers of parts supplied in an average quantity less than 300.

There's a trap here: A part that isn't supplied at all has an average quantity that's *undefined*. So the following putative solution is in fact inadequate:

```
( ( SUMMARIZE SP BY P [ P# ] ADD AVG ( QTY ) AS AQ )
    WHERE AQ < 300 ) [ P# ]
```

Because of problems like the one illustrated here, the expression in the ADD clause needs some extension. In the example, instead of ADD AVG(QTY), we need to be able to say something like:

```
ADD ( IF EXISTS ( MATCHING SP ) THEN AVG ( QTY ) ELSE 0 )
```

Given this specification, the value of AQ for a part that isn't supplied at all will be zero.

THE CARDS PROBLEM

Source: "Quota Queries (Part 1 of 3)" (see Installment 47).

Problem statement: Fig. 1 represents four cards displayed on a table. You're told that each card has either a blue or a yellow back, and either a square or a triangle on the front. What's the minimum number of cards you need to turn over in order to give a guaranteed correct answer to the question: Does every card with a blue back have a square on the front?

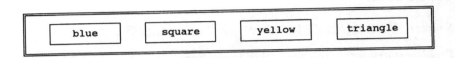

| blue | square | yellow | triangle |

Fig. 1   The cards as displayed

Solution: Let's number the cards 1 to 4 from left to right. Then:

1. Card 2 is irrelevant; regardless of its back color, it doesn't help with the specified question.
2. Card 3 is irrelevant because its back color isn't blue.
3. We must turn over Card 1 to see whether it has a square on the front. If it doesn't, the specified question is answered in the negative.
4. Otherwise, we must turn over Card 4 to see whether its back is blue. If it is, the specified question is answered in the negative. Otherwise, the specified question is answered in the affirmative.

Thus, the *minimum* number of cards we need to turn over in order to answer the specified question is one! In general, however, *two* cards need to be turned over (if turning the first card over doesn't help).

QUOTA QUERIES

Source: "Quota Queries (Part 2 of 3)" (see Installment 48).

Problem statement: There were two problems in this installment. The first was as follows. Given the parts relation P of Fig. 2:

a. Rank the parts by decreasing weight.
b. Show all corresponding quotas, underquotas, and overquotas.

P	P#	PNAME	COLOR	WEIGHT	CITY
	P1	Nut	Red	12	London
	P2	Bolt	Green	17	Paris
	P3	Screw	Blue	17	Rome
	P4	Screw	Red	14	London
	P5	Cam	Blue	12	Paris
	P6	Cog	Red	19	London

Fig. 2   The parts relation

Solution: The ranking is as follows:

```
P1   5=
P2   2=
P3   2=
P4   4
P5   5=
P6   1
```

Rearranging as explained in the original column:

```
P6   P2   P3   P4   P1   P5   *
0    1    1    3    4    4    6
```

Exact quotas:

```
0-quota  :  { }
1-quota  :  { P6 }
3-quota  :  { P6, P2, P3 }
4-quota  :  { P6, P2, P3, P4 }
6-quota  :  { P6, P2, P3, P4, P1, P5 }
```

Underquotas:

```
0-underquota  =  0-quota : { }
1-underquota  =  1-quota : { P6 }
2-underquota  =  1-quota : { P6 }
3-underquota  =  3-quota : { P6, P2, P3 }
4-underquota  =  4-quota : { P6, P2, P3, P4 }
5-underquota  =  4-quota : { P6, P2, P3, P4 }
6-underquota  =  6-quota : { P6, P2, P3, P4, P1, P5 }
```

The q-underquota is the same as the 6-quota for all q greater than 6.

Overquotas:

```
0-overquota  =  0-quota : { }
1-overquota  =  1-quota : { P6 }
2-overquota  =  3-quota : { P6, P2, P3 }
3-overquota  =  3-quota : { P6, P2, P3 }
4-overquota  =  4-quota : { P6, P2, P3, P4 }
5-overquota  =  6-quota : { P6, P2, P3, P4, P1, P5 }
6-overquota  =  6-quota : { P6, P2, P3, P4, P1, P5 }
```

The q-overquota is not defined for q greater than 6. ∎

The second problem was as follows. Given a relation EMP with columns EMP# and HEIGHT, the following sequence of relational algebra operations computes the q-overquota of employees by increasing height ("the q shortest employees"):

```
T1   :=   EMP RENAME HEIGHT AS HX ;
T2   :=   EMP RENAME HEIGHT AS HY ;
T3   :=   EXTEND T1
          ADD COUNT ( T2 WHERE HY < HX )
          AS #_SHORTER ;
T4   :=   T3 WHERE #_SHORTER < q ;
```

(Assume for simplicity that q does not exceed the cardinality of the EMP relation.) Can you find an analogous sequence of algebraic operations for the corresponding q-underquota?

Solution: The following solution, obtained from the foregoing sequence of operations by simply replacing the two "<" symbols by "≤" symbols, is probably the most straightforward:

```
T1   :=   EMP RENAME HEIGHT AS HX ;
T2   :=   EMP RENAME HEIGHT AS HY ;
T3   :=   EXTEND T1
          ADD COUNT ( T2 WHERE HY ≤ HX )
          AS #_SHORTER ;
T4   :=   T3 WHERE #_SHORTER ≤ q ;
```

(It might be preferable from an intuitive point of view to change the name #_SHORTER in this solution to #_SAME_HEIGHT_OR_SHORTER.)

Another approach to a solution is based on the fact that—loosely speaking—if N is the cardinality of the complete EMP relation, then the q-underquota by increasing height is what's left if we remove the *(N-q)-over*quota by *decreasing* height from that relation. Hence:

```
T1   :=   EMP RENAME HEIGHT AS HX ;
T2   :=   EMP RENAME HEIGHT AS HY ;
T3   :=   EXTEND T1 ADD COUNT ( T2 WHERE HY > HX ) AS #_TALLER ;
T4   :=   EXTEND T3 ADD COUNT ( EMP ) - q AS CARD_LESS_q ;
T5   :=   T4 WHERE #_TALLER < CARD_LESS_q ;
T6   :=   EMP MINUS T5 ;
```

In fact, this sequence of operations yields the true underquota even if $q > N$ (where N is the cardinality of the original relation). By contrast, the first sequence does *not* yield the "true overquota" (which is undefined) if $q > N$; instead, it yields the entire EMP relation. This latter result is, of course, intuitively preferable anyway.

QUOTA EXPRESSIONS

Source: "Quota Queries (Part 3 of 3)" (see Installment 49).

Problem statement: Given the usual suppliers-and-parts database, use the constructs introduced in this month's column to formulate the following queries.

1. Get the two highest-status suppliers.
2. Get the first four parts by weight within city.
3. Get all parts whose weight is one of the three greatest.
4. Get all shipments whose quantity is the second lowest.
5. For each part, get the highest-quantity shipment.

Solution: Note that every one of these queries is actually ambiguous as stated! However, the following solutions "probably" best represent the requirement in each case.

```
1. S QUOTA ( 2, STATUS DESC )

2. P QUOTA ( 4, CITY ASC, WEIGHT ASC )

3. P JOIN ( P [ WEIGHT ] QUOTA ( 3, WEIGHT DESC ) )

4. SP : IS_NTH_SMALLEST ( 2, QTY )

5. EXTEND ( P [ P# ] )
     ADD ( ( MATCHING SP ) QUOTA ( 1, QTY DESC ) ) AS HQS
```

Note that a part that has no shipments will still be represented in the result here (with an HQS value that is an empty relation).

Faults and Defaults (Part 1 of 5)

*Missing information and default
values: the truth at last (?)*

Regular readers of this column will know that I reject the idea of using nulls and three-valued logic—or, more generally, *N*-valued logic for any *N* greater than two—as a basis for dealing with missing information in databases. Instead, I've argued for years that **default values** represent a much better approach to the problem. In my book *An Introduction to Database Systems* [2], I buttressed this argument with the claim that "default values are what we use in the real world." (Indeed, defaults, not nulls, are often the logically *correct* treatment in the real world. The following quote illustrates the kind of mistake made all too often in this regard: "[The employee's] total sales will be null until the employee files his or her first sales report" [6]. That null should of course be zero.) And *The Third Manifesto,* by Hugh Darwen and myself [1], includes a "very strong suggestion" that the system should incorporate support for the default values idea.

However, the default values idea has itself been attacked and criticized on many occasions. One comparatively recent example appeared in the pages of *Database Programming & Design,* in Tom Johnston's two-part article on many-valued logic [7]. Johnston's attack incorporates most of the objections that critics usually raise in this connection; for that reason, it's worth quoting from it at length here (see the next section), in order to provide a useful summary of the opposition's point of view.

Originally published in *Database Programming & Design 9,* No. 11, November 1996. Reprinted by permission of Miller Freeman Inc.

Before going any further, I must make it clear that most of what I have to say on this subject isn't really new: It just seems to need saying one more time, albeit at greater length than previously. In particular, I must acknowledge my debt to David McGoveran's thinking in this area, especially as articulated in Part 4 of his paper "Nothing from Nothing" [8]. David argues strongly that we should design our databases in such a way as to avoid the need, or apparent need, to clutter them up with nulls. In what follows, I argue that—for somewhat similar reasons—we shouldn't clutter them up with default values either. However, even if we do manage to design our databases in such a way, and thereby avoid the need for default values in *base* relations, we'll still need them in certain *derived* relations (as we'll see), so they can't be avoided entirely.

Another preliminary remark: This is a big subject; that's why I've had to present it as a "miniseries" spread over several installments. All I can really hope to do this month is set the scene for the more detailed discussions to follow in subsequent installments. Please accept my apologies, therefore, if this first installment seems a little light on technical substance. It'll get heavier next time, I promise you.

Finally, please note that this whole miniseries on the default values scheme—which might (unlike the nulls scheme) be regarded as a **relational** approach to the missing information problem—should be considered as amplifying and superseding my own earlier writings on this same subject [3].

JOHNSTON'S ARGUMENTS

As promised, this section presents arguments *against* the default values idea. The text consists of an edited and condensed version of the section "Default Values *vs.* MVL" from Part II of Johnston's article [7] (MVL = "many-valued logic"). I've numbered the paragraphs for ease of subsequent reference. Throughout those paragraphs, please understand that the personal pronoun "I" refers to Tom Johnston and not myself.

1. From the semantic perspective, what's wrong with defaults is that they aren't what we mean. When we say that Joe doesn't have an hourly rate, we don't mean that he has some special hourly rate—the $0.00 rate, for example; what we mean is that he doesn't have any hourly rate. And when we say that we don't know which department Joe works in, we don't mean that he works in some department with an unusual designation—the UNK (unknown) department, for example; we mean that we don't know the department to which he is assigned.

2. Because default values don't represent what we mean, no logical apparatus can recognize what we do mean when we use them. As a result, normal

queries issued against a relational database that uses default values will give us misleading information.

3. Suppose the database shows 15 employees as being assigned to the Human Resources department and six employees whose department is given as the default value UNK. Suppose further that three of these six employees are actually assigned to the Human Resources department. If we pose the query "How many employees are in the Human Resources department?" to this database, we will get back the reply 15. Now if we were querying a person who had the same information, then—in the situation just described—we would regard the answer 15 as misleading, to say the least. The informative answer, of course, is something like "15 known to be in the Human Resources department, but six whose assignment to a department is not known." A database that uses defaults could not be this informative.

4. This is what's wrong with the default values approach from a semantic perspective: It has the semantics wrong, and so the ability of a database using default values to inform the inquirer fully is correspondingly hampered.

5. From the formal perspective, what's wrong with default values is that they're not the same thing as domain values, yet they're represented in the same way as domain values. The presence of a value from a domain in a particular instance of an attribute represents the ascription of a particular predicate to an individual. However, UNK does not represent a predicate descriptive of an individual: It represents the absence of any such predicate value. It cannot, therefore, be a member of any domain.

6. Date asserts that default values are what we use in "the real world," and he uses the symbol "NA" (not applicable), as entered on a form, as an example. What I dispute is his claim that "NA" *is* an example of a default value. I don't think it is. Instead, I think we all understand that "NA" doesn't represent a value from the domain for that entry on the form, but rather represents the fact that no such value is applicable! "NA" is an assertion about that entry on the form, not a value to be put into that entry.

7. As a final practical point, I note that for numeric-based domains in particular, the domain is often coextensive with the range of values expressible by the underlying data type. When this is the case, whatever value is chosen to represent "unknown" will be a homonym since its other meaning will be the normal meaning it can express. In Joe's case earlier, for example, we suggested that $0.00 might be the value chosen to represent "unknown." But if it is, that value is a homonym, since its other interpretation is as an hourly rate of $0.00—the known value assigned, for example, to volunteers working for a nonprofit organization.

In my original response to Johnston [5], I said:

There are so many points I want to make regarding [the default values issue] that I think it best to save them for a separate article—perhaps a column in my regular *Database Programming & Design* series.

This miniseries is that promised "separate article" (I was optimistic to think it would all fit into a single column).

CONCEPTS AND TERMINOLOGY

Before I can respond to Johnston's arguments in detail—indeed, before I can explain exactly how the default values scheme works—there are a couple of important preliminaries to get out of the way.

First of all, the term **default values** is itself perhaps a little misleading, because it suggests something that was never intended: namely, that the value in question occurs so frequently that it might as well be the default. Rather, the intent was simply to use an appropriate "default" value, distinct from all possible regular values, when no regular value can be supplied. For example, if regular values of the SALARY column are dollar and cent amounts, the default value "UNK" might be used to mean that no regular value is known for some reason. (Note, therefore, that the domain here is *not* just dollar and cent amounts; it's dollar and cent amounts *plus* the "UNK" value. I'll have a lot more to say on this particular point over the next couple of months.)

Now—speaking purely for myself here, and not necessarily for any other advocates of the approach—I was sidetracked into the default values terminology by a simple syntactic (hence merely psychological) concern, to wit: A default value is what you get if you don't supply anything else; and if "the information is missing" (see below) you *can't* supply anything else! For example, suppose we're given the relvar EMP { EMP#, SALARY }. In SQL, then, we might write the following INSERT statement:

```
INSERT INTO EMP ( EMP# ) VALUES ( 'E3' ) ;
```

Since we haven't supplied a salary value, employee E3's salary will be set to the applicable default value in the database, and then we'll probably interpret that default value to mean that employee E3's salary is unknown. (In SQL in particular, of course, that default value will typically, though not necessarily, be null. For the sake of the present discussion, let's assume it isn't.)

But this justification for the default values terminology is certainly not a very good one. What's more, a given column can have, by definition, *at most one* associated default value, yet there might be many different reasons—value unknown, value not applicable, value undefined, and so on—for not being able to supply a regular value for that column, each of them requiring a different "default" value. And so those "defaults" aren't really *defaults,* as such, at all!

Perhaps a better term would be simply **special** value; at least this term doesn't carry the unwanted connotation that the value occurs very frequently (in fact it pretty much conveys the opposite), and it overcomes the objection that a given column can't have more than one of them. Let's agree, therefore, to switch to the special values terminology in our discussions from this point forward.

Second, the term **missing information** is misleading too. To take Tom Johnston's example, if we say that the hourly rate property doesn't apply to employee Joe, we're saying, quite specifically and explicitly, that Joe is not paid by the hour. No information is missing here. Likewise:

- If we say the value of *a/b* is undefined for *b* = 0, we're not saying the expression yields a value but that value is unknown or otherwise missing—we're simply saying the expression yields no value. Again, no information is missing here.

- If I fill out a hotel registration form and mark the "Newspaper" box NONE, I'm not saying the name of the newspaper I want is unknown or otherwise missing, I'm saying I don't want a newspaper. Once again, no information is actually missing.

- And one more example (acknowledgments to Hugh Darwen for this one): In contract bridge and other card games, the correct answer to the question "What are trumps?" is often "No trumps." This answer doesn't mean some suit is trumps but we don't know which it is; it means no trumps are in effect. Yet again, no information is actually missing.

  As Hugh has pointed out to me (in a private communication), this last example makes the valuable point that bridge players have clearly discovered that SUITS is *not* the same domain as the domain that contains all possible answers to the question "What are trumps?" The domain SUITS contains four values; the other domain, which bridge players call DENOMINATION, contains five.

In fact, it seems that the only case in which information can truly be said to be missing is, precisely, the case we call *value unknown.* For example, if we say that Joe's salary is unknown, we mean that Joe does have a salary (because all employees have a salary), but we don't know what it is—the information is literally missing, for some reason.

CONCLUDING REMARKS

This concludes the necessary scene-setting. Next month, we'll take a detailed look at a concrete example of how the special values scheme might work in practice. Until then, let me leave you as usual with a puzzle corner problem. Since I'm engaged in presenting what I believe to be a preferable alternative to the nulls scheme, it seems appropriate to set a problem that points up some of the difficulties with that latter scheme . . . The following example is based on a discussion in the book *A Guide to the SQL Standard* [4], by Hugh Darwen and myself. We're given the usual suppliers-and-parts database, and the query: "Get parts whose weight is greater than that of every blue part." Two possible SQL formulations of this query are proposed:

```
1. SELECT  PX.*
   FROM    P AS PX
   WHERE   PX.WEIGHT >ALL  ( SELECT PY.WEIGHT
                             FROM    P AS PY
                             WHERE   PY.COLOR = 'Blue' ) ;

2. SELECT  PX.*
   FROM    P AS PX
   WHERE   NOT EXISTS
         ( SELECT *
           FROM    P AS PY
           WHERE   PY.COLOR = 'Blue'
           AND     PY.WEIGHT ≥ PX.WEIGHT ) ;
```

Are these two formulations equivalent? Is either one correct? If either is incorrect, state as precisely as you can the conditions under which it produces the wrong answer.

REFERENCES

1. Hugh Darwen and C. J. Date: "The Third Manifesto," *ACM SIGMOD Record 24*, No. 1 (March 1995). See also the book-length version *Foundation for Object/ Relational Databases: The Third Manifesto*. Reading, Mass.: Addison-Wesley (1998).

2. C. J. Date: *An Introduction to Database Systems* (6th edition). Reading, Mass.: Addison-Wesley (1995).

3. C. J. Date: "The Default Values Approach to Missing Information," in C. J. Date and Hugh Darwen, *Relational Database Writings 1989–1991*. Reading, Mass.: Addison-Wesley (1992).

4. C. J. Date and Hugh Darwen: *A Guide to the SQL Standard* (4th edition). Reading, Mass.: Addison-Wesley (1997).

5. C. J. Date, Hugh Darwen, and David McGoveran: "Nothing to Do with the Case" (Chapter 9 of the present book).

6. Stephen Ferg: Technical correspondence, in C. J. Date, *Relational Database Writings 1991–1994* (page 356). Reading, Mass.: Addison-Wesley (1995).

7. Tom Johnston: "MVL: Case Open," *Database Programming & Design 8*, No. 2 (February 1995); "The Case for MVL," *Database Programming & Design 8*, No. 3 (March 1995).

8. David McGoveran: "Nothing from Nothing (Part 4 of 4)" (Chapter 8 of the present book).

Faults and Defaults
(Part 2 of 5)

*Avoiding explicit "missing
information" through good
database design*

Last month I introduced the basic idea of default values or—as we agreed to call them from now on—*special* values as a basis for dealing with the missing information problem. (I also pointed out that the term *missing information* is something of a misnomer, but it'll serve for present purposes.) This month, I want to consider a concrete example of a database in which certain information happens to be "missing"; in particular, I want to show how good design techniques can be used to exclude all *explicit* representation of that "missing" information from the database. Next month I'll consider some sample queries against that same database.

THE EXAMPLE

Suppose we have a database of employees, each identified by an employee number (EMP#). Suppose further that, in general, each employee has a salary (SALARY), a bonus (BONUS), and a salary-to-bonus ratio (RATIO), defined as the result of dividing SALARY by BONUS. For simplicity, let's agree

---

Originally published in *Database Programming & Design 9,* No. 12, December 1996. Reprinted by permission of Miller Freeman Inc.

that—in accordance with the entity integrity "rule" (*guideline* would be a better term [1])—every employee known to the system does always have a system-known employee number. Let's assume too that every employee earns a salary, but not every employee gets a bonus. For any given employee, then, any of the following might be the case:

1. SALARY is known and BONUS is applicable (and known and nonzero). This is "the normal case."

2. BONUS is not applicable, in which case RATIO is not applicable (regardless of whether SALARY is known).

3. BONUS is applicable but unknown, in which case RATIO is applicable but unknown (regardless of whether SALARY is known).

4. BONUS is applicable but zero, in which case RATIO is applicable but undefined (regardless of whether SALARY is known).

5. BONUS is applicable (and known and nonzero) and SALARY is unknown, in which case RATIO is applicable but unknown.

THE FIRST DESIGN

A conventional design for this database would typically consist of a single base relvar, ALL_IN_ONE say:

```
ALL_IN_ONE { EMP#, SALARY, BONUS, RATIO }
           PRIMARY KEY { EMP# }
```

Fig. 1 shows a set of sample rows for this relvar. With respect to the five possibilities identified in the previous section, observe that the row for employee E1 illustrates Case 1 (the normal case); the rows for employees E2 and E3, Case 2; the rows for E4 and E5, Case 3; the rows for E6 and E7, Case 4; and the row for E8, Case 5. Observe too that the data includes three different special values, namely NA, UNK, and UNDEF. (Note in passing that ALL_IN_ONE is not in third normal form—RATIO is functionally dependent on the combination of SALARY and BONUS.)

Before I go any further, there's one point I must make crystal clear: Although Fig. 1 shows the special values as explicit strings—"UNK" and the rest—it is certainly *not* my intention that users should have to know the actual values (strings or otherwise) that happen to be used. In particular, it is *not* my intention that such actual values should be hard-coded into queries or application programs. Rather, an (open-ended) series of *operators* should be provided that allow the special values to be referenced symbolically. For example, let *dom* denote an arbitrary domain. Then we might define operators as follows:

ALL_IN_ONE			
EMP#	SALARY	BONUS	RATIO
E1	40000	10000	4
E2	55000	*NA*	*NA*
E3	*UNK*	*NA*	*NA*
E4	35000	*UNK*	*UNK*
E5	*UNK*	*UNK*	*UNK*
E6	72000	0	*UNDEF*
E7	*UNK*	0	*UNDEF*
E8	*UNK*	13000	*UNK*

Fig. 1 Design 1 (sample data, special values in italics)

- UNK (*dom*): Denotes the "unknown" special value for the specified domain (it's an error if no such special value exists—a compile-time check).
- NA (*dom*): Denotes the "not applicable" special value for the specified domain (again it's an error if no such special value exists—another compile-time check).

And so on—one such operator for each domain and each corresponding special value. (Note in passing that these operators effectively provide a means of writing special-value literals.) In other words, the definition of domain *dom* might look something like this:

```
CREATE DOMAIN dom ...
       UNK ( value1 )
       NA  ( value2 ) ... ;
```

Explanation: The UNK and NA special values for domain *dom* are represented by *value1* and *value2,* respectively; no UNDEF special value is defined for that domain. As a consequence, UNK(*dom*) and NA(*dom*) can be used as "UNK" and "NA" literals for *dom;* UNDEF(*dom*), by contrast, will raise a compile-time error.

Analogous operators should also be provided for testing for the presence of special values. For example, let *exp* denote an arbitrary scalar expression. Then:

- IS_UNK (*exp*): Returns *true* if the value of *exp* is the "unknown" special value for the applicable domain, *false* otherwise. (It's an error if no such special value exists—a compile-time check.)
- IS_NA (*exp*): Returns *true* if the value of *exp* is the "not applicable" special value for the applicable domain, *false* otherwise. (Again it's an error if no such special value exists—another compile-time check.)

And so on. *Note:* It's worth pointing out that (for example) IS_UNK(*exp*) is
semantically identical to the comparison *exp* = UNK(*dom*), where *dom* is the
applicable domain. However, we haven't yet discussed the semantics of the
"=" operator! I'll get to this latter point next month.

It's convenient to assume also that the system supports CASE expressions
along the following lines:

```
CASE
   WHEN cond-1 THEN exp-1
   WHEN cond-2 THEN exp-2
   .................
[ ELSE exp-n ]
END CASE
```

(where *cond-1, cond-2, . . .* are conditional expressions and *exp-1, exp-2, . . . ,*
exp-n are scalar expressions; note in particular that CASE expressions are
themselves scalar expressions and so can be arbitrarily nested). CASE
expressions have many uses, of course, but the particular use that's most
relevant to the topic at hand is their ability to replace a special value by an
ordinary "nonspecial" value (I'm speaking rather loosely here). For example, the expression

```
CASE
   WHEN NOT ( IS_UNK ( SALARY ) ) THEN SALARY
   ELSE MONEY ( 0̄ )
END CASE
```

returns the specified salary value, unless that value happens to be the applicable UNK value, in which case it returns zero instead; in other words, it effectively replaces the UNK by zero. Various syntactic shorthands could be
supported too if desired, analogous to the NULLIF and COALESCE shorthands provided in SQL/92 [2].

Note 1: The example assumes that column SALARY is defined on domain
MONEY; "MONEY(0)" is a **money literal**—it effectively converts the numeric value 0 to a money value (a value from the MONEY domain). I show
the literal as MONEY(0) rather than just plain 0 for reasons of clarity; I don't
necessarily mean to suggest that plain 0 shouldn't be permitted as a shorthand.
It's important to understand, however, that any such shorthand would merely
mean that the conversion to a money value is done implicitly instead of
explicitly; the conversion still has to occur.

Note 2: CASE expressions themselves are subject to a certain amount of
controversy. Some would argue that such expressions introduce an undesirable degree of procedurality into an otherwise nonprocedural language
(because, of course, the WHEN clauses are evaluated in sequential order as
written). Please understand, therefore, that the special values idea is in no way
dependent on CASE expressions as such; I use them here merely because it's
convenient to do so.

AN IMPROVED DESIGN

Let's refer to the single-relvar design illustrated in Fig. 1 as *Design 1*. Can we improve on that design? Well, first of all, let's agree to ignore RATIO until further notice. Then it seems to me that the following design, *Design 2*, involving three base relvars, is superior to Design 1 in several respects:

```
EMP            { EMP#, BONUS_APPLIC }
               PRIMARY KEY { EMP# }

EMP_SALARY    { EMP#, SALARY }
               PRIMARY KEY { EMP# }
               FOREIGN KEY { EMP# } REFERENCES EMP

EMP_BONUS     { EMP#, BONUS }
               PRIMARY KEY { EMP# }
               FOREIGN KEY { EMP# } REFERENCES EMP
```

Explanation: EMP contains a row for every employee; the BONUS_ APPLIC column indicates whether the property of getting a bonus applies ("Y") or not ("N") to the corresponding employee. EMP_SALARY contains a row for every employee represented in EMP, except where the corresponding salary is unknown. EMP_BONUS contains a row for every employee represented in EMP where BONUS_APPLIC is "Y", except where the corresponding bonus is unknown. Fig. 2 shows what this design would look like for the sample data from Fig. 1 (ignoring RATIO values, as agreed).

EMP			EMP_SALARY			EMP_BONUS	
EMP#	**BONUS_ APPLIC**		**EMP#**	**SALARY**		**EMP#**	**BONUS**
			E1	40000		E1	10000
E1	Y		E2	55000		E6	0
E2	N		E4	35000		E7	0
E3	N		E6	72000		E8	13000
E4	Y						
E5	Y						
E6	Y						
E7	Y						
E8	Y						

Fig. 2   Design 2 (sample data)

One reason Design 2 is preferable to Design 1 is that the relvars in Design 2 *never* contain anything other than regular data values; that is, they never contain any special values such as NA or UNK. An employee's salary is unknown if and only if that employee is represented in EMP and not in EMP_SALARY.

An employee's bonus is inapplicable if and only if that employee is represented in EMP with a BONUS_APPLIC value of "N". An employee's bonus
is applicable but unknown if and only if that employee is represented in EMP
with a BONUS_APPLIC value of "Y" and not represented in EMP_BONUS.
Exercise for the reader: Check these remarks for the eight employees E1
through E8.

There's another, subtler reason why Design 2 is preferable to Design 1.
Refer back to Fig. 1 and consider the row for employee E3 (in which the
SALARY value is UNK), and observe that:

1. For that row, the "obvious" predicate *employee EMP# earns salary SALARY*
   doesn't apply! More accurately, that "obvious" predicate IS IN FACT NOT
   THE CORRECT PREDICATE—and the "obvious" meaning of SALARY
   is likewise not correct either. The correct meaning of SALARY is, rather,
   "this value *either* specifies the known salary *or* indicates that the salary is
   unknown" (and the predicate needs adjusting accordingly).[*]

2. Because of the foregoing point, it might be preferable to change the name
   of the column from SALARY to (say) SALARY_OR_UNK. It's certainly
   misleading to call it just SALARY, at least from an intuitive point of view.

3. Note further that *the domain of that column is not just MONEY.* Rather,
   it's the domain (say) MONEY_OR_UNK, a domain consisting of all legal
   money values plus the special UNK value. (By the way, don't be surprised
   at the suggestion that some elements of a domain might be represented as
   numeric values—which is presumably how regular money values are represented—and others as nonnumeric values, perhaps strings, which might
   be how the UNK value is represented. There's nothing in the relational
   model to prohibit such a possibility. It's true that today's SQL products
   might have difficulties with such a notion, but that's their problem.)

Analogous remarks apply, of course, to every ALL_IN_ONE row in which the
SALARY value is UNK, and to every ALL_IN_ONE row in which BONUS
is NA or UNK. All of these possibilities complicate the interpretation of relvar ALL_IN_ONE considerably! *Exercise for the reader:* State the predicate
for ALL_IN_ONE as precisely as you can.

In sharp contrast to the foregoing, Design 2 is intuitively much cleaner and
much easier to understand:

1. The obvious predicates—for instance, *employee EMP# earns salary
   SALARY,* in the case of EMP_SALARY—are indeed the correct ones, and
   the obvious meanings of the columns are correct too.

---

[*]In this connection, see the section entitled "Relations with Nulls Aren't Relations" in
Installment 28.

2. The column names SALARY, BONUS, and so on, are therefore intuitively correct as well.

3. The domain of the SALARY column *is* just MONEY (and similarly for the other columns).

Incidentally, now that we've switched our terminology from *default* to *special* values, we can reinstate the term "default value" to mean what it always should have meant: merely the value that is assumed if no explicit value is supplied on INSERT. For instance, the default value for the SALARY column might be the company's defined minimum salary, say $10,000. This kind of default value has nothing to do with the topic of "missing information," of course; it's merely a syntactic convenience, serving as a shorthand for a commonly occurring case.

"MISSING" FOREIGN KEY VALUES

Suppose now that employees are assigned to departments, such that each employee has exactly one department (at any given time), but the department might be unknown for some employees. The "Design 1" approach to this situation is really *not* very satisfactory; we can invent a special value, "???" say, to stand for the department number for an employee whose department is unknown, but then we have to keep a kind of dummy row for department "???" in the departments relvar in order not to violate referential integrity. (I use "???" instead of UNK just to reduce monotony.) An example is shown in Fig. 3; for simplicity I've dropped the salary, bonus, and ratio information from ALL_IN_ONE, but I've added a new DEPT relvar. Note that—in accordance with our discussion of such matters in the previous section—both DEPT# columns should really be called DEPT#_OR_??? (or some such name).

	ALL_IN_ONE			DEPT	
	EMP#	DEPT#		DEPT#	BUDGET
	E1	D1		D1	100000
	E2	D2		D2	150000
	E3	D2		???	NA
	E4	D2			
	E5	???			
	E6	D2			
	E7	???			
	E8	D1			

Fig. 3   Using special values in a foreign key position (example)

A much better design, using a "Design 2" approach, is illustrated in Fig. 4. The basic idea is to move the employee-to-department cross-reference information out into another relvar, EMP_DEPT, thereby once again avoiding the need to include the explicit special values. Detailed consideration of the advantages of the Fig. 4 design is left as another exercise for the reader. *Note:* David McGoveran refers to cross-reference relvars such as EMP_DEPT as *association tables* [3].

EMP			EMP_DEPT			DEPT	
EMP#	....		EMP#	DEPT#		DEPT#	BUDGET
E1	....		E1	D1		D1	100000
E2	....		E2	D2		D2	150000
E3	....		E3	D2			
E4	....		E4	D2			
E5	....		E6	D2			
E6	....		E8	D1			
E7	....						
E8	....						

Fig. 4   Using a cross-reference relvar

Let me now change the semantics slightly and suppose that the property of having a department doesn't apply to certain employees. Then we need to extend the Fig. 4 design to include a DEPT_APPLIC column in relvar EMP, analogous to the BONUS_APPLIC column of Fig. 2. Omission of a given employee from EMP_DEPT would then mean that the department for that employee is (a) unknown if DEPT_APPLIC is "Y", (b) not applicable if DEPT_APPLIC is "N".

Note: David McGoveran argues [3] that the "Y" and "N" values in columns such as BONUS_APPLIC and DEPT_APPLIC are really *metadata,* not ordinary data, and argues further that metadata and ordinary data shouldn't be mixed together in the same relvar. "Just as exception processing should be separated from normal processing in applications, metadata should be maintained in separate *exception tables* and not interspersed with unexceptional production data" (slightly paraphrased). I tend to agree with this position, but see it as somewhat orthogonal to the main thrust of the present series of articles.

CONCLUDING REMARKS

Next month I want to consider the implications of the two design approaches for various kinds of queries. For now, let me leave you with another puzzle corner problem (nothing to do with databases this month): Can you find three integers x, y, and z, not necessarily distinct and not necessarily positive, such that the sum of their cubes is 100?

REFERENCES

1. C. J. Date: "Notes Toward a Reconstituted Definition of the Relational Model Version 1 (RM/V1)," in C. J. Date and Hugh Darwen, *Relational Database Writings 1989–1991*. Reading, Mass.: Addison-Wesley (1992).

2. C. J. Date and Hugh Darwen: *A Guide to the SQL Standard* (4th edition). Reading, Mass.: Addison-Wesley (1997).

3. David McGoveran: "Nothing from Nothing" (Chapters 5–8 of the present book).

Faults and Defaults
(Part 3 of 5)

*"Database management would be
simpler if missing values didn't exist"*

Last month I gave two possible designs, Design 1 and Design 2, for a simple employees database involving various kinds of missing information. Design 1 included explicit representation of the missing information and Design 2 didn't. This month, I want to consider, or at least begin to consider, the implications of the two designs for the task of formulating queries. Almost always, Design 2 will turn out to be superior to Design 1, as we'll see. For convenience, Figs. 1 and 2 repeat from last month a set of sample values for the two designs (except that the RATIO column is omitted from Fig. 1; the question of RATIO values remains on the back burner—I'll get to it eventually). Also, I've changed the column names in Fig. 1 in accordance with our discussions last month; the corresponding domains are MONEY_OR_UNK (for SALARY_OR_UNK) and MONEY_OR_UNK_OR_NA (for BONUS_OR_UNK_OR_NA).

Originally published in *Database Programming & Design 10,* No. 1, January 1997. Reprinted by permission of Miller Freeman Inc.

ALL_IN_ONE		
EMP#	SALARY_OR_UNK	BONUS_OR_UNK_OR_NA
E1	40000	10000
E2	55000	*NA*
E3	*UNK*	*NA*
E4	35000	*UNK*
E5	*UNK*	*UNK*
E6	72000	0
E7	*UNK*	0
E8	*UNK*	13000

Fig. 1   Design 1 (sample data, special values in italics)

EMP

EMP#	BONUS_APPLIC
E1	Y
E2	N
E3	N
E4	Y
E5	Y
E6	Y
E7	Y
E8	Y

EMP_SALARY

EMP#	SALARY
E1	40000
E2	55000
E4	35000
E6	72000

EMP_BONUS

EMP#	BONUS
E1	10000
E6	0
E7	0
E8	13000

Fig. 2   Design 2 (sample data, no explicit special values)

A SAMPLE QUERY

Suppose the user wants to get employee numbers for employees who earn a salary of more than $45,000. The first thing we have to do is understand *exactly* what it is that the user wants here; specifically, what are we supposed to do about employees whose salary is unknown?

Of course, we can never actually ask the system queries about the real world *per se,* only about its knowledge of the real world as represented by the contents of the database. Thus, the query as stated actually can't be answered (from the database, that is). By contrast, the following query (Q1) certainly can:

Q1: Get employee numbers for employees who **are known to the system to** earn a salary of more than $45,000.

Let's assume for the moment that query Q1 is indeed what the user really meant. Given Design 2, then, this query can be expressed straightforwardly as follows:

```
( EMP_SALARY
    WHERE SALARY > MONEY ( 45000 ) ) [ EMP# ]
```

(Let me remind you from last month that column SALARY is defined on domain MONEY; MONEY(45000) is a *money literal*. This formulation assumes that the operator ">" is defined in the obvious way for the MONEY domain. I'll get to this question of defining operators for domains in just a moment.)

The analogous formulation for Design 1 is a little more complex. Here's the obvious first attempt:

```
( ALL_IN_ONE
    WHERE SALARY_OR_UNK > MONEY_OR_UNK ( 45000 ) ) [ EMP# ]
```

However, *this formulation doesn't work*. Why not? Well, notice that the comparison in the WHERE clause involves an application of the ">" operator to values from the MONEY_OR_UNK domain. So the question is: What does that operator mean for that domain?—in particular, what does it mean if either comparand is UNK?

In order to answer this question, let me first remind you that (as I explained in an earlier installment in this series [4]), the task of defining a domain does indeed necessarily include the task of defining the operators—in particular, the comparison operators—that apply to values from that domain. How then might we define the comparison operators for a domain like MONEY_OR_UNK? Well, let a and b be arbitrary values from that domain. Then the "=" and "≠" operators are easy:

- The comparison "$a = b$" is defined to return *true* if and only if a and b are the same member of the domain (as is in fact required by the prescriptions of *The Third Manifesto* [1]).

- The comparison "$a \neq b$" is defined to return *true* if and only if the comparison "$a = b$" returns *false*.

Note that this definition implies that the comparison "UNK = UNK"—more precisely, the comparison "UNK(MONEY_OR_UNK) = UNK(MONEY_OR_UNK)"—returns *true*. It also implies that the comparison "UNK = a"—more precisely, the comparison "UNK(MONEY_OR_UNK) = a"—returns *false* if a is any value other than UNK. No three-valued logic here!

So what about the ">" operator? Well, we might try the following:

- The comparison "$a > b$" is defined to return *true* if neither a nor b is unknown and the money amount a is greater than the money amount b, and *false* otherwise.

This definition would imply that the comparisons "$a > \text{UNK}$" and "$\text{UNK} > b$"—more precisely, the comparisons "$a > \text{UNK}(\text{MONEY\_OR\_UNK})$" and "$\text{UNK}(\text{MONEY\_OR\_UNK}) > b$"—always return *false*.

The trouble with this definition, however, is that there's nothing special about "$>$"; symmetry would dictate that we must adopt an exactly analogous definition for the operators "$<$", "$\leq$", and "$\geq$". But then we run into the problem that, for any value a other than UNK, $false = (a > \text{UNK}) = \text{NOT}\ (a \leq \text{UNK}) = \text{NOT}\ (false) = true$. Contradiction!

So the suggested definition doesn't work very well. In fact, I would argue that—always assuming that we want to be able to apply the "$>$" operator at all, itself a debatable question (see later)—the only reasonable definition is the following:

- The comparison "$a > b$" is defined to return *true* if neither a nor b is unknown and the money amount a is greater than the money amount b; *false* if neither a nor b is unknown and the money amount a is not greater than the money amount b; and an exception if either a or b is unknown.

And similarly for "$<$", "$\leq$", and "$\geq$". In other words, comparison operators other than "$=$" and "$\neq$" on the MONEY_OR_UNK domain work as expected if the comparands are both regular money values, but raise an exception if either comparand is UNK.

Returning to our attempted Design 1 formulation of query Q1, therefore, we see that it will fail at run time as soon as it encounters an UNK in the SALARY_OR_UNK column. Thus, what we need to do is rephrase the query in order to eliminate the rows with UNKs before doing the "$>$" comparison. Let's examine this possibility.

First, the expression

```
ALL_IN_ONE WHERE NOT ( IS_UNK ( SALARY_OR_UNK ) )
```

clearly "eliminates the UNKs"—that is, it evaluates to just those rows of ALL_IN_ONE that don't have UNKs in the SALARY_OR_UNK position. Let *exp1* denote this expression. Then it might seem that the overall query could be expressed as follows:

```
( ( exp1 )
WHERE SALARY_OR_UNK > MONEY_OR_UNK ( 45000 ) ) [ EMP# ]
```

Let *exp2* denote this overall expression. Now, to show that *exp2* does in fact achieve the desired result, we argue as follows: Because *exp1* eliminates the rows with UNKs, the SALARY_OR_UNK comparand to the ">" comparison in *exp2* is guaranteed to be a regular money value, and hence the comparison works as desired and produces the desired result.

However, *this argument is incorrect* (and the overall formulation *exp2* is incorrect too). It's instructive to see exactly why this is so. The problem is as follows. For simplicity, let's agree to ignore the final projection over EMP#. Then expression *exp2* is of the basic form

```
( R WHERE c1 ) WHERE c2
```

(*R* is ALL_IN_ONE, *c1* is the condition that eliminates the UNKs, and *c2* is the condition that checks for salaries of more than $45,000). The trouble is, the expression just shown is semantically identical to—and can therefore logically be transformed into—the expression

```
R WHERE c1 AND c2
```

(see the discussion of expression transformations in an earlier installment [3]). And, of course, given the expression *c1* AND *c2*, the system is free to evaluate the conditions *c1* and *c2* in either order (because *c1* AND *c2* is semantically identical to *c2* AND *c1*)—which means that *c2* might actually be evaluated first after all. In the case at hand, therefore, there's still a possibility that the SALARY_OR_UNK comparand to the ">" comparison in *exp2* is an UNK instead of a regular money value. And if it is, of course, we'll get a run-time error.

How do we get over this difficulty? Well, let's think about the domains MONEY and MONEY_OR_UNK a little more carefully. As I've already pointed out, the task of defining a domain necessarily includes the task of defining the operators that apply to values from that domain. In the case at hand, we would probably want to define **conversion** or "cast" operators for converting MONEY values into MONEY_OR_UNK values and *vice versa:*

- Casting MONEY values to MONEY_OR_UNK values is easy, of course, since every MONEY value is a legal MONEY_OR_UNK value as well. The syntax might be:

```
CAST_TO_MONEY_OR_UNK ( exp )
```

  Here *exp* is a scalar expression representing a value of type (domain) MONEY.

- The opposite direction is slightly more complicated. Presumably we would want to say that every regular money value in MONEY_OR_UNK maps to its counterpart in MONEY in the obvious way, but attempting to cast the MONEY_OR_UNK "unknown" value to a MONEY value raises a run-time error. Syntax:

```
CAST_TO_MONEY ( exp )
```

Here *exp* is a scalar expression representing a value of type MONEY_ OR_UNK.

Given the existence of such cast operations, we can now introduce some new *relational* operators, of the following generic form:

```
rel : TO_dom ( col )
```

Here *rel* is an arbitrary relational expression, *col* is the name of a column of the relation represented by that expression, and *dom* is the name of a domain. The overall value of the expression is defined to be a relation with:

- A heading the same as that of *rel*, except that the domain corresponding to column *col* in that heading is *dom;*
- A body consisting of those rows of *rel* in which *col* contains a value that can be cast to domain *dom*, except that the *col* values in those rows are replaced by their *dom* counterparts.

For example, the expression

```
ALL_IN_ONE : TO_MONEY ( SALARY_OR_UNK )
```

yields the relation shown in Fig. 3 (note that the domain of column SALARY_ OR_UNK in that relation is MONEY, not MONEY_OR_UNK).

EMP#	SALARY_OR_UNK	BONUS_OR_UNK_OR_NA
E1	40000	10000
E2	55000	NA
E4	35000	UNK
E6	72000	0

Fig. 3 ALL_IN_ONE : TO_MONEY (SALARY_OR_UNK)

Query Q1 thus becomes:

```
( ( ALL_IN_ONE : TO_MONEY ( SALARY_OR_UNK ) )
    WHERE SALARY_OR_UNK > MONEY ( 45000 ) ) [ EMP# ]
```

Explanation: The inner expression ALL_IN_ONE : TO_MONEY (SALARY_OR_UNK) evaluates—loosely speaking—to a relation containing just those rows of ALL_IN_ONE that have regular money values in the

SALARY_OR_UNK position (and the domain of that column of that relation is MONEY, not MONEY_OR_UNK). The overall expression thus (at last!) evaluates to the desired result.

Note 1: Since we agreed that ">" on the MONEY_OR_UNK domain should raise an exception if either comparand is UNK, we might just as well not have defined ">" for that domain at all, defining it instead (in the usual way) only for the simple MONEY domain. I'll leave it to you to verify that this change would effectively make no difference to the question of how to formulate query Q1.

Note 2: It might be thought that much of the complexity we've been discussing could be avoided by defining the UNK value for domain MONEY_ OR_UNK to be a numeric value, say -1, instead of a string such as "UNK." The comparison operators could then be defined to work in the usual way on such a value, and it might not even be necessary to distinguish between the domains MONEY and MONEY_OR_UNK.

However, to argue thus is *to confuse type and representation.* It's true that the **representation** chosen for the unknown special value could indeed be numeric; but, of course, the representation is irrelevant to the discussion at hand. *Semantically,* the unknown special value is completely different from regular values, and it makes no sense to say that (for example) such a special value is "greater than" (or "less than" or whatever) some regular value.

It seems to me that the net of all of the foregoing is that Design 2 is clearly preferable to Design 1, at least insofar as query Q1 is concerned.

THE SAMPLE QUERY CONTINUED

There is, of course, the possibility that what the user really meant was not query Q1 but query Q2:

Q2: Get employee numbers for employees who **either are known to the system to** earn a salary of more than $45,000 **or have salaries that aren't known to the system at all.**

Since we've already discussed the first part of this requirement (it's basically just query Q1), let's ignore it, thereby simplifying query Q2 to query Q3:

Q3: Get employee numbers for employees **whose salaries aren't known to the system at all.**

Here's the Design 2 formulation:

```
EMP [ EMP# ] MINUS EMP_SALARY [ EMP# ]
```

And a Design 1 counterpart:

```
( ALL_IN_ONE WHERE IS_UNK ( SALARY_OR_UNK ) ) [ EMP# ]
```

Although there's little difference in complexity between these two formulations, I have to say that the Design 2 version is more to my taste, since it eschews all mention of special values.

DISCUSSION

Let me now point out one very nice feature of the scheme I'm advocating here. Specifically, observe that the scheme does *not* rely on any kind of builtin semantics for the special values ("unknown" and "not applicable" and all the rest), nor for the comparison operators ">" and so forth. The problem with builtin semantics—that is, the problem with prescribing specific semantics that the system *must* support—is that we'll probably get that prescription wrong, as SQL did. The advantage of not usurping such decisions but leaving them to the DBA or database designer is precisely that the system can thus be tailored to whatever specific requirements seem appropriate to the situation at hand. Of course, it does mean that the DBA or database designer must understand the data properly . . . but I don't think I'd trust a database that wasn't designed without such an understanding anyway. More important, it also means that **the system must support domains properly!** Such support is something I and other relational advocates have been calling for, in other contexts, for a long time now [4].

ANOTHER SAMPLE QUERY

Let's leave these philosophical musings and consider another example. The query is:

Q4: Get employee numbers for employees who are known to get a bonus that is less than their salary.

Note that I've deliberately phrased this query in such a way that it can be answered from the database. In practice, of course, we don't usually bother to be so precise—but maybe we should. Indeed, an argument can be made that it was a lack of such precision that led us into the nulls quagmire in the first place. But I digress . . .

With Design 2, a correct formulation of the query is again fairly simple:

```
( ( EMP_SALARY JOIN EMP_BONUS )
  WHERE BONUS < SALARY ) ) [ EMP# ]
```

With Design 1, what we'd *like* to write is probably something like this:

```
( ALL_IN_ONE
  WHERE BONUS_OR_UNK_OR_NA < SALARY_OR_UNK ) [ EMP# ]
```

The trouble is, columns BONUS_OR_UNK_OR_NA and SALARY_OR_
UNK are defined on different domains (as mentioned earlier, the domains are
MONEY_OR_UNK_OR_NA and MONEY_OR_UNK, respectively). We
might consider the possibility that the "<" operator could be defined to operate appropriately across these two domains. However, this idea is essentially
a nonstarter (it runs into the same kind of difficulties over special values as
our first attempt to define the ">" operator did in the section "A Sample
Query"). Instead, what we'll have to do is rephrase the query along the following lines:

```
( ( ( ALL_IN_ONE : TO_MONEY ( BONUS_OR_UNK_OR_NA ) )
            : TO_MONEY ( SALARY_OR_UNK ) )
    WHERE BONUS_OR_UNK_OR_NA < SALARY_OR_UNK ) [ EMP# ]
```

Once again I conclude that Design 2 is the preferable design.

TOO MANY JOINS?

There's one potential objection I must address before closing this month's
column—namely, doesn't the design discipline I'm advocating lead to an
excessive number of base relvars, and hence to an excessive number of joins
(and other dyadic operations) at run time?

Well, it's undeniable that the Design 2 formulation of query Q4 involves
a join that the Design 1 formulation doesn't, and the Design 2 formulation
of query Q3 involves a difference (MINUS) that the Design 1 formulation
doesn't. But the argument that the design discipline is therefore bad news is
precisely analogous to the argument that normalization (to third normal form
or whatever) is bad news! Normalization too tends to lead to "lots of base
relvars and lots of joins"; however—as I've argued in this series before [2]—
this latter state of affairs is bad news only in a product that provides an inadequate degree of physical data independence. (It's true, of course, that just
about every product currently on the market suffers from this defect. No excuse!) I conclude that, in a properly architected system, the objection is not
valid. What's more, I'm pleased to be able to say that on this particular
point—his overall objections to the special values scheme notwithstanding—Tom Johnston seems to agree with me [5].

PUZZLE CORNER

Give "Design 1" and "Design 2" formulations of the following queries:

- Get employee numbers for employees whose bonus is greater than $5000.
- Get employee numbers for employees whose bonus is at least half their total pay.

REFERENCES

1. Hugh Darwen and C. J. Date: "The Third Manifesto," *ACM SIGMOD Record 24*, No. 1 (March 1995). See also the book-length version *Foundation for Object/ Relational Databases: The Third Manifesto*. Reading, Mass.: Addison-Wesley (1998).

2. C. J. Date: "The Importance of Closure," *Database Programming & Design 5*, No. 10 (October 1992). Republished in *Relational Database Writings 1991–1994*. Reading, Mass.: Addison-Wesley (1995).

3. C. J. Date: "Expression Transformation (Part 1 of 2)," *Database Programming & Design 6*, No. 6 (June 1993). Republished in *Relational Database Writings 1991–1994*. Reading, Mass.: Addison-Wesley (1995).

4. C. J. Date: "Domains, Relations, and Data Types," *Database Programming & Design 7*, Nos. 6–7 (June–July 1994). Republished in *Relational Database Writings 1991–1994*. Reading, Mass.: Addison-Wesley (1995).

5. Tom Johnston: "MVL: Case Open," *Database Programming & Design 8*, No. 2 (February 1995); "The Case for MVL," *Database Programming & Design 8*, No. 3 (March 1995).

•

Faults and Defaults
(Part 4 of 5)

Continuing our investigation
into special values and queries

Last month, we looked at some simple queries against two possible designs, Design 1 and Design 2, for a simple employees database involving various kinds of missing information. This month I want to examine some more complicated queries against those two designs. For convenience, the two designs and corresponding sample values are repeated in Figs. 1 and 2. I remind you that columns SALARY_OR_UNK and BONUS_OR_UNK_OR_NA are defined on domains MONEY_OR_UNK and MONEY_OR_UNK_OR_NA, respectively, and columns SALARY and BONUS are defined on domain MONEY.

ALL_IN_ONE		
EMP#	SALARY_OR_UNK	BONUS_OR_UNK_OR_NA
E1	40000	10000
E2	55000	*NA*
E3	*UNK*	*NA*
E4	35000	*UNK*
E5	*UNK*	*UNK*
E6	72000	0
E7	*UNK*	0
E8	*UNK*	13000

Fig. 1   Design 1 (sample data, special values in italics)

Originally published in *Database Programming & Design 10*, No. 2, February 1997. Reprinted by permission of Miller Freeman Inc.

EMP	
EMP#	BONUS_APPLIC
E1	Y
E2	N
E3	N
E4	Y
E5	Y
E6	Y
E7	Y
E8	Y

EMP_SALARY	
EMP#	SALARY
E1	40000
E2	55000
E4	35000
E6	72000

EMP_BONUS	
EMP#	BONUS
E1	10000
E6	0
E7	0
E8	13000

Fig. 2   Design 2 (sample data)

SPECIAL VALUES IN THE RESULT

In the previous installment I briefly discussed the following query (Q2):

Q2: Get employee numbers for employees who either are known to the system to earn a salary in excess of $45,000 or have salaries that aren't known to the system at all.

However, this query is rather unrealistic as stated, because, for a given employee number in the result, the user won't be able to tell whether the employee in question has an unknown salary or a known salary in excess of $45,000. A more realistic requirement would be:

Q5: Get employee numbers **and corresponding salaries** for employees who either are known to the system to earn a salary in excess of $45,000 or have salaries that aren't known to the system at all.

(I'm continuing the query numbering from the previous installment.)
    Note that, once again, the requirement is still not very precisely stated. A more precise statement would look something like the following:

For employees who are known to the system to earn a salary in excess of $45,000, get employee numbers and corresponding salaries; for employees whose salaries aren't known to the system at all, get employee numbers only (we obviously can't ask the system to get their *salaries*).

This more precise version makes it clear that Query Q5 is really *two separate queries rolled up into one*. In terms of Design 2, for example, the two queries correspond to the following two relational expressions:

```
EMP_SALARY WHERE SALARY > MONEY ( 45000 )

EMP [ EMP# ] MINUS EMP_SALARY [ EMP# ]
```

X1	EMP#	SALARY		X2	EMP#
	E2	55000			E3
	E6	72000			E5
					E7
					E8

Fig. 3 Result relations X1 and X2

(see Fig. 3 for the corresponding result relations, X1 and X2 say).

Now, we might imagine some extensions to the relational algebra—some new relational operators, that is—that would allow us to write a single expression that evaluates to a *set* of relations (instead of just to a single relation, which is all the existing operators allow). However, the relational algebra doesn't include any such operators at the time of writing. Therefore, *either* we'll have to write two separate queries, as already discussed, *or* we'll have to write a single query that yields a single relation (X, say) that includes some explicit UNKs, as shown in Fig. 4. (My own preference would be to go with the first of these options, but I suspect I'm in a minority here.)

So let's consider the question of writing a query to produce relation X. Now, it might be thought that Design 1 will prove superior to Design 2 for this task, since explicit special values are required in the result and in Design 1 such values already exist in the database, whereas for Design 2 they'll have to be generated dynamically. Despite this state of affairs, however, Design 1 displays no significant superiority over Design 2, as we'll see.

It turns out that the query is rather more complicated than it might appear at first glance (were you surprised?). For this reason, I'll approach its

X	EMP#	SALARY_OR_UNK
	E2	55000
	E3	UNK
	E5	UNK
	E6	72000
	E7	UNK
	E8	UNK

Fig. 4 Result relation X

formulation a step at a time, instead of just presenting one great big nested expression "out of the blue," as it were. Here first is a Design 1 formulation. You might want to work through this sequence of steps, using the sample data from Fig. 1.

```
T1   :=   ALL_IN_ONE : TO_MONEY ( SALARY_OR_UNK ) ;
T2   :=   T1 WHERE SALARY_OR_UNK > MONEY ( 45000 ) ;
T3   :=   T2 : TO_MONEY_OR_UNK ( SALARY_OR_UNK ) ;
T4   :=   T3 [ EMP#, SALARY_OR_UNK ] ;
T5   :=   ALL_IN_ONE WHERE IS_UNK ( SALARY_OR_UNK ) ;
T6   :=   T5 [ EMP#, SALARY_OR_UNK ] ;
ANS  :=   T4 UNION T6 ;
```

Explanation:

- Step 1 yields a relation T1 consisting of just those rows of ALL_IN_ONE for employees whose salary is known (and column SALARY_OR_UNK in T1 is defined on domain MONEY, not MONEY_OR_UNK).

- Step 2 then restricts T1 to just those rows for employees whose salary is greater than $45000.

- Step 3 then casts the salary values in those rows back to type (domain) SALARY_OR_UNK. This step is necessary in order to ensure that the UNION operands in the final step are of the same type.

- Step 4 projects the output from Step 3 over columns EMP# and SALARY_OR_UNK.

- Step 5 yields a relation T5 consisting of just those rows of ALL_IN_ONE for employees whose salary is unknown.

- Step 6 projects the output from Step 5 over columns EMP# and SALARY_OR_UNK.

- Finally, Step 7 yields the desired overall result.

Now let's turn to a Design 2 formulation of the query. Again I suggest you work through the following sequence of steps, using the sample data from Fig. 2.

```
T1   :=   EMP_SALARY WHERE SALARY > MONEY ( 45000 ) ;
T2   :=   T1 : TO_MONEY_OR_UNK ( SALARY ) ;
T3   :=   T2 RENAME SALARY AS SALARY_OR_UNK ;
T4   :=   EMP [ EMP# ] ;
T5   :=   EMP_SALARY [ EMP# ] ;
T6   :=   T4 MINUS T5 ;
T7   :=   EXTEND T6 ADD UNK ( MONEY_OR_UNK ) AS SALARY_OR_UNK ;
ANS  :=   T3 UNION T7 ;
```

Explanation:

- Step 1 restricts EMP_SALARY to just those rows for employees whose salary is greater than $45000; Step 2 then casts those salary values to domain MONEY_OR_UNK, and Step 3 renames the SALARY column as SALARY_OR_UNK.

- Steps 4 and 5 yield, respectively, a relation T4 consisting of all employee numbers and a relation T5 consisting of employee numbers for all employees whose salary is known. Step 6 thus yields a relation T6 consisting of employee numbers for all employees whose salary is unknown.

- Step 7 extends T6 to add a new column called SALARY_OR_UNK (with domain MONEY_OR_UNK), containing an UNK in every row. (By the way: How does the system know the domain is MONEY_OR_UNK?)

- Finally, Step 8 produces the desired overall result.

As you can see, the Design 1 and Design 2 solutions are both a little complicated! Note carefully, however, that:

- The complexity is *caused,* in large part, by the desire to bundle what are really two separate queries together into a single query. As we saw near the beginning of this section, formulating the two queries separately is very easy, in fact almost trivial.

- Even if we agree that the bundling is desirable (in itself a moot point), the fact that Design 1 includes explicit special values in the database, while Design 2 doesn't, doesn't seem to make the Design 1 solution significantly simpler than the Design 2 formulation.

Aside: We might, following Darwen [1], define a "respectable" version of outer join to help in the formulation of queries such as Q5 against designs such as Design 2. Let *exp* denote the expression

```
( ( EMP_SALARY WHERE SALARY > MONEY ( 45000 ) )
        : TO_MONEY_OR_UNK ( SALARY ) )
              RENAME SALARY AS SALARY_OR_UNK
```

In other words, *exp* represents a relation containing just employee-number/salary rows for those employees whose salary is known to be greater than $45,000. The heading of that relation is { EMP#, SALARY_OR_UNK }, and column SALARY_OR_UNK in that relation is defined on domain MONEY_OR_UNK. Then the following expression will produce something like the required result:

```
EMP [ EMP# ]
    LEFT_JOIN exp
          FILL UNK ( MONEY_OR_UNK )
```

Note, however, that:

- Missing information in the result of this "respectable" outer join is represented, not by nulls, but by special "fill" values—and exactly which special values are used as such fill values is under user control.
- The discussions of this section might help to convince you that outer join is actually a very complicated operation!—much more complicated than is usually thought.

End of aside.

SCALAR COMPUTATIONAL OPERATIONS

Here's another sample query:

Q6: For each employee, get the employee number and corresponding total pay (defined as salary plus bonus).

Once again, this query is actually much more complex than it seems—or, at least, the requirement is considerably underspecified. The basic problem is, what should we do for an employee where either the salary or the bonus is unknown, or where the bonus is not applicable? We certainly don't want the system to *guess* what the user might want in such cases. (I note in passing that, in general, guessing is EXACTLY what the nulls scheme does.) So let's try to pin the requirement down more precisely. Perhaps we can agree that the following definitions are reasonable:

1. If either the salary or the bonus is unknown, the total pay is unknown. (Though if just one of the two is unknown, we do at least know that the total pay must be equal to or greater than the other. We could extend the query to retrieve the salary and bonus as well, to enable the user to deal with this eventuality.)

2. Otherwise, if the bonus is inapplicable, the total pay is just the salary.

3. Otherwise, the total pay is indeed just the sum of the salary and the bonus, as stated.

Query Q6 thus actually represents a bundling of three distinct queries, each of which is easily formulated in terms of either Design 1 or Design 2 (exercise for the reader). However, if—again—the user really insists on writing a single query to generate a single relation that contains explicit special values, well, of course it can be done. Here's a possible Design 1 formulation. (I make the reasonable assumption that the "+" operator is defined in the obvious way for

the MONEY domain and is not defined at all for the domains MONEY_OR_
UNK and MONEY_OR_UNK_OR_NA.)

```
( EXTEND ALL_IN_ONE
  ADD CASE
        WHEN IS_UNK ( SALARY_OR_UNK ) OR
             IS_UNK ( BONUS_OR_UNK_OR_NA )
             THEN UNK ( MONEY_OR_UNK )
        WHEN IS_NA ( BONUS_OR_UNK_OR_NA )
             THEN SALARY_OR_UNK
        ELSE CAST_TO_MONEY ( SALARY_OR_UNK ) +
             CAST_TO_MONEY ( BONUS_OR_UNK_OR_NA )
     END CASE
  AS PAY ) [ EMP#, PAY ]
```

A Design 2 formulation might look like this:

```
( EXTEND EMP
  ADD CASE
        WHEN IS_EMPTY ( MATCHING EMP_SALARY ) OR
           ( IS_EMPTY ( MATCHING EMP_BONUS ) AND
             BONUS_APPLIC = 'Y' )
             THEN UNK ( MONEY_OR_UNK )
        WHEN BONUS_APPLIC = 'N'
             THEN ext ( ( MATCHING EMP_SALARY ) [ SALARY ] )
        ELSE     ext ( ( MATCHING EMP_SALARY ) [ SALARY ] )
             + ext ( ( MATCHING EMP_BONUS ) [ BONUS ] )
     END CASE
  AS PAY ) [ EMP#, PAY ]
```

Once again, the Design 1 and Design 2 formulations turn out to be of ap-
proximately the same degree of difficulty. (Note, however, that the Design 2
formulation does make use of an operator, here shown as *ext,* that extracts the
single scalar value from a one-row, one-column relation. I haven't discussed
this operator previously, but something like it is clearly going to be needed in
any real relational language. Of course, it might be possible—though almost
certainly undesirable—to conceal it in the concrete syntax, as SQL does.)

> *Important aside:*   One thing neither of the foregoing formulations
> does is rely on prescribed behavior for the "+" operator—for exam-
> ple, a prescription that x + UNK must give UNK for all x (another dif-
> ference from SQL, of course). I reject the idea of relying on such a
> prescription for the following reason. First, such an approach would
> suggest (for consistency) that we would have to insist that x – UNK
> must also give UNK for all x. This requirement in turn would mean
> that $x - x$ must give UNK, instead of zero, if x is UNK. And this last
> state of affairs leads to all kinds of anomalies, details of which are be-
> yond the scope of the present discussion. Suffice it to say that they
> resemble some of the anomalies that arise over nulls—and that way
> madness lies. *End of aside.*

WHAT ABOUT THE RATIO VALUES?

Now (at last!) I can turn my attention to the question of RATIO values. Recall that—ignoring all the special cases—RATIO is defined as SALARY divided by BONUS. In other words, RATIO values are **derived,** and thus probably shouldn't be part of the base design at all; that is, RATIO probably shouldn't be included as a column in any base relvar (but see the note at the end of this section). Instead, what we need is a *derived* relvar (a view, if you prefer), say EMP_RATIO, with columns EMP# and RATIO, defined by means of the following relational expression:

```
( EXTEND
( EMP_SALARY JOIN ( EMP_BONUS WHERE BONUS ≠ MONEY ( 0 ) ) )
  ADD SALARY / BONUS AS RATIO ) [ EMP#, RATIO ]
```

This relvar contains a row for every employee represented in both EMP_SALARY and EMP_BONUS, except where the corresponding bonus is zero. In other words, it contains a row for every employee *except* those for whom one of the following is true:

- The bonus is inapplicable (BONUS_APPLIC in EMP is "N").

- The bonus is applicable but zero (in which case the ratio is undefined).

- The bonus is applicable but unknown (no matching row in EMP_BONUS).

- The salary is unknown (no matching row in EMP_SALARY).

Of course, one question we do need to consider is how to construct the relation ALL_IN_ONE shown in Fig. 5 (with its RATIO column) from the relations of Fig. 2 (exercise for the reader).

ALL_IN_ONE			
EMP#	**SALARY_OR_UNK**	**BONUS_OR_UNK_OR_NA**	**RATIO**
E1	40000	10000	4
E2	55000	NA	NA
E3	UNK	NA	NA
E4	35000	UNK	UNK
E5	UNK	UNK	UNK
E6	72000	0	UNDEF
E7	UNK	0	UNDEF
E8	UNK	13000	UNK

Fig. 5   ALL_IN_ONE, including the RATIO column

Note: Actually it's a slight oversimplification to say that ratios are derived and salary and bonus aren't. The fact is, if we know any two of salary, bonus, and ratio, then we can derive the third. So long as we limit our attention to the normal case, therefore, it's arbitrary which of the three we consider to be derived and which "base." The other cases complicate the picture considerably, however; for example, if we know the bonus (and therefore the ratio) to be "not applicable," there's no way we can derive the salary. In practice, therefore, regarding ratios specifically to be the derived values seems a reasonable thing to do.

AGGREGATE OPERATIONS

What about aggregate operators such as SUM? Consider the query:

Q7: Get the total salary for all employees.

Again, the first thing we have to do is pin down the exact requirement. What if some employees have an unknown salary? It seems to me there are two possibilities:

1. The query means "Get the total salary for all employees whose salary is known."

2. The query means "Try to get the total salary for *all* employees—but, if any of those employees has an unknown salary, return an appropriate UNK value."

Both possibilities are easily expressed in terms of Design 2:

```
1. SUM ( EMP_SALARY, SALARY )

2. CASE
       WHEN IS_EMPTY ( EMP [ EMP# ] MINUS EMP_SALARY [ EMP# ] )
            THEN SUM ( EMP_SALARY, SALARY )
       ELSE UNK ( MONEY_OR_UNK )
   END CASE
```

The Design 1 analogs are left as an exercise for the reader.

Aside: A Design 2 formulation of the first interpretation that yields a relation as a result (instead of a scalar as the expression SUM (EMP_SALARY, SALARY) does) would be

```
EXTEND TABLE_DEE ADD SUM ( EMP_SALARY, SALARY ) AS TOTAL
```

An analogous remark applies to the second interpretation also, of course.   *End of aside.*

Observe that the one thing I *don't* want to do with this query is what SQL does—namely, usurp the user's decision by defining the aggregate operator SUM to "ignore UNKs" (or nulls, rather). Instead, I want SUM to be properly defined, essentially as an iterated "+" (whatever "+" happens to mean for the domain in question). In other words, one thing I do want to prescribe is that SUM and the other aggregate operators be properly defined!

CONCLUDING REMARKS

We're approaching the end of this miniseries on the "missing information" problem. In the final installment, I want to address some of the objections that have been leveled at the approach I've been advocating—that is, the approach based on the use of special values and two-valued logic, instead of nulls and three-valued logic. For now, let me just leave you with this month's puzzle corner problem (a nondatabase problem once again):

> A cylindrical hole 6″ long is drilled straight through the center of a wooden sphere. What's the volume of the sphere without the hole?

(This is one of those nice problems where it seems we don't have enough information to solve it, but in fact we do.)

REFERENCES

1. Hugh Darwen: "Outer Join with No Nulls and Fewer Tears," in C. J. Date and Hugh Darwen, *Relational Database Writings 1989–1991*. Reading, Mass.: Addison-Wesley (1992).

Database Graffiti

Scribbles from The Askew Wall

Many congratulations to *Database Programming & Design* on reaching its tenth birthday! To mark the occasion, I've decided to interrupt my miniseries on special values and "missing information" (I'll return to those topics next month); instead, I thought I'd share some gems from my own private collection of quotations, aphorisms, and anecdotes that are relevant—albeit pretty loosely, in some cases—to the subject of database management. My aim is partly to edify, partly just to amuse.

NORMALIZATION, NETWORKS, AND NULLS

I'll begin with a couple of items having to do with normalization. I overheard the following in the hallway as I was hurrying to my session at the December 1995 *Database and Client/Server World* conference in Chicago: "Well, he *said* the tables were all in fifth normal form, but I think he must have meant sixth." I wish I'd had time to stop for further enlightenment . . . When I told Hugh Darwen this story, he countered by telling me of someone he met in the UK who, on first meeting the term *normalization,* inquired: "Normalization? What's that? Is it sort of the opposite of denormalization?"

These two anecdotes remind me of one of my favorite definitions (it appeared in an early IBM PL/I reference manual, back in the 1960s): "Normal: *see* abnormal." Which unavoidably reminds me of the old chestnut: "Recursion: *see* recursion." And that one in turn reminds me of the following maxim, due I

Originally published in *Database Programming & Design 10,* No. 3, March 1997 (the tenth anniversary issue). Reprinted by permission of Miller Freeman Inc. *Note:* The appendix to the present book contains a greatly expanded version of this article.

believe to Jim Gray: "Anything in computer science that's not recursive is no good" (how true).

Talking of "old chestnut" definitions, it would be very remiss of me not to include this one (from Dr. Johnson's Dictionary—where else?):

- **Network:** Any thing reticulated or decussated, with interstices between the intersections.

And networks bring me to distributed databases . . . I hope I'm not the only one to find humor in the following (a lightly edited excerpt from the references section of a paper on distributed query processing, in *ACM Computing Surveys 16,* No. 4, December 1984):

- Yu, C. T., *et al.* 1982a. "Promising approach to distributed query processing." In . . . (etc.).
- Yu, C. T., *et al.* 1982b. "Two surprising results in processing simple queries in distributed databases." In . . . (etc.).

The description of some line of investigation first as promising, later as surprising, could probably be applied to a lot of research activity, if the truth be known.

To close this section, here are a few items having to do with missing information and nulls:

- "Database management would be simpler if missing values didn't exist" (one of my favorites!—E. F. Codd, in "Much Ado about Nothing," *Database Programming & Design 6,* No. 10, October 1993).*
- "It all makes sense if you squint a little and don't think too hard" (anon; quoted by David Maier in his book *The Theory of Relational Databases,* Computer Science Press, 1983).
- "Everything should be made as simple as possible—but *no simpler*" (Albert Einstein, quoted in *Newsweek,* April 16th, 1979); the point here is that nulls, at least as usually understood, represent an oversimplistic approach to a complex problem. Oversimplifying can be harmful to your health.

SQL AND OTHER MYSTERIES

Another rich source is the SQL/92 standard, which is chock-a-block with quotable material. A personal favorite—I included it in the book I wrote with Hugh Darwen, *A Guide to the SQL Standard,* 4th edition (Addison-Wesley, 1997), but it certainly bears repeating here—is this one:

---

*I used this quote as the subtitle to Installment 53, as you might recall.

- "However, because global temporary table contents are distinct within SQL-sessions, and created local temporary tables are distinct within <module>s within SQL-sessions, the *effective* <schema name> of the schema in which the global temporary table or the created local temporary table is instantiated is an implementation-dependent <schema name> that may be thought of as having been effectively derived from the <schema name> of the schema in which the global temporary table or created local temporary table is defined and the implementation-dependent SQL-session identifier associated with the SQL-session."

This sentence (yes, it's all one sentence!) is taken from a section of the standard entitled—and intended to explain the SQL concept of—"Tables." I never realized tables were so complicated. It reminds me of the beautiful, but unfortunately anonymous, saying: "If you're not confused by all this, it just proves you're not thinking clearly."

Of course, it's not just SQL; our entire industry is plagued by bad terminology and graceless prose. By way of example, consider the following, which is one of the reviewer options that used to appear (I don't know if it still does) on ANSI standard release forms:

- "I nonconcur with the subject release for announcement for the following reasons and understand that under the rules of dissent, I am obligated to escalate my nonconcurrence for a timely resolution."

To redress the balance a little, perhaps I should give an example to show that other disciplines—if I might be allowed a little poetic license in the use of such a term—can yield sentences that are just as bad as the ones quoted above. The following excerpt from the UK Scrap Metal Dealers Act of 1964 was quoted in a letter to *The Times* (of London), April 5th, 1995:

- "For the purposes of this Act a person carries on business as a scrap metal dealer if he [*sic*] carries on a business which consists wholly or partly of buying and selling scrap metal whether the scrap metal sold is in the form in which it was bought or otherwise, other than a business in the course of which scrap metal is not bought except as materials for the manufacture of other articles and is not sold except as a by product of such manufacture or as surplus materials bought but not required for such manufacture, and 'scrap metal dealer' (where the expression is used in this Act otherwise than in reference to carrying on business as a scrap metal dealer) means a person who (in accordance with the preceding provisions of this subsection) carries on business as a scrap metal dealer."

OBJECTS AND OBJECTIONS

Back to databases. In my book *An Introduction to Database Systems* (6th edition, Addison-Wesley, 1995), in a chapter on object-oriented (OO) systems, I said this:

- *"Caveat:* Before we start getting into details, it is as well to warn readers not to expect the kind of precision they are accustomed to in the relational world. Indeed, many OO concepts . . . are quite imprecise, and there is very little true consensus and much disagreement, even at the most basic level."

Naturally enough, I wasn't all that surprised when one reviewer complained—quite hotly!—that my characterization of OO concepts here was unfair. However, I *was* surprised by what he actually said: "No, no, no, no, no! OO *concepts* aren't fuzzy and imprecise at all. It's only their *definitions* that are sometimes fuzzy and imprecise." I was tempted to say "I rest my case." Though perhaps it would be more diplomatic to say, with Mark Twain, merely that "The logic of our adversary resembles the peace of God" (from *Roughing It;* Twain was quoting Thomas Fitch, editor of the *Union* newspaper in Virginia City, Nevada).

More diplomatically still (or at least more charitably), I might have responded in the words of Sidney Smith, who, on seeing two women leaning out of their respective houses and arguing across the street, observed: "Those two ladies will never agree, for they are arguing from different premises."

While on the subject of disagreements, here's another quotation I like very much—a serious one this time:

- "Whenever you find yourself getting angry about a difference of opinion, be on your guard; you will probably find, on examination, that your belief is going beyond what the evidence warrants" (from Bertrand Russell, "An Outline of Intellectual Rubbish," in *Unpopular Essays,* Simon & Schuster, 1950).

Still on the same subject, I recently came across the following beautiful piece of criticism (of one professor's work by a rival academic):

- "It seems to me that [my esteemed colleague], by avoiding the issue of the concrete historical reality lying behind the various similarities between cultural forms which he seeks to recognize, has allowed himself a much freer hand and perhaps a less disciplined methodology than might have been prudent" (from Colin Renfrew, *Archaeology and Language,* Cambridge University Press, 1988).

The understatement here ("allowed himself a much freer hand" . . . "perhaps a less disciplined methodology" . . . "than might have been prudent") is quite delightful.

Back to databases again, or at least computers. Here's another serious quotation, this one from Maurice Wilkes (*Communications of the ACM 34,* No. 5, May 1991):

- "I would like to see computer science teaching set deliberately in a historical framework . . . Students need to understand how the present situation has come about, what was tried, what worked and what did not, and how improvements in hardware made progress possible. The absence of this element in their training causes people to approach every problem from first principles. They are apt to propose solutions that have been found wanting in the past. Instead of standing on the shoulders of their precursors, they try to go it alone."

It is indeed sad to see how often the wheel gets reinvented in our industry. In particular, I think OO database technology is a case in point. There's almost nothing about it that's truly new!—and much that has indeed been "tried [and] found wanting in the past." However, to get into *that* discussion here would take us much too far afield; perhaps I'll come back to it in some future column, or columns.

THE ROLE OF SIMPLICITY

Here are some more beautiful quotations, these ones all having to do with *the role of simplicity in science*. Database professionals (and other computer professionals, and scientists in general, come to that) could do a lot worse than take all of them to heart.

- "For what is clear and easily comprehended attracts; the complicated repels" (David Hilbert).
- "Sometimes one has to say difficult things, but one ought to say them as simply as one knows how" (G. H. Hardy).
- "Most of the fundamental ideas of science are essentially simple, and may, as a rule, be expressed in a language comprehensible to everyone" (Albert Einstein).
- "Even for the physicist the description in plain language will be a criterion of the degree of understanding that has been reached" (Werner Heisenberg).
- "If you cannot—in the long run—tell everyone what you have been doing, your doing has been worthless" (Erwin Schrödinger).

BOOKS AND BOOK REVIEWS

Here now are a couple of nice typos. First, a White Paper from a few years back, describing a new SQL product, had the term "referential integrity" set throughout as *reverential* integrity . . . I like it. Second, a certain review, again from a few years back, of a book by James Martin entitled *System Design from Provably Correct Constructs* (Prentice-Hall, 1985) was headed "How to Write Programs that are *Probably* Correct" (emphasis added). Again, very nice! (Actually, I think we all know how to write programs that are *probably* correct.)

While I'm on the topic of book reviews, I can't resist mentioning one of the best I know:

- "The covers of this book are too far apart" (Ambrose Bierce, review, quoted by Matthew Parris in *Scorn with Added Vitriol,* Hamish Hamilton Ltd., 1995).

And another:

- "This is not a [book] to be tossed aside lightly. It should be thrown with great force" (Dorothy Parker, of course).

I can name several database books to which the foregoing remarks apply only too well. Though I'd better be careful what I say here, having published a few books on the topic myself . . .

THE GREAT DATABASE LIMERICK COMPETITION

I thought a literary "puzzle" would be appropriate this month, given the somewhat literary flavor of the column overall. Thus, you're invited to complete any or all of the following limericks—or, indeed, to contribute a wholly original database limerick of your own. I *might* award a small prize for the best entry, if the quality of submissions warrants it.*

1. The last DB2 ever sold . . .
2. The debate between Bachman and Codd . . .

(This one refers to the famous Great Debate "Data Models: Data Structure Set *vs.* Relational," held at the ACM SIGMOD Workshop on Data Description, Access, and Control in Ann Arbor, Michigan, May 1st–3rd, 1974.)

---

*It didn't.

   3. What database language can equal
      The query expressions of SQL . . .

(You can substitute " The glory and grandeur," or " The flaws and the failures," or indeed anything else that makes sense, for " The query expressions" in this last one.)

    I'd also like to request any further database quotations, anecdotes, etc., that you might be aware of and think I might like to add to my collection. Thanks in advance!

    Let me close by acknowledging the many people—far too many to mention individually—who've drawn my attention over the years to one or other of the items included in this month's column. In particular, I should say that the opening lines of the third limerick above are due to an old friend and ex-colleague of mine, the late Bob Engles of IBM. I must also thank Hugh Darwen for letting me use his coinage "The Askew Wall" in my column subtitle (see his chapter "The Askew Wall: A Personal Perspective" in our joint book *Relational Database Writings 1989–1991,* Addison-Wesley, 1992).

Faults and Defaults
(Part 5 of 5)

Responding to criticisms of the
special values approach

This is the final installment of my miniseries on the special values approach to dealing with "missing information" (I explained in the first installment that "missing information" is really not a very apt term, but never mind). I want to devote my column this month to responding to criticisms of the special values idea.

SPECIAL VALUES *vs.* NULLS

As we saw in Installments 53 and 54, queries involving "missing information" can become quite complicated—at least at first blush—if we're determined not to use nulls. And an advocate of nulls might well argue that one advantage of the nulls approach is precisely that it avoids such complexities. Let's investigate this claim.

Fig. 1 shows what our usual sample data would look like if we decided to use nulls instead of special values to represent unknown, inapplicable, and undefined data. Note that (as is customary) I show the nulls as being "in" certain row-and-column slots, but they really aren't; rather, the slots in question actually contain **nothing at all** (and the "relation" is thus not a relation!). Detailed

Originally published in *Database Programming & Design 10,* No. 4, April 1997. Reprinted by permission of Miller Freeman Inc.

```
  ALL_IN_ONE
  ┌───────┬───────────────┬────────────────────┬───────┐
  │ EMP#  │ SALARY_OR_UNK │ BONUS_OR_UNK_OR_NA │ RATIO │
  ├───────┼───────────────┼────────────────────┼───────┤
  │ E1    │         40000 │              10000 │     4 │
  │ E2    │         55000 │               null │  null │
  │ E3    │          null │               null │  null │
  │ E4    │         35000 │               null │  null │
  │ E5    │          null │               null │  null │
  │ E6    │         72000 │                  0 │  null │
  │ E7    │          null │                  0 │  null │
  │ E8    │          null │              13000 │  null │
  └───────┴───────────────┴────────────────────┴───────┘
```

Fig. 1   The sample data with nulls instead of special values

consideration of these points would get us too far away from the topic at hand, however, so let's just ignore them for present purposes; the interested reader can find detailed discussion of such matters in many other places (for example, in David McGoveran's paper "Nothing from Nothing" [5]).

Note next that we can't tell from Fig. 1 exactly what the nulls *mean;* for example, does the null RATIO value for employee E2 mean that the ratio is unknown? Or inapplicable? Or undefined? Or something else? **What's the relation predicate for ALL_IN_ONE?** Again, detailed consideration of these issues would take us too far afield, so unfortunately we're going to have to ignore them also.

Let's now revisit queries Q1–Q7 from Installments 53 and 54 and see how they'd look against the design of Fig. 1 (I'll ignore query Q2, however, since it's just a combination of queries Q1 and Q3). *Note:* Since we're switching from two-valued logic (2VL) to three-valued logic (3VL), let's also switch from relational algebra, which doesn't support 3VL, to SQL, which does (or tries to).

Q1: Get employee numbers for employees who are known to the system to earn a salary in excess of $45,000.

```
SELECT EMP#
FROM   ALL_IN_ONE
WHERE  SALARY > 45000 ;
```

At first sight, this formulation does seem considerably simpler than the relational algebra Design 1 analog (though not the Design 2 analog). *That increased simplicity is spurious, however;* it's a direct result of the fact that SQL is very cavalier about the niceties of distinguishing between domains such as MONEY and MONEY_OR_UNK. (In fact, of course, as I explained in an earlier installment [3], SQL doesn't properly support domains at all.) *Note:* I suppose I

ought to say MONEY_OR_NULL, not MONEY_OR_UNK, but the whole
question of whether nulls belong to domains is yet another of those Big Issues
we're unfortunately going to have to ignore here.

Q3: Get employee numbers for employees whose salaries aren't known to the
system at all.

```
SELECT  EMP#
FROM    ALL_IN_ONE
WHERE   SALARY IS NULL ;
```

This one is at about the same level of simplicity (or complexity) as its relational algebra analog. "IS NULL" in SQL corresponds to the operators
IS_UNK, IS_NA, IS_UNDEF (and so on) that I introduced a few installments back.

Q4: Get employee numbers for employees who are known to get a bonus that
is less than their salary.

As stated, this query too is easily expressed (and this formulation is not too different from its relational algebra analog):

```
SELECT  EMP#
FROM    ALL_IN_ONE
WHERE   BONUS < SALARY ;
```

But suppose we extend the requirement to include employees who don't get a
bonus at all (in effect, treating an inapplicable bonus as zero for comparison purposes). This extended query is readily expressible using special values but *cannot* be expressed against the SQL design of Fig. 1, because we can't tell which
employees the property of getting a bonus applies to and which it doesn't.

> *Aside:*   Of course, we could follow Codd's suggestion and introduce
> a different kind of null and *four*-valued logic [1]. But then what do we
> do about "undefined" values?—move to *five*-valued logic? And then
> what about "not supplied" values . . . ? And "empty set" values . . . ?
> And . . . ? This argument can be extended indefinitely, of course.
> *End of aside.*

Q5: Get employee numbers and corresponding salaries for employees who
either are known to the system to earn a salary in excess of $45,000 or
whose salaries aren't known to the system at all.

```
SELECT  EMP#, SALARY
FROM    ALL_IN_ONE
WHERE   SALARY > 45000
OR      SALARY IS NULL ;
```

Comments analogous to those under query Q1 above apply here also. Note
moreover that even if you believe the result of this query is a relation (it isn't),

the "obvious" predicate *employee EMP# earns salary SALARY* is not the correct one for that "relation."

Q6: For each employee, get the employee number and corresponding total pay (defined as salary plus bonus).

The obvious formulation is:

```
SELECT EMP#, ( SALARY + BONUS ) AS PAY
FROM   ALL_IN_ONE ;
```

On the face of it, this formulation does again seem simpler than its relational algebra analog, but again that increased simplicity is spurious. What's more, the formulation is incorrect!—it misses employees where the bonus is inapplicable (for whom the total pay is just the salary).

Q7: Get the total salary for all employees.

If this query means "Get the total salary for all employees whose salary is known," an appropriate SQL formulation is:

```
SELECT SUM ( SALARY ) AS TOTAL
FROM   ALL_IN_ONE ;
```

(though this "obvious" formulation in fact gives the wrong answer if there are no employees at all, as I explained in an earlier installment [4]). However, if the query means "Try to get the total salary for *all* employees—but, if any of those employees has an unknown salary, the result is unknown too," an appropriate SQL formulation looks quite different:

```
SELECT CASE
          WHEN EXISTS ( SELECT *
                        FROM   ALL_IN_ONE
                        WHERE  SALARY IS NULL )
             THEN CAST ( NULL AS DECIMAL )
             ELSE ( SELECT SUM ( SALARY )
                    FROM   ALL_IN_ONE )
       END
       AS TOTAL
FROM   ALL_IN_ONE ;
```

Note 1: This formulation still gives the wrong answer if there are no employees at all.

Note 2: I'm assuming that column SALARY is defined to be of data type DECIMAL and that SUM applied to that column produces a result of that same data type.

Note 3: Actually the last line (the FROM clause, that is) could equally well refer to any other table in the database; I use ALL_IN_ONE only because I happen to know it exists!

To summarize: I've included this brief discussion of nulls *vs.* special values in a probably vain attempt to stop readers from responding "Well, there you are, you see, this whole special values idea is hopelessly complex—we're much better off staying with good old nulls." It's my position, however, that:

1. "Papering over the cracks" and pretending that certain complexities—*inherent* complexities, too—don't exist is not a good idea. It's usually dangerous to oversimplify.

2. The simplification achieved in query formulation by the nulls approach encourages bad database designs! The queries we've been discussing are mostly straightforward under Design 2; it's only Design 1 that gets us into difficulties.

3. In any case, the problems caused by nulls are, in my opinion, *complete showstoppers*. This isn't the place to go into those problems in detail; they've been more than adequately documented, by myself and other writers, in many other places, including the pages of *Database Programming & Design* [2,5].

RESPONSE TO TOM JOHNSTON

Let me now return to Tom Johnston's criticisms [6] as documented in the first installment in this miniseries and address them one by one. For the reader's convenience I'll repeat each criticism before giving my response to it.

1. From the semantic perspective, what's wrong with defaults is that they aren't what we mean. When we say that Joe doesn't have an hourly rate, we don't mean that he has some special hourly rate—the $0.00 rate, for example; what we mean is that he doesn't have any hourly rate. And when we say that we don't know which department Joe works in, we don't mean that he works in some department with an unusual designation—the UNK (unknown) department, for example; we mean that we don't know the department to which he is assigned.

Response: Johnston's criticisms are certainly typical in this respect: They misrepresent, or misconstrue, the default values approach, and then proceed to attack their own misrepresentation. "When we say that Joe doesn't have an hourly rate, we don't mean that he has some special hourly rate—the $0.00 rate, for example." Indeed we don't. Instead, what we do mean is that the domain for the HOURLY_RATE column is—let's say—RATE_OR_NA, where RATE_OR_NA consists of all legal hourly rates *plus* the special NA value. This value is made known to the system via the CREATE DOMAIN operation, as we saw a few installments back. Thus, the system *is* capable of

234 Part I / Theory Is Practical!

recognizing this special value as meaning "not applicable" and acting accordingly; indeed, it should do so. (Though I must point out that if the Design 2 approach is followed as recommended, such domains will probably be used, and such special values will probably appear, only in derived relations. And they might not appear even there, if the preferred approach of breaking "bundled" queries into distinct component queries is followed as well.)

2. Because default values don't represent what we mean, no logical apparatus can recognize what we do mean when we use them. As a result, normal queries issued against a relational database that uses default values will give us misleading information.

Response: I think this point is adequately addressed by the previous response and the next response in combination.

3. Suppose the database shows 15 employees as being assigned to the Human Resources department and six employees whose department is given as the default value UNK. Suppose further that three of these six employees are actually assigned to the Human Resources department. If we pose the query "How many employees are in the Human Resources department?" to this database, we will get back the reply 15. Now if we were querying a person who had the same information, then—in the situation just described—we would regard the answer 15 as misleading, to say the least. The informative answer, of course, is something like "15 known to be in the Human Resources department, but six whose assignment to a department is not known." A database that uses defaults could not be this informative.

Response: First of all, let me point out that the answer that Johnston here claims is "misleading" is *exactly* the answer SQL would give—assuming, of course, that those six UNKs would be replaced by nulls in an SQL database. Second, as I stated a few months back, we can never actually ask the system queries about the real world *per se,* only about its knowledge of the real world as represented by the contents of the database. Johnston's query would better be phrased: "How many employees are *known to be* in the Human Resources department?" The correct answer to this query is indeed 15—and this answer can be obtained just as easily with special values as it can with nulls. And exactly the same is true of the query "How many employees have an unknown department?" In other words, a database that uses "defaults" (special values) certainly can be just as "informative" as one that uses nulls.

4. This is what's wrong with the default values approach from a semantic perspective: It has the semantics wrong, and so the ability of a database using default values to inform the inquirer fully is correspondingly hampered.

Response: I completely disagree. See the previous response.

5. From the formal perspective, what's wrong with default values is that they're not the same thing as domain values, yet they're represented in the same way as domain values. The presence of a value from a domain in a particular instance of an attribute represents the ascription of a particular predicate to an individual. However, UNK does not represent a predicate descriptive of an individual: It represents the absence of any such predicate value. It cannot, therefore, be a member of any domain.

Response: Johnston here overlooks the point that (as I've tried to make plain throughout this miniseries) there is all the difference in the world between, say, the domain MONEY and the domain MONEY_OR_UNK. UNK and the other special values most certainly can *and must* be members of some domain; the point is, however, that they're not members of the domains that contain only regular values of the columns in question.

6. Date asserts that default values are what we use in "the real world," and he uses the symbol "NA," as entered on a form, as an example. What I dispute is his claim that "NA" *is* an example of a default value. I don't think it is. Instead, I think we all understand that "NA" doesn't represent a value from the domain for that entry on the form, but rather represents the fact that no such value is applicable! "NA" is an assertion about that entry on the form, not a value to be put into that entry.

Response: I agree that describing "NA" as a *default* value is misleading. It's a *special* value. And I agree it's not a value from "the domain for that entry on the form" (X, say)—it's a value from the domain "X_OR_NA," as previously discussed.

7. As a final practical point, I note that for numeric-based domains in particular, the domain is often coextensive with the range of values expressible by the underlying data type. When this is the case, whatever value is chosen to represent "unknown" will be a homonym since its other meaning will be the normal meaning it can express. In Joe's case earlier, for example, we suggested that $0.00 might be the value chosen to represent "unknown." But if it is, that value is a homonym, since its other interpretation is as an hourly rate of $0.00—the known value assigned, for example, to volunteers working for a nonprofit organization.

Response: Actually, Johnston suggested that $0.00 might be the value chosen to represent "not applicable," not "unknown." The point is irrelevant, however; the crux of the issue, once again, is understanding the distinction between (say) the domain MONEY and the domain MONEY_OR_UNK. It might indeed be the case that the domain MONEY is "coextensive with the range of values expressible by the underlying data type." If "the underlying data type"—that is, the *representation*—for regular money values is DECIMAL, say, then every possible value of that data type might well represent a legal MONEY value. But the "unknown" special value for money is represented by (say) the string "UNK"—*not* by a DECIMAL value. Johnston's argument is not valid.

CONCLUDING REMARKS

This brings us to the end of this miniseries on the special values approach to "missing information." To reinforce the ideas I've been describing, I suggest the following exercise as this month's puzzle corner problem: Take any database with which you're familiar and redesign it to eliminate all nulls (assuming you haven't done so already!). Then consider what's involved in rephrasing queries against that revised design.

REFERENCES

1. E. F. Codd: *The Relational Model for Database Management Version 2.* Reading, Mass.: Addison-Wesley (1990).
2. E. F. Codd and C. J. Date: "Much Ado about Nothing," *Database Programming & Design 6,* No. 10 (October 1993). Republished in C. J. Date, *Relational Database Writings 1991–1994.* Reading, Mass.: Addison-Wesley (1995).
3. C. J. Date: "SQL Domains Aren't Domains!" (see Installment 38).
4. C. J. Date: "Aggregate Operators" (see Installment 44).
5. David McGoveran: "Nothing from Nothing" (Chapters 5–8 of the present book).
6. Tom Johnston: "MVL: Case Open," *Database Programming & Design 8,* No. 2 (February 1995); "The Case for MVL," *Database Programming & Design 8,* No. 3 (March 1995).

Answers to Puzzle Corner Problems (Installments 51–56)

Here they are at last: solutions to all the latest puzzle corner problems

My column this month is devoted once again to answering the various outstanding "puzzle corner" problems from previous installments. Thanks as always to those readers who wrote in with their own solutions.

SQL QUERIES AND NULLS

Source: "Faults and Defaults (Part 1 of 5)" (see Installment 51).

Problem statement: You're given (a) the usual suppliers-and-parts database, (b) the query "Get parts whose weight is greater than that of every blue part," and (c) two proposed SQL formulations for that query:

```
1. SELECT PX.*
   FROM   P AS PX
   WHERE  PX.WEIGHT >ALL ( SELECT PY.WEIGHT
                           FROM   P AS PY
                           WHERE  PY.COLOR = 'Blue' ) ;

2. SELECT PX.*
   FROM   P AS PX
   WHERE  NOT EXISTS
          ( SELECT *
            FROM   P AS PY
            WHERE  PY.COLOR = 'Blue'
            AND    PY.WEIGHT ≥ PX.WEIGHT ) ;
```

Originally published under the title "Return to Puzzle Corner" in *Database Programming & Design 10,* No. 5, May 1997 (the subtitle was contributed by *DBP&D* too). Reprinted by permission of Miller Freeman Inc.

Are these two formulations equivalent? Is either one correct? If either is incorrect, state as precisely as you can the conditions under which it produces the wrong answer.

Solution: Before I try to answer these questions in detail, I think it's relevant to mention that in the book [2] from which they're taken, I got them at least partly wrong myself (thanks to Ed Dee of Edinburgh University for setting me straight here). It's also important to understand that the two formulations are indeed equivalent, and correct, in the absence of nulls; the whole point of the exercise, of course, is to illustrate some of the difficulties that nulls can cause, at least in SQL.

Now to the details. The fact is that, in the presence of nulls, (a) the two formulations are *not* equivalent, and (b) *neither* of them is correct! (Were you surprised?)

In order to demonstrate the truth of these two assertions, we first have to agree on exactly what the original query is supposed to mean. I propose the following interpretation:

> *Get part names for parts known to have a weight greater than that of every part that both (a) is known to be blue and (b) has a known weight.*

We also have to be clear on the semantics of the SQL operators ">ALL" and "EXISTS." The following definitions are based on ones given in reference [2]:

- The conditional expression

```
x  >ALL  ( table-expression )
```

evaluates to *true* if the expression

```
x  >  y
```

evaluates to *true* for every y in the result of evaluating the table expression (or if that result is empty); it evaluates to *false* if the expression

```
x  >  y
```

evaluates to *false* for at least one y in the result of evaluating that table expression; and it evaluates to *unknown* otherwise.

- The conditional expression

```
EXISTS ( table-expression )
```

evaluates to *false* if the table expression evaluates to an empty table, the value *true* otherwise.

Note: As I've explained elsewhere [1], this latter definition means that the SQL EXISTS operator cannot be regarded as a faithful implementation of the existential quantifier of three-valued logic (3VL). Specifically, the 3VL quantifier sometimes yields *unknown,* whereas the SQL operator never does. This failure in turn serves to show that it's not just ordinary users who find 3VL confusing—language designers can make mistakes in this area as well.

Back to the query. Let's refer to the two proposed SQL formulations shown for that query as *exp1* and *exp2,* respectively. I now present a series of scenarios under which at least one of *exp1* and *exp2* gives the wrong answer.

Scenario 1: Suppose there exists at least one part known to be blue, but every such part has a null weight. Then *exp1* correctly yields an empty result; *exp2,* by contrast, incorrectly yields a result consisting of all parts. (It follows that *exp1* and *exp2* are not equivalent.) This scenario shows that *exp2,* at least, is an incorrect formulation.

Scenario 2: Suppose there exists at least one part known to be blue, and every such part has a known weight; suppose there also exists at least one part *p* with a null weight. Then *exp2* (though not *exp1*) yields a result incorrectly including all such parts *p*. (Again, it follows that *exp1* and *exp2* are not equivalent.) This scenario shows (again) that *exp2,* at least, is an incorrect formulation.

Scenario 3: Suppose there exists at least one part known to be blue with a known weight and at least one part known to be blue with a null weight. Then *exp1* yields an empty result, which is (in general) incorrect; *exp2* yields a result incorrectly including all parts *p* with a null weight. (Yet again, it follows that *exp1* and *exp2* are not equivalent.) This scenario shows that *exp1* is also an incorrect formulation, like *exp2.*

I make no claim that the foregoing discussions are exhaustive, but they should be more than sufficient to make the point. A subsidiary question for you: Suppose there are no parts known to be blue, but there is at least one part with a null weight. What do *exp1* and *exp2* yield in this case? Are the results correct?

THE SUM OF THREE CUBES

Source: "Faults and Defaults (Part 2 of 5)" (see Installment 52).

Problem statement: Can you find three integers x, y, and z, not necessarily distinct and not necessarily positive, such that the sum of their cubes is 100?

Solution: One possible answer (not the only one) is $x = 7$, $y = -6$, $z = -3$. Incidentally, note that if the problem had asked for *four* integers whose cubes add up to 100, a simple answer consists of the set of integers 1, 2, 3, 4.

QUERY FORMULATIONS INVOLVING "MISSING INFORMATION"

Source: "Faults and Defaults (Part 3 of 5)" (see Installment 53).

Problem statement: Give "Design 1" and "Design 2" formulations of the following queries:

1. Get employee numbers for employees whose bonus is greater than $5000.
2. Get employee numbers for employees whose bonus is at least half their total pay.

Solution: Here first are Design 1 formulations of the two queries:

```
1. ( ( ALL_IN_ONE : TO_MONEY ( BONUS_OR_UNK_OR_NA ) )
         WHERE BONUS_OR_UNK_OR_NA > MONEY ( 5000 ) ) [ EMP# ]

2. ( ( ( ALL_IN_ONE : TO_MONEY ( BONUS_OR_UNK_OR_NA ) )
                    : TO_MONEY ( SALARY_OR_UNK ) )
          WHERE BONUS_OR_UNK_OR_NA ≥ SALARY_OR_UNK ) [ EMP# ]
```

As usual, the Design 2 formulations are more straightforward:

```
1. ( EMP_BONUS WHERE BONUS > MONEY ( 5000 ) )   [ EMP# ]

2. ( ( EMP_SALARY JOIN EMP_BONUS )
              WHERE BONUS ≥ SALARY ) ) [ EMP# ]
```

THE HOLE IN THE SPHERE

Source: "Faults and Defaults (Part 4 of 5)" (see Installment 54).

Problem statement: A cylindrical hole 6″ long is drilled straight through the center of a wooden sphere. What's the volume of the sphere without the hole?

Solution: Let the radius of the sphere be R and that of the cylindrical hole be r (refer to Fig. 1). Let the height of each of the two caps at the end of the hole be h. Clearly $h = R-3$ and $r = \sqrt{(R^2-9)}$. Now, the volume of the sphere is $4\pi R^3/3$, the volume of the hole is $6\pi r^2$, and the volume of each of the caps is $\pi h^2(3R-h)/3$ [3]. So the required volume, V say, is equal to the volume of the sphere, minus the volume of the hole, minus the volume of the two caps:

$$V = (4/3)\pi R^3 - 6\pi r^2 - 2\pi h^2 (3R-h)/3$$

Substituting for h and r and evaluating this expression, we discover that all terms involving R disappear and the final result is simply 36π cubic inches. ∎

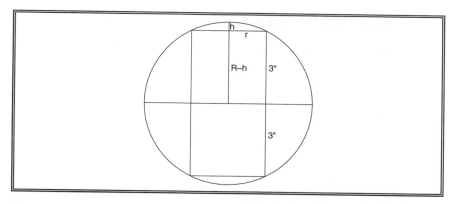

Fig. 1 The hole in the sphere

How interesting that the answer doesn't depend in any way on the radius of the hole or the radius of the sphere! Given that this is the case, in fact, we can tackle the problem in a different way and "spot" the answer, as follows. Presumably the problem-setter wouldn't even have bothered to set the problem in the first place unless there was a unique answer, independent in particular of the radius of the hole. So let's consider the extreme case, in which that radius is zero. In this case, we're simply looking for the volume of a sphere of diameter six inches. And that volume is readily seen (again) to be 36π cubic inches. ∎

THE GREAT DATABASE LIMERICK COMPETITION

Source: "Database Graffiti" (see Installment 55).

Problem statement: I gave you the opening lines for certain database limericks and asked you to complete them, and/or to contribute some original database limericks of your own.

Solution: *DBP&D* deadlines mean I'm writing this "solution" before the problem itself has appeared in print, so readers have had no chance to submit their limericks yet. For that reason, I'll hold this problem over to a future installment.* For now, let me just remind you that I *might* award a small prize for the best entry . . .

---

*See Installment 62.

AVOIDING NULLS BY DESIGN

Source: "Faults and Defaults (Part 5 of 5)" (see Installment 56).

Problem statement: Take any database with which you're familiar and re-design it to eliminate all nulls. Then consider what's involved in rephrasing queries against that revised design.

Solution: It's obviously not possible to give a "solution" to this problem here. But I'd like to ask some follow-up questions:

1. How many different kinds of "missing information" did you find being represented by that single catchall null?
2. How many queries did you find that were giving the wrong answer (or, perhaps, represented the wrong real-world question) because of that over-loading of meanings?
3. How sure are you of your answers to the first two questions?
4. How sure are you of your answer to the previous question?
5. Go back to question 4 and repeat until satisfied.

REFERENCES

1. C. J. Date: "EXISTS Is Not Exists!", in *Relational Database Writings 1985–1989*. Reading, Mass.: Addison-Wesley (1990).
2. C. J. Date and Hugh Darwen: *A Guide to the SQL Standard* (3rd edition). Reading, Mass.: Addison-Wesley (1993). *Note:* The errors in this book noted in the section "SQL Queries and Nulls" of the present installment were corrected in the revised (4th) edition, which appeared in 1997.
3. William H. Beyer (ed.): *CRC Standard Mathematical Tables and Formulae* (29th edition). Boca Raton, Fla.: CRC Press (1991).

Why Is It Important to Think Precisely? (Part 1 of 4)

Some fundamental distinctions that lie at the heart of the database field

One of Codd's objectives when he introduced the relational model was to bring some clarity of thinking and expression into a field, *viz.* database management, that was in sore need of it at the time—and evidently still is. Confusion is rife; confusion leads to mistakes; and we can't even *discuss* those mistakes sensibly if we're confused over basic concepts! This month, therefore, I want to begin another miniseries, this one having to do with certain fundamental distinctions that lie at the heart of the database management field. What I want to do is:

- First, explain exactly what the distinctions are;
- Second, quote examples from the literature where writers have failed to make the distinctions properly;
- Third, discuss some of the consequences of such failure.

SOME GUIDING PRINCIPLES

Let me begin with a couple of quotations that have served me well over the years as guiding principles in my own endeavors in this field. The first is taken from Bertrand Russell (boldface added):

Originally published in *Database Programming & Design 10,* No. 6, June 1997. Reprinted by permission of Miller Freeman Inc.

Clarity, above all, has been my aim. I prefer a clear statement subsequently disproved to a misty dictum capable of some profound interpretation which can be welcomed as a "great thought." It is not by "great thoughts," but by careful and detailed analysis, that the kind of technical philosophy which I value can be advanced. [9]

These wonderful remarks need no further elaboration by me.

My second quotation is from Wittgenstein (I believe—though, as I've said elsewhere, to my regret I don't know the source of this quote, and I'd be grateful to any reader who could track it down for me):

All logical differences are big differences.

Hugh Darwen and I bore this particular dictum in mind throughout our work on *The Third Manifesto* [5], and Hugh uses it to draw an interesting corollary:

All logical mistakes are big mistakes!

He justifies this position by observing that a mistake is certainly a difference—namely, a difference between what's right and what's wrong. He further conjectures that the reverse implication is true as well:

All nonlogical differences are small differences.

In other words, differences that are merely psychological or syntactic in nature are not very important (at least in the context at hand).

SOME LOGICAL DIFFERENCES

Here then are four major logical differences that I want to examine in this series of columns:

- model *vs.* implementation
- values *vs.* variables
- domains *vs.* relations
- types *vs.* representations

I've at least touched on most of these issues in earlier installments; however, I think it's a good idea to bring all the material together in this way, and in any case I also think there's quite a bit more that can usefully be said. Hence the present series.

As I've already indicated, much of the literature seems to be confused over these issues (among others). The confusions in question stretch back many years—indeed, they continue to this day. My thesis, therefore, can be summed up as follows:

1. Computers are very precise in their operation—they don't have much tolerance for error.
2. In the field of computing above all, therefore, clarity, accuracy, and precise thinking are surely paramount.
3. These remarks are true of database management in particular.
4. Thus, I claim that any endeavor having to do with database management, if it's confused over issues as basic as those I'll be discussing in what follows, is *doomed to eventual failure.*

AN OVERRIDING DISTINCTION

One of the most familiar and fundamental distinctions of all—albeit one that people still do often get confused over—is that between *logical* and *physical* concepts (some of the other distinctions I'll be discussing are special cases of this overriding one). I define this distinction in terms of *what users need to know* in order to do their job ("users" here meaning both end users and application programmers):

- **Logical** concepts are ones the user needs to know about.
- **Physical** concepts are ones the user doesn't need to know about (in other words, ones that are, at least potentially, hidden from the user).

Now let's move on to examine the first of the more specific distinctions listed in the previous section, namely model *vs.* implementation (I defer the others to future installments for space reasons).

MODEL *vs.* IMPLEMENTATION

The distinction between model and implementation can be summarized as follows:

- The **model** is an abstract, self-contained, *logical* definition of the data objects, data operators, and so forth, that together constitute the abstract machine with which the user interacts.
- By contrast, an **implementation** is the *physical* realization on a real computer system of the components of the model.

As you can see, this distinction is indeed a special case of the overriding logical *vs.* physical distinction; the user certainly *does* have to know about the model, and does *not* have to know about the implementation (at least in principle).

By way of example, consider the logical construct *relation* in the relational world. That construct *per se* is certainly part of the model; by contrast, how relations are physically represented on the disk is a matter of implementation. Likewise, the logical construct *join* is again part of the model; by contrast, how joins are physically performed (by means of indexes, physical I/O operations, and so on) is, again, a matter of implementation. Note in particular, therefore, that everything to do with *performance* is, first and foremost, an implementation matter, not part of the model!

> *Aside:*   It's worth pointing out in passing that the relational model was actually the *first* data model to be defined. In other words, Codd has some claim to being the inventor, not just of the relational model in particular, but of the data model concept in general. Earlier "data models" (hierarchic, network) were defined *after the fact* by a process of induction from existing implementations—in other words, by *guesswork*. And it would be a pity to repeat such a *logical mistake . . .* yet that seems to be exactly what some people want to do! Here's an excerpt from *The Object-Oriented Database System Manifesto* [1]: "We are taking a Darwinian approach: We hope that, out of the set of experimental prototypes being built, a fit model will emerge." In other words, let's write the code first and see what happens! I don't much care for this approach.   *End of aside.*

Here now are some examples of confusion over the model *vs.* implementation distinction, with commentary.

1. "COBOL can no more access a relational database than a circle can have corners. It's simply a contradiction in terms . . . There's no such thing as a relational database. When you get right down to it, 'relational database' is as meaningless as 'plaid music' or 'scratchy color.' The adjective describes languages or processes, not data. The database itself, the pool of shared business data, can be neither procedural nor relational." [10]

What this paragraph seems to be saying is that the "real" database (the "database itself") is simply bits and bytes, and bits and bytes aren't relational. But to argue thus is akin to arguing that human beings are never really *thinking,* because what's "really" happening inside their heads is simply that neurons are firing! In other words, I would say that what we have here is *a total failure to abstract.*

2. "[The relational model] has proved to be a poor model for the internal schema . . . because of performance problems (at least with standard hardware organizations)." [4]

But the relational model was—*obviously* and *explicitly* and *deliberately!*—never intended as a "model for the internal schema" (not with "standard hardware organizations" and not with any "nonstandard" hardware organizations either). The phrase "because of performance problems" reveals a hopeless confusion over model *vs.* implementation issues (see my earlier remarks on performance near the beginning of this section).

3. ". . . one prophet of the relational model claims that a database must avoid . . . physical access mechanisms to be relationally pure. The gentleman becomes irate with those of us who make a living writing programs—rather than just talking about it—when we point out that the inescapable consequence of such ideological purity is grinding inefficiency." [11]

I don't think this one needs any further comment from me.

4. ". . . we are compelled to choose between supporting Codd's rules with a toy or building a real DBMS that breaks the rules. Such theological purity is pointless, of course. All serious DBMSs employ links . . . They must, if they are to work. In practice, they follow Charles Bachman's network model, not Codd's relational model." [12]

Again, no further comment seems necessary.

5. ". . . only an object's methods may examine or update [the private memory of the object]; the methods are public." [3]

This quotation is taken from a textbook on object-oriented databases (more specifically, from a chapter entitled "Object Data Management Concepts"). Observe that "methods are public" means they're part of the *model,* while "methods may examine or update the private memory" means they're part of the *implementation.* Quotations like this one lend weight to my suspicion that object-oriented advocates often fail to make a clear distinction between model and implementation.

6. "[A deficiency of the relational model is the] join-based retrieval of a collection of related data (even when the need to retrieve the collection of data is known at the time of database design)." [7]

I've discussed this one in detail elsewhere [6]. To summarize that discussion: I'm pretty sure that *join* here means a foreign-to-primary-key join; from the context, the argument is that joins are slow and pointer chasing is faster. But if you think pointers are a good idea, *then there's absolutely no reason why foreign-to-primary-key relationships shouldn't be implemented by pointers on the disk!* (At least one system, the IBM Starburst prototype, does provide such an implementation [2].) In other words, (a) *implementing* relationships by pointers is very different from (b) exposing such pointers in the *model*. The writer is confusing two very different things.

7. "To run through the rows [of a relation] in . . . sequence requires the relational DBMS to sort the rows." [8]

Well, of course the desired *logical* sequence might be *physically* represented by an index . . . or a pointer chain . . . or even physical contiguity (all implying no need for a run-time sort). *Note:* Since this particular quotation is taken from a discussion that purports to show the superiority of object systems over relational ones for sequential processing, let me add the following: Regardless of whether the system is relational or object-oriented, the options available for *physically* implementing some *logical* sequence are, at least in principle, exactly the same in the two cases. But in an object system, whatever representation is chosen is (typically) made visible to the user, thereby causing distress and unrest among the user community; in a relational system, by contrast, the representation is—as it should be—*hidden*.

8. "An object DBMS builds these relationships into the object database and can use them directly at run time . . . By contrast, a relational DBMS must recreate relationships at run time using joins, based upon instructions from an application." [8]

The confusion here is very similar to that found in Quotation 6. Again, note how something that ought really to be part of the *implementation*—namely, the representation of certain "relationships" by means of pointers—becomes part of the *model* in an object system (because those pointers are visible to the user).

That's probably enough quotations for now—but you might try looking for further examples of such confusions for yourself. Indeed, I'd be interested in seeing any you might come up with.

CONSEQUENCES OF SUCH CONFUSIONS

A general failure to appreciate the model *vs.* implementation distinction has plagued the database industry for years, and remains widespread to this day. Confusion has arisen above all in relational contexts!—which has led to the following consequences, among others:

- An unfortunate loss of physical data independence in most current SQL products (and, as a direct result, the stupid debates—which should never have been necessary—over whether to *denormalize* at the logical level);
- A general "more heat than light" level of discourse in the industry as a whole, to the detriment of all;

- Misleading advertising and marketing claims (for example, "relational can't handle complex information," "relational has a builtin performance barrier," and so on);

- Blaming the relational model for the shortcomings of SQL (I'll return to this particular issue later in this series);

- A failure to understand that many "new" requirements—for example, "complex objects"; "multidimensional data"; "on-line analytical processing" (OLAP); "temporal data"; and so on—*can* all perfectly well be handled in a relational framework, at least in principle;

- Accordingly, a rash of *ad hoc* solutions to these problems that serve only to increase confusion, don't work together terribly well (owing to lack of a common model), and—in my opinion—will ultimately wind up costing us all a great deal (and I don't just mean financially, either).

PUZZLE CORNER

Since this series is very much concerned with logical thinking, the puzzle corner problems will all be simple logic problems instead of database problems as such. Here's the first one. Consider the following list of statements:

S1: The number of the first true statement in this list plus the number of the second false statement equals the number of a true statement.

S2: There are more true statements than false ones.

S3: The number of the first false statement in this list plus the number of the second true statement equals the number of a true statement.

S4: No two adjacent statements are both true.

S5: At most three statements are false.

S6: If this statement were deleted, the solution to the problem would remain unchanged.

Which statements are true?

CONCLUDING REMARKS

This brings me to the end of the first installment in my "fundamental distinctions" series. Let me close by explaining my overall title ("Why Is It Important to Think Precisely?"). As some readers will know, I've been teaching seminars on database topics for several years now. But it doesn't matter how many times you teach a given seminar, you can always get questions you've never heard before . . . On one occasion, I was claiming that one of the virtues of the relational model was that it enabled you to *think precisely*—in particular, it helped you to articulate problems in a precise manner. Whereupon one student asked: "Why is it important to think precisely?" (a question right out of left field, so far as I was concerned!—certainly not one I'd ever heard before). I replied: "Well, I don't know exactly." Which I thought was a pretty good response, off the top of my head.

REFERENCES

1. Malcolm Atkinson *et al.*: "The Object-Oriented Database System Manifesto," Proc. First International Conference on Deductive and Object-Oriented Databases, Kyoto, Japan (1989). New York, N.Y.: Elsevier Science (1990).

2. Michael Carey, Eugene Shekita, George Lapis, Bruce Lindsay, and John McPherson: "An Incremental Join Attachment for Starburst," Proc. 16th Int. Conf. on Very Large Data Bases, Brisbane, Australia (August 13th–16th, 1990).

3. R. G. G. Cattell: *Object Data Management*. Reading, Mass.: Addison-Wesley (1994).

4. Robert M. Curtice and William Casey: "Database: What's in Store?", *Datamation 31,* No. 23 (December 1st, 1985).

5. Hugh Darwen and C. J. Date: "The Third Manifesto," *ACM SIGMOD Record 24,* No. 1 (March 1995). See also the book-length version *Foundation for Object/Relational Databases: The Third Manifesto*. Reading, Mass.: Addison-Wesley (1998).

6. C. J. Date: "Objects and Relations: Forty-Seven Points of Light" (Chapter 12 of the present book).

7. Won Kim: "On Marrying Relations and Objects: Relation-Centric and Object-Centric Perspectives," *Data Base Newsletter 22,* No. 6 (November/December 1994).

8. Mary E. S. Loomis: *Object Databases: The Essentials*. Reading, Mass.: Addison-Wesley (1995).

9. Bertrand Russell: Preface to *The Bertrand Russell Dictionary of Mind, Matter and Morals* (ed., Lester E. Denonn). New York, NY: Citadel Press (1993).

10. Frank Sweet: "What, if Anything, Is a Relational Database?", *Datamation 30,* No. 14 (July 15th, 1984).

11. Frank Sweet: "The Trouble with SQL," *Database Programming & Design 1,* No. 6 (June 1988).

12. Frank Sweet: "Techniques For Physical Data Modeling," *Database Programming & Design 1,* No. 8 (August 1988).

Why Is It Important to Think Precisely? (Part 2 of 4)

The distinction between values and variables

Last month I discussed (in general terms) the importance of "thinking precisely" in connection with certain issues that lie at the heart of the database management field. I then went on to discuss the significance of the fundamental distinction between *model* and *implementation* in particular. This month I want to turn my attention to another crucial distinction, *viz.* that between *values* and *variables.*

VALUES *vs.* VARIABLES

It's hard to believe that people could get confused over a distinction as elementary and obvious as the one between values and variables. As it turns out, however, it's very easy to fall into traps in this area. Let me begin, therefore, by spelling out just what the distinction is as I see it (the following definitions are based on definitions given by Cleaveland [2]):

- A **value** is an "individual constant" (for example, the individual constant "3"). A value has no location in time or space; however, it can be *represented* in memory by some encoding, and of course such representations

Originally published in *Database Programming & Design 10,* No. 7, July 1997. Reprinted by permission of Miller Freeman Inc.

do have locations in time and space (see below). By definition, a value cannot be updated (if it could, then after such an update it would no longer be that value).

- A **variable** is a holder for the representation of a value. A variable does have location in time and space. Moreover, a variable can be updated or changed; that is, the current value of the variable in question can be replaced by another value, probably different from the previous one.

Of course, I don't mean to suggest that only simple things like the integer "3" are legitimate values. On the contrary, values can be arbitrarily complex; for example, an array is a value, a stack is a value, a list is a value, a polygon is a value, a document is a value, and so on. (I'll be discussing this point in more detail over the next couple of months.) Analogous remarks apply to variables too, of course.

In the relational world, relations themselves provide a good example of the importance of the value *vs.* variable distinction. (*Note:* The discussion that follows is taken from an earlier article by Hugh Darwen and myself [3]. A similar discussion also appeared in my regular column a couple of years back [7]. However, the concept is important, and I think it's worth discussing one more time.) Suppose we say, in some programming language:

```
DECLARE N INTEGER ... ;
```

We all understand that N here isn't an integer as such; rather, it's an integer *variable*—that is, a variable whose *values* are integers (different integers at different times). In exactly the same way, if we say, in SQL:

```
CREATE TABLE T ... ;
```

There isn't a relation (SQL would say "table") as such; rather, it's a relation *variable*—that is, a variable whose *values* are relations *per se* (different relations at different times).

Now, in the past we've tended to use the term *relation* when we really meant *relation variable* (as well as when we meant a relation *per se*—that is, a relation *value*). But the practice is unfortunate, and historically has led to a certain amount of confusion (I'll give some examples in the next section). In *The Third Manifesto* [4], therefore, Hugh Darwen and I introduced the term **relvar**—short for relation variable—and we tried to distinguish as carefully as we could between relvars and relations *per se*.

Here now are some examples of confusion in the literature over the value *vs.* variable distinction. The first three are all taken from a tutorial on object-oriented databases [9]:

1. "We distinguish the declared type of a variable from . . . the type of the object that is the current value of the variable . . . we distinguish objects

from values . . . a *mutator* [is an operation such that it's] possible to observe its effect on some object."

Let's examine this quotation a piece at a time.

- The phrase "the object that is the current value of the variable" clearly implies that a value is an object (more precisely, that some objects are values and some values are objects).

- The phrase "we distinguish objects from values" clearly implies that a value isn't an object (more precisely, that no objects are values and no values are objects).

- And the existence of mutators—that is, operations that have an "effect on some object," or in other words update some object—clearly implies that the object in question is a variable; so some objects, at least, are variables.

What *is* one to make of such a muddle?

2. ". . . the extension [of a class is] all current instances of the corresponding [class] . . . some [classes] support operations that will alter the state of [their] instances."

Instance here is a synonym for *object*. The first part of the quotation implies an object is a value. The second implies it's a variable.

3. "An [object class] is a template specifying all possible objects with a given structure . . . [objects have] an *object identity* . . . that remains invariant across all possible modifications of the object's value."

The phrase "all possible objects" implies (to me, at least) that an object is a value. The phrase "all possible modifications of the object's value" implies that an object is a variable. (By the way, the phrase "objects with a given structure" also confuses *type* and *representation!* I'll be discussing this particular confusion in my column the month after next.)

This next one is taken from *The Object Database Standard: ODMG-93* [1]:

4. ". . . the type *Denotable_Object* [has subtypes] *Object* and *Literal* . . . Objects are mutable; literals are immutable . . . Literals are objects . . ."

Again let's examine this quotation a piece at a time. Note first that a denotable object isn't necessarily an object (in other words, some objects aren't objects!). "Objects are mutable, literals are immutable" is fine: It means objects are variables and literals are values. But then what are we to make of "Literals are objects"?

5. "[Some] relational database systems . . . assign tuple identifiers to tuples in relations . . ." [8]

No, they don't. Like a relation, a tuple is a *value*. A case *might* be made—though not by me!—that the systems in question think of relvars—not relations!—as containing tuple *variables* or "tuplevars," and that they then assign identifiers to those tuplevars; however, they certainly don't assign identifiers to tuples *per se*. *Note:* I'd like to point out too that the systems in question assign such identifiers within *base* relvars only—not within any other kind of relvar. Forgetting that other kinds of relvars (and relations) exist is, regrettably, a ubiquitous error, both in the relational world itself and in the object world.

CONSEQUENCES OF SUCH CONFUSIONS

In the relational world, the historical lack of a clear distinction between relations and relvars has led to some confusion over *normalization*. In the second edition of my own book *An Introduction to Database Systems* [5], for example, I wrote:

6. "Given a relation R, we say that attribute Y of R is functionally dependent on attribute X of R if and only if each X-value in R has associated with it precisely one Y-value in R (at any one time)."

I should have said *relvar,* not *relation!*—then I could (and should) have deleted "(at any one time)." To put the point another way: If we call a relvar a relation, what do we call a relation? (The situation here is reminiscent of another of my pet peeves—namely, the all too common use of the term "database" to mean *database management system*. If we call the DBMS a database, what do we call a database?)

Confusions have also arisen over *update*. In the first printing of the sixth edition of that same book [6], I wrote:

7. "Tuple assignments are performed (implicitly) during INSERT and UPDATE operations."

No, they're not! INSERT and UPDATE operations—and DELETE operations too, of course—are really shorthands for certain *relational* assignments, which replace the current value (a relation) of the target relvar by another value (another relation). The target of the assignment is *not* a "tuplevar," as it would have to be in a genuine *tuple* assignment.

To be fair, however, I think issues such as the ones just discussed (concerning normalization and update) have usually been pretty well understood in the relational world—they just haven't always been very well articulated. In other words, I don't think such confusions have caused too much of a problem in practice in the relational world. Do analogous remarks apply to the object world? Frankly, I don't think they do. *Au contraire,* I find a widespread lack of genuine understanding in the object world (not least in connection with the concept of type inheritance); and confusions over basic issues such as the value *vs.* variable distinction must surely be held accountable for that lack, at least in part.

A good illustration of this thesis is provided by the concept, mentioned in Quotation 3 in the previous section, of *object identity* ("object ID"). In my opinion, it's precisely a confusion over the value *vs.* variable distinction that leads to the introduction of this unnecessary and undesirable concept into the object database world. *The Third Manifesto* [4], by contrast, quite deliberately rejects the object ID concept. We—that is, the authors of the *Manifesto*—justify our position as follows:

- By definition, every value is distinct from every other value (is in fact self-identifying).

- Values thus do not need to carry around some hidden, secret identifier that is somehow separate from the value itself, and indeed do not do so.

- Variables, by contrast, do need some identity that is separate from their value, and that identification is provided, precisely and sufficiently, by the variable's **name.**

Note: This is as good a place as any to try heading another confusion off at the pass. Throughout my discussions so far, I've used the term "variable" in its conventional programming language sense. You should be aware, however, that some object languages and systems use the term to mean, very specifically, a variable *whose value is an object ID*—that is, a variable whose value is (at least conceptually) a pointer to some object. You can get into some very confusing conversations if you're unaware of this fact.

CONCLUDING REMARKS

The difference between values and variables is a *major* logical difference. (To repeat last month's quotation from Wittgenstein: *All logical differences are big differences.*) If you're like me, therefore, and sometimes have difficulty in understanding an article or presentation on object databases, it's a good idea to ask: "What does the writer or speaker here mean by the term *object?* Is it a *value* or a *variable?*" In my experience, this question can lead to considerable enlightenment (of one kind or another).

As usual, I'll close with a small puzzle—a simple logic problem again (as promised last month). Individuals *A, B,* and *C* make statements as indicated:

A: *B*'s statement is false.
B: *C*'s statement is false.
C: *A*'s statement and *B*'s statement are both false.

Who's telling the truth?

REFERENCES

1. R. G. G. Cattell (ed.): *The Object Database Standard: ODMG-93.* San Mateo, Calif.: Morgan Kaufmann (1994). *Note:* This book has been superseded by R. G. G. Cattell and Douglas K. Barry (eds.): *The Object Database Standard: ODMG 2.0.* San Francisco, Calif.: Morgan Kaufmann (1997).

2. J. Craig Cleaveland: *An Introduction to Data Types.* Reading, Mass.: Addison-Wesley (1986).

3. Hugh Darwen and C. J. Date: "Introducing . . . The Third Manifesto," *Database Programming & Design 8,* No. 1 (January 1995). See also Chapter 3 in the present book.

4. Hugh Darwen and C. J. Date: "The Third Manifesto," *ACM SIGMOD Record 24,* No. 1 (March 1995). See also the book-length version *Foundation for Object/ Relational Databases: The Third Manifesto.* Reading, Mass.: Addison-Wesley (1998).

5. C. J. Date: *An Introduction to Database Systems: Volume I* (2nd edition). Reading, Mass.: Addison-Wesley (1977).

6. C. J. Date: *An Introduction to Database Systems* (6th edition). Reading, Mass.: Addison-Wesley (1995).

7. C. J. Date: "Domains Aren't Relations!" (see Installment 37).

8. Won Kim: "On Marrying Relations and Objects: Relation-Centric and Object-Centric Perspectives," *Data Base Newsletter 22,* No. 6 (November/December 1994).

9. Stanley B. Zdonik and David Maier: "Fundamentals of Object-Oriented Databases," in Zdonik and Maier (eds.), *Readings in Object-Oriented Database Systems.* San Mateo, Calif.: Morgan Kaufmann (1990).

Why Is It Important to Think Precisely? (Part 3 of 4)

*More on the distinction between
domains and relations*

This month I want to discuss the fundamental distinction between *domains* and *relations* (again!—I've discussed this distinction in my regular column before [3]; I don't intend to repeat the same points here, but I think there's more that can usefully be said).

DOMAINS *vs.* RELATIONS

I'll begin with a couple of definitions:

- A **domain** is a *data type,* either system- or user-defined. The definition of a given domain includes a specification of the set of permissible values for that domain. The internal representation of those values can be arbitrarily complex, but is hidden from the user; values from a given domain, and variables defined on a given domain, are operable upon solely by means of the operators defined for the domain in question.

- A **relation** is a *value,* consisting of a *heading* and a *body.* The heading is a set of attribute-name/domain-name pairs; the body is a set of rows that conform to that heading.

Originally published in *Database Programming & Design 10,* No. 8, August 1997. Reprinted by permission of Miller Freeman Inc.

Let me remind the reader of some of the most important points from my earlier discussion of the domain *vs.* relation distinction [3]:

- Domains *are* types, relations *have* types.
- Domains contain scalars, relations contain tuples.
- Domains encapsulate, relations don't.*

And the truly crucial—in fact, overriding—*conceptual* distinction is this:

- Domains (or, rather, values in domains) are *the things we can talk about;* relations (or, rather, tuples in relations) are *the truths we utter about those things.*

Thus, it's very clear in the relational model that the domain and relation concepts are distinct, and I think database professionals in the 1990s ought at least to know what they *are*. But not all of them do.

1. ". . . simply defining a domain as having a data type and rules is not enough. For example, assume you have . . . a domain of length in feet and a domain of weight in pounds . . . [You] can add pounds with pounds and get a result of pounds, and you can add feet with feet and get a result in feet. You cannot multiply pounds by pounds and get a meaningful result—there are no such things as square pounds. However, you can multiply feet by feet and get a result in square feet. How does the database [*sic*] disallow the operation in the first case and create an entire new domain in the second case? These rules get more and more complex as you add domains to the database. When you multiply feet by pounds, you get work expressed in foot-pounds. But not always—a man's height multiplied by his weight is nonsense, not foot-pounds. The relation or entity where the attributes reside matters quite a bit." [1]

This passage betrays confusion over what a domain is on so many levels at once that I think I'm going to have to discuss it—at length!—elsewhere [4]. So I'm afraid you'll have to wait for that discussion for the specifics.

2. "In relational theory the ordering of rows in a table is explicitly immaterial . . . This is a valid perspective, unless the ordering itself is supposed to convey information." [9]

These remarks seem to me simply fatuous—like criticizing a cat because it isn't a dog, or red wine because it isn't white. A relation is a relation, and there's an end on't! (Perhaps I should point out that—of course—any information "the ordering itself is supposed to convey" can certainly be *represented* relationally, without any need for the "rows in a table" to be ordered themselves.)

---

*See the footnote on this point in Installment 37.

3. "Though Columbus proved [*sic*] the world is round more than 500 years ago, relational database professionals still view the world as flat. For them, [object-oriented databases] come as a revelation. When you're well-trained in relational modeling, you begin to believe the world is two-dimensional. You think you can get anything into the rows and columns of a table." [10]

The criticism that "relations are flat" is another of my pet peeves, and I'll have more to say about it following Quotation 4. But given that "the world is round" and that object-oriented databases are, apparently, better suited to deal with that round world than are "flat relations," am I supposed to conclude that objects are round? The phrase "round objects" make just about as much sense as "flat relations." (Some of you might be aware that in UK English "round objects" is a well known synonym for *nonsense.*)

More to the point, you *can* "get anything into the rows and columns of a table"!—as I've explained on many occasions and in many places, including earlier installments of this column. To spell it out one more time: Values in domains, and therefore values in relations, can be *as complex as you like,* provided only that the representation of those values is hidden from the user (I'll be discussing this point in detail next month). Thus, you can have relations containing engineering drawings, relations containing legal contracts, relations containing geometric figures, even relations containing other relations . . . and on and on.

4. "There is simply no way to mask the complexities involved in assembling two-dimensional data into a multi-dimensional form." [5]

I'm getting very tired of hearing claims to the effect that relations are "flat"—that is, two-dimensional—and real data is "multi-dimensional." Anyone who thinks such claims constitute a valid criticism of relations is seriously confused. Of course it's true that a relation *looks* flat when pictured in tabular form on paper. But a picture of a thing isn't the thing! (This is another logical difference, in fact, and a very big one.) Rather, the point is this: If the relation has *n* attributes, then *each tuple in that relation represents a point in* n-*dimensional space*—and the relation as a whole represents a set of such points. In other words, a relation of *n* attributes is *n*-dimensional, not two-dimensional! **Let's all vow never to say "flat relations" ever again.**

5. ". . . it is desirable to treat domains as just another type of relation—because it allows us to apply the . . . relational operators to domains." [6]

How could you possibly apply, say, the *projection* operator to the domain of integers? (Remember in particular that "domains encapsulate, relations don't.") *Note:* Actually, I suspect that the author of this quotation wants to treat domains as *relvars,* not relations (not that this revision would make the confusion any more justified). For a detailed discussion of the "domains as a special kind of relvar" heresy, again I refer the reader to my earlier column [3].

FURTHER CLARIFICATION OF THE DOMAIN CONCEPT

Before we go on to consider some of the consequences of confusions such as those illustrated in the previous section, let me say a few more words regarding domains specifically. First of all, note that domains—or, rather, the values belonging to any given domain—don't really belong to any particular database! (What database does the set of integers belong to?) Rather, such sets of values, just like individual values themselves, *have no location in time or space*.

It follows that CREATE DOMAIN doesn't really create a domain!—rather, it simply creates a *name* that can be used to *refer* to the relevant set of values. Of course, that name, unlike the set of values it refers to, can and does belong to some particular database, in the sense that it can be referenced in (for example) relvar definitions for that database. Analogous remarks apply to DROP DOMAIN and (especially) ALTER DOMAIN. *Note:* The fact that it might be possible, by performing some kind of ALTER DOMAIN operation, to "change the set of values in" the domain in question—thereby making it look as if the domain in question is a variable—is probably one of the sources of the domain *vs.* relvar confusion. (ALTER DOMAIN really just means "let this name now be used to refer to a different set of values than before.")

CONSEQUENCES OF SUCH CONFUSIONS

The most important consequence of the domain *vs.* relation (or domain *vs.* relvar) confusion is what I've referred to elsewhere [2] as *The Great Blunder*[*]—namely, an attempt to integrate relational and object-oriented concepts on the basis of the fundamentally flawed equation *relvar = object class* (instead of the logically correct equation *domain = object class*). Let me repeat the definition I gave earlier for *domain:*

■ A **domain** is a data type, either system- or user-defined. The definition of a given domain includes a specification of the set of permissible values for that domain. The internal representation of those values can be arbitrarily complex, but is hidden from the user; values from a given domain, and

---

[*]Or, rather, The *First* Great Blunder. The second is mixing pointers and relations (see Chapters 3 and 13, later in this book).

variables defined on a given domain, are operable upon solely by means of the operators defined for the domain in question.

And here is a definition for *object class:*

- An **object class** (*class* for short) is a data type, either system- or user-defined. The definition of a given class includes a specification of the set of permissible values for that class. The internal representation of those values can be arbitrarily complex, but is hidden from the user; values from a given class, and variables defined on a given class, are operable upon solely by means of the operators defined for the class in question.

As you can see, a domain in the relational world and an object class in the object world are *exactly the same thing.* Hence, domains are the key to integration between the two technologies. *Note:* For simplicity I ignore the point that some data types (domains, classes) might be *subtypes* (subdomains, subclasses) of other *supertypes* (superdomains, superclasses). This point doesn't materially affect the argument in any way, of course.

To repeat, I claim that domains are the key to integrating the two technologies; and many writers (and some products) agree with this claim—but not all! One recent book on object-oriented databases devotes just one paragraph to this issue:

6. "There have been claims . . . that the relational model as originally conceived is as powerful semantically as an [*sic*] object model. These claims are based on equating the relational notion of domain with the object notion of [class]. By allowing a relational table to include [*sic*] a rich set of domains, rather than the relatively restricted set of builtin types offered by most relational DBMSs today, the ability of relational databases to handle more kinds of data would certainly be enhanced. However, these domains [*sic*] need to be able to be extensible [*sic*] by application type definers. The domain notion also needs to be enhanced with the ability to specify operations. Note that most object DBMS products today do little with operations either [*sic*]." [9]

In my opinion, this extract "dismisses the theory without fully engaging it." (I also find the final sentence somewhat telling.)

As for the equation that I referred to just now as "fatally flawed," here are a couple of quotations that espouse that equation:

7. "Now, let us change the relational terms as follows. Change *relation* to *class, tuple* . . . to *instance* [that is, object] . . . , *column* to *attribute* . . . [Then the] data model . . . is an object-oriented data model!" [7]

A relation **is not** the same thing as a domain. A domain **is** the same thing as an object class. Therefore, a relation **is not** the same thing as an object class.

Note: Of course, this simple syllogism is equally valid if we replace *relation* by *relvar* throughout.

8. "A relation is . . . a class [that includes] a system-defined column for tuple identity (i.e., object identifier) . . . A relation is the extent of this type of class." [8]

This particular quotation is even *internally* confused! Apparently, a relation is both a class and an extent; yet these two constructs aren't the same thing (?).

CONCLUDING REMARKS

The difference between domains and relations is another major "logical difference"! Domains and relations are very different things, and you should beware of anyone who tries to tell you otherwise. Analogous remarks apply to domains *vs.* relvars also.

I'll close with another simple logic problem. *A, B, C,* and *D* are defendants in a criminal case. The following facts are known:

1. If *A* is guilty, then either *B* was an accomplice or *C* is innocent.
2. If *D* is innocent, then *B* is innocent and *C* is guilty.
3. If *C* is guilty, then *A* was an accomplice.
4. If *D* is guilty, then so is *C*.

Who's guilty and who's not?

REFERENCES

1. Joe Celko: *SQL Explorer, DBMS 8,* No. 8 (July 1995).

2. Hugh Darwen and C. J. Date: "Introducing . . . The Third Manifesto," *Database Programming & Design 8,* No. 1 (January 1995). See also Chapter 3 in the present book.

3. C. J. Date: "Domains Aren't Relations!" (see Installment 37).

4. C. J. Date: "Types, Units, and Type Design" (Chapter 4 of the present book).

5. Richard Finkelstein: "MDD: Database Reaches the Next Dimension," *Database Programming & Design 8,* No. 4 (April 1995)

6. Douglas W. Hubbard: Response to a letter to the editor, *DBMS 7,* No. 10 (September 1994).

7. Won Kim: "Object-Oriented Database Systems: Promises, Reality, and Future," Proc. 19th Int. Conf. on Very Large Data Base Systems, Dublin, Ireland (August 24th–27th, 1993).

8. Won Kim: "On Marrying Relations and Objects: Relation-Centric and Object-Centric Perspectives," *Data Base Newsletter 22,* No. 6 (November/December 1994).

9. Mary E. S. Loomis: *Object Databases: The Essentials.* Reading, Mass.: Addison-Wesley (1995).

10. Alan Radding (quoting Douglas Barry, executive director of the Object Database Management Group): "Strike While the Iron Is Hot," *Computerworld* (October 17th, 1994).

Why Is It Important to Think Precisely? (Part 4 of 4)

More on the distinction between types and representations

The last "fundamental distinction" I want to discuss in this miniseries is that between *types* and *representations*. Once again this is a topic I've discussed before [4,8], but not I think at sufficient length. As usual, I'll begin with some brief definitions.

- A **type**—usually called a *domain* in relational contexts—is a named set of *values*. Every type has an associated set of *operators* that apply to values of that type.

- Given a type, a **representation**—also known as a *structure*—for that type is an *encoding in memory* for (appearances of) values of that type.

Thus, types are a *model* consideration, representations are an *implementation* consideration. It follows that the type *vs.* representation distinction is a special case of the general and familiar logical *vs.* physical distinction; in other words, types are important to the user, representations aren't (or shouldn't be, anyway).

As a trivial example, consider the data type REAL in SQL. The representation of REAL numbers is not specified in the SQL language, and users don't

---

Originally published in *Database Programming & Design 10,* No. 9, September 1997. Reprinted by permission of Miller Freeman Inc.

need to know what it is; what they do need to know is the operations they can perform on REAL numbers—"+", "*", "<", and so on. And that's *all* they need to know. To quote Cardelli and Wegner [1]: "A major purpose of type systems is to avoid embarrassing questions about representations, and to forbid situations in which these questions might come up."

In general, the internal representation of values (of any given type) can be arbitrarily complex. As indicated, however, that representation must be *hidden from the user;* values of a given type must be operable upon *solely* by means of the operators defined for the type in question. To repeat, whatever "structure" values might possess is purely an implementation matter—it's not part of the model, and it's not visible to the user. In object terminology, values are said to be *fully encapsulated;*[*] there are *no* "public instance variables" or "public attributes," there are only "methods" (the object term for operators).

EXAMPLES OF CONFUSION

Let's take a look at some examples of confusion over the type *vs.* representation distinction. The first is taken from the current SQL standard, SQL/92 [10]. As I explained in an earlier column [9], "domains" in SQL/92 aren't really domains at all—they're just a way of defining a shorthand name for a primitive (builtin, system-defined) data type. Consider the following SQL/92 example:

```
CREATE DOMAIN S#_DOM AS CHAR(5) ;
CREATE DOMAIN P#_DOM AS CHAR(6) ;

CREATE TABLE SP ( S# S#_DOM, P# P#_DOM, ... ) ;

SELECT *
FROM   SP
WHERE  S# = P# ;
```

The comparison S# = P# here does *not* fail on a type error!—though logically it should. Instead, the comparison is performed on the basis of the *representations* (which are both character strings, so the comparison "works"). Analogous remarks apply to all other scalar operations, of course.

As a consequence of this failure on the part of SQL, critics of the relational way of doing business have been able to get away with complaints such as this one:

1. "SQL . . . poses [*sic*] no limitations on [what comparisons] can be [performed] . . . Even bizarre requests can be easily stated." [12]

---

[*]More precisely, *scalar* values are encapsulated (as noted in Installment 37, nonscalar values aren't).

This quotation—which is taken from a book on object databases, in a section entitled (of all things!) "Relational DBMS Principles"—leads into an example involving an equality comparison between "customer's number of children" and "zoo animal's number of legs." And the author goes on to say:

> This request [joins customers and zoo animals] based on relationships [between number of children and number of legs] . . . The meaning of these relationships is not entirely clear.

The tone here ("not entirely clear," indeed) is, I think, a trifle gratuitous. The whole passage is an example—one of all too many, I fear—of criticizing the relational model for not having been implemented! As such, it is *very annoying*. As I've stated elsewhere [6], the biggest problem with SQL is precisely that it doesn't implement the relational model. If SQL supported domains properly, criticisms such as the one just discussed wouldn't be possible.

> *Aside:* The SQL/92 standard actually defines the syntax for CREATE DOMAIN as follows (in part):
>
> ```
> CREATE DOMAIN <domain name> [AS] <data type>
> ```
>
> In other words, it actually uses the term *data type* to refer to what would more accurately be called the *representation*. However, it would be hypocritical of me to make too much of this point, since I made the same mistake myself (for historical reasons) on page 83 of my book *An Introduction to Database Systems* [7] . . . This error will be corrected in future editions!   *End of aside.*

Let's get back to the quotations.

2. "When comparing . . . a computed value with a database value [as opposed to comparing two database values directly] . . . , the DBMS [merely] checks that the basic data types [that is, the *representations*] are the same." [3]

Taken at face value, these remarks mean that we would have to agree that if, for example, attributes WEIGHT and QUANTITY were defined on different domains that just happened to have the same representation (NUMERIC, say), then the comparison

```
WEIGHT = QUANTITY
```

would (quite correctly) be regarded as invalid, whereas the comparison

```
WEIGHT - QUANTITY = 0
```

would be regarded as valid! There is, of course, no *logical* difference between these two comparisons.

3. "The SALARY variable should contain a numeric value because [salaries are] measured using numbers and computation using the variable must be possible." [2]

"Computation . . . must be possible": So we're allowed to multiply two salaries? I don't think so! If I'd been the author here, I would have written:

> The SALARY variable should be declared to be of type MONEY because [salaries are] money values and computations appropriate to such values must be possible.

Here's another example:

4. "[Inheritance is] the . . . use of operations *and representation* of one type in the implementation of another type." [11]

I disagree. I would say rather that:

> If *B* is a subtype of *A,* then—*by definition!*—all operators that apply to values of type *A* are inherited, necessarily, by values of type *B*.

In other words, the operators (only) are inherited; representations are irrelevant. (Operators are part of the model, representations aren't.) Whether values of type *B* have the same representation as values of type *A* is, or should be, of no interest whatsoever to the user.

(Incidentally, there's no logical reason why all values of the *same* type *A* need to have the same representation—let alone values of type *A* and values of type *B*. This point is discussed further in *The Third Manifesto* [5].)

5. "I want to represent [*sic*] temperatures. Degrees Kelvin is one possible scale. I could use Celsius or Fahrenheit instead; they all use numeric values. Or I could use the scale ('hot,' 'warm,' 'cool,' 'cold'); the data type is character string. What is the right choice? [Given a certain application area,] I will probably prefer Kelvin because it is expressed with a numeric data type. I can use arithmetic operators with numeric data types, and I will need to do calculations." [2]

Points to note:

- First, the data type is *not* character string for "the scale ('hot,' 'warm,' 'cool,' 'cold')"; the *representation* is character string. We're not going to perform substring or concatenate operations on temperatures!

- Likewise, it's not the data type, it's the *representation,* that is numeric for the Kelvin and Celsius and Fahrenheit designs. We're not going to multiply temperatures. Rather, the operations we're going to perform on temperatures are, precisely, the operations that are defined for the temperature *type,* whatever those might be.

CONSEQUENCES OF SUCH CONFUSIONS

If the type *vs.* representation confusion shows up *in the system itself*—as it must do in any faithful implementation of SQL/92!—then one consequence is *a loss of data independence*. For if the representation shows through to the user, then we're not free to change that representation without causing applications to fail (in general). Consider, for example, an application that relies on the fact that the supplier numbers and part numbers are both represented as character strings, or one that relies on the fact that temperatures are represented in degrees Kelvin.

A second consequence in such a system is *the weakened ability for the system to do type checking* (regardless of whether we're talking about compile-time or run-time checking). Again, supplier numbers and part numbers in SQL/92 provide an illustration (see the example discussed earlier). Indeed, as I pointed out in a previous installment [9], SQL/92 systems in particular must effectively behave as if there were *exactly eight* true types (or domains): numbers, character strings, bit strings, dates, times, timestamps, year-month intervals, and day-time intervals. That is, type checking *is* performed, but only on the basis of these eight builtin types. Net effect: More errors—possibly undetected ones!

While I'm on the subject of SQL, by the way, I'd like to add a few remarks on another common confusion (perhaps not so fundamental as those we've been discussing over the past four installments, but important nevertheless): namely, the confusion between SQL on the one hand and the relational model on the other. Here are a couple of examples:

6. "SQL . . . defines the type system supported by a relational DBMS. These are the only types allowed in a relational database. The relational type system is not the type system of any programming language . . ." [12]

SQL does *not* define "the type system supported by a relational DBMS"—it defines the type system supported by an *SQL* DBMS. This is a logical difference.

7. "Relationships have been acknowledged by the database research literature . . . for many years, but they were not incorporated formally into the relational model until the SQL/92 specification." [12]

It's clear from context that what the author means here by "relationships" is foreign-to-primary-key relationships specifically. To claim that such a concept was "not incorporated formally into the relational model until the SQL/92 specification" is particularly outrageous, given that the concept was *invented* (in 1969) in the context of the relational model. The whole quotation is another example—a very offensive one, too—of criticizing the relational model for not having been implemented.

CONCLUDING REMARKS

This brings me to the end of this short series on "fundamental distinctions." Now, obviously we all get confused from time to time—in itself, this is nothing to be ashamed of! To quote Bertrand Russell again (boldface added):

> I have been accused of a habit of changing my opinions . . . I am not myself in any degree ashamed of [that habit]. What physicist who was already active in 1900 would dream of boasting that his [*sic*] opinions had not changed during the last half century? . . . new discoveries can make the admission of former error inevitable to any candid mind. For what I have said . . . I do not claim the kind of truth which theologians claim for their creeds. I claim only, at best, that the opinion expressed was a sensible one to hold at the time . . . I should be much surprised if subsequent research did not show that it needed to be modified. [Such opinions were intended] only as the best I could do at the time towards the promotion of clear and accurate thinking. **Clarity, above all, has been my aim.** [14]

In other words, it's natural to be confused from time to time. However, we should constantly strive to overcome such confusions—in particular, in the fundamental areas of:

- model *vs.* implementation
- values *vs.* variables
- domains *vs.* relations
- types *vs.* representations

To close, here are three simple logic problems, all of them based on ideas taken from Raymond Smullyan's wonderful book *What Is the Name of this Book?* [13]. A certain island is inhabited entirely by *knights* (who always tell the truth) and *knaves* (who always tell the opposite of the truth). First of all, inhabitants *A* and *B* make the following statements about themselves and a third inhabitant *C:*

A: *B* is a knight.
B: If *A* is a knight, then so is *C*.

Can you tell whether *A*, *B*, and *C* are knights or knaves?

Second, inhabitant *A* makes the following statement: "This isn't the first time I've said this." Is *A* a knight or a knave?

Third, imagine you've been given the task of choosing among three closed boxes, one of which contains a million dollars (the other two being empty). Five inhabitants *A*, *B*, *C*, *D*, and *E* are trying to help you, as follows:

A: The money's in Box 1.
B: No, it's in Box 2.
C: Either *A*'s a knight or *B*'s a knight.
D: Either *A*'s a knave or *B*'s a knight.
E: Either *C* and *D* are both knaves or both knights, or I'm a knave.

Assuming you want the money, which box should you pick?

REFERENCES

1. Luca Cardelli and Peter Wegner: "On Understanding Types, Data Abstraction, and Polymorphism," *ACM Comp. Surv. 17,* No. 4 (December 1985).

2. Joe Celko: Letter to the editor, *DBMS 8,* No. 11 (October 1995).

3. E. F. Codd: *The Relational Model for Database Management Version 2*. Reading, Mass.: Addison-Wesley (1990).

4. Hugh Darwen and C. J. Date: "Introducing . . . The Third Manifesto," *Database Programming & Design 8,* No. 1 (January 1995). See also Chapter 3 in the present book.

5. Hugh Darwen and C. J. Date: " The Third Manifesto," *ACM SIGMOD Record 24,* No. 1 (March 1995). See also the book-length version *Foundation for Object/ Relational Databases: The Third Manifesto*. Reading, Mass.: Addison-Wesley (1998).

6. C. J. Date: "How We Missed the Relational Boat," in C. J. Date, *Relational Database Writings 1991–1994*. Reading, Mass.: Addison-Wesley (1995).

7. C. J. Date: *An Introduction to Database Systems* (6th edition). Reading, Mass.: Addison-Wesley (1995).

8. C. J. Date: "Domains Aren't Relations!" (see Installment 37).

9. C. J. Date: "SQL Domains Aren't Domains!" (see Installment 38).

10. International Organization for Standardization (ISO): *Database Language SQL*. Document ISO/IEC 9075:1992. Also available as American National Standards Institute (ANSI) Document ANSI X3.135-1992.

11. Bruce G. Lindsay: Presentation at Database World, Boston, Mass. (June 1994).

12. Mary E. S. Loomis: *Object Databases: The Essentials*. Reading, Mass.: Addison-Wesley (1995).

13. Raymond Smullyan: *What Is the Name of this Book?* New York, NY: Penguin Books (1981).

14. Bertrand Russell: Preface to *The Bertrand Russell Dictionary of Mind, Matter and Morals* (ed., Lester E. Denonn). New York, NY: Citadel Press (1993).

Answers to Puzzle Corner Problems (Installments 55–61)

Put down your pencils—the answers are in

My column this month is devoted once again to answering the various out-standing "puzzle corner" problems from previous installments. Thanks as usual to those readers who wrote in with their own solutions. *Note:* The problem from Installment 56 was discussed in Installment 57; Installment 57 itself did not include a puzzle corner problem.

THE GREAT DATABASE LIMERICK COMPETITION

Source: "Database Graffiti" (see Installment 55).

Problem statement: I gave you the opening lines for certain database limericks and asked you to complete them, and/or to contribute some original database limericks of your own.

Solution: Of course, there's no "right" solution to this problem. I'll content myself with showing just one limerick (one that I happened to like) for each of the given opening lines. The given opening lines are shown in **bold.**

Originally published under the title "Last Piece of the Puzzle" in *Database Programming & Design 10,* No. 10, October 1997 (the subtitle was contributed by *DBP&D* too). Reprinted by permission of Miller Freeman Inc.

What database language can equal
The flaws and the failures of SQL?
    Well designed it is not
    And your brain it will rot
If you try to use it to speak well.

The last DB2 ever sold
Was a horrible sight to behold
    With its S-Q-L-4
    And objects galore
And tables quite out in the cold.

I note that the reference to "SQL4" threatens not to be a joke for much longer!

The debate between Bachman and Codd
Was a highlight of that year's SIGMOD
    And when everyone said
    That tabular Ted
Was the winner, none thought it odd.

TRUE AND FALSE (I)

Source: "Why Is It Important to Think Precisely? (Part 1 of 4)" (see Installment 58).

Problem statement: Consider the following list of statements:

S1: The number of the first true statement in this list plus the number of the second false statement equals the number of a true statement.

S2: There are more true statements than false ones.

S3: The number of the first false statement in this list plus the number of the second true statement equals the number of a true statement.

S4: No two adjacent statements are both true.

S5: At most three statements are false.

S6: If this statement were deleted, the solution to the problem would remain unchanged.

Which statements are true? *Note:* This problem is taken from *The Penguin Book of Curious and Interesting Puzzles* [3].

Solution: First of all, if *S6* were true, deleting it certainly would change the overall solution to the problem: *contradiction!* Hence *S6* must be false.

Next, if *S4* is true, then:

- *S5* must be false (because *S4* and *S5* are adjacent);
- *S3* must be false (because *S3* and *S4* are adjacent);
- At least one of *S1* or *S2* must be false (because *S1* and *S2* are adjacent);
- Hence there are at least four false statements (*S6, S5, S3,* and at least one of *S1* and *S2*);
- Hence there are at most two true statements;
- Hence *S2* is false;
- If *S1* were false, it would mean that the only true statement out of *S1–S5* would be *S4*. But then *S6* would be true! Hence *S1* is true.

So we have *S1* and *S4* true and the rest false. Are these conclusions consistent with what the statements actually say?

S1: The number of the first true statement is 1, the number of the second false statement is 3, their sum is 4, which is the number of a true statement; so *S1* is indeed true.

S2: Is indeed false.

S3: The number of the first false statement is 2, the number of the second true statement is 4, their sum is 6, which is *not* the number of a true statement; so *S3* is indeed false.

S4: Is indeed true.

S5: Is indeed false.

S6: Is indeed false.

So one possible solution is that the only true statements are *S1* and *S4*. Is this solution unique? Well, let's see what happens if we reverse our initial assumption and take *S4* to be false. Then:

- Either the pair *S1* and *S2* must both be true or the pair *S2* and *S3* must both be true (since these are the only pairs of adjacent statements not already accounted for);
- Hence *S2* must be true;
- Hence *S1, S3,* and *S5* must all be true (because *S2* says there must be more true statements than false ones);
- But then the number of the first true statement is 1, the number of the second false statement is 6, their sum is 7, which is *not* the number of a true statement, so *S1* is false: *contradiction!*

So the solution that the only true statements are *S1* and *S4* is indeed the only one possible. ∎

Part I / Theory Is Practical!

TRUE AND FALSE (II)

Source: "Why Is It Important to Think Precisely? (Part 2 of 4)" (see Installment 59).

Problem statement: Individuals *A, B,* and *C* make statements as indicated:

A: *B*'s statement is false.

B: *C*'s statement is false.

C: *A*'s statement and *B*'s statement are both false.

Who is telling the truth?

Solution: Let me use *SA, SB,* and *SC* to refer to the statements of *A, B,* and *C,* respectively. Then, if *SA* is true, *SB* is false, so *SC* is true, so *SA* is false: *contradiction!* Hence *SA* is false. It follows that *SB* is true, and hence that *SC* is false, whence either *SA* is true or *SB* is true (or both). But we already know that *SA* is false and *SB* is true, so there's no contradiction. So *B* is telling the truth and *A* and *C* are not. ∎

Incidentally, this particular puzzle is due to Lewis Carroll [1].

COPS AND ROBBERS

Source: "Why Is It Important to Think Precisely? (Part 3 of 4)" (see Installment 60).

Problem statement: *A, B, C,* and *D* are defendants in a criminal case. The following facts are known:

1. If *A* is guilty, then either *B* was an accomplice or *C* is innocent.
2. If *D* is innocent, then *B* is innocent and *C* is guilty.
3. If *C* is guilty, then *A* was an accomplice.
4. If *D* is guilty, then so is *C*.

Who's guilty and who's not?

Solution: From 2. and 4., we see that *C* is guilty, regardless of whether *D* is guilty. From 3., therefore, we see that *A* is guilty too. From 1., therefore, we see that either *B* is guilty or *C* isn't; since the second of these possibilities has already been ruled out, it follows that *B* is guilty. Finally, from 2. we see that if *D* is innocent then *B* is too; since *B* is *not* innocent, *D* can't be either. Thus, all four defendants are guilty. ∎

Note: We ought really to go back and check that all four of the given statements do evaluate to true if all four are guilty (subsidiary exercise for the reader).

KNIGHTS AND KNAVES

Source: "Why Is It Important to Think Precisely? (Part 4 of 4)" (see Installment 61).

Problem statement: Actually there were three problems in this installment, all of them set on Raymond Smullyan's island [2] that's inhabited entirely by *knights* (who always tell the truth) and *knaves* (who always tell the opposite of the truth). The first problem was as follows: Inhabitants A and B make the following statements about themselves and a third inhabitant C:

A: B is a knight.

B: If A is a knight, then so is C.

Can you tell whether A, B, and C are knights or knaves?

Solution: If A is a knight, then A's statement is true, which means that B is a knight, which means that B's statement is true too, and hence all three of A, B, and C are knights. If A is a knave, then A's statement is false, which means that B is a knave, which means that B's statement is false too. But if A is a knave, then B's statement is *not* false (remember that "if p then q" is true if p is false or q is true or both), so we have a contradiction. Hence all three of A, B, and C must be knights. ∎

The second problem was as follows. Inhabitant A makes the following assertion: "This isn't the first time I've said this." Is A a knight or a knave?

Solution: If A's a knight, then the assertion is true, so A has made the same assertion before. But then it must have been true that time too, which means that A must have made the assertion *twice* before. But then A must have made it *three* times before . . . and so on, forever. In other words, if A's a knight, then A must have lived for an infinite length of time (in order to make the assertion an infinite number of times). Since this latter is impossible, A must be a knave. ∎

For the third problem, you had to imagine that you'd been given the task of choosing among three closed boxes, one of which contained a million dollars (the other two being empty). Five inhabitants A, B, C, D, and E are trying to help you, as follows:

276 Part I / Theory Is Practical!

A: The money's in Box 1.

B: No, it's in Box 2.

C: Either *A*'s a knight or *B*'s a knight.

D: Either *A*'s a knave or *B*'s a knight.

E: Either *C* and *D* are both knaves or both knights, or I'm a knave.

Assuming you want the money, which box should you pick?

Solution: If *E* is a knave, the second part of *E*'s statement is true, and hence *E*'s overall statement is also true: *contradiction!* So *E* is a knight. *E*'s overall statement is therefore true. Since the second part of that statement is false, the first part must be true; in other words, *C* and *D* are of the same kind (both knights or both knaves).

If *C* is a knave, then *C*'s statement is false, so *A* and *B* must both be knaves. But then *D*'s statement is true, so *D* is a knight: *contradiction!* So *C* and *D* are both knights.

Since *C* and *D* are both knights, their statements are both true. Since *A* cannot be both a knight and a knave, and *C*'s statement and *D*'s statement contradict each other regarding *A*, exactly one of them must be incorrect regarding *A*. Whichever it is, the second part of the statement must be true in order to make the overall statement true. But the second part of the statement is the same in both cases (namely, "*B* is a knight"). It follows that *B* must be a knight, in which case the money's in box 2 (and *A* is a knave). ∎

CONCLUDING REMARKS

From this point forward, I've decided to drop the "puzzle corner" as a regular feature of my column (owing mainly to what seems to be a falling off in interest on the part of the readership!). I still plan to include suitable problems from time to time—when the opportunity presents itself—but they won't be a regular feature any longer.

REFERENCES

1. Charles L. Dodgson: *The Diaries of Lewis Carroll*. Oxford, England: Oxford University Press (1954).

2. Raymond Smullyan: *What Is the Name of this Book?* New York, NY: Penguin Books (1981).

3. David Wells: *The Penguin Book of Curious and Interesting Puzzles*. New York, NY: Penguin Books (1992).

RELATIONAL DATABASE MANAGEMENT

INTRODUCTION

This part of the book contains four papers. The first, by Hugh Darwen, considers the question of what a database really is; in fact, it articulates a position that can be seen as a common thread that runs through this entire book (in this connection, see especially Installments 28 and 37 in Part I).

The second paper, by David McGoveran, was written to mark the 25th anniversary of the relational model. It considers the question of how well the industry at large has managed to implement various features of that model, concluding (sadly enough) that in fact it has not done a very good job at all. To quote: "I have to say that I have never seen a relational DBMS" (!).

The third paper is a joint effort by Hugh Darwen and myself. It consists of an introduction to some of the key ideas of *The Third Manifesto*, which consists (among other things) of an attempt to lay the foundation for a true *rapprochement* between object-oriented and relational database technology.

The fourth and last paper is an attempt to clarify certain aspects of the relational *domain* concept (though it uses the terminology of *types* rather than *domains* as such, the two concepts being in fact one and the same).

What a Database *Really* Is: Predicates and Propositions

An open letter to Open University database students

ABSTRACT

Despite the name, a database is best thought of as a repository not just for data, but rather for *facts*—that is, for *true propositions*. The article that follows explains this remark in lay terms and begins to explore some of its many implications.

COMMENTS ON REPUBLICATION

This first chapter is by Hugh Darwen. By way of introduction, I cannot do better than repeat what I wrote when the paper first appeared:

(Begin quote)

The article that follows is an essay by Hugh Darwen, addressed to the students he tutors on a database course offered by the Open University in the UK. When he showed it to me for review, I was very pleased, for I had long felt

---

Originally published in *Database Programming & Design 11*, No. 7, July 1998. Reprinted by permission of Hugh Darwen and Miller Freeman Inc.

such an article was sorely needed; indeed, I had thought of trying to write one myself. Hugh's explanation for writing it intrigued me:

> Almost every year, about halfway through the course, some student or other asks, in a manner that suggests the question has been burning: *What's a predicate?* I'm always so pleased that anybody has even realized this might be an important question that I take pains over my careful but *ad hoc* answer. And then I think: Why didn't we get this out of the way right at the very beginning? This year, I'm giving it a try.

Well, I hope it works for Hugh's students, for I sincerely believe that if only more people—especially DBMS implementers—thought this way about databases, then we might stand a chance of seeing the emergence of respectable database systems that people could enjoy and not have to fight with.

(*End quote*)

INTRODUCTION

Hello. Let me introduce myself. My name is Hugh Darwen, and I am the tutor (staff number 44525) in region 4 for certain students on course M357, which is entitled *Data Models and Databases*.

   The foregoing paragraph contains three sentences, and those sentences are different in kind as well as in content:

- The first, "Hello," is a mere signal, establishing contact.
- The second is in the form of an imperative, demanding something of you, the reader (though of course we all know that it's really just a common courtesy in this particular instance).
- The third is a plain statement of fact.

Each of these three kinds of sentence has an analog in communications between people and computers. We often have to do something special to *establish contact* with a computer; we often use the imperative style to give *commands* to the computer; and sometimes such a command includes a *statement of fact* that we want the computer to remember (because that fact is both true and relevant), or forget (because it is now either false or irrelevant). I focus for the rest of this article on this "statement of fact" kind of sentence.

STATEMENTS OF FACT

How do we distinguish statements of fact from other kinds of sentences, such as greetings, imperatives, and questions? Well, here's another example that might help:

- I am writing this article in my study at home in Warwickshire on February 9th, 1997.

Now, you cannot tell whether what I've just told you is a true statement of fact or a false one, but you do know, from its very form, that it *is* either true or false. By contrast, we cannot say of utterances such as "Hello," "Let me introduce myself," or "What's the time?" that they must be either true or false.

By the way, you will observe that I do entertain the notion that a "statement of fact" might be false. If you think that the very term *statement of fact* connotes undeniable truth, please don't worry too much—I could have chosen an alternative term, such as *assertion* or *declaration*. As always, the concept is more important than the terminology, and sometimes it's difficult to choose the most appropriate term in everyday speech to match a concept one is trying to communicate, especially when that concept is a very precise one. I'll continue to use *statement of fact* in this article, but I'm about to introduce an alternative term also, one that is conventionally used to mean precisely the concept I'm trying to convey. That term is *proposition*.

PROPOSITIONS

The term *proposition* is the one logicians use for the "statement of fact" concept. Aristotle (384–322 BC) understood the importance of propositions, and he worked out a formal system of reasoning whereby, from an assumption of the truth of certain given propositions, the truth of certain other derived propositions can be concluded. The given propositions are called *axioms* and the method of reasoning is called *logic*. The axioms and the derived propositions concluded from those axioms are collectively called *theorems*. For example, given certain propositions already discussed in this article, you could use logic to obtain the following *logical consequence* (i.e., derived proposition):

- The home of the Open University tutor identified by staff number 44525 is in Warwickshire.

Further, if the given propositions are in fact true, then you can be sure the logical consequence (the conclusion) is true, too.

Note: Why might you bother to obtain a derived proposition (or logical consequence) such as the one just shown? I suggest that you would be very unlikely to do so unless somebody asked you a question to which that derived proposition would be an appropriate answer.

A DATABASE IS A SET OF TRUE PROPOSITIONS

It's useful to view a database as a set of propositions (assumed to be true ones) concerning some enterprise of which the database is supposed to provide some kind of record.[*] If we do take that view, there are some important questions that immediately arise:

- How do we choose which propositions should be stated to form the record of our enterprise?

- In what form should those propositions be stated?

- How can we instruct the computer to remember or forget a given proposition or set of propositions?

- Can we get the computer to prevent us from stating propositions that are ridiculous or contradictory? A ridiculous proposition might be one that states that a certain person is 200 years old; contradictory ones might state that a person is both male and female, or that a tutor in region 4 is— contrary to Open University rules—tutoring a student in region 5.

- In what form can we present a question (or "query") to the computer, the response to which would be a proposition or a set of propositions derived by logic from a given database? And in what form should we expect to find that response?

Course M357 answers these questions. Indeed, there's little in that course that's not related to at least one of them, though you might note that I didn't bother to mention certain subsidiary matters, such as who's allowed to access a database, how the computer checks authorizations, how databases might be protected from accidental loss or damage, and so on.

PREDICATES

There's a word in my title that I haven't used yet, and I come to it now: *predicate*. The concept of predicates is very important, for an understanding of them could underpin everything you will be asked to learn on course M357.

---

[*]I'm using the term *record* here in its generic sense, not the special sense in which it's often used in computer contexts (in database contexts in particular).

Consider two things:

- First, logicians from Aristotle onwards found that reasoning based just on the notion of propositions had certain severe limitations, which they eventually overcame by studying certain *generalized forms* of such propositions. They found that, when several propositions are of the same generalized form, various impressive shortcuts could be taken by reasoning in terms of those general forms instead of in terms of individual propositions *per se*.

- Second, commercial databases can contain billions of propositions; if propositions of the same general form cannot somehow be lumped together, such databases will surely be unmanageable and unusable.

Logicians use the term *predicate** for the "general form" in question—and it's predicates that have made databases, database management, and database queries tractable to computerization. Consider once again the proposition from my opening paragraph, which I'll now restate in a very slightly different way:

- Hugh Darwen is the name of a tutor (staff number 44525) in region 4 for certain students on course M357, which is entitled *Data Models and Databases*.

It's easy to see that this statement has a certain form that could be common to a whole set of propositions one might wish to state in some record of the enterprise called the Open University. For example, we could replace the course number M357 by M355, thereby obtaining a proposition which makes the same kind of sense as the original one, and might even be true. (In fact it's not true, for two reasons: First, I'm not a tutor for any students on course M355; second, course M355 is not entitled *Data Models and Databases*.)

Here's what is probably the most general form of the original proposition that we might all agree on:

- . . . is the name of a tutor (staff number . . .) in region . . . for certain students on course . . . , which is entitled . . . .

And *that's* a predicate!†

---

*Some authorities use the alternative term *propositional function,* which does have a certain attraction to it for reasons too deep for the present article.

†In the database literature you'll sometimes find the term *predicate* used in some more restrictive sense; you might even find it used in some subtly different sense. For example, quite often it's used where the term *condition* would be appropriate. I prefer to keep *predicate* for the sense agreed by logicians.

Here then are some important points to note and questions to be asked:

1. The predicate as shown can be broken down in various ways into smaller pieces, each of which is a predicate in turn. For example, ". . . is the name of a tutor" is a predicate, and so are ". . . is the name of a tutor (staff number . . .)" and "course . . . is entitled . . ." (and so on).

2. It might be useful to give the predicate a name, such as TUTOR_INFO. Such names are used a great deal in database designs, as you will discover in course M357. Indeed, many of the names used in databases are really predicate names, even if they aren't often referred to as such.

3. The holes marked by ". . ." are known as *placeholders*. It might be useful to give them names, too. In fact, predicates are often written using such names. For example:

   - TUTOR is the name of a tutor (staff number STAFF#) in region REGION# for certain students on course COURSE#, which is entitled TITLE.

4. Notice that the placeholder names are often accompanied by text indicating the kind of thing they stand for: "TUTOR is the **name**," "**staff number** STAFF#," "**region** REGION#," and so on. **Staff number** and **name** here are both *common nouns,* standing for anything or everything of the kind indicated. **Region** is perhaps a little sloppy, considering that what follows is really a region *number,* not a region *per se,* but "the region identified by region number REGION#" seemed just a little heavy-handed for my present purpose.

   Now, if those "indicators of kind" are common nouns, then the accompanying placeholders themselves can be thought of as *pronouns.* For example, consider the statement "He is her father." This statement contains two pronouns, *he* and *her; he* stands for some unspecified person who is the father of some other unspecified person, *her.* Now, in normal discourse the context would provide referents for these pronouns, and we would know precisely who is being asserted to be whose father. Because there are no referents here, we can't tell which people they actually stand for. However, imagine a context in which the referents are Tom and Jane, respectively. Then we will understand that we need to substitute Tom and Jane for the pronouns to obtain "Tom is Jane's father." In a like manner, when we substitute an appropriate name or *proper noun* for each placeholder in a predicate, we obtain a *proposition.* For example, if we substitute Hugh Darwen for TUTOR and 44525 for STAFF# (and so on) in the TUTOR_INFO predicate, we obtain once again the proposition:

- Hugh Darwen is the name of a tutor (staff number 44525) in region 4 for certain students on course M357, which is entitled *Data Models and Databases*.

    In general, if there are *n* placeholders and we substitute a proper noun for one of them, we obtain a predicate with *n*–1 placeholders (and so on). When there are no placeholders left at all, the predicate degenerates to a pure proposition—it is now true or false, unequivocally.

5. The presence of at least one placeholder in a predicate means it cannot be the kind of statement of which we can say categorically that "it is true" or "it is false." Although we can make propositions out of predicates, a predicate is not, in general, a proposition (the exception is the degenerate case of a predicate with no placeholders at all).

6. It's important to agree on what proper nouns, in general, are appropriate for each placeholder. For example, we might not wish to form propositions such as:

    - 3.14159 is the name of a tutor (staff number Camembert) in region CV35 7AY for certain students on course Aintree, which is entitled Jurassic Park.*

    Indeed, the proper nouns agreed upon will almost certainly bear a close relationship to the kind of thing the placeholder represents, often indicated by the presence of a common noun in the predicate (as discussed in point 4).

7. The connectives *and* and *or* can be used with predicates, to make longer predicates, just as they can be used with propositions to make longer propositions. *Not* can be used, too.

8. Would it actually be a good idea to use the suggested form, TUTOR_ INFO, to hold information about tutors in the Open University database? Can you think of any problems that might arise if we did?

9. The form of some predicate might also be used to formulate a question ("query") to be presented to the computer. The answer to that question would be the set of all propositions that (a) can be formed by substitution of proper nouns for placeholders in the form and (b) can be shown to be true. Of course, if the database itself uses the form of that same predicate to hold the original given statements of fact, then "showing to be true" will be, for the computer, a trivial task of mere regurgitation.

---

*I hope you'll bear with my suggestion to treat, e.g., 3.14159 and CV35 7AY as proper nouns—logically, they are.

QUANTIFICATION

In point 4 in the previous section I showed how to make a proposition out of a predicate by substitution of a proper noun for each placeholder. However, there's another way of disposing of a placeholder; it goes by the name of *quantification,* meaning "saying how many." Consider for example the simple predicate:

- ARTIST painted a portrait of PERSON.

Instead of just substituting appropriate names for both ARTIST and PERSON (as in, e.g., "Holbein painted a portrait of Henry VIII"), I can obtain propositions by saying *how many* artists painted a portrait of a certain person, or *how many* people had their portraits painted by a certain artist.

Now, there's one particular form of quantification that is both fundamental and very common: It's called *existential* quantification, and it involves replacing the placeholder in question by a phrase involving something like "at least one" or "some" or "there exists." For example, the following are all propositions that can be obtained from the predicate "ARTIST painted a portrait of PERSON":

- Holbein painted a portrait of some person.
- Some artist painted a portrait of Henry VIII.
- Some artist painted a portrait of some person.

Aristotle studied propositions of a certain form that includes quantifiers. He realized that if propositions of the form "*a* is *x*" and "*a* is not *x*" are interesting, then we might also want to consider the truth of "Some *a* is *x,*" "Every *a* is *x,*" and "No *a* is *x.*" "Some" (as we have seen) is the existential quantifier. "Every" is what we now call the *universal* quantifier. "No" is a *negated* form of the existential quantifier, for "No *a* is *x*" clearly means the same as "It is not the case that some *a* is *x.*" However, while these observations might justify a claim that Aristotle started the study of predicates, that study did not come to fruition until the late 19th century, with the contributions of Frege, Boole, Peirce, and others.

CONCLUDING REMARKS

The M357 course material does use the term *predicate* a little, but not a lot, for there are other ways of saying what's going on in databases—ways that are often more appealing, in their own special contexts, than always talking in terms of predicates. However, if you have difficulty understanding those other ways, try referring them back to the predicates and simple logic that really underpin the whole subject.

To end, here are three observations to give you a feel for that universal underpinning:

- In *Block I* of the course we study a method of analysis known as "Entity-Attribute-Relationship modeling," this activity being a common preliminary step in database design. Deciding what entity types to describe and what types of relationship might exist among instances of those entity types is really just deciding what kinds of statements of fact one would like to use to make a formal record of the enterprise being modeled. Kinds of statements of fact, as we have seen, are otherwise known as predicates. The concept known as *attribute* in this modeling method is just *placeholder* by another name.

- In *Block II* we study a theory called "The Relational Model of Data" and a simple computer language called RAS based on that theory. We will discover how the ideas of predicate names and placeholder names are used in the formulation of such languages, and we will discover how queries can be presented to the computer by constructing predicates from predicates, using substitution, quantification, and the "connectives" *and, or,* and *not.* Incidentally, in this theory we will discover that the mathematical term *relation* is used to refer collectively both to the general form of a predicate and to the set of true propositions that can be formed from it.

- RAS is not a commercially used language—it has been designed especially for the Open University for tutorial purposes. In *Block III* we will study the industry's most widely accepted attempt to implement the theory we learned in Block II, a database language called SQL. SQL has become so prevalent since its first commercial appearance in 1979 as to have been characterized by one rather flamboyant authority as "intergalactic dataspeak." Alas, the industry's most widely accepted attempt is not a very good one, as we shall see, but a good understanding of predicates will help us to use SQL wisely in spite of its traps and shortcomings.

ACKNOWLEDGMENTS

Thanks to Adrian Larner, who first taught me to think this way, and for the observation that a database is not really a model of an enterprise, but a record or *account* of it; thanks also to Mike Newton of the Open University, Chris Date, and Adrian Larner again, for reviews of early drafts of this article and valuable suggestions.

The Relational Model Turns 25

. . . and we're still trying to get it right

ABSTRACT

Codd's first paper on the relational model [1] was published in 1969, so this year (1994) marks the relational model's 25th birthday. It thus seems appropriate to take stock and consider whether the theoretical benefits promised by the relational model all those years ago have in fact been realized in practice.

COMMENTS ON REPUBLICATION

The paper that follows was written by David McGoveran in 1994. About a year earlier, I wrote an article myself ("How We Missed the Relational Boat," reprinted in this book's predecessor), which opened with the following quote from *The Hollow Men*, by T. S. Eliot:

> *Between the idea*
> *And the reality . . .*
> *Falls the Shadow*

As David's paper shows, there is indeed—sadly—a very wide gap between the relational idea and the SQL reality.

By the way, the paper's subtitle (contributed by *DBMS*) says "we're still trying to get it right." I agree, in the sense that the SQL products available some four years later are still not all that relational (so much so, in fact, that I prefer not to call them relational DBMSs at all but, much more specifically, *SQL* DBMSs); but I also disagree, in the sense that I don't see many signs that the vendors are really trying to make their products any more faithful to the relational model. (With one exception: As I've argued elsewhere—see, e.g., Chapter 3 of the present book—the current crop of "object/relational" systems can at least be seen as trying to implement *domains* properly.) Indeed, it's partly this very lack of true relational support that led Hugh Darwen and myself to write *The Third Manifesto,* which can be seen in part as an attempt to move the industry back to its relational roots.

I should say too that it might be possible to quibble with David's paper on one or two points of detail (especially with the benefit of four more years of hindsight). For my own part, I don't fully agree with every last detail of Figs. 1–4, *q.v.* But I don't think these disagreements are very important; they don't change the big picture at all, and on that big picture David and I are in 100 percent agreement.

INTRODUCTION

Codd's famous 1970 paper on the relational model [2]—which was based on a less well known but no less significant 1969 paper [1]—begins with the words: "[Users] . . . must be protected from having to know . . . the internal representation [of data] . . . Activities of users at terminals and most application programs should remain unaffected when the internal representation . . . is changed." This *physical data independence* was the key goal of the relational model.[*]

At that time, application code (including control flow structure) was tightly coupled to the physical implementation of data structures. In addition, there was little uniformity in that physical implementation: The data structures and access methods were often specific to each application. This approach resulted in high maintenance costs, slow development, and error-prone code. Sharing data among applications was difficult and file oriented. The very concept of database

---

[*]*Note added on republication:* In fact, reference [2] also asserts that terminal users and application programmers should remain unaffected "even when some aspects of the *external* representation are changed" (italics added). Thus, Codd had logical data independence in mind as a goal as well.

consistency was ill defined. The relational model promised to solve these problems, as well as provide other business benefits.

Nonetheless, many applications today are still suffering from the same old problems—and some of the applications in question are even so-called relational ones. Although the data processing world has progressed greatly in the last 25 years, the industry continues to pay for the sins of the past. Legacy and heritage systems still place a burden and a constraint on businesses. In this 25th year since the introduction of the relational model, therefore, it seems appropriate to ask a few questions:

- Why are we still fighting these problems?
- What should we expect of an implementation of the relational model?
- Has the relational model delivered, and, if not, why not?

In summary, just what is the state of attempts to implement the relational model?

GOALS

I am sometimes asked "Why should anyone care whether DBMS vendors implement the relational model?" I find this question both amusing and sad. To me, the question is exactly like asking "Why should anyone care whether automobile manufacturers follow the laws of physics?" The answer is the same in both cases: We want a product that works—one we can understand, one that performs, one that meets user needs, and one we can continue to improve upon.

The relational model promises numerous benefits. (If you are a DBMS user who does not want these benefits, please raise your hand!) Those benefits include:

- *Minimization of application code and improvements in code reliability:* Services are provided through a nonprocedural language, thereby eliminating the most common sources of coding errors.

- *Isolation of performance and resource management issues:* The relational model guarantees that database performance and resource management problems can be fixed without modifying the application.

- *An active repository for business rules, processes, and integrity constraints:* The database can represent relationships among business entities, including management policies, workflow precedence, and definitions of business functions and objects, all in a consistent fashion. As the business evolves, the business model also evolves, becoming an accessible repository for maintaining business consistency and making training of new employees more efficient.

- *Guaranteed data consistency:* The DBMS can ensure that no user or application makes a change to the database that is inconsistent with the business rules; it can also detect existing inconsistencies and periodically check database consistency.

- *Guaranteed accuracy without programmatic effort:* The result of any query or update is predictable and meaningful (this property is perhaps most essential for transaction processing).

- *Guaranteed expressive completeness without programmatic effort:* The relational language can access every fact, whether physically stored or derivable (this property is perhaps most essential for decision support and *ad hoc* query).

- *Freedom to distribute both data and processing:* The physical location of data is independent of and hidden from the application, permitting physical distribution of data, database processing, and application processing.

- *The ability to grow:* We can modify database designs and their physical implementations without modifying applications.

- *Concurrent user support:* Data can be maximally shared, without loss of integrity, among all types of users (and processes), including batch, OLTP, decision support, read-only, ad hoc query, and report writing.

- *Guaranteed recovery:* Hardware failures need never cause a loss of data or of database consistency.

- *Algorithmic (and therefore highly automatable) logical database design:* The relational model differs from other models in that there are objective criteria for determining whether a logical relational database design is correct. It is important to understand that any physical database design that can be mapped into this logical view of the database is therefore an acceptable physical design. Physical design has to do with performance, not with relational correctness.

- *High performance, limited only by physical resources:* The relational model is an abstraction of the physical implementation that permits automatic optimization of throughput, concurrency, response time, and physical resource consumption (CPU utilization, memory, disk space, disk I/O, network I/O, and so on). There is no type of data (including object data), query, or transaction that the relational model cannot handle as well as any other model, because the relational model guarantees that it can exploit the techniques used by those other models to enhance performance.

However, controversy continues over the efficiency that is possible with the relational model. Some end users still maintain that relational systems can't handle real mission-critical OLTP systems because they require too much I/O ("a situation that is only made worse by normalization"). Some well-known consultants claim that the data model itself is unsuitable for tasks such as decision support. Object database proponents claim that the relational system can't support anything but simple data types. And so on.

Relational DBMS (RDBMS) vendors build great products that violate the model, claiming their products must address "the real world." If such claims were the only evidence to be considered, I would have to conclude that the relational model is not worth much. At the same time, I must stand by the claims I have already made in this article in favor of the relational model. So, what's wrong? Let's look at what RDBMS vendors have accomplished (and how), and try to see if we can discover what, if anything, has gone wrong.

WE'VE COME A LONG WAY, MAYBE

Since the first commercial RDBMS products began to ship in the late 1970s, users have reaped many benefits. Vendors such as Computer Associates, Cincom, Digital, Hewlett-Packard, IBM, Informix, Ingres, Oracle, Sybase, and Tandem should be praised for these achievements, which would not have been possible without the relational model.* There are several shining examples of relational technology's success, including the following:

- Relational DBMSs are the *de facto* "open systems" database solution at all levels of business. Each year, RDBMSs support a wider variety of platforms and configurations. Indeed, the idea of an "open systems" DBMS is hard to imagine without the relational model.

- There is now a single, standard language—namely, SQL—for data access. As a result, RDBMS applications have achieved some degree of portability and interoperability, and training costs have dropped.

- Because of the high-level nature of relational operations, we now write and debug less code than we used to with nonrelational systems. In particular, we no longer need to write sort, merge, or filter routines, and we have a guarantee of accurate, expected results.

Note added in 1998: To keep the record straight, we should say that (a) the Cincom product is no longer commercially available, (b) the Digital product has been acquired by Oracle, (c) the Ingres product has been acquired by Computer Associates, and (d) Tandem has been acquired by Compaq.

- Database integrity and transaction consistency can be managed outside of the application to a degree not possible with nonrelational DBMSs.

- DBMSs are significantly more reliable, recoverable, available, and functional than ever before.

- Data modeling is now a science (though analysis is not): We can identify mixes of transactions and data structures that cause data anomalies or conflicts, and fix the problems.

- DBMS performance can often be improved without requiring modification of application code (and, in many cases, without human intervention). Parallelization of DBMS operations has made great leaps forward in recent years.

- Distribution of applications and databases is rapidly becoming a viable approach, with features such as asynchronous replication, triggers, and stored procedures greatly improving both performance and ease of use.

- Enterprise-wide database designs and implementations are now feasible (though they are still in their infancy).

Despite these improvements, some applications are still being developed using low-level, record-at-a-time database or file access. Some RDBMS vendors have even designed their products to facilitate such nonrelational access, claiming that their products "must work in the real world" or that the industry demands that they "deliver what customers want and need."

RDBMS users are still frustrated by product deficiencies. Although relational has clearly won the database model battle for industry acceptance and, in some ways, dominance, many users still find reasons to avoid an RDBMS solution. Among the more common reasons I hear for this state of affairs are:

- RDBMSs use more I/O than their nonrelational counterparts in performing the same function.

- RDBMSs do not support complex data structures (including objects, multidimensional arrays, hierarchies, and so on) or inheritance.

- RDBMSs can't manipulate certain data types (for example, text).

- SQL is too difficult to use.

- RDBMS operations are inherently just too slow.

For the most part, such users tend to equate commercial RDBMS technology with the relational model, which is a serious error. RDBMS marketing, sales, and engineering personnel often make the same error. In some cases, so-called experts and vendors equate commercial RDBMS products with the relational model as an excuse for omitting important functionality and as a motivation for promoting the next product release, which will be "postrelational."* By contrast, I believe the problems assigned to the relational model are actually caused by violations of the model, either in product implementation or in use.

THE RELATIONAL MODEL, VINTAGE 1969–70

Recently, I reviewed Codd's 1969 and 1970 papers [1–2], writing down each of the features he specified for the relational model (by Codd's count there are about 50). Each time I read them, I am impressed by the depth of the articles and their succinctness. I almost always find a gem I had previously overlooked. If you haven't read the papers, please do so, but be forewarned that they can be a little "difficult"; Codd didn't take much space to explain all of the features he was proposing.

Conceptually, we can divide the 1969–70 features into three categories: *structure, manipulation,* and *integrity.* Let's look at each in turn, commenting on the status of today's RDBMSs.

First of all, the structural features specify a clean separation between the external view of the database and the internal view of the database, each supported by its own language. The external view includes how data is viewed and manipulated by users, programmers, and those who specify and maintain the logical content of the database. This is the place where relations, integrity constraints, and relational operations reside.

The internal view of the database includes how the data is physically stored, placed, and manipulated by the DBMS software—e.g., the disk, tape, or memory data structure and access methods, degree of redundancy, and so on. Only vendors are intended to have direct control over manipulations performed at the internal level. At most, users specify which of several vendor-supplied physical storage structures and index types are to be used to support some structure defined in the external view. Users must not be permitted to mix references to the internal and external views, except as needed to map named structures in the external view to their implementation in the internal view (and that mapping must exist outside the application as well, being the province of the DBMS).

Chris Date adds: I don't know if the *DBMS* editorial staff were just trying to cause unrest, but it's interesting to note that, in the issue in which it originally appeared, David's article was *immediately* followed by a four-page advertisement for a "postrelational" product. The lead-in to that advertisement read "Beyond RDBMS: PostRelational Database Technology." And at the time of writing (1998), another product is also being advertised as a "postrelational database" (that *database* should more properly be *DBMS,* of course): "Now you can develop . . . applications without the limitations of relational technology." Indeed.

Today's RDBMSs consistently fail to exploit relational's powerful separation of the internal and external views. For the most part, they provide only a single physical storage structure that closely mimics tables, giving physical database designers few choices. In particular, users seldom have the choice of how to store a relational table (for example, as an array, linked list, or tree structure); of storing multiple tables together (for example, to optimize joins or access to repeating groups) or storing single tables in separate partitions (horizontal or vertical); of storing multiple copies of the data; of creating multitable or functional indexes; and so forth.

Even worse, in today's RDBMSs, the separation is *corrupted.* Users ought to be able to modify physical storage structures without affecting the external view; instead, however, RDBMS storage options, which properly belong to the internal view, are often offered as clauses on the SQL CREATE TABLE statement, which properly belongs to the external view. This entanglement of internal and external views makes it impossible to restructure the storage of a table (its internal implementation) without dropping its external definition. Likewise, when redundancy in physical storage is supported, the external view fails to hide that redundancy from users, who have to be aware of the copies. A similar problem exists with respect to physical partitions of a table being stored separately on disk.

This mixing of internal and external levels has many negative consequences, not the least of which is a perverted understanding of the relational model. Specifically, most users think the relational model forces data to be stored as tables, altogether failing to recognize the distinction between internal and external. Furthermore, in many implementations where internal and external issues are confused, both error behaviors and restrictions on integrity constraints depend on the physical implementation (such as the existence of certain indexes).

Without separation, vendors cannot support new storage structures and access methods in new versions of their products without affecting applications. Worse, users cannot implement both a conceptual data model (defined by logical relationships) and a distinct physical data model (defined by resource and performance requirements). Consequently, database administration and system management are much more difficult than necessary. This problem becomes even more apparent when vendors try to implement distributed database functionality.

Vendor implementation of the external view is only moderately successful. Certainly, users perceive data as rows and columns. However, RDBMSs violate many of Codd's specifications: They permit duplicates, do not require primary key identification, place significance on column order, limit row width according to physical page size, do not label columns with domain names, do not support domains (active, simple, and nonsimple), do not support a generation identifier, and often do not support a general naming scheme. *Note:* The concept of domain, a collection of atomic data values and legal operations on those values, is intended to hide data element complexities that are not relevant to an application or user. All columns should be defined as drawing their values from a particular domain, much in the way a mathematical function $y = f(x)$ maps values from a domain of values x into a range of values y. Domains can be either fundamental or derived, and need not be restricted to simple data types such as integers, character strings, floating point numbers, and so on.[*]

Codd required that the language to be used in defining and manipulating the external view should be based on the first-order predicate calculus. It should support logical inference and various restricted set operations (intersection, union, set difference, and Cartesian product). Other operations it should support include projection, column permutation, restriction, join, and composition. The language should permit declaration of relations and primary keys and should support queries, insertions, deletions, and updates. The language should allow the user to form expressions in which any combination of columns could be either known (the values being specified by the user in the expression) or unknown (the values being determined by the system as part of the result).

He noted that this language would suffice if all relations were in at least *first normal form* (primary keys, no duplicates or repeating groups, with every row representing the same kind of fact; it is assumed that operations remove duplicates from their results). Codd also recognized that some deletions and updates would trigger others automatically, based on update dependencies (referential integrity enforcement). The language should be able to invoke arithmetic and other functions defined in another language, but should not itself contain these functions.

While SQL does implement most of the first-order predicate calculus and set operations, it fails in the most crucial ways to be a relational language. In particular, it treats both relations and nonrelations indiscriminately and tends to produce nonrelations as results (e.g., it doesn't automatically remove duplicates). It does not directly implement the universal quantifier, which would let you state that a property is true of all rows in a table (essentially an iterated logical AND over all values of a logical variable). It also contains arithmetic and other functions directly, rather than allowing arbitrary functions to be implemented in another language and invoked from SQL. This last feature permits the expression of paradoxical statements while inhibiting user extensions to the language that would reduce complexity.

---

[*]Incidentally, Codd noted that some nonsimple domains might have relations as elements, although these would be normalized away if the DBMS knew about their nonsimple character.

Codd also realized the need for declaration of time-independent integrity constraints within the language. He deemed batch constraint checking necessary, in addition to dynamic constraint enforcement (which implies dynamic constraint checking). Part of his concern was that the DBMS should be able to recognize and enforce state consistency, and deduce the redundancies applicable to a named relation.

As implemented in today's products, SQL's support for integrity constraints between relations (multitable or database constraints) remains weak. Despite the recent (and optional!) addition of declarative referential integrity to the SQL standard and subsequently to most products, SQL's concept of integrity is crippled. It simply does not enforce the use of primary keys or the integrity of domains as needed to provide explicit support of active domains.

THE 1979 PAPER

In 1979 (about the time the first commercial RDBMS products began to ship), Codd clarified and extended the relational model [3]. In his 1979 paper, he made it clear that relations could be either fundamental or derived and that some derived relations, called views, should be explicitly named. He discussed how many capabilities were either inherent in the 1969–70 explanation of the relational model or were natural extensions to it, the following among them:

- 3VL (three-valued logic, with internal and external forms) and versions of the relational operations to support 3VL. This aspect is the one serious error in Codd's work, in my opinion, because many-valued logics introduce numerous logical anomalies and nonintuitive results without adding value to the model [4].
- The divide operation (first defined in 1971)
- Surrogate keys (system-generated and maintained primary keys)
- Types and subtypes
- Association relations
- Generalization and specialization
- Single and multiple inheritance
- Cover aggregation
- Graph operations
- Domain operations
- Operations on collections of relations
- Event-type relations, with predecessor and successor functions
- Various types of integrity to support the new functionality

Chapter 2 / The Relational Model Turns 25   **299**

Of this list, partial support has been provided in commercial RDBMSs for Codd's 3VL (much to the detriment of the products, in my opinion). Also, a weakened version of surrogate keys, called system-generated keys, has been added to some of the RDBMS products during the intervening years. All of the other features explained in 1979 are still lacking.

RELATED TECHNICAL WORK

Almost all of the massive amount of work done on transaction isolation, database recovery, database consistency, database design (dependency theory and normalization theory), and query optimization since 1969–70 has benefited from—and been a benefit to—the relational model. Academic and industrial research have together made it possible to implement most of the relational features in practical ways. The viability of Codd's early goal of logical data independence continues to improve; with most views and derived tables now being updatable [5–6], there is little operational reason to differentiate derived tables from base tables. To the user, all derived tables (including query results and views) should work the same way as base tables.

These advances have found only limited implementation in SQL DBMSs. For example, commercial query optimizers lag far behind the theory, partially because the theory deals with relations while commercial products deal with nonrelational tables. Lack of support for the relational model is a crippling disease that vendors and users should not tolerate.

THE TWELVE RULES AND BEYOND

In 1985, Codd gave a popular summarization of the relational model in his now famous "Twelve Rules" paper [7]. Those rules gave the user community, in the context of the technology of the day, a set of guidelines for quickly determining whether a DBMS deserved to be called relational. Unfortunately, but predictably, vendors seized upon the paper as a marketing tool and gave it a variety of simplistic, self-serving interpretations. Suffice it to say that the twelve rules should not be considered the technical definition of the relational model. Beware of those who define the model so simplistically. Tell them to read Codd's 1969–70 and 1979 papers.

Nonetheless, the rules did serve as a rallying point. They were probably responsible for emphasis in the late 1980s on referential integrity and primary keys. They also served as a platform to spread a better understanding of the prohibition against subversion of the relational language and the need for relational closure. (The prohibition against subversion requires that users be allowed to access and manipulate data only through the relational interface; closure requires that the result of any relational operation be another relation, thereby guaranteeing that such operations can be nested.)

Given that Codd defined 333 rules in his 1990 book [8], vendors often complain that the number of requirements for their products to qualify as relational keeps growing. But this complaint is not well founded. Version 2 of the relational model consists primarily of the features of the 1969–70 papers, along with a few features from the 1979 paper, with considerable detail added. In other words, vendors should have been able to implement the greater portion of Version 2 based on the 1969–70 and 1979 papers. Reading the preface to Codd's 1990 book, you can detect considerable frustration and disappointment in Codd's perception of the state of the industry. I heartily sympathize with those feelings.

WELL, WHAT DO YOU KNOW?

Perhaps the greatest failure of the RDBMS industry is inadequate training. Throughout the commercial existence of relational products, there has never been a time when either users or vendors have had access to a good supply of trained relational professionals. Neither vendors nor users can be held fully responsible for this problem. In a sense, its existence is a measure of just how successful even the partial implementation of the relational model has been.

Vendors, in their quest to bring products to market quickly, have been forced to hire individuals who do not understand the model. These well-meaning individuals have marketed, defined, and designed products, changing forever the market's understanding of what is relational. Similarly, users have had to obtain training from these vendors, resulting in applications designed to use anything but the relational model. Few so-called relational professionals really understand the theory; they therefore cannot assess the root cause of product or application failures. This situation, ultimately caused by the premature success of pseudorelational products, has led to considerable dissatisfaction among users. The result is cries for denormalization, navigational access, and object databases.

THE NEORELATIONAL MODEL

I have to admit that I have never seen a relational DBMS. I have seen many great pseudorelational (or SQL) DBMSs; that is, products labeled relational that implement a few of the ideas in the relational model, but simply ignore many of the crucial ones. Nonetheless, I can't say I want to go back to the days of the "prerelational" DBMSs. Writing and maintaining applications with those DBMSs was just too hard and too uncertain. Designing and maintaining the database was worse.

It is amazing that, after 25 years, RDBMS vendors have heeded so little of Codd's original papers (see Figs. 1–4). However, the reason becomes clear when I ask database professionals if they have ever read Codd's original papers. Most say they have not.

A word of explanation regarding Figs. 1–4 is in order. The figures are based on the typical features and functionality found in the major RDBMS

FEATURE	IMPLEMENTATION STATUS
"host" language *H*	N
physical implementation defined in *H*	N
arithmetic (and other) functions defined in *H*	N
data independence	P
partial redundancy permitted in internal view	N
consistency enforced in internal view	N
connections distinct from relationships	P
independence of internal orderings	Y
independence of indexing	P
independence of access path	P
storage declaration in *H*	N
uncontrolled external redundancy forbidden	N

Fig. 1 State of the art (selected 1969–70 relational features)—separation of internal and external levels

FEATURE	IMPLEMENTATION STATUS
model based on *n*-ary relations	N
first normal form enforced	P
each row represents an *n*-tuple of an *n*-ary relation	P
order of rows is immaterial	Y
order of columns is immaterial	N
all rows are distinct	N
domain name labeling of columns	N
no practical limit on relation degree	N
support for names of relationships	P
active domains	N
simple domains	N
nonsimple domains	N
relations as domain elements	N
primary keys required	N
foreign keys supported	P
generation identifiers for relations	N
general naming scheme	P

Fig. 2 State of the art (selected 1969–70 relational features)—structural aspects

FEATURE	IMPLEMENTATION STATUS
universal data sublanguage *R*	P
nonsubvertible	Y
based on first-order predicate calculus	P
relational operators with duplicate removal:	
join (various types)	N
project	N
restrict	Y
product	P
composition	N
column permutation	Y
universal and existential operators	P
R used to declare relations and primary keys	P
user-defined functions invoked in *R*	N
supports high-level retrieve, insert, update, delete	Y
triggered deletions and updates based on dependencies	P
any aspect of a relation can be a known or unknown	Y
time-dependent constraints between relations	P
relational closure	P

Fig. 3   State of the art (selected 1969–70 relational features)—manipulative aspects

FEATURE	IMPLEMENTATION STATUS
system-captured semantic information	N
system deduction of applicable redundancies	N
constraint statements	N
system-determined state consistency	P
dynamic constraint checking	N
batch constraint checking	N
user-accessible journal of state changes	P

Fig. 4   State of the art (selected 1969–70 relational features)—integrity aspects

products (as of about 1994), including Computer Associates' OpenIngres, Cincom's Supra, IBM's DB2, Hewlett-Packard's Allbase/SQL, Informix's Informix-OnLine, Oracle's Oracle7, and Sybase's SQL Server System 10. If the feature is not implemented in a manner consistent with the definitions of the relational model, if it is implemented in the internal view when it should be in the external view (or *vice versa*), or if the implementation impairs the relational promise, I have given them an evaluation of either N (not supported) or P (partially supported), depending on the degree of support; otherwise I have given them a Y (yes, the feature is supported). *Please note that the list should not be used for "scoring" RDBMS products.* The evaluation was done solely for the purpose of illustrating the lack of support for the relational model, not for defining it or its constituent features.

Perhaps we need a new name for the relational model. Let the existing products have the old name. We'll certify them as "truly relational." They can advertise as such. Then we'll explain to them that what we want and need, and what they will profit from the most, is something called the "neorelational model." The neorelational model will solve most, if not all, of the problems we have with products that are merely "truly relational." Best of all, this great model was invented back in 1969 by a guy named Codd. We can even show them his definitive research papers! They are publicly available.

REFERENCES

1. E. F. Codd: "Derivability, Redundancy, and Consistency of Relations Stored in Large Data Banks," IBM Research Report RJ599 (August 19th, 1969).

2. E. F. Codd: "A Relational Model of Data for Large Shared Data Banks," *CACM 13*, No. 6 (June 1970). Republished in "Milestones of Research," *CACM 26*, No. 1 (January 1982).

3. E. F. Codd: "Extending the Database Relational Model to Capture More Meaning," *ACM TODS 4*, No. 4 (December 1979).

4. David McGoveran: "Nothing from Nothing" (Chapters 5–8 of the present book).

5. C. J. Date and David McGoveran: "Updating Union, Intersection, and Difference Views" and "Updating Joins and Other Views," *Database Programming & Design 7*, Nos. 5 and 7 (May and July 1994). Republished in C. J. Date, *Relational Database Writings 1991–1994*. Reading, Mass.: Addison-Wesley (1995).

6. David McGoveran and C. J. Date: "A New Database Design Principle," *Database Programming & Design 7*, No. 6 (June 1994). Republished in C. J. Date, *Relational Database Writings 1991–1994*. Reading, Mass.: Addison-Wesley (1995).

7. E. F. Codd: "How Relational Is Your Database Management System?", *Computerworld* (October 14th and 21st, 1985).

8. E. F. Codd: *The Relational Model for Database Management* Version 2. Reading, Mass.: Addison-Wesley (1990).

The Third Manifesto: **Foundation for Object/Relational Databases**

The view from 20,000 feet

ABSTRACT

The Third Manifesto [3] is a detailed and rigorous proposal for the future of data and database management systems. The present article consists of an informal discussion of certain of the key technical ideas underlying the *Manifesto*, including in particular the idea that domains in the relational world and object classes in the object world are really the same thing.

COMMENTS ON REPUBLICATION

Some readers will be aware that Hugh Darwen and I have been working on what we call *The Third Manifesto* for some considerable time. The first "official" version appeared in *ACM SIGMOD Record 24,* No. 1, March 1995 (though we had

Originally published (in somewhat different form) in C. J. Date and Hugh Darwen: *Foundation for Object/Relational Databases: The Third Manifesto* (Addison-Wesley, 1998). A version of this paper can also be found on the World Wide Web at *http://www. alternativetech.com.* Reprinted by permission of Hugh Darwen and Addison-Wesley.

been thinking about the ideas for several years prior to that time). A rather longer version, including in particular an appendix on type inheritance, appeared in this book's predecessor (*Relational Database Writings 1991–1994*, Addison-Wesley, 1995). A gentle introduction to some of the major themes, entitled "Introducing . . . *The Third Manifesto*," appeared in *Database Programming & Design 8*, No. 1 (January 1995). Most recently, a book-length version of the *Manifesto* was published by Addison-Wesley in 1998. The article that follows is basically a late draft of one chapter from that book, edited somewhat to make it more self-contained. It can also be regarded as a drastically revised and extended version of the introductory article from January 1995.

Note: The book's full title is the very similar to that of the present article— *viz., Foundation for Object/Relational Databases: The Third Manifesto.* There's a subtitle too: *a detailed study of the impact of objects and type theory on the relational model of data, including a comprehensive proposal for type inheritance.*

By the way, you might notice that there's some degree of overlap between this article and certain of the installments of my regular column that appear in Part I of this book (especially Installments 37, 59, and 60). There's also some overlap with Hugh Darwen's article on "what a database really is" (Chapter 1 of the present book). I apologize for such duplication, but felt it was better to keep the article as self-contained as possible.

INTRODUCTION

There is much current interest in the database community in the possibility of integrating objects and relations. However (and despite the fact that several vendors have already announced—in some cases, even released—"object/ relational" products), there is still some confusion over the question of the right way to perform that integration. Since part of the purpose of *The Third Manifesto* [3] is to answer this very question, the idea of bringing the *Manifesto* to the attention of a wider audience than hitherto seems timely.

The *Manifesto* is meant as a foundation for the future of data and database management systems (DBMSs). Because of our twin aims in writing it of comprehensiveness and brevity, however, it is—unfortunately but probably inevitably—rather terse and not very easy to read; hence this introductory article (which, as the subtitle suggests, might be characterized as "the view from 20,000 feet"). Our aim is to present some of the key technical ideas underlying the *Manifesto* in an informal manner, thereby paving the way for a proper understanding of the *Manifesto* itself. In particular, as already indicated, we would like to explain what we believe is the right way to integrate objects and relations. More precisely, we want to address the following question:

> *What concept in the relational world is the counterpart to the concept "object class" in the object world?*

There are two equations that can be proposed as answers to this question:

1. domain = object class
2. relation = object class*

In what follows, we will argue strongly that the first of these equations is right and the second is wrong.

WHAT PROBLEM ARE WE TRYING TO SOLVE?

Databases of the future will contain much more sophisticated kinds of data than current commercial ones typically do. For example, we might imagine a biological database that includes a BIRD relation like that shown in Fig. 1. Thus, what we want to do is extend—dramatically—the range of possible kinds of data that we can keep in our databases. Of course, we want to be able to manipulate that data, too; for example, we might want to find all birds whose migration route includes Italy:

```
SELECT NAME, DESCR, VIDEO
FROM   BIRD
WHERE  INCLUDES ( MIGR, COUNTRY ( 'Italy' ) ) ;
```

Note: We use SQL here for familiarity, though in fact the *Manifesto* expressly proscribes it (see the next section).

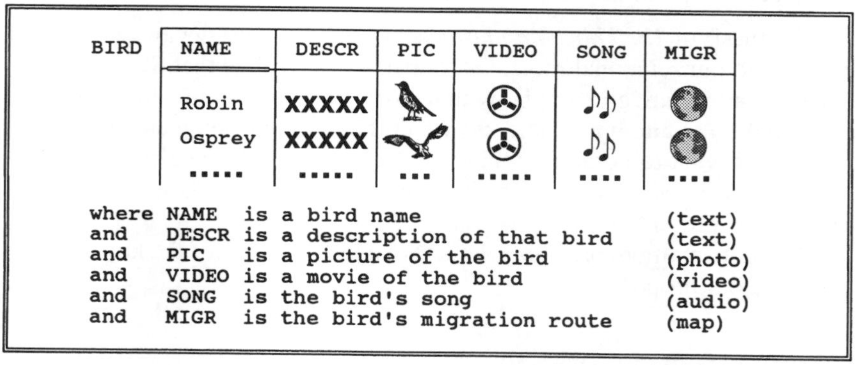

Fig. 1   The BIRD relation

---

*More correctly, *relvar* = object class. See the section "Relations *vs.* Relvars," later.

Thus, the question becomes: How can we support new kinds of data within the relational framework? Note that we do take it as axiomatic that we want to stay in the relational framework!—it would be unthinkable to walk away from nearly 30 years of solid relational R&D. We mustn't throw the baby out with the bathwater.

WHY THE *THIRD* MANIFESTO?

Before going any further, we should explain that "third" in our title. In fact, our *Manifesto* is the third in a series (of a kind). Its two predecessors are:

1. *The Object-Oriented Database System Manifesto* [1]
2. *The Third Generation Database System Manifesto* [7]

Like our own *Manifesto,* each of these documents offers a proposed basis for future DBMSs. However:

1. The first essentially ignores the relational model! In our opinion, this flaw is more than enough to rule it out immediately as a serious contender.
2. The second does agree that the relational model must not be ignored, but assumes that SQL (with all its faults) is an adequate realization of that model and hence an adequate foundation for the future. By contrast, we feel strongly that any attempt to move forward, if it's to stand the test of time, must *reject SQL unequivocally.* Our reasons for taking this position are many and varied, far too much so for us to spell them out in detail here; in any case, we've described them in depth in other places (see, e.g., references [2] and [4]), and readers are referred to those publications for the specifics.

A major thesis of *The Third Manifesto* is thus that we must get away from SQL and back to our relational roots. Of course, we do realize that SQL databases and applications are going to be with us for a very long time—to think otherwise would be quite unrealistic. So we do have to pay some attention to the question of what to do about today's SQL legacy, and *The Third Manifesto* does include some proposals in this regard. Further details are beyond the scope of the present article, however.

Without any more preamble, let's take a look at some of the key technical aspects of our proposal.

RELATIONS *vs.* RELVARS

The first thing we have to do is clear up a confusion that goes back nearly 30 years. Consider the bill of materials relation shown in Fig. 2. As that figure suggests, every relation has two parts, a *heading* and a *body;* the heading is a

MAJOR_P# : P#	MINOR_P# : P#	QTY : QTY
P1	P2	2
P1	P3	4
P2	P3	1
P2	P4	3
P3	P5	9
P4	P5	8
P5	P6	3

Fig. 2   A bill of materials relation

set of column-name/domain-name pairs, the body is a set of rows that conform to that heading.* For the relation in Fig. 2:

- The column names are MAJOR_P#, MINOR_P#, and QTY (where P# means *part number*);
- The corresponding domain names are P#, P# again, and QTY, respectively;
- Each row includes a MAJOR_P# value (from the P# domain), a MINOR_P# value (also from the P# domain), and a QTY value (from the QTY domain).

Informally, of course, we often ignore the domain-name components of the heading (as indeed we did in Fig. 1).

Now, there's a very important (though perhaps unusual) way of thinking about relations, and that's as follows. Given a relation *R,* the heading of *R* denotes a certain *predicate* (or truth-valued function), and each row in the body of *R* denotes a certain *true proposition,* obtained from that predicate by substituting certain arguments—more precisely, certain domain values—for that predicate's parameters ("instantiating the predicate"). In the case of the bill of materials example, the predicate looks something like this:

part MAJOR_P# contains QTY of part MINOR_P#

(the three parameters are MAJOR_P#, QTY, AND MINOR_P#, corresponding of course to the three columns of the relation).

And the corresponding true propositions are

part P1 contains 2 of part P2

---

*It could be argued that it would be slightly more correct, and preferable, to regard the body alone as the relation proper and the heading not as part of the relation per se but as "metadata" that defines the relation type.

(obtained by substituting the domain values P1, 2, and P2);

```
part P1 contains 4 of part P3
```

(obtained by substituting the domain values P1, 4, and P3); and so on. In a nutshell:

- *Domains* **comprise the things we can talk about;**
- *Relations* **comprise the truths we utter about those things.**

It follows that:

- First, domains and relations are both essential (without domains, there's nothing we can talk about; without relations, there's nothing we can say).
- Second, they aren't the same thing (beware anyone who tries to tell you otherwise!).

In fact, there's a third implication as well, which is that, between them, domains and relations are *sufficient,* as well as necessary—i.e., we don't need anything else, logically speaking.

By the way, there's a nice analogy here (albeit a slightly loose one) that might help you appreciate and remember these important points:

Domains are to relations as nouns are to sentences.

Now we can get back to the main theme of the present section. Historically, there's been much confusion between relations *per se* (i.e., relation *values*) and relation *variables.* Suppose we say in some programming language:

```
DECLARE N INTEGER ...
```

N here isn't an integer *per se,* it's an integer *variable* whose values are integers *per se*—different integers at different times. Likewise, if we say in SQL:

```
CREATE TABLE T ...
```

T here isn't a relation (or table) *per se,* it's a relation *variable* whose *values* are relations *per se*—different relations at different times. And when we "update T" (e.g., by "inserting a new row"), what we're really doing is *replacing the old relation value of T en bloc by an entirely new relation value.* Of course, it's true that the old value and the new value are somewhat similar—the new one just has one more row than the old one—but conceptually they are different values.

Now, the trouble is that, very often, when people talk about relations, they really mean relation variables, not relations *per se.* This distinction—or, rather, the fact that this distinction is usually not clearly made—has been a rich source of confusion in the past. For example, the overall value of a given relation, like the overall value of a given domain, doesn't change over time, whereas of course the value of a relation variable certainly does. Despite this obvious difference, some people—we suppress the names to protect the guilty—have proposed that domains and relations (meaning relation variables) are really the same kind of thing! See the section "Relvars *vs.* Object Classes," later.

In *The Third Manifesto,* therefore, we've tried very hard to be clear on this point (and the same goes for the rest of the present article). Specifically, we've introduced the term *relvar* as a convenient shorthand for *relation variable,* and we've taken care to phrase our remarks in terms of relvars, not relations, when it's really relvars that we mean.

DOMAINS *vs.* OBJECT CLASSES

It's an unfortunate fact that most people have only a rather weak understanding of what domains are all about; typically they perceive them as just conceptual pools of values, from which columns in relations draw their actual values (to the extent they think about the concept at all, that is). This perception is accurate so far as it goes, but it doesn't go far enough. The fact is, a domain is really nothing more nor less than a *data type*—possibly a simple system-defined data type like INTEGER or CHAR, more generally a user-defined data type like P# or QTY in the bill of materials example.

Now, it's important to understand that the data type concept includes the associated concept of the *operators* that can legally be applied to values of the type in question (values of that type can be operated upon solely by means of the operators defined for that type). For example, in the case of the system-defined INTEGER domain (or type—we use the terms interchangeably):

- The system defines operators "=", "<", and so on, for comparing integers;
- It also defines operators "+", "*", and so on, for performing arithmetic on integers;
- It does *not* define operators "||". SUBSTRING, and so on, for performing string operations on integers (in other words, string operations on integers aren't supported).

Likewise, if we had a system that supported domains properly (but most of today's systems don't), then we would be able to define our own domains—say the part number domain P#. And we would probably define operators "=", "<", and so on, for comparing part numbers. However, we would probably *not* define operators "+", "*", and so on, which would mean that arithmetic on part numbers would not be supported.

Observe, therefore, that we distinguish very carefully between a data type *per se* and the *representation* or *encoding* of values of that type inside the system. For example, part numbers might be represented internally as character strings, but it doesn't follow that we can perform string operations on part numbers; we can perform such operations only if appropriate operators have been defined for the type. And (in general) the operators we define for a given domain will depend on that domain's intended *meaning,* not on the way values from that domain happen to be represented or encoded inside the system.

By now you might have realized that what we've been talking about is what's known in programming language circles as *strong typing.* Different writers have slightly different definitions for this term; as we use it, however, it means, among other things, that (a) everything *has* a type, and (b) whenever we try to perform an operation, the system checks that the operands are of the right type for the operation in question. And note carefully that—as already indicated—it's not just *comparison* operations that we're talking about here (despite the emphasis on comparisons in much of the database literature). E.g., suppose we're given the well known suppliers-and-parts database, with relvars S (suppliers), P (parts), and SP (shipments), and consider the following expressions:

```
1. P.WEIGHT + SP.QTY   /* part weight plus shipment quantity */

2. P.WEIGHT * SP.QTY   /* part weight times shipment quantity */
```

The first of these expressions makes no sense, and the DBMS should therefore reject it. The second, on the other hand, does make sense—it denotes the total weight for all parts involved in the shipment. So the operators we would define for weights and quantities would presumably include "*" but not "+".

Observe now that so far we've said nothing at all about the nature of the values that can belong to a domain. In fact, those values can be *anything at all!* We tend to think of them as being very simple (numbers, strings, and so forth), but there's absolutely nothing in the relational model that requires them to be limited to such simple forms. Thus, we can have domains of sound recordings, domains of maps, domains of videos, domains of engineering drawings, domains of legal documents, domains of geometric objects (and so on and so on). The only requirement is that—to say it one more time—the values in the domain must be manipulable solely by means of the operators defined for the domain in question.

The foregoing message is so important that we state it again in different words:

> **The question as to what data types are supported is orthogonal to the question of support for the relational model**

To sum up, therefore: What we're saying is that, in the relational world, a domain is a data type, possibly user-defined, of arbitrary internal complexity, whose values are manipulable solely by means of the operators defined for the type in question. Now, if we turn to the object-oriented (OO) world, we find that what is arguably the most fundamental OO concept of all, the *object class,* is a data type, possibly user-defined, of arbitrary internal complexity, whose values are manipulable solely by means of the operators defined for the type in question . . . In other words, domains and object classes are *the same thing!* Thus, we have here the key to integrating the two technologies—and, of course, this position is exactly what we espouse in *The Third Manifesto.* Indeed, we believe that a relational system that supported domains properly would be able to deal with all of those "problem" kinds of data that (it's often claimed) OO systems can handle and relational systems cannot: time-series data, biological data, financial data, engineering design data, office automation data, and so on. Accordingly, we also believe that a true "object/relational" system is nothing more than a true *relational* system—which is to say, a system that supports the relational model, with all that that entails.

RELVARS *vs.* OBJECT CLASSES

In the previous section we equated object classes and domains. Many people, however, equate object classes and *relvars* instead (see reference [6] for an example). We now argue that this latter equation is a serious mistake. Indeed, the *Manifesto* includes a categorical statement to the effect that *relvars are not domains.*

Consider the following example. First, here's part of a simple object class definition, expressed in a hypothetical OO language (the keyword PUBLIC is meant to indicate that the specified items are "public instance variables"):

```
CREATE OBJECT CLASS EMP
PUBLIC ( EMP#       CHAR(5),
         ENAME      CHAR(20),
         SAL        NUMERIC,
         HOBBY      CHAR(20),
         WORKS_FOR  CHAR(20) ) ... ;
```

And here's part of a simple relational—or at least SQL—table (relvar) definition:

```
CREATE TABLE EMP
       ( EMP#       CHAR(5),
         ENAME      CHAR(20),
         SAL        NUMERIC,
         HOBBY      CHAR(20),
         WORKS_FOR  CHAR(20) ) ... ;
```

It's very tempting to equate these two definitions!—which is in effect what certain systems (both prototypes and commercial products) have already done. So let's take a closer look at this equation. More precisely, let's take the CREATE TABLE just shown, and let's consider a series of possible extensions that (some people would argue) make it more "OO"-like.

First, we allow column values to be *tuples from some other relvar* ("tuple" here being just another word for *row,* loosely speaking). In the example, we might replace the original CREATE TABLE by the following collection of definitions:

```
CREATE TABLE EMP
         ( EMP#       CHAR(5),
           ENAME      CHAR(20),
           SAL        NUMERIC,
           HOBBY      ACTIVITY,
           WORKS_FOR  COMPANY ) ;

CREATE TABLE ACTIVITY
         ( NAME  CHAR(20),
           TEAM  INTEGER ) ;

CREATE TABLE COMPANY
         ( NAME      CHAR(20),
           LOCATION  CITYSTATE ) ;

CREATE TABLE CITYSTATE
         ( CITY   CHAR(20),
           STATE  CHAR(2) ) ;
```

Fig. 3 shows the structure of relvar EMP at this point.

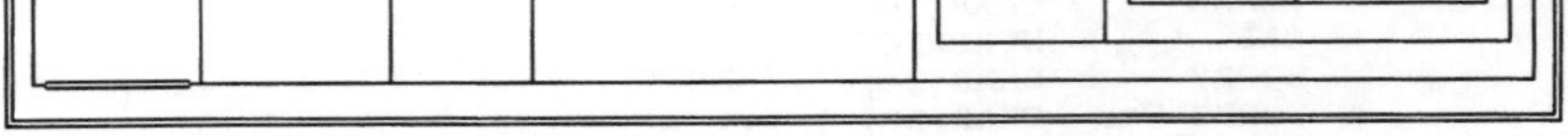

Fig. 3 Columns containing (pointers to) rows—deprecated

Explanation: Column HOBBY in relvar EMP is declared to be of type ACTIVITY. ACTIVITY in turn is a relvar of two columns, NAME and TEAM, where TEAM gives the number of players in the corresponding team—for instance, a possible "activity" might be (Soccer, 11). Each HOBBY value is thus actually a *pair* of values, a NAME value and a TEAM value (more precisely, it's a pair of values that currently appear as a row in relvar ACTIVITY). Note that we've already violated the dictum that relvars aren't domains!

Similarly, column WORKS_FOR in relvar EMP is declared to be of type COMPANY, and COMPANY is also a relvar of two columns, one of which is defined to be of type CITYSTATE, which is another two-column relvar, and so on. In other words, relvars ACTIVITY, COMPANY, and CITYSTATE are all considered to be *types* as well as relvars (as is relvar EMP itself, of course).

This first extension is thus roughly analogous to allowing objects to contain other objects, thereby supporting the concept sometimes known as a *containment hierarchy.*

Note: As an aside, we remark that we have characterized this first extension as "columns containing rows" because that's the way advocates of the "relvar = class" equation themselves characterize it. It would be more accurate, however, to characterize it as "columns containing *pointers* to rows"—a point that we will be examining in a few moments. (In Fig. 3, therefore, we should really replace each of the three appearances of the term *tuple* by the term *pointer to tuple.*) Analogous remarks apply to the second extension also.

That second extension, then, is to add *relation-valued columns.* E.g., suppose employees can have an arbitrary number of hobbies, instead of just one (refer to Fig. 4):

```
CREATE TABLE EMP
      ( EMP#        CHAR(5),
        ENAME       CHAR(20),
        SAL         NUMERIC,
        HOBBIES     SET OF ( ACTIVITY ),
        WORKS_FOR   COMPANY ) ;
```

Fig. 4   Columns containing sets of (pointers to) rows—deprecated

Explanation: The HOBBIES value within any given row of relvar EMP is now (conceptually) a set of zero or more (NAME,TEAM) pairs—i.e., rows—from the ACTIVITY relvar. This second extension is thus roughly analogous to allowing objects to contain "aggregate" objects (a more complex version of the containment hierarchy).

The third extension is to permit relvars to have associated *methods* (i.e., operators). E.g.:

```
CREATE TABLE EMP
       ( EMP#       CHAR(5),
         ENAME      CHAR(20),
         SAL        NUMERIC,
         HOBBIES    SET OF ( ACTIVITY ),
         WORKS_FOR  COMPANY )
METHOD RETIREMENT_BENEFITS ( ) : NUMERIC ;
```

Explanation: RETIREMENT_BENEFITS is a method that takes a given EMP instance as its argument and produces a result of type NUMERIC. The code that implements the method is written in a language such as C.

The final extension is to permit the definition of *subclasses.* E.g. (refer to Fig. 5):

```
CREATE TABLE PERSON
       ( SS#       CHAR(9),
         BIRTHDATE DATE,
         ADDRESS   CHAR(50) ) ;

CREATE TABLE EMP
    AS SUBCLASS OF PERSON
       ( EMP#       CHAR(5),
         ENAME      CHAR(20),
         SAL        NUMERIC,
         HOBBIES    SET OF ( ACTIVITY ),
         WORKS_FOR  COMPANY )
METHOD RETIREMENT_BENEFITS ( ) : NUMERIC ;
```

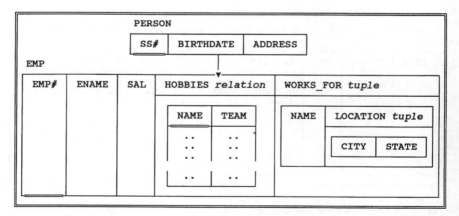

Fig. 5   Relvars as superclasses and subclasses—deprecated

Explanation: EMP now has three additional columns (SS#, BIRTHDATE, ADDRESS) inherited from PERSON. If PERSON had any methods, it would inherit those too.

Along with the definitional extensions sketched above, numerous manipulative extensions are required too, of course—for instance:

- Path expressions—e.g., EMP.WORKS_FOR.LOCATION.STATE (and note that such expressions can return scalars or rows or relations, in general; note further that in the latter two cases the components of those rows or relations might themselves be rows or relations in turn, and so on)

- Row and relation literals (possibly nested)—e.g.,

```
( 'E001', 'Smith', $50000,
        { ( 'Soccer', 11 ), ( 'Bridge', 4 ) },
                        ( 'IBM', ( 'San Jose', 'CA' ) ) )
```

- Relational comparison operators—e.g., SUBSET, SUBSETEQ, and so on
- Operations for traversing the class hierarchy
- The ability to invoke methods within expressions—e.g., in WHERE clauses
- The ability to access individual components within column values that happen to be rows or relations

So much for a quick overview of how the "relvar = class" equation is realized in practice. What's wrong with it?

Well, first of all, a relvar is a variable and a class is a type; so how can they *possibly* be the same thing? (We showed in the section "Relations *vs.* Relvars" that relations and domains aren't the same thing; now we see that relvars and domains aren't the same thing either.)

The foregoing argument should be logically sufficient to stop the "relvar = class" idea dead in its tracks. However, there is more that can usefully be said on the subject, so let us agree to suspend disbelief a little longer . . . Here are some more points to consider:

- The equation "relvar = class" implies that "objects" are *rows,* and the corresponding (public) "instance variables" are *columns.* It follows that, whereas a pure OO class has methods and no public instance variables, a relvar "class" has public instance variables and only optionally has methods. So, again, how can the two possibly be the same?

- There's a major difference in kind between the column definitions (e.g.) SAL NUMERIC and WORKS_FOR COMPANY. NUMERIC is a true data type (equivalently, a true—albeit primitive—domain); it places a time-independent constraint on the values that can appear in column SAL.

By contrast, COMPANY is *not* a true data type; the constraint it places on the values that can appear in column WORKS_FOR is *time-dependent* (it depends, obviously, on the current value of relvar COMPANY). In fact, as pointed out earlier, the relvar *vs.* domain distinction has been muddied.

- As we saw, row "objects" can contain other such "objects"; e.g., EMP "objects" (apparently) contain COMPANY "objects." But they don't— not really; instead, they contain *pointers* (object IDs, to use the OO term) to those "contained" objects, and users must understand this point clearly. E.g., suppose the user updates one particular COMPANY row in some way (refer back to Fig. 3). Then that update will immediately be visible in all EMP rows that correspond to that COMPANY row.

    It follows that we're not really talking about the relational model any more. The fundamental data object isn't a relation containing values, it's a "relation" (actually not a proper relation at all) containing values *and pointers*.

- Suppose we define view V to be the projection of EMP over (say) just ENAME. V is a relvar too, of course (a *derived* one, whereas EMP is a *base* relvar). Thus, if "relvar = class" is a correct equation, V is also a class. *What class is it?* Also, classes have methods; *what methods apply to V?*

    Well, "class" EMP had just one method, RETIREMENT_BENEFITS, and that one clearly doesn't apply to V. In fact, it hardly seems reasonable that *any* methods that applied to "class" EMP would apply to V—and there certainly aren't any others. So it looks as if (in general) *no methods at all* apply to the result of a projection; i.e., the result, whatever it is, isn't really a class at all. (We might *say* it's a class, but that doesn't make it one!—it will have public instance variables and no methods, whereas we've already observed that a true class has methods and no public instance variables.)

    In fact, it's clear that when people equate relvars and classes, it's specifically *base* relvars they're referring to—they're forgetting about the *derived* ones. (Certainly the pointers discussed above point to rows in base relvars, not derived ones.) As we've argued elsewhere [5], to distinguish base and derived relvars in this way is a mistake of the highest order, because the question as to which relvars are base and which derived is, to a very large degree, arbitrary. For further discussion of this important issue, see that same paper [5].

- Finally, *what domains are supported?* Those who espouse the "relvar = class" equation never seem to have much to say about domains, presumably because they cannot see how domains fit into their overall scheme. And yet (as we saw in the section "Relations *vs.* Relvars" earlier) domains are essential.

A NOTE ON INHERITANCE

You might have noticed that we did briefly mention the possibility of *inheritance* in the previous section but not in the earlier section "Domains *vs.* Object Classes." And you might therefore have concluded that support for inheritance does constitute at least one point in favor of the "relvar = class" equation. Not so, however; we do indeed want to include inheritance as part of our "domain = class" approach, and thus (e.g.) be able to define domain CIRCLE as a "subdomain" of "superdomain" ELLIPSE. The problem is, however, there doesn't seem to be a clearly defined and generally agreed model of inheritance at the time of writing. As a consequence, *The Third Manifesto* includes *conditional* support for inheritance, along the lines of "if inheritance is supported, then it must be in accordance with some well defined and commonly agreed model." We do also offer some detailed proposals toward the definition of such a model.

CONCLUDING REMARKS

We have discussed the question of integrating relational and object-oriented (OO) database concepts. In our opinion, OO contains exactly one unquestionably good idea: user-defined data types (which includes user-defined operators). It also contains one *probably* good idea: type inheritance (though the jury is still out on this one, to some extent). A key technical insight underlying *The Third Manifesto* is that these two ideas are completely *orthogonal to the relational model.* In other words, the relational model needs no *extension,* no *correction,* no *subsumption*—and, above all, no *perversion!*—in order for it to accommodate these orthogonal ideas.

To sum up, therefore: What we need is simply for the vendors to give us *true relational DBMSs* (and note that "true relational DBMSs" does *not* mean SQL systems) that include *proper domain support.* Indeed, an argument can be made that the whole reason OO systems (as opposed to "O/R" systems) look attractive is precisely the failure on the part of the SQL vendors to support the relational model adequately. But this fact shouldn't be seen as an argument for abandoning the relational model entirely (or at all!).

ACKNOWLEDGMENTS

This article is an updated version of "Introducing . . . *The Third Manifesto*" by Hugh Darwen and C. J. Date, which appeared in *Database Programming & Design 8,* No. 1 (January 1995); it appears here by permission of Miller Freeman Inc. We would also like to thank the many people who have reviewed drafts of *The Third Manifesto* and offered constructive criticism and helpful comments on those drafts.

REFERENCES

1. Malcolm Atkinson *et al.:* "The Object-Oriented Database System Manifesto," Proc. First International Conference on Deductive and Object-Oriented Databases, Kyoto, Japan (1989). New York, N.Y.: Elsevier Science (1990).

2. Hugh Darwen: "Adventures in Relationland," in C. J. Date and Hugh Darwen, *Relational Database Writings 1985–1989*. Reading, Mass.: Addison-Wesley (1990).

3. Hugh Darwen and C. J. Date: "The Third Manifesto," *ACM SIGMOD Record 24*, No. 1 (March 1995). See also the book-length version *Foundation for Object/ Relational Databases: The Third Manifesto*. Reading, Mass.: Addison-Wesley (1998).

4. C. J. Date: *An Introduction to Database Systems* (6th edition). Reading, Mass.: Addison-Wesley (1995).

5. C. J. Date: "Objects and Relations: Forty-Seven Points of Light" (Chapter 13 of the present book).

6. Won Kim: "On Marrying Relations and Objects: Relation-Centric and Object-Centric Perspectives," *Data Base Newsletter 22*, No. 6 (November/December 1994).

7. Michael Stonebraker *et al.:* "Third Generation Database System Manifesto," *ACM SIGMOD Record 19*, No. 3 (September 1990).

Some Remarks on Types, Units, and Type Design

Clarifying certain aspects of the data type concept

ABSTRACT

There seems to be some confusion in the industry over the question of exactly what a data type is. This short paper presents some examples of such confusion and makes an attempt at clarification.

COMMENTS ON PUBLICATION

In Installment 60 (see Part I of this book), following a certain quoted passage, I wrote: "This passage betrays confusion over what a [type] is on so many levels at once that I think I'm going to have to discuss it—at length!—elsewhere . . . So I'm afraid you'll have to wait for that discussion for the specifics." The paper that follows is that promised discussion.

Previously unpublished.

INTRODUCTION

The Third Manifesto [3], by Hugh Darwen and myself, includes the following definitions and prescriptions:

- A **domain,** also known as a **data type,** is a named set of values. Note that we treat the terms *domain* and *data type—type* for short—as equivalent and interchangeable.

- Values from a given domain, and variables whose values are constrained to be from a given domain, can be operated upon solely by means of the operators explicitly defined for that domain.

- The definition of each such operator must include a specification of the type of the result (if any) of that operator.

And it also says: "Because values and variables can be operated upon solely by means of the operators defined for the applicable type, the internal structure or representation of such values and variables is always *hidden from the user;* in other words, we draw a sharp distinction between **types** and **representations.**"

The overall intent of these extracts from the *Manifesto* (all of which are slightly edited here) is, of course, to try to pin down the notion of *data type* precisely. In this short paper, I want to elaborate on this notion somewhat; after all, the notion *is* absolutely fundamental, and a clear understanding of it is essential—especially in these days of "universal database servers," which among other things allow users to define types of their own.

CONFUSION IN THE INDUSTRY

There does seem to be a certain amount of confusion in the industry over the type concept. The following quote from a recent article is not atypical [1]:

The part I don't agree with in *The Third Manifesto* is that simply defining a domain as having a data type and rules is not enough.

Actually this sentence is a little hard to construe, but what I think it means is that domains should be more than just "data types and rules"—and I think "rules" is supposed to mean *operators.* If this interpretation is correct, however, I confess myself puzzled right away, since domains don't *have* data types, they *are* data types; in fact, as already indicated, the two concepts are identical, and the terms "domain" and "data type" are, or should be, completely interchangeable. Further (again as already indicated), the data type notion *includes* the notion that values of the type in question can be operated upon solely by means of the operators defined for that type, so to speak of "data types *and* operators" (my italics) makes little sense. Well, never mind; let's see if we can understand the writer's position a little better by examining his arguments in a little more detail.

> *Aside:*   Part of the confusion discussed in the previous paragraph might perhaps be due to the current SQL standard SQL/92. SQL/92 does include something it calls a domain, and SQL/92 domains do "have data types and rules" (where—very unfortunately, in my opinion!—"data types" really means *representations* and "rules" really means *constraints*). As I've explained elsewhere, however [6], SQL/92 domains have almost nothing to do with true relational domains. If indeed it is the case that the writer has been confused by SQL/92, then that fact only serves to support my contention that it would have been a good idea not to have called the SQL/92 construct a "domain" in the first place.   *End of aside.*

LENGTHS AND WEIGHTS

In that same recent article [1], the writer gives an example involving the domains "length in feet" and "weight in pounds" (let's agree to refer to these domains as L and W, respectively), and goes on to say:

> You cannot multiply pounds by pounds and get a meaningful result— there are no such things as square pounds. However, you can multiply feet by feet and get a result in square feet. How does the database [*sic*] disallow the operation in the first case and create an entire new domain in the second case?

This passage unfortunately displays several confusions at once:

1. First of all, it's confused over **types** *vs.* **units;** the question is not whether we can multiply pounds by pounds or feet by feet, but rather whether we can multiply weights by weights or lengths by lengths.

2. Let's agree for the sake of the discussion that multiplication does make sense for two lengths (domain L) but not for two weights (domain W). Very well: Whoever defines domain L will specify that the multiplication operation is legal between two values of type L, and will specify that the type of the result of such an operation is, say, A ("area"). By contrast, whoever defines domain W will *not* specify that the multiplication operation is legal between two values of type W.

3. Now, of course, the DBMS (*not* "the database," please) can indeed "disallow the operation" for weights but allow it for lengths. But it certainly

doesn't "create an entire new domain in the second case"! On the contrary, the domain of the result, namely A ("area"), has already been defined to the DBMS, just as domains L and W were.

(At the risk of beating the point to death, let me add that the problem of how to allow the multiplication of two lengths but not two weights is precisely analogous to the problem of how to allow the multiplication of two integers but not two strings. Today's SQL products do at least handle this latter problem reasonably well.)

Anyway, reference [1] continues:

These rules get more and more complex as you add domains to the database. When you multiply feet by pounds, you get work expressed in foot-pounds. But not always—a man's height multiplied by his weight is nonsense, not foot-pounds. The relation or entity where the attributes reside matters quite a bit.

This passage too is rife with confusions, the most significant of which is, of course, the one already mentioned regarding types *vs.* units. **There is no such thing as a domain of feet or a domain of pounds** (what could such domains possibly contain?)—there are only domains whose values are *measurements* in feet or pounds. Thus, the question of multiplying feet by pounds doesn't arise; rather, what does arise is the question of multiplying feet *measurements* by pound *measurements*.

- Thus, for example, we might reasonably define domains PERSON_ HEIGHT and PERSON_WEIGHT, containing feet measurements and pound measurements respectively, and disallow multiplication between PERSON_HEIGHT and PERSON_WEIGHT values.

- At the same time, we might also define domains DISTANCE and FORCE, again containing feet measurements and pound measurements respectively, and *allow* multiplication between DISTANCE and FORCE values (to produce WORK values).

TEMPERATURES

The commonest (and indeed most basic) confusion displayed in the industry on this general topic has to do with the fundamental distinction between types and representations.* Before going any further, therefore, let me try to restate

---

*A good example of that confusion is provided by the concept usually called *domain check override*. The very idea of domain check override stems from a failure to make a clear distinction between types and representations; as such, it makes no logical sense at all.

my position on this point (or the position of *The Third Manifesto*—it's the same thing):

- A *type*—usually called a *domain* in relational contexts—is a named set of *values*. Every type has an associated set of *operators* that apply to values of that type.

- Given a type, a *representation*—also known as a *structure*—for that type is an *encoding in memory* for values of that type.

It follows that types are a **model** consideration, while representations are an **implementation** consideration. As a trivial example, consider the type REAL in SQL. The representation of REAL numbers is not specified in the SQL language, and users don't have to know what it is; what they do have to know is the operations they can perform on REAL numbers—"+", "*", "<", and so on. And that's *all* they need to know. To quote Cardelli and Wegner [2]: "A major purpose of type systems is to avoid embarrassing questions about representations, and to forbid situations in which these questions might come up."

At one point, the author of the various extracts quoted earlier does seem to agree with the foregoing position, because he asserts forthrightly that "numbers . . . and numerals . . . are [not the same thing]" (I interpret this assertion to mean that numbers are the type, while numerals are the representation). Unfortunately, however, he uses the term *type* to mean *representation!*—which is presumably why he says elsewhere that he doesn't see "how domain and data type can [possibly] be the same" [1]. *Note:* As suggested earlier, the source of this terminological mix-up is probably SQL, which is thoroughly confused in this whole area—my REAL example above notwithstanding.

However, the writer also gives an extensive example that suggests that he does *not* properly understand the type *vs.* representation distinction after all (and I know from experience that he's not alone in this regard):

> I want to represent [*sic*] temperatures. Degrees Kelvin is one possible scale. I could use Celsius or Fahrenheit instead; they all use numeric values. Or I could use the scale ('hot,' 'warm,' 'cool,' 'cold'); the data type is character string. What is the right choice? [Given a certain application area,] I will probably prefer Kelvin because it is expressed with a numeric data type. I can use arithmetic operators with numeric data types, and I will need to do calculations. [But] you cannot add temperatures . . .

I have two major observations on this example. The first has to do with the type *vs.* representation distinction and is fundamental. The second is not fundamental but has to do with the question of good type design.

1. The data type is *not* character string for "the scale ('hot,' 'warm,' 'cool,' 'cold')"; the *representation* is character string. We're not going to perform string operations, such as substring or concatenate, on temperatures! Likewise, it's not the data type, it's the *representation,* that's numeric for the Kelvin and Celsius and Fahrenheit designs; as the writer himself points out, we're not going to add temperatures.

   No: The operations we're going to perform on temperatures are, precisely, the operations that are defined for the temperature *type*—whatever those might be.

2. The author also asks, rhetorically, which of the various designs he mentions is the right one. Presumably he's saying we could have a domain called, say, K_TEMP, whose values are measurements on the Kelvin scale; or a domain called, say, C_TEMP, whose values are measurements on the Celsius scale; or several other analogous possibilities.

   Personally, I think *none* of these proposals is the best choice. Rather, I would have a single "temperature" domain, with operators to expose temperature values as "number of degrees Kelvin," "number of degrees Celsius," "number of degrees Fahrenheit"—possibly even as the strings "hot," "warm," and so on, if desired. One advantage of this design is that it avoids the need for explicit conversion operators from one scale to another (all such conversions would be completely under the covers). Another is that it affords a greater degree of data independence—we can change the representation from, say, Kelvin to Fahrenheit with complete logical impunity.

LENGTHS AGAIN

Elsewhere, the same writer returns to the question of length as a type:

> Viewing each entity-attribute combination as a separate domain/data type seems unworkable to me. Take the number of entities in the universe that can have a length and make a type for it [*sic*], and you will see that there is just too much work involved. Then build an array to show all the possible allowed pairs of entities whose lengths can be multiplied together (real estate, but not people, and so on) and it [*sic*] is a very unnatural model. Why not carry it down to all particular entities and say a John-person-height cannot be multiplied by a Mary-person-height and so forth?

To these remarks I respond as follows:

1. First of all, I've never suggested that "each entity-attribute combination" should be "viewed as" (*defined on* would be more apt) "a separate domain/data type," and I don't see how a reading of any of my remarks on this subject could possibly be construed otherwise.

2. "Too much work involved"? It seems to me that the number of domains required in the writer's "lengths" example would almost certainly be *two*—LENGTH1 and LENGTH2, say. The multiplication operator would be defined for one of these domains but not for the other.

3. In any case, it's not a matter of considering the number of entities (*entity types* would be more accurate) "in the universe" that can have a length, but only the number of such entity types to be dealt with in *one particular database*. So even if the criticisms discussed in the previous two paragraphs were accurate, the problem wouldn't be nearly as intractable as the writer suggests.

CONCLUDING REMARKS

Let me end on a positive note. The same writer does make one point on which—I think—we are partly in agreement: He suggests that it might be possible to express a given calculation in two distinct but equivalent ways, one involving an explicit multiplication of two weights and the other not. So if we've "disallowed the operation weight times weight at the data type level," as he puts it, one of these two distinct but equivalent expressions might be legal and the other not.

I agree this is a valid concern (at least in general, though I'm not sure it's valid in the case of weights in particular). I've pointed out elsewhere [4] that, for example, if we can't add two dates together, we obviously can't go on to divide that sum by two to obtain the date midway between the given ones—yet this latter would be a useful and valid thing to do. (This criticism applies to SQL, incidentally [5].) But the moral isn't that types should simply "inherit" operations from their representations (which is what the writer suggests), but rather that data type definition needs to be done carefully. What's more, this moral applies at least as much to builtin types as it does to user-defined ones.

ACKNOWLEDGMENTS

I'm grateful to Hugh Darwen for his helpful comments on an earlier draft of this paper.

REFERENCES

1. All quotes in this paper are taken (unless otherwise noted) from an exchange between Joe Celko and myself that originally appeared in the magazine *DBMS*. The exchange began in Celko's *SQL Explorer* column in *DBMS 8,* No. 8, July 1995, and continued in the letters column in *DBMS 8,* Nos. 10–12 (October–December 1995), and *9,* No. 1 (January 1996).

2. Luca Cardelli and Peter Wegner: "On Understanding Types, Data Abstraction, and Polymorphism," *ACM Comp. Surv. 17,* No. 4 (December 1985).

3. Hugh Darwen and C. J. Date: "The Third Manifesto," *ACM SIGMOD Record 24,* No. 1 (March 1995). See also the book-length version *Foundation for Object/ Relational Databases: The Third Manifesto.* Reading, Mass.: Addison-Wesley (1998).

4. C. J. Date: "Defining Data Types in a Database Language," in *Relational Database Writings 1985–1989.* Reading, Mass.: Addison-Wesley (1990).

5. C. J. Date: "Dates and Times in the SQL Standard," *Database Programming & Design 10,* Nos. 2–3 (February–March 1997). See also C. J. Date and Hugh Darwen: *A Guide to the SQL Standard* (4th edition). Reading, Mass.: Addison-Wesley (1997).

6. C. J. Date: "SQL Domains Aren't Domains!" (Installment 38 in Part 1 of the present book).

THE PROBLEM OF MISSING INFORMATION

INTRODUCTION

Part III of this book's predecessor, *Relational Database Writings 1991–1994*, was also entitled "The Problem of Missing Information," and I think I had better repeat what I said there:

(*Begin quote*)

Part IV of this book's predecessor, *Relational Database Writings 1989–1991*, was also entitled "The Problem of Missing Information," and I think I had better repeat what I said there:

> *[This part of the book] addresses, once again, the subject of missing information. This topic has already been discussed in two papers in the first book in this series and three in the second; indeed, in that second book I wrote that I was "a little embarrassed to be dredging up [this] hackneyed topic . . . yet again"—but here we go once more, with* five *papers this time. The topic is endless, it seems.*

Well, at least it's only two papers this time . . .

(*End quote*)

Well, I'm afraid it's three papers this time, and one of those (by David McGoveran) is in four parts.

Nothing from Nothing (Part 1 of 4): What's Logic Got to Do With It?

Success of relational database is endangered by
a misunderstanding of its true foundation—
the ageless logic behind the relational model

ABSTRACT

This article is Part 1 of a four-part series. The series as a whole addresses a crisis (and a *scandal*) in the relational model: namely, the use of many-valued logic as a mechanism for handling "missing information." This first part is essentially a tutorial on logic for database practitioners; it lays the required foundation for Parts 2–4 by defining and explaining, in database terms, some important concepts in formal logic.

Originally published in *Database Programming & Design 6,* No. 12, December 1993 (the subtitle was contributed by *DBP&D*). Copyright © 1993–1998, Alternative Technologies. All rights reserved. Reprinted by permission of David McGoveran.

COMMENTS ON REPUBLICATION

The arguments for rejecting many-valued logic as a basis for dealing with "missing information" in databases are much deeper than are often supposed—though the implications and ramifications of those arguments are important and (for the most part) intuitively fairly obvious.* David McGoveran has thought about these issues more deeply than most database professionals, and his thoughts on the subject deserve close attention and very careful consideration. In this four-part series, he brings the focus of a trained logician *and* an "in the trenches" database practitioner to bear on the question.

Perhaps I should add that in some respects, the articles that follow might be thought a little "difficult." I've read the whole series myself several times now; it's certainly comprehensive, and I can vouch for the fact that it certainly does repay repeated rereading. To be frank, however, I'm still not sure I've grasped every last detail (which is, perhaps, a coward's way of saying that specific questions on the content are best directed to David himself in the first instance). I should mention also that—along with certain other writings by Hugh Darwen and myself—these articles of David's led to a certain amount of controversy in the literature (see in particular Chapters 9 and 10 of the present book).

Note: Despite this book's overall title, this first article in David's series actually appeared at the end of 1993.

INTRODUCTION

The relational model might not be dead, but it suffers from incapacitating wounds at the hands of DBMS vendors, standards and benchmark committees (not necessarily distinct from vendors), and certain "experts" who insist on explaining what they never bothered to understand. Of course, not all the blame can be laid on these innocents; despite the genius of many of his contributions, Codd himself must take some responsibility for the confusion that surrounds certain issues, especially those having to do with the use of many-valued logics.

As noted in the abstract, this article is Part 1 of a four-part series. The series as a whole addresses a crisis (and a *scandal*) in the relational model: namely, the use of many-valued logic as a mechanism for handling missing information. Before embarking on our journey into the world of many-valued

---

*The reason we often put the phrase "missing information" in quotes is explained in Installment 51 in Part I of the present book (in fact, it would probably be no bad thing *always* to put that phrase in quotes).

logics (and their attendant problems), however, it is necessary to consider exactly what a *logical system* is and how such systems relate to the question of DBMS implementation. The goal of Part 1, therefore, is to provide a brief tutorial on such matters and thereby to lay the necessary logical foundation for the remaining parts.

Before I start on that tutorial, let me say a brief word regarding the other three parts. *Part 2* will use the concepts introduced and defined in Part 1 to explain why many-valued logics are not appropriate for practical database use. *Part 3* will then go on to examine the pragmatic motivations that impel database designers to use nulls* or other indicators of missing information. These discussions will lead us to a conundrum: If many-valued logics are inappropriate for handling missing information, yet database designers have legitimate reasons for wanting to represent such missing information, what can we use in place of many-valued logic? Part 3 sets the stage for, and *Part 4* provides, a comprehensive answer to this question, with practical solutions for the most common situations in which nulls appear in current database implementations.

The articles are neither as formal nor as complete as I would like them to be. There are known issues I must pass over due to space limitations, and I am sure there are formal issues and developments of which I am unaware. Nonetheless, I have tried to assure myself (through extensive research and study) that the key issues are discussed accurately and that the reader will be prepared to understand the essential problems, discussed in Part 2, that arise from real-world database use of many-valued logics. However, I do suggest that you read this first article several times if you find it necessary; the concepts are difficult, so be patient, and read carefully and slowly.

DBMS GOALS

The overall purpose of a DBMS is to provide sharable, reusable, and efficient services for the definition, capture, organization, and manipulation of data. The DBMS should carry out this function in such a manner as to ensure the integrity of the data, regardless of user actions or system failures. An additional goal drives much of what differentiates an RDBMS (relational DBMS) from

---

*By "null" here I mean an argument placeholder—not a value—that, typically, forces the applicable relation predicate to be neither *true* nor *false* (SQL's NULL construct is a particularly bad implementation of such a placeholder). Note that nulls are distinct from the *unknown* truth value and can be of various kinds ("not applicable," "applicable but unknown," and so on). *Note:* See the section "Predicate Calculus" for an explanation of *arguments,* the section "Implementation" for an explanation of *relation predicates,* and Part 2 of this series for an explanation of *unknown truth values.*

other DBMSs: Changes to the data should not require changes to applications and *vice versa*. Adherence to this goal reduces the amount of code that must be written for a given application and reduces application maintenance. Curiously, however, this goal is often forgotten, although it has had a strong impact on the features needed in an RDBMS.

If applications are to be independent of data organization and access methods, the data definition and manipulation language must be declarative (sometimes called "nonprocedural"). Otherwise, a change to data organization or access methods, such as might be required as the database grows or is tuned for performance, will require a compensating change in applications. In addition, much of the data access code found in structured applications involves sorting and selecting data, typically using numerous control loops. If this code can be moved out of individual applications and shared by all applications, obvious gains can be obtained with respect to maintenance and performance optimization. Of course, if application developers have to choose from many data access routines, the gains will not be very great. For example, having one data access routine for each data structure would defeat the purpose.

The foregoing discussion implies that we should try to minimize the number of distinct data access routines, at least as seen by applications. In other words, we need a special *language* (the "data sublanguage" or "query language"), one that uses the smallest number of operations. At odds with the "smallest number of operations" goal, however, is the requirement that the language be capable of expressing every possible request for the intended set of applications (including *ad hoc* queries, unforeseen applications, and so forth). This latter requirement is known formally as **expressive completeness**.

Also at odds with the idea of minimizing the number of data access routines is the fact that the most efficient method of access *does* depend on physical data organization. So the question is: How can we map the few data access routines seen by the user to the possibly many routines existing under the covers, each one optimized for some particular physical data organization and some particular type of data? The answer is, of course, *automatic data access code optimization*. Such optimization requires knowledge of the physical organization of the data—and if the database is changing rapidly, that knowledge must be up to the minute. So where in the structure of a business system is this information available? Where should shared data access code be maintained, and where should this optimization take place? The obvious answer to all of these questions is: "In the DBMS."

This line of argument leads us to a fundamental problem: What algorithms should the DBMS optimizer (the code that performs data access optimization) use? The techniques used by compilers for optimization of conventional procedural code are comparatively straightforward—in the sense that, for the most part, they do not alter the algorithm as coded by the application developer—and are therefore inappropriate for the task at hand. What we need is a different kind of optimization, one that substitutes an equivalent but more efficient algorithm (a data "access method") for a standard data access routine. This difference implies that the optimizer must be able to identify algorithm equivalences (and be able to evaluate the relative cost of available algorithms); in particular, therefore, it must have *provably correct rules* by which it can determine such algorithm equivalences.

The foregoing considerations lead us inevitably to one conclusion: **The query language must be an implementation of a formal logical system.** In order to see what is possible in this connection, we need to take a brief look at the components and properties of formal logical systems in general.

FORMAL LOGICAL SYSTEMS

I will begin with some definitions, which will be used extensively as we proceed. A **logical system** consists of four types of objects:

- A **vocabulary**—i.e., a collection of symbols, used to represent truth-valued variables (e.g., P, Q, x), grouping indicators (e.g., "(", ")", "{", "}"), truth values (e.g., T for *true* and F for *false*), and connectives (e.g., OR, AND, NOT).

- A collection of **formation rules**—i.e., rules for governing the creation of **well-formed formulas** (*wffs*, pronounced "wiffs").

- A collection of **axioms**—i.e., an initially given set of wffs, each of which is guaranteed to be *true*. Ideally, the axioms should all be *independent* (that is, it should not be possible to prove any given axiom from the others).

- A collection of **rules of inference** (also called *deductions*)—i.e., rules by which a new wff can be derived from existing wffs. If the given wffs are *true* then the new one is *true* also and is called a **theorem**. A finite sequence of wffs, each of which is either an axiom or can be inferred from an earlier wff in the sequence via a rule of inference, is called a **proof;** to be more specific, it is a proof of the final wff in the sequence.

For example, SQL (without nulls!) can be regarded—loosely speaking—as a formal logical system. Refer to Fig. 1.

It is important to understand that the definition of a logical system is meant to be applied *in a purely mechanical fashion;* that is, the process of determining whether a given object belongs to the vocabulary, or a given expression is a wff, or a given wff is an axiom, cannot be based on judgment or on the outcome of some random event. Determining whether or not a rule of inference has been properly applied must also be purely mechanical.

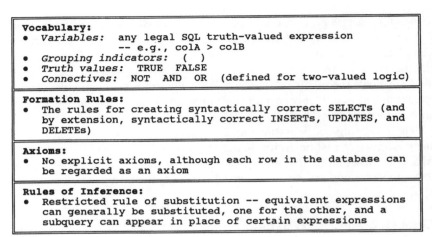

Vocabulary:
- *Variables:* any legal SQL truth-valued expression
  -- e.g., colA > colB
- *Grouping indicators:* ( )
- *Truth values:* TRUE FALSE
- *Connectives:* NOT AND OR (defined for two-valued logic)

Formation Rules:
- The rules for creating syntactically correct SELECTs (and by extension, syntactically correct INSERTs, UPDATES, and DELETEs)

Axioms:
- No explicit axioms, although each row in the database can be regarded as an axiom

Rules of Inference:
- Restricted rule of substitution -- equivalent expressions can generally be substituted, one for the other, and a subquery can appear in place of certain expressions

Fig. 1   SQL (without nulls) as a logical system

The connectives are often defined in terms of **truth tables**. A truth table is a tabular representation of a formation rule, and possibly certain rules of inference, that together specify the truth value of the compound given the truth value of the components (see Fig. 2). We say that a set of connectives is *independent* if no connective in the set is such that its truth table can be expressed in terms of those for the other connectives in the set. For example, the SQL connectives AND, OR, and NOT together with the connective called *material implication* (truth table shown in Fig. 3) do not form an independent set, since material implication has the same truth table as (NOT P) OR Q (as the reader can show by substitution, using the truth tables for NOT and OR). In fact, AND, OR, and NOT also fail the test of independence (see the "Exercises" section at the end of this article).

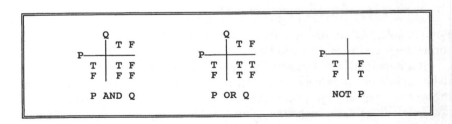

Fig. 2   Two-valued truth tables for SQL connectives

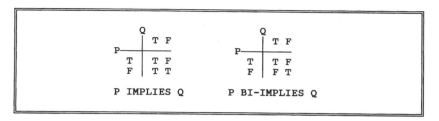

Fig. 3   Two-valued material implication and material equivalence
(these operators are not directly suported in SQL)

When the truth value of a wff can be evaluated in a purely mechanical manner from the truth values of its components, the logical system is said to be **truth functional**. This concept is very important, as we will soon see.

Each possible choice for the objects that make up a logical system results in a different system. Certain logical systems can be shown to be equivalent in some sense, but only in trivial cases (usually involving mere differences of notation—e.g., using Greek letters in place of English ones for symbols—or swapping the identification of axioms and theorems). Not all logical systems are equally powerful.

For a particular logical system, a rule that assigns a truth value to every truth-valued variable in a set of wffs is called an **interpretation** of that set of wffs. For example, given the set of wffs consisting of just P AND Q and P OR Q, one particular interpretation of that set consists of the assignment of *false* to P and *true* to Q.* Note that in some logical systems—including in particular the one supposedly underlying SQL—a wff might consist of a truth-valued expression *x* that contains variables *v* that are not themselves truth-valued, but whose assigned values imply the truth or falsity of the containing expression *x* (an example might be the SQL expression "colA > colB"). The interpretation of such a wff then includes the (nontruth) values assigned to those variables *v*.

An important further illustration is provided by the familiar example of relational tables (hereinafter simply "tables"). Any such table defines a truth-valued expression, in which each column represents a variable. Consider the suppliers table S from the familiar suppliers-and-parts database. That table has four columns: supplier number (S#), supplier name (SNAME), status (STATUS), and city (CITY). The corresponding truth-valued expression is:

---

*E.g., P might represent the proposition "Ill-defined many-valued logics are useful for relational databases" and Q the proposition "SQL is an ill-defined many-valued logic" (what inferences do you draw?). *Note:* The term *proposition* is explained in the next section.

"There exists a supplier with S# = w and SNAME = x and STATUS = y and CITY = z" (where w, x, y, and z are variables). A given row, say the row <'S1','Smith',20,'London'>, represents that truth-valued expression with particular values substituted for w, x, y, and z. And if substituting particular values for w, x, y, and z produces a row that does actually appear in the table, the expression with those substitutions is said to evaluate to *true;* otherwise, it is said to evaluate to *false.*

PROPOSITIONAL CALCULUS

Perhaps the most familiar logical system is the (two-valued) **propositional calculus**. This system treats each (necessarily truth-valued) variable as a **proposition*** that must be evaluated independently of all others, and each such variable can be assigned exactly one value in a proof. The connectives include the familiar AND, OR, and NOT, together with IMPLIES (implication) and BI-IMPLIES (equivalence); these latter two are defined in terms of the base connectives (AND, OR, and NOT) in a manner called *material implication* and *material equivalence,* respectively—see Fig. 3 again. (*Note:* I use BI-IMPLIES in place of the more usual EQUIVALENCE for reasons of readability and intuitive understanding.) Among the rules of inference are:

- The rule of *substitution*—e.g., given P IMPLIES Q and Q BI-IMPLIES R, we can infer that P IMPLIES R;
- The rule of *modus ponens*—i.e., given P and P IMPLIES Q, we can infer Q (in particular, if the first two of these wffs are *true,* then the third is *true* as well).

Now, a logical system is generally intended for some practical use. For convenience, we will say that our understanding of the subject of that practical use (it might be accounting, for example) is **an informal theory** of that subject (consisting typically of some informal collection of rules, requirements, descriptions, etc.). The scope of the informal theory is sometimes called **the universe of discourse**. The practical use of a logical system is implemented by assigning meaning to the elements of the vocabulary. From this intended meaning, it should be possible to assign to each truth-valued variable an obvious truth value. The resulting interpretation is said to be **the intended interpretation**. For example, if we designed a database with an ACCOUNTS table, our intended interpretation of the column ACCOUNT# would be the set

---

*A proposition in logic is simply something that is either *true* or *false,* unequivocally. For example, "The sun is a star" and "The sun is a planet" are both propositions (the first of which evaluates to *true,* of course, and the second to *false*).

of permissible account numbers for the actual business; we would not intend users of the database to substitute PRODUCT# for ACCOUNT#, a substitution that would always make *false* the truth-valued expression that the ACCOUNTS table represents.

We try to set up a logical system in such a way that:

a. Any interpretation that makes all the axioms *true* also makes all the theorems *true*—the property of **correctness;**

b. All statements of the informal theory can be expressed in the system—the property of **expressive completeness;** and

c. Any truth expressible in the system is provable—the property of **deductive completeness.**

In other words, we intend that the set of true expressions of the system, under any interpretation that makes the axioms true, will be identical to the set of provable expressions (i.e., theorems). A system is said to be **truth functionally complete** if, given a set of connectives defined by truth tables, one can express all possible truth tables by various combinations of the given truth tables. As will be seen, this property is extremely important: It implies that all possible connectives can be expressed via suitable combinations of the given ones.

When a logical system has more than two truth values, it is said to be *a many-valued logic*. Generally, at least one truth value is called *true* and another is called *false*, reflecting our commonly held understanding of those words. The meaning of the other values depends on the intended interpretation of the logical system. In order to understand better the role being played by those other values, logicians classify them as being "true-like," "false-like," or neither. A truth value is said to be **designated, anti-designated,** or **undesignated,** according to whether it is treated as true-like, false-like, or neither. These subtleties are necessary for many-valued logics in which the notions of "degrees of truth" and "degrees of falsity" might be intended.

Within any logical system, a **tautology** is a wff that always evaluates to a true-like truth value. For example, according to our usual understanding of two-valued logic, P OR (NOT P) is a tautology because it is always *true,* regardless of whether P is *true* or *false*. Similarly, a **contradiction** is a wff that always evaluates to a false-like truth value. For example, according to our usual understanding of two-valued logic once again, P AND (NOT P) is a contradiction because it is always *false,* regardless of whether P is *true* or *false*. Note that the axioms of a logical system are tautologies under the intended interpretation.

In a *correct* logical system (i.e., one with the property of correctness), if every wff that is a theorem is also a tautology, logicians say the system is

consistent; that is, the theorems that are provable from the axioms are always tautologies. Otherwise, they say the system is **inconsistent.** *Note:* The logician's concepts of consistency and inconsistency are related to, but distinct from, our common notions of being consistent or inconsistent (i.e., contradictory). Logicians refer to those common notions as **negation** consistency and inconsistency, respectively.

If every tautology in a correct system is guaranteed to be provable, then (as already noted) we say the system is **deductively complete.** Further, we say that a system is deductively complete **in a strong sense** if there is no wff that can be added to its axiom set that would be independent of the other axioms. In fact, it can be shown that adding a new independent axiom to a system that is deductively complete in a strong sense will have the effect of making a previously consistent system inconsistent. We say that a system is **decidable** if there exists an algorithm by which it can be determined whether or not an arbitrary wff is a theorem.

To get back to the (two-valued) propositional calculus *per se:* It turns out that the propositional calculus is *deductively complete, negation consistent* (i.e., it is impossible for a wff and its negation both to be *true*), and *decidable.* Despite these positive properties, however, the propositional calculus is expressively weak. In particular, it is incapable of recognizing when two propositions share a common subject. Therefore, deductions that rely on such sharing must be performed outside of the intended interpretation. For example, the Greek Stoics recognized the problem with the following (invalid) argument, called *The Nobody:*

Premise: If someone is here, then he is not in Rhodes.

Premise: Someone is here.

Conclusion: Therefore it is not the case that someone is in Rhodes!

This line of reasoning would, of course, be valid if we replaced the word "someone" by the name of an individual, say "Ted." But the word "someone" is ambiguous: It is being used to refer to a specific individual for part of the time and to some nonspecific individual for the rest of the time. The propositional calculus cannot help us determine what is wrong here because it has no way of representing the concept of propositions that share a common subject.

PREDICATE CALCULUS

The **first-order predicate calculus** is an extension of the propositional calculus. It is intended (among other things) to help with the kind of reasoning that does rely on sharing subjects across propositions. It addresses the problem by introducing the notion of **arguments**[*] (formally called "predicate variables"), much as algebra extends arithmetic by introducing variables. An argument is interpreted by assigning it a particular value from a domain of possible values. (We have already seen examples of such arguments in our discussion of the truth-valued expressions that are represented by relational tables.) A **predicate** is a statement that the argument possesses a certain property; a predicate without uninterpreted arguments performs essentially the same function as a proposition, and is truth-valued. A predicate can have zero or more arguments, and arguments can be shared among numerous predicates. Note that all occurrences of an argument must uniformly take on the same value for any given interpretation. Thus, in the compound predicate "x is red AND x is angry," it is not permissible to replace the first x with "Joe" and the second with "Jim."

Given arguments, it is possible to introduce **quantifiers**. Two quantifiers of the first-order predicate calculus are particularly important: the *existential* (a claim that at least one value of the argument has the specified properties) and the *universal* (a claim that all values of the argument have the specified properties). The existential quantifier EXISTS x can be thought of (but only informally) as the propositional connective OR iterated over the domain of the argument x and the truth value *false*. Similarly, the universal quantifier FORALL x can be thought of (but again only informally) as the propositional connective AND iterated over the domain of the argument x and the truth value *true*.

Now, the first-order predicate calculus, unlike the propositional calculus, is capable of handling infinite domains, such as the domain of natural numbers. This fact accounts for the "but only informally" qualifications in the foregoing paragraph: Any attempt to write an algorithm for EXISTS over an infinite domain must fail, since the evaluation might never terminate (we might never find the one value that makes the predicate *true*); likewise, any attempt to write an algorithm for FORALL over an infinite domain must also fail, since again the evaluation might never terminate (we might never find the one value that makes the predicate *false*). It is therefore important to understand that the predicate calculus EXISTS and FORALL quantifiers are *not* (in general) identical to simple iterated propositional OR and AND, respectively. The substitution is permissible only when the number of possible values each quantified argument can take is guaranteed to be finite.

The first-order predicate calculus is *deductively complete* (though not in the strong sense) and *consistent*. It is not decidable; i.e., there is no algorithm for determining whether an arbitrary wff is a first-order predicate calculus theorem or not. However, if a restricted version of the first-order predicate

---

[*]It might help to point out that the computer science term would be *parameters,* not arguments ("arguments" then being the values substituted for such parameters). In Chapter 1, Hugh Darwen referred to them as *placeholders.*

calculus is constructed in which (a) the number of arguments permitted in any expression is always finite and (b) the domains for those arguments are also finite, then that restricted (finite) version is indeed *decidable*. Note that imposing these restrictions changes the intended meaning of the quantifiers and reduces certain rules of inference to the corresponding rules for the *propositional* calculus. This fact will be important in the discussion that follows. Thus, although we often say the relational model is built on the first-order predicate calculus, in practice any implementation of that model will be more like the finite version described here (i.e., at any given point in time, any real database will have a finite number of tables, columns, domains, actual values, and so on).

IMPLEMENTATION

When we design a relational database, we define a set of predicates (the defining predicates for tables), which we call **relation predicates**. A permissible row in a table is one that has values that satisfy the appropriate domain constraints and the appropriate relation predicate. Each permissible row in these tables is taken to represent a true instance of the relation predicate. The resulting set of true propositions can be understood as the axioms of the system (in effect, we assert that the rows represent the true instances of the relation predicates; together, they constitute the intended interpretation of the system).

   Normalization is a process that is meant to remove redundancy given the relational operations; that is, the purpose of the normalization process is to help ensure that no relation predicate actually consists of a combination of several independent relation predicates. It thus contributes to (but does not guarantee) the independence of the axiom set. The attributes of a table can be understood as arguments, which are functions over the defining domains.

   By establishing a set of database domains (with their domain constraints), we effectively constrain the universe of discourse. Domains, along with column and table constraints, are used to implement the relation predicate for each table. When we insert a row into a table, we are implicitly claiming that substituting values from that row for the appropriate arguments in that table's relation predicate results in a "fact" (i.e., a true proposition). We can regard each such row as a premise from which conclusions can be drawn using the formal axioms and rules of inference. If a row could exist in a given table (i.e., the values are legal and would otherwise satisfy the relation predicate) but actually does not, the meaning of the fact that it does not depends on whether we take a closed or open world interpretation.

   The *closed world* interpretation states that the proposition corresponding to a missing row is *false;* the *open world* interpretation states that it is either *false* or *unknown*. For example, suppose we have a table MANAGERS, with columns EMP# and MGR# and relation predicate " The manager of employee

EMP# is employee MGR#." Suppose too that the row <'E2,' 'E1'> does not appear in the table. The closed world interpretation says we can assume that the statement "The manager of employee E2 is employee E1" is *false*. By contrast, the open world interpretation says we can assume only that that same statement is either *false* or *unknown*. For the remainder of this article I will assume the closed world interpretation.

When you write a query, you are attempting to write a wff (a predicate in its own right). It is the job of the parser to verify that the query you write is a wff—i.e., that it is syntactically correct. The optimizer can be understood as using the rules of inference, various axioms, and various provable theorems to produce a set of equivalent wffs, each of which uses only operations having a physical access method associated with them. Each of the rows returned by the DBMS represents a tuple of values that, on proper substitution into the predicate, result in propositions that evaluate to *true* in the logical system. The result set is a provable theorem of the system (see Fig. 4). The important point to

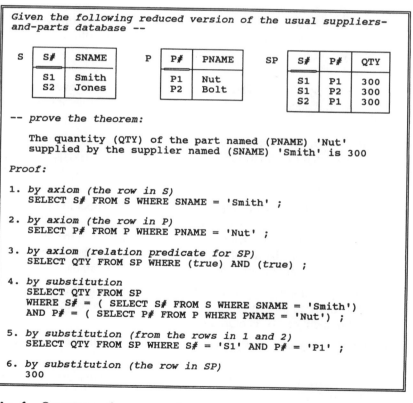

Fig. 4   Querying as theorem proving

remember is this: Whenever you execute a series of statements in a transaction or application, issue a sequence of decision support queries, or embed a subquery in a query (or decompose it into a sequence of queries), you are using the axioms and rules of inference of the logical system to prove theorems!

OBJECTIVES

From the foregoing discussions, it should be clear that certain properties are desirable of any logical system on which a DBMS is based. In particular, the DBMS should be a logical system that is familiar, uniformly interpretable, truth functional, truth functionally complete, expressively complete, deductively complete, consistent, and (ideally) decidable. These objectives can be explained intuitively as follows:

- *Familiar:* The common understanding of the truth values, connectives, rules of inference, and accepted tautologies should apply. That is, the user should not have to learn an unfamiliar or counterintuitive logical system, one that contains surprising theorems and tautologies or denies commonly held rules of inference (and thereby leads to the likelihood of user error).

- *Uniformly interpretable:* The intended interpretation of every symbol, truth value, and query should be unambiguous, irrespective of the state of the database.

- *Truth functional:* The evaluation of a query (i.e., a wff) can proceed mechanically from the evaluation of its components. Similarly, queries of arbitrary complexity can be written and understood from an understanding of the connectives alone.

- *Truth functionally complete:* The set of initially given operations and connectives in the query language suffice to express any logical connective definable via a truth table. Thus, for every possible fact in the universe of discourse, there will be a truth-valued expression to determine whether that fact is represented in or can be derived from the database.

- *Expressively complete:* All queries that are meaningful in the context of the application can be expressed, and all relevant facts about the application environment can be captured in the database.

- *Deductively complete:* Every fact represented by the database, either implicitly or explicitly, can be obtained via a query.

- *Consistent:* The result of every query represents facts that can be inferred from the database.

■ *Decidable:* Although not strictly required, a decidable and consistent system would have the advantage that a query could be checked via an algorithm to determine whether it were: (a) a tautology (in which case every row would satisfy the query); (b) a contradiction (in which case no rows would satisfy the query); or (c) neither.

LOGIC AND THE DATABASE

I hope this article will have made the relationship between formal logic and databases a little clearer for database practitioners. I have stated the goals that make it advantageous to use a logical system as the basis for database management, and I have presented the desirable properties of that logical system in database terms. At the very least, I would hope that database professionals will now be able to use some of these logical concepts in evaluating the strengths and weaknesses of a given RDBMS. While errors of implementation are sometimes to blame, the causes of many performance, integrity, and maintenance problems lie in much more serious design flaws involving failure to capitalize on the logical foundation of relational theory. With a little practice, logical concepts will prove useful in identifying such database and application design problems. You can start by insisting that DBMS vendors meet the logical objectives outlined in this article.

In Part 2 of this series, I will examine many-valued logics in light of those objectives. We will find those logics lacking, and therefore unsuitable for representing and manipulating "missing information." In Part 3, I will discuss what seem to me to be the main reasons people want to include nulls in the database. Certain of those reasons do have some degree of validity; this fact, along with the fact that many-valued logic is inappropriate, leaves us with a dilemma. That dilemma will be resolved in Part 4.

EXERCISES

1. Using the truth tables for AND, OR, NOT, and material implication (IMPLIES), give the truth tables for the following wffs:

   a. `NOT (P AND (NOT P))`

   b. `NOT (P AND Q)`

   c. `(NOT P) OR (NOT Q)`

   d. `(NOT Q) IMPLIES (NOT P)`

2. Show that the truth table for (NOT P) OR Q is the same as that for IMPLIES in Fig. 3.

3. Show that AND, OR, and NOT are not independent.
4. Show that the following wff is a tautology:

    ```
    ((NOT P) AND (P OR Q)) IMPLIES Q
    ```

5. Show that the following wff is a contradiction:

    ```
    (P IMPLIES Q) IMPLIES (NOT ((NOT Q) IMPLIES (NOT P)))
    ```

6. Would a logical system with the formulas in Exercises 3 and 4 as axioms be consistent? Explain your answer.
7. State an interpretation for propositional calculus, restricted to the variables P and Q.
8. For the database of Fig. 4, prove the following theorem:

    ```
    The supplier named (SNAME) 'Smith' supplies parts named
    (PNAME) 'Nut' and 'Bolt'.
    ```

ACKNOWLEDGMENTS

I would like to thank Chris Date, Hugh Darwen, and Ron Fagin for their helpful comments and criticisms. I would also like to apologize to Billy Preston and Tina Turner for the abuse of their song titles.

BIBLIOGRAPHY

Note: The books and papers listed below are not referenced in the body of this article. They are listed here as suggestions for background reading.

1. E. F. Codd: "A Relational Model of Data for Large Shared Data Banks," *CACM 13*, No. 6 (June 1970). Republished in "Milestones of Research," *CACM 26*, No. 1 (January 1982).
2. E. F. Codd: "Extending the Database Relational Model to Capture More Meaning," *ACM TODS 4*, No. 4 (December 1979).
3. H. Delong: *A Profile of Mathematical Logic*. Reading, Mass.: Addison-Wesley (1970).
4. G. Massey: *Understanding Symbolic Logic*. Harper & Row (1970).
5. Patrick Suppes: *Introduction to Logic*. Princeton, N.J.: Van Nostrand (1957).

CHAPTER **6**

Nothing from Nothing (Part 2 of 4) Classical Logic: Nothing Compares 2 U

If the true power of the relational model is its foundation in classical logic, why do RDBMSs use multivalued logic—and betray that strength?

ABSTRACT

Part 2 of this four-part series classifies many-valued logics into three categories—*fragments, extensions,* and *deviants*—and explains how certain intrinsic properties in each case render logics in that category unsuitable as a foundation for a DBMS. It also offers a few critical comments on Codd's and SQL's many-valued logics in particular.

COMMENTS ON REPUBLICATION

See the "Comments on Republication" in the previous chapter.

Originally published in *Database Programming & Design 7,* No. 1, January 1994 (the subtitle was contributed by *DBP&D*). Copyright © 1993–1998, Alternative Technologies. All rights reserved. Reprinted by permission of David McGoveran.

INTRODUCTION

In Part 1 of this series, I provided a brief tutorial on logic for database practitioners. Having thus laid the necessary foundation and defined some key terminology, I can now explain why the current handling of "missing information" via many-valued logic is misguided. Although there are numerous systems of many-valued logic, it is my central thesis that *none* of them is suited to the needs of a DBMS. By contrast, the (two-valued) propositional logic does meet all of the objectives established in Part 1 (repeated for convenience in the sidebar, opposite).

For convenience, I also repeat here from Part 1 the definition of a formal logical system. Such a system consists of four types of objects:

- A **vocabulary**—i.e., a collection of symbols, used to represent truth-valued variables (e.g., P, Q, x), grouping indicators (e.g., "(", ")", "{", "}"), truth values (e.g., T for *true* and F for *false*), and connectives (e.g., OR, AND, NOT).

- A collection of **formation rules**—i.e., rules for governing the creation of **well-formed formulas** (*wffs*, pronounced "wiffs").

- A collection of **axioms**—i.e., an initially given set of wffs, each of which is guaranteed to be *true*. Ideally, the axioms should all be *independent* (that is, it should not be possible to prove any given axiom from the others).

- A collection of **rules of inference** (also called *deductions*)—i.e., rules by which a new wff can be derived from existing wffs. If the given wffs are *true* then the new one is *true* also and is called a **theorem.** A finite sequence of wffs, each of which is either an axiom or can be inferred from an earlier wff in the sequence via a rule of inference, is called a **proof;** to be more specific, it is a proof of the final wff in the sequence.

For example, SQL (without nulls!) can be regarded—loosely speaking—as a formal logical system.

I remind you too that it is important to understand that the definition of a logical system is meant to be applied *in a purely mechanical fashion;* that is, the process of determining whether a given object belongs to the vocabulary, or a given expression is a wff, or a given wff is an axiom, cannot be based on judgment or on the outcome of some random event. Determining whether or not a rule of inference has been properly applied must also be purely mechanical.

OBJECTIVES

A DBMS should be a logical system that is familiar, uniformly interpretable, truth functional, truth functionally complete, expressively complete, deductively complete, consistent, and (ideally) decidable. These objectives can be explained intuitively as follows:

- *Familiar:* The common understanding of the truth values, connectives, rules of inference, and accepted tautologies should apply. That is, the user should not have to learn an unfamiliar or counterintuitive logical system, one that contains surprising theorems and tautologies or denies commonly held rules of inference (and thereby leads to the likelihood of user error).

- *Uniformly interpretable:* The intended interpretation of every symbol, truth value, and query should be unambiguous, irrespective of the state of the database.

- *Truth functional:* The evaluation of a query (i.e., a wff) can proceed mechanically from the evaluation of its components. Similarly, queries of arbitrary complexity can be written and understood from an understanding of the connectives alone.

- *Truth functionally complete:* The set of initially given operations and connectives in the query language suffice to express any logical connective definable via a truth table. Thus, for every possible fact in the universe of discourse, there will be a truth-valued expression to determine whether that fact is represented in or can be derived from the database.

- *Expressively complete:* All queries that are meaningful in the context of the application can be expressed, and all relevant facts about the application environment can be captured in the database.

- *Deductively complete:* Every fact represented by the database, either implicitly or explicitly, can be obtained via a query.

- *Consistent:* The result of every query represents facts that can be inferred from the database.

- *Decidable:* Although not strictly required, a decidable and consistent system would have the advantage that a query could be checked via an algorithm to determine whether it were: (a) a tautology (in which case every row would satisfy the query); (b) a contradiction (in which case no rows would satisfy the query); or (c) neither.

In order to support my thesis, I need to show that many-valued logics do not and cannot meet all of these objectives. For simplicity, I will limit my attention to many-valued propositional logics specifically. Such a simplification is legitimate for three reasons:

- First, any many-valued predicate logic can be understood as a generalization of a corresponding many-valued propositional logic; hence, certain problems with the propositional logic version carry over to the predicate logic version.

- Second, as pointed out (though not much stressed) in Part 1, real databases are finite. At worst, therefore, only a very limited version of the first order predicate calculus need be used, one with a finite number of finite domains. In other words, real DBMSs support only (a) a finite number of types of variables and a finite number of possible values for each of those types and (b) well-formed formulas (wffs) of some finite maximum length. As a result, the number of propositions that can be expressed against a real database is necessarily finite (as everyone knows who has ever written a query that the DBMS found too big to parse).

- Third, the formal investigation of many-valued predicate logic is immature anyway (there are comparatively few such investigations in the literature).

Whereas Date has written extensively about problems associated with Codd's and SQL's many-valued logics, the discussion that follows is more general, for the most part. In particular, I will show that Codd's so-called four-valued logic and (worse) SQL's "three-valuedness" are both ill defined; as a result, I cannot give formal arguments against any specific formal flaws they might possess! My arguments are forced to be more general and apply to formal and informal problems that arise in using *any* many-valued logic for database work.

LEAVING NOTHING

First I should explain how distinct many-valued logics are similar and how they differ. Most three-valued systems are identical in their definitions of AND, OR, and NOT; typically, however, they differ with respect to (a) the truth table definitions for other connectives, (b) which connectives they take as primitive, and (c) which rules of inference apply.

For purposes of informal explanation, a three-way classification of propositional many-valued logics will be useful, allowing us to take a divide-and-conquer approach in our investigation. The classification scheme is based on the following **reduction procedure:**

Permit the components of every wff in the logic to take only *true* or *false* as truth values and compare the resulting logical system to conventional propositional logic.

The classes, slightly nonstandard and informal, are as follows:

1. *Fragment:* A many-valued logic will be classified as a **fragment** if, under the reduction procedure, it reduces to a fragment of the propositional logic (that is, some propositional logic connectives or rules of inference are missing, or some propositional logic theorems or tautologies no longer hold, in the reduced version).

2. *Extension:* A many-valued logic will be classified as an **extension** if it reduces to the propositional logic under the reduction procedure.

3. *Deviant:* A many-valued logic will be classified as a **deviant** if it is so different from the propositional logic that it cannot be understood as either an extension or a fragment. A number of well known (and often referenced) many-valued logics fall into this category; they are entirely different from the conventional propositional logic and thus certainly do not satisfy our familiarity objective. Furthermore, they are either not truth functionally complete or have semantics that are difficult to understand, as we will see later in this article.

It is important to understand that the foregoing classification is exhaustive—*all* many-valued logics fall into one or other of the three classes. I now proceed to examine each class in turn.

FRAGMENTS

Fragments are generally not truth functionally complete; in addition, they generally require that users understand which portions of the propositional logic do not apply. This fact means that fragments necessarily violate the familiarity objective. To see why this is so, we consider a special one-place connective called *the Slupecki T-function.* This operator converts every possible truth value to some particular truth value that is neither true-like nor false-like (that is, to *unknown,* if the logic is three-valued). A many-valued logic must include such a connective in order to be truth functionally complete. Thus, if the logic does not include this connective, it is not truth functionally complete; however, if we then add the connective to such a logic, the effect is to convert the fragment into an extension at best, or possibly into a deviant.

In any case, a meaningful interpretation of the T-function for database use is hard to imagine; this fact alone should be sufficient to show that it is unreasonable to expect a many-valued logic to meet our needs. That is, the fact that the T-function must be included, and the importance of certain tautologies implied by it, together mean that the logical system clearly violates the familiarity objective.

EXTENSIONS

The familiarity objective requires that the truth tables for the many-valued propositional connectives of an extension reduce to those for the two-valued propositional logic under the reduction procedure (see Fig. 1). Clearly, this property is highly desirable in a logic used by a DBMS. However, a many-valued logic can reduce to classical propositional logic if and only if it is not truth functionally complete! Indeed, this fact is easy to see:

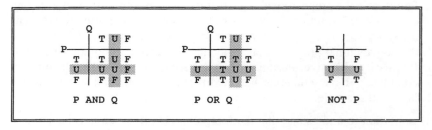

Fig. 1   The three-valued truth tables for AND, OR, and NOT reduce to their two-valued counterparts if shaded portions are removed

- By definition, every connective in a truth functionally complete logical system must be expressible, either directly (as a primitive operator) or indirectly (by composing primitive connectives).
- In particular, the T-function must be so expressible.
- But the T-function has no counterpart in two-valued logics, even under the reduction procedure.

So if the logic is truth functionally complete it is not an extension, and if it is an extension it is not truth functionally complete. It follows that an extension *must* violate either the familiarity objective or the truth functional completeness objective.

EXTENSIONS AND DEVIANTS

The familiarity objective is actually more difficult to satisfy than the foregoing discussions might suggest. Extensions and deviants both violate the uniform interpretability objective. Under the reduction procedure, few many-valued logics preserve those tautologies and rules of inference most commonly relied upon by database users to reason about queries (see Fig. 2). (Of course, users might not realize how much they depend on those tautologies and rules!) There are two important implications:

```
Law of Detachment               P & (P → Q) → Q
Modus Tollendo Tollens          ¬Q & (P → Q) → ¬P
Modus Tollendo Ponens           ¬P & (P | Q) → Q
Law of Simplification           P & Q → P
Law of Adjunction               P & Q → P & Q
Law of Hypothetical Syllogism   (P → Q) & (Q → R) → (P → R)
Law of Exportation              (P & Q → R) → (P → (Q → R))
Law of Importation              (P → (Q → R)) → (P & Q → R)
Law of Absurdity                (P → Q & ¬Q) → ¬P
Law of Addition                 P → P | Q

Law of Double Negation          P → ¬¬P
Law of Contraposition           (P → Q) ↔ (¬Q → ¬P)
De Morgan's Laws                ¬(P | Q) → (¬P & ¬Q)
                                ¬(P & Q) → (¬P | ¬Q)
Commutative Laws                P & Q → Q & P
                                P | Q → Q | P
Law of Equivalence for
   Implication and Disjunction  (P → Q) ↔ (¬P | Q)
Law of Negation for Implication ¬(P → Q) ↔ P & ¬Q
Laws for Biconditional          (P ↔ Q) ↔ (P → Q) & (Q → P)
   Sentences                    (P ↔ Q) ↔ (P & Q) | (¬P & ¬Q)

Law of the Excluded Middle      P | ¬P
Law of Contradiction            ¬(P & ¬P)
```

```
┌──────────────────────────────────────────────────────────┐
│ ¬ means NOT (highest precedence)                           │
│ & and | mean AND and OR (medium precedence)                │
│ → and ↔ mean IMPLIES and BI-IMPLIES (lowest precedence)    │
└──────────────────────────────────────────────────────────┘
```

Fig. 2   Some useful tautologies of two-valued propositional logic (from reference [9])

- First, the violated propositional tautologies must never be used, either implicitly or explicitly, when working with a database using such a logic. Thus, extensions and deviant logics are less intuitive than the propositional logic, and, for practical purposes at least, are thus less deductively powerful as well.

- Second, the permissible rules of inference (used both by the user and the optimizer) must be sensitive both (a) to whether or not the database permits nulls and (b) to whether or not it actually contains nulls.

Let me elaborate on this latter point.

- If the database does not permit nulls, the familiar propositional logic can be used and the many-valued logic need never be learned. If it does permit nulls, however, the many-valued logic rules of inference must be used from the beginning. The meanings of query results are then definite so long as nulls do not actually appear in the database, and the uniform interpretability objective can be preserved.

- But if nulls do actually appear, all queries become indefinite in meaning—even if the nulls appear in tables not accessed in the query under consideration! (I exclude here the rather bizarre possibility that the table containing the null has no relationship whatsoever to the tables accessed.) One null, anywhere in the database, changes the meaning of all related tables, and thereby violates the uniform interpretability objective. Why? Because we can no longer think of the accessed tables as if they simply contain rows representing facts about the universe of discourse; instead, each row now represents a fact that has some relationship to information that is missing.

By way of example, consider the familiar suppliers-and-parts database (see Fig. 3). If the database could not contain the shaded row in table P, the results of all queries would have a definite and fairly intuitive meaning. But with that row permitted, the very meaning of both "parts" and "suppliers" changes! "Parts" are no longer things that are definitely located in a known city. And since "suppliers" are defined as supplying parts, by extension they are no longer suppliers of parts that are definitely located in a known city. Thus, even querying the suppliers table S—which contains no nulls—results in a fundamentally different kind of answer when the parts table P is permitted to contain nulls!

Now consider the distinction between the shaded row merely being permitted and actually appearing in the database. As we have just seen, the row being permitted changes the meaning of the entities represented by the tables; by contrast, the actual appearance of the row changes the meaning of query

S	S#	SNAME	STATUS	CITY
	S1	Smith	20	London
	S2	Jones	10	Paris

SP	S#	P#	QTY
	S1	P1	300
	S2	P1	300
	S2	P2	400

P	P#	PNAME	COLOR	WEIGHT	CITY
	P1	Nut	Red	12	London
	P2	Bolt	Green	17	\<null\>

Fig. 3   Troublesome rows in the suppliers-and-parts database

results—even when that row is deliberately excluded! For example, suppose we try to follow a "no nulls" discipline and so want to see only those suppliers "not affected by" the shaded row. To select those suppliers I must first presume the existence of a relationship to rows like the shaded one and then use that relationship to exclude affected suppliers. In SQL, I must issue a query something like the following:

```
SELECT *
FROM   S
EXCEPT (SELECT S.*
        FROM   S, SP, P
        WHERE  S.S# = SP.S#
        AND    SP.P# = P.P#
        AND    P.CITY IS NULL) ;
```

If the shaded row does not exist, this query gives suppliers who supply (if anything at all) parts that might or might not be definitely located in a known city. But if the shaded row does exist, it gives suppliers who definitely do not supply those parts that are indefinitely located! As strange as it seems, when a row like the shaded one actually appears in the database, the results to our "null avoiding" queries become more definite regarding the indefinite!

The reader might object that I have chosen a particular interpretation of null to illustrate these problems, but I invite consideration of other interpretations as an exercise. No matter what the interpretation, the net effect is that many-valued logic means that database designers, developers, and users must all learn a whole new way of thinking. The practical costs of this approach are hard to assess; certainly they do violence to the goals we set out to satisfy with an RDBMS.

What about the objective of truth functional completeness? Sometimes we can make a many-valued logic truth functionally complete by adding a new axiom or a new connective (e.g., the T-function mentioned earlier). But adding a new axiom or new connective has at least one of three undesirable consequences:

a. It leads to theorems that have no counterpart in two-valued logic; or

b. It makes the system inconsistent; or

c. It makes the system incomplete.

In fact, so long as the system does not contain certain types of undesirable theorems (i.e., ones having no propositional logic counterpart, thereby violating the familiarity objective), we can say, based on work by the logician Rose (see reference [6], page 166), that at least one of two consequences must result: Either the new axiom makes the system inconsistent, or the new axiom is a tautology of the propositional logic (i.e., it's something we intuitively thought was already true but actually wasn't).

- The first of these alternatives (inconsistency) is clearly undesirable—it means that every wff becomes a tautology, even ones that would otherwise be contradictions (in an inconsistent system, you can prove anything). Suppose an SQL SELECT were issued against a database managed by a DBMS based on such a system. Regardless of the predicate in the WHERE clause, that predicate would be treated as *true* for every row examined and would therefore never restrict the result set (i.e., every query would return all rows!).

- As for the second alternative (the new axiom is a tautology): In this case, the system cannot be an extension of the propositional logic (since an extension requires adding a many-valued tautology and results in an inconsistent system). Thus, it is either a fragment or a deviant and is subject to the problems discussed earlier for such many-valued logics.

MORE ROPE, PLEASE!

Suppose we are willing to violate the truth functional completeness objective, under the assumption that the theorems that cannot be expressed (owing to the unavailability of certain connectives) are, in some sense, "obscure." Perhaps we are even willing to give up on part of the familiarity objective, under the assumption that learning new tautologies and rules of inference is not an excessive task. Even so, a many-valued logic introduces further undesirable complexities, having to do with (among other things) the number of connectives, the number of meaning assignments for connectives, meanings of query results, arbitrariness in the number of truth values, loss of deductive power, and unusual or nonintuitive semantics. I will discuss each of these additional complexities in turn.

- *Number of connectives:* The number of connectives in a logic depends exponentially on the number (n, say) of permissible truth values and therefore grows rapidly with n. In the familiar two-valued logics, there are four one-place and 16 two-place connectives (see Fig. 4). For a three-valued logic, the corresponding figures are 27 and 19,683 respectively!— see reference [6], page 63. Fig. 5 shows the number of one- and two-place connectives for many-valued logics in general.

    Of course, even in the two-valued case we don't normally need to remember or use all of the connectives explicitly because a few suffice to express all the others. This fact gets at the essence of truth functional completeness. Likewise, not all possible connectives in a many-valued logic need be memorized if the primitive set is truth functionally complete. That primitive set can be very small [1].

```
      | T F            | T F            | T F            | T F
  T   | T T        T   | F F        T   | F T        T   | T F
  F   | T T        F   | F F        F   | F T        F   | T F

      | T F            | T F            | T F            | T F
  T   | F T        T   | T F        T   | T T        T   | T T
  F   | T T        F   | T T        F   | F T        F   | T F

      | T F            | T F            | T F            | T F
  T   | F F        T   | T T        T   | F T        T   | T F
  F   | T T        F   | F F        F   | T F        F   | F T

      | T F            | T F            | T F            | T F
  T   | T F        T   | F T        T   | F F        T   | F F
  F   | F F        F   | F F        F   | T F        F   | F T
```

Fig. 4   The 16 two-place connectives of two-valued logic

truth values	1-place connectives	2-place connectives
2	4	16
3	27	19,683
4	256	4,294,967,296
...	...	....
n	n^2	n^{n^2}

Fig. 5   Number of connectives *vs.* number of truth values

But if, as assumed, the system is not truth functionally complete, both users and the optimizer must be prepared to use and understand all 27 one-place and 19,683 two-place connectives (in the three-valued case) individually! Such complexity is beyond the grasp of most users; not only would they find it frustrating, but they would almost certainly make mistakes, using the wrong connective for a desired result. This same complexity also applies to the design of the optimizer and the amount of code required to implement it [2].

■ *Number of meaning assignments:* In addition to increases in complexity due to the number of connectives, the number of distinct meaning assignments for connectives increases as well. As noted in Part 1, any truth

P	NOT P		P	NOT P		P	NOT P
+T	F		+T	F		+T	F
U	U		+U	U		-U	U
-F	T		-F	T		-F	T

P	NOT P		P	NOT P		P	NOT P
+T	F		+T	F		+T	F
U	F		+U	F		-U	F
-F	T		-F	T		-F	T

P	NOT P		P	NOT P		P	NOT P
+T	F		+T	F		+T	F
U	T		+U	T		-U	T
-F	T		-F	T		-F	T

Fig. 6   Possible meaning assignments of three-valued NOT
("+" = designated, "−" = anti-designated)

value can be treated as true-like ("designated"), false-like ("anti-designated"), or neither ("undesignated"); these distinctions are necessary for identifying tautologies and contradictions in many-valued logics. For example, in a three-valued logic, there are three distinct one-place connectives that could be called negation.* But if *unknown* can be designated, anti-designated, or undesignated, the number of possible meaning assignments for negation expands to nine (see Fig. 6)! This complexity violates one of the motivations for using a logical system in the first place. Surely users do not wish to work with such a DBMS.

■ *Meanings of query results:* If the users and designers of a database do not agree on the meanings of query results, confusion is inevitable; furthermore, that confusion will eventually lead to a loss of data integrity (users will eventually update the database in ways that violate the intended, but unenforceable, meaning of the data). In order to assign truth values to propositions or arguments (which is, of course, the process of defining an intended interpretation), the designer of the database must have a consistent understanding of what each truth value means (our uniform interpretability objective). That meaning must be (a) understandable to users and (b) consistent with the connectives and rules of inference. Although

---

*All three map *true* to *false* and *false* to *true*, of course; they differ in their treatment of *unknown*, however, mapping it to *true, false,* and *unknown,* respectively.

the meaning of individual truth values (as used in, for example, Codd's relational model with three-valued logic) might appear to be reasonable, they can have nonintuitive consequences and can lead to incorrect results. Codd [7] categorizes such results as either "mildly" incorrect (meaning an expression has evaluated to *unknown* when it should have been either *true* or *false*) or "severely" incorrect (meaning an expression has evaluated to *true* or *false* when it should have been *unknown*). But either way, the fact that the DBMS is capable of giving incorrect results means "Don't trust the DBMS!" It is like saying of a certain calculator that 1 plus 1 sometimes equals 2 and sometimes doesn't [7], so check it yourself (in which case, why use the calculator in the first place?).

- *Arbitrary number of truth values:* A many-valued logic can have an arbitrary number of truth values (that is, the number of truth values needed cannot be definitively established). If we think of *unknown* as intermediate between *true* and *false* in a three-valued logic, there is no intuitive reason to stop at three; in fact, there are some immediate motivations not to. For example, Codd suggests a *four*-valued logic in order to deal with both "unknown" and "inapplicable" missing values. But what if we need to insert a row with a missing value into a table but don't know whether that missing value is "unknown" or "inapplicable"? Clearly, we need yet another kind of "missing value" and a fifth truth value [3,8]. Where does this process end?

- *Loss of deductive power:* Two-valued logical systems can sometimes be uniformly extended to handle an arbitrary number of truth values, assuming that properties such as completeness are not important. However, as the number of truth values increases, the number of tautologies generally decreases. But tautologies are essential tools of deduction, so this decrease means a practical loss in deductive power (if not a formal one). And let us not forget the implications for the optimizer—which is, of course, the DBMS component that not only offers performance improvements but also facilitates data independence! Among other things, an optimizer that uses many-valued logic is less likely to recognize when expressions are semantically equivalent, and less likely to be able to simplify complex expressions via rules of inference and tautologies, than one that uses standard two-valued logic.

What makes matters worse is the particular tautologies that typically tend to be lost [6,8]. For example, the expression

```
( P IMPLIES P ) BI-IMPLIES ( ( NOT P ) OR P )
```

is not a tautology in some many-valued logics, even though intuitively it should be.

The impact of this loss in deductive power is serious. Most optimizers effectively just give up when faced with many-valued logic and make no expression transformations whatsoever.* Some even fail to use an index if the indexed columns can contain nulls, regardless of whether they actually do or not! And the reduction in deductive power implied by such failures makes it much more difficult for users to reason toward a desired answer using a sequence of queries. The poorer the optimizer in this regard, the more the user must "optimize by hand," carefully selecting the exact manner in which a query should be expressed (two expressions are not likely to be equivalent except for specific values of arguments). And this fact means the user must understand the logical system very well indeed and be willing to give up logical data independence.

- *Unusual semantics:* Although perhaps interesting from a formal perspective, the many-valued logics proposed by Codd (and related proposals by Vassiliou, Lipski, Biskup, and others) leave much to be desired from the perspective of understandable semantics. In Codd's scheme (as elaborated by Grahne [13]), a table that contains one or more "A-marks"† can be seen as shorthand for a set of tables, one such table for each combination of legally substitutable values for the A-marks in the original table. In order to construct understandable queries in such a system, the user must somehow keep in mind all of the possible substitutions. Such semantics make the systems nonintuitive and error-prone. In an informal survey of some 30 database designers and administrators, all of the parties concerned expressed amazement at this interpretation and felt it was unacceptable.

OTHER MANY-VALUED LOGICS

The most common many-valued logics are variations on systems developed by Łukasiewicz, Post, and Kleene. In particular, variations on the systems of Łukasiewicz are sometimes said to be the basis for SQL's three-valued logic. While this claim cannot be correct [4], it is worth taking a moment to examine the properties of the Łukasiewicz systems.

- First of all, Łukasiewicz systems are not truth functionally complete (so the system would not be able to verify some facts using the available operators).

---

*Or they make invalid ones (i.e., ones that would be valid in two-valued logic but not in many-valued logic).

†Codd's "A-marks" are similar to SQL's nulls (the "A" stands for "applicable but unknown").

- They are also not natural extensions of the classical propositional logic (certain tautologies of propositional logic cease to be true in the Łukasiewicz systems, and, conversely, certain tautologies of the Łukasiewicz systems have no counterpart in propositional logic).*

These properties are sufficient to eliminate Łukasiewicz systems from further consideration. They are not candidates for use as the logical system of a DBMS.

Some many-valued logics are truth functionally complete (all are consistent by definition if at least one truth value is undesignated) but have semantics that are clearly inappropriate for a DBMS. Here are a few examples.

- In the systems of Post, truth valuations apply only to sets of propositions (i.e., sets of rows), not to individual propositions *per se*.

- Kleene had in mind the truth valuations of propositions involving mathematical functions that were undefined for certain ranges of predicate values.

- Bochvar created a system with a set of "internal" truth tables and a set of "external" truth tables, treating *unknown* as "undecidable" or "meaningless." This scheme resembles SQL in the sense that SQL effectively returns *false* (the external system) to the user when the answer is *unknown* (the internal system), but it differs from SQL in other respects.

"RELATIONAL" THREE-VALUED LOGIC

The arguments presented thus far are generic: They apply to many-valued logics in general. The problems I have raised cannot be fixed (indeed, formal logicians do not perceive them as "problems" that *need* to be fixed!). Now I want to consider (briefly) the specific three- and four-valued logics described by Codd and the three-valued logic implemented in SQL. Although it is my thesis that *no* many-valued logic is suitable for the needs of a DBMS, I feel compelled to point out a few specific problems that apply to these pragmatically important cases.

- As noted in the introduction earlier, my discussion of the problems associated with using a many-valued logic in an RDBMS was forced to be general, because Codd's three-valued logic is not completely defined.

---

*In other words, they are deviants, to use our terminology. They were originally intended to treat contingent (especially future contingent) propositions as being "temporarily unknown." For example, the truth value of "It will rain tomorrow" would initially be *unknown*, but would eventually be determined to be either *true* or *false*. Thus, the Łukasiewicz *unknown* is a temporary placeholder for a standard truth value.

The situation is even worse in SQL, in part because the definition is only implicit (rules of inference, axioms, and primitive connectives are all unspecified). In particular, as explained in the previous section, the system is definitely not a Łukasiewicz system [4]; it is also not one of the systems defined by Post or Kleene or Bochvar. What, exactly, *is* the definition of this logical system?

- The rules of inference are unspecified. Now, we can assume that (since subqueries are supported) a limited rule of substitution is supposed to hold, but what about other standard rules such as *modus ponens* (if P IMPLIES Q and P, then Q)? Note that in a many-valued logic there are many forms of this rule (two forms if the logic is three-valued); if *modus ponens* is supposed to hold, therefore, it is obviously important to say which form is intended. Similar remarks apply to other rules of inference, such as *modus tollens* and De Morgan's Laws.

- Although most many-valued logics are based on an extension to the propositional logic, the relational model is supposedly based on first-order *predicate* logic. Certainly SQL "supports" the EXISTS quantifier, and the FORALL quantifier can be simulated (though they both get into trouble over nulls). Unfortunately, however, there is no discussion of a many-valued first-order predicate logic in the relational model, nor of how the relational model fares without appeal to first-order predicate logic. How the formal system should treat quantifiers and what special rules of inference apply are both left largely to the imagination. However, we do know that the relational model and SQL both treat EXISTS as a finite iteration of OR; in practice, therefore (and assuming that nulls are not permitted), the logical system is at best the finite version of the first-order predicate calculus mentioned in Part 1 [5].

WHAT SHOULD WE DO?

The criticisms of many-valued logics in this article as they apply to DBMS use have simple, practical consequences. Based on these results, I recommend adherence to the following guidelines:

- Avoid nulls and many-valued logic.
- Don't use SQL operations like outer join and outer union that generate nulls.
- Until you can implement these first two actions, review the meanings of queries and query results carefully. The more complex the query, the more important this review process becomes.

- Lobby vendors to drop support for nulls and many-valued logic from their products.

- Ask vendors to make full use of first-order predicate calculus in their optimizers.

- Demand that DBMS vendors place high priority on the goals and objectives outlined in Part 1. To this end, they must recommend against the use of many-valued logic in their products and must oppose it in the SQL standard.

- Demand that, until vendors can comply with these guidelines, they supply a configuration option to disable the use of nulls and many-valued logic at the system level.

To summarize this part of the paper (somewhat glibly), the key conclusion readers should draw from this technical discussion is that "nothing" is to be gained from "nothing"; nothing compares to the two-valued approach. In fact, a great deal of knowledge, power, usability, performance, and maintainability is at risk if many-valued logic is used in a DBMS. Apply Occam's Razor: Eliminate all the nothing from your databases.

In the next part of this series, I will consider the main reasons why people think they want to include nulls (both I-marks* and A-marks) in a database and discuss their validity. Certain of those reasons will be found to be valid. That conclusion, along with the conclusion that many-valued logic is inappropriate, leaves us with a dilemma. That dilemma will be addressed in Part 4.

ACKNOWLEDGMENTS

I would like to thank Chris Date, Hugh Darwen, and Ron Fagin for their helpful comments and criticisms. I would also like to apologize to Billy Preston (again) and Sinead O'Connor for the abuse of their song titles.

NOTES AND REFERENCES

Note: Items 10–14 are not referenced in the body of the article.

1. In fact, a single two-place connective w suffices. In a system with n truth values, if the truth values are represented by the natural numbers from 1 to n, the connective w is defined as:

```
/P w Q/ = 1 + [max (/P/,/Q/) mod n]
```

---

*An "I-mark" indicates that some property is inapplicable.

where /R/ is the truth valuation of the truth-valued expression R and "mod" is the modulo operation (see reference [6], page 65).

2. Contrary to Codd's position on this issue [7], the number of distinct logical connectives in the absence of a specified number of primitive connectives that satisfy truth functional completeness is not comparable to the infinite number of distinct arithmetic functions that can be defined in ordinary arithmetic. Instead, it is properly compared to the number—*N*, say—of distinct operations (e.g., addition and multiplication) that are needed to *define* that infinite number of arithmetic functions. For arithmetic, that number *N* is not very large.

3. Codd replied to this criticism by saying, essentially, that an I-mark is a "catchall" and therefore terminates the process [7]. This response is incorrect. The system requires a mechanical procedure by which it can determine which wffs should be evaluated as corresponding to the truth value for a simple predicate with an I-marked variable *vs.* one with an A-marked variable. At the very least, if A-marks are to be distinguished from I-marks, the need for such a procedure is implied by the distinction. Thus Codd's four-valued logic is not substantially different from that described by Date [8], and it is susceptible to the same problems.

4. Łukasiewicz gave IMPLIES and NOT as his primitive connectives, deriving OR and AND from them. His definition of IMPLIES is different from that used in the propositional and predicate calculus, which define P IMPLIES Q as NOT P OR Q (see Fig. 7). In fact, Łukasiewicz's version of IMPLIES cannot be derived from NOT, AND, and OR. The reason is that NOT, AND, and OR each preserve *unknown* from the inputs (and therefore so do all possible combinations of these operators), whereas Łukasiewicz's IMPLIES does not. Since SQL does not define IMPLIES, claims that it is based on a variant of Łukasiewicz's three-valued logic must be invalid.

```
              Q                              Q
          ┌─ T U F                       ┌─ T U F
        P─┤                            P─┤
        T │  T U F                     T │  T U F
        U │  T U U                     U │  T T U
        F │  T T T                     F │  T T T

         MATERIAL                      ŁUKASIEWICZ
        IMPLICATION                    IMPLICATION
```

Fig. 7   Three-valued material *vs.* Łukasiewicz implication

5. It would be good if this logical system were the intended one, since such a system has the desirable properties of being both complete and decidable.

6. Nicholas Rescher: *Many-Valued Logic*. New York, N.Y.: McGraw-Hill (1969).

7. E. F. Codd and C. J. Date: "Much Ado About Nothing." *Database Programming & Design 6,* No. 10 (October 1993). Republished in C. J. Date, *Relational Database Writings 1991–1994.* Reading, Mass.: Addison-Wesley (1995).

8. C. J. Date: "NOT Is Not "Not"! (Notes on Three-Valued Logic and Related Matters)," in *Relational Database Writings 1985–1989.* Reading, Mass.: Addison-Wesley (1990).

9. Patrick Suppes: *Introduction to Logic.* Princeton, N.J.: Van Nostrand (1957).

10. E. F. Codd: "A Relational Model of Data for Large Shared Data Banks," *CACM 13,* No. 6 (June 1970). Republished in "Milestones of Research," *CACM 26,* No. 1 (January 1982).

11. E. F. Codd: "Extending the Database Relational Model to Capture More Meaning," *ACM TODS 4,* No. 4 (December 1979).

12. L. Bolc and P. Borowik: *Many-valued Logics 1: Theoretical Foundations.* New York, N.Y.: Springer-Verlag (1992).

13. G. Grahne: *The Problem of Incomplete Information in Relational Databases.* New York, N.Y.: Springer-Verlag (1991).

14. H. Delong: *A Profile of Mathematical Logic.* Reading, Mass.: Addison-Wesley (1970).

CHAPTER **7**

Nothing from Nothing (Part 3 of 4): Can't Lose What You Never Had

Null support in RDBMS applications implies multivalued logic support—with all its attendant problems. What are designers really looking for?

ABSTRACT

Part 3 of this four-part series addresses the question of why database users and designers think they need nulls in their databases anyway. It approaches this question by classifying the motivations of those users and designers into a number of categories, and concludes that some of those motivations, at least, do seem to be valid. So what is to be done?

COMMENTS ON REPUBLICATION

See the "Comments on Republication" in Chapter 5.

Originally published in *Database Programming & Design 7,* No. 2, February 1994 (the subtitle was contributed by *DBP&D*). Copyright © 1993–1998, Alternative Technologies. All rights reserved. Reprinted by permission of David McGoveran.

INTRODUCTION

Professional DBMS users are of various kinds: database administrators, database designers, application developers, end users. But I doubt whether any of them thinks very much about whether or not the DBMS supports a many-valued logic. (Indeed, I doubt whether DBMS designers and implementers examine this issue much either, if the products themselves are any evidence.) However, they do often ask whether the DBMS (or a given database) supports *nulls.* For most users, "SQL nulls" have become a catchall means of addressing a variety of different problems. Even end users, who used to be interested in application support for "don't know" or "not applicable" responses during data entry, now treat these issues as a matter of null support.

But why exactly are such users asking for "null support" (which, even if they do not realize it, implies support for many-valued logic)? In Part 2 of this series, I explained why many-valued logics were inappropriate as a foundation for a DBMS. In Part 3, I will examine the key reasons why database designers and users nevertheless think they want such support.

For this analysis to make sense, it is important to review our understanding of the semantics of a database. First of all, a database design constitutes a model or representation of some portion of the world of experience, called the *universe of discourse.* It defines the set of permissible facts that can legally be represented in the database. At any given time, only some of those permissible facts will actually appear in the database (in the form of rows in relational tables). If a permissible fact does *not* appear in the database, the closed world interpretation lets us say it is *false.* If you think about your own database application, you will readily see that the presence or absence of a given row in the database represents a statement about your knowledge of the application domain. Specifically, let T be a table with corresponding predicate $P(x)$. Then the presence of row r in table T means something like "We know $P(r)$ is *true,*" while its absence means "We know $P(r)$ is *false.*" Under the closed world interpretation, a row of column values that is not permissible (that is, does not correspond to anything in the universe of discourse) cannot be used to form a predicate—the result would not be a well-formed formula (wff).

Given this understanding of database semantics, it is my position that every appearance of a null in a database represents some form of *conditioned knowledge.* By "conditioned knowledge," I mean knowledge that can be made precise (e.g., by choosing a particular value to replace a null) only by satisfying some condition that *cannot* be satisfied. For example, when a data entry field on the screen is allowed to be "not applicable," the appearance of that field on the screen in the first place could be conditioned on whether a value is applicable; i.e., some condition exists that, if satisfied, would determine whether the data entry operator would be asked for a field value.

Now, we have long known that some facts about the world are conditional, as in (e.g.) "some, but not all, instances of x have property P." We have also long understood that some relationships are conditional, as in (e.g.) "some, but not all, instances of x are in relationship $R(x,y)$ to some instances of y."[*] In the remainder of this article, I will examine various kinds of conditioned knowledge, each of which typically leads to the appearance of nulls in the database.

I will first examine those types of conditioned knowledge that encourage database designers to specify columns as permitting nulls, including:

- Conditional relationships
- Conditional properties
- Conditional operations
- Conditional constraints

I will then examine the various types of nulls that data entry operators might invoke (called *conditional information* here), and relate those various nulls to the kinds of conditionality handled by database designers. In the absence of maliciousness, carelessness, or ignorance (as due to, for example, lack of training), these situations, inclusively, account for the appearance of nulls in a database and therefore for the perceived need for many-valued logic.

CONDITIONAL RELATIONSHIPS

Relationships can be characterized in many ways. When the relationship is not computed by a function or transformation, it is usually specified as a simple mapping; such mappings are then typically characterized by the ratio of the cardinalities of the entity types involved. For example, a mapping involving just two entity types is often characterized via the notation $m:n$, meaning that m entities of the one type have the designated relationship to n entities of the other type (m and n here both being interpreted as "one or more"; we will use the notation $0/m$ or $0/n$ to stand for "zero or more"). Observe that the notion of a $m:0$ or $0:n$ relationship makes little sense, since it says the relationship holds for no entities at all of one of the two types.

Perhaps the mapping most familiar to relational database designers is the "parent-child" or, more precisely, the $1:0/n$ relationship, in which, for each instance of the "parent" entity type, there are zero or more instances of the

---

[*]Indeed, it was considerations such as these that led to the introduction of the so-called "necessity" and "possibility" quantifiers, thereby creating *modal logic*.

"child" entity type. Such a relationship is generally modeled by means of a foreign key in the child relation that refers to the primary key of the corresponding parent relation. This foreign key technique also works for 1:1 and 1:0/1 relationships, both of which are, of course, just special cases of 1:0/n. (Of course, it is a little strange to think of a "parent" who has no "children": How can something be a "parent" by virtue of its relationship to nonexistent children?)

Suppose now that not every child instance has a corresponding parent instance, meaning the relationship is now 0/1:0/n. I will refer to such a relationship as "conditional" because it represents a situation in which (in general) each of the entity types involved is such that some instances of that type are related to no instances of the other type. For example, consider the case of real children generally. Not all children have identifiable parents; it is an unfortunate fact that the parents of some children are forever unknown due to the inhumanities of wars, kidnapings, and other causes. It is not uncommon to find a conditional relationship modeled using foreign keys, with the special case of zero references (as in case of the child with no parent) being modeled by a null in place of a foreign key value.

CONDITIONAL PROPERTIES

In logic, an entity type (or class) is said to have *defining properties* and *meaning criteria* [1]. **Defining properties** are properties an instance *must* possess if it is of the entity type in question. By contrast, **meaning criteria** are properties an instance *might* possess: Any individual meaning criterion counts only as evidence that the instance might be of the entity type (though the exhaustive disjunction of all meaning criteria is a defining property). For example, one defining property of an insect is that it has six legs. By contrast, having wings is a meaning criterion: Some insects have wings and others do not. As another example, the definition of a poem abounds with meaning criteria: Some poems have meter, others rhyme, still others use metaphor, and so on.

I will use the term "conditional properties" to refer to meaning criteria. Conditional properties are often modeled by permitting nulls in the applicable columns. Thus, a table representing insects might have a column regarding wings that would be set to null for insects with no wings. Similarly, a table about poems might have a column to specify its meter, which would be set to null for poems that had no meter. By extension, a compound foreign key might be entered as partially null if a part of the referenced primary key is, in fact, a meaning criterion.

CONDITIONAL OPERATIONS

Various operations supported in relational DBMSs operate on operands of different types. For example, the conventional inner join operates on relations that are (in general) of different types. However, those types are related in a certain manner. By contrast, the *outer* join operates on relations that are (again in general) of types *that are only conditionally related.* Similarly, the outer union operates on relations that only conditionally satisfy the union compatibility relationship. In a sense, then, the operands of these operations are conditionally defined. I will refer to such operations as "conditional operations."

Because the relationship among operands is not uniform for all instances of the operands, the result of a conditional operator is not a uniquely defined relation. Specifically, the result of an outer join or outer union does not, in general, have a unique relation predicate. Instead, it is a collection of possible relations, one relation for columns without nulls plus one for each combination of columns containing nulls.

For example, suppose we had an employees table EMP and a managers table MGR with primary keys EMP# and MGR#, respectively, both from the same domain. An outer join of these tables on EMP# and MGR# should logically return at least two tables—one with the relation predicate "employee EMP# has properties $P(\text{EMP\#})$ and manager MGR#" and one with the simpler relation predicate "employee EMP# has properties $P(\text{EMP\#})$." However, since operations in the relational algebra always return just one relation, the various result relations are "unified"—i.e., "made uniform"—by creating extra columns containing nulls. Those nulls are of the kind "value is the empty set."

CONDITIONAL CONSTRAINTS

For certain constraints it is impossible to specify in advance exactly when they are to be satisfied. In particular, we cannot say they must be satisfied at statement completion time (immediate) or commit time (deferred). For example, if an investor "sells short," there is an implied commitment to buy back the stock at some future, unspecified time. Selling short thus involves an integrity constraint—balancing the amount of stock sold short with the amount purchased—with a conditional timing (the time will depend on some other event or condition). I will refer to such constraints as "conditional constraints."

Conditional constraints imply the existence of entity instances that would satisfy them. Those instances are sometimes modeled by including instances in the database in advance of the time at which the constraint is satisfied in reality. This tactic creates entity instances for which the values of certain properties cannot be known. The missing information is often modeled with nulls, to be replaced at some later time by real values. In the interim, the conditional constraint is satisfied by defining it to accept either real values or nulls. For example, a stock trade might be modeled by a transaction that inserts into a STOCK_SALES table a row containing the stock identifier, its sell price, date, and buyer, and into a STOCK_BUYS table the stock identifier, buy price, date, and seller. Selling short would then insert the appropriate information into STOCK_SALES; it would also insert a row into STOCK_ BUYS for the stock identifier, setting the buy information to nulls. The constraint would be defined to accept the existence of such a row, thus effectively deferring the real integrity check indefinitely.

CAPTURING NOTHING: CONDITIONAL INFORMATION

Having considered the various data modeling issues that contribute to a perceived need for nulls, we now need to take a look at those situations in which the database designer must anticipate incomplete data entry. What are end users trying to convey when they enter a null into a field during data entry? Date [2] has listed some of the more common possible meanings that might be attributed to a null. Suppose we had a DBMS that was capable of distinguishing all of those flavors of null. Let's examine each in turn.

- *Value not applicable:* For example, a data entry form might contain fields for an employee's name and spouse's name. If the employee has no spouse, the user might enter "N/A" for "not applicable" or might simply skip the field, leaving it empty. The application program might then enter the spouse's name into the database as a null. However, a little thought shows that no entry into the database should be made at all, unless there is an integrity constraint that requires employees to have spouses. In this latter case, the spouse's name would be required and failure to enter a value from the domain of possible spouse names would be a constraint violation. "Value not applicable" is the data entry operator's way of handling either a conditional relationship or a conditional property.

- *Value unknown (temporarily):* Suppose the same data entry form is used, but this time the user simply does not know the name of the spouse—the employee is known to have a spouse, but the name has not been obtained. In other words, the field is "applicable, but value temporarily unknown." This situation can occur quite legitimately; it is often the case that not all necessary information for a given task is gathered at one time. Of course, not all information relating to a task can be deferred; for example, some unique designation of the employee is essential, even if that designation is just an arbitrary employee identification number. In the spouse name example, there is a need to recognize the existence of a spouse without necessarily knowing the name of that spouse.

The "value unknown" kind of null does not quite succeed here; it captures the existence of a relationship, but does not capture the fact that there exists a unique designation for that spouse. In particular, it cannot treat two particular occurrences of the "value unknown" designation as the same and all others as different. For example, if the data entry form also had a place for children of the spouse (as, for example, from a different marriage), it would be very difficult to capture this information in a database without resorting to repeating groups. Few people would make this mistake on paper: Some means would be invented to establish which person had which children, even for persons whose name is currently unknown!

"Value unknown" is another way data entry operators handle a conditional property, while at the same time conveying the belief that a value will become known at some time in the future.

- *Value does not exist:* Suppose employees normally have social security numbers, but a particular employee does not. Although it might reasonably be expected that the employee would get a social security number eventually, some foreign employees might never do so. Thus, the data entry operator might understand, not just that the social security number was currently unknown, but that no such number would ever be assigned. "Value does not exist" is thus another way of handling a conditional property, while conveying the belief that the value can never be known.

- *Value undefined:* Some fields are defined in such a way that the value is "undefined" in certain circumstances. For example, consider a field defined as the quotient of two numbers, such as the percentage of departmental sales revenues contributed by a particular salesperson. If the departmental sales revenues are zero (for example, at the beginning of the sales period), this number is undefined. Now, we might be dealing here with a case of bad design—the quotient is not entirely functionally dependent on either the salesperson or the department; instead, it is a value derived from two other values, one of which is functionally dependent on salesperson and the other on department. "Value undefined" is one data entry version of a conditional constraint.

- *Value not valid:* Suppose the value a data entry operator enters violates a constraint, such as a domain constraint. We might still want to record the fact that such an error has occurred in the information gathering process. "Value not valid" is another data entry version of a conditional constraint.

- *Value rejected:* It might happen that a value is rejected by the system and yet the data entry operator knows it to be correct. Such a state of affairs means a change is required to the applicable domain definition (or to some other aspect of the underlying system design). In other words, the data entry operator has uncovered a system design error. "Value rejected" is another data entry version of a conditional constraint, but with the added attempt to convey a belief that the constraint being violated is incorrect.

- *Value not supplied:* Sometimes a value is not supplied during data entry. This situation often arises when the processes of data entry and data collection are combined into a single operation. It can also arise when the data is collected from uncooperative users or unreliable sources. For example, the US census survey contains certain optional questions that certain US residents might prefer not to answer. It is also possible that the data entry operator simply chooses not to enter a particular field. No matter what the reason for the omission, there are two cases to consider when data is not supplied: Either the missing information is the value of a property (and so a way of handling conditional properties or conditional relationships), or it is the value of an identifier (for the entity in question). In the latter case, we have the problem of capturing information about an improperly identified entity, possibly violating primary key discipline. I will claim in Part 4 that this case represents a database design error, and will reduce the problem to that of dealing with a conditional property.

Each of the foregoing situations can cause nulls to be placed in a "relational" database as part of the data entry process. In fact, of course, each of these types of missing information can also be found in legacy (prerelational) databases. The importance of understanding all of these different "null flavors" should not be underestimated; in particular, the process of migrating legacy data to a relational database requires proper identification and handling of each possible case.

WHAT ABOUT DEFAULTS?

It is unfortunate that most SQL DBMSs make it far easier to specify the default for a given column as null instead of something meaningful. As a result, SQL nulls are sometimes used as an improper substitute for defaults. Indeed, the relationship between defaults and nulls is so entwined that Date [3] has suggested a systematic use of defaults as an alternative for all types of null, a position with which I have some sympathy. Certainly a systematic use of defaults would result in a far better DBMS than the many-valued logic alternative that I have criticized in Part 2 of this series. However, I do not believe systematic defaults can or should be used in place of every possible occurrence of nulls. An alternative and more restricted systematic use of defaults will be among the proposed solutions to the problem of "missing information" that I will be discussing in Part 4.

CONCLUSIONS

Ralph Waldo Emerson once said (*Journals,* 1866) "If I cannot brag of knowing something, then I brag of not knowing it." By accident or by design, database practitioners often find themselves in this unfortunate position. The existence of a null in a database is ultimately a statement about what we don't know—i.e., about something that is not part of the defined (and hopefully agreed upon) universe of discourse for that database.

A database designer's motivations for incorporating or allowing nulls in a database are sometimes valid, representing a valiant attempt to deal with conditional relationships, conditional properties, conditional operations, conditional constraints, and conditional information. This fact, along with the conclusion of Part 2 that many-valued logics—and therefore nulls—are not an appropriate solution to the problem of "missing information," leaves us with a dilemma. In Part 4, I will propose a set of solutions to that dilemma.

ACKNOWLEDGMENTS

I would like to thank Chris Date and Hugh Darwen for their helpful comments and criticisms on this series of articles. I would also like to apologize to Billy Preston (again) and the Allman Brothers for the abuse of their song titles.

REFERENCES

1. R. G. Olson: *Meaning and Argument: Elements of Logic.* Harcourt, Brace, and World (1969).

2. C. J. Date: "NOT Is Not "Not"! (Notes on Three-Valued Logic and Related Matters)," in *Relational Database Writings 1985–1989.* Reading, Mass.: Addison-Wesley (1990).

3. C. J. Date: "The Default Values Approach to Missing Information," in C. J. Date and Hugh Darwen, *Relational Database Writings 1989–1991.* Reading, Mass.: Addison-Wesley (1992). *Note:* This paper is superseded by Installments 51–54 and 56 (in Part I of the present book).

Nothing from Nothing (Part 4 of 4): It's in the Way That You Use It

Database designers and users need to represent missing information: Can it be done without resorting to many-valued logic? Yes—here's how

ABSTRACT

In the final part of this four-part series, we consider a variety of design and other techniques by which "missing information" can be handled without the need for many-valued logic.

COMMENTS ON REPUBLICATION

See the "Comments on Republication" in Chapter 5.

Originally published in *Database Programming & Design 7*, No. 3, March 1994 (the subtitle was contributed by DBP&D). Copyright © 1993–1998, Alternative Technologies. All rights reserved. Reprinted by permission of David McGoveran.

INTRODUCTION

In Part 3 of this series of articles, I reviewed and categorized the key reasons why database designers and users both seem to find themselves wanting some kind of many-valued logic support. In this final part of the series, I propose a number of methods by which "missing information" can be handled without the need for many-valued logic.

The emphasis is on using logical design principles to eliminate the perceived need for nulls. *Logical design* is defined here as that design that can be inferred from logical concerns alone. It is not affected by physical design issues such as denormalization or index creation or space allocation, nor is it affected by the manner in which data is perceived by individual users. It is my firm position that all design should be logical *first*, with the physical design then being derived from that logical design. Moreover, the physical design should be allowed to deviate from a simple augmentation of that logical design only when there is no other alternative (in which case the reasons for deviation should be documented and the impact on data integrity thoroughly assessed).

Several database design principles will be invoked in this article. An important one is what I call the "Knowledge Principle." Just as Codd's well known Information Principle requires that all information be captured by values in columns, the Knowledge Principle *precludes disinformation* by stating:

> *All columns must contain values that convey knowledge about the universe of discourse (and must not contain metadata).*[*]

Both the Knowledge Principle and the Information Principle extend trivially to the system catalog, which contains (a definition of) the structure of the database. That is, both in the database itself and in the catalog that describes the database, we record what we know and we do not attempt to record what we do not know.

In the sections that follow, I will address each of the key sources of "missing information" and describe techniques for handling each. These logical design techniques eliminate the need for nulls and many-valued logic. Note carefully, however, that they are not meant to be applied separately; they constitute an *integrated* and systematic approach to the overall problem. In overview, the techniques proposed are:

- *Separating metadata from data:* Part of the means for dealing with conditional information
- *Association tables:* Take care of conditional relationships
- *Enforcing relation predicate uniqueness:* Deal with one apparent case of conditional properties (*viz.*, conditional entities)

---

[*]See the next section for an extensive discussion of what is meant by the term *metadata* in this context.

- *Modeling subtypes:* Handle both conditional properties and conditional operations

- *Abstract entities:* Convert some apparently conditional relationships into ordinary relationships and handle conditional constraints

- *Meaningful defaults:* Eliminate nulls as defaults, without confusing data and metadata

Because these techniques lead to a more accurate representation of the application domain, the resulting logical design inherently contains more structure. That additional structure serves to reduce the amount of application code needed to support database access, and it makes the necessary SQL statements more meaningful and easier to write. On the other hand, it also serves to highlight certain weaknesses of SQL (it sometimes means more SQL statements are needed), and physical design might sometimes be less than optimal. To address these concerns, I propose a few enhancements to relational products:

- *User-extensible audit trails:* Declarative support for user-defined metadata

- *Cross-table and computed indexes:* Better support for association tables

- *Set operation support:* Better support for types and subtypes

- *Declarative relation predicates:* Automatic recognition and distinction of tables based on relation predicates (type and subtype support is a special case)

- *Surrogate keys:* Better support for certain conditional properties

CONDITIONAL INFORMATION

In Part 3, I introduced the term *conditional information* as a convenient catchall phrase for various types of missing information encountered during data entry:

- On the one hand, such "data entry nulls" were found to reflect conditional properties, conditional constraints, conditional relationships, and so on, depending on the variety of null. These different cases are addressed one at a time in subsequent sections.

- On the other hand, those nulls also reflect an attempt to record information about the data entry process itself. In other words, the classification into "value not applicable," "value temporarily unknown," "value undefined," and so on, is based on *why* data is missing; i.e., the various categories give *information about the data*, or *metadata*. For example, "value temporarily unknown" tells us the data entry operator believes a value does exist, but the value is currently unknown (it is temporarily unavailable). Until the value is actually obtained, however, it remains possible that the data entry operator is wrong in this belief; it might be the case that no value is applicable or no value exists.

Let's examine why we might be interested in such metadata. In the example just given, we might want to know the data entry operator's opinion so that we can, at a later time, locate those instances of "value temporarily unknown." We could then actively seek the real values to replace those unknowns. (A similar reasoning applies to instances of "value not supplied" and "value rejected.") But this latter activity is quite distinct from the activity of modeling the state of our knowledge about the entities represented in a logical design—it is, rather, the activity of modeling our knowledge about the data collection and entry process.

Distinguishing between data about the application and "data about the data" (i.e., metadata) in this way makes it easier to understand how we can improve on our efforts. We can model both data and metadata more carefully, thereby obtaining more utility than is possible using nulls and many-valued logic. After all, we often keep track of metadata such as exceptions and errors in application processing; why should we not do the same kind of thing in the database as well? And, just as exception processing should be separated in applications from normal processing, so metadata should be maintained in separate "exception tables" in the database and not interspersed with regular production data.

Of course, the system catalog contains metadata, but that data is generally not related to the specifics of data entry. The kind of metadata we are concerned with here is most commonly encountered in *audit trails*, in which the source of the data, data entry operator ID, time of entry, and so on are captured. Extending the audit trail concept to include metadata about missing information would seem natural. To accomplish this goal, we would need to capture the table identifier, the primary key of the row involved, a code classifying the data entry operator's belief, and an identifier for the column involved (but not a column value). This metadata can be recorded in separate lookup tables (see Fig. 1 for an example). While this solution can be implemented manually, why should not RDBMS products support audit trails in which the information to be captured is declaratively specified by the user?*

Some people might complain that this solution implies planning for additional information about every value in the database. In reality, however, rows in which nulls fulfill a functional purpose are the exception when the database is designed along the principles outlined in this article. Few database administrators actually scan their databases for nulls, attempting to replace them with real values. Likewise, few applications provide meaningful information about

---

*In order to implement this approach properly, support for *subtypes* will also be required, as described later in this article.

EMP	EMP#	FNAME	LNAME
	1	Minnie	Mouse
	2	Bill	Clinton
	3	Daffy	Duck

METADATA	TABLE	PK_VALUE	COLUMN	STATUS
	EMP	2	SPOUSE	temp unk
	EMP	3	SPOUSE	n/a

Fig. 1   Keeping metadata in lookup tables

nulls to data entry operators; a field containing a null in the database is usually displayed as empty or some other noninformative value such as the string "NULL." No information is conveyed as to the *kind* of null.

However, note that, if RDBMS products did support differentiated nulls as metadata (i.e., if nulls affected neither DBMS logic nor the user's view of the data), something very like the current physical implementation of nulls could be used for tracking "missing information" metadata. For users who already have tables containing nulls, I recommend creating views that implement the database design principles I am describing in this article. Those views will not contain nulls and should be used for all data manipulation. To obtain metadata, the base tables (which do contain nulls) can be accessed. See Fig. 2 for an example.

EMP	EMP#	FNAME	LNAME	SPOUSE
	1	Minnie	Mouse	Mickey
	2	Bill	Clinton	*<null>*
	3	Daffy	Duck	*<null>*

VIEW1 (restriction)	EMP#	FNAME	LNAME	SPOUSE
	1	Minnie	Mouse	Mickey

VIEW2 (restriction and projection)	EMP#	FNAME	LNAME
	2	Bill	Clinton
	3	Daffy	Duck

Fig. 2   Views of null-bearing tables

One last point to close this section: In addition to dealing with "data entry nulls" as discussed above, designers might also have to take into account metadata about missing information captured in legacy or nonrelational databases. Given the fact that SQL's nulls are undifferentiated, however, this metadata is often lost when the nonrelational database is migrated to a relational one, unless the designer is very careful.

CONDITIONAL RELATIONSHIPS

Recall from Part 3 that conditional relationships are relationships in which not all instances of the entity types in question actually participate. Such relationships are characterized in general as "$0/m:0/n$" (with $0/m:n$, $0/1:n$, etc., being special cases). A common approach to modeling conditional relationships uses foreign keys. Where the instance does not participate, the foreign key is set to null. This approach treats all instances uniformly, imposing a table structure that represents noninformation for some rows and violates the Knowledge Principle.

For example, the traditional employees table EMP often contains a foreign key MGR# referencing its own primary key EMP# (corresponding to the traditional—and conditional—"employee to manager" relationship). Typically, at least one employee has no manager, and this fact is often modeled by means of a null in the foreign key position within the applicable row (see Fig. 3).

The solution is to model all conditional relationships by means of *association tables*. An association table is one in which the entire primary key consists of foreign keys to other tables, thereby capturing an association among the applicable entity types. By creating an association table EMP_MGR consisting of EMP# and MGR#, we can remove the MGR# foreign key from the original EMP table (see Fig. 4). With this design, no row in any table need have any nulls in any foreign key column; instead, the lack of a manager for a particular employee is modeled correctly by the lack of a corresponding row in the association table.

EMP	EMP#	FNAME	LNAME	MGR#
	1	Minnie	Mouse	2
	2	Bill	Clinton	4
	3	Daffy	Duck	2
	4	Hillary	Clinton	<null>

Fig. 3 Foreign key column containing a null (example)

EMP	EMP#	FNAME	LNAME	EMP_MGR	EMP#	MGR#
	1	Minnie	Mouse		1	2
	2	Bill	Clinton		2	4
	3	Daffy	Duck		3	2
	4	Hillary	Clinton			

Fig. 4   Using an association table (example)

It is worth noting that this procedure also breaks referential cycles, thereby eliminating the various performance and design problems associated with such cycles (this benefit was noted by Date [1]). Likewise, modeling relationships via an association table is often easier for users to understand and control. For example, if we wish to represent a 0/1:4 relationship (where the "4" is to be interpreted as "no more than four," as in, e.g., "no manager manages more than four employees"), the cardinality constraint can be expressed in terms of the association table in a rather straightforward manner. For example (SQL):

```
... CHECK ( NOT EXISTS ( SELECT *
                         FROM   EMP_MGR
                         GROUP  BY MGR#
                         HAVING COUNT (*) > 4 ) )
```

Because association tables eliminate so many anomalies—including special-case handling of referential cycles, difficult integrity constraint enforcement, even restrictions on constraint definition in some cases—performance often improves when association tables replace the embedded foreign key approach. Certainly tuning becomes easier: Since access to all tables is by primary key, we need not be concerned about foreign key index creation and maintenance. The optimizer can become more efficient and predictable as well. Of course, performance losses are a potential disadvantage that must be addressed. By using simple surrogate keys (especially integers) for associated entities in place of possibly nonsimple primary keys, association tables can be kept quite small, can be fully indexed, and can often be cached. Note too that the foreign key index on the original EMP table can now be dropped, improving the update performance of that table.

Indexing an association table can improve performance but does require some care. There are several possibilities. A single B-tree index on the primary key might suffice; this case requires that the leading index keys be specified in queries so they are known in most lookups. A small number of B-tree indexes with different index key orders might be appropriate otherwise. Alternatively, if the DBMS supports index-only join strategies, separate indexes on each of the foreign keys will permit any key to be unknown, and the additional index access need represent little additional overhead. Ideally, DBMSs would support cross-table indexes for this purpose. Such indexes could sometimes implement the association table itself and could even be a better implementation of foreign keys (Computer Associates' CA-DB was an example of a product that used this technique for managing referential integrity).

Now, you have probably realized that *m:n* relationships effectively *must* be implemented by means of association tables. However, I am arguing here that 1:*n* relationships should be handled in the same way, even though it is clearly possible to implement them in the more conventional "embedded foreign keys" approach. (That more traditional approach can then be treated as a possible performance optimization.) Adopting such a uniform approach can greatly improve database understanding, and can also eliminate many anomalies arising from the standard embedded approach. With proper support for association tables in RDBMSs, any conceivable performance penalties for their use will most likely be eliminated. Even without such support, you might be surprised to find that they can actually improve performance.

CONDITIONAL ENTITIES

Even if we use association tables as recommended in the previous section, we might be overlooking the source of other problems. The very existence of a null in place of a value for some foreign key (as in Fig. 3, for example) makes it clear that the table is mixing together two distinct types of entities. Indeed, they have very different relation predicates, because they have different *defining properties* (see Part 3 of this series).

I refer to such mixtures of entity types (somewhat loosely) as "conditional entities." For example, we might say that every employee is conditionally also a manager, meaning that (in the traditional employees table) the rows represent two rather different types of entities—some employees are managers, while every manager is probably (though not necessarily) an employee. The distinction becomes immediately apparent if we recognize that managers have defining properties (budget, for example) not shared by nonmanagers. The columns representing such properties are typically set to null for nonmanagers; nonmanagers are not the same kind of entity as managers. (As if we didn't already know that!)

Instead of trying to represent both entity types in a single table, we should model them with two distinct tables: an employees table EMP with primary key EMP# and a managers table MGR with primary key MGR#. Any other approach violates an important design principle: *Each table should have a single relation predicate that specifies the represented entity type's defining properties* [2]. An association table representing the relationship between them can then be established, having a primary key composed of two foreign keys, EMP# and MGR#.

CONDITIONAL PROPERTIES

Whenever a value in a nonkey base table column is optional (i.e., permits nulls), that column represents a conditional property or *meaning criterion* (again, see Part 3 of this series). The existence of such columns indicates that (again) several entity types are being mixed together in a single table. Each of the entity types in question should be given a separate table (they have distinct relation predicates).

For example, if a table describing vehicles contains a "paint color" column, that column will typically be set to null for vehicles that have not been painted (see Fig. 5). In the case of painted vehicles, the predicate is something like "the vehicle identified by vehicle identification number VIN has paint color COLOR(VIN) and other properties P(VIN)." By contrast, the predicate for unpainted vehicles is something like "the vehicle identified by vehicle identification number VIN has properties P(VIN)."

Following the simple principle that entity types should be differentiated by their relation predicates leads to the design illustrated in Fig. 6.* Of course,

VEHICLE	VIN	MAKE	MODEL	COLOR
	1	Ford	Escort	Green
	2	Pontiac	Gd Prix	Red
	3	Porsche	Carrera	<null>
	4	Chrysler	LeBaron	<null>

Fig. 5   Mixing painted and unpainted vehicles

a. PAINTED_ VEHICLE	VIN	MAKE	MODEL	COLOR
	1	Ford	Escort	Green
	2	Pontiac	Gd Prix	Red

b. UNPAINTED_ VEHICLE	VIN	MAKE	MODEL
	3	Porsche	Carrera
	4	Chrysler	LeBaron

Fig. 6   Differentiating tables by relation predicates

---

*Another design (preferable in some respects) would put VIN, MAKE, and MODEL in one table and VIN and COLOR in another; all vehicles would be represented in the first table, while only painted vehicles would be represented in the second.

abiding by this principle does mean that entity types with large numbers of meaning criteria can cause the database design to become quite complicated, involving a combinatorial explosion of additional tables. This concern would properly be addressed through DBMS support for types and subtypes as described in the next section but one. In any case, experience suggests that such a combinatorial explosion does not often occur, and the gains of creating the additional tables far outweigh the inconvenience.

CONDITIONAL OPERATORS

Even if its operands do not contain nulls, a conditional operator such as outer join can *generate* them. As with base tables, the appearance of nulls in a derived (i.e., result) table is an indication that the table represents a mixture of entity types, each with its own distinct relation predicate. For example, consider the outer join of the EMP table from Fig. 3 with itself (based on matching the MGR# foreign key and the EMP# primary key). Fig. 7 shows the result, USUAL_RESULT (more accurately, a projection of that result—employee first and last names are not shown, and nor are manager last names).

USUAL_RESULT	EMP#	MGR#	MGR_FNAME
	1	2	Bill
	2	4	Hillary
	3	2	Bill
	4	<null>	<null>

Fig. 7   Usual result of an outer join (example)

As you can see, most rows in table USUAL_RESULT contain information about the employee together with information about that employee's manager. Those rows have a predicate something like "the employee identified by EMP# has properties *P*(EMP#) and manager identified by MGR# with properties *P*(MGR#)." By contrast, those rows in which the MGR# is null have a predicate something like "the employee identified by EMP# has properties *P*(EMP#) and is such that there does not exist a manager identified by MGR# with properties *P*(MGR#)."

Conditional operations can be simulated as the union of the results of several ordinary SELECTs, one for each distinct relation predicate, as suggested

RESULT1	EMP#	MGR#	MGR_FNAME	RESULT2	EMP#
	1	2	Bill		4
	2	4	Hillary		
	3	2	Bill		

Fig. 8 Breaking outer join into separate queries (example)

in Fig. 8. (*Note:* By "union" here, I mean a general set union, not the usual more limited relational union—see the next paragraph.) Of course, this approach can become quite cumbersome if there are more than a few relation predicates involved in the desired result, which is one of the reasons why users want outer join support in SQL. Unfortunately, however, outer join is (intrinsically) *logically flawed*, since it produces a result in which entities of different types are presented as though they were all of the same type.

As just indicated, the manual solution to the problem—the problem, that is, that outer join is supposed to solve—is to query each entity type separately, an approach that requires the user to be explicitly cognizant of the differences in meanings of different rows. A better solution would involve DBMS support for general set operations—in particular, for the general set union, which (unlike its relational counterpart) does not require its operands to be of the same type. When a set union is performed, it is understood that the result is not of the type of either of the operands; rather, it is some supertype of those types (thus, e.g., the union of a set of apples and a set of oranges is a set of apples and oranges, or perhaps a set of fruit). As with conditional properties, this capability would properly be addressed through DBMS support for types and subtypes (see the section immediately following).

TYPES AND SUBTYPES

Each table should have a unique relation predicate, thereby representing one and only one entity type; by contrast, a table that permits nulls corresponds to several distinct predicates, and logically is therefore several distinct tables all rolled up into one. Those distinct tables should be broken out by successively restricting the table and projecting away the null-bearing columns [3]. The various tables created in this way are each supertypes of the source table. Referring to Fig. 6, for example, we can say that vehicles that are not differentiated by COLOR (because paint color is not a relevant property) are more general than vehicles that are painted. Incidentally, note that projecting away a null-bearing column differs from ordinary projection in that it does not append an EXISTS to the relation predicate. For example, it is meaningless to say that "vehicle VIN has properties P(VIN) and there exists some color COLOR(VIN) for vehicle VIN in the domain of colors" if color is not a relevant property for the vehicle in question.

Ideally, DBMSs would support supertypes, types, and subtypes directly. It should not be necessary to create supertypes explicitly by user-written projection operations: The lack of a value for a property should automatically imply an appropriate modification of the relation predicate. If the DBMS kept track of supertypes automatically, it could present separate relations to the user with appropriate identification of the relation predicate on demand. Furthermore, conditional operators would then be understood as operations on several relationships at once (masquerading as a single relationship), yielding a result involving several entity types (masquerading as a single entity type).

The possibility of such results suggests some extensions to the relational algebra to support more general versions of the relational operators. In particular, relational union is a restricted version of the general set union. I propose that the system should automatically create several tables in the output (when appropriate), grouping like rows together by performing the "restrict and project away nulls" operation in the user's behalf. This capability would help users distinguish the entity types and recognize their interrelationships. In effect, such set operations would be many-table-result versions of existing relational operations; they would avoid the need for users to simulate such operations manually, via several SQL statements. Whether many-table *operands* (as opposed to results) should be permitted deserves additional and careful consideration, however. **For the time being, I propose that such many-table values be supported only for output.**

Note: Whereas the relational model *per se* does not permit the union of operands of distinct types (such as apples and oranges), the outer union operation does, and so does the proposal I am making here. The difference is that outer union creates a bizarre kind of combined result in which every apple is given orange properties and every orange is given apple properties. By contrast, my proposal creates a result in which apples and oranges retain their respective identity and the user is not encouraged to confuse them. Similar remarks apply to the other set operations.

Some readers might be concerned that complexity will arise because of the number of tables that might appear in a result. However, such complexity is at once bounded and unlikely to be very great in the majority of queries—in most cases, there are few entity types involved in a query result (even the more complex outer joins usually produce fewer than four). Certainly the complexity is no greater than that caused by nulls, since it is essentially only the presentation of results that changes! Users need not be burdened with collecting together rows having nulls in the same columns, and understanding the result is more straightforward.

CONDITIONAL CONSTRAINTS

Conditional constraints, such as those implied by "selling short" (see Part 3), involve an anticipated ability to comply with some constraint at some future time. They differ from normal constraints in that it can be very hard to specify exactly when they are to be satisfied. In a sense, conditional constraints attempt to enforce *desired* states of the database, while normal constraints enforce *necessary* states. Conditional constraints require special consideration if the common approach involving nulls (e.g., creating an entry in a "STOCK_BUYS" table with nulls in place of the buy information) is to be avoided.

The solution is to create status or *bookkeeping* tables, whose purpose is to represent the abstract instances that are needed to "balance the books." For example, consider a simplified version of selling short. As noted in Part 3, the requirement that stock sales balance stock purchases in any transaction is a conditional constraint. Instead of making special entries (with nulls) in the STOCK_BUYS table, we create a PENDING_STOCK_BUYS table; then, for each instance of selling short, we insert a row into that table (see example in Fig. 9). The table will contain those columns that suffice to constrain the purchase that must be made in the future and satisfy the conditional constraint. It is sometimes useful to include a general STATUS column in the table as

STOCK_SALES

STOCK_ID	BUYER	SELL_PRICE	SELL_DATE	SHARES
1	Rockefeller	100.00	10/12/97	5000
2	Hearst	400.00	2/01/98	10000

STOCK_BUYS

STOCK_ID	SELLER	BUY_PRICE	BUY_DATE	SHARES
1	J.P.Morgan	100.00	10/12/97	5000

PENDING_STOCK_BUYS

STOCK_ID	STATUS	SHARES
2	SOLD SHORT	10000

Fig. 9 Satisfying the "selling short" conditional constraint

well. The conditional constraint would then be rewritten in terms of the STOCK_SALES, STOCK_BUYS, and PENDING_STOCK_BUYS tables (essentially to say that, for any given stock, the total shares in STOCK_SALES is equal to the total shares in STOCK_BUYS plus the total shares in PENDING_STOCK_BUYS).

ABSTRACT ENTITIES

Some occurrences of nulls are due to a perceived lack of an appropriate entity. This problem arises when the database designer insists on modeling only concrete entities when, in fact, the business process involves both concrete and abstract entities. In fact, the problem is most prevalent when some of the instances of a given entity type are concrete and others are abstract. For example, suppose every employee is supposed to be assigned to a department, with the result that the EMP table contains a DEPT# column (I ignore here the fact that this column might be a foreign key, since it is not germane to the present discussion). From time to time, however, a row might be entered into table EMP for a new hire before that new hire is assigned to a department. Typically, this problem is handled by setting the DEPT# in that row to null.

A little careful thought will show that this problem occurs because the modeling process is too simplistic. Although the new hire has not been explicitly assigned to any department, some aspect of the company is likely to perform the function of a department for that employee nonetheless. You can discover the identity of that *abstract entity* by analyzing the business function of departments and the business processes that affect employees. For example:

- A department serves as the collective unit for a group of employees;
- Typically, the manager of an employee's department has hire and fire authority and might sign off on paychecks;
- Sometimes the department determines the physical location where the employee is to report at the beginning of work.

For an unassigned employee, one entity that could carry out these functions might well be the human resources department—but as an *abstract* entity, distinct from the *concrete* entity to which personnel actually belonging to the human resources department are assigned. The trick is to assign the abstract entity instance a unique department identifier from the appropriate domain.

SURROGATE KEYS

In Part 3, I pointed out that conditional information sometimes involves the primary key. If there is no candidate key for which the data entry operator *must* enter a value, no primary key can be selected without violating the entity integrity rule. This problem can be solved by having the system create an artificial identifier, called a *surrogate key*, to serve as the primary key. For example, suppose that table EMP originally contained FNAME and LNAME columns (first name and last name), but not EMP#. It is possible that an employee is always identified uniquely by the combination of a first name and a last name, but sometimes the first name is missing and sometimes the last name is missing. In such a case, creating a system-assigned employee number (EMP#) eliminates the problem by converting FNAME and LNAME to conditional properties.

MEANINGFUL DEFAULTS

As noted in Part 3, Date [4] has recommended a systematic use of defaults as being better than the use of nulls. While this article should make it clear that I believe better logical design would eliminate nulls, I do believe that systematic use of defaults is an essential part of the solution and agree with much of Date's proposal. Although the details are too involved to expound here, Date recommends (among other things) the following:

- DBMSs should support the declaration of user-defined defaults for columns.
- Various builtin functions should be defined to support defaults, including IS_DEFAULT (returning *true* if and only if its argument evaluates to the default value for the applicable domain) and DEFAULT (returning the default value for the domain of its argument).

To this proposal I would add a few embellishments:

- Nulls should never be used in place of default values.
- Defaults should always be meaningful values from the domain. That is, they should not be artificially created values (including such values as "N/A" or "UNKNOWN"). Otherwise, default values no longer convey knowledge about the entities to which they apply, and the Knowledge Principle is thereby violated.
- Default values should be defined only in the catalog and not physically stored with the data itself. Of course, such an implementation requires the ability to mark a stored field as having the default value. Then, if the system administrator or DBA chooses to change the default for some domain, no data need be physically rewritten.
- During data entry, users (including data entry operators) should be required to distinguish between entry of a default value and entry of a value that happens to be the same as the declared default. For example, it must be possible to distinguish between an actual value of "Blue" and a default that happens to be set to "Blue."

- We must distinguish between data entry defaults and database defaults. Data entry defaults are usually associated with a particular application and quite possibly a particular data entry operator or even a session; their purpose is to save the data entry operator time and effort by "preentering" the most probable value of a field. By contrast, the purpose of database default values is to reflect the "standard" value of an attribute for all possible instances. For example, if we had a table containing information about rooms, we might like.to set the database default ceiling color to white, under the hypothesis that white is the most likely color of any ceiling. If a particular data entry operator were entering information about rooms in a particular building that tended to have light gray ceilings, however, the data entry default for ceiling color would be different from the database default and would most likely be set by the data entry operator and maintained by the application. In fact, it is possible to have an entire hierarchy of default values, but only the one at the "root" of the hierarchy corresponds to the database default value.

While database default values can and should be used to represent our "best guess" about missing information, they should not be used for conditional properties, conditional relationships, conditional constraints, or conditional operations. In such cases, the assertion of a value where there is none conveys false information about the universe of discourse.

CONCLUSIONS

By representing missing information structurally and recognizing "information about information" (i.e., metadata) as the separate class it is, we eliminate the need to put nothing in our databases. Moreover, in accordance with the new presentation of conditional operators in this article, there is also no need to permit the automatic generation of nulls in results. As a result, there is no need to support many-valued logic in a DBMS. These changes have a number of positive influences:

- The DBMS can rely on classical logic. In doing so, it can meet the goals we established for a DBMS (see Part 1).
- Performance can improve because (a) the entire power of classical logic can be brought to bear on the problem of optimization and (b) the many anomalies due to the existence of nulls do not have to be treated.
- Integrity can be enforced more directly without having to worry about restrictions (such as disallowing cascade delete on a self-referencing table).
- The structure of the database can be easier to understand, and queries therefore easier to write.

- The results of relational operations can be more consistent with expectations and easier to interpret.
- Meanings of tables (both base and derived) no longer depend on whether or not nulls can or do exist in the database.
- Without the need for null support, the SQL standard could be simplified, as could many applications.

In this series of articles we have (1) reviewed the motivations for using a formal logical system as a foundation for a DBMS; (2) translated certain important properties of logical systems into database terminology, thereby motivating the need for database professionals to understand logic; (3) examined the use of many-valued logics as a formal foundation for DBMSs and found them wanting; (4) reviewed the key reasons why users and database designers seem to require DBMS support for many-valued logic; and (5) provided a set of alternatives that meet user requirements without doing violence to the logical properties we desire of a DBMS. While most of these alternatives can be implemented through careful database design and use, a couple of them do require additional support by vendors. In particular, vendors need to improve their support for default values; they also need to add support for types and subtypes, domains, general set operations [5], and relation predicates.

ACKNOWLEDGMENTS

I would like to thank Chris Date and Hugh Darwen for their helpful comments and criticisms on this series. I would also like to apologize to Billy Preston (again) and Eric Clapton for the abuse of their song titles.

NOTES AND REFERENCES

1. C. J. Date: "A Note on One-to-One Relationships," in *Relational Database Writings 1985–1989*. Reading, Mass.: Addison-Wesley (1990).

2. A relation predicate states all of the necessary conditions for row membership in a table (all of the conditions, that is, that are independent of other tables). There is much more to be said about the definition and importance of relation predicates; I omit an extended discussion here for space reasons.

3. I recently became aware of a similar treatment by Codd [7], which he refers to as "[normalization to] Conceptual Normal Form." Codd uses projection to create supertypes, eliminating all but some arbitrarily determined percentage of nulls. By contrast, I treat all null-bearing rows as evidence of mixed relation predicates in the table and therefore an indication of bad table design.

4. C. J. Date: "The Default Values Approach to Missing Information," in C. J. Date and Hugh Darwen, *Relational Database Writings 1989–1991*. Reading, Mass.: Addison-Wesley (1992). *Note:* This paper is superseded by Installments 51–54 and 56 (in Part I of the present book).

5. The relational model would have to be extended to handle collections of tables as single operands, while guaranteeing that results are the same as they would be from some sequence of relational operations.

6. Codd discussed association tables, surrogate keys, and types/subtypes in reference [8].

7. E. F. Codd: "A Practical Approach to Combining Two or More Relational Databases," *The Relational Journal 2*, No. 3 (June/July 1990).

8. E. F. Codd: "Extending the Database Relational Model to Capture More Meaning," *ACM TODS 4*, No. 4 (December 1979).

Nothing to Do with the Case

A response to a two-part paper by Tom Johnston entitled "MVL: Case Open" (Part 1) and "The Case for MVL" (Part 2)

ABSTRACT

This paper presents a detailed set of arguments against the use of many- or multi-valued logic (MVL) as a means of dealing with missing information. As the subtitle indicates, the paper is in fact a response to another, by Tom Johnston [1]; however, we—i.e., Date, Darwen, and McGoveran—believe it does stand on its own and is therefore worth including here.

COMMENTS ON REPUBLICATION

As I said in the introduction to this part of the book, the topic of missing information seems to be endless . . . Reference [1], the two-part paper by Tom Johnston to which the present paper was a response, was itself a response to all of the following:

- Comments by myself in my debate with E. F. Codd [10];
- "Several articles by Date and Hugh Darwen that advise against using MVL with relational databases" (to quote reference [1]); and

Originally published in *Database Programming & Design 8,* No. 9, September 1995. Reprinted by permission of Hugh Darwen and David McGoveran and Miller Freeman Inc.

■ David McGoveran's four-part paper "Nothing from Nothing" [6] (reprinted as Chapters 5–8 of the present book).

See also the next chapter of this book (Chapter 10) and the remarks in the opening section "Background" immediately following.

BACKGROUND

Note: The material in this section consists of a lightly edited version of Database Programming & Design's *own introduction to the article as originally published.*

The debate over the use of many-valued logic (MVL) in relational databases has been scorching a path through the pages of *Database Programming & Design* for several years now. The latest round began with C. J. Date's *DBP&D* columns of December 1992 through February 1993 (as well as other writings of his, published elsewhere). Those columns prompted a searing reply from none other than Dr. E. F. Codd, father of the relational model. Codd, who supports certain forms of MVL, countered Date's criticisms and clarified his own views on the topic. Codd's commentary, along with rebuttals from Date, were featured as a "debate" in *DBP&D* two years ago [10].

For two months, all was quiet. Then, beginning in the December 1993 issue and carrying on into early 1994, *DBP&D* carried an important series of articles by David McGoveran entitled "Nothing from Nothing" [6]. McGoveran's series described, first, the logical problems with MVL; second, why today's relational (or, rather, SQL) DBMSs do not support the relational model's underlying logic; and finally, how designers can avoid having to use MVL. Date and McGoveran took these ideas further, teaming up to describe a "New Database Design Principle" in a series of articles in the summer of 1994.*

By 1995, it was about time for a counterpunch. That punch was provided by Tom Johnston's "MVL: Case Open" and "The Case for MVL" in February and March of that year [1]. Johnston, using extensive examples regarding underlying logic and relational database design, defended Codd's views and strongly countered those of McGoveran, Date, and Hugh Darwen.

Given the extent of Johnston's articles, we felt that Date and his colleagues deserved a chance to defend their views and offer a critique of John-

---

*Actually the articles in question [19–20] had little to do with MVL and nulls as such (except insofar as they did assume that nulls weren't being used!). They did—as stated—have to do with the "New Database Design Principle" (subsequently christened *The Principle of Orthogonal Design*), but they had to do even more with *a theory of updating* (a theory that applied to updating views in particular).

ston's articles: Hence the present article. In the name of fairness, we will provide Johnston with an opportunity to rebut this article (his comments will appear in the November 1995 issue). With that, we'll all shake hands and end this chapter of The Great MVL Debate.*

INTRODUCTION

Tom Johnston's article [1] strongly criticizes the published views of myself and, to a lesser extent, Hugh Darwen and David McGoveran on the subject of many-valued logic and its suitability as a basis for dealing with missing information in databases. Since it's my writings that seem to be Johnston's primary target, it seems appropriate that I should be the primary author of this response. However, I'll use the first person plural when making statements that reflect the joint position of all three of us (almost always, in other words!). Also, Hugh and David have reviewed this response in its entirety and both have some comments of their own to add at the end.

OVERVIEW

The problem of how best to deal with missing information in databases has long been a thorny one. Johnston's article doesn't move us any closer to solving that problem. In particular, it totally ignores most of our documented objections to the idea of using three-valued logic (3VL) as a basis for any such solution. Those objections are discussed in detail elsewhere [2–6]; there's no point in repeating the specifics here, but I will at least give a list of some of our more serious objections later in this response. We remain convinced that the database field must look elsewhere for possible solutions to the missing information problem.

Johnston makes three claims in support of his contention that DBMSs should be based on many-valued logic (MVL) instead of two-valued logic (2VL) [7]:

1. 2VL is just as "flawed" with problems of interpretation as MVL is (a discussion of this use of the term *flawed* appears in the next section).

2. "Basic" logic sacrifices a great deal of expressive power (an explanation of the term basic logic appears in the next section but one).

3. Many of "Date's objections" to MVL are inconclusive. A discussion of the term *Date's objections* follows immediately!

---

*Some wishful thinking here!

Note: While I do understand Johnston's reasons for using expressions such as "Date's objections," and "Date's arguments," and "Date's recommendations," and so on and so forth, I have to say that I'm not very comfortable with them; they give the impression that I'm the only one who believes in those objections and arguments and all the rest. On the contrary, the positions I've articulated in my various writings on this subject are supported quite widely in the database community, and (I believe) with good reason.

I now proceed to examine Johnston's three claims. *Note:* In what follows, all otherwise unattributed quotations are from Johnston's article [1].

2VL FLAWS *vs.* 3VL FLAWS

I've argued elsewhere that, in 3VL, NOT is not *not*—meaning that the NOT of 3VL isn't the same as the *not* of ordinary English [4]. This claim is undeniably true and has demonstrably led to errors, both in vendor DBMS implementations and in user queries—even, in the latter case, when the user in question was or should have been thoroughly familiar with 3VL [8]. In Part 1 of his article, Johnston devotes a very great deal of space to arguing what we all know—namely, that even in ordinary *two*-valued logic, AND is not *and,* OR is not *or,* and IMPLIES is not *implies.* He concludes that:

> To paraphrase Quine, . . . AND is merely the truth functional distillate of *and* [*and similarly for OR and IMPLIES, presumably*] . . . No significant difference exists between 2VL and MVL in point of counterintuitivities of interpretation . . . 2VL is just as logically flawed as any MVL . . . MVL is actually *less* misleading than 2VL, because with MVL, the counterintuitivities are so obvious . . . Just because [those counterintuitivities] are so startling, they are less likely to trip us up than [the] subtler counterintuitivities [of 2VL].

Now, we can surely all agree that the operators (also known as *connectives*) AND, OR, and IMPLIES are indeed open to being misunderstood, even in 2VL; they are indeed "distillates" of their natural language counterparts. (It's worth pointing out, however, that the reason for this state of affairs is that the meanings of the logical operators are required to be *context-free,* as David McGoveran explains later in this response.) Nevertheless, I would contend precisely that these operators *are* distillates of their natural language counterparts in a way that the 3VL NOT operator is not! (if you see what I mean). In 3VL, moreover, AND, OR, and IMPLIES also seem to depart further from their natural language counterparts. As already mentioned, it's undeniable that DBMS *implementers** (not just users) have made mistakes over the 3VL

---

*Not to mention language designers . . .

operators that they didn't make with the 2VL versions. Johnston's claim that MVL is "less likely to trip us up" than 2VL isn't supported by the evidence.

Furthermore, if the 2VL operators were as much a problem as Johnston suggests, the whole business of computing would never have gotten off the ground in the first place. 2VL is relevant to the entire computing field, not just to that particular subfield we happen to call database management. (I'm not saying that no mistakes have ever been made in 2VL, but those mistakes haven't been nearly as pervasive as those in 3VL have been.) To put the point another way: I'm quite comfortable with the idea of having to teach "naive end users" how to use 2VL correctly; I'm not at all comfortable with the idea of having to teach them how to use 3VL correctly (and I speak from experience here).

As a further conclusion to his first argument, Johnston also claims to "have demonstrated that 2VL is just as logically flawed as any MVL," and hence that MVL is "just as secure a mathematical foundation for relational theory as 2VL." Here I'd just like to point out that even if we accepted these claims—which we don't [9]—of course it wouldn't follow that MVL is a *good* foundation, nor that MVL is better than 2VL for such purposes.

Incidentally, Johnston repeatedly accuses me of, and takes me to task for, referring to the difficulties with 3VL (and MVL) as *logical flaws:* "If . . . Date is referring to MVL as a system of *mathematical* logic, then neither Date, Darwen, nor McGoveran have pointed out a single logical flaw in MVL." Actually I can find only one remark in all my writings on this subject that could reasonably be construed as suggesting that I think that 3VL is *logically* flawed. In my published debate on the subject with Codd [10], I said the following:

> It seems to me that there is all the difference in the world between:
>
> - Building a system—i.e., one based on 3VL—in which we *know* errors will occur, because the system has logical flaws in it, and
>
> - Building a system that is at least logically correct but is open to misuse. *Any* system is open to misuse. That's why we have to have discipline.

This remark was perhaps a little hasty; certainly I realize that it would be possible to define a 3VL that is logically self-consistent, and I never meant to suggest otherwise. What I did mean was that, in a system based on such a 3VL, certain conclusions will follow that are "logically incorrect" *in the real world*. The most obvious example is the well-known fact that the expression *p* OR NOT *p* is not a tautology (that is, it's not identically *true*) in 3VL. Other examples abound.

(To head another objection off at the pass, I should perhaps point out that I certainly have claimed that *SQL's attempt to implement* 3VL suffers from logical flaws [11]. But this claim is very different from the claim that 3VL itself is logically flawed, and I still stand by it.)

STAYING WITH BASIC LOGIC

Johnston uses the term *basic logic* to refer to "the logic on which the original version of relational theory was based"—namely, two-valued propositional (and first-order predicate) logic. And he claims that "Date apparently wants to remain within the confines not just of 2VL, but of [basic logic]"—though he does also go on to say that he doesn't "know whether [Date] has ever said this" but has "never seen an example [in which Date] went beyond these confines." This disclaimer seems a little perfunctory, however, or even disingenuous, since Johnston then devotes virtually the whole of Part 2 of his article to criticizing my imputed position that DBMSs should "remain within the confines . . . of basic logic."

In response to this broadside, I observe first that Johnston is quite right to say that "basic logic" is the logic on which relational theory was originally based. Thus, it would be more accurate to say that "remaining within the confines" of that logic was *Codd's* original position, rather than ours (or mine).

Be that as it may, I feel bound to say that it's very distressing to be criticized so roundly for something I didn't do. I never intended to rule out the possibility of exploiting such disciplines (advocated by Johnston) as modal logic and the rest, and I don't believe any of my writings suggest otherwise. However, I do believe strongly that any attempt to incorporate such concepts into our DBMSs should be approached with considerable circumspection; the price for making mistakes in such matters is far too high. In other words, I subscribe to *The Principle of Cautious Design* [12] (and so do my colleagues).

Much more to the point: All of this discussion of modal logic and so forth is *a complete red herring!* It has nothing whatsoever to do with the matter at hand—which is, to repeat, the suitability or otherwise of MVL as a basis for dealing with missing information in databases. Most of our publications in this field have dealt, very specifically, with the clear *UN*suitability of the brand of 3VL (and 4VL) advocated by Codd [10,14,15]—and supported, in a flawed fashion, by SQL—for this purpose. We certainly don't see anything in Johnston's article as a valid defense for this particular brand of 3VL (or 4VL).

Incidentally, Johnston says at one point that he "will venture a guess . . . as to what Date and company's philosophical principle might be." There's no need to guess!—our principle is well documented and is a matter of public record; it's *The Principle of Cautious Design* already mentioned [12]. In other words, Johnston is quite right in suggesting that our position on this whole topic is "conservative" rather than "liberal." Perhaps the point needs spelling out that we're not talking about politics here, we're talking about the best way to design and implement software systems—systems of a rather fundamental nature, too, systems in which errors of design can have calamitous consequences. Liberalism might be laudable in the political arena, but it doesn't follow that it's a good position to adopt in the arena under discussion.

INCONCLUSIVE OBJECTIONS?

To repeat from Johnston's article: "Date's objections to MVL are not as con-
clusive as they may appear at first glance." Since Johnston doesn't even address most of those objections, the most charitable thing that can be said about
this claim is that it remains unproven. Here for the reader's benefit is a list (not
annotated, for reasons of space) of some of those unaddressed objections. For
further discussion, see our previous publications on this subject [2–6].

- Mathematically speaking, a "relation" that "contains a null" isn't a relation (and so relation theory doesn't apply).

- A "relation" that "contains a null" violates Codd's own Information
  Principle.

- If TABLE_DEE represents *true* and TABLE_DUM represents *false,* what
  represents *unknown?*

- What's the relation predicate for a "relation" that permits nulls in one or
  more of its columns?

- The fundamental theorem of normalization breaks down in 3VL.

- What's the justification for treating nulls as duplicates of one another for
  the purposes of union and projection but not for the purposes of restriction and join?* (In other words, are two nulls equal or aren't they?)

- Even if such a justification can be found, why is it necessary for the relational algebra to suffer such complication?

- Expressions that evaluate to *true* in 3VL are not necessarily true in the real
  world (in other words, "3VL doesn't match reality").

And so on (this isn't an exhaustive list).

DEFAULT VALUES *vs.* MVL

Now here I really do object, vehemently. Johnston misrepresents, or misconstrues, the default values approach and then attacks his own misconstruction. "When we say that Jones doesn't have an hourly rate, we don't
mean that he has some special hourly rate—the $0.00 rate, for example." I
agree, we don't. What we do do is this: We say that the domain for the
HOURLY_RATE column is—let's say—X, where X consists of all possible

---

Note added on republication: It's worth pointing out that Codd's 3VL treats nulls as
duplicates of one another for intersection, too, which means that (using that logic) intersection is no longer a special case of join. Of course, it *is* a special case of join in conventional 2VL.

valid hourly rates *plus* the default value "N/A". The system certainly *IS* capable of recognizing this default value as meaning "not applicable" and acting accordingly (and indeed should do so).

There are so many points I want to make regarding this particular issue that I think it best to save them for a separate article—perhaps a column in my regular *DBP&D* series.* For now, I'll just have to refer readers to my own published description of the default values approach [13].

MISCELLANEOUS COMMENTS

In this section I want to respond to a number of miscellaneous claims and observations in Johnston's article.

- "One of [Date's] arguments—the *infinite regress of truth values* argument—does not apply to many standard versions of MVL."

  I never claimed that the MVL approach (more accurately, the idea of using "nulls" instead of values to represent the fact that information is missing) implied an infinite regress of truth values; rather, I claimed that it implied "an infinite regress" of *nulls* [4]. These two claims aren't the same thing at all! In fact, Johnston's error here might well be called a howler. Though it's not irrelevant to point out that many other writers, including both Codd himself [14] and the authors of the draft "SQL3" proposals [16], have fallen into this same trap of equating nulls and truth values at one time or another.

- "When *p* represents any of several different kinds of self-referential statement, . . . tautologies [such as *p* OR NOT *p*] become contradictions."

  Actually, they become *paradoxes*—they are neither *true* nor *false*. (A contradiction is a statement that's identically *false;* it's the opposite of a tautology, which is a statement that's identically *true* [17].)

- "It should be an object lesson to those who dream of relational databases as contemporary versions of such self-evident systems that Frege actually got it wrong!"

  In connection with this remark, Johnston imputes to us the claim that we would like to realize an "ancient [but unachievable] philosophical dream." We've never made such a claim; indeed, we've shown clearly that we know that the "philosophical dream" in question can't be realized [18].

- The "proof" that basic logic is nonmonotonic is specious. What it boils down to is the following:

---

*It was more than one column. See Installments 51–54 and 56 in Part I of this book, which in fact supersede reference [13].

1. Queries produce results from database states.

2. "Adding an axiom" means changing the database state (it's just a fancy way of saying "update the database").

3. Changing the database state will certainly change the answers to some queries (it'd be pretty useless if it didn't!).

- The penguin example is specious too, for similar reasons. (I can't resist the temptation to refer to it as *a red penguin;* perhaps it subsists on red herrings.)

- "Standard two-valued, first-order predicate logic is *not* truth-valued!"

  This claim is correct as stated, because "standard two-valued, first-order predicate logic" permits infinite sets and quantification over them. In databases, however, we deal only with finite sets, and Johnston's point is irrelevant.

- "It may surprise some to realize that MVL is consistent with bivalence."

  It certainly surprises me! (and it's a very strange remark to tuck away in the references, if it's really as significant as it seems to be). "Bivalent" means two-valued; the "MV" in MVL means, well, *many*-valued, where *many* means "greater than two."

  Perhaps Johnston is referring to a system in which every truth value except *true* itself is (at some point) effectively converted to *false*. SQL's 3VL might be thought of as behaving in this way, since (for example) SQL queries retrieve only rows for which the defining condition evaluates to *true*, not rows for which it evaluates to *false* or *unknown* (in other words, SQL effectively converts *unknown* to *false* just before the retrieval is done). If this is all that Johnston's remark means, then his point is irrelevant, and our criticisms of 3VL are still germane.

- "I think it is clear that the supervaluational approach is not at all unwieldy."

  This conclusion is far from clear to me, and I suspect it isn't valid. Is it always possible to recognize tautologies and contradictions? Even if it is possible, how feasible is it to do so? (In this connection, it might be worth mentioning that—as a correspondent, Ceuan Clement-Davies from Frankfurt, West Germany, pointed out to me in a letter following the publication of my debate with Codd [10]—such a proposal seems to mean that the DBMS "should use *two*-valued logic to detect tautologies, and *three*-valued logic for everything else. This would be a curious mixture.")

- "That RDBMSs could eliminate these [join] costs, or at least keep them to a manageable level, is a misconception put forward by vendors and, I regret to say, by Date himself."

  Here I cry *FOUL!* This comment is gratuitous at best (it has nothing to do with our complaints regarding 3VL, nor with Johnston's objections to those complaints); moreover, the part that refers to me is untrue—I've criticized the vendors for years, not least in the columns of *Database Programming & Design,* for delivering products that provide inadequate levels of independence between the base and stored table levels. (Such lack of independence is the crux of the issue here; if the vendors provided a greater degree of such independence, then join costs could indeed be "eliminated or kept to a manageable level.") And I cry *FOUL* again, for much the same reason, in connection with the second paragraph of annotation to Johnston's reference [8] in Part 2 of his article.*

CONCLUSION

Johnson's article concludes: "By restricting ourselves to basic logic, we spurn a logic that wears its difficulties on its sleeve for one that hides its difficulties up its sleeve" (implying that we should indeed opt for MVL instead of 2VL). We find this conclusion prettily phrased but unsupported by the arguments that precede it. Our own conclusion, by contrast, is that we find absolutely no reason in Johnston's article for modifying our position.

HUGH DARWEN ADDS:

Chris Date has already said nearly everything I wanted to say and more, and I agree with it all. Above all, Johnston hasn't risen to the biggest challenge of all facing those who would promote MVL as a foundation for database systems: He hasn't given us a replacement for, or a suggestion for a replacement for, the relational model of data (including abstract machines to replace the relational calculus and algebra, and a database design methodology to replace the relational methodology based on dependency analysis, especially functional dependency analysis). He writes, in his conclusion to Part 1, "I believe that there is not adequate reason to enshrine basic logic as *the* logic for relational database access languages." But relations just do "enshrine basic logic," *by definition,* so this statement makes about as much sense as would "I believe there is not adequate reason to enshrine the basic operators *plus, minus, times,* and *divide* as *the* set of operators for doing arithmetic." If Johnston has in mind some alternative structure, analogous in some sense to the relation but enshrining MVL, then could he please tell us about it?

---

*That paragraph read in part: "I think [Date] should add his voice to mine in recommending that vendors rearchitect their products to solve this fundamental [performance] problem and forever eliminate the need to denormalize a relational database!"

Does he perchance have in mind something close to what SQL pretends (in both senses of that word) to support? Take the example of the EMPLOYEE_ EARNINGS relation in which certain symbols appearing in the BONUS column are to be severally interpreted as "a bonus of $1000," "a bonus of $2000," "some bonus," "no bonus," "a bonus of $0," "some level-3-security-classified bonus," and so on. I'm a simple soul. I can't see any way of preventing the DBA from designing the database in such a manner, and I would have to change hats before I could comment on the advisability of doing such a thing. I would just observe that the *data type* (domain) of that BONUS column is *not* MONEY (though I can imagine an operator that would easily map a certain proper subset of that domain to values in the MONEY domain). I do understand that something called "modal logic" *might* help us to handle such domains in a general way, but it isn't clear to me that such a mechanism would necessitate a departure from 2VL.

Johnston rolls out the old problems of interpretation that arise with the logical operators *and, or,* and *implies.* We've never denied that these problems exist, but they aren't remedied by MVL. Besides, logical *and* really does mean one of the things human "and" means, and logical *or* really does mean one of the things human "or" means, and it's not difficult to explain to human beings which of the meanings is the applicable one in both cases. Logical *implies* means everything that human "implies" means, too; it's just that humans use only half of what the logical operator means, and are sometimes a little puzzled as to why logicians bother with the other half. (I, an amateur in the field of logic, have sometimes been surprised to find myself defending the logician's position in hot debate with *mathematicians!*) These "counterintuitivities" should be put into perspective against those that arise with 3VL.

By the way (and contrary to what reference [1] alleges), I don't believe I've ever used the phrase "counterintuitivities of interpretation," which, personally, I can't make sense of. I *did* use the phrase "difficulty of interpretation," arising from the "traps and counterintuitivities" in MVL, which does make reasonable sense (to me). And I *might* have written, if only I had been bold enough, "*errors* of interpretation," but then our gainsayers would probably have accused me of below-the-belt rhetoric. But our gainsayers are mostly silent ones, in public, so I am at at least very grateful to Tom Johnston for his efforts in reopening the debate.

DAVID MCGOVERAN ADDS:

While I am sure Tom Johnston is well intentioned, I think he has missed numerous important points and misinterpreted many statements from my series of articles [6]. Comments 1–7 apply to Part 1 of Johnston's article, comments 8–12 to Part 2.

1. Johnston's use of the term "interpretation" is very different from mine. I have consistently used this term in the Tarskian sense (except in writings where I have explicitly referred to "semantic interpretation"). My concern has always been with providing a consistent formal interpretation along with a semantic interpretation having some relevance to database work. Users of logic need to understand that arbitrary assignments of meaning to logical operators and truth valuation symbols can completely destroy the value of a logical system; some assignments work and others do not. I have yet to see an explicit 3VL (or 4VL, 5VL, . . .) that has the required properties, and indeed argued in my earlier articles [6] that such a logic was impossible.

2. Throughout his article, Johnston confuses the need for a computational apparatus with the issue of the ambiguities of the English language. He proposes the use of such logics as *quantification over propositions, second-order predicate logic, modal logic, relevance logic, epistemic logic, deontic logic,* and *nonmonotonic logic* for a DBMS. But such logics are, in general, either incomplete or inconsistent, have esoteric interpretations (and are therefore very hard to use at all), and/or are completely noncomputational. They cannot be used for automated query optimization and therefore do not provide logical data independence! We can reasonably assert that they are inconsistent when lumped together in a single logical system.

3. My usage of *true* and *false* differs from Johnston's, particularly in that I do not equate propositions and statements (and certainly not utterances), nor do I use the terms "proposition" and "statement" interchangeably.

4. The issues raised by Johnston regarding the interpretation of English statements into formulas of logic has no relevance to the issues at hand. English is context-sensitive and, as such, beautifully ambiguous. It is precisely this ambiguity that allows us to carry on conversations, as I learned as a graduate student from Jim McCawley (see Johnston's reference [6] in Part 2 of his article). But in any particular context, English statements are translatable into logical formulas. Even future contingents such as "It will rain tomorrow" can be formulated logically; for example, we often understand this statement to mean "So and so claims it will rain tomorrow," but we rarely construe it to mean something so simplistic and Aristotelian as "Rain happens tomorrow"! The first of these two construings is classifiable as *true* or *false,* while the second can only be classified as some kind of nonsense. Databases are holders of assertions made by reasonable people; each row inserted in the database is *an assertion of* a fact, not an absolute fact. Nothing can be done about this state of affairs, as knowledge is always somewhat relative. You can never *logically prove* that you know anything.

5. Every child studying simple set theory at elementary school learns that AND does not mean English "and then" and that INCLUSIVE OR is to be distinguished from EXCLUSIVE OR. Yet Johnston seems to think these are subtle issues. Logical OR, AND, and IMPLIES are not simply distillates of their natural language counterparts, since logical connectives had to be made context-free. This freeing of the connectives from context has always been a major aspect of the evolution of 2VL. By contrast, I have never seen any evidence that the development of 3VL was due to an attempt to make the meanings of the connectives more "natural-language-like"; rather, it seems always to have been a matter of circumventing the restriction that connectives apply only to propositions and well-formed formulas!

6. Johnston wrongly asserts that P0 IMPLIES (P1 OR . . . OR Pn) somehow means that any false proposition P0 implies the truth of all disjunct propositions Pi. Instead, it is the entire proposition "P0 IMPLIES (P1 OR . . . OR Pn)"—and *not* the disjunction P1 OR . . . OR Pn, nor any individual Pi alone—that is *true*. Perhaps Johnston is confusing this issue with the more common concern of being able to prove anything from a contradiction. The proper understanding of IMPLIES would be "accepting the truth of a false proposition implies the truth of all other propositions." Expressed colloquially: "If you'll accept a falsehood, you'll accept anything." Or even: "If you believe *that,* you'll believe anything."

7. The exercise at the end of Part 1 of Johnston's article consists solely of problems with ambiguities of English statements presented without a clarifying context. They have nothing to do with logic!

8. The reference to Russell's Paradox—"Is the set of all sets a member of itself?"—and Frege is gratuitous and irrelevant.

9. Johnston's definition of the Closed World Assumption* is correct for systems involving quantifiers over predicate variables having domains that are nonfinite sets, but is not correct if all predicate variable domains are finite. In this latter case, it is crucial to define the finite domain of discourse for all predicate variables. The Closed World Assumption then means that if P is neither an axiom nor a theorem of the system, then either it is outside the domain of discourse or we may add NOT P as an axiom. Johnston's definition leads to logical systems that are infinitely extensible with new axioms.

10. Johnston gives an argument against truth functionality, asserting that "basic logic" is not even truth functional. Unfortunately, the implied definition of truth functional is simply wrong.

---

*Also called the Closed World Interpretation.

11. Contrary to Johnston's implication, standard 2VL first-order predicate logic *is* truth functional as long as quantification is over predicate variables defined on finite domains (which entails a special version of the Closed World Assumption). Regarding Johnston's alternative supervaluational approach, I would love to see an algorithm for identifying tautologies and contradictions, or a proof that any such algorithm either is or is not NP-complete.

12. Claims that RDBMSs cannot optimize for the join I/O problem are ludicrous. I'd be pleased to consult for any vendor interested and would even offer a discounted rate if they would implement the algorithm in question!

There are so many other errors in Johnston's article that I would have to spend a great deal of time correcting and explaining all of them. Some of them represent failures to understand myself, Date, and Darwen; others are due to incorrect application of formal logic; still others are simply false assertions about the history of logic; others are due to a lack of understanding of what McCawley referred to as "linguistic logic" and natural languages.

It is unclear to me how best to help readers understand the negative impact of such articles and avoid the dangerous conclusions they draw. All I can do is suggest that, before you support esoteric bases for your DBMS, you should be sure that your company can afford to risk the validity of your applications and the integrity of your data. At least with 2VL, we know what needs to be taught, we know what needs to be included in DBMS query languages and optimizers, and we know how to avoid any mechanical (i.e., automatic or computational) errors. Thus, we do at least have some hope of identifying other errors as human and striving for better use of the products. The whole point of computerization is not to automate errors, but to automate correct (possibly complex) procedures—thereby leaving to people the noncomputational tasks involving judgment, intuitive recognition, and creativity, and (hopefully) more time for these enjoyable activities.

NOTES AND REFERENCES

1. Tom Johnston: "MVL: Case Open," *Database Programming & Design 8,* No. 2 (February 1995); "The Case for MVL," *Database Programming & Design 8,* No. 3 (March 1995).

2. Hugh Darwen: "Into the Unknown," in C. J. Date, *Relational Database Writings 1985–1989.* Reading, Mass.: Addison-Wesley (1990).

3. C. J. Date: "Null Values in Database Management," in *Relational Database: Selected Writings.* Reading, Mass.: Addison-Wesley (1986).

4. C. J. Date: "NOT Is Not "Not"! (Notes on Three-Valued Logic and Related Matters)," in *Relational Database Writings 1985–1989*. Reading, Mass: Addison-Wesley (1990).

5. C. J. Date: "Three-Valued Logic and the Real World" and "Oh No Not Nulls Again," both in C. J. Date and Hugh Darwen, *Relational Database Writings 1989–1991*. Reading, Mass.: Addison-Wesley (1992).

6. David McGoveran: "Nothing from Nothing" (Chapters 5–8 of the present book).

7. This contention on Johnston's part notwithstanding, our published papers on this subject have been primarily concerned with three-valued logic specifically, rather than with many-valued logic in general. (David McGoveran's paper [6] is an exception.) However, most of our criticisms of 3VL apply to MVL also, often with even more force. Following Johnston, however, I will talk in terms of MVL in this response, except where I want to say something regarding 3VL specifically.

   Incidentally, we do realize that Johnston doesn't limit his discussions to the applicability of MVL to the problem of missing information solely. However, it's our position that even if MVL can be shown to be useful for other problems, it is *not* useful—in fact, it's worse than useless—for the missing information problem in particular. And it's specifically this latter notion (that MVL might be useful for dealing with the missing information problem) that has been the subject of our published criticisms; hence the emphasis on this particular issue in this response.

8. An example of an incorrect "expert" query can be found in the correspondence following publication of my column in *Database Programming & Design 5*, No. 12 (December 1992). Alternatively, see C. J. Date, *Relational Database Writings 1991–1994* (pages 26–29). Reading, Mass.: Addison-Wesley (1995).

9. In fact, David McGoveran explicitly rebuts this claim in Part 2 of his four-part article, "Classical Logic: Nothing Compares 2 U" (Chapter 6 of the present book).

10. E. F. Codd and C. J. Date: "Much Ado about Nothing," *Database Programming & Design 6*, No. 10 (October 1993). Republished in C. J. Date, *Relational Database Writings 1991–1994*. Reading, Mass.: Addison-Wesley (1995).

11. C. J. Date: "EXISTS Is Not "Exists"! (Some Logical Flaws in SQL)," in *Relational Database Writings 1985–1989*. Reading, Mass: Addison-Wesley (1990).

12. C. J. Date: "The Principle of Cautious Design," in C. J. Date and Hugh Darwen, *Relational Database Writings 1989–1991*. Reading, Mass.: Addison-Wesley (1992).

13. C. J. Date: "The Default Values Approach to Missing Information," in C. J. Date and Hugh Darwen, *Relational Database Writings 1989–1991*. Reading, Mass.: Addison-Wesley (1992). *Note:* This paper is superseded by Installments 51–54 and 56 (in Part I of the present book).

14. E. F. Codd: "Extending the Database Relational Model to Capture More Meaning," *ACM TODS 4*, No. 4 (December 1979).

15. E. F. Codd: *The Relational Model for Database Management Version 2*. Reading, Mass.: Addison-Wesley (1990).

16. International Organization for Standardization: *(ISO working draft) Database Language SQL3*. Document ISO/IEC JTC1/SC21/WG3 DBL OTT-003 (May 1992). Also available as American National Standards Institute (ANSI) Document ANSI X3H2 1992-109 (May 1992).

17. Robert R. Stoll: *Sets, Logic, and Axiomatic Theories*. San Francisco, Calif.: W. H. Freeman and Company (1961).

18. C. J. Date: "Putting the Pieces Together," *Database Programming & Design 7,* No. 2 (February 1994). Republished in *Relational Database Writings 1991–1994* (the relevant discussion appears on pages 118–119). Reading, Mass.: Addison-Wesley (1995).

19. C. J. Date and David McGoveran: "Updating Union, Intersection, and Difference Views," *Database Programming & Design 7,* No. 6 (June 1994); "Updating Joins and Other Views," *Database Programming & Design 7,* No. 8 (August 1994). Both republished in C. J. Date, *Relational Database Writings 1991–1994*. Reading, Mass.: Addison-Wesley (1995).

20. C. J. Date and David McGoveran: "A New Database Design Principle," *Database Programming & Design 7,* No. 7 (July 1994). Republished in C. J. Date, *Relational Database Writings 1991–1994*. Reading. Mass.: Addison-Wesley (1995).

Up to a Point,
Lord Copper

A response to a paper by
Tom Johnston entitled
"More to the Point"

ABSTRACT

Tom Johnston's recent article "More to the Point" [2] was a response to a critique by the present authors [3] of an earlier two-part article by Johnston [4] in support of many-valued logic. What follows is a response to that response. *Note:* Despite this fact, we believe that what follows—like reference [3], reprinted as the previous chapter in this book—does stand on its own and is worth including here.

COMMENTS ON REPUBLICATION

The debate continues . . . See the "Introduction" section immediately following for more specifics.

Originally published on the *Database Programming & Design* website: *http://www. dbpd.com* (November 1996). A version of this paper can also be found at *http://www. alternativetech.com.* Reprinted by permission of Hugh Darwen and David McGoveran and Miller Freeman Inc.

INTRODUCTION

As the subtitle indicates, this paper is a response to Tom Johnston's recent article "More to the Point" [2]. In fact, it is our second such; our first, much briefer, was intended as a letter to the editor of *Database Programming & Design* [5]. We begin with a slightly edited excerpt from that letter. *Note:* Following normal convention, we use MVL, 2VL, 3VL, . . . throughout this paper to stand for many-valued logic, two-valued logic, three-valued logic (and so on). Our comments tend to focus on 3VL specifically, though most do also apply, sometimes with even more force, to 4VL, 5VL, and the rest.

(Begin quote)

Probably many readers are bored to tears with this whole subject. Certainly the editor of *Database Programming & Design* seems to think so; in his introduction to our previous critique, he wrote: "[Johnston's response to this critique] will appear [soon] . . . With that, we'll all shake hands and end this chapter of The Great MVL Debate."

Would that we could! But Johnston's response simply cries out for further rebuttal. The sad truth is that the topic of our debate is *fundamentally important*. What's more, it isn't going to go away (indeed, nor should it), so long as MVL advocates such as Johnston fail even to address—let alone answer—our many serious and well-founded objections to their position. We stand by our contention that MVL is not only not a good approach to the problem at hand, but has the potential to be a disastrously bad one.

This isn't the time or place for a detailed response to Johnston's latest comments. Suffice it to say that we find them almost entirely without merit, and that we plan to respond in detail as soon as we can.

(End quote)

The present article is that promised—perhaps *threatened* would be a more appropriate word—detailed response.

OVERVIEW

Given that we've already admitted that readers are likely to be heartily fed up with this whole topic, we obviously need to justify our decision to contribute yet another episode to the saga. The plain fact is that we simply can't leave Johnston with the last word. To do so would be to suggest that we acquiesce in the opinions he expresses in his latest article, and indeed that we accept his position as a valid one. *Au contraire,* we find nothing in that article to undermine our own position (in fact, we find nothing new in it at all). But to leave it unrefuted would be to give the dangerous impression that the whole debate *is* just a matter of opinion, not one of science and logic.

Let's get down to specifics. Our overriding criticisms of the article in question are twofold:

1. Portions of it are simply irrelevant—they have nothing to do with the problem at hand.

2. Those portions that do pertain to the problem at hand don't say anything new (actually, nor do the others), and they don't address our fundamental objections.

To elaborate:

1. The "problem at hand" is—to spell it out one more time—the question of whether MVL is suitable as a basis for dealing with missing information. Much of Johnston's article, by contrast, concerns itself not with this question but with the question of using certain "extended" logics for purposes that have little or nothing to do with missing information *per se.* In the blow-by-blow response that follows, we choose not to bother much with points of Johnston's that seem to us irrelevant to the problem at hand.

2. By his own admission, Johnston does not really address—let alone answer satisfactorily—our major objections to MVL. (Those objections, and Johnston's failure to address them, are **The Big Issue,** of course.) To quote: "I will attempt to answer [those objections] in a future article. I simply ask that [Date, Darwen, and McGoveran] provide me with a list of [those objections]" (presumably to facilitate preparation of a corresponding list of responses).

    Well, as we point out in our letter [5], such a list did in fact appear in our earlier critique [3]. However, we repeat it here for convenience:[*]

    - Mathematically speaking, a "relation" that "contains a null" isn't a relation (and so relation theory doesn't apply).

    - A "relation" that "contains a null" violates Codd's own Information Principle.

    - If TABLE_DEE represents *true* and TABLE_DUM represents *false,* what represents *unknown?*

    - What's the relation predicate for a "relation" that permits nulls in one or more of its columns?

    - The fundamental theorem of normalization breaks down in 3VL.

---

[*]Apologies for the duplication.

- What's the justification for treating nulls as duplicates of one another for the purposes of union and projection but not for the purposes of restriction and join? In other words, are two nulls equal or aren't they?
- Even if such a justification can be found, why is it necessary for the relational algebra to suffer such complication?
- Expressions that evaluate to *true* in 3VL are not necessarily true in the real world (in other words, "3VL doesn't match reality").

To this list David McGoveran now adds the following further challenges [1]:

- Many benefits have been claimed for MVL. Please give a solid definition of an MVL that is supposed to provide these benefits, including its vocabulary, axioms, connectives (logical operators, including quantifiers), rules of inference, truth valuation semantics (including a definition of which truth values are designated, which anti-designated, and which neither), and an explanation of how the user is to understand the meaning of each of those truth values.
- Prove that this MVL either is or is not (a) truth functional, (b) truth functionally complete, (c) deductively complete, (d) expressively complete, (e) negation consistent, (f) relatively or absolutely consistent, (g) decidable.
- Provide a consistent (that is, uniform) interpretation of this MVL. In other words, explain the intended meaning *in database terms* of each and every axiom, operator, and rule of inference in this MVL.
- If the MVL is not truth functionally complete, then how many connectives does the user have to learn? Specify precisely which ones those are, and prove that what is lost by ignoring the others is unimportant.
- If it is claimed that SQL implements some such MVL, then repeat all of the above for that particular MVL, and show that SQL/92—or some vendor's dialect thereof—implements that MVL consistently. (It would be particularly nice to pin down the meanings of IMPLIES and BIMPLIES in such an "SQL MVL.")

McGoveran further adds: If Johnston cannot respond adequately to the foregoing requests, then he cannot substantiate his claims that MVL is useful in the field of database management. Nobody can evaluate the costs and benefits of a system of logic that isn't adequately defined.

The remainder of the present paper consists of a blow-by-blow rebuttal of various points in Johnston's article [2]. The structure of the paper (such as it is) thus mirrors that of that article. All otherwise unattributed quotations are taken from that source; we've numbered them for ease of reference. The section headings are also taken from that same source. *Note:* We're very conscious that such a blow-by-blow rebuttal, by getting heavily into details of various kinds, might serve to obscure **The Big Issue**. But Johnston's article contains so many errors and misleading remarks that we felt that a blow-by-blow response had to be attempted, despite that risk [6].

AN AGREEMENT WITH DATE: SCOPE AND LIMITS

1. "For example, it is precisely the counterintuitivity of IMPLIES, in *basic* logic, that motivated . . . C. I. Lewis's formalization of modal logic . . . In fact, [Lewis] pointed out that if you take any two statements from the newspaper, at random, either the first IMPLIES the second, or *vice versa*. This is very different from our commonsense notion of implication!"

    So what? We believe we adequately addressed the question of "the counterintuitivity of IMPLIES" (in conventional 2VL) in our previous critique; we also pointed out that the problem isn't remedied by MVL. In any case, Lewis's systems of logic suffer from counterintuitivities of their own. For example, in all of those systems, if you take any two statements from the newspaper, at random, either the first implies the second or it implies the negation of the second [7]. This is very different from our commonsense notion of implication!

    David McGoveran adds: If Johnston wants to see modal logic used in a DBMS, I invite him to convince a vendor to implement such a system. Let the market decide this one; it has nothing to do with the problem at hand. Much more to the point: Johnston criticizes the 2VL version of IMPLIES, but neither he, nor Codd, nor the SQL standards committee, nor any RDBMS vendor has defined a 3VL or 4VL version! We might assume that *material implication* is intended (meaning that p IMPLIES q is defined as (NOT P) OR q), but several other definitions are possible; just which one does Johnston assume? He is very willing to make claims for MVL in general, but he has never, so far as I know, specified a particular MVL (by defining its vocabulary, rules of inference, logical operators, and so forth) that we might thereby examine and criticize scientifically.

2. ". . . to minimize errors . . . due to using relational DBMSs, we must (a) minimize ambiguities in our assertions that are recorded in those databases [*sic*], (b) minimize errors in manipulating the formal language with which we query the DBMSs [*sic*], and (c) minimize misinterpretations of the databases' [*sic*] responses to our queries . . . I claim that it is *more to the point* to adopt this wider focus than to adopt Date's narrower focus on (b) alone."

    We have several comments on this extract. First, some minor editorial points: The phrase "databases' responses" would be better shortened to just "responses," and the two occurrences of "DBMSs" should be replaced by "databases." (Perhaps these points aren't so minor. The difference between a database and a DBMS is most certainly a *logical* difference, and hence a *big* one [8].)

Anyway, to continue:

a. "Assertions . . . recorded in databases" are unambiguous by definition (see David McGoveran's further remarks on this point under Quotation 29). Thus, we contend rather that what we need to "minimize" here are ambiguities—and ideally errors too, of course—in *real-world* assertions, before trying to enter counterparts to those real-world assertions into our formal databases. We believe 3VL hinders rather than helps us in our attempts to meet this goal.

b. We also contend that errors are demonstrably more likely to occur in "manipulating the formal query language" if that language is based on 3VL instead of 2VL. Moreover, such errors can be—and historically have been, and still are to this day!—committed both by the user *and by the DBMS*.

c. We further contend that "misinterpretations of query responses" are, again, demonstrably more likely to occur in a 3VL context than a 2VL one.

d. Finally, it's not at all clear to us that Johnston's article has much of a constructive nature to say regarding "this wider focus" anyway.

DATE'S POSITIONS AND DATE'S OBJECTIONS

3. "[Although Date's] position may have 'wide support' in some sense, it is certainly not a *consensus* position . . . Many approaches to handling missing information are still being put forward in the academic journals . . . Many authors have extensively studied the relevance of various kinds of null values to functional and other dependencies . . . Indexing nulls, in order to distinguish null values which are known to be distinct, has been studied by several different authors . . . If Date's default values alternative were accepted, these investigations would be moot."

By *moot* here, Johnston presumably means not *debatable* but *irrelevant*. But if so, why does he act so surprised?—it wouldn't be the first time some research direction or other has later turned out to be a dead end. Readers can surely provide plenty of examples of their own [9].

4. "A second issue Date raises is why I suggested that he apparently 'wants to remain within the confines not just of 2VL,' but also of propositional and first-order predicate logic. Was this a 'disingenuous' or 'perfunctory' attribution on my part? I don't think so . . ."

Here Johnston has misconstrued our original critique. Our original text read as follows:

(*Begin quote*)

[Johnston] claims that "Date apparently wants to remain within the confines not just of 2VL, but of [basic logic]"—though he does also go on to say that he doesn't "know whether [Date] has ever said this" but has "never seen an example [in which Date] went beyond these confines." This disclaimer seems a little perfunctory, however, or even disingenuous, since [he] then devotes virtually the whole of Part II of his article to criticizing [our] imputed position that DBMSs should "remain within the confines . . . of basic logic."

(*End quote*)

In other words, it was the *disclaimer,* not the *imputation* (or "attribution"), that we suggested might be disingenuous or perfunctory. Another logical difference! Furthermore, we went on to point out that it would be more accurate to say that "remaining within the confines . . . of basic logic" was *Codd's* original position, rather than ours. Of course, we certainly support Codd in this regard.

5. "Date objects to MVL because, among other things, it would be difficult to teach to 'naive end users.' Well, let him try to teach those users basic modal logic, or temporal modal logic! Tarskian semantics—which is the semantics for first-order predicate logic—is difficult enough for beginning students of logic to grasp. How well, then, would Date's 'naive end user' understand Kripkean semantics—the semantics for modal logic—which subsumes Tarskian semantics as merely intra-possible world semantics?"

   We find this excerpt puzzling on at least two counts. First, it seems, if anything, to be arguing in favor of *our* position (that is, that we should stay with simple 2VL). Second, it was Johnston, not us, who raised the question of "exotic logics" (modal logic and the rest); at the risk of beating a dead horse, we point out once again that they have *nothing to do with the case!*—they do not represent an attack on the missing information problem.

   There is a useful expression in logic: *ignoratio elenchi*—defined in Chambers Twentieth Century Dictionary as "ignoring the point in question; the fallacy of arguing to the wrong point." (There is also a more familiar expression: *blinding with science.*)

6. "The third and final point on which Date feels I have misrepresented him is my statement: 'That RDBMSs could eliminate these (join) costs, or at least keep them to a manageable level, is a misconception put forward by vendors and, I regret to say, by Date himself.' To this statement, Date cries 'FOUL!' . . . My comment was based on two related observations . . .

[First,] far from *criticizing* 'the vendors . . . for delivering inadequate levels of independence between the base and stored table levels,' Date has claimed that 'relational technology . . . *decouples* the logical and physical levels of the system to a greater extent than did previous technologies' . . . [Second,] in none of [Date's] publications have I been able to find these criticisms . . . [Although Date has described] two of the . . . techniques that are part of my proposed solution to this problem, [he has] said nothing about the fact that no vendor has provided an implementation of either technique."

There are several points to be made by way of response here:

a. We (especially Date) certainly have criticized the vendors in print for "delivering inadequate levels of independence between the base and stored table levels." Examples of such criticism—not the only ones—can be found in references [10–12].

b. Regarding "[Date's claim] that relational technology . . . *decouples* the logical and physical levels of the system to a greater extent than did previous technologies": Not only is this claim 100 percent true, but in fact such decoupling is 100 percent *required* for Johnston's "proposed solution to this problem."

c. It's incorrect to say that "no vendor has provided an implementation of either technique." Oracle provides what is probably the best-known counterexample (though we hasten to add that Oracle's implementation is very far from perfect, and we can agree with Johnston that vendors could do much better in this area).

7. "Date, however, publicly *accepted* the need for denormalization when he said . . . that: 'Sometimes, in order to improve retrieval performance, it may be desirable to put two facts in one place, or one fact in two places.' It seems to me, therefore, that instead of criticizing vendors on this point, Date has actually *acquiesced* in the architectural flaw that imposes these join costs!"

The quotation attributed to Date here is correct as stated. However, it was made—admittedly tacitly!—in the context of the implementations that existed at the time (1983, when SQL products were very new). In any case, this seems to be a good place to quote Bertrand Russell once again [13]:

(*Begin quote*)

I have been accused of a habit of changing my opinions . . . I am not myself in any degree ashamed of [that habit]. What physicist who was already active in 1900 would dream of boasting that his [*sic*] opinions had not changed during the last half century? . . . The kind of philosophy that I value and have endeavoured to pursue is scientific, in the sense that there is some definite knowledge to be obtained and that new discoveries can make the admission of former error inevitable to any candid mind. For what I have said, whether early or late, I do not claim the kind of truth which theologians claim for their creeds. I claim only, at best, that the opinion expressed was a sensible one to hold at the time ... I should be much surprised if subsequent research did not show that it needed to be modified. [Such opinions were not] intended as pontifical pronouncements, but only as the best I could do at the time towards the promotion of clear and accurate thinking. Clarity, above all, has been my aim.

(*End quote*)

A LOGICAL HOWLER?

8. "... the phrase 'infinite regress of truth values' is fairly common in the philosophical literature on MVL. And although Date did not use that phrase, and instead used the phrase 'infinite regress of nulls,' I believe that Date is quite wrong to imply that these are very different concepts."

Nulls aren't truth values. Truth values are, by definition, values; as such, they belong to a certain domain (sometimes called the *boolean* domain). Nulls are not values [14]; they do not belong to any domain. This is a logical difference with a vengeance! It follows that an infinite regress of truth values is not the same thing as an infinite regress of nulls (and any contributor to "the philosophical literature on MVL" who thinks otherwise is thoroughly confused). We stand by our original claim.

9. "Null markers play the same role that the traditional 'T' and 'F' markers play; that is, nulls belong, with 'T' and 'F', in the characteristic matrices for sentential connectives ... If a metalinguistic marker for null is actually stored in the database, one might wonder ... why the two other metalinguistic markers—'T' and 'F'—are not stored in the database. The answer is that 'F' isn't needed so long as the Closed-World Assumption is used, since that assumption designates all and only those assertions not stored in the database, [and not] deducible from assertions stored in the database, as false assertions. And 'T' isn't needed either ... since any atomic assertion in the database in which the null marker does not appear can be assumed to have the 'T' marker."

Johnston seems to be seriously confused here. "Null markers" apply to row-and-column intersections within relations. "T" markers, if there were such a thing, would apply to whole rows. Of course, one might imagine a "U" ("unknown") marker that would also apply to whole rows—presumably it would be used to mark all and only those rows that included one or more nulls—but that "U" marker would not itself *be* a null. Once again: *Nulls aren't truth values.*

DOES DR. CODD UNDERSTAND WHAT A RELATION IS?

10. "Hugh Darwen's basic response to my arguments appears to be that 'relations just do enshrine basic logic *by definition* . . . Well, if this is true, then we must apparently conclude that Dr. Codd himself does not understand what a relation is! . . . Darwen's position seems to be that of a neighbor of his good friends, Tweedledum and Tweedledee: 'When I use a word,' Humpty Dumpty said, in a rather scornful tone, 'it means just what I choose it to mean—neither more nor less.' In fact, it is only on the basis of Date's 'own Version 1 of the relational model' (or that version extended by numerous essays by Date and Darwen) that relations enshrine basic logic by *definition*."

It's hard to know how to respond to these truly extraordinary claims! Surely Johnston agrees that the real numbers together with the operators "+", "−", "*", and so on, "just do enshrine" basic arithmetic by definition. Well, in a precisely analogous manner, relations together with the operators union, join, difference, and so on, just do enshrine basic logic by definition—and that's the end of the matter. It's not a question of our *asserting, à la* Humpty Dumpty, that this is so; it *is* so.

By the way, the "numerous essays by Date and Darwen" that Johnston refers to here have been aimed not so much at "extending" the relational model as *explaining* it.

Hugh Darwen adds: My co-initialee, Humpty Dumpty, is indeed one of my favorite literary characters, and I've often used Carroll's joke at my own expense when I've felt a need to confess to some possible abuse of a word. But I can think of nothing more galling than to have the HD jibe thrown at me in connection with the one word whose precise meaning I value above (perhaps) all others: *relation*. The tenor of Johnston's jibe is "Who does Darwen think he is, claiming to know better than Dr. Codd what a relation is?"—a kind of adhominery that I find is often resorted to by people who are running short of good technical argument [15].

Well, in Codd's book [22] I find (a) a perfectly acceptable definition of *relation* in Chapter 1, but also (b) much text in Chapter 8, "Missing Information," that is inconsistent with that definition. The definition runs like this:

> Given sets S1, S2, . . . S*n* (not necessarily distinct), R is a relation on these *n* sets if it is a set of *n*-tuples each of which has its first element from S1, its second from S2, and so on.

To repeat, I have no quarrel with this slightly informal definition (except that I would have written what I'm sure Codd intended, namely "if and only if," in place of just "if"). What I mean by *relation* is also completely consistent with Chapter 4, Section 5 ("Properties of Relations"), of *Beginning Logic,* by E. J. Lemmon, first published by Thomas Nelson and Sons in 1965—four years before Codd's first paper on the subject.

11. "Dr. Codd, of course, does *not* think that he has misunderstood what a relation is. According to him, 'Chris (Date) has said that a relation is not a relation if it contains missing values. This, of course, is not true at all.'"

    By definition, "a relation that contains missing values"—we take this expression to mean, more specifically, a relation that contains *nulls,* because of course missing values as such (again by definition) don't exist, and so can hardly be contained in anything!—is an object that contains something that does not come from any of the applicable domains. A true relation, by contrast, contains only values that do come from the applicable domains. This is a logical difference.

12. ". . . Darwen is certainly right that I haven't 'given us a replacement for . . . the relational model of data.' And I take Date to be making the same point when he says that 'Johnston's articles . . . totally ignore most of our documented objections to the idea of using three-valued logic.'"

    Yes, it's the same point. To repeat, this is **The Big Issue!**—see the second of our "overriding criticisms" in the "Overview" section, earlier. It is, accordingly, the issue that we desperately want readers not to lose sight of as they wade through the point-counterpoint arguments of the present paper.

    Hugh Darwen adds: Johnston actually goes on to say that ". . . it would have been foolhardy to attempt to provide an alternative version of the relational model in the space of two articles." **ALTERNATIVE VERSION???** I said *replacement!* The relational model might have needed some clarification over the years, but it's not up for versioning (*pace* Codd). Perhaps I should have been a little less demanding and asked not for a replacement *per se,* but merely for some indication as to what Johnston's replacement might look like (in other words, some idea as to what sort of abstract machine he envisages). And he could make a good start on a response by giving acceptable answers to our specific questions, instead of beating about the bush.

    He might make an even better start by justifying the decision to use "null markers" in place of values in the first place. What he actually does instead is try to justify a certain *consequence* of that decision—namely, many-valued logic. And it is precisely because he concentrates on what is really a secondary effect that I find so much of Johnston's contribution to be beside the point. To justify the idea of "null markers," you would have to show them to be an improvement over *values* as a way of dealing with the problem at hand. The great advantage of using values is that (a) we already have a highly acceptable abstract machine based on nothing but values, and (b) we've had technology capable of delivering much of the promise of that abstract machine for at least two decades. Beat that!

McGOVERAN'S POINTS

13. "I challenge McGoveran to name a *single* example of a system of modal or multivalued logic that is inconsistent. I assure our readers that logicians don't waste time creating *inconsistent* systems of logic!"

    David McGoveran responds:

    a. Actually, logicians do create inconsistent logics on occasion. Initial attempts at axiomatizing a system often include inconsistences. Johnston himself provides us with an excellent example—namely, Frege's attempt to axiomatize arithmetic.

    b. But Johnston missed my point, which was as follows. First, logicians have proved that a large class of MVLs are not truth functionally complete (a point Johnston concedes). Second, they have also proved that if such an MVL is made complete (for instance, by adding the Slupecki T-function), it becomes inconsistent! Therefore, for this class of MVLs— which includes ones that Johnston apparently advocates—we can have either truth functional completeness or consistency, but not both. I invite Johnston to read one of the best known texts on this issue [16].

    c. As an aside, I note that an inconsistency in one of the MVL systems Johnston cites was pointed out* at the very conference where it was first presented [17]. That system has the bizarre (and inconsistent) property that $(R$ WHERE $p)$ UNION $(R$ WHERE NOT $p) \neq (R$ WHERE p OR NOT $p)$!

14. ". . . McGoveran is correct that several systems of 3VL are truth functionally *incomplete* . . . However, this assumes that truth functional completeness is a *sine qua non* of a system of logic. But professional logicians don't make this assumption . . . For example, modal logic is not truth functionally complete, lacking finite characteristic matrices entirely. Intuitionist logic, and supervaluational logic, are also not truth functionally complete."

---

*In fact, it was pointed out by none other than Codd himself.

David McGoveran responds: I can't fathom why Johnston has so much trouble in understanding the importance of truth functional completeness. First of all, I never claimed such completeness was "a *sine qua non* of a system of logic." But I did claim it was essential to a logical foundation for a DBMS! As I noted in my original articles on this topic [18], such completeness guarantees that there will be a truth-valued expression for every fact that can be deduced, under the intended interpretation, from the primitive assertions (that is, rows) in the database. Without this property, there is no guarantee that the system will be able to derive, mechanically, the answer to any query! Imagine telling your end users that— occasionally, and unpredictably—the DBMS might respond to a syntactically correct query with "Huh?" and a shrug of the shoulders! I wouldn't run *my* business on such a system.

Let's get something straight here. Human beings can use systems of logic that aren't computational, but computers can't (though you can fake it for them with heuristics). If you want to use such a noncomputational logic, then you'll have to exercise human judgment as an integral part of such use. Human judgment is *not* a basis for automation.

15. "[McGoveran asserts] that 'Johnston confuses the need for a computational apparatus with the issue of the ambiguities of the English language' . . . On this issue, I disagree with McGoveran. It is, perhaps, the very crux of our disagreement. I stated repeatedly in my original articles what the relevance of natural-language ambiguities to 'formulas of logic' is. I will defer my last attempt to [a later section of the present article]."

    David McGoveran responds: Johnston doesn't seem to understand that the value of automated systems is that they *compute.* In particular, RDBMSs compute results from stated assertions. (Those stated assertions are *rows,* in database terms.) Of course an assertion *per se* is noncomputational. Of course the natural language in which an assertion is expressed "in the outside world" is context-sensitive, and therefore ambiguous when taken out of context. But the person making the assertion knows what the assertion means! Once a row is inserted into the database—that is, once an assertion has been made—the human element is removed from the picture. The *system* can now *compute* (in a predictable and optimizable fashion) results from those assertions without human interference. This is precisely the value of nonprocedural processing: Human beings don't have to tell the computer what to do each step of the way.

16. "McGoveran has 'never seen any evidence that the development of 3VL was due to an attempt to make the meanings of the connectives more [natural]' . . . But the evidence is there. The desire to develop a logical system more in accordance with ordinary discourse modes of reasoning was clearly Aristotle's and Łukasiewicz's motivation for three-valued

logic. Both believed that in ordinary discourse, statements about future contingent events do not have any truth value until those events actually occur. And Bochvar's three-valued logic 'was intended to supply a solution to the semantic paradoxes' that appear in natural language when a 2VL is assumed."

David McGoveran responds: Here Johnston seems to be equating two very different things—connectives (logical operators) on the one hand, and future contingent statements on the other. Try a simple grammatical diagramming of the future contingent statement "It will rain in 2001." I'm sorry, but I don't see any connectives here! Of course logicians have been concerned with "ordinary discourse," but *my* claim was that redefining the connectives had nothing to do with the evolution of logical systems, 3VL included.

17. "[McGoveran claims that my] 'reference to Russell's Paradox—Is the set of all sets a member of itself?—and Frege is gratuitous and irrelevant.' First of all, that's not Russell's Paradox, which concerns, instead, the set of all sets *that are not members of themselves*. More to the point, my argument was that usage errors are likely to occur with familiar logics precisely because they are familiar . . . I therefore reject McGoveran's familiarity objective, and the emphasis Date puts on the unfamiliarity of NOT's multi-valued interpretation. Instead of being 'gratuitous and irrelevant,' my reference to Russell and Frege illustrates why I do not agree that familiarity . . . is a *sine qua non* of a logical apparatus for relational DBMSs."

David McGoveran responds: Johnston has correctly stated Russell's Paradox; I simply stated the crux of the issue it raised without going into the original construction. Anyway, I fail to see what the discovery by Russell of a paradox (inconsistency) in Frege's very complex logical system has to do with familiarity, and I fail to see how it supports Johnston's argument that familiarity is unnecessary. The 2VL system we support is known to be free of such inconsistencies—by the way, SQL isn't!—and is *very simple;* Frege's system is and was *very complex* (just as MVLs are very complex). Familiarity is a *sine qua non* for simplicity. Simplicity in turn is highly desirable in the foundations of a DBMS, since a DBMS is a system that must be used and understood by many people.

18. "[McGoveran claims that my] 'definition [of the Closed World Assumption] leads to logical systems that are infinitely extensible with new axioms.' Huh? And, so what?"

David McGoveran responds: Each time we add a new axiom, we'll have a new logical system, with new logical properties (consistency, completeness, . . .), and probably a new intended interpretation as well. How in the world does Johnston expect users to deal with such a wildly dynamic notion of logic? How can we expect to run our businesses using such a system?

19. "... basic logic is not truth functional because the quantifiers are not. [Date says this] claim is 'correct as stated' but is 'irrelevant' because 'in databases ... we deal only with finite sets.' Well, at the same time that I made that comment, I said that my point was 'to provide some motivation for keeping an open mind about truth functionality.' In order to call my point 'irrelevant,' Date would have had to miss this passage, which occurred just one line before the challenged point."

    We didn't miss the passage. We continue to find the point irrelevant.

20. "... here's the algorithm McGoveran requested [*for identifying tautologies and contradictions in the supervaluational approach*]. Start with a standard two-valued interpretation. ... If the statement in question is a tautology or a contradiction under the two-valued interpretation, then proceed no further ... Otherwise, evaluate it using the multivalued characteristic matrix ..."

    David McGoveran responds: Here I fear I didn't express myself clearly, and I apologize to both Johnston and the readership. What I wrote was: "I would love to see an algorithm for identifying tautologies and contradictions." Johnston understood me to be asking for a mechanical test for whether *a particular expression* was a tautology or a contradiction, but what I wanted was an algorithm that would *generate* all tautologies or all contradictions for a given MVL. Such an algorithm (a) is required to meet the needs of a logical foundation for a DBMS, (b) does indeed exist for the form of 2VL we support, but (c) *is known not to exist* for the brands of MVL Johnston apparently advocates.

    In any case, Johnston's "algorithm" doesn't do what he says it does. In fact, it isn't an algorithm, since it begins by *assuming* part of what it's supposed to be (algorithmically) specifying—namely, that we can identify the class of expressions that will be tautologies or contradictions under a 2VL interpretation. Further, it also assumes that the MVL under consideration has a characteristic matrix—but most MVLs don't.

21. "[McGoveran says my] 'claims that RDBMSs cannot optimize for the join I/O problem are ludicrous.' On the contrary, they aren't even wrong. Optimization techniques optimize the *access path* to data, whereas the join I/O problem exists because *frequently co-referenced* rows are not *physically co-located* on DASD ... Furthermore, *no* RDBMSs today can maintain such co-location over a series of updates, even if they permit procedurally specified loading that initially establishes such co-location. In addition, no extensions to SQL DDL (other than those that I have proposed) exist to permit the declarative specification of such co-location."

    David McGoveran responds: There are two aspects to relational optimization, logical and physical. Johnston's remark that "optimization techniques optimize the *access path*" has to do purely with physical optimization. If the optimizer did logical optimization too, it would recognize join as a logical operation and separately recognize that no I/O was necessary for tables that were to be joined but were in fact co-located. This separation of logical and physical aspects is a key element of the optimizer: Data can be physically stored wherever makes the best performance sense (witness Oracle's clustering keys and Rdb's support for hashing multiple tables to the same storage area), without the user having to be aware of such physical issues at all.

DATE'S POINTS

22. "[Date claims that] 'Johnston misrepresents, or misconstrues, the default values approach and then attacks his own misconstruction' . . . My assertion that Date's default values approach may sometimes require a value to take on two meanings *was* in error, and I retract the faulty criticism. But what is the difference between 'misrepresents' and 'misconstrues' that leads Date to use both terms . . . ? In ordinary language, the difference is one of intention; one *intentionally* misrepresents, but only *inadvertently* misconstrues."

   We thank Johnston for the retraction. As for "misrepresents" *vs.* "misconstrues," our intent was merely to give Johnston the benefit of the doubt (though it could be argued that misrepresentation can be inadvertent too!). *Note:* A full description of the default values scheme does now exist in draft form. We hope to publish it soon.*

23. ". . . when Date claims that a system using basic logic and a default value 'certainly *is* capable of recognizing this default value as meaning not applicable and acting accordingly,' I disagree."

   Let's consider the example from our previous critique, in which the property "hourly rate" doesn't apply to certain employees. In the default values scheme, the domain for the HOURLY_RATE column would be—let's say—X, where X consists of all possible valid hourly rates *plus* the default value—let's say—"N/A". And, of course, the system is informed of these facts (that the domain and the "not applicable" value for HOURLY_RATE are X and "N/A", respectively) by means of the database definition. Now the system can obviously deal appropriately with queries such as:

   ■ Find all employees for whom the hourly rate property applies

---

*See Installments 51–54 and 56 in Part I of this book.

- Find the average hourly rate for those employees
- Find all employees with an hourly rate in excess of some specified value

and so on. Doesn't this kind of behavior on the part of the system effectively mean that the system is recognizing that the default value means "not applicable" and acting accordingly? If not, in what sense does it not?

24. "The whole purpose of a logical system is to compute a meta-value assignment for a wff [*i.e., well-formed formula*] based on the meta-value assignments for other wffs, using the syntactic patterns and the given assignments."

We don't see that this remark in any way contradicts or undermines our claims regarding the system's ability to "deal appropriately" with default values.

25. "It is precisely this poverty of formal expressiveness that is the cost of adopting the logical conservatism Date recommends—a cost which he appears not to recognize."

We believe the cost of embracing MVL is much greater, and our various publications on the subject have tried to show why. (Perhaps we should stress the point yet again that our concern here is *solely* with the suitability of MVL as a basis for dealing with missing information—not with the possibility of using "extended logics" as a basis for dealing with temporal data and the like, which we see as a totally separate and orthogonal issue.)

26. ". . . McGoveran has proposed an elaborate framework for dealing with missing information . . . However, he [makes] no reference to the dozens of publications in the academic journals on the topic of missing information, indicating that his proposals are either unresearched or else based on unacknowledged previous work by others. It does seem to me a very *selective* use of the 'Principle of Cautious Design' to (a) reject even a modest three-valued logic, whose mechanics were developed well over half a century ago, while (b) recommending this elaborate and possibly unresearched framework . . ."

But the whole point of that "framework"—which, by the way, we do not see as particularly "elaborate"—is to stay firmly within the boundaries of the relational model and 2VL! It seems to us, therefore, that it rests on a very solidly researched foundation indeed and needs no further apology on our part.

Of course, it's true that that "framework" might lead to, or possibly even require, the development of certain new database design principles. If so, however, such new principles are in all probability to be welcomed. And in any case, the question of database design has little to do with research into the relational foundation *per se*. (By the way, it's also true that nulls tend to encourage *bad* database designs, in our opinion.)

David McGoveran adds:

a. It is incorrect to state, as Johnston does, that in my original articles [18] I "make no reference to . . . publications in the academic journals on the topic of missing information" (as readers can readily verify for themselves).

b. My proposal did reference the work of others (e.g., Date's default values approach), but I was unable to find a description anywhere in the literature of an approach that was exactly similar to mine. If it turns out after all that my proposal isn't "original" (but see point c. below), I apologize to those on whose shoulders I unwittingly stand.

c. Nothing in my approach is unresearched. Each and every database design recommendation is a part of the standard database design framework; all I did was to point out how that framework can deal with "missing information," *without* needing an MVL. I have used these techniques for years, and the only criticisms anyone has been able to bring have to do either with physical issues (performance or storage space, both of which I addressed in my original articles [18]) or with administration issues (current products could be more user-friendly with regard to physical design, a point I've addressed elsewhere [19]).

d. Using such familiar techniques to address the problem of "missing information" will very likely lead to new understanding in the field of database design and to further clarification of the relational model, and thereby to better (more elegant and more consistent) presentation of the ideas in my articles.

27. "I said in my second article that 'It may surprise some to realize that MVL is consistent with bivalence.' Date says 'It certainly surprises me!' Bivalence is the principle that every statement is either true or false. To make a long story about a peripheral issue short, Susan Haack states that *'the use of a many-valued system needn't even require denial of bivalence.'* She goes on to add that a four-valued interpretation she described 'entails that every *wff* is either true or else false.'"

This seems to be "an explanation that doesn't explain." Here is a slightly edited version of what we said in our earlier critique:

(Begin quote)

"Bivalent" means two-valued; the "MV" in MVL means, well, many-valued, where "many" means greater than two . . . [The standard version of the principle of bivalence refers to two-valuedness.] Perhaps Johnston is referring to a system in which every truth value except *true* itself is (at some point) effectively converted to *false*. SQL's 3VL might be thought of as behaving in this way, since (for example) SQL queries retrieve only those rows for which the defining condition evaluates to *true*, not those for which it evaluates to *false* or *unknown* (in other words, SQL effectively converts *unknown* to *false* just before the retrieval is done). If this is all that Johnston's remark means, then his point is irrelevant, and our criticisms of 3VL are still germane.

(End quote)

Simple dogmatic assertions such as those attributed to Haack in Johnston's response here do not in our opinion constitute an adequate refutation of these arguments, nor are they an adequate explanation or justification of what still seems to us a rather surprising remark on Johnston's part.

David McGoveran adds: It is truly frustrating to be presented with a quotation (from Susan Haack's book) that shows such little understanding of context. As the Bard has it: "The devil can cite Scripture for his purpose." Haack reviews many nonstandard logics in her book and discusses their characteristics in the large. In particular, she discusses the complexities of an MVL extension to the principle of bivalence. She doesn't say that all MVL systems can avoid the denial of bivalence, only that some can. Those that do, like Bochvar's, usually have an internal MVL and an external 2VL. Johnston takes Haack's statement and a grab-bag of properties of numerous MVLs and uses them to argue that *some particular MVL* can exist that has all the nice properties he would like to see. By contrast, I've tried to show that *no single MVL can exist that does have all those properties*.

In fact, if Johnston will reread my articles [18], he'll find that even if we agree to forgo the familiarity requirement, those systems that satisfy the other requirements defy description in business terms. For example, I'm certain he can't even explain to a business person what Post's third truth value means *in terms that business person could use!* I took a comprehensive approach in my articles by classifying every MVL into one of three categories and then demonstrating the properties of each.

NOTHING TO DO WITH THE CASE?

28. "In my first article, I argued that there is no sense in which MVL is 'logically flawed' but basic logic is not. In his response, Date retracted 'logically flawed,' and substituted the notion of being conducive to generating

'conclusions that are logically incorrect . . . *in the real world*' . . . Like its predecessor—'logically flawed'—Date's new phrase seems to me to have no more cash value than 'somewhat puzzling, on first sight'; and its forcefulness, and air of authority (*'logically incorrect!'*), therefore seem to me very misleading. Nonetheless, given this retrenchment [*sic*], my argument can be rephrased as follows: There are no grounds for saying that MVL is conducive to generating such erroneous conclusions while basic logic is not."

We have published examples of queries in which the answer that is correct according to 3VL is incorrect in the real world [20]. (Yes, *logically* incorrect! We're talking about another logical difference.) We continue to disagree with the position Johnston articulates in the final sentence of this excerpt.

29. ". . . at the beginning of my first article . . . I distinguished between mathematical logic and philosophical logic. I granted that McGoveran's articles were full of impressive stretches of mathematical logic, but stated that the real issue was one of philosophical logic."

David McGoveran responds: The real issue is most emphatically *not* one of philosophical logic (though it's clear that it would be to Johnston's advantage if it were). The whole point of automation is to eliminate the need for the human element (or at least to relegate it to a realm outside that of the system), and the situation is no different when it comes to automating database management. *Every* system of logic is subject to problems of human error in translating between human discourse and logical expressions. Most of those problems arise because human discourse is context-sensitive and ambiguous; indeed, much of its flexibility (in terms of linguistic evolution and expressiveness) derives from these very qualities. Human reasoning is often nonlinear; it can even capitalize on its errors without acknowledging them (much as a genetic mutation can create DNA coding errors with positive benefits).

What Johnston fails to comprehend is that all of these problems are *confined to the mind of the user*—as indeed they must be! *No* system of logic can choose its own axioms or provide an intended interpretation of its own symbols. The insertion of a row into a database—by definition, an operation performed by the *user*—establishes an axiom (possibly redundant). The user must understand the intended subject of the database (certainly no computer can) and should be honest in efforts to make assertions that others can rely upon. But once a row is in the database, the DBMS simply relies upon the truth of the corresponding assertion (axiom) and computes from it. Johnston's ambiguities are not visible to the system of logic: They are completely encapsulated in the meanings assigned to atomic domain values by users.

Claiming that the issues surrounding MVL are issues of philosophical, not mathematical, logic is rather like claiming that a program used for accounting is bad because users can't understand how to represent "three-ness" within it. We, on the other hand, would say that the program is bad because it's not an accounting program!—but (perhaps) a drawing program. And we could support our position, using mathematical logic, by showing how the drawing program fails to meet the accounting need. (Analogously, I tried to show in my original article [18] that MVL fails to meet the database management need.) In other words, using "philosophical logic," one can make philosophical *claims* regarding such issues, but one would be very hard pressed to supply philosophical *proofs*.

30. "Date also claimed that my discussion of extended logics, such as modal and temporal logic, was *'a complete red herring!'* . . . But the point of that discussion was to illustrate how much expressive power lay within the range of formal logic, but beyond the range of the basic logic that Date and company advocate."

   David McGoveran responds: If Johnston wants nothing more than expressive power, he should stick to English or some other natural language. Alternatively, he might try to prove (not just claim) that some modal or temporal logic is more expressive than predicate logic. (Such logics *are* two-valued, by the way; "red herring" was right.)

   Be that as it may: What I want is correct (accurate), reliable, computational, predictable, understandable, complete, consistent systems that produce results I can capitalize on. If Johnston thinks some particular system of logic does all this better than a finite propositional 2VL (with equality and quantifiers that iterate AND and OR over finite sets of values), he should write the papers that prove it. His philosophy be damned if he can't prove that two plus two will still be equal to four in his chosen system of logic.

WHAT SHOULD WE DO?

31. "I believe that we should give up the idea of query formulation as a 'one-shot' process. Instead . . . the interface should use artificial intelligence techniques . . . which would present other formal queries back to the user, queries that he or she *might have meant*."

   On the face of it, these remarks are quite astounding. Is Johnston really arguing that we should give up the benefits (so dearly achieved) of nonprocedurality? Surely not! Perhaps he is merely asking for an interactive "query helper" layer on top of an underlying interface that is indeed nonprocedural. If so, we agree this could be a fruitful path to explore. However, database technology and the database industry clearly aren't there yet, and we would have to question the wisdom of designing and building systems *now*—systems, that is, that are based on MVL—if the success of those systems were conditional on research, as yet unperformed, into new kinds of interfaces and "artificial intelligence techniques."

32. "... a good illustration of the danger of unassisted query formulation is the many 'SQL puzzles' that have appeared in Date's columns in this magazine. I seldom get them right! So I thank Date for these examples, because I certainly could not come up with better ones to show that *basic logic* itself is quite conducive to generating conclusions that are 'logically incorrect *in the real world*,' and therefore just as in need of AI expert assistance as any extended logic."

    Do we detect a slight hint of "gotcha" in this extract? In any case, it seems likely to us that the difficulties Johnston has encountered in solving these puzzles are due as much to the quirks and idiosyncrasies of SQL as they are to the difficulties of "basic logic." Certainly such has been our own experience.

33. "I think that an initial foray into an implementation of three-valued logic is warranted."

    Do we understand this suggestion correctly as implying that—in Johnston's opinion—none of today's SQL products constitutes such a "foray"?

34. "And I would call that third [truth] value simply 'null.'"

    If you call some truth value "null," what do you call a null? (See our comments on Quotations 8 and 9.) We say it one last time: *Nulls aren't truth values!*

35. "Indeed, because of the many business rules that involve temporal notions . . . I think that a real *need* exists to introduce propositional modal logic into database administration."

    Why? Why not just treat time as another domain? (Also, why the emphasis on *administration?*)

36. "What Should We Do About Using Extended Logics With Relational Databases?"

    David McGoveran responds: Johnston can do whatever he likes with extended logics. But until he can conclusively demonstrate—using formal arguments—that their costs do not outweigh their benefits, I sincerely hope no commercial DBMS will use them as a foundation. When vendors demonstrate that they've used 2VL correctly, I'll even support research into extended logics. At this time, however, I do want to caution users: If Johnston can't show that the proposed system of logic is truth functionally complete, don't buy it, unless you want to do a lot of work manually; the query language will, of necessity, be more procedural, and the optimizer won't be able to do very much for you.

CONCLUSION

By way of conclusion, we cannot do better than paraphrase some remarks from our previous critique:

(*Begin quote*)

The problem of how best to deal with missing information in databases has long been a thorny one. Johnston's articles don't move us any closer to solving that problem . . . We find absolutely nothing in those articles to cause us to modify our position . . . At least with 2VL, we know what needs to be taught, we know what needs to be included in DBMS query languages and optimizers, and we know how to avoid mechanical errors. Thus, we do at least have some hope of identifying other errors as human and striving for better use of database products.

(*End quote*)

Of course, we're not so naive as to think this will be the end of the debate;* doubtless we'll be hearing from other MVL defenders in due course. We ask only that any such future defenses be couched—if possible—in the form of cogent, rational, and technical arguments, so that we can respond to them in a like manner.

NOTES AND REFERENCES

1. Portions of this paper directly contributed by Hugh Darwen or David McGoveran are so flagged.

2. Tom Johnston: "More to the Point," *Database Programming & Design 8,* No. 11 (November 1995).

3. C. J. Date, Hugh Darwen, and David McGoveran: "Nothing to Do with the Case" (Chapter 9 of the present book).

---

*How right we were . . . Johnston himself produced yet another article, "The Faults with Defaults," which can be found on the World Wide Web at *http://www.dbpd.com.* That article consisted in large part of an attack on the special values scheme as described in Installments 51–54 and 56 in Part I of the present book. In a letter to the editor of *Database Programming & Design* concerning that article, however (*DBP&D 11,* No. 2, February 1998), Johnston did very graciously also say the following: "[This is] my swansong in this debate . . . and I leave the last word to Date. But before readers decide who has had the best word, I ask that they look at my articles in their entirety and not rely on Date's paraphrases and quotations from them." We choose not to prolong the agony by responding in detail to Johnston's swansong.

4. Tom Johnston: "MVL: Case Open," *Database Programming & Design 8,* No. 2 (February 1995); "The Case for MVL," *Database Programming & Design 8,* No. 3 (March 1995).

5. C. J. Date, Hugh Darwen, and David McGoveran: Letter to the editor of *Database Programming & Design* (unpublished as of the time of writing).

6. We note in passing that certain arguments made by us in our previous critique— for example, our argument that Johnston's "proof" that basic logic is nonmono- tonic was specious—are simply ignored in his latest article. Are we to infer that Johnston now agrees with us on all such points?

7. James D. McCawley: *Everything that Linguists Have Always Wanted to Know about Logic* (page 297). Chicago, Ill.: University of Chicago Press (1981).

8. Ludwig Wittgenstein (attrib.; quoted in Hugh Darwen and C. J. Date: "The Third Manifesto," *ACM SIGMOD Record 24,* No. 1, March 1995, and elsewhere).

9. The results reported in some of the references cited by Johnston on research into nulls and MVL specifically are most certainly moot (i.e., debatable). Reference [17] is a case in point.

10. C. J. Date: *An Introduction to Database Systems* (6th edition, page 72). Reading, Mass.: Addison-Wesley (1995).

11. C. J. Date: *Relational Database Writings 1991–1994* (page 11). Reading, Mass.: Addison-Wesley (1995).

12. *Ibid.,* pages 85–86.

13. Bertrand Russell: Preface to Lester E. Denonn (ed.): *The Bertrand Russell Dictionary of Mind, Matter and Morals.* New York, N.Y.: Citadel Press (1993).

14. Despite the fact that Johnston uses the term "null *values*" (emphasis added) sev- eral times in his article; see Quotation 3, for example. Incidentally, it's worth noting that Codd himself has frequently stated that a null is not a value; see, for instance, reference [22], page 179 and elsewhere.

15. Humpty Dumpty defines *adhominery* as the practice of indulging in *ad hominem* remarks.

16. Nicholas Rescher: *Many-Valued Logic.* New York, N.Y.: McGraw-Hill (1969). Page 163.

17. Yannis Vassiliou: "Functional Dependencies and Incomplete Information," Proc. 6th International Conference on Very Large Data Bases, Montreal, Canada (October 1st–3rd, 1980).

18. David McGoveran: "Nothing from Nothing" (Chapters 5–8 of the present book).

19. David McGoveran: "The Relational Model Turns 25" (Chapter 2 of the present book).

20. C. J. Date: "Three-Valued Logic and the Real World," in C. J. Date and Hugh Darwen, *Relational Database Writings 1989–1991.* Reading, Mass.: Addison- Wesley (1992).

21. Nicholas Rescher: *Op. cit.*

22. E. F. Codd: *The Relational Model for Database Management Version 2*. Reading, Mass.: Addison-Wesley (1990).

23. *For the benefit of readers who have had the endurance to stay with us this far and might be wondering about our choice of title:* Lord Copper is an all-powerful and overbearing newspaper tycoon in Evelyn Waugh's novel *Scoop;* Mr. Salter is his foreign editor. Mr. Salter's contribution to any conversation with his employer is "limited to expressions of assent. When Lord Copper was right he said, 'Definitely, Lord Copper'; when he was wrong, 'Up to a point.' " The phrase "Up to a point, Lord Copper" has since passed into the language as an elegant variation on "I disagree," or, more simply, *NO*.

RELATIONAL *vs.*
NONRELATIONAL
SYSTEMS

INTRODUCTION

This part of the book consists of a series of papers that examine various aspects of the "objects *vs.* relations" controversy. Chapter 11 suggests that "the object model" is not really a *data* model at all, in the traditional sense of that term. Chapter 12 compares and contrasts object IDs and relational keys, and goes on to suggest that the former have no place in a good logical data model. Chapter 13 is a response to an article by Won Kim criticizing the position of *The Third Manifesto* that the equation "domain = class" is correct and the equation "relvar = class" is not. Finally, Chapters 14 and 15 both have to do with what I now regard as *The Second Great Blunder*—namely, mixing pointers and relations (the first great blunder being the adoption of the wrong equation "relvar = class").

Why "The Object Model" Is Not a Data Model

A contribution to the debate over objects and relations

ABSTRACT

Arguments over the relative merits of objects and relations are often of the "more heat than light" variety. Why is this? This paper suggests an answer to this question. Specifically, it suggests that the underlying models are more different than is usually realized—one, the relational model, being a true data model and the other not. One consequence is that, perhaps without fully realizing the fact, object proponents and relational proponents are likely to be arguing from different premises.

COMMENTS ON REPUBLICATION

It can often be helpful to challenge assumptions, especially unstated ones—and it seems to me that "object *vs.* relational" debates do often rely on certain unstated assumptions. I originally wrote the paper that follows in an attempt to get some of those particular assumptions out into the light, so that we could take a careful look at them. Reactions at conferences where I've presented the ideas of this paper have generally been favorable to such an approach, and indeed to my conclusions also.

Originally published in *InfoDB 10,* No. 4 (August 1996). Reprinted by permission of Database Associates International Inc.

INTRODUCTION

In this paper, I want to discuss an idea that I believe can help shed some light on the debate over the relative merits of objects and relations. The idea is this:

The "object model" is a storage model, not a data model.

Let me immediately explain why I place the term "object model" in quotation marks. I do so because, as is well known, there's actually no such thing as a universally agreed, abstract, formally defined "object model" (nor is there even consensus on an *in*formal model)—despite the fact that several attempts have been made to define such a thing over the past few years; see, for example, references [1], [4], and [14]. Indeed, there's very little agreement in the object world even on *terminology*. However, it is at least safe to say that every candidate "object model" does include, under one name or another, all of the features we need to examine in this paper—see the next section but one—and so this lack of consensus need not concern us too much here.

As indicated by my opening sentence, I hope this paper will serve to clarify certain aspects of the objects *vs.* relations debate. To this end, I invite anyone who disagrees with the thesis adopted in this paper to take up a dissenting position in public, so that we can at least get the arguments out into the open and thereby stand a better chance of assessing their relative worth—and, perhaps more importantly, a better chance of deciding how best to move forward in our field.

One final preliminary remark: Please note that, at least so far as this paper is concerned, I'm interested in object orientation *solely* as it pertains to database management. Thus, I don't want to discuss object-oriented interfaces, or applications, or programming languages, or analysis, or design (etc., etc.). Indeed, I suspect that another reason why the objects *vs.* relations debate sometimes seems so confusing is that the arguments themselves sometimes confuse these very different issues. Throughout this paper, therefore, all references to objects, or object orientation, or just "OO"—which I use here generically as an abbreviation for either "object-oriented" or "object orientation," as the context demands—are to be understood *from a database perspective specifically,* barring explicit statements to the contrary.

DATA MODELS AND STORAGE MODELS

Perhaps I should begin by explaining what I mean by the terms "data model" and "storage model"—especially as the first of these terms, at least, is used in the literature to denote two quite different things. So here goes:

■ First of all, a model (of anything) is basically a construction, as concrete or as abstract as we please, that captures certain aspects of the thing being modeled—where by "capturing certain aspects" I mean that features or properties of the model mimic, in certain specific ways, features or properties of the thing being modeled. Study of the model can thereby lead to improved understanding of the thing being modeled.

■ In particular, therefore, a model of *data* is a construction—necessarily somewhat abstract, since data itself is already a fairly abstract concept—that captures certain aspects of data. What aspects? Well, the aspects we're interested in are clearly those that are *intrinsic,* as opposed to those that are mere artifacts of some particular representation or implementation. We want to study data in its pure form and not be distracted by irrelevancies. To use the usual jargon, we're interested in the logical aspects of data, not the physical aspects.

■ It follows that a *good* model of data will be one that (like the relational model) is "logical, not physical"—i.e., one that captures only logical aspects, not physical aspects. (Ideally it would capture *all* of those logical aspects, of course, but this goal I take to be unachievable.) Moreover, it shouldn't include anything else!—i.e., there should be no properties or features that don't correspond to anything intrinsic. In IMS, for example, the very same data item can be interpreted either as a character string or as a packed decimal number; but this oddity is merely an artifact of "the IMS model" (if I might be permitted to use such a term)—it certainly isn't something that's intrinsic to data *per se.**

■ To be more specific, a good data model will include a set of *objects* (using the word here in its generic sense, not its OO sense), together with a set of *operators* for operating on those objects. The objects allow us to model the *structure* of data. The operators allow us to model its *behavior.* Taken together, therefore, the objects and operators effectively constitute an *abstract machine*†—and we can thus usefully distinguish the model from its *implementation,* which is the physical realization of that abstract machine on some underlying real machine. In a nutshell: The model is what users have to know about; the implementation is what users don't have to know about.

---

*In fact, of course, it's a consequence of a failure to distinguish adequately between type and representation.

†One seminar attendee suggested strongly that I should go further here and demand that the objects and operators form an *algebra* specifically (as they do in the case of the relational model, of course)—and I have to say I'm very sympathetic to this suggestion.

- Next, the objects and operators of the model serve as a basis for further investigations into the nature of data. For example, what does it mean for data to be secure? consistent? redundant? (and so on). And those investigations in turn can lead to (compatible!) extensions to the original model; that is, the model can grow over time to become an ever more faithful abstraction of data "as it really is." In other words, a model of data is really a *theory* of data (or at least the beginnings of one), and it's not a static thing.

   (As an aside, I remark that it might have been better if, right back in the early days of database research, we had spoken in terms of a data *theory* instead of a data *model*. There would then have been less likelihood of confusion with the other common interpretation of the term "data model"—namely, as a model of some enterprise or business. *Note:* It might help to observe in passing that the relationship between the two interpretations of the term "data model" is analogous to that between (a) some given programming language *P* and (b) some given program written in that language *P*. It's also worth mentioning in passing that the familiar activity of "data modeling" refers to the second meaning of the term, not to the meaning that's the principal focus of this paper.)

- Finally, a model of *storage* is, of course, a model that captures certain aspects of storage, not data. In the remainder of this paper I will elaborate on this distinction and explain it in more detail.

AN OVERVIEW OF "THE OBJECT MODEL"

This section summarizes those components of the object model that are relevant to the thesis of this paper (it ignores aspects, such as inheritance, that might be important in themselves but aren't relevant to that thesis). *Note:* In the interests of readability, I'll drop the quotation marks surrounding "object model" from this point forward. Too much repetition quickly becomes tiresome.

First of all, we need to understand exactly what objects themselves are. In a typical object model:

- Every object is an *instance* of some **object class** (*class* for short).
- Objects can be either **mutable** or **immutable.**

In more conventional terms:

- A *class* is essentially just a **data type** (*type* for short). The type in question can be either system-defined (i.e., builtin) or user-defined; either way, however, the only way objects of the type in question can be operated upon is by means of the **operators** (also known as *methods*) defined for the type. In other words, the *representation* of those objects—which can be arbitrarily complex—is always *hidden from the user.*

Note: In the case of a user-defined type, of course, the representation might be visible to the user who actually defines the type. However, it will definitely be hidden from other users.

- A *mutable object* (instance) of type (class) *T* is essentially just a **variable** of type *T.**

- An *immutable object* (instance) of type (class) *T* is essentially just a **value** of type *T.*

Thus, for example, the system might provide a builtin type called REAL, with operators "+", "*", "<", and so on. Users would then be able to declare REAL variables and specify REAL literals, perform arithmetic and comparison operations on REAL values, and so on; but they would not know, nor would they need to know, how REAL values were represented internally.[†] As another example, some suitably authorized user might provide a user-defined type called CIRCLE, with operators GET_CENTER, GET_RADIUS, SET_CENTER, SET_RADIUS, and so on; users would then be able to declare CIRCLE variables and specify CIRCLE literals, operate on CIRCLE centers and radii, and so on, but again they would not know how CIRCLE values were represented internally, nor would they need to know.

Next, the operators associated with any particular class (type) are required to include at least one **constructor,** the purpose of which is to "construct" a new object (instance) of the class (type) in question. In Smalltalk, for example, the constructor for a given class is invoked by sending a message to that class asking it to create a "new" object of the class in question, as here:

```
CIRCLE NEW
```

Constructing an object causes the system to return an object **identifier** (*object ID,* or just *OID* for short) for the new object. That OID can be thought of as a *pointer* to, or *address* for, the new object. Thus, the Smalltalk message just shown can be regarded as an *expression* that evaluates to a pointer to a newly constructed circle. (Of course, when I say "pointer" here, I mean some kind of *logical* pointer—I'm not talking about physical disk addresses. At least, I hope not.)

---

*Be warned, however, that object systems typically usurp the general term "variable" and give it a very specific meaning—namely, a variable whose legal values are object IDs (see later). In this paper, we use the term in its more traditional general sense.

[†]It's interesting to note that a builtin type called REAL is in fact included in the SQL standard and that not a single word of this example need be changed for it to be fully applicable to SQL.

Note: Before going any further, I ought really to consider the question of what it might mean to "construct a circle" (or any other kind of object)—I certainly don't think it's obvious. However, I choose to defer discussion of that question to the next section; for now, please just assume that it does in fact have a sensible answer.

To continue with the overview: Next, it's important to understand that constructing an object does not necessarily **initialize** that object to any particular value. If it does not, such initialization will have to be performed as a separate, follow-on step. For example (Smalltalk again):

```
C_PTR   :=   CIRCLE NEW .
C_PTR SET_CENTER : CENTER_PTR .
C_PTR SET_RADIUS : RADIUS_PTR .
```

The first step here, the assignment statement, constructs a new circle and assigns its OID to the variable C_PTR. The second and third steps then send messages to the object whose OID is contained in that variable C_PTR—in other words, to the circle just constructed. Those messages cause two further operations to be performed, the effect of which is to set the center and radius of that new circle to certain initial values. More precisely, the effect is:

- To set the center of the new circle to the value that is the current value of the object whose OID is contained in the variable CENTER_PTR;
- To set the radius of that circle to the value that is the current value of the object whose OID is contained in the variable RADIUS_PTR.

Note that, as the example suggests, all references to objects are by means of the corresponding OIDs;[*] in other words, OIDs provide *addressability*— that is, *logical* addressability—to the objects they identify. Thus, for instance, a request to get the center (GET_CENTER) of a given circle will actually return, not the relevant point *per se,* but rather the OID of that point (I assume for the sake of the example that POINT is another user-defined type).

Finally, the object model requires support for a full complement of **type generators** (also known as type *constructors;* I use the term "generator" in order to avoid confusion with the constructor operators already discussed). Examples of such generators include STRUCT (or TUPLE), LIST, ARRAY, SET, BAG, and so on. These generators can be combined in arbitrary ways; thus, for example, an array of lists of bags of arrays of real numbers might constitute a single ("complex") object in suitable circumstances. Along with the

---

[*]This fact explains why—as is well known—OO systems typically provide (a) two different equality comparison operators, equal OID *vs.* equal value, and (b) two different assignment operators, assign OID *vs.* assign value. The two forms (of both assignment and comparison) are sometimes referred to as "deep *vs.* shallow," though authorities disagree as to which of the two is which.

OID mechanism already discussed, the availability of these type generators essentially means that *any data structure that can be created in an application program can be created as an object in an OO database*—and further that the structure of such objects is *visible to the user.* For example, consider the object, EX say, that is (or rather denotes) the collection of employees in a given department. Then EX might be implemented either as a linked list or as an array, and users will have to know which it is (because the access operators will differ accordingly).

Note: This "anything goes" approach to what can be stored in the database is a major point of difference between the object and relational models, of course, and it deserves a little further discussion here. In essence:

- The object model says we can store anything we like—any data structure we can create with the usual programming language mechanisms.

- The relational model effectively says the same thing, but then goes on to insist that whatever we do store be presented to the user in pure relational form.

More precisely, the relational model—quite rightly—says *nothing* about what can be physically stored (it's a logical model only). It therefore imposes no limits on what data structures are allowed at the physical level; the only requirement is that whatever structures *are* in fact physically stored must be mapped to relations at the logical level and so hidden from the user. Relational systems thus make a clear distinction between logical and physical (data model *vs.* implementation), while OO systems don't. One consequence is that—contrary to conventional wisdom!—OO systems might very well provide less data independence than relational systems. For example, suppose the implementation in some object database of the object EX mentioned above (denoting the collection of employees in a given department) is changed from an array to a linked list. What are the implications for existing code that accesses that object EX?

OBJECT CONSTRUCTION

Now I return to the question of what it means to construct an object. Let me begin by reminding you that there are basically two kinds of objects, *values* ("immutable objects") and *variables* ("mutable objects"). So what exactly do I mean by the terms *value* and *variable?* The following definitions are based on ones given by Cleaveland in reference [5]:

- A **value** is an "individual constant" (e.g., the individual constant "3"). A value has *no location in time or space*—in effect, it simply exists. What's more, a value can't be updated—for if it could, then after such an update it wouldn't be that value any more (by definition!). However, values can be *represented* by some encoding, and such representations can be used to denote "current values" of *variables,* which do have locations in time and space and can be updated. See the next bullet item.

Note: I don't mean to suggest that only simple things like integers are legitimate values. On the contrary, values can be arbitrarily complex; for example, a point is a value, a circle is a value, an array is a value, a list is a value, and so on.

- A **variable** is a holder for a representation of a value. As already stated, a variable does have location in time and space, and of course it can be updated; that is, the current value of a variable can be replaced by another, probably different from the previous one.

From the foregoing definitions, it is clear that:

- The idea of constructing a **value** makes no sense. Consider integers, for example. Nobody ever "constructs" the integer 3; that value simply exists, logically speaking. It's true that a given user at a given time might happen to become *interested* in that value (for example, in order to be able to specify the number of employees in a given department), but that user doesn't suddenly "construct" that value out of thin air; rather, he or she *makes use of* a value that already exists. And exactly the same argument applies to *all conceivable values,* no matter how complex they might happen to be—integers, strings, points, circles, lists or arrays of any of the foregoing . . . whatever.

- By contrast, the idea of constructing a **variable** does make sense—it means, precisely, constructing a *holder* into which we can put values (or, rather, representations of values). In other words, it means *declaring,* or *creating,* or *defining,* the variable in question.

Let's agree, then, that from this point forward "constructing an object" means constructing a *mutable* object (i.e., a variable) specifically. Thus, for example, execution of the PL/I statement

```
DECLARE N INTEGER ;
```

might be thought of as "constructing" a "mutable object" called N, of "class" INTEGER. And, once that mutable object has been constructed, we know we can go on to place (representations of) various "immutable objects" into that mutable object (different immutable objects at different times, in general). For example, the PL/I assignment

```
N = 3 ;
```

places (a representation of) the immutable object "3" in the mutable object N.

Now, all I've done so far is introduce certain terms (terms that might possibly be novel to some readers) for concepts that aren't really novel at all. And if matters stopped there—if that were all there were to it—everything would be just fine (well, reasonably fine, anyway; we don't really want too many different terms for the same thing). The trouble is, in OO matters don't stop there, as I now explain.

First of all, no matter what language we're talking about, a variable—i.e., a holder for values—has to be implemented under the covers as an area of storage. That is, one of the things the system has to do in order to implement an operation like the PL/I DECLARE statement shown earlier is **allocate storage** for the variable under "construction." But, of course, the whole point of traditional programming languages is precisely that users shouldn't have to worry about implementation-level details like storage allocation; to put it another way, the goal of such languages is *to raise the level of abstraction.* Thus, users of such a language should be able to ignore the physical details of the underlying real machine and focus instead on the logical details of the abstract machine defined by the language at hand. In particular, they should be able to ignore the idiosyncrasies of physical computer storage and operate in terms of the "variable" abstraction instead.

Next, of course, the goal of data models too is to raise the level of abstraction, in an exactly analogous fashion; in many respects, in fact, a data model really is a kind of high-level programming language (except that it doesn't prescribe any specific concrete syntax). Thus, all of the remarks in the previous paragraph apply equally well, *mutatis mutandis,* to data models as well as to programming languages.

I now claim that the OO notion of "constructing an object" is much closer to the *implementation* notion of allocating storage than it is to the more abstract *data model* notion of declaring a variable, and hence that the object model is really a *storage* model, not a data model. In the next two sections, I present arguments in support of this claim.

OBJECT IDENTIFICATION

My first argument goes like this:

- In a traditional programming language (or in a data model), when a variable is declared, a *name* is typically specified for that variable, and that variable can then be referenced by that name from that point forward.

- At the implementation level, by contrast, when an area of storage is allocated, it isn't given a name; instead, the system returns the *address* of that storage, and that storage can then be referenced by that address from that point forward.

What happens in an OO system? When an object is constructed, it isn't given a name; instead, the constructor operation returns an OID—which is to say, an address—for the new object.* I conclude that, as already suggested, an OO "object" is more like an area of storage than it is like a conventional variable.

Note: Earlier, I said that a mutable object was "essentially just a variable." I would have preferred to have said that it was *nothing more nor less* than a variable. However, as we now see, it lacks one very important feature of a typical variable (to wit, a name); in that respect, at least, therefore, it is indeed less than a true variable. (On the other hand, it is also more than just plain storage, inasmuch as it is at least usually *typed.*)

My second point is related to my first. Given a type (class), OO systems permit the construction of *any number* of individual objects of that type (class). For example, given the type CIRCLE introduced in the overview section earlier, the user is at liberty to construct as many CIRCLE "variables" (mutable objects) as he or she desires: one, two, a hundred, a million, possibly even none at all. As a direct consequence of this fact, individual CIRCLE "variables" do not—in fact, cannot—have names in the usual sense but are distinguished by address (OID) instead, as we've already seen.

Now, it's interesting, and relevant, to note that a close parallel to the foregoing state of affairs can be found in PL/I once again, in the form of *based variables.* Consider the following PL/I code fragment (I've numbered the lines for purposes of subsequent reference):

```
1. DECLARE 1 CIRCLE BASED ,
2.             2 CENTER ... ,
3.             2 RADIUS ... ;
4. DECLARE C_PTR POINTER ;

5. ALLOCATE CIRCLE SET ( C_PTR ) ;
6. C_PTR -> CENTER = some center value ;
7. C_PTR -> RADIUS = some radius value ;
```

Explanation:

■ Lines 1–3 declare a "based" variable—actually a based *structure* variable—called CIRCLE, with components CENTER and RADIUS. The specification BASED means that the declaration is really just a *template;* no storage will be allocated at compilation time (it will be allocated at run time instead, presumably).

---

*Remember that "object" here means a *variable* (mutable object) specifically. *Values* (immutable objects), which are never "constructed" but simply exist, can be thought of as serving as their own OIDs; in other words, they are *self-identifying.* (Though I ought to mention in passing that the OO literature often talks, confusingly, as if address-style OIDs refer not to variables *per se* but rather to the values those variables happen to have. See the section "Values *vs.* Variables," later.)

- Line 4 declares a "regular" (nonbased) variable, a pointer variable called C_PTR. Storage *is* allocated for this variable.

- Line 5 allocates storage for an unnamed CIRCLE variable—that is, an unnamed variable whose structure conforms to the template defined in lines 1–3. It also returns a pointer to that storage—equivalently, to that unnamed variable—in the pointer variable C_PTR.

- Lines 6–7 assign values to the CENTER and RADIUS components of the particular CIRCLE variable that the pointer variable C_PTR currently happens to point to.

The parallels to OO are obvious: The based variable declaration for CIRCLE corresponds to an object class definition; ALLOCATE CIRCLE is the corresponding constructor; access to a given CIRCLE variable by means of its address corresponds to access to a given object by means of its OID; "construction" and initialization are logically distinct operations. And, of course, any number of individual unnamed CIRCLE variables can be allocated, each with its own address, just as any number of individual unnamed objects can be constructed, each with its own OID.

Why bother with these OO-PL/I parallels? Well, in his book *Concepts of Programming Languages* [13], Robert Sebesta refers to variables like the allocated CIRCLE variable in the foregoing example as *explicit dynamic variables:* "Explicit dynamic variables are *nameless objects* whose *storage is allocated . . . by explicit run-time directives . . .* These variables *can only be referenced through pointer variables*" (my italics). And he goes on to say: "Explicit dynamic variables [and the corresponding pointers] are often used for dynamic structures, such as linked lists and trees, which need to grow and shrink during execution. Such structures can be conveniently built using pointers and explicit dynamic variables."

So the point is this: Just as pointers and explicit dynamic variables can be used to build and maintain "dynamic structures" in programming languages like PL/I, so OIDs and objects can be used to build and maintain such structures in OO. In particular, OO databases do frequently include such dynamic structures.

Is this, then, a serious logical distinction between OO and relational systems? **No.** Relational systems can, and often do, involve dynamic structures also. The difference is that in the relational case those structures are built and maintained using, not pointers, but rather the mechanisms—mainly primary and foreign keys—prescribed by the relational model. There is no logical need to use pointers instead of keys for such a purpose. And there are good reasons not to! To quote Sebesta again [13]: "The disadvantages of explicit dynamic variables [and pointers . . . include] *the difficulty of using them correctly*" (my italics again). To be specific, pointers lead to pointer chasing, and pointer chasing is notoriously error-prone.[*]

It's worth mentioning in passing that Codd certainly agrees with the foregoing. When he first defined the relational model, he very deliberately excluded pointers. And in his book *The Relational Model for Database Management Version 2* [6], he explains why:

> It is safe to assume that all kinds of users [including end users in particular] understand the act of comparing values, but that relatively few understand the complexities of pointers. The relational model is based on this fundamental principle . . . [The] manipulation of pointers is more bug-prone than is the act of comparing values, even if the user happens to understand the complexities of pointers.

In view of the foregoing, it's curious that so many people seem to regard OIDs as the *sine qua non* of the object model.[†] For example, *The Object-Oriented Database System Manifesto* [1] says "Thou shalt support object identity"—but it doesn't give any *logical* justification for such an edict. Likewise, Jim Melton [12] says "References in the form of object identifiers are the key [*sic!*] to the object-oriented paradigm," but he provides no evidence in support of this strong claim. And in a useful annotated and comprehensive anthology of writings on the subject [2] compiled by Declan Brady (containing "the substance of everything I've managed to unearth on the [subject] of OIDs"), numerous similar assertions can be found. So far as I can see, however, none of those assertions is accompanied by any *logical* supporting arguments.

Of course, OO advocates will probably counter with the argument that OIDs are needed for *performance* reasons. As I've written elsewhere, however [8], everything to do with performance is, first and foremost, an implementation matter!—it shouldn't be part of a data model. Anyone who thinks otherwise is seriously confused over the distinction between a data model and its implementation. Let me elaborate:

- The argument that pointers (or OIDs) are needed is usually based on a claim that following a pointer from some referencing data to some referenced data is more efficient than performing a foreign-to-primary-key join.

---

[*]Indeed, it is this aspect of OO systems that gives rise to the criticisms, sometimes heard, to the effect that such systems "look like CODASYL warmed over."

[†]Personally, I would have said **user-defined types** were the *sine qua non*. For the record, therefore, let me say here that in *The Third Manifesto* [7], Hugh Darwen and I take the position that user-defined type support can be achieved without OIDs. Further, we concur with Sebesta and Codd that OIDs can be positively harmful and therefore expressly proscribe them. We see no need to burden users with obsolete technology.

- For the sake of the argument, let's agree that "following pointers" is efficient (though I think there are situations in which this claim is almost certainly invalid). But the point is—again as I've said elsewhere [9]—*there's absolutely no reason why foreign-to-primary-key relationships shouldn't be implemented by pointers at the physical level.* (I know they typically aren't implemented that way in today's SQL products, but that's a criticism of those products, not a criticism of the relational model. At least one system, the IBM Starburst prototype, does provide such a pointer-based implementation [3].)

In other words, (1) *implementing* relationships by pointers is very different from (2) *exposing* such pointers in the data model. The fact that (1) might be a good idea doesn't imply that (2) is a good idea, and of course it categorically isn't. We *must* keep logical and physical concepts distinct, and not get confused over the two levels in our debates; we've learned the hard way—or at least some of us have—what happens when this principle is violated.

VALUES *vs.* VARIABLES

The fact that, at least in some object models, object construction and object initialization are separate operations lends further weight to my thesis that objects more closely resemble storage areas than they do variables. In fact, an argument could be made that—like assembler language!—the object model is rather unclear on the distinction between a value and a variable. The following quotation, which is taken from a tutorial on object databases [15], is not atypical:

- "We distinguish the declared type of a variable from . . . the type of the object that is the current value of the variable . . . we distinguish objects from values . . . a *mutator* [is an operation such that it's] possible to observe its effect on some object."

Observe that:

- The phrase "the object that is the current value of the variable" clearly implies that a value is an object (more precisely, that at least some objects are values and at least some values are objects).

- The phrase "we distinguish objects from values" clearly implies that a value isn't an object (more precisely, that no objects are values and no values are objects).

- And the existence of mutators—that is, operations that have an "effect on some object," or in other words update some object—clearly implies that the object in question is a variable; so at least some objects are variables (and at least some variables are objects).

So what *is* an object? The sad fact is that the picture is not nearly as clearcut as my earlier characterizations (of mutable objects as variables and immutable ones as values) would suggest. For this reason, I recommend in all sincerity that if you ever find yourself embarking on a discussion of objects, you should spend some time up front making sure that all parties to the discussion agree on exactly what the term "object" means. Otherwise, quite frankly, you're likely to be wasting your time.

Let me now explain my remark to the effect that the object model resembles assembler language in its lack of clarity over the "value *vs.* variable" distinction. For definiteness, I'll take IBM System/360 Assembler Language as the basis for my discussion. That language provides two instructions, DC and DS, that might be thought of, loosely, as "specify value" and "declare variable," respectively. But what they really do, both of them, is *allocate storage;* the only difference is that DC ("define constant") places a specified initial value in the allocated storage area, whereas DS ("define storage") doesn't. Subsequently, however, the contents of the allocated storage area can be changed at any time, regardless of whether it was allocated via DC or DS. Once again, I think the parallels with the object model are obvious; once again, in other words, I think the object model is closer to a storage model than it is to a data model.

Note: Assembler language and the object model do both include the notion of a *literal,* of course (called a "self-defining term" in IBM System/360 Assembler Language). But a literal isn't a value!—it's a *symbol* that *denotes* a value. Thus, to say that assembler language and the object model do at least have a clear notion of literals is not to say that they have a clear notion of values *per se* (and in the case of some object models, at least, they certainly don't [4]).

A LITTLE SPECULATION

Note: The material of this section previously appeared, in somewhat different form, in my book *An Introduction to Database Systems* [10].

Perhaps I should digress for a moment and consider the question of just why the object model and the relational model are so different—i.e., why the object model is really, as I've said, a storage model rather than a data model *per se*. I think the difference reflects a difference in origins between object technology on the one hand and database technology on the other. It seems to me that OO databases grew out of a desire on the part of OO application programmers—for a variety of application-specific reasons—to keep their application-specific objects in persistent memory. That "persistent memory" might perhaps be regarded as a database, but the important point is that **it was indeed application-specific;** it wasn't a shared, general-purpose database, intended to be suitable for applications that might not even have been foreseen at the time the database was defined. As a consequence, many features that database professionals regard as essential were simply not requirements in the OO world, at least not originally. Thus, there was little perceived need for:

- Data sharing across applications
- Physical data independence
- *Ad hoc* queries
- Views and logical data independence
- Application-independent, declarative integrity constraints
- Data ownership and a flexible security mechanism
- Concurrency control
- A general-purpose catalog
- Application-independent database design

These requirements all surfaced later, after the basic idea of storing objects in a database was first conceived, and thus all constitute "add-on features" to the original object model. (I might mention in passing too that some of those features—for example, views and *ad hoc* queries—turned out to be quite difficult to add to the original model. The reasons for this state of affairs are beyond the scope of the present discussion, however.)

One important consequence of all of the foregoing is that there really is a *difference in kind* between an object DBMS and a relational DBMS. In fact, I would argue that an object DBMS is not really a DBMS at all!—at least, not in the same sense that a relational DBMS is a DBMS. For consider:

- A relational DBMS comes *ready for use;* in other words, as soon as the system is installed, users (application programmers and end users) can start building databases, writing applications, running queries, and so on.
- An object DBMS, by contrast, can be thought of as a kind of *DBMS construction kit.* When it's originally installed, it's *not* available for immediate use by application programmers and end users. Instead, it must first be *tailored* by suitably skilled technicians, who must define the necessary classes and methods, etc. (the system provides a set of building blocks— class library maintenance tools, method compilers, etc.—for this purpose). Only when that tailoring activity is complete will the system be available for use by application programmers and end users; in other words, the result of that tailoring will indeed more closely resemble a DBMS in the more familiar sense of the term.

■ Note further, however, that the resultant "tailored" DBMS will be *application-specific;* it might, for example, be suitable for CAD/CAM applications, but be essentially useless for, e.g., medical applications. In other words, it still won't be a general-purpose DBMS, in the same sense that a relational DBMS is a general-purpose DBMS.

Please understand that I'd be the first to admit that the foregoing speculations might be wide of the mark—but they do seem to explain some of the differences in emphasis that can be observed between the object and relational models, and between object and relational DBMSs and databases.

SUMMARY

In this paper, I've tried to show that the object model can usefully be thought of as a storage model rather than a data model. I've also speculated on some of the reasons for this state of affairs. Among other things, I've tried to show that:

■ Although mutable objects can be thought of in some ways as variables, they also behave in other ways more like areas of storage.

■ Unlike variables (but like storage), mutable objects are nameless and so must be distinguished or identified by addresses (OIDs).

■ Object constructors are basically storage allocators. OIDs are addresses or pointers. Constructing an object might not even initialize that object— suggesting, again, that it's really just storage that's being "constructed."

■ However, OIDs are logically unnecessary (as is obvious, in fact, since the relational model manages perfectly well without them).

■ The object model doesn't distinguish clearly between values and variables (as is perhaps to be expected of a storage model, but not of a data model).

■ The object model allows the database to contain arbitrarily complex data structures but *exposes them to the user,* thereby undermining data independence.

With respect to this last point, I have to ask (as I did earlier in connection with OIDs): What's the **logical** justification for this "anything goes" approach? In fact, let me close with one final observation that touches on this very issue (taken from a review by Adrian Larner [11] of a collection of papers on OO):

> [In a contribution to the collection,] Zdonik states, correctly, that in the OO paradigm, "data and programs are not . . . separate . . . they are designed, implemented, and used together." Yes: and *maintained* together, any change to shared data requiring modification of all the

programs that use it, however irrelevant to them the data change might be. We were originally driven to use databases to avoid the costs of this unproductive maintenance . . . *OO and database are incompatible* (my italics).

ACKNOWLEDGMENTS

I'm grateful to Declan Brady and Hugh Darwen for their careful review of earlier drafts of this paper and their many helpful comments.

REFERENCES

1. Malcolm Atkinson *et al.*: "The Object-Oriented Database System Manifesto," Proc. First International Conference on Deductive and Object-Oriented Databases, Kyoto, Japan (1989). New York, N.Y.: Elsevier Science (1990).

2. Declan Brady: Private communication (July 1st, 1996).

3. Michael Carey *et al.*: "An Incremental Join Attachment for Starburst," Proc. 16th Int. Conf. on Very Large Data Bases, Brisbane, Australia (August 13th–16th, 1990).

4. R. G. G. Cattell (ed.): *The Object Database Standard: ODMG-93*. San Mateo, Calif.: Morgan Kaufmann (1994). *Note:* This book has been superseded by R. G. G. Cattell and Douglas K. Barry (eds.): *The Object Database Standard: ODMG 2.0*. San Francisco, Calif.: Morgan Kaufmann (1997).

5. J. Craig Cleaveland: *An Introduction to Data Types*. Reading, Mass.: Addison-Wesley (1986).

6. E. F. Codd: *The Relational Model for Database Management Version 2*. Reading, Mass.: Addison-Wesley (1990).

7. Hugh Darwen and C. J. Date: "The Third Manifesto," *ACM SIGMOD Record 24*, No. 1 (March 1995). See also the book-length version *Foundation for Object/ Relational Databases: The Third Manifesto*. Reading, Mass.: Addison-Wesley (1998).

8. C. J. Date: "Why Is It Important to Think Precisely? (Part 1 of 4)" (Installment 58 in Part I of the present book).

9. C. J. Date: "Objects and Relations: Forty-Seven Points of Light" (Chapter 13 of the present book).

10. C. J. Date: *An Introduction to Database Systems* (6th edition). Reading, Mass.: Addison-Wesley (1995).

11. Adrian Larner: *Review of* Asuman Dogac *et al.* (eds.), *Advances in Object-Oriented Database Systems, BCS Computer Journal 38*, No. 10 (October 1995).

12. Jim Melton: "A Shift in the Landscape (Assessing SQL3's New Object Direction)," *Database Programming & Design 9,* No. 8 (August 1996).

13. Robert W. Sebesta: *Concepts of Programming Languages.* Redwood City, Calif.: Benjamin/Cummings (1989).

14. Michael Stonebraker *et al.*: "Third Generation Database System Manifesto," *ACM SIGMOD Record 19,* No. 3 (September 1990).

15. Stanley B. Zdonik and David Maier: "Fundamentals of Object-Oriented Databases," in Zdonik and Maier (eds.), *Readings in Object-Oriented Database Systems.* San Mateo, Calif.: Morgan Kaufmann (1990).

CHAPTER **12**

Object Identifiers *vs.* Relational Keys

Object IDs considered harmful

ABSTRACT

It's my opinion that "object identifiers" (object IDs) have no place in the data model as seen by the user. In this paper, I present arguments in support of that opinion.

COMMENTS ON PUBLICATION

No further commentary seems necessary; the title and (especially) the subtitle say it all.

INTRODUCTION

I recently taught one of my regular seminars on objects, relations, and object/relational databases [8]. During that seminar, the question arose (as it usually does): What's the *logical* argument for object IDs? In other words, if we try to come up with an abstract, formal, logical, rigorous, and coherent definition of some kind of "object model," what part do object IDs (OIDs for short) have to play in that model? *Do* they have a part to play? *Note:* I assume for the purposes

---

Previously unpublished.

457

of this paper that the term *object* is well defined and well understood. My reasons for placing the term "object model" in quotation marks are explained in reference [10].

Well, it's clear that if—as many authorities believe—OIDs are effectively just *pointers* in another guise, then there's certainly a performance argument that can be made for them. But, of course, performance is an implementation matter, it's nothing to do with the model; in other words, the performance argument is really an argument for including OIDs (or something like them) in the *implementation,* not the *model.* So are there any other arguments in favor of OIDs, apart from the performance one?

USER KEYS

In my seminar [8], I approached this question by first taking a look at how data is identified and referenced in the relational world (since, of course, object IDs are used for identifying and referencing data in the object world). Now, in a relational context, we use primary keys* as identifiers, and we use matching foreign keys to serve as references to the data identified by those primary keys. And, typically, the actual values assumed by those primary and foreign keys are (a) initially assigned by human users, and (b) subsequently controlled and maintained—i.e., possibly even updated—by human users. Let's agree, therefore, to call such keys *user keys* for short.

Now, it's well known that (in the absence of suitable discipline) user keys can suffer from certain problems. To be specific:

- User keys might be "intelligent."
- User keys might be nonuniform.
- User keys might be subject to change.
- User keys might be composite.
- An "obvious" user key might not exist.
- More than one "obvious" user key might exist.

To elaborate:

- *User keys might be "intelligent":* The term "intelligent key" is used to refer to a user key that doesn't act just as a unique identifier but additionally carries certain encoded information about the thing identified. For example, the International Standard Book Number (ISBN) includes a publisher ID,

---

*I've argued elsewhere [12] that it would be better to talk in terms of *candidate* keys rather than primary keys, but the point isn't important for the purpose at hand.

a code indicating the language in which the book is written, and various other information [13]. And the problem with such intelligent keys, of course, is that application programs can come to rely on their internal structure—possibly even on their specific values as well. Consequently, a change in the structure or values of such a key can lead to program failures, or significant program maintenance efforts, or both.

- *User keys might be nonuniform:* Distinct user keys can be—in fact, usually are!—of different types, sizes, or formats. (How often are the primary keys of distinct relations defined on the same domain?) This fact can cause difficulties whenever it becomes necessary, for whatever reason, to construct a relation containing a column containing references to (rows in) two or more distinct relations. For example, consider a relation that gives the IDs of all components—CDs, cassette tapes, LP albums, etc.—in a certain music collection.

- *User keys might be subject to change:* The relational model deliberately includes no prohibition against updating primary keys, because there are occasions when such updates *must* be done. For example, such an update might be necessary in order to reflect a change in the real world; e.g., in biology, the scientific names of plants and animals do change from time to time. As another example, such an update might be necessary in order to correct a past error; e.g., a person's name might have been spelled incorrectly.

  The trouble is, of course, that a primary key update will often require one or more cascaded foreign key updates as well, in order to maintain the integrity of the data, and—for a variety of reasons—those cascaded updates might not get done. As a consequence, the database can be in a state that, despite the fact that it's internally consistent (in the sense that it satisfies all system-known integrity constraints), *doesn't reflect reality.* For example, a change to a company's product numbering scheme might cause the database to show, incorrectly, that customer *C* owns product *Y* instead of product *X* (I've been a victim of this particular error myself).

- *User keys might be composite:* A composite key is a key that involves two or more columns. Though legal, such keys can give rise to a variety of problems, problems that I've discussed in detail in several other places [14–16]. One such problem is caused by the fact that composite keys can *overlap;* for example, the column combinations {*A,B*} and {*B,C*} might each constitute a foreign key, with the result that updating one of the two can have the side effect of updating the other as well (and side effects, of course, are usually best avoided).

- *An "obvious" user key might not exist:* Sometimes we need to record information (possibly just existence information) for certain real-world entities that don't have any "obvious" user key. For example, a person's name is not unique, in general (nor even is the combination "name plus birthday"). What then is the "obvious" user key for identifying persons?

■ *More than one "obvious" user key might exist:* Some real-world entities have more than one "obvious" user key (this problem is the inverse of the previous one, of course). As a trivial example, the very same entity might be identified as "C. J. Date" in some contexts and "Chris Date" in others. One consequence is that the system might not be able to recognize that two distinct key values in fact identify the same entity (hence the well-known junk mail problem, in which the unfortunate person receives numerous copies of the same irritating piece of marketing material).

SURROGATE KEYS

As hinted near the beginning of the previous section, there's a way to avoid the problems associated with user keys (or most of them, anyway), and that's to use *surrogate keys* instead. A surrogate key is a key in the usual relational sense, but one that has the following specific properties:

■ It's not composite—i.e., it's defined on a single underlying domain, not a combination of such domains.

■ Its values serve *solely* as surrogates (hence the name) for the real-world entities they stand for. In other words, such a value serves merely to represent the fact that the corresponding entity exists—it carries no additional information or meaning whatsoever.

■ When a new entity is inserted into the database, it's assigned a surrogate key value that's never been used before and will never be used again, even if the entity in question is subsequently deleted. *Note:* I'm speaking a little loosely here! This isn't meant to be a very formal paper.

In addition, it would be nice if the operation of assigning a surrogate key value to a new entity could be performed by the system instead of the user (at "create entity" time), in order to save the user from the burden of having to invent the necessary "meaningless" values. However, whether they're system- or user-generated has nothing to do with the basic idea of surrogate keys as such.*

> *Aside:* I note in passing that an argument could be made that many of the identifiers we use in the real world are essentially just surrogates anyway. For example, think of employee numbers, department

---

*In Chapter 8 of the present book David McGoveran uses the term "surrogate key" to mean a system-generated key specifically.

numbers, musical opus numbers, and so forth. Of course, these surrogates are certainly user-generated, not system-generated. *End of aside.*

Now let's take a look at how surrogate keys can help with the problems identified with user keys in the previous section:

- *Intelligent keys:* Surrogate keys aren't intelligent, so this problem goes away by definition. *Note:* Perhaps I should point out in passing that the arguments against "intelligent keys" apply with only minor changes to *all columns,* not just key columns! Thus, to say that "the problem goes away" with surrogate keys is a little misleading, in a sense. Further discussion of this issue would take us too far away from the main point of this paper, however.

- *Nonuniformity:* Since they're not intelligent, there doesn't seem to be much reason to have more than one domain of surrogate values. And, of course, if there's only one, then all surrogate values in the entire database will be "uniform," so the problems caused by lack of such uniformity won't arise. (Even if there's more than one, those problems can still be avoided by careful design—e.g., by ensuring that at least the primary keys of the CD, cassette, and LP relations are all defined on the same surrogate domain.)

- *Subject to change:* Since surrogate primary keys represent existence and nothing else, there's no reason ever to update them, and hence no need ever to perform cascaded updates on matching foreign keys. Thus, the problems caused by such updates don't arise. (The point here is that even if there are still user keys in the database—which, as we'll see below, there almost certainly will be in practice—those keys need never be used as *foreign* keys. That is, all referencing inside the database can always be done in terms of surrogates, and if it is, then there's never any need to cascade a primary key update to a matching foreign key.)

- *Composite keys:* Surrogate keys aren't composite, so these problems go away by definition.

- *No "obvious" key:* Surrogate keys take care of this problem, obviously.

- *Too many "obvious" keys:* Surrogate keys can help with this problem as well, but only to some extent. To be specific, if (a) entity *e* is given surrogate *s,* and (b) we adopt the discipline that all foreign key references within the database to entity *e* are via surrogate *s,* then (c) the system will certainly be able to recognize that two such references do in fact identify the same entity. On the other hand, if the end user (a) asserts on one occasion that there's an entity "C. J. Date" (assigned surrogate *s1*), and (b) asserts on another occasion that there's an entity "Chris Date" (assigned surrogate *s2*), then (c) there's no way the system can tell, unaided, that *s1* and *s2* do in fact identify the same entity. But this problem is *intrinsic:* It's nothing to do with the question of whether we use surrogate or user keys (or OIDs!—see later).

To sum up: Surrogate keys are a good idea (frequently, if not invariably—see below). More specifically, surrogate keys can help avoid many of the problems that occur with ordinary undisciplined user keys. It follows that if OIDs are basically just surrogate keys, nothing more and nothing less, then there's a good *prima facie* case for including them in our "object model"; in other words, we will have found some logical arguments for object IDs. So the question becomes: *Are* OIDs in fact the same thing as surrogate keys?

Aside: Before trying to answer this question, there are a few further points I'd like to clarify.

- First, surrogate keys, even when they're a good thing, *do not make user keys unnecessary.* For one thing, even if all identification and referencing *inside the database* is in terms of surrogate keys, it's still typically user keys that we use *outside* the database (i.e., in the real world). So at the very least there needs to be some way of mapping between user and surrogate key values (unless those user keys are themselves the surrogates, of course, a possibility noted earlier), and of course that mapping is performed inside the system. In other words, user keys are still needed for interaction with the outside world.

- Second, consider the familiar suppliers-and-parts database. Suppose relations S (suppliers) and P (parts) have primary keys S# and P#, respectively, and suppose S# and P# are both surrogates. Now consider relation SP ("shipments"), which indicates which suppliers supply which parts. What's the primary key for relation SP? If we take it (as we usually do) to be the combination {S#,P#}, then that key, though it does *involve* two surrogates, is not itself a surrogate key, it's a user key. As such, it might need updating!—e.g., consider what happens if all shipments from supplier S*x* are taken over by supplier S*y* instead. Of course, there's nothing to stop us *introducing* a surrogate, SP# say, to act as the primary key for shipments.

- Finally, you should be aware that there are sometimes good arguments—*logical* arguments, that is—for not using surrogate keys inside the database after all [14]. It's relevant to observe that those arguments apply to OIDs, too.

The whole question of user *vs.* surrogate keys is explored in depth in references [16], [18], and (especially) [14]. *End of aside.*

OBJECT IDENTIFIERS

Back to our question ("Are OIDs the same thing as surrogate keys?"). Well, here are some logical differences between the two concepts (please note that I make no claim that what follows is an exhaustive list):

- Surrogates in a relational database are (of course) represented in the same way as everything else: namely, as values in columns in relations. By contrast, OIDs in an object database are represented *differently* from everything else—with the result that (regardless of the advantages, if any, that might accrue from that difference) there is the inevitable *dis*advantage that object data is more complicated than relational data, involving as it does at least one additional concept.

- As a consequence of the previous point, access to relational data by surrogate is performed in exactly the same way as access by any other column: namely, associatively. By contrast, access to object data by OID is quite different from access by any other property (if indeed such "access by any other property" is even supported, which it might well not be in practice). In other words, surrogates are visible to the user, whereas OIDs aren't (that is, the user never sees OID values, and OID "columns"—if I might be permitted to use such a term—do not behave at all like regular columns).

- Following on from the previous point: In fact, of course, OIDs are really *values of type address*—in other words, they're *pointers*—and object databases necessarily support the data type *address*. Relational databases, of course, do not. *Note:* By *address* here, I don't necessarily mean a hardware address, of course. The idea is just that every object can be thought of as having a location of some kind, and that location in turn has some kind of unique identifier which we call the object's OID. However, we can certainly *think* of that OID as an address, in the usual sense of that term.

- It follows from the previous point that the "object model" fundamentally requires two operators, usually called *referencing* and *dereferencing,* that the relational model doesn't need. The referencing operator takes an object and returns its address (OID). The dereferencing operator takes an address (OID) and returns the object addressed by that OID. Incidentally, note the *programming-oriented nature* of these two operations; they aren't the kind of thing we'd expect the average end user to be able to use (or even understand). *Note:* In practice referencing and dereferencing are often implicit, but this fact doesn't materially affect the argument, of course.

- Indeed, OIDs really are pointers, at least conceptually. And the trouble with pointers is that they *point;* that is, they have *directionality,* and they have a single, specific target. Surrogates, by contrast, are *regular data values*: A given surrogate is simultaneously connected—logically speaking—not only to the entity in question but also to *all references* to that entity, no matter where in the database those references happen to be. In other words, surrogates (like all values in a relational database, but unlike pointers) are "multiway associative." For example, the department row for department *d* is logically connected to all employee rows for employees in department *d,* and each of those employee rows is logically connected to all the others and also to the department row for department *d* (where *d* is a surrogate, of course).

- To repeat, OIDs really are pointers, at least conceptually. And so we have here a major difference between the "object model" and the relational model! When Codd first defined the relational model, he very deliberately excluded pointers. To quote reference [5]: "It is safe to assume that all kinds of users [including end users in particular] understand the act of comparing values, but that relatively few understand the complexities of pointers. The relational model is based on this fundamental principle . . . [The] manipulation of pointers is more bug-prone than is the act of comparing values, even if the user happens to understand the complexities of pointers." (To be specific, pointers lead to pointer chasing, and pointer chasing is notoriously error-prone. Indeed, it is this aspect of object systems that gives rise to the criticisms, sometimes heard, to the effect that such systems "look like CODASYL warmed over.")

In other words, OIDs do perform some of the same functions as surrogates, but they're most certainly not just "surrogates pure and simple"—they carry a lot of additional baggage with them. Furthermore, I don't think anyone can seriously argue with the claim that the baggage in question is strongly motivated by performance considerations (i.e., by considerations that are more properly part of the implementation, not the model). And so we're still faced with our original question: What's the *logical* argument for object IDs?

IDENTITY vs. EQUALITY (?)

One answer sometimes offered in response to this latter question is that OIDs allow us to make a distinction between *identity* and *equality*. Two objects are said to be identical if and only if they have the same OID (in other words, if and only if they are in fact the very same object); two objects are said to be equal if and only if they have the same value, regardless of whether they have the same OID. Thus, identity implies equality, but the converse is not true.

So the next question we have to ask is: Is this identity vs. equality distinction a useful one? Note that—bearing in mind the fact that OIDs are hidden from the user—the distinction implies that two objects that look the same to the user (meaning the user has no way to tell them apart) might in fact be distinct. In other words, the objects in question are precisely analogous to those *duplicates* that—for very good reasons [6,17]—the relational model categorically prohibits! Why do supporters of the "object model" think duplicates are a good idea?

One of the attendees on my seminar [8], Tony Blair (not his real name), posted a couple of questions to this effect on the Internet that evening, and I'd like to present (and offer some brief comments on) the responses he got. First let's take a look at the exact form of those questions.

BLAIR'S QUESTIONS

Here's the text of Blair's original message:

> The primary difference between OIDs and relational keys seems to be that OIDs allow one to make a distinction between object equivalence and object identity. I have two questions:
>
> 1. Of what logical significance is such a distinction?
> 2. Of what practical significance is such a distinction?
>
> Thanks for any and all opinions.

These questions drew responses from two well-known figures in the object world, both of them members of the Object Data Management Group, ODMG [4]. I will call them Member X and Member Y, respectively.* The next two sections below consist largely of text from those responses, together with comments of my own (so marked) where such comments seem warranted.

RESPONSE BY ODMG MEMBER X

Member X's response begins thus:

> "To make sure we're using words the same way, relational keys can be used as a secondary data structure, managed by the user, with (very slow) joins to find related rows. The relationship is by values stored in the rows."

---

*I originally planned to refer to the two respondents by their real names, but decided not to because I didn't want what follows to be taken as any kind of *ad hominem* attack. I want to discuss concepts, not personalities.

Comment: Joins aren't necessarily slow, even in today's typically somewhat limited SQL products. Furthermore, of course, there's no reason why, if we accept the point (for the sake of the argument) that "pointers are fast," joins couldn't be *implemented* by pointers. As I've written elsewhere [9]: ". . . (1) *implementing* [joins] by pointers is very different from (2) *exposing* such pointers in the data model. The fact that (1) might be a good idea doesn't imply that (2) is a good idea, and of course it categorically isn't. We *must* keep logical and physical concepts distinct, and not get confused over the two levels in our debates."

Anyway, Member X continues:

"OIDs are system-created and -managed (unlike keys), are independent of values of the object (unlike keys), and of the location/address of the object, and relate objects (rather than rows . . . often an application's object, to be force-fitted into tables, will be split into multiple rows). Also they're much faster (than joins), sometimes by orders of magnitude."

Comment: "Independent of the location/address"? I think this claim just means OIDs aren't hardware disk addresses (i.e., there's a level of indirection between the two, such as is classically provided by "page and offset"-style addresses). I still think OIDs are essentially just pointers; for if not, the performance claims don't make much sense.

Member X then goes on to offer the following responses to Blair's first question ("Of what logical significance is the distinction between identity and equality?"):

(Begin quote)

- [OIDs] can connect higher-level abstractions (objects, not rows).
  Comment: There seems to be some confusion here over what "higher-level" means. Surely objects are a lower-level abstraction than rows, not a higher-level one, since they correspond (loosely speaking) to *components* of a row. See *The Third Manifesto* [7], where this position is articulated and substantiated.
- [OIDs] can maintain an identity concept independent of value and location.
  Comment: This point basically just means that OIDs can be thought of (in part) as surrogates.
- [OIDS] are automatically managed.
  Comment: "Automatic management" is an implementation detail, which in any case might apply to surrogate keys too (as noted earlier).

- [OIDs] are always present, and therefore can be relied upon for other parts of the DBMS or application.

    Comment: A colleague, Declan Brady, observes in reference [2] that "it's a fundamental mistake not to bother to distinguish objects *logically* just because the system does it *physically* . . . [The object community] fails to take account of how *users* distinguish objects" (somewhat paraphrased).

(*End quote*)

Member X then offers the following responses to Blair's second question ("Of what practical significance is the distinction between identity and equality?"):

(*Begin quote*)

- [OIDs are] faster (sometimes orders of magnitude).

    Comment: This response betrays confusion between model and implementation (quite apart from the fact that in any case it seems to have nothing to do with Blair's question).

- [OIDs] often support many-to-many relationships.

    Comment: So do keys (I think they do it better, too).

- [OIDs] often support bidirectional relationships.

    Comment: So do keys (I think they do it better, too).

- [OIDs are] easier to use (no need to create, insert, manage foreign keys, do joins, write stored procedures for referential integrity, etc.).

    Comment: I dispute this claim, strongly! See Chapter 23 ("A Cradle-to-Grave Example") of my book *An Introduction to Database Systems* [11] for evidence in support of my position here.

- [OIDs] allow direct mapping of software objects to real-world entities that have identity (customers, products, etc.).

    Comment: I dispute the suggestion that (e.g.) customers have identities that look anything like OIDs. To quote Brady again [2]: "I for one don't know where the chassis number is stamped on a human being!"

- [OIDs] form the basis of several other features often found in ODBMSs, including:

    - Distribution (transparent access to objects in any database on any server, even as objects are moved)
    Comment: Keys support distribution too, and I think they do it better.

    - Relationships (see above)
    Comment: Keys support relationships too, and I think they do it better.

- Versions (the entire concept of versioning is to take an application-meaningful unit, or object, and track the changes of its state . . . so it requires a concept of identity independent of state)
  Comment: I would have said rather that the concept of versioning depends on a clear concept of *time,* together with (of course) support for that concept. The versioning issue is orthogonal to the question of OIDs *vs.* keys (and orthogonal to the question of objects *vs.* relations, come to that).

- Composite objects (multiple objects, linked by relationships, that act as a single object)
  Comment: The idea of treating combinations (of objects or rows or whatever) as a single aggregate construct might certainly be useful in certain contexts, but (again) it's orthogonal to the question of OIDs *vs.* keys. In fact, I think that, once again, keys do it better.

- Schema evolution (essentially versioning of types, plus migration [of] instances)
  Comment: "Schema evolution" is not only considerably more complex in the object world than it is in the relational world, it's more of a *requirement* [20]. (It's more complex because the schema itself is more complex, and it's more of a requirement because of the model *vs.* implementation confusion.) Thus, the suggestion that OIDs are somehow more suited to supporting such evolution is founded on a faulty premise.

- [OIDs] can provide integration across the features above (e.g., behavior of relationships as one of the objects versions [*sic*]) and with traditional database capabilities (e.g., management of relationships or composites across recovery, concurrency, etc.)
  Comment: ???

(End quote)

It seems to me that Member X nowhere answers either of Blair's questions! (Actually Member X seems to interpret those questions as referring to the distinction between OIDs and keys, not to that between identity and equality. For that reason many of my comments on Member X's responses were framed in terms of that interpretation, as you might have noticed.)

RESPONSE BY ODMG MEMBER Y

In contrast to Member X, Member Y does at least try to answer the questions asked. His response begins thus:

"Great question.

"When considering this problem . . . [we termed it] the 'starry, starry night problem.' Consider: You are a painter and you paint a picture of a starry, starry night. Someone comes along and puts it on the copying machine and creates 100 identical copies of it. How do you distinguish the original from the copies? And what value is placed on being able to identify the original from the copies? When is it useful?"

Comment: Distinguishing the original from the copies is trivial, of course (unless you think the copying machine produces paintings, not photocopies). The more interesting question is: How do you distinguish one copy from another? Or, rather, *can* you distinguish one copy from another? The answer to this question, of course, is *yes*— for otherwise you couldn't know that there were 100 of them! (In order to count them, you have to know which ones you've already counted. See reference [17] for an extensive discussion of this particular issue.) And this observation is the key to answering Member Y's two subsidiary questions, too.

Member Y continues:

"Couldn't some collection of properties of the picture identify it as unique? Or is there some 'starry, starry night' essence that makes one unique and the other [*sic*] copies (and thus each copy also unique)? Some people argued that if a value-based comparison of all the properties is done and they are all equal they are equivalent, and if they are equivalent, what matter is it if they are unique—you can't tell them apart anyways!!! If you changed one of the properties, e.g., changed a color of a star from white to yellow, then it wouldn't be equivalent and each could be distinguished. So what is identity anyway? What makes 'that copy,' 'that copy'? Thus, this question of Object Identity and its value is one of the oldest in the OO domain . . ."

Comment: There seems to be some confusion here. The fact that we can distinguish—somehow—between distinct copies (as previously discussed) means, by definition, that each copy certainly does have its own *identity*. However, it could be argued that those copies are *equal* to one another in some sense (and so we are, perhaps, beginning to get at the distinction between identity and equality). The question is, in just what sense are they equal? In order to answer this question, what we need, first, is a *criterion* of equality: a criterion, that is, by which we can determine whether or not two given objects are equal. That is, there's no such thing as *absolute* equality! For example, are or are not the following equal to one another:

6   6.0   VI   six   6E0   2+4

(etc.)? I hope it's obvious that, given any two of these expressions, it would be possible to define one criterion of equality according to which they would be equal and another according to which they would not. (Perhaps a more telling example is the following. Let object *a* be "ODMG Member Y in 1996" and object *b* be "ODMG Member Y in 1997." Are or are not objects *a* and *b* equal?)

Anyway, Member Y continues:

"The theory is: that an OID is independent of the data contained in the object. It provides the unique identity for the object independent of the characteristics or specific properties of any instance. Regardless of how the object changes or even 'dies' (is deleted) the OID is never changed and never reused. If two OIDs are compared and are the same then the two objects are said to be identical. If they don't but the contents of the objects are the same, then the objects are said to be equivalent (this distinction is for the readers as you already know this . . .)."

Comment: Regarding this portion of Member Y's response, Brady remarks in reference [2]: "I remain unable to reconcile the two ideas that (a) objects correspond closely to the real world and (b) objects have identity independent of their characteristics. In the real world, an object's identity *is* one of its characteristics. Also, in the relational model, we can easily cope with the idea of not updating identifier attributes—just because it's *possible* to update a column doesn't mean we have to" (somewhat paraphrased).

Member Y continues:

"The theory for keys is: A key is a unique value or values that when taken together uniquely identify the entity. Now note that I didn't identify tuples or objects, because in fact you can have keys for both . . . (a point to discuss in a moment). A key can either be natural and implicit to the data (e.g., a social security number) or can be generated (e.g., department number). OIDs are always generated by the 'system' but are 'natural' and 'implicit' to the object.

"In the relational model the values must be a column or a series of columns which form a compound key. Thus in the relational model, the actual key is physically derived from the properties (columns) of the tuple. Contrast this with an OID, which in every object database, is independent of the contents of the object. This is a critical point. In a relational database, a key is actually used for two things: relationship and, possibly, identity. Two keys (or more specifically a key and a foreign key) can be compared to determine if there is a relationship between the two rows. However, it is also possible, and in fact quite common, that two rows in the same table will have the same key value. If two rows in the same table have the same key but different other columns they are not identical, nor are they equivalent, but they have the same key. If the keys are rich enough compound keys and the data normalized enough, then possibly you can also use the key to uniquely identify a specific tuple. OIDs don't have this problem. Because they are a separate entity but implicit to the object OIDs can be used for identification, for establishing uniqueness, and for creating direct relationships."

Comment: Actually I find this extract quite difficult to follow— the reference to normalization in particular is puzzling—but I *think* Member Y is blaming the relational model for not having been properly implemented. "Duplicate keys" don't exist in the relational model! Of course, SQL departs from the prescriptions of the relational model in this respect (it permits tables to have no primary key and hence to contain duplicate rows), but this fact is an indictment of SQL—it's nothing to do with the relational model. In any case, and perhaps more to the point, it seems to me that the analogous problem of two objects that should be identical but are in fact merely equal can arise just as easily in an object context. OIDs do not and cannot help with this problem.

Member Y continues:

"In fact, in either model, you could determine equivalence by comparing all the properties or columns of two objects and rows respectively. That is useful in some applications, especially where value-based comparison is required (lots of queries are exactly that). So now we get into that 'starry, starry night' question above (is there a value in identity?) but from a pragmatic side: can you compare 'all' the properties—how long will that take? Space and time (performance) are issues in the nontheoretical world."

Comment: Of course I agree performance is an issue, but I certainly don't agree it's an issue "in the nontheoretical world" only! The relational model *per se* deliberately doesn't address the performance issue, but much of the theory of relational technology does (think of optimization theory in particular). There's much more to relational theory than just the relational model, and some of that extra theory is aimed specifically at the performance question. However, the whole point (or a large part of the point, anyway) of the model *vs.* implementation separation is precisely to keep performance issues where they belong: namely, out of the model and in the implementation.

Furthermore, I have to say that expressions like "the nontheoretical world" really make me gnash my teeth . . . "Theoretical" does *not* mean "nonpractical"! In this connection, I'd like to offer the following wonderful quotation from Leonardo da Vinci's *Notebooks:*

> Those who are enamored of practice without theory are like a pilot who goes into a ship without rudder or compass and never has any certainty where he [*sic*] is going. Practice should always be based upon a sound knowledge of theory.

Anyway, Member Y continues:

"While in a relational database you're not supposed to change key values, you can and often need to in order to change the relationship. In an object database, you can't change the OID and generally don't want to anyway. Relationships are expressed and changed in a different manner. Keys, however, cannot distinguish identity *per se*. That depends on how well you normalize the data.

"In an [*sic*] object model, you can also create keys for objects based on unique properties. This is very useful, especially for value-based processing (comparing) of object instances (by their properties). The same rules apply for objects as for keys, and a similar object-like 'join' can be performed over the values. So one pragmatic difference is that OIDs are largely used for relationship and identity processing and keys are largely used for relationships."

Comment: It's interesting that Member Y refers to the possibility of joining objects. What type or class of object results from such an operation? In particular, classes have "methods" or operators; what methods apply to the result? And what's the OID of that result?

Member Y continues:

"The value of OIDs is:

1. Objects can directly refer to or reference other objects by knowing their OID or storing it as a value for a property. One side effect of this is that no intermediate entities (tables, objects, etc.) [are required] to define the relationship and no additional processing [is] required to compute what it relates to. Relationships between objects can be 'navigated' by following the chain of properties and OIDs contained in them. Overall, for multivalued relationships, and in navigation in general, the performance is orders of magnitude faster than using keys and joins. This reduces space (no intermediate tables), improves performance (especially in highly interrelated or 'complex'—that is usually what complex means—models), and enhances understanding of the relation-

ships (they can be more easily visualized). This is a practical and fundamental point.

2. Only one copy of the specific object exists. Thus if we are talking about the 'Tony Blair person instance' there is only one of it, and all objects will refer to that one instance. It is semantically accurate: 'that one!' 'not this one!' This . . . improves model accuracy, reduces data redundancy, eliminates most if not all of the normalization process (as there is in the relational model—all data, no context . . .). It also lines up with how we think about people in the real world: There is only one instance of Tony Blair; when he dies there won't be another exactly like him.

3. Having a notion of unique identity in the software model seems natural, as it seems to correspond to the same notion that we have about things in the real world. Object identity is an abstraction. It allows us to easily, naturally, and directly map real-world entities to . . . some entity we're modeling in software. This has great value: ease of programming, simplicity of expression, comprehension, enhanced communication, and more accurate software models."

Comment: I'm very tempted to offer a small prize for the maximum number of confusions found in the foregoing. Myself, I gave up on trying to formulate a blow-by-blow response . . . I'd just like to comment on the remarks concerning navigation. Navigation essentially means pointer chasing, which in turn means we're talking about *programmer* access, not end user access. What the object community seems so often to overlook is that databases aren't supposed to be built for the convenience of programmers but rather for the convenience of end users!

Member Y concludes:

"Value-based comparisons are still required and valid for determining a different kind of relationship (e.g., all RED cars) not based on unique identity. OIDs guarantee unique identity. Keys do not."

Comment: Clearly, Member Y doesn't understand the relational key concept.

CONCLUDING REMARKS

If the responses by ODMG Members X and Y can be considered indicative of what the object community has to say in defense of OIDs, I think we can safely conclude that there *is* no logical argument for them. I'd like to close, therefore, by repeating some remarks I made on the same topic in an earlier paper [10]: "[It's] curious that so many people seem to regard OIDs as the *sine qua non* of the object model. For example, *The Object-Oriented Database System Manifesto* [1] says 'Thou shalt support object identity'—but it doesn't give any *logical* justification for such an edict. Likewise, Jim Melton [19] says 'References in the form of object identifiers are the key [*sic!*] to the object-oriented paradigm,' but he provides no evidence in support of this strong claim. And in a useful annotated and comprehensive anthology of writings on the subject [3] compiled by Declan Brady (containing 'the substance of everything I've managed to unearth on the [subject] of OIDs'), numerous similar assertions can be found. So far as I can see, however, none of those assertions is accompanied by any *logical* supporting arguments."

ACKNOWLEDGMENTS

I'd been meaning to write something on the topic of OIDs *vs*. keys for a long time, but it was Tony Blair's questions on the Internet, and the responses to those questions from ODMG Members X and Y, that finally made me get down to producing something concrete. So I'm grateful to these three individuals for providing the necessary impetus . . . I'd also like to thank Declan Brady for his helpful comments on the original responses by ODMG Members X and Y, and Hugh Darwen and Declan Brady (again) for their careful review of earlier drafts of this paper.

REFERENCES

1. Malcolm Atkinson *et al.*: "The Object-Oriented Database System Manifesto," Proc. First International Conference on Deductive and Object-Oriented Databases, Kyoto, Japan (1989). New York, N.Y.: Elsevier Science (1990).

2. Declan Brady: Private communication (May 23rd, 1997).

3. Declan Brady: Private communication (July 1st, 1996). See also Declan Brady: "Relational *vs*. Object-Oriented Database Systems: An Approach to Rapprochement," MSc thesis, School of Computer Applications, Dublin City University, Ireland (January 1997).

4. R. G. G. Cattell (ed.): *The Object Database Standard: ODMG-93*. San Mateo, Calif.: Morgan Kaufmann (1994). *Note:* This book has been superseded by R. G. G. Cattell and Douglas K. Barry (eds.): *The Object Database Standard: ODMG 2.0*. San Francisco, Calif.: Morgan Kaufmann (1997).

5. E. F. Codd: *The Relational Model for Database Management Version 2*. Reading, Mass.: Addison-Wesley (1990).

6. Hugh Darwen: "The Duplicity of Duplicate Rows," in C. J. Date and Hugh Darwen, *Relational Database Writings 1989–1991*. Reading, Mass.: Addison-Wesley (1992).

7. Hugh Darwen and C. J. Date: "The Third Manifesto," *ACM SIGMOD Record 24*, No. 1 (March 1995). See also the book-length version *Foundation for Object/Relational Databases: The Third Manifesto*. Reading, Mass.: Addison-Wesley (1998).

8. C. J. Date: "Object-Oriented Database Technology" (live seminar), Washington DC (April 7th–8th, 1997).

9. C. J. Date: "Objects and Relations: Forty-Seven Points of Light" (Chapter 13 of the present book).

10. C. J. Date: "Why 'The Object Model' Is Not a Data Model" (Chapter 11 of the present book).

11. C. J. Date: *An Introduction to Database Systems* (6th edition). Reading, Mass.: Addison-Wesley (1995).

12. C. J. Date: "The Primacy of Primary Keys: An Investigation," in *Relational Database Writings 1991–1994*. Reading, Mass.: Addison-Wesley (1995).

13. C. J. Date: "Don't Encode Information into Primary Keys!", in C. J. Date and Hugh Darwen, *Relational Database Writings 1989–1991*. Reading, Mass.: Addison-Wesley (1992).

14. C. J. Date: "Composite Keys," in C. J. Date and Hugh Darwen, *Relational Database Writings 1989-1991*. Reading, Mass.: Addison-Wesley (1992).

15. C. J. Date: "Composite Foreign Keys and Nulls," in C. J. Date and Hugh Darwen, *Relational Database Writings 1989–1991*. Reading, Mass.: Addison-Wesley (1992).

16. C. J. Date: "Referential Integrity and Foreign Keys. Part I: Basic Concepts; Part II: Further Considerations," in *Relational Database Writings 1985–1989*. Reading, Mass.: Addison-Wesley (1990).

17. C. J. Date: "Why Duplicate Rows Are Prohibited," in *Relational Database Writings 1985–1989*. Reading, Mass.: Addison-Wesley (1990).

18. P. Hall, J. Owlett, and S. J. P. Todd: "Relations and Entities," in G. M. Nijssen (ed.): *Modelling in Data Base Management Systems*. Amsterdam, Netherlands: North-Holland / New York, N.Y.: Elsevier Science (1975).

19. Jim Melton: "A Shift in the Landscape (Assessing SQL3's New Object Direction)," *Database Programming & Design 9*, No. 8 (August 1996).

20. C. M. Saracco: "Writing an Object DBMS Application," Part 1, *InfoDB 7*, No. 4 (Winter 1993/1994); Part 2, *InfoDB 8*, No. 1 (Spring 1994).

CHAPTER **13**

Objects and Relations: Forty-Seven Points of Light

A response to a paper by Won Kim entitled
"On Marrying Relations and Objects:
Relation-Centric and Object-Centric Perspectives"

ABSTRACT

This paper is intended as a contribution, both general and specific, to the continuing debate over objects *vs.* relations. It consists principally of a detailed response to Won Kim's recent article "On Marrying Relations and Objects: Relation-Centric and Object-Centric Perspectives" [10–11]. It also addresses a number of more fundamental issues. *Note:* Like certain earlier papers in this collection, this paper is—as indicated—basically a response to another, but once again I believe it does stand on its own and is worth including here.

COMMENTS ON REPUBLICATION

The article to which the present paper was a response was (for the most part) an attack on the position adopted in *The Third Manifesto* [4] to the effect that "domain = class" is the right equation and "relvar = class" is the wrong one (see Chapter 3 of the present book). When that article first appeared in *Data*

Originally published in *Data Base Newsletter 23*, No. 5 (September/October 1995). Reprinted by permission of Database Research Group Inc.

Base Newsletter [10], Hugh Darwen and I immediately wrote a letter to the editor of that publication, and by way of introduction to the present paper I cannot do better than reproduce the substance of that letter here [5].

(*Begin quote*)

Dear Editor:

We have studied the article "On Marrying Relations and Objects: Relation-Centric and Object-Centric Perspectives," by Won Kim [10]. We note that it comments on our own work in what might be the same field as Kim's. This commentary includes several inaccuracies that are so gross as to require the record to be put straight. In the interests of brevity, we will be selective:

1. "Chris Date (and Hugh Darwen) recently observed that there are two perspectives to adding objects to relations: What they call the **relational bigot's perspective,** and the **object bigot's perspective** [*here Kim gave a reference to Data Base Newsletter 22, Nos. 3–4, which contained an interview entitled "Marrying Objects and Relational" (republished in this book's predecessor)*] . . . [Some] readers may find these terms objectionable . . .."

   We are among those readers. That is possibly why we have not used those terms ourselves, especially not in the referenced interview. It is true that some years ago one of us (Darwen) did give a lecture to British audiences entitled "OObservations of a Relational Bigot." The jocular title was directed at himself.

2. With further reference to the extract from Kim's text cited above, we do not use the term "perspective" for the various approaches to what we have called the *rapprochement* of objects and relations, nor do we think it appropriate. We are not interested in mere points of view.

3. "Recently, Chris Date (and Hugh Darwen) proposed a simple scheme to extend the relational model with arbitrary data types and inheritance."

   No, we didn't. We have both made it abundantly clear that we do not propose to extend the relational model. Data types have always been orthogonal to the relational model, and our PRIME AIM is to keep them so.

4. "The relation-centric perspective holds that the object-centric perspective equates a relation with a class. The fact is that no object database systems ever have equated a relation with a class. In this sense, the relation-centric perspective offers criticism of a nonexistent perspective."

   Here Kim is being disingenuous, to say the least. *Object* database systems as such don't talk about relations at all; however, the newer "object/relational" systems certainly do, and many of those systems—Kim's own UniSQL product included—do indeed equate relations and classes.

Thus, our criticism of that equation is both relevant and, we believe, valid.

In addition to the foregoing, we have to say that we find confusion in various forms pervading Kim's article. This is not the time or place for a blow-by-blow critique; rather—and with additional reference to another recent article by Kim entitled "Observations on the Current SQL3 Object Model Proposal (and Invitation for Scholarly Opinions)," available from UniSQL Inc.—we invite study of our own proposal entitled *The Third Manifesto* [4]. We would like that *Manifesto* to be considered as providing some of the scholarly opinion Kim seeks.

(*Signed*) Hugh Darwen (and Chris Date)

(*End quote*)

What follows, by contrast, *is* a blow-by-blow critique (for the most part).

INTRODUCTION

This paper grew in the writing. It began as a letter to the editor of *Data Base Newsletter;* in that form, it was meant as a straightforward follow-up to a previous letter to that same publication from Hugh Darwen and myself [5]. That previous letter in turn was a reaction to Won Kim's *Data Base Newsletter* article "On Marrying Relations and Objects: Relation-Centric and Object-Centric Perspectives" [10]. In our letter, we claimed to "find confusion in various forms pervading Kim's article," but went on to say that "this [was] not the time or place for a blow-by-blow critique." We therefore limited ourselves at that time to an attempt to set the record straight on a few really major inaccuracies.

However, subsequent conversations with other database professionals convinced us both that a more detailed critique was needed. Certainly it is the case that people tend to get confused over the issue at hand—i.e., objects *vs.* relations—and articles like Kim's must be held to blame for some of that confusion. Moreover, Kim has since published a slight variant of his article elsewhere [11], thereby making his ideas available to a new and wider audience, and accordingly increasing the desirability of making a detailed response to those ideas available too. Following the publication of reference [11], therefore, I began work on such a response.

It soon became clear that a simple blow-by-blow commentary on reference [10] would not be sufficient. For one thing, the various confusions pervading that paper seemed to be based on a number of underlying, but unstated, fundamental assumptions that were themselves in error. (Reference [10] is not alone in this respect, by the way; much of the object literature seems to be confused over those same fundamental issues. I can cite chapter and verse if need be.) It therefore seemed worthwhile to bring those issues out into the open, even if space did not permit them to be examined in any great depth.

I also felt it would be desirable to make the paper stand alone as a useful contribution to the objects *vs.* relations debate, even for readers who might not have seen Kim's original article. This fact too meant that the paper soon became much longer than a mere "letter to the editor" had any right to be. The net result was that I found myself with a whole new paper on my hands.

Before going any further, I would like to make my own general position on this topic absolutely clear. I'm not "opposed" to objects. I don't see objects as a "threat" to relations. I don't wish that objects would "just go away." Quite the contrary, in fact: I've stated in many places and on many occasions that object technology does include some good ideas, and that we should try to incorporate those good ideas into our database systems (without, I hasten to add, at the same time giving up on any of the good ideas of relational technology). The trouble is, there's no consensus on just what those good object ideas are. The work Hugh Darwen and I have recently been engaged in (*The Third Manifesto* in particular—see the next section) has been aimed, in part, at trying to answer exactly this question.

SOME FUNDAMENTAL DISTINCTIONS

Some months ago, Hugh Darwen and I published a paper entitled *The Third Manifesto* [4] (the *Manifesto* for short). The *Manifesto* consists of a detailed proposal for the future of data and data management; as indicated in the previous section, it addresses the topic of the present paper, namely objects *vs.* relations, in particular. (I should mention too that a gentle introduction to the basic ideas of the *Manifesto* appears in another paper by Hugh Darwen and myself [3].)

Now, the *Manifesto* is informed throughout by certain crucial and fundamental principles, and its proposals are rigorously based on those principles. More specifically, it draws a number of very clear and sharp distinctions:

- between *model* and *implementation;*
- between *values* and *variables;*
- between *domains* and *relations;*
- between *types* and *representations.*

In my opinion, it is precisely a failure to make these distinctions that characterizes a number of the writings in the object literature. And that failure in turn, I believe, accounts for the lack of coherence and logical consistency that is the hallmark of such writings. It therefore seems worth elaborating briefly on these four fundamental issues in the present section.

Note: It goes without saying that each of these issues could easily be the subject of a very lengthy discussion, much longer than time and space considerations permit here.* But I hope I can at least make the reader aware that confusion does exist—and should not!—over each of these issues, so that later in the paper I can point out the source of some of the mistakes in reference [10].

- Model *vs.* implementation

    This is probably the most fundamental distinction of all, yet for some reason it seems very difficult for some people to comprehend. Basically, it is just the familiar distinction between *logical* and *physical* (at any rate, it's closely related to this latter distinction). To be more specific:

    a. The *model* is what the user sees; it consists of an abstract logical definition of the data constructs,† data operators, and so forth, that together constitute the abstract machine with which the user interacts.

    b. By contrast, the *implementation* is—at least potentially—hidden from the user; it consists of the physical realization on a real computer system of the components of the model. Note in particular, therefore, that everything to do with *performance* is, first and foremost, an implementation matter, not part of the model!

So, for example, the concept *relation* in the relational world is a construct in the model; how relations are physically represented on the disk is a matter of implementation. Likewise, the concept *join* is a construct in the model; how joins are actually performed (by means of indexes, physical I/O operations, etc.) is, again, a matter of implementation.

- Values *vs.* variables

    It's hard to believe that people could get confused over such an elementary distinction as this one, but in fact it's very easy to fall into traps in this connection. I won't bother to spell out exactly what the distinction is, since I think it's obvious, but later on in the paper I'll point out some specific examples of the confusion. For the record, though, I will say that object writings do often seem to be confused over whether an object is a value or a variable.

- Domains *vs.* relations

    In the relational model, it's very clear that domains and relations are different things. To state the distinction briefly: A domain is a data type; a relation is a construct that has columns that are "defined on" certain

---

*See Installments 58–61 in Part I of this book.
†I would have preferred to say data *objects,* but "objects" is a loaded term.

domains (i.e., are "of" certain data types). It follows immediately that the object notion of *object class*—which is also basically a data type—is equivalent to the domain notion and not the relation notion. Yet many writers, Kim included, persist in equating classes and relations.

Note: In *The Third Manifesto,* we took great pains to distinguish carefully between relations *per se* (i.e., relation *values*) and relation *variables* or "relvars." In preparing this paper, however, I decided—out of deference to readers who might not be familiar with the *Manifesto*—to stay with the generic and more familiar term "relation," even when "relvar" would have been more strictly correct. But note the value *vs.* variable confusion that decision entails!

■ Types *vs.* representations

This last distinction is an important special case of the general and familiar logical *vs.* physical distinction already touched on above. To quote reference [1]: "A major purpose of type systems is to avoid embarrassing questions about representations, and to forbid situations in which these questions might come up." In other words, types are *logical,* representations are *physical.*

In *The Third Manifesto,* we allow the internal representation of values of any given type to be arbitrarily complex, but we also require that representation to be hidden from the user. Thus, we insist that values of a given type be manipulable *solely* by means of the operators that are defined for the type in question. In other words, whatever "structure" values might possess is purely an implementation matter—it's not part of the model, and it's not visible to the user. In object terminology, values are *fully encapsulated;* there are *no* "public instance variables" or "public attributes," there are only "methods."[*] *Note added on republication:* As explained elsewhere in this book, it would be more accurate to say rather that *scalar* values are fully encapsulated (nonscalar values are not); for present purposes, however, this refinement need not concern us very much.

As a trivial example of the idea that structure (representation) of values is not part of the model, consider the data type REAL in SQL. The representation of REAL numbers is not specified in the SQL language and is typically not known to users. What users do know is the operations they can perform on REAL numbers—"+", "*", "<", etc. And that's all they *need* to know.

---

[*]In the *Manifesto* we favor the term *operator* over the term *method.* Likewise, we favor the terms *domain* and *type,* which we use interchangeably, over the term *class.*

FURTHER PRELIMINARIES

I'm almost ready to begin my blow-by-blow commentary on reference [10]. There are just a couple of additional preliminary remarks I need to get out of the way before I can start getting into detail. First of all, I have to say that, quite frankly, it's difficult to criticize something coherently when what you're trying to criticize is itself not very coherent in the first place! Thus, if some of my criticisms don't always seem as crystal clear as they might, then I apologize, but I don't accept full responsibility.

Second, I suppose I should also apologize for the fact that parts of the text that follows might seem to smack slightly of "angels on the head of a pin" arguments (not to mention being thought a trifle self-indulgent), consisting as they do of comments by me on comments by Kim on comments by Hugh Darwen and myself on ideas of Kim's . . . Given the context, however, such a nastily self-referential state of affairs seems unavoidable.

All otherwise unattributed quotations in what follows are taken from reference [10]; I have numbered those quotations for ease of reference. The section headings are taken from that same source, except for the one immediately following. Also, Hugh Darwen has asked me to say that, while this paper—unlike our letter [5]—is not exactly a joint effort, he has reviewed it very carefully and fully agrees with my commentary.

WHY MARRY OBJECTS AND RELATIONS?

1. "The ANSI X3H2 (SQL-3) standards committee has been working to formulate object-oriented extensions to the SQL-92 relational database standard."

   The point is worth emphasizing that, so far as I know, the SQL/92 standard makes no claim whatsoever to being a *relational* standard. In fact, I don't believe the word "relation" appears anywhere in the official standard document [12]. This point is significant, because *The Third Manifesto* takes the position that what we should be trying to do is marry objects and *relational technology,* not objects and SQL.

2. ". . . why marry objects and relations? . . . The first reason is to eliminate several deficiencies in the relational model . . . [the first of which is] the limited data types supported in relational database systems. (It should be noted that this is a problem in the implementation of the relational model, rather than a problem of the relational model itself.)"

   So Kim's first "relational model deficiency" is, by his own admission, actually not a relational model deficiency at all, and his first criticism of the relational model is thereby self-contradictory and invalid.

Please understand that I don't mean to nitpick here—there's a significant point at stake. To be specific, it's very important to understand that:

a. The relational model has *absolutely nothing* to say regarding what data types should be supported. Indeed, the question as to what types are supported is *completely orthogonal* to the question of support for the relational model *per se*.

b. It is precisely the type concept that is the key to marrying objects and relations! We don't have to do *anything* to the relational model in order to obtain object functionality—we only have to build a relational system that includes the ability for users to define their own types (as well as providing certain system-defined types, of course, as today's SQL products do).

Note: The more usual relational term for *type* is *domain*. As noted in the previous section, however, the concepts are identical, and we use the terms interchangeably.

3. "[The second relational model deficiency is the] join-based retrieval of a collection of related data (even when the need to retrieve the collection of data is known at the time of database design)."

Just what it is that's being criticized here isn't fully clear to me, but presumably what Kim means is something like the following:

a. According to the relational model, the only way to combine logically related pieces of data is by doing a join.

b. Such joins are required even when the need to perform them is known at design time.

c. Joins are inherently slow.

Let's analyze these points one by one.

a. There are of course many ways of "combining" data in the relational model—join, union, and so forth—but for the sake of the argument I'm prepared to accept that join is the most important.

b. I suppose the reference here is to joins that are based on foreign-to-primary-key matching. It's a slight stretch to say that the existence of a foreign-to-primary-key relationship between two relations implies that it's "known at design time" that those two relations will need to be joined at run time, but again I'm prepared to accept the point for the sake of the argument. (Though I'd like to remind readers that making assumptions at design time about the way the data will be used at run time is, in general, a dangerous thing to do—as we've learned, or ought to have learned, from past experience.)

c. This third point is completely specious! Anyone who advances this argument is seriously confused over the model *vs.* implementation distinction. Let me elaborate.

First of all, the "joins are slow" claim usually serves as lead-in to an argument that "pointers are faster"; that is, advocates of this position usually argue that following a pointer from the referencing relation to the referenced relation (or *vice versa)* is a good—i.e., efficient—implementation mechanism for "combining the data." Fine: I'll agree to this point too, for the sake of the argument.* *But there's absolutely no reason why foreign-to-primary-key relationships shouldn't be implemented by pointers on the disk.* (I know they typically can't be implemented that way in today's SQL products, but that's a defect in those products, not a "relational model deficiency." At least one prototype system, the IBM Starburst prototype, does provide such a pointer-based implementation [2].)

In other words, (1) *implementing* relationships by pointers is very different from (2) *exposing* such pointers in the model. The fact that (1) might be a good idea doesn't imply that (2) is a good idea, and of course it categorically isn't. We *must* keep logical and physical concepts distinct, and not get confused over the two levels in our debates; we've learned the hard way (or at least some of us have) what happens when this principle is violated.

Note: It has belatedly occurred to me that perhaps it is Kim's contention, not that joins are slow, but that they're *cumbersome.* If so, then I respond by observing that the alleged cumbersomeness is, first and foremost, a mere syntactic matter (and thus easily fixed), and in any case the joins can often be hidden from the user by means of the relational view mechanism.

4. "[The third relational model deficiency is the] duplication of records to work around the first-normal-form restriction."

Again I don't quite understand the criticism. Let me just offer the following observations:

a. I don't know why Kim thinks first normal form (1NF) leads to "duplication of records," but I note that *higher* normal forms—third normal form (3NF), Boyce/Codd normal form (BCNF), etc.—are intended precisely to avoid such duplication. (Or, at least, to avoid duplication of *data;* I don't know what Kim means by "duplication of *records.*")

---

*Please don't infer that I think that pointers are the *best* way of "combining the data." They might not even be a *good* way. It all depends!

   b. The problems that those higher normal forms address—*viz.*, data redundancy and update anomalies—don't suddenly go away just because we happen to be dealing with objects instead of relations. In other words, those higher normal forms are still relevant, even in a world of objects.

   c. **(Important!)** The 1NF requirement does *not* mean that we can't have "complex objects" in relations. On the contrary, a relation in which (say) one column contains audio recordings, another video recordings, another images, and so on, is a perfectly respectable 1NF relation. So too is a relation in which each row contains an employee number, a department number, a salary, and a set of names of the employee's dependents*—because a set too can be regarded as a single "complex object" in the right context, as I have explained elsewhere (see, e.g., references [6] and [7]). See my comments under Quotations 20 and 22 for further discussion.

5. "The second reason [for marrying objects and relations] is to bring the productivity benefits in object-oriented programming to database design and application development. These include inheritance . . . and support [for] object-oriented programming languages . . . The relation-centric view has important additions to the original relational model, but still is missing important modeling facilities necessary to satisfy the two reasons mentioned above . . ."

   a. I'm not sure I accept the premise that objects provide "productivity benefits . . . to database design"; in fact, I think they make the job harder, because they open up many more design alternatives without providing dependable guidelines for choosing among those alternatives. I would also argue that, first, object designs tend to be harder to change, precisely because they tend to muddle logical and physical considerations; second, they *need* to be changed more often, for exactly the same reason.

   b. The "relation-centric view"—this is Kim's term for the approach advocated in *The Third Manifesto*—does *not* "[have] important additions to the original relational model." The whole point of our approach is to do *nothing* to the relational model!

   c. Our approach is not "still missing important facilities necessary to satisfy the two reasons mentioned above." Regarding the first of those reasons ("eliminating deficiencies in the relational model"), see my

---

*I'm not saying this relation is well *designed* (indeed, it probably isn't)—I'm just saying it's a legal 1NF relation.

remarks under Quotations 2–4 above. Regarding the second "reason" (*objective* might be a better word), I would argue that any language that conforms to the specifications of *The Third Manifesto* would in fact *be* an object-oriented programming language, so Kim's claim is incorrect.

As for inheritance, it's true that the *Manifesto's* support for inheritance is conditional at this time (in fact, the topic is currently relegated to an appendix), but the reason for this slight hesitancy on our part is that we have yet to find a good *model* of inheritance in the literature. Let me add, however, that we are ourselves actively working on such a model, and are cautiously optimistic about the outcome of that work.[*]

Perhaps I should elaborate briefly on the basic inheritance idea. The kind of inheritance we're interested in is the kind we mean when we say, for example, that every circle is an ellipse, and hence that all properties that apply to ellipses in general apply to—i.e., are *inherited by*—circles in particular (e.g., every circle has an area, because every ellipse has an area). To use the usual nomenclature, we say we have two types, ELLIPSE and CIRCLE, such that ELLIPSE is a *supertype* of CIRCLE and CIRCLE is a *subtype* of ELLIPSE; we also say (a trifle loosely) that all properties that apply to the supertype apply *a fortiori* to the subtype. Of course, the converse is not true; that is, the subtype might have properties of its own that do not apply to the supertype (e.g., circles have a radius, which ellipses in general do not).

Given that inheritance applies—by definition—to *types,*[†] it follows that the "properties" that are inherited by the subtype are—by definition—precisely the *operators* that apply to the supertype. In object terms, in other words, we're talking about "behavioral" inheritance, not "structural" inheritance. There's no structural inheritance in our model, because there's no *structure!*—see the discussion of the type *vs.* representation distinction in the section "Some Fundamental Distinctions."

6. "Chris Date (and Hugh Darwen) recently observed that there are two perspectives to adding objects to relations: What they call the 'relational bigot's perspective,' and the 'object bigot's perspective' . . . [Some] readers may find these terms objectionable . . ."

See the section "Comments on Republication," earlier.

---

[*] We are now (1998) much more optimistic concerning our proposed inheritance model than we were when the present paper was first written.

[†] The possibility of additionally supporting some kind of inheritance that applies to relations (more accurately, relvars) is not precluded; in fact, our book-length version of *The Third Manifesto* [4] does explore that possibility. However, we have to say too that we don't find the idea very appealing, for reasons beyond the scope of the present paper.

THE RELATION-CENTRIC PERSPECTIVE

7. "The domain of a column of a relation may be not only the alphanumeric data types (e.g., integer, float, string) that relational database systems currently allow, but also any arbitrary user-defined data type (e.g., point, polygon, document, image). A user-defined data type consists of 'all possible values for the type,' and 'functions that perform operations on each value of the type.' A user-defined data type, not the relation, is equivalent to [an object] class . . ."

   This characterization of our approach is roughly correct so far as it goes, but it doesn't go far enough.

   a. It's correct when it implies that we regard the three concepts *domain, type,* and *class* as one and the same, and when it states that we don't equate classes and relations. It's also correct when it suggests that we permit data types to be "arbitrarily complex." Note, however, that the qualification "user-defined" should be deleted from (at least) the second and third sentences.

   b. More important, it omits to mention the fact that (as explained in the section "Some Fundamental Distinctions") we make a strong and clean distinction between *type* and *representation*—a distinction that is often *not* properly made in the object world, at least in a database context (see Quotation 34).

8. ". . . the structure of a . . . data type . . . is not inherited."

   That's right!—because, as explained in the section "Some Fundamental Distinctions," there's no such thing as "structure of a data type" *in the model* ("structure" here being just another word for *representation*).* *The Third Manifesto* is concerned with the model, not the implementation, and structure has to do with the implementation, not the model. On this point, incidentally, we find ourselves in full agreement with both (1) a "purist" view of object orientation, as found in, e.g., Smalltalk, and (2) the classical view of data types, or domains, as understood in a relational context.

9. "All queries (i.e., projection, selection and join) . . . are directed to relations, and never to . . . data types."

   I'll comment on the idea of "querying data types" under Quotation 31. Here I just want to point out that the wording in this extract is very imprecise, to say the least. First of all, projection, selection, and join aren't

---

Note added on republication: This response is a little glib. I should have said, more specifically, that there's no such thing as "structure of a *scalar* data type." The slight inaccuracy is not too important for present purposes, however.

queries, they're *relational operations*. Second, relational operations—which are, of course, not limited to just the three mentioned—can be used in the construction of *relational expressions*. Third, such expressions can be used for *formulating* queries—as well as for formulating lots of other important things, such as view definitions, integrity constraints, security constraints, and so forth.

Now, I dare say some readers will dismiss these criticisms as mere pedantry and terminological quibbling, but I don't think they are. In my opinion, imprecise wording often betrays imprecise thinking. And it's very distressing to find such imprecision in writings dealing with, of all things, relational technology, given that one of Codd's objectives in introducing the relational model was precisely to bring some clarity of thinking and expression into a field (*viz.*, database management) that was in sore need of it at the time—and evidently still is.

10. "In an object-oriented model, a class includes instances . . . [By contrast,] a data type is simply a domain that includes 'all possible values' for the type."

I'm glad to see that Kim uses the indefinite article here ("an" object-oriented model). Because the sad fact is that, so far as I can tell, there *is* no single universally accepted object model, and there's no consensus on the meaning of *any* of the terms commonly used in the object world. (Consider the many differences between the—implicit!—models underlying C++ and Smalltalk, for instance.) So if Kim wants to use the term "class" to include instances (meaning the set of instances that are currently of interest), he is certainly at liberty to do so. And he is then correct to conclude that our "data type" is not the same as his "class." But then what term does he use for that part of a class that's *not* the set of instances? Whatever it is, that's what our "type" is equivalent to. Kim's objection is invalid and irrelevant.

Note, incidentally, that Kim does find a need to introduce a separate term (*viz.*, "extent") for that part of a class that *is* the set of instances—see Quotation 11 immediately following.

11. "A class . . . has . . . instances that users have created and inserted into the extent of the class . . ."

The idea that instances are "created" seems to be one of the most fundamental tenets of the entire object-oriented approach (creating instances is supposed to be what "constructor functions" do).* This fact notwithstanding, it's my opinion that the idea is confused, ill conceived, and very misleading. Consider the class INTEGER, for example. No user ever "creates" the integer 3; that value simply *exists*, logically speaking. It's

---

* See Chapter 11 of the present book.

true that a given user at a given time might happen to become *interested* in that value (for example, in order to be able to specify the number of dependents for a given employee), but that user doesn't suddenly "create" the value out of thin air; rather, he or she *makes use of* a value that already exists. And exactly the same argument applies to *all conceivable classes,* no matter how "complex" the "instances" (values) of that class might happen to be—integers, strings, polygons, vehicles, whatever.

Thus, instead of thinking of instances being "created" (and "destroyed" too, presumably), what we should be doing is *clearly distinguishing* between the following two notions:

a. The set of all *possible* instances (e.g., the set of all possible integers), and

b. The set of all *currently interesting* instances (e.g., the set of all integers currently appearing in some column in some relation).

And then we might reasonably argue that the first of these notions corresponds to the *class* and the second to the *extent.** (As an aside, I remark that Kim's own UniSQL/X product is confused over these two notions.)

12. " The relation-centric [view] does not include any notion of object identity . . . A tuple of a relation does not have a unique identifier . . . (It should be noted that relational database systems do assign tuple identifiers to tuples in relations . . .)"

a. It's correct to say, as is implied by Kim's first sentence here, that *The Third Manifesto* excludes the notion of object identity (at least as that notion is usually understood in the object world). But of course that exclusion is deliberate; we see nothing to be gained, and much to be lost, from the inclusion of such a concept in the model. See Quotation 21 for further discussion.

b. *The Third Manifesto* also VERY EXPLICITLY rejects the notion, implicit in Kim's second sentence, that objects and tuples are the same thing!

c. As for Kim's third sentence: Some SQL systems do assign tuple identifiers to tuples *in base relations,* but I'm not aware of any that assigns identifiers to tuples in arbitrary *derived* relations. (More accurately, those systems assign tuple identifiers to tuple *variables,* not to tuples *per se.* What we're seeing here is another example of the values *vs.* variables confusion.†)

---

*Though I can't help pointing out that the relational model manages very well without any direct equivalent to that *extent* notion.

†In this connection, see also the next two chapters of the present book.

This last point touches on an all too pervasive error, to wit: Those who argue in favor of the equation "tuples = objects" typically (but tacitly) take "tuples" to mean *base* tuples only, and forget about derived tuples! This is a mistake of the highest order, because the question as to which relations, and hence which tuples, are base and which derived is, in a very important sense, arbitrary. For example, in a personnel database, we might define

```
EMP { EMP#, DEPT#, SALARY }
```

to be a base relation, and then define

```
EMPX { EMP#, DEPT# }
EMPY { EMP#, SALARY }
```

as two projection views of that base relation. Alternatively, we might define

```
EMPX { EMP#, DEPT# }
EMPY { EMP#, SALARY }
```

to be two base relations, and then define

```
EMP { EMP#, DEPT#, SALARY }
```

as a join view of those two base relations. And given that the decision between these two approaches is largely arbitrary (it's a database design decision, in fact!), the one thing we *mustn't* do is have arbitrary distinctions between base and derived data—for example, a distinction that says that base tuples have tuple identifiers but derived tuples don't.

13. "In an object-oriented model, a subclass (or subtype) inherits not only methods from superclasses (or supertypes), but also attributes (i.e., structure). The relation-centric model expressly excludes the structure of a data type from inheritance. Why this restriction is imposed is not stated."

    a. First of all, I think Kim is moving the goalposts here. If the distinction he previously drew between class and type is accepted (see Quotation 10), he surely can't now equate subclass and subtype, or superclass and supertype.

    b. More important, we "exclude structure from inheritance" for the reason—*pace* Kim, the *stated* reason!—that (as I explained in my comments under Quotation 8) there *is* no structure in our model, and therefore there's no structure to inherit. Inheritance, if supported at all, applies to "behavior" *only*—necessarily so.

14. ". . . proponents of the relation-centric view take the confusing stance that methods should not be associated with a class (data type), but rather should be free-floating . . ."

Yes, we do adopt this position—not, however, because it's "relation-centric" to do so (this particular issue has nothing to do with being "relation-centric" or "object-centric"); rather, we do so because, although the idea of an operator (or "method") being bundled in with an object class works fine so long as the operator in question has just one parameter, it breaks down as soon as it has two or more.

Let me put the point another way. Every operator has a set of parameters. If that set happens to be of cardinality one, then little harm is done by bundling the operator with the class to which that single parameter belongs. But as soon as two parameters are involved (or more than two), an unpleasant degree of artificiality, arbitrariness, awkwardness, and asymmetry inevitably arises. For example, does the method "multiply velocity by time" (to yield a distance) belong to the VELOCITY class or the TIME class? Or the DISTANCE class, come to that? The best answer is surely "None of the above." In other words, some operators *have* to be "free-floating"; it therefore seems best (i.e., most consistent) to make them *all* so, for reasons of simplicity.

Incidentally, it's sometimes claimed that methods have to be bundled with classes in order to achieve proper encapsulation—the idea being that method *M* can access the internal representation for objects (values) of class *C* only if *M* is bundled with *C*. But to argue thus is to confuse logical and physical once again! Encapsulation does *not* imply bundling. It's true that certain methods do require privileged access to the internal representation of objects of certain classes. But it's surely preferable to use the system's security mechanism, instead of the *ad hoc* notion of bundling, to control such access (just as we use the security mechanism to control access to everything else).

15. "In an object-oriented model, if a data type is specified as the domain of an attribute, the domain often actually is meant not only to be the specified data type, but also all its subtypes. The relation-centric model is not capable of supporting this, since the structure of a data type cannot be inherited."

It's not easy to see exactly what Kim is getting at here, but what I think he means is that (for example) he wants to be able to define some column of some relation to contain VEHICLEs, and then permit that column actually to contain CARs, TRUCKs, etc., where CAR, TRUCK, etc., are subtypes of the VEHICLE supertype. If this is in fact what he means, then I assure him that our inheritance model certainly does permit such a capability. (The final remark concerning lack of inheritability of *structure* is—as should be apparent by now—a pure red herring.)

16. "The relation-centric model is certainly more powerful than the conventional relational model."

    No, it isn't. It is, however, more powerful than SQL. The "conventional relational model" has never been implemented.

Object Configuration

17. "The extended relational model does not provide a natural means to model an object configuration (often called a complex object . . .)"

    a. What we're proposing isn't an extended relational model.

    b. Moreover, we do provide what Kim would call a "natural" means to "model an object configuration," as a careful reading of *The Third Manifesto* should make clear. (Exactly what constitutes a "natural" way to model things is a separate question, of course. See my further comments on this topic following Quotation 20.)

18. "An object configuration may be a physical configuration or a logical configuration."

    I feel bound to say here that the terminology of physical *vs.* logical configurations here is just about as ill-chosen as it possibly could be. Abstracting from Kim's own explanation of the terms, they refer merely to one-to-many and many-to-many relationships respectively, but they thoroughly confuse model and implementation considerations once again. (The significance—such as it is—of the terminology is that one-to-many relationships are implemented by containment of objects *per se*, while many-to-many relationships are implemented by containment of *pointers to* objects. It has nothing to do with the usual distinction between logical and physical!—but it does have something to do with the distinction between model and implementation, because users will need to know whether a given relationship is "logical" or "physical.")

19. "Database application developers . . . have been baffled by the intolerable performance [incurred] . . . by performing joins . . ."

    I think I've addressed this point adequately under Quotation 3.

20. "A natural way to model an object configuration is by having an object recursively . . . point to . . . its constituent objects . . . (In fact, the primary-key/foreign-key construct is merely a longwinded means to express this simple referencing from one tuple to related tuples.)"

    When Codd excluded pointers from the relational model, he didn't do so as a matter of mere caprice!—and I don't think he'd take kindly to the suggestion that keys are a "longwinded" substitute for pointers. Surely no database professional could possibly believe that pointers are superior to keys *at the model level*. It's true that pointers might be a good idea at the implementation level, but (to repeat) anyone who uses that fact as an argument for exposing them at the model level is—to put the most charitable complexion on the matter—confusing logical and physical once again.

The entire remainder of this subsection on object configurations in Kim's article displays this same fundamental confusion. In order to avoid wearying the reader with highly repetitive comments on my part, therefore, I will omit a blow-by-blow rebuttal here. But I would like to say a few words regarding one common example of an "object configuration": namely, the familiar bill of materials structure, which is often used to demonstrate that object database systems can dramatically outperform today's SQL products.

The point I want to make is this. *The Third Manifesto* would permit *an entire bill of materials structure* to appear as a single "atomic value" at a row-and-column intersection in some relation (if desired). Further, the internal representation of that structure would very likely make heavy use of pointers. However, *those pointers would not be visible to users,* and users would not have to indulge in pointer-chasing in order to traverse the structure. Instead, they would of course be provided with appropriate *operators*—"explode part *p*," "implode part *p*," "get immediate components of part *p*," and so on. And, presumably, the performance of those operators would be directly comparable to that of their counterparts in a pure object system (in which the pointer-chasing would be done by the user).

Note: In case it's not obvious, let me make it clear that I'm not saying the foregoing approach is the *best* relational solution to the bill of materials problem—I'm just saying it's a possible one.

Object-Oriented Programming Languages

21. "The extended relational model . . . does not provide a basis for efficiently supporting object-oriented programming languages. The reason . . . is that the model does not include object identity. There is no object identity for each tuple of a relation . . . [The extended relational model omits] support for an important emerging application domain—namely, applications that are written in C++ or Smalltalk."

    a. What we're proposing isn't an extended relational model.

    b. Yes, we do exclude object identity (at least as that notion is usually understood in the object world), for what we believe are good reasons—essentially the same reasons as those Codd used for excluding pointers from the relational model. (To elaborate: Object identities are used as pointers in object systems. They lead to pointer-chasing. We see no need to burden users with obsolete technology.)

    c. I've already pointed out that we reject the "object = tuple" equation, very strongly!

    d. I've also claimed that any language that conforms to the proposals of *The Third Manifesto* would in fact *be* an object-oriented programming language, so the point about not supporting object-oriented languages is not completely valid. However, it's true that we might have a problem over C++ and Smalltalk specifically, owing to the pointer-based semantics of those languages. We haven't studied this issue very thoroughly, but one thing I will say: We're certainly not going to let the tail wag the dog and use the issue of support for C++ or Smalltalk serve as a back door for the introduction of pointers into our model.

First Normal Form

22. "Although the extended relational model allows a set of values in a row/column entry in a relation, it insists that the set be treated as a single atomic value . . . In other words, [the system] should not provide any means to access and manipulate individual elements of [such] a set."

    a. What we're proposing isn't an extended relational model.

    b. As for "treating the set as a single atomic value": Kim has misunderstood us here. The relevant text from *The Third Manifesto*—which actually talks about *relations* in "row/column entries," but does not preclude more general sets—reads as follows: ". . . it shall be possible to . . . [define columns of relations whose values are relations in turn] . . . The applicable operators shall include . . . an operator for extracting a specified tuple . . . ." In other words, the system certainly must provide a means to "access and manipulate individual elements" of row-and-column values that happen to be relations, and analogous remarks apply to row-and-column values that happen to be more general sets. It is our position (and we're prepared to defend this position at length) that providing access to individual elements of such values in this manner does not in any way undermine the benefits (such as they are) of encapsulation.

23. ". . . it is unreasonable to retain some theoretical restrictions in the face of the serious practical problems they precipitate."

    The idea of rejecting "theoretical restrictions" that "precipitate serious practical problems" is not in itself "unreasonable." But when the theory in question has proven itself to be of great *practical* value (not just theoretical value), it's incumbent on anyone who wishes to jettison it to show first that it does indeed "precipitate serious practical problems." In the case at hand, this has most categorically NOT been shown—not least because the theoretical ideas have never been implemented, at least not in their entirety.

Of course, it's true that today's SQL products are subject to "serious practical problems," *but the biggest such problem is the failure on the part of those products to implement the relational model!* We've tried to show with *The Third Manifesto* that the database industry—if it wants—can have its cake and eat it too, by enjoying what benefits objects might have to offer, *without* having to reject one iota of the relational model.

Let me add too that rejecting "theoretical restrictions" is very likely to lead us back to the bad old days of IMS, IDMS, and other prerelational anarchy, chaos, and general adhocery. The industry needs to be VERY sure of what it's doing if it decides to depart from the theoretical prescriptions of something as solid as the relational model.

24. "After all, a data model is not a religion. If the relational calculus cannot explain everything, then it is time either to extend the theory, or to find another that is more encompassing. Telling users that they must not demand things that may disrupt the simple elegance of an old mathematical theory is not acceptable."

Yes, but we mustn't rush into believing that the "old mathematical theory" is no longer applicable, just because today's SQL products (which in fact don't conform to that theory!) suffer from certain problems. In my experience, people who claim that the relational model cannot handle some new requirement, such as "complex objects" (or several other "new requirements" I might mention), *usually don't understand the relational model.* And—probably for that very reason—their criticisms of the relational model usually don't hold water.

THE OBJECT-CENTRIC PERSPECTIVE

25. "The relation-centric perspective holds that the object-centric perspective equates a relation with a class. The fact is that no object database systems ever have equated a relation with a class. In this sense, the relation-centric perspective offers criticism of a nonexistent perspective."

As already noted in the section "Comments on Republication," here Kim is being disingenuous to say the least. *Object* database systems as such don't talk about relations at all; however, the newer "object/relational" systems certainly do, and many of those systems—Kim's own UniSQL product included—do indeed equate relations and classes. Let me hansardize!—here's a quotation from one of Kim's own papers [9]:

". . . let us change the relational terms as follows. Change *relation* to *class, tuple of a relation* to *instance of a class, column* to *attribute, procedure* to *method, relation hierarchy* to *class hierarchy, child relation* to *subclass,* and *parent class* to *superclass.* The UniSQL/X data model . . . is an object-oriented data model!" (exclamation point in the original).

    Our criticisms of the "relation = class" equation are thus both relevant and, we believe, valid.

26. "[In the object-centric perspective, a] user-defined data type consists of 'all possible values for the data type,' and 'functions that perform operations on each value of the type.' A user-defined data type is equivalent to a class in object-oriented programming or object-oriented database systems."

    But didn't Kim previously say that a data type *wasn't* "equivalent to a class"? His precise words were (to repeat from Quotation 10): "In an object-oriented model, a class includes instances . . . [By contrast,] a data type is simply a domain that includes 'all possible values' for the type." *Someone* is confused here, and I don't think it's me.

    By the way: If a *user-*defined type is "equivalent to" a class (i.e., "class" means the same as "user-defined type"), what's a *system*-defined type?

27. "A relation is augmented to a class by including a system-defined column for tuple identity (i.e., object identifier), and optionally, functions (i.e., methods) that operate on each tuple of the relation. A relation is the extent of this type of class. Queries (i.e., projection, selection and join) and data manipulation statements (i.e., insert, update and delete) may be directed to the relations that are the extents of the classes. A class is regarded as a data type that belongs in the type hierarchy."

    I don't think it's worth trying to subject this particular extract to a blow-by-blow analysis. The alert reader will observe that it manages to combine in one paragraph several (at least six!) of the confusions already addressed earlier in this paper; but at least I don't think it introduces any new ones. I could be wrong.

28. "A class augmented from a relation may contain an attribute that 'references' another class augmented from a relation. The reference is to the extent of the class."

    A careful contextual analysis of what he's saying here will show that, among other things, Kim is confusing the two very different concepts *foreign key* and *domain* (to use the relational terms). Another confusion to add to the list!

29. "The above object-centric model summary fully subsumes the extended relational model of the relation-centric view."

    a. What we're proposing isn't an extended relational model.

b. Kim's object-centric model doesn't "fully subsume" the proposals of *The Third Manifesto,* it categorically violates them. (Indeed, if it did "fully subsume" those proposals, that fact in itself would constitute a violation!)

30. "Contrary to the implied concern in the relation-centric perspective that [the object-centric model] may cause chaos, these [ideas] are well-founded on research and engineering work conducted around the world during the past ten years."

   Just because a certain model seems to work well for a while doesn't mean it's *right.* The flat earth model was widely accepted for quite a long time. To take another example, perhaps more directly germane: SQL-style nulls are founded on research on many-valued logic that reaches back over the past *70* years, yet those nulls certainly do "cause chaos" in real databases and real applications.

   Let me add too that the proposals of *The Third Manifesto* are founded on "research and engineering work" that has been "conducted around the world" for very much more than a mere 10 years: The relational model itself is over 25 years old, predicate logic and set theory are each well over 100 years old, and propositional logic dates back to the ancient Greeks (4th century BC).

Closure

31. "Proponents of the relation-centric view are troubled by the idea of issuing a query against a class. Their primary objection seems to be that the result of a query against a class is not a class. A class has methods, but the result of a SELECT * query against a class will lose the methods . . . This concern is not well-founded. A query against a class is really against the extent of a class . . . If the query result needs to be saved as the extent of a new class, the user may add to the new class any useful methods defined in the original class."

   Again I don't think it's worth trying to respond blow-by-blow to every single one of the errors in this particular extract, but I do want to say this: It's not the idea of issuing a query against a class (type, domain) that "troubles" us; on the contrary, we understand that idea very well, and as a consequence see little utility in providing such a capability. What does "trouble" us is the fact that some people in our industry don't seem to understand the difference between a domain and a relation!

32. ". . . properties [of a relation] may include integrity constraints (UNIQUE, primary key, foreign key), and domain, length, and integrity (NULL allowed) specification for each column."

I hope Kim doesn't think the integrity constraints he mentions are the only ones possible, though a literal reading of the quoted extract would suggest that he does.

33. "For example, the result of a join . . . does not necessarily have all the integrity constraints [of the two input relations]."

    The meaning of this extract is not very clear, but it *sounds* wrong. The result of a join—or any other relational operation, come to that—certainly does "have all the integrity constraints" of the applicable input relation(s). For an accurate characterization of the situation in the case of join in particular, see reference [8].

Encapsulation

34. "If a rigorous view of encapsulation is adopted for attributes in a class, two methods must be written for each attribute in order to make them public . . . For a database, this is an unproductive exercise. The simple view that the attributes in a database class are all public attributes is preferable."

    More confusion! First of all, pure object classes don't have public attributes. Second, "writing two methods" for *private* (i.e., implementation-level) attributes doesn't make them public—the whole point of writing those methods is to keep the attributes private. Third, making private attributes public as Kim suggests undermines data independence; indeed, it constitutes a very high-handed dismissal of one of the most fundamental aspects of the entire object-oriented idea—namely, encapsulation.* Doesn't Kim believe in objects after all?

35. "The relation-centric perspective . . . observes that sometimes methods are needed that operate on values of more than one data type. A very simple solution exists for this problem . . . 'free-floating' methods . . . should be supported, which belong to the entire database, rather than any particular class."

    Yes, that's why we adopted this solution in *The Third Manifesto*. So why did Kim earlier refer to our approach as a "confusing stance" (see Quotation 14)?

    By the way, I'm not sure I agree that free-floating methods "belong to the database." What database does the method "+" ("add") belong to? Or the method "=" ("test for equality")?

Note added on republication: Since this paper was first published, I've changed my mind somewhat regarding the real meaning and importance of encapsulation anyway. See the footnotes concerning this issue in Installment 37 in Part I of this book.

References

36. "[Allowing a class to contain an attribute that references another class] represents the result of theoretical research and engineering work that has been undertaken during the past ten years to overcome serious limitations of the relational model."

   a. Note first that "allowing a class to contain an attribute that references another class" really means that *individual objects* of the first class contain an attribute value that is a pointer to an *individual object* of the second class. It's an unfortunate fact that object writings often use "class" to mean "object" and *vice versa*.

   b. Second, those pointer-valued attributes are *publicly visible*. I've already made it clear that I don't think pointers have any place at the model level at all, and further that I don't think attributes, pointer-valued or otherwise, should be publicly visible in any case.

   c. As for the "theoretical research and engineering work that has been undertaken during the past ten years to overcome serious limitations of the relational model," see my comments under Quotations 2–4 and 30.

37. "It appears that proponents of the relation-centric view have three areas of concern with respect to [the idea of allowing a class to contain an attribute that references another class:] *querying nested objects, breaking encapsulation,* and *pointer swizzling*."

   See my comments on Quotations 38–42 immediately following.

38. *"Querying nested objects:* . . . For example, if a class Automobile has an attribute Manufacturer that 'references' a class Company, a resulting path is of the form 'Automobile.Manufacturer' . . . Automobile.Manufacturer. Name = 'General Motors' is a [valid] query predicate . . ."

   Kim's discussion here concerns itself merely with matters of syntax, not substance. It doesn't address the point that restricting users to such "path queries" is reminiscent of the situation that obtained in prerelational systems, where users were restricted to traversing predefined paths in the database and true *ad hoc* query was difficult or even impossible.

39. *"Breaking encapsulation:* One common complaint about a path query is that encapsulation may be violated in evaluating a query. There is no harm done, however, as long as it is the database system, rather than a random user, that violates encapsulation."

   I don't know what it means to talk about encapsulation being violated in *evaluation* of a query. Encapsulation is violated as soon as private attributes are made public (i.e., visible to users)—see my earlier comments on this point under Quotation 34. If the user can write an expression such as Automobile.Manufacturer, that expression had better resolve to something, or user programs and queries will fail. What freedom do we now have to change the representation of Automobile?

40. "An obvious means to implement the 'reference' attribute is to store the identifiers of the [objects] in the referenced class as the values of the attribute. For example, if a class Automobile has an attribute Manufacturer that 'references' a class Company, the value stored in an instance of the class is the identifier of a particular instance of the class Company."

    Yes, and users had better understand this point very well!—because of such issues as update propagation to shared subobjects. In other words, we're definitely talking about the model here, not just the implementation; but I don't get the impression that Kim agrees with me on this point. On the contrary, I think he thinks he's talking about mere implementation matters (especially in view of his lead-in sentence, also in view of what he has to say in Quotation 41 immediately following).

41. "For simplicity, in the UniSQL database system, the notion of 'reference to a class' is implicit. No special syntax is provided to distinguish between a class and a reference to a class, when the class is specified as the domain of an attribute."

    On the face of it, these remarks are staggering. Is Kim really asking us to believe that not distinguishing between distinct things is a good idea? Especially since the things in question are part of the *model?*

42. "*Pointer swizzling:* . . . the identifiers of instances may be mapped (by the database system) to memory pointers when the instances are fetched into memory."

    We have no objection to pointer swizzling *per se*—how could we? It's purely a performance (i.e., implementation) issue. What we do object to is the inclusion of pointers in the *model.*

43. "A database system . . . generally must provide *ad hoc* query facilities."

    Yes, but this is very difficult to do with proper encapsulation!—which is perhaps why Kim seems not to believe in proper encapsulation (see Quotation 34), though he never actually admits as much.

44. ". . . it also must be recognized that some important applications absolutely require pointer traversal."

    I'm not aware of any evidence that supports this very strong claim. And I think the industry should *demand* to see such evidence before countenancing the idea of extending—or destroying—the relational model by including such a throwback as "pointer traversal."

45. ". . . *ad hoc* query facilities and pointer traversals can be combined in a single database system, and users can use either or both data access mechanisms."

    We don't dispute the *possibility* of supporting both styles of access; what we do dispute is the *wisdom* of supporting both.

Type Hierarchies

46. "A class . . . consists of user-created instances only."
    One of the things that makes Kim's position so confusing is that he keeps changing his mind!—or at least changing the definitions his arguments seem to be based on. I think I need to see a precise definition of what he means by the term "class" (probably "instance" too); then perhaps I might be able to criticize his position more coherently.

CONCLUSION

47. "Recently, Chris Date (and Hugh Darwen) proposed a simple scheme to extend the relational model with arbitrary data types and inheritance."
    NO, WE DIDN'T. We have both made it abundantly clear that we do not propose to extend the relational model. Data types have always been orthogonal to the relational model, and our PRIME AIM is to keep them so. *Note:* Again this quotation and response are copied from the section "Comments on Republication;" I repeat them here because they seem to form a fitting coda to this detailed commentary and review.

ACKNOWLEDGMENTS

I would like to thank Hugh Darwen, Herb Edelstein, Fabian Pascal, and Ron Ross for their thoughtful and helpful comments on earlier drafts of this paper.

REFERENCES

1. Luca Cardelli and Peter Wegner: "On Understanding Types, Data Abstraction, and Polymorphism," *ACM Comp. Surv. 17,* No. 4 (December 1985).

2. Michael Carey, Eugene Shekita, George Lapis, Bruce Lindsay, and John McPherson: "An Incremental Join Attachment for Starburst," Proc. 16th Int. Conf. on Very Large Data Bases, Brisbane, Australia (August 13th–16th, 1990).

3. Hugh Darwen and C. J. Date: "Introducing . . . The Third Manifesto," *Database Programming & Design 8,* No. 1 (January 1995). See also Chapter 3 in the present book.

4. Hugh Darwen and C. J. Date: "The Third Manifesto," *ACM SIGMOD Record 24,* No. 1 (March 1995). See also the book-length version *Foundation for Object/ Relational Databases: The Third Manifesto.* Reading, Mass.: Addison-Wesley (1998).

5. Hugh Darwen (and Chris Date): "Response to Won Kim, UniSQL," *Data Base Newsletter 23*, No. 2 (March/April 1995).

6. C. J. Date: "Domains, Relations, and Data Types," in *An Introduction to Database Systems* (6th edition). Reading, Mass.: Addison-Wesley (1995).

7. C. J. Date: "Domains, Relations, and Data Types," in *Relational Database Writings 1991–1994*. Reading, Mass.: Addison-Wesley (1995).

8. C. J. Date and David McGoveran: "Updating Joins and Other Views," *Database Programming & Design 7*, No. 8 (August 1994). Republished in C. J. Date, *Relational Database Writings 1991–1994*. Reading, Mass.: Addison-Wesley (1995).

9. Won Kim: "Object-Oriented Database Systems: Promises, Reality, and Future," Proc. 19th Int. Conf. on Very Large Data Base Systems, Dublin, Ireland (August 24th–27th, 1993).

10. Won Kim: "On Marrying Relations and Objects: Relation-Centric and Object-Centric Perspectives," *Data Base Newsletter 22*, No. 6 (November/December 1994).

11. Won Kim: "On Marrying Relations and Objects: Relation-Centric and Object-Centric Perspectives," Proc. 4th Int. Conf. on Database Systems for Advanced Applications (DASFAA'95), World Scientific Publishing Co., Singapore (April 10th–13th, 1995).

12. International Organization for Standardization (ISO): *Database Language SQL*. Document ISO/IEC 9075:1992. Also available as American National Standards Institute (ANSI) Document ANSI X3.135-1992.

CHAPTER **14**

Don't Mix Pointers and Relations!

A criticism of (among other things) SQL3

ABSTRACT

It's sometimes suggested that relational databases should be allowed to include pointers to data as well as data *per se*. This paper argues against that idea.

COMMENTS ON REPUBLICATION

In reference [5], Hugh Darwen and I identified what we called **The Great Blunder**—*viz.*, using (or attempting to use) the mistaken equation "relvar = class" as a basis on which to build an object/relational DBMS. I'm glad to be able to report in 1998 that many object/relational systems are now avoiding that blunder—though unfortunately not all; adherence to the "relvar = class" equation is still fairly widespread in the industry at large (in object-to-relation mapping tools, for example), if not so much in object/relational DBMSs as such.

Subsequently, however, I came to realize that there was a **Second Great Blunder** as well, one that was at least as serious as the first—*viz.*, introducing pointers into relations. And it seems to me that just about every object/relational DBMS is committing this one, even those that are avoiding the first!

Originally published in *InfoDB 10,* No. 6 (April 1997). Reprinted by permission of Database Associates International Inc.

What's more, the proposed follow-on to the current SQL standard, codenamed "SQL3" [8], is also currently going down the same path, more or less. I wrote the paper that follows, and the companion paper that appears in the next chapter, in an attempt to explain just why it would be a good idea *not* to commit this second blunder.

INTRODUCTION

The idea that databases should be allowed to include pointers to data as well as data *per se* has been around for a long time. Certainly it was a *sine qua non* in the old prerelational (IMS and CODASYL) world, and—in the shape of "object IDs"—it permeates the object world as well. And, despite the fact that Codd very deliberately excluded pointers from the relational model when he first defined it, the same idea also rears its head from time to time in the relational world. One of the most recent manifestations of the idea in a relational context occurs, not surprisingly, in connection with current "SQL3" attempts to extend the SQL standard to include support for objects [8]. In this paper, I want to explain why, in my opinion, mixing pointers and relations (if I might be allowed to characterize the scheme in such a manner) is a very bad idea.

  Note: Given that there are no pointers in the relational model, it follows immediately that "relational" databases that include pointers are—by definition—not relational! So what are they? One aim of this paper is to explore this question in some detail.

  Now, before we can dismiss the idea of mixing pointers and relations in any depth, we need to agree on a number of important preliminaries. Specifically, we need to pin down:

- The distinction between *values* and *variables* in general;
- The distinction between *relation* values and variables in particular;
- The concepts of *referencing* and *dereferencing*.

The next three sections therefore discuss these background matters in some detail (of course, readers already familiar with the material can skip those sections if they wish*). Subsequent sections then give an overview of the basic idea of mixing pointers and relations, followed by an analysis and detailed

---

*The first section in particular duplicates material found at various other points in the present book.

criticisms of that idea. The final section speculates on the origin of what is, after all, a very strange notion indeed from a relational point of view.

VALUES AND VARIABLES

The distinction between values and variables is fundamental. It's also very simple!—yet people do get confused over it (quite often, in fact), so let me spell it out in detail here. *Note:* The following definitions are based on ones given by Cleaveland [2].

- A **value** is an "individual constant" (for example, the individual constant "3"). A value has *no location in time or space*. However, values can be represented in memory by some encoding, and of course such representations do have locations in time and space (see the next paragraph). Note that—by definition!—a value cannot be updated (if it could be, then after such an update it wouldn't be that value any more).

- A **variable** is a holder for a representation of a value. A variable does have location in time and space. Moreover, variables (unlike values) can be updated; that is, the current value of the variable in question can be replaced by another value, probably different from the previous one.

Of course, I don't mean to suggest that only simple things like the integer "3" are legitimate values. On the contrary, values can be arbitrarily complex; for example, a value might be an array, or a stack, or a list, or a polygon, or a document, or an X-ray, or a fingerprint (and so on). Analogous remarks apply to variables too, of course.

Incidentally, it's worth noting that confusion over values *vs.* variables seems to be rife in the object world. For instance, consider the following, which is taken from a tutorial on object databases [9] (the italicized portions in square brackets are comments by myself):

> We distinguish the declared type of a variable from . . . the type of the object that is the current value of the variable [*so an object is a value*] . . . we distinguish objects from values [*so an object isn't a value after all*] . . . a **mutator** [*is an operation such that it's*] possible to observe its effect on some object [*so in fact an object is a variable*].

So what exactly *is* an object? Is it a value or a variable? Or both? Or something else entirely? *Note:* In fact, it's precisely this object world confusion over values *vs.* variables that seems to be one of the principal sources of the "mixing pointers and relations" idea, as I hope to make clear.

RELATION VALUES AND RELATION VARIABLES

Relations themselves provide a good example of the importance of the values *vs.* variables distinction. (The following discussion is an extended version of one given in an earlier paper by Hugh Darwen and myself [5].) Suppose we say, in some programming language:

```
DECLARE N INTEGER ... ;
```

We all understand that N here isn't an integer as such; rather, it's an integer *variable*—that is, a variable whose *values* are integers (different integers at different times). In exactly the same way, if we say, in SQL:

```
CREATE TABLE EMP ... ;
```

EMP here isn't a relation (SQL would say "table") as such; rather, it's a relation *variable**—that is, a variable whose *values* are relations (different relations at different times).

For example, suppose the relation variable EMP currently has the value— the *relation* value, that is—shown in Fig. 1, and suppose we "INSERT the row"

```
{ EMP#:'E4', ENAME:'Saito', DEPT#:'D2', SALARY:45K }
```

into EMP, yielding the result shown in Fig. 2. (The reason for placing the phrase "INSERT the row" in quotation marks will become clear in a moment.)

Conceptually, what has happened is that *the old (relation) value of EMP has been replaced* en bloc *by an entirely new (relation) value.* Of course, it's

EMP	EMP#	ENAME	DEPT#	SALARY
	E1	Lopez	D1	25K
	E2	Cheng	D1	42K
	E3	Finzi	D2	30K

Fig. 1   Relation variable EMP: initial value

EMP	EMP#	ENAME	DEPT#	SALARY
	E1	Lopez	D1	25K
	E2	Cheng	D1	42K
	E3	Finzi	D2	30K
	E4	Saito	D2	45K

Fig. 2   Relation variable EMP: value after INSERT

---

*In his original paper on the relational model [3], Codd called relation variables *time-varying relations*.

true that the old value (involving three rows) and the new value (involving four) are somewhat similar, but conceptually they *are* different values. Indeed, the INSERT operation in question is basically just shorthand for the following **relational assignment** operation :[*]

```
EMP  :=  EMP UNION { { EMP#:'E4', ENAME:'Saito',
                       DEPT#:'D2', SALARY:45K } } ;
```

As in all assignments, what's happening here, conceptually, is that (a) the expression on the right hand side is evaluated, and then (b) the result of that evaluation is assigned to the variable on the left hand side. As already stated, the net effect is thus to replace the "old" EMP value (a relation value) by a "new" one (another relation value).

In analogous fashion, of course, DELETE and UPDATE operations are also basically shorthand for certain relational assignments.

Now, it's an unfortunate fact that in the past we've tended to use the term *relation* when what we really meant was a relation *variable* (as well as when we meant a relation *per se*—that is, a relation *value*). Historically, however, this practice has led to a certain amount of confusion (over normalization, for example). In *The Third Manifesto* [6], therefore, Hugh Darwen and I introduced the term **relvar**—short for relation variable—and we tried to distinguish as carefully as we could between relvars and relations *per se*. *Note: The Third Manifesto* is a proposal for the future direction of data and database management; in particular, it proposes a *rapprochement* between objects and relations (as does SQL3, of course, but SQL3's approach to the issue is very different). Further details of the *Manifesto* are beyond the scope of this paper.

REFERENCING AND DEREFERENCING

Many programming languages support *pointers.* That is, they recognize that the concept of a variable is really an abstraction of the concept of an *area of storage;* accordingly, they recognize that variables have *addresses;* they therefore support address or "pointer" values and variables (in other words, they support an address **type**). Thus, a pointer value is an address, and a pointer variable is a variable whose permitted values are addresses.[†]

---

[*] It's a slight oversimplification to say the INSERT is shorthand for the exact assignment shown; for example, we'd probably want to include a check to make sure that the previous value of EMP didn't already include a row for employee E4.

[†] By *address* here, I don't necessarily mean a hardware address, of course. The idea rather is just that every variable has a location of some kind, and of course the address of that location is independent of the current value of the variable in question (it stays constant while the value of the variable changes). Some writers use the term *reference* for this concept; I find this term too broad, and prefer the more suggestive term *address.*

The type *address* has two fundamental operations associated with it, usually called *referencing* and *dereferencing.*

- **Referencing:** Given a variable V, the referencing operator applied to V returns the address of V. For example, here's the syntax used for the referencing operator in C, Pascal, and PL/I:

```
C       --   &V
Pascal  --   ^V
PL/I    --   ADDR(V)
```

For example, the following PL/I code fragment has the effect of assigning the address of the integer variable N to the pointer variable P:

```
DECLARE N INTEGER ... ;
DECLARE P POINTER ... ;

P  =  ADDR ( N ) ;
```

Or if you prefer C:

```
INT N ;
INT *P ;

P  =  &N ;
```

Note carefully that the argument to the referencing operator must be specified as a *variable,* not as a literal or more general expression. The reason is, of course, that values don't have addresses, variables do (recall that values have no location in time or space). Thus, for example, ADDR(3) and ADDR(N+1) are both illegal in PL/I. (After all, if they were legal, the best the system could do with them would be to return the address of the *system-generated* variable that holds the result of evaluating the argument expression—surely a useless thing to do.)

- **Dereferencing:** Given a variable A of type address, the dereferencing operator applied to A returns the variable whose address is currently contained in A. Here's the syntax for dereferencing in C, Pascal, and PL/I:[*]

```
C       --   *A
Pascal  --   A^
PL/I    --   A -> V
```

For example, the following PL/I code fragment has the effect of assigning the integer value "3" to the integer variable N that pointer variable P currently points to:

```
P -> N  =  3 ;
```

---

[*]The PL/I syntax assumes that V is a "based" variable and the address in A identifies a certain "generation" of that based variable. Further details of these niceties are irrelevant for our purposes, and I omit them here.

C analog:

```
*P = 3 ;
```

Note carefully that the dereferencing operator returns a *variable*, not a value. The reason is, again, that values don't have addresses, variables do. (Of course, if the dereferencing operation occurs in a source position instead of a target position—in particular, if it occurs on the right hand side instead of the left hand side of an assignment—it can be regarded, harmlessly, as returning the value of the variable in question instead of returning that variable *per se*. This point isn't very significant for the purposes of the present paper, however.)

Before going any further, I have to say that personally I find the "referencing and dereferencing" terminology quite confusing. In particular, I think it would be very reasonable to regard the PL/I expression "P -> N" as *referencing* the particular integer variable N that pointer variable P currently points to; yet as we've seen, that expression is really an example of **de**referencing. For such reasons, I'll try to avoid the referencing/dereferencing terminology as much as possible in what follows. (I should mention too that several languages, PL/I included, support *implicit* dereferencing, which can serve to make the concepts even more confusing to the uninitiated. In what follows, all dereferencing will be explicit.)

MIXING POINTERS AND RELATIONS: THE BASIC IDEA

Now (at last) we're equipped to examine the central issue of this paper. As noted in the introductory section, there have been suggestions to the effect that "relational" databases should be allowed to include pointers to data as well as data *per se*. For example, the current SQL3 proposals [8] introduce a new data type, REF, which—loosely speaking—allows values of a column in one relation to be addresses of rows in another relation (or possibly the same relation). As already indicated, I refer to this scheme as "mixing pointers and relations." Is it a good idea? Can it be made to work?

Well, let's look at an example. Fig. 3 shows what such a scheme might look like in the case of an employees-and-departments database. Note the EMP column DADDR, which might have been defined to be of type REF (or POINTER, or ADDR, or something else of that same general nature), with the further constraint that values—that is, addresses—in that column must be, very specifically, addresses of DEPT rows. The intent of the example, of course, is that the EMP rows for employees E1 and E2 point to the DEPT row for department D1, and the EMP rows for employees E3 and E4 point to the DEPT row for department D2.

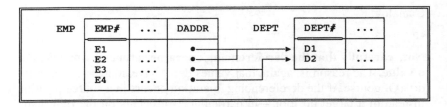

Fig. 3   Mixing pointers and relations (example)

Now let's consider some sample queries involving this database. *Note:* Naturally I assume for the moment that the database makes sense, and therefore that queries and other operations involving it make sense also. In my opinion, however, they *don't* make sense, and the examples that follow don't stand up under careful scrutiny. But my objective for the moment is simply to give an idea of what the "mixing pointers and relations" scheme might look like in practice, in order that I might have a concrete target for subsequent analysis and criticism. Note too that (for familiarity) I use an SQL-like syntax for my examples, even though it's not to my own taste; I choose not to use the exact SQL3 syntax [8], however, for reasons that aren't important here.

Example 1: Get the department number for employee E1.

```
SELECT  ex.DADDR -> DEPT#
FROM    EMP ex
WHERE   ex.EMP# = 'E1' ;
```

Note the dereferencing operation in the SELECT clause (the expression *ex.*DADDR –> DEPT# returns the DEPT# value from the DEPT row that the DADDR value in question points to). Note too the slightly counterintuitive nature of the FROM clause!—the DEPT# value to be retrieved comes from DEPT, not EMP, but *DADDR* values come from EMP, not DEPT. I suppose we might extend the FROM clause, harmlessly, to mention DEPT as well as EMP, thus:

```
FROM EMP ex, DEPT dx
```

Though if we did, we'd probably want to specify DISTINCT in the SELECT clause as well!

It's interesting to note that the very same query can logically be formulated in terms of *referencing* (in the WHERE clause) rather than dereferencing (in the SELECT clause):

```
SELECT  dx.DEPT#
FROM    DEPT dx
WHERE   'E1' = ( SELECT ex.EMP#
                 FROM   EMP ex
                 WHERE  ex.DADDR = ADDR ( dx ) ) ;
```

Here I've assumed that the referencing operation ADDR(*dx*) in the inner SELECT–FROM–WHERE returns the address of the DEPT row *dx* currently being processed by the outer one.

Yet another formulation (again using referencing rather than dereferencing) might look like this:

```
SELECT  dx.DEPT#
FROM    EMP ex, DEPT dx
WHERE   ex.EMP# = 'E1'
AND     ex.DADDR = ADDR ( dx ) ;
```

Note: SQL has long been known (and criticized) for supporting many different ways of doing the same thing. In the case at hand, however, the fact that there are so many possible formulations is due, at least in part, not to the idiosyncrasies of SQL *per se,* but rather to the basic idea of mixing pointers and relations in the first place. To be specific (albeit simplifying simply), the expressions

```
ex.DADDR -> DEPT#
```

and

```
dx.DEPT# WHERE ex.DADDR = ADDR ( dx )
```

(where *ex* and *dx* represent a particular EMP row and DEPT row respectively) are logically equivalent by definition, and hence lead to distinct formulations of the same query.

Now let's look at an example illustrating *dereferencing* in the WHERE clause.

Example 2: Get employee numbers for employees in department D1.

```
SELECT  ex.EMP#
FROM    EMP ex
WHERE   ex.DADDR -> DEPT# = 'D1' ;
```

Note: The following expression (using referencing rather than dereferencing) might possibly be thought to be an alternative formulation of this query:

```
SELECT  ex.EMP#
FROM    EMP ex
WHERE   ex.DADDR = ADDR ( SELECT dx.*
                          FROM   DEPT dx
                          WHERE  dx.DEPT# = 'D1' ) ;
```

The thinking behind this putative formulation is that the ADDR invocation in the outer WHERE clause will return the address of the DEPT row for department D1. But of course that thinking is mistaken! As explained earlier, the argument to ADDR must be a variable, not a more general expression. The ADDR invocation just shown is illegal, and so therefore is the overall expression.

Example 3: What does the following query do?

```
SELECT  ex.DADDR
FROM    EMP ex
WHERE   ex.EMP# = 'E1' ;
```

Presumably it simply returns the DADDR value (that is, an *address*) for employee E1. What does this address look like if it's returned to the user? Do we have to support address *literals* of some kind? (The answer to this question is *yes,* of course. Note that if it were *no,* certain *relation* values—namely, those that contain addresses—wouldn't be expressible as *relation* literals!)

Here's another example of a query that returns an address:

```
SELECT  ADDR ( dx )
FROM    DEPT dx
WHERE   dx.DEPT# = 'D1' ;
```

To close out this section, here are a couple of update examples.

Example 4: Insert an employee.

```
INSERT INTO EMP ( EMP#, DADDR )
       VALUES ( 'E5', ( SELECT ADDR ( dx )
                        FROM    DEPT dx
                        WHERE   dx.DEPT# = 'D2' ) ) ;
```

If (as the example suggests) DADDR values are provided by the user by means of ADDR invocations, instead of by means of address literals or address-valued variables, then presumably it won't be possible to insert an EMP row that points to a nonexistent DEPT row.

Example 5: Delete a department.

```
DELETE
FROM    DEPT dx
WHERE   dx.DEPT# = 'D1' ;
```

Clearly, we'll need some rules—ON DELETE CASCADE and the like—to cater for the possibility that there might be pointers elsewhere in the database to the row(s) being deleted. Analogous remarks apply to UPDATE, of course.

A CLOSER LOOK AT THE BASIC IDEA

Having sketched the basic idea of mixing pointers and relations, I now want to ask the question: Does the idea really stand up? Let's take a closer look.

First of all, note that—as pointed out several times already—*values* don't have addresses, *variables* do. It follows that, for example, the addresses in column DADDR in the example of Fig. 3 must be addresses, not of row *values,* but of row *variables.*

But there's no such thing as a row variable in the relational model. The relational model deals with relation values, which are (loosely speaking) sets of row values, which are in turn (again loosely speaking) sets of scalar values. It also deals with relation variables, which are variables whose values are relations. However, it does *not* deal with row variables (which are variables whose values are rows) or scalar variables (which are variables whose values are scalars). In other words, the **only** kind of variable included in the relational model is, very specifically, the *relation* variable. *It follows that the idea of mixing pointers and relations constitutes a MAJOR departure from the relational model, introducing as it does an entirely new kind of variable.*

Why exactly would the introduction of row variables constitute such a major departure? Well, orthogonality would dictate that we'd have to allow such variables to appear in the database as well as relation variables. And then we'd have to define a whole new query language for rows—that is, a set of row operators (a "row algebra"?), analogous to the operators already defined for relations (*viz.,* the relational algebra). We'd also have to define row-level update operators, analogous to the existing relational ones. We'd have to be able to define row-level integrity and security constraints, and row-level views. The catalog would have to describe row variables as well as relation variables. (And what would the catalog itself consist of?—row variables? or relation variables? or a mixture of both?) We'd need a row-level design theory, analogous to the existing body of relational design theory. We'd also need guidelines as to when to use row variables and when relation variables. And so on (I'm sure this list of issues isn't exhaustive).

The net of all this is:

- Assuming that a "row algebra" can be defined, and all of the other questions raised in the previous paragraph answered satisfactorily, we will now have two ways of doing things, where one sufficed before. In other words, adding a new kind of variable certainly adds *complexity,* but it doesn't add any *power* (there's nothing useful that can be done with a mixture of row and relation variables that can't be done with relation variables alone).

- Thus, the user interface will now be more complex and involve more choices (most likely without good guidelines as to how to make such choices).

- As a direct consequence of the foregoing, database applications—including in particular general-purpose applications or "frontends"—will become more difficult to write and more difficult to maintain.

- Those applications will also become more vulnerable to changes in the database structure. That is, some degree of logical data independence will be lost (consider what happens, for example, if the representation of some piece of information is changed from relation to row variables, or the other way around).

In my opinion, the foregoing arguments should be sufficient to stop the "mixing pointers and relations" idea dead in its tracks.* Nevertheless, there are several further criticisms of the idea that are also worth articulating. Before I can get to those, however, I want to take a look at one suggestion that's sometimes made in an attempt to rescue the basic idea.

CAN THE IDEA BE RESCUED?

The suggestion I refer to is as follows: Instead of insisting that addresses such as those in column DADDR in the example of Fig. 3 must point to row variables *per se,* can't we think of them as somehow pointing to *components* of *relation* variables—thereby retaining relation variables specifically as the only kind of variable permitted in the model? In PL/I, for example, the expression ADDR (S.C), where S is a structure variable and C is a component of S, is perfectly legitimate. As another example, the expression ADDR (A(3)), where A is an array variable and that parenthesized "3" is a subscript, is likewise perfectly legitimate. So why not dispose of the row variable argument in the same kind of way? Let's examine this idea.

- First of all, of course, those "component pointers" (meaning pointers to components of some relation variable) obviously can't be *absolute* addresses, for all the usual reasons.

- Nor can they be *relative* or "offset" addresses, because of course a given relation variable contains different rows at different times; thus, even if it

---

*It's worth noting in passing that precisely analogous arguments apply to the idea of introducing *any* new kind of variable into the relational model. Further discussion of this point would take us much too far afield, however.

contains "the same" row at different times, there can be no guarantee that the offset remains the same, because of insert/delete activity. (Note carefully that this argument doesn't apply to the PL/I examples mentioned above.)

- Hence, they must be purely *symbolic* or *associative* in nature. In other words, they must be key values! (or something logically equivalent to key values)—where by "key" I mean some *candidate* key of the relation variable in question. And so the "pointers" we're dealing with are really conventional *foreign* keys in a different guise.

If we adopt the "component pointers" suggestion, in other words, we're not really dealing with pointers (in the generally accepted sense of that term) at all. As a consequence, the entire idea of mixing pointers and relations reduces to nothing more than a different syntax* for something the relational model already gives us—namely, candidate and foreign keys, together with certain foreign key rules such as ON DELETE CASCADE—and is therefore fundamentally uninteresting from a logical point of view. *Note:* I feel bound to point out too that, in my opinion, using keys to implement pointers is 100 percent upside down! (not to say perverse in the extreme). By contrast, the inverse idea—that is, using pointers to implement keys—might sometimes be useful, as I've indicated elsewhere [7].

As an aside, let me point out that the discussions of this section should go some way to show why (contrary to what's sometimes claimed) foreign key values aren't pointers, and why (unlike the proposed pointer mechanism) foreign keys don't violate the spirit of the relational model.

FURTHER ISSUES

From the discussions of the previous section, I conclude that the pointers that people—at least, some people—want to mix with relations really are genuine pointers and really do point to variables (albeit variables that are somehow "contained within" relation variables, though I find it hard to make any sense of this latter notion). In this section I want to point out a number of further implications of this state of affairs.

---

*Not a very nice syntax, either, because of the asymmetry inherent in referencing *vs.* dereferencing. For example, the process of stepping from EMP to DEPT is syntactically quite different from that of stepping from DEPT to EMP (contrast the situation with key value matching, which involves no such syntactic asymmetry).

More on Values *vs.* Variables

Regardless of whether we agree that the notion of relation variables containing row variables makes no sense, we must surely agree that *values* can't contain variables, and hence that relation values in particular can't contain variables (neither row variables, nor any other kind). It follows that the pointers we're talking about always "point into" relation *variables* specifically, not into relation *values*. As a consequence, we're dealing with a system in which certain operators work for variables but not for values!* Consider the following example, which is intended to show an SQL-like representation of what we might call a *pointer join* (more precisely, a projection of such a join).

Example 6: For all employees, get the employee number and corresponding department number.

```
SELECT  ex.EMP#, dx.DEPT#
FROM    EMP ex, DEPT dx
WHERE   ex.DADDR = ADDR ( dx ) ;
```

EMP and DEPT here are relation variables, and the pointer join "works" just fine. But suppose we were to replace DEPT by a relation literal, representing the current *value* of relation variable DEPT, as follows (note the use of the SQL/92 VALUES construct, which—among other things—allows us to write relation literals):

```
SELECT  ex.EMP#, dx.DEPT#
FROM    EMP ex, ( VALUES ( 'D1', ... ),
                         ( 'D2', ... ) ) dx ( DEPT#, ... )
WHERE   ex.DADDR = ADDR ( dx ) ;
```

This latter query (if it works at all, a moot point in itself) will necessarily return an empty result!—because the ADDR invocation in the WHERE clause refers to the *system-generated* relation variable, DUMMY say, that contains the result of evaluating the VALUES expression in the FROM clause, while DADDR values refer to the relation variable DEPT.[†] Thus, the comparison in the WHERE clause can never evaluate to *true*.

If you're having difficulty appreciating the significance of this point, the following analogy might help. Let X and Y be variables of type INTEGER, with current values 4 and 5, say. Then it's as if the "+" operator were defined for integers in such a way that the expression $X + Y$ gave 9, but the expression $X + 5$ gave zero! (The expressions $X + (Y + 1)$, and $X + (Y + 0)$, and even $X + (Y)$, would also all give zero, presumably.)

---

*Of course, this remark is already true of update operators. But the operators I'm talking about here are not update operators but *read-only* operators.

[†]Analogous remarks would apply if we were to replace DEPT by a more general relational expression, representing (say) the join of two other relations.

A related point—perhaps the same point in a different guise—is the following. The operators of the relational algebra are defined to work on *relations* (that is, relation *values*); in particular, of course, they work on the values that happen to be the current values of relation *variables*. But none of those operators works on relation variables specifically; that is, none of those operators *requires* some operand to consist of a relation variable specifically. The "pointer join," by contrast, certainly does require one operand (the "pointed to" operand) to be a relation variable specifically. **And so we're talking about another major departure from the classical relational model.** To spell it out: The classical relational algebra has no concept of a relation variable; the "pointer join," by contrast, necessarily does.

Yet another related point is as follows. When people talk of "pointers to rows in relations," it's quite clear that what they mean is pointers to rows in *base* relations specifically. (I deliberately blur the values *vs.* variables distinction here.) In other words, they forget about *derived* relations! As I've argued elsewhere [7], this is a mistake of the highest order, because the question as to which relations are base and which derived is, in a very important sense, arbitrary. For further discussion of this issue, see that earlier paper [7].

More on the Pointer Join

Let's take another look at the pointer join example from the previous subsection:

```
SELECT ex.EMP#, dx.DEPT#
FROM    EMP ex, DEPT dx
WHERE   ex.DADDR = ADDR ( dx ) ;
```

Note the tacit assumption that each EMP row has just one corresponding DEPT row (the DADDR value in any given EMP row obviously points to just one DEPT row); in other words, the pointer join is inherently a many-to-one operation. What happens if the situation changes, such that the same department can be represented in several DEPT rows?—for example, if departments are spread across several locations, and DEPT contains one row for each valid DEPT#-LOCATION combination? Clearly, the pointer join operation won't work any more—or, rather (and more fundamentally), the database design won't be valid any more! By contrast, the conventional relational design, in which EMP contains a DEPT# column instead of a DADDR column, would still be valid after the change, and the conventional relational join—

```
SELECT ex.EMP#, dx.DEPT#
FROM    EMP ex, DEPT dx
WHERE   ex.DEPT# = dx.DEPT# ;
```

—would still work.

Orthogonality

If we're allowed to deal with addresses of row variables, orthogonality dictates that we must be allowed to deal with addresses of other kinds of variables too. And since the "mixing pointers and relations" idea does entail at least one other kind of variable—*viz.*, relation variables—it follows that we should be able to write expressions of the form

```
ADDR ( R )
```

and

```
P -> R
```

where R is a relation variable. I certainly haven't explored all of the implications of this point, but I'd be willing to wager that some of them, at least, are undesirable.*

The Information Principle

Codd has stated his **Information Principle** in various forms and various publications over the years; indeed, I believe he has referred to it on occasion as "the fundamental principle of the relational model." It can be stated as follows:

All information in the database must be cast explicitly in terms of values in relations and in no other way.

In his book [4], Codd gives a number of arguments in support of this principle (arguments with which I agree, of course). And he goes on to point out that one consequence of the principle is that all "interrelating" between different parts of the database must be "achieved by comparisons of values" (where by *values* he means, essentially, values at row-and-column intersections in relations).

I now want to argue that a comparison such as the following (which appeared in several earlier examples) clearly violates the spirit, if not the letter, of the foregoing:

```
ex.DADDR = ADDR ( dx )
```

It's true that this comparison does involve scalar values, but it seems to me that the right hand comparand is special. To be specific, the value of that comparand *cannot be derived from the value of the ADDR argument* (because, to say it one more time, values don't have addresses, variables do). By contrast, a comparison such as (say)

---

*One implication—a serious one, too—is that the system will now have to support *second-order logic,* whereas the classical relational model is based on the simpler *first-*order logic only.

```
X = LOG ( Y )
```

isn't subject to the same kind of criticism, because the value of LOG(Y) certainly can be derived from the value of Y. In the first comparison, in other words, we're dealing with a scalar value—namely, the result of the ADDR invocation—that *cannot* be derived from the scalar values in the database. And so there's apparently some "information in the database" that's *not* "cast explicitly in terms of values in relations," and the principle is thereby violated.*

I would argue further that this violation of the Information Principle—indeed, the whole idea of mixing pointers and relations in the first place—can be seen as **undermining the conceptual integrity of the relational model.**† And conceptual integrity is a serious matter! In his classic *The Mythical Man-Month* [1], Fred Brooks says:

> . . . conceptual integrity is *the* most important consideration in system design. It is better to have a system omit certain anomalous features [and] to reflect one set of design ideas, than to have one that contains many good but independent and uncoordinated ideas (italics in the original).

And writing 20 years later, he adds:

> A clean, elegant programming product must present . . . a coherent mental model . . . [Conceptual] integrity . . . is the most important factor in ease of use. . . . **Today I am more convinced than ever.** Conceptual integrity *is* central to product quality (boldface and italics in the original).

Redundancy

My final criticism of the idea of adding pointers to the relational model is simply that they're unnecessary! The relational model has managed perfectly well without them for over a quarter of a century; thus, any "relational" pointer mechanism—*if* it could be made to work in such a way as to overcome all of the objections already articulated in this paper—would still be 100 percent redundant. Also, of course, pointers lead to pointer chasing, and pointer chasing is notoriously error-prone (which is basically why Codd rejected pointers in the first place).

---

*In case you might be thinking that LOG(Y) isn't "cast explicitly as a value in a relation" either, let me point out that it can easily be made so by means of the EXTEND operation [6].

†In fact, one reviewer of the original paper (Declan Brady) went so far as to suggest that it's "the conceptual integrity of the whole future of data" that's being undermined.

CONCLUDING REMARKS

So where did this strange idea of mixing pointers and relations come from? It seems to me that what we have here is (as so often) *a fundamental confusion between model and implementation.* To be specific, it has been observed that certain SQL products don't perform very well on certain joins, and it has further been conjectured that performance would be improved if we could follow a pointer instead of doing a join. As I've written elsewhere [7], however, such thinking is seriously confused:

> ... (1) *implementing* relationships by pointers is very different from (2) *exposing* such pointers in the model. The fact that (1) might be a good idea doesn't imply that (2) is a good idea, and of course it categorically isn't. We *must* keep logical and physical concepts distinct, and not get confused over the two levels in our debates; we've learned the hard way—or at least some of us have—what happens when this principle is violated [7].

Of course, I'm aware that another driving force behind the idea of exposing pointers in the model is a strong desire to bring object and relational technologies closer together. In itself, this is a worthy objective. However, as Hugh Darwen and I have argued elsewhere [5], there's a right way and a wrong way to approach such a goal. The wrong way, which we refer to as *The Great Blunder,** involves a mistaken understanding of the true nature of objects—relations too for that matter—and seems to lead inevitably to the heresy of mixing pointers and relations. The analyses of the present paper tend to reinforce our position that this blunder is indeed a very great one! By contrast, in *The Third Manifesto* [6], we've tried to show what would be involved in approaching this same goal in the "right" way, which (among other things) doesn't lead to that same heresy.

ACKNOWLEDGMENTS

I'm grateful, first of all, to Don Chamberlin, whose original question "So what's wrong with having REF values in a relational database?" (I'm quoting from memory) led directly to the production of this paper. I'd also like to thank Nelson Mattos for his more detailed explanation of the "REF type" idea. I'm also grateful to Hugh Darwen for numerous discussions, for his careful review

---

*As noted in the section "Comments on Republication," we now regard it as the *first* great blunder. The topic of the present paper (mixing pointers and relations) is the second.

of an earlier draft of this paper, and for providing me with a copy of the current SQL3 proposals [8]. Finally, I'm grateful to my other reviewers Declan Brady and Don Chamberlin (again) for further helpful comments.

REFERENCES

1. Frederick P. Brooks, Jr.: *The Mythical Man-Month* (20th anniversary edition). Reading, Mass.: Addison-Wesley (1995).

2. J. Craig Cleaveland: *An Introduction to Data Types.* Reading, Mass.: Addison-Wesley (1986).

3. E. F. Codd: "Derivability, Redundancy, and Consistency of Relations Stored in Large Data Banks," IBM Research Report RJ599 (August 19th, 1969).

4. E. F. Codd: *The Relational Model for Database Management Version 2.* Reading, Mass.: Addison-Wesley (1990).

5. Hugh Darwen and C. J. Date: "Introducing . . . The Third Manifesto," *Database Programming & Design 8,* No. 1 (January 1995). See also Chapter 3 of the present book.

6. Hugh Darwen and C. J. Date: "The Third Manifesto," *ACM SIGMOD Record 24,* No. 1 (March 1995). See also the book-length version *Foundation for Object/ Relational Databases: The Third Manifesto.* Reading, Mass.: Addison-Wesley (1998).

7. C. J. Date: "Objects and Relations: Forty-Seven Points of Light" (Chapter 13 of the present book).

8. International Organization for Standardization: *Database Language SQL—Part 8: SQL/Object* (Committee Draft). Document ISO/IEC JTC1/SC21 N10491 (July 1996). *Note:* After the present paper was first written, Part 8 of the SQL specification was dropped as a separate part and the material moved into other parts of the document (primarily *Part 2, SQL Foundation*).

9. Stanley B. Zdonik and David Maier: "Fundamentals of Object-Oriented Databases," in Zdonik and Maier (eds.), *Readings in Object-Oriented Database Systems.* San Mateo, Calif.: Morgan Kaufmann (1990).

CHAPTER **15**

Don't Mix Pointers and Relations—*Please!*

*A response to a paper by Don Chamberlin entitled
"Relations and References—Another Point of View"*

ABSTRACT

It's sometimes suggested that relational databases should be allowed to include
pointers to data as well as data *per se*. In reference [2], I presented arguments
against this idea. In reference [1], Chamberlin offered a rebuttal to some of
those arguments. The present paper is a rebuttal to reference [1]. *Note:* Like
several other papers in this collection, this paper is—as indicated—basically
a response to another one, but once again I believe it does stand on its own and
is worth including here.

COMMENTS ON PUBLICATION

See the "Comments on Republication" in the previous chapter.

Previously unpublished.

INTRODUCTION

References [1] and [2] don't merely disagree, they seem to be at complete cross purposes. In my original paper [2], I explained that the idea of "mixing pointers and relations" could be interpreted in two quite different ways, which might loosely be characterized as follows:

- *Interpretation 1:* The pointers are really just keys.
- *Interpretation 2:* The pointers are really pointers, not keys.

If *Interpretation 1* is the correct one, then we're not really talking about pointers at all, we're just talking about a syntactic shorthand, and the whole debate becomes a nonissue (at least from a logical point of view, though there are certainly some psychological questions that need to be addressed—I'll get to those later). In other words, *Interpretation 2* is the interesting one. Throughout reference [2], therefore (with the minor exception of a section entitled "Can the Idea Be Rescued?"), I assumed *Interpretation 2,* and I tried to explain why I thought it would be a mistake for the industry to embrace such a radical idea.

   In reference [1], however, Chamberlin incorrectly assumes that my principal concern is with *Interpretation 1*. Noting that he accuses my original paper [2] of containing a number of red herrings, therefore, I think that, *au contraire,* his entire response [1] is one huge red herring! Nevertheless, I do also think that many of the points he raises need to be refuted—hence the present paper.

RED HERRINGS?

Chamberlin's incorrect assumption that I was addressing *Interpretation 1* is, I believe, the main reason why he thinks some of my points are red herrings. I claim, contrariwise, that the points I was making are both germane and important. Let me address some of Chamberlin's specific comments in this regard.

- "One [red herring] is the observation that the ADDR operator . . . is not meaningful when applied to a constant or an expression. This is an unremarkable fact, and has a direct analogy in every programming language that has a similar operator . . . So we should not be surprised that if a similar operator is introduced into SQL, it is undefined for constants and expressions—indeed, we should be surprised if this were not the case."

   The fact is not unremarkable! Rather, the point is that "every programming language that has a similar operator" also has *variables,* and the operand to ADDR is required to be a *variable* specifically. Thus, when we talk of the ADDR of a "row," we have to mean, specifically, the ADDR of a row *variable*. The relational model doesn't have row variables, and neither does SQL. So we're talking about a major extension!—and in reference [2] I showed that the extension in question has a number of undesirable consequences.

As for "we should not be surprised that if a similar operator is introduced into SQL, it is undefined for constants and expressions": What *should* surprise us is the idea that someone might suggest introducing such an operator into a language that doesn't include the kind of thing that the operator needs to operate on. Chamberlin's second and third sentences are the real red herring here.

By the way: Statements like "the ADDR operator . . . is not meaningful when applied to . . . an expression" illustrate the difficulty of talking about subjects like this one with clarity and precision, and the consequent difficulty of getting the language specifications right (whatever "right" might mean in the present context). After all, the SQL3 draft [7] certainly does propose that we should be able to write something like ADDR(*x*), and *x* here certainly is an expression (a variable name is certainly a special case of an expression). In other words, ADDR *does* apply to expressions; the only question is, which ones?

And by the way again: Note that, as far as SQL3 is concerned, the *x* in ADDR(*x*) is required to denote a *row* specifically (SQL3 uses the syntax REF ROW *x* in place of my ADDR(*x*), which perhaps makes this point a little more explicit). I observe, however, that once the idea of "addressing" or "referencing" or "pointing" is introduced (no matter what term or syntax we use), then—as I said in reference [2]—orthogonality would surely dictate that it be available for *all* variables, of all kinds. But it isn't, in SQL3.

- "In Example 2 [Date] writes a putative formulation [of a certain query] which applies ADDR to an expression, which is invalid in SQL3 and has never been proposed by anybody."

I've already noted that in fact ADDR does apply to expressions; what Chamberlin means is that I was trying to apply ADDR to an expression that wasn't valid as an ADDR operand. Anyway, all I was trying to do with my Example 2 was draw the reader's attention to a trap that SQL users in particular might be likely to fall into. The query was "Get employee numbers for employees in department D1," and the "putative formulation" included the following ADDR invocation (slightly simplified):

```
ADDR ( SELECT * FROM DEPT WHERE DEPT# = 'D1' )
```

As I tried to explain in my original paper [2], the (incorrect) thinking here is that the ADDR invocation will return the address of the DEPT row for department D1. This thinking is incorrect because, as already discussed, the operand to ADDR must be a variable, not a more general expression. The point I was trying to make, though, is that SQL users in particular might be likely to fall into this trap (as indeed I did myself, on my first attempt!), because SQL already makes the mistake of regarding an expression such as

```
SELECT * FROM DEPT WHERE DEPT# = 'D1'
```

as denoting a row rather than a table—and indeed very likely a *base* row at that—in certain contexts. Let me elaborate:

- If the expression appears in a *row subquery,* it effectively denotes a row. (More precisely, it denotes a one-row table, and that table then gets implicitly converted—i.e., *coerced*—to the row in question.)
- If the expression appears in a *cursor definition,* it effectively denotes a *base* row specifically. (More precisely, it denotes a one-row table, and the row in question can then be directly retrieved, updated, or deleted via that cursor. The fact that it can be updated or deleted in this way effectively means the row in question must be a base row specifically.)

Thus, since the expression can be regarded—at least in certain contexts—as denoting a row (and a base row at that), I stand by my contention that it might easily be thought that ADDR could be applied to it.

- "In Example 6 [Date] attempts to apply ADDR to a constant relation . . . [and] then writes that the failure . . . to produce any meaningful result is as if the "+" operator were defined . . . in such a way that the expression X + Y [where X and Y have current values 4 and 5, respectively] gave 9, but the expression X + 5 gave zero. This analogy is clearly invalid, since "+" is defined for both variables and constants but ADDR is not."

  Chamberlin has missed my point here. The analogy isn't between "+" and ADDR, it's between "+" and **join.** The "+" operator is indeed defined "for both variables and constants" (as Chamberlin puts it), **and so is join**—at least, the join that's part of the relational algebra. But the operator I called (for want of a better term) the "pointer join" does *not* work "for both variables and constants," it works for variables (that is, *relation* variables) only. The relational algebra doesn't have relation variables. So we're talking about another major extension (to the relational algebra this time).

  Incidentally, this criticism applies regardless of whether we're talking about *Interpretation 1* or *Interpretation 2.*

- "[Date observes that] the classical relational algebra has no concept of a relation variable. The consequences of this argument are interesting to consider. The concept of a relation variable (or table, as it is called in SQL) is, of course, essential to INSERT, DELETE, UPDATE, and any other operation that modifies the database. While it is true that these operations are missing in the classical relational algebra, I believe that they have proved their worth to the database industry."

Again Chamberlin has missed my point. My observation that the relational algebra has no concept of a relation variable isn't an argument, it's a fact. I'm certainly not trying to suggest—though the functional programming community might!—that we don't *need* relation variables and update operators; rather, I'm saying that we shouldn't muddy up the relational algebra *per se* with such concepts. The operators of the relational algebra are (by definition) *read-only* operators, and they operate on **values;** operators such as INSERT, UPDATE, and DELETE are, by contrast (and again by definition), *update* operators, and they operate on **variables.** But (regardless of whether we're talking about *Interpretation 1* or *Interpretation 2*) the idea of mixing pointers and relations introduces a totally new kind of construct— namely, an operator, ADDR, that, although read-only, nevertheless requires its operand to be a variable, not a value. I claim, therefore, that this construct introduces muddle where there was none before.

By the way: Unlike the relational algebra, SQL does include the concept of a relation variable. However, I observe that, in most languages, the syntax for the operation that returns the value of a given variable—be it a relation variable or any other kind—consists simply of the *name* of the variable in question; thus, e.g., we write the expression *V* to refer to the value of the variable *V*. But this simple convention is violated in SQL! In SQL, in order to refer to the value of relation variable *R,* we usually have to write an expression of the form "SELECT * FROM *R*"—or something along such lines. This fact, I believe, lends additional weight to my earlier contention that people might easily (albeit incorrectly) expect certain SELECT expressions to be valid as an ADDR operand.

And by the way again, I have to ask: If (as Chamberlin says) the SQL term for "relation variable" is *table,* then what's the SQL term for "relation value"?

THE SQL3 PROPOSALS

In a section of reference [1] entitled "Reality" (!), Chamberlin describes *Interpretation 1* (or, rather, his interpretation of *Interpretation 1*) by sketching certain "small extensions" to SQL that are currently proposed as part of "the SQL3 Standard." He claims, essentially, that those SQL3 proposals correspond to *Interpretation 1*—though he isn't quite correct in this claim, as I will show.

Before getting into details, incidentally, I think it should be made quite clear that SQL3 is *not* a standard, at least not at the time of writing. While it's

530 Part IV / Relational vs. Nonrelational Systems

true that some version of SQL3 might *become* a standard at some future time, we should certainly not assume that any such future standard will look exactly like the current SQL3 draft [7]. Thus, I think we should avoid the use of misleading expressions like "the SQL3 standard."[*]

Be that as it may, Chamberlin's first SQL3 extension is really two separate extensions rolled up into one, namely "the idea of a system-generated unique identifier for a row," and "a syntax that can be used to refer to this identifier." I'll come back to the syntax extension later. Regarding the "system-generated unique identifiers" extension: I have no objection to the basic idea of system-generated identifiers, if done properly—in fact, I think they could be very useful[†]—so long as:

1. In accordance with Codd's Information Principle, those identifiers aren't hidden from the user; and

2. In accordance with The Principle of Interchangeability of Base and Derived Relations—see reference [3] for a discussion of this principle—they're available for derived relations as well as base ones.

However:

1. In SQL3, system-generated identifiers can be hidden from the user.[‡] Chamberlin says such hiding is "much like hiding a column by a view" (slightly paraphrased). No, it isn't! The analogy is a complete red herring! If the identifiers for table *T* are hidden, then it's not as if the "column" that contains those identifiers is somehow "hidden"; rather, *no such column exists* (i.e., the identifiers aren't in a column at all). And there's fundamentally only one way those identifiers can be accessed—namely, via the new SQL3 "reference operation" REF ROW *T*. And there's simply **no way** such an operation can be regarded as syntactic shorthand for any previously available SQL expression.

    ("Hiding a column by a view," by contrast, doesn't mean the information in that column has to be accessed by some new and special operation like REF ROW *T*, it merely means the information can't be accessed via that view. Of course, that information *can* be accessed via the underlying table, and that access is performed by means of conventional SQL operations.)

---

[*] The fact that SQL3 has changed considerably at the detail level since this paper was first written (see later) lends additional weight to my argument here, I believe.

[†] See Chapter 12 of the present book.

[‡] No longer true (1998). This is one of the details of SQL3 that has changed since this paper was first written. I decided to leave my original text unchanged, however, because the arguments as such are themselves still valid, and they would need to be invoked again if— as could easily happen—someone proposed the reintroduction of hidden identifiers.

In other words—and contrary to Chamberlin's repeated assertions—what's being proposed for SQL3 is *not* mere syntactic shorthand (i.e., it's not just *Interpretation 1*). And yes, it does violate the Information Principle. In particular, it means that two rows that are in fact distinct might appear to the user to be duplicates (e.g., in a display of the table in question).

I note in passing too that if, e.g., department (DEPT) identifiers are hidden, then—at least as SQL is currently specified—the employees (EMP) column that contains DEPT references can't be defined as a foreign key. As a consequence, referential actions such as ON DELETE CASCADE can't be specified for that column, either. Implications of this fact are left as something for the reader to meditate on.

2. In SQL3, system-generated identifiers apply to **base relations only.** As I wrote in reference [2], this is a mistake of the highest order, because the question as to which relations are base and which derived is, in a very important sense, arbitrary. Again, see reference [3] for further discussion of this important point. (I note in passing that this particular issue is one of several raised in reference [2] that reference [1] doesn't address at all.)

As a matter of fact, I do have another objection to the idea of system-generated identifiers—at least, to the specific manner in which that idea is currently realized in SQL3 per se. The point is, those system-generated identifiers involve a brand new data type, called a "REF type" in SQL3 (and so it isn't possible to request, e.g., system-generated identifiers of type INTEGER). This fact means, again, that what's being proposed for SQL3 is not mere syntactic shorthand (again, it's not just Interpretation 1); there's no way those system-generated identifiers, or references to them, can be expressed in terms of existing SQL constructs.

I now move on to Chamberlin's next SQL3 extension, which is "a phrase [*i.e., mere syntax again*] that is used [to declare that a] column is defined on the same domain as the [system-generated identifiers] of some target table." Again I have no major problems with the basic idea here, but:

1. I feel bound to say once again that it's a big mistake to introduce arbitrary distinctions, as this extension does, between base and derived relations.

2. It's also a big mistake to permit base relation *R2* to include a column *C,* as this extension does, that's "defined on the same domain as" the system-generated identifiers of some base relation *R1* if those identifiers are "hidden" in *R1*. Note in particular that we can't perform a join of *R2* and *R1* on the basis of column *C* and those hidden identifiiers.

3. I remark too that the term *domain* must be understood here in its relational sense, not its SQL sense!

4. I remark further that the domain in question must be, not just any domain but, very specifically, one whose values are values of the new REF type.

5. I do agree with Chamberlin that the actual syntax proposed for SQL3 is awkward (though my reasons are probably not the same as his).

Chamberlin's final SQL3 extension is the dereferencing operator, which he says is "nothing more than a syntactic shortcut . . . If column D contains references to [rows within] the DEPT table, then [the dereferencing operation] D–>LOCATION is defined [to be equivalent to] the following scalar sub-query: (SELECT LOCATION FROM DEPT X WHERE ADDR(X) = D)."

Well, yes, the SQL3 dereferencing operator might be just shorthand, but only for another SQL3 construct—it's not shorthand for anything that can be expressed in existing SQL, because of the reliance already noted on the new REF type. Moreover—perhaps precisely because it *is* supposed to be shorthand for a scalar subquery specifically—an expression such as D –> LOCATION *cannot appear in a target position within an UPDATE operation*. Thus, e.g., the following is illegal in SQL3:

```
UPDATE ...
SET     D -> LOCATION = 'New York'
WHERE   ... ;
```

By contrast, most other languages (if they support the concept of dereferencing at all) certainly do permit dereferencing in target positions. I gave this PL/I example in reference [2]:

```
P -> N  =  3 ;
```

("assign the value 3 to the variable N that pointer variable P currently points to"). This omission in SQL3 looks like a serious lack of orthogonality to me.

Note: Oddly enough, the current SQL3 draft [7] does permit the following *sequence* of operations:[*]

```
SELECT ex.DADDR
INTO    D
FROM    EMP ex
WHERE   ex.EMP# = 'E1' ;

SET D -> LOCATION = 'New York' ;
```

(The SELECT operation assigns the address of a certain DEPT row to the pointer variable D, and the SET operation then assigns the value "New York" to the LOCATION component of the row that pointer variable D points to.)

---

[*]No longer true (1998). This is another detail of SQL3 that has changed since this paper was first written. Again I decided to leave my original text unchanged, however, for essentially the same reasons as before.

The fact that the SET operation in particular is legal here suggests that perhaps dereferencing isn't just shorthand for a scalar subquery after all! (And so, once again, we're not really talking just about *Interpretation 1*.) The SQL3 draft [7] defines the effect of the SET operation in this example to be equivalent to that of the following UPDATE:

```
UPDATE DEPT
SET    LOCATION = 'New York'
WHERE  REF ROW DEPT = D ;
```

Aside: The possibility that the database might be updated by means of a simple assignment (i.e., SET) operation raises all kinds of additional questions! However, further discussion of those questions would take us much too far away from the topic at hand; I'll have to leave them for another day. *End of aside.*

Chamberlin goes on to accuse me of objecting to the idea that dereferencing might be just a shorthand: "The introduction of an operator that is defined in terms of other operators is presented by Date as a disadvantage, since it conflicts with the idea that there should be One True Way to formulate each query. But redundant operators can be found in almost all languages . . . Modern database optimizers often take advantage of this fact to transform queries into equivalent forms that they find more manageable."

Well, I've never argued that there should be "One True Way" to formulate a query, nor do I necessarily believe we can design languages that meet such a goal. However, I do think the goal is worth striving for as an ideal. I think we should try to design languages, as far as possible, in such a way as to exclude features with overlapping functionality—except where a feature is *expressly defined* to be shorthand for some other combination of features. In other words, I have nothing against syntactic shorthands *per se,* so long as they're properly defined to *be* such shorthands. As I've already pointed out, however, SQL3's referencing operation is not so defined, and now it seems its dereferencing operation isn't, either.

Aside: I feel bound to note in passing that the *existing* SQL language—never mind SQL3—already includes far too many constructs (e.g., EXISTS, GROUP BY, HAVING, range variables, and many others) that were not originally defined to be shorthands but later turned out to be redundant. As a result, saying just what it is that might be equivalent to such constructs—thereby showing that the construct in question is indeed redundant—can certainly be done, but the process is fairly messy. Surely it would have been better to define a kernel language with as little redundancy as possible *first,* and then define appropriate shorthands, in a systematic manner, *later.* Because this procedure wasn't followed with SQL, however, the business of "optimizers [transforming] queries into equivalent forms that they find more manageable" is made much more difficult than it ought to have been; indeed, numerous *incorrect* SQL transformations have appeared in the literature! References [18.35–18.39] in Chapter 18 of my book [4] contain several examples.   *End of aside.*

Chamberlin also asks, rhetorically: "If ADDR(*x*) is an operator [invocation] that returns a system-generated key [value], what is *x?*" And he answers, in effect, that *x* is the name of a range variable, and states correctly that range variables are an integral part of the relational calculus. True: but they're not part of the relational algebra, and in fact (as I noted in the previous paragraph) they're 100 percent redundant in SQL today. So something that is redundant and unnecessary in SQL today might become nonredundant and necessary in SQL3!—a state of affairs that should, I think, give us some pause.

One last point on SQL3. As already indicated, Chamberlin sees the SQL3 proposals as a realization of *Interpretation 1*—but I'm not sure the SQL3 committee members see them the same way. Indeed, it's quite clear that at least some of those members see SQL3 as a vehicle for introducing "true object orientation" into SQL (see, e.g., references [5–6]; the fact that the portions of SQL3 under discussion have been moved into a separate part of the specification with the suggestive name *SQL/Object* [7] seems relevant here, too).* And "true object orientation" strongly implies, at least to me, that what those committee members really want to do is make SQL3 a realization of *Interpretation 2*, And All That That Entails. Indeed, this objective probably accounts for the introduction of the new REF data type; REF values look suspiciously like what the object community calls *object IDs*. Given all of these points taken together, it follows that I reject the arguments Chamberlin propounds in the final section ("What About Objects?") of reference [1].

REFERENTIAL INTEGRITY

Under this heading, Chamberlin points out, correctly, that SQL3-style "references" provide strictly less functionality than foreign keys (a strange argument, to my mind, for wanting to support them!). And he takes me to task for "confusion" over the differences between SQL3-style references, on the one hand, and the familiar relational concept of referential integrity, on the other.

Well, I plead guilty as accused . . . but such confusions seem to me inevitable, given the considerable overlap in functionality and the unfortunate

---

*The name "SQL/Object" has since been dropped [8].

terminological clashes (note that the term *reference* now means two quite different things!). Whoever was it who thought it would be a good idea to introduce a new feature whose functionality duplicates so extensively that of something that already exists? Whoever was it who took the familiar relational term "reference" and gave it this brand new (additional but overlapping) meaning? How many times will similar confusions arise in the future? How many *people* will get confused? Has any thought been given to the concomitant problems of teaching, and learning, and communication, and documentation (and so on, and so on)?

Under the same heading, Chamberlin also criticizes another of my examples. The example in question involves the following query (which makes use of a "pointer join"):

```
SELECT  ex.EMP#, dx.DEPT#
FROM    EMP ex, DEPT dx
WHERE   ex.DADDR = ADDR ( dx ) ;
```

In my original paper [2], I pointed out the tacit assumption here that each EMP row had just one corresponding DEPT row, and asked what would happen if the situation changed, such that the same department were now represented in several DEPT rows (e.g., if departments were spread across several locations, and DEPT had one row for each valid DEPT#-LOCATION combination). I claimed that after such a change, the pointer join wouldn't work any more— or, rather (and more fundamentally), the database design wouldn't be valid any more. I also claimed that, by contrast, the conventional relational design, involving a DEPT# foreign key instead of a DADDR "reference," would still be valid after the change, and the conventional relational join would still work (it would now be a many-to-many join instead of a many-to-one join, of course). Here are Chamberlin's comments on this example:

> After [the] change, each reference [i.e., DADDR] value in EMP will still identify a single row in DEPT, perhaps representing the department and location of the given employee. Joining a row of the EMP table to the DEPT row that represents the employee's department and location is a perfectly reasonable thing to do, and there's nothing about Date's example query that won't work any more.

Well, let me just observe that this approach of Chamberlin's:

- Involves a mass update to EMP to change all EMP.DADDR values appropriately (I'll be charitable and assume no similar mass update is required to DEPT, though in practice I think this assumption probably wouldn't be valid);

- Makes an unwarranted semantic assumption (that each employee has just one corresponding department location); and

- Changes the semantics of EMP (or at least of EMP.DADDR).

None of these actions and assumptions would be necessary if the design were key- instead of "reference"-based.

WHY WE DON'T NEED "REFERENCES"

In reference [1] (in a section entitled "Why Do We Need References?"), Chamberlin says: "The Information Principle . . . has served us well over the years. [It] is not compromised by the introduction of [system-generated identifiers]." Yes, it is, if those identifiers are hidden!—as already discussed in the section "The SQL3 Proposals" earlier.

Anyway, Chamberlin goes on to say: "I believe [the sole purpose of] references [is] to simplify the expression of an important class of queries." In support of this position, he presents two examples—one involving outer join (which I don't propose to discuss here at all because I think it's a *major* red herring) and the other the well-known query "Find the names and salaries of employees who make more than their managers." Here is Chamberlin's "references"-style formulation of this latter query:

```
SELECT  ex.NAME, ex.SALARY
FROM    EMP ex
WHERE   ex.SALARY > ex.DEPTREF -> MANAGER -> SALARY ;
```

But—my goodness!—if **that's** what all the fuss is about (*viz.*, merely simplifying the expression of certain queries), well, we can certainly achieve *that* objective without all this baggage of a new data type and "references" (or pointers, or addresses, or whatever you want to call them). Let me illustrate.

First, let's revert to a conventional relational design (i.e., one not involving any SQL3-style "references" at all). Thus, let's assume that table DEPT has a conventional primary key column called DEPT#; also, let's replace the "references" columns EMP.DEPTREF and DEPT.MANAGER by conventional foreign key columns EMP.DEPT# and DEPT.MGR#, respectively. Now consider the following expression:

```
SELECT  ex.NAME, ex.SALARY
FROM    EMP ex
WHERE   ex.SALARY > ex.DEPT# ► DEPT.MGR# ► EMP.SALARY ;
```

I've just invented this syntax, and I make no great claims for it, and it probably has problems, but I'd be willing to wager I could clean it up satisfactorily. Anyway, for what it's worth, I explain it as follows. First, let *ex* denote some row within the current value of relation variable EMP. Then the expression *ex*.DEPT# ▶ DEPT

means the unique row within the current value of relation variable DEPT that's referenced by the value of the DEPT# foreign key in that EMP row *ex*. Let's call that DEPT row *dx*. Then the expression on the right hand side of the ">" comparison in my SELECT statement is logically equivalent to the expression

dx.MGR# ▶ EMP.SALARY

which means, analogously (more or less), the SALARY value in the unique row in the current value of relation variable EMP that's referenced by the value of the MGR# foreign key in the DEPT row *dx*.

In other words, we don't need pointers as such (or a new REF data type, or SQL3-style "references") in order to achieve the desired simplification of expressions; all we need is an operator ("▶") that represents traversal of a foreign-to-matching-candidate-key relationship. I suppose—if you really insist, though I don't think I'd recommend it—I might even let you use the arrow syntax "–>" instead of my "▶" notation, but (again) we certainly don't have to buy into the whole pointers idea just to use that syntax!

This paper is already much longer than I wanted it to be, and I apologize to the reader on that account. Let me close by taking this syntactic shorthand issue just a tiny bit further. Don't you think it's odd that even though the SQL3 proposal is supposed to be "just shorthand" (at least, that's what Chamberlin claims), the whole business of referencing and dereferencing applies only to tables that are *defined in a certain way?* I complained earlier that it applied only to *base* tables and not to derived ones; now I point out (and complain further) that it doesn't even apply to *all* base tables, it applies only to certain special ones—basically those that are defined to make use of the new REF type (the exact details are a little complex and not too relevant to the overall message of this paper). In other words:

- I indicated at the beginning of this paper that I don't think the *Interpretation 1* idea is all that interesting;

- On the other hand, I don't have major objections to it, either;

- But I do at least think that if we decide to go for it, then it should be done properly;

- And it *isn't* being done properly in the current SQL3 draft [7].

Don't let the SQL3 committee do this to us! Let's stop this crazy idea before it's too late!

ACKNOWLEDGMENTS

As with this paper's predecessor [2], I'm grateful, first of all, to Don Chamberlin for forcing me to get my thinking straight on this subject and to get that thinking down on paper. I've always had the greatest respect for Don personally and for his very great contributions to our field, and I hope nobody will take my criticisms of SQL3 (either in this paper or in its predecessor) as any kind of *ad hominem* attack. I'm also grateful to Declan Brady and Hugh Darwen for their comments on earlier drafts of this paper.

REFERENCES

1. Donald D. Chamberlin: "Relations and References—Another Point of View," *InfoDB 10*, No. 6 (April 1997).

2. C. J. Date: "Don't Mix Pointers and Relations!" (Chapter 14 of the present book).

3. C. J. Date: "Objects and Relations: Forty-Seven Points of Light" (Chapter 13 of the present book).

4. C. J. Date: *An Introduction to Database Systems* (6th edition). Reading, Mass.: Addison-Wesley (1995).

5. Jim Melton: "The 'What's What' of SQL3," *Database Programming & Design 9*, No. 12 (December 1996).

6. Jim Melton: "A Shift in the Landscape," *Database Programming & Design 9*, No. 8 (August 1996).

7. International Organization for Standardization: *Database Language SQL—Part 8: SQL/Object* (Committee Draft). Document ISO/IEC JTC1/SC21 N10491 (July 1996). *Note:* After the present paper was first written, Part 8 of the SQL specification was dropped as a separate part and the material moved into other parts of the document (primarily *Part 2, SQL/Foundation*).

APPENDIX

DATABASE GRAFFITI
(script for a live presentation)

Scribbles from The Askew Wall

satis eloquentia, sapientiae parvum

ABSTRACT

This is a greatly extended version of one of my regular columns in *Database Programming & Design* (the earlier version appeared in the March 1997 issue of that magazine and is republished as Installment 55 in Part I of the present book). It consists of a series of quotations, aphorisms, and anecdotes—along with a few personal comments, where appropriate—that are (mostly) relevant to the general subject of database management. The presentation is not meant to be technically deep, but a number of serious messages do lie not too far below the surface, I believe. My aim is partly to edify, partly just to amuse.

COMMENTS ON PUBLICATION

Since this is a script for a live presentation rather than a formal (or even informal) paper, the style is a a good deal chattier than usual. I hope you don't find it too offensive . . . Also, I apologize once again for the degree of overlap with the material of certain portions of the body of the book (especially Installment 55, of course).

INTRODUCTION

Hello! I'm very pleased to welcome you to this perhaps rather self-indulgent presentation. What I want to do is this. For many years now, I've been maintaining a private collection of quotations, aphorisms, anecdotes, etc. that are relevant—sometimes pretty loosely, I must confess—to the overall subject of database management and database technology. And today I'd like to share some gems from that collection with you . . . So this isn't exactly a technically

539

deep session!—though I do have some important points to make, I think. My aim is partly to edify, partly just to amuse.

I should perhaps begin by explaining the background. Some of you will know that I do a regular column in one of the trade magazines, *Database Programming & Design*. Well, that magazine celebrated its tenth anniversary in March of 1997, and I dedicated my column in that issue to this same topic, as a way of marking the occasion and saying "many happy returns" to the magazine on its tenth birthday. By the way, I think you'll be getting a copy of that original column as a handout later. Anyway, I called that column *Database Graffiti* . . . And this presentation is essentially a greatly expanded version of that original column.

I must also explain my subtitle ("Scribbles from The Askew Wall"). The term *The Askew Wall* is due to Hugh Darwen . . . I presume it's pretty obvious where he gets it from! As he explains:

- Basically, the Askew Wall is an ugly construction that surrounds *Relationland*.

- And it acts as a major BARRIER TO COMMUNICATION between Relationland and the rest of the world. It really gets in the way!—people look for Relationland and see only the Wall.

- Because of the Wall, indeed, some people don't even realize that Relationland exists. In other words, they think the Wall, with all its warts and blemishes, is all there is—with the result, of course, that the relational model gets blamed for the shortcomings and mistakes of S-Q-L (sorry, I mean the Wall). This one really makes me gnash my teeth!—because the biggest problem with SQL is precisely that it doesn't implement the relational model. But I digress . . .

- Others have tried to enter Relationland but have lost their way and become inextricably stuck *inside* the Wall itself.

- Still others who were once honest Relationlanders have also since become immured (I could name a few names here, but it's probably better if I don't).

I don't think I'd better push this metaphor any further! But I just couldn't resist the idea of my *graffiti* being scribbled on Hugh's *wall* . . .

Onward. I've divided the rest of my talk—somewhat arbitrarily in some cases—into the following sections:

- Introduction (we're in this right now)
- The prehistoric era
- Objects and objections
- Normalization, networks, and nulls

- The role of simplicity
- The joy of self-reference
- Some fundamental principles
- Relational database: further misconceptions number 4
- Some *good* quotes
- Books and book reviews
- Miscellany
- The great database limerick competition
- Concluding remarks

Without further ado, let's get started. I'll begin with ancient history—that is, the world before relational databases (or at least SQL databases) became a commercial reality.

THE PREHISTORIC ERA

We're so used to relational databases these days, and think of them as so "obvious" and "natural" and "right," that I suspect many people don't even know what the database scene was like before Ted Codd published his original papers in the 1970s. So I think it's worth taking a look . . . Indeed, the obvious first quote is:

- *Those who don't know history are doomed to repeat it* [George Santayana, somewhat paraphrased].

(The actual quote is: *Those who cannot remember the past are condemned to repeat it.*)

Of course, some cynic did once say that the only thing we learn from history is that we learn nothing from history! (Actually, the cynic was Hegel. The exact quote is: *What experience and history teach is this—that people and governments never have learned anything from history, or acted on principles deduced from it.*)

Incidentally—as I expect some of you know—I do have a real concern here regarding **object databases.** The object database people really do seem to be repeating a lot of history, a lot of *bad* history at that. But that's a whole separate topic!—we can't get into it now, it would take us much too far afield. Some of my other presentations do deal with this issue—e.g., my full-length seminar on object databases.

Let's have a look at the historical context, then. What was going on in the database world before relational databases came along? Well, here's a quote that might give some idea:

- *Logically deleting a logical child prevents further access to the logical child using its logical parent. Unidirectional logical child segments are assumed to be logically deleted. A logical parent is considered logically deleted when all its logical children are physically deleted. For physically paired logical relationships, the physical child paired to the logical child must also be physically deleted before the logical parent is considered logically deleted.*

   Physical Parent of a Virtually Paired Logical Child: *When . . . all physical children that are virtually paired logical children are logically deleted, the physical parent segment is physically deleted.*

No prizes for guessing where this deathless prose comes from! (actually it's from the IMS/ESA Database Administration Guide). But you see the garbage we used to have to put up with?

(I won't pursue this one any further in case—as I've sometimes had reason to believe—the author happens to be here in the room with us right now . . .)

Mind you, I'm not sure matters have improved all that much. Here's a much more recent quote:

- *However, because global temporary table contents are distinct within SQL-sessions, and created local temporary tables are distinct within <module>s within SQL-sessions, the* **effective** *<schema name> of the schema in which the global temporary table or the created local temporary table is instantiated is an implementation-dependent <schema name> that may be thought of as having been effectively derived from the <schema name> of the schema in which the global temporary table or created local temporary table is defined and the implementation-dependent SQL-session identifier associated with the SQL-session* [from the current SQL standard, "SQL/92"].

I beat up on this one in the book I wrote on SQL/92 with Hugh Darwen, *A Guide to the SQL Standard* (4th edition, Addison-Wesley, 1997), but I certainly think it bears repeating here. The entire sentence (yes, it's all one sentence!) is taken from a section of the standard entitled—and intended to explain the SQL concept of—"Tables." I never realized tables were so complicated. It reminds me of that great line:

- *If you're not confused by all this, it just proves you're not thinking clearly* [anon.].

I don't know where this quote comes from originally, but I got it from Nagraj Alur.

   Of course, it's not just SQL; our entire industry is plagued by bad terminology and graceless prose. By way of example, consider the following:

- *I nonconcur with the subject release for announcement for the following reasons and understand that under the rules of dissent, I am obligated to escalate my nonconcurrence for a timely resolution* [one of the options that used to appear—I don't know if it still does—on ANSI standard review forms].

To redress the balance a little, perhaps I should give an example to show that other disciplines—if I might be allowed a little poetic license in the use of such a term—can yield sentences that are just as impenetrably bad as the ones just quoted:

- *For the purposes of this Act a person carries on business as a scrap metal dealer if he* [sic] *carries on a business which consists wholly or partly of buying and selling scrap metal whether the scrap metal sold is in the form in which it was bought or otherwise, other than a business in the course of which scrap metal is not bought except as materials for the manufacture of other articles and is not sold except as a by product of such manufacture or as surplus materials bought but not required for such manufacture, and "scrap metal dealer" (where the expression is used in this Act otherwise than in reference to carrying on business as a scrap metal dealer) means a person who (in accordance with the preceding provisions of this subsection) carries on business as a scrap metal dealer* [excerpt from the UK Scrap Metal Dealers Act of 1964, quoted in a letter to the London *Times,* April 5th, 1995].

Back to databases and the historical context. In 1975, while he and I were both still in IBM, Ted Codd wrote an internal IBM memo suggesting that relational database should be seriously considered as part of IBM's longterm database strategy. I still have in my possession a copy of the reply he received from the IBM manager concerned:

- *My staff and I have found your comments interesting. In order to provide a more thorough and in-depth analysis on their applicability as a requirement for future database systems, we respectfully request that you provide the following:*

(I love that "respectfully." It reminds me of *Yes Minister:* You know, Sir Humphrey says, "With the deepest respect, Minister, . . . ," and the Minister replies "Don't use that filthy language to me!" Of course, "with the deepest respect" really means "with the deepest *dis*respect.")

  1. *A clear definition of relational databases: their structure, access technique, programming methods, compatibility, and comparison with our current database standard DL/I*
  2. *Economic justification of a business case*

3. *Account scenarios and experience of users in today's environment, with names, descriptions, performance, and function provided*

4. *Account of application descriptions of users in the future, by industry and application type, if possible*

5. *Description of compatibility with CODASYL*

This, in 1975 . . . !

Actually, while I'm talking about history: Did you know that in fact some people dispute Ted Codd's claim to be the originator of the relational model? . . . Indeed, there is considerable evidence to suggest that the true originator was *William Shakespeare:*

> *Thy gift, thy tables, are within my brain*
> *Full charactered with lasting memory,*
> *Which shall above that idle rank remain*
> *Beyond all date, even to eternity;*
> *Or at the least so long as brain and heart*
> *Have faculty by nature to subsist,*
> *Till each to razed oblivion yield his part*
> *Of thee, thy record never can be missed.*
> *That poor retention could not so much hold,*
> *Nor need I tallies thy dear love to score;*
> *Therefore to give them from me was I bold,*
> *To trust those tables that receive thee more.*
> > *To keep an adjunct to remember thee*
> > *Were to import forgetfulness in me.*

This is Shakespeare's Sonnet 122 (acknowledgments here to Pam McFarland—at that time with a company called VM Software Inc.—who first brought my attention to the fact that the Bard was relational-hip).

Actually, if you take a closer look, you can see that Shakespeare isn't really making a claim to prior *ownership* of the relational model—in fact, he's *addressing* Ted, and admitting that it was all really Ted's doing—

Thy *gift,* **thy** *tables, are within my brain . . .*

So now we've solved another mystery!—the Dark Lady of the Sonnets is obviously Ted Codd.

I'm not sure about that "beyond all Date," however!

On a more serious note—here's a quote from Maurice Wilkes (grand old man of British computing) that I really like:

■ *I would like to see computer science teaching set deliberately in a historical framework . . . Students need to understand how the present situation has come about, what was tried, what worked and what did not, and how improvements in hardware made progress possible. The absence of this element in their training causes people to approach every problem from first principles. They are apt to propose solutions that have been found wanting in the past. Instead of standing on the shoulders of their precursors, they try to go it alone [CACM 34, No. 5, May 1991].*

Indeed, I do think it's sad to see how often the wheel gets reinvented in our field. I also think object databases are a case in point! As I've already suggested, there's almost nothing about them that's truly new, and much that has indeed been "tried [and] found wanting in the past." Again, however, I really don't want to get into that discussion here. Let me just say that, in my opinion, there's EXACTLY ONE *good* idea in object databases—namely, abstract data types—and that's not new.

OBJECTS AND OBJECTIONS

Although I've already said I don't want to get into detail here on why I think object databases are so misguided, there's just one item I *would* like to show you . . . In my book *An Introduction to Database Systems* (6th edition, Addison-Wesley, 1995), in a chapter on object databases, I said this:

- **Caveat:** *Before we start getting into details, it is as well to warn readers not to expect the kind of precision they are accustomed to in the relational world. Indeed, many [object-oriented] concepts . . . are quite imprecise, and there is very little true consensus and much disagreement, even at the most basic level.*

Of course, I wasn't all that surprised when one reviewer complained—quite hotly!—that my characterization of objects here was unfair. But I *was* surprised by what he actually said:

- *No, no, no, no, no! Object* **concepts** *aren't fuzzy and imprecise at all. It's only the* **definitions** *that are sometimes fuzzy and imprecise* [source suppressed here to protect the guilty].

I'm tempted to say "I rest my case."

Though perhaps it would be more diplomatic to say, with Mark Twain, merely that:

- *The logic of our adversary resembles the peace of God* [from *Roughing It;* Twain was quoting Thomas Fitch, editor of the *Union* newspaper in Virginia City, Nevada].

(A wonderful example of an insult that sounds like a compliment! Good old Sam Clemens.)

More diplomatically still—or at least more charitably—I might have responded in the words of Sidney Smith, who, on seeing two women leaning out of their respective houses and arguing across the street, observed:

- *Those two ladies will never agree, for they are arguing from different premises.*

(And, I might add, different foundations.)

Still on objects: Despite the phenomenal success of relational technology in the marketplace, we are—predictably enough—seeing something of a "relational backlash" right now. Mind you, I'm not quite sure what the term "relational backlash" means, but it was the headline on the *Computerworld* article I got this quote from:

- *It is hard for relational advocates, having been on the leading edge for 10 to 12 years, to wake up and find that fashion has moved on to something else. The temptation is to tell the upstarts they don't know what they're talking about* [Charles Babcock, Computerworld, June 28th, 1993].

He's referring, of course, to the new wave of hype regarding object systems . . . It reminds of the old line "But am I paranoid if everyone really *is* out to get me?"—Oh . . . an aside . . . a great quote I came across recently:

- *Paranoia is having all the facts* [this one is from William Burroughs; it's kind of the flip side of "ignorance is bliss," I suppose].

Because, of course, the upstarts—that is, the object folks—*don't* know what they're talking about, at least as regards database technology in general and relational databases in particular. Indeed, that's the problem: We've got the object community over *here* and the database community over *there,* and these two communities really don't seem to communicate with each other very well. At least I can tell you this: Those object people I've spoken to do *not* understand the relational model. And it does seem to me that if you're claiming that technology *A* should be replaced by technology *B,* it's incumbent on you to understand technology *A* first, and to show conclusively that it can't handle whatever problem you say technology *B* can. In the case of objects and relations, I don't think anyone has shown any such thing.

Anyway, objects are indeed *fashion*—fashion really is the *mot juste* here—as Babcock effectively admits. I have a nice quote on this point; it comes from the end of a long letter that I got from a friend in the UK, Adrian Larner, when I was learning all about objects for myself (the letter—I think it was 27 pages—gave Adrian's own take on the subject). Anyway, this was Adrian's closing paragraph:

- *I am, I regret to say, resigned to the transient triumph of object orientation: Fashion is more powerful than reason, for reason is not the property of any vested interest. We should count ourselves lucky that for some while now, fashion and reason have coincided in relational. But—once again—we have failed to learn from our successes* [Adrian Larner, private communication].

Very elegant, and very eloquent . . . But, you see, *I* am NOT so resigned! However, that's (once again) a topic for another day . . .

By the way, why exactly do we talk about object *orientation* [*sic*]? Is it because that's all it is—just an *orientation? A leaning?* Is this an admission that objects (unlike relations) don't rest on any solid model or theory?

While I'm on the subject of disagreements, here's another quote I like very much—a serious one again:

- *Whenever you find yourself getting angry about a difference of opinion, be on your guard; you will probably find, on examination, that your belief is going beyond what the evidence warrants* [from Bertrand Russell, "An Outline of Intellectual Rubbish," in *Unpopular Essays,* Simon & Schuster, 1950].

I really wish people would take this one to heart . . . (it reminds me of Wittgenstein, who said *Whereof one cannot speak, thereon one must remain silent*— or words to that effect).

Still on the subject of objections and disagreements, I recently came across the following beautiful quote. It's a criticism of a certain professor's work by a rival academic:

- *It seems to me that [my esteemed colleague], by avoiding the issue of the concrete historical reality lying behind the various similarities between cultural forms which he seeks to recognize, has allowed himself a much freer hand and perhaps a less disciplined methodology than might have been prudent* [from Colin Renfrew, *Archaeology and Language,* Cambridge University Press, 1988].

I love this! The understatement ("allowed himself a much freer hand" . . . "perhaps a less disciplined methodology" . . . "than might have been prudent") is perfectly delightful.

In fact I have another (similar) example from the same source:

- *The methods of comparative linguistics have much to offer in the study of these processes, but the construction of a protolexicon may not be their most important contribution.*

Obviously the words "may not be their most important contribution" here really mean the work in question—i.e., the construction of a protolexicon, whatever that might be—is complete nonsense. It's the academic's way of saying "you *turkey,* how could you *possibly* believe anything so stupid" (etc., etc.).

NORMALIZATION, NETWORKS, AND NULLS

Now let's move on to some quotes that are a bit more directly relevant to modern (that is, relational, or at least SQL) databases . . . They're a bit of a miscellany, but (as I say) they are at least somewhat related to modern database technology.

The first has to do with normalization. I overheard this snippet in the hallway as I was hurrying to my session at the DCI *Database and Client/Server World* conference in Chicago (December 1995):

- *Well, he **said** the tables were all in fifth normal form, but I think he must have meant sixth.*

I wish I'd had time to stop for further enlightenment . . . (I mean, we do all know that *fifth* is the final normal form, right? I mean, there's nowhere else to go after fifth. Right?)

When I told Hugh Darwen this story, he countered by telling me of someone he had dealings with in the UK who, on first hearing the term *normalization,* inquired:

- *Normalization? What's that? Is it sort of the opposite of denormalization?*

I believe the person in question had previously served some kind of apprenticeship with a certain well known SQL vendor . . .

All this talk of normal forms and normalization reminds me of one of my favorite definitions:

- *Normal:* see *abnormal* [from an early IBM PL/I reference manual, *circa* 1969].

And *that,* of course, unavoidably reminds me of the old chestnut:

- *Recursion:* see *recursion.*

Which in turn reminds me of the following maxim, due I believe to Jim Gray:

- *Anything in computer science that's not recursive is no good.*

How true!

(Incidentally—if anyone wants to argue that *relations* are therefore no good, because they can't contain relations nested inside themselves, and so aren't recursive—let me just say that this criticism is in fact incorrect, though it might come as a surprise to some people to hear me say this! Again I don't have time to go into detail; suffice it to say that relations *can* contain other relations, as I explain at length in various other presentations, including my *Introducing . . . The Third Manifesto* and my full-length seminar *Relational Remodeled,* among others.)

Talking of "old chestnut" definitions, it would be very remiss of me not to include this one:

- **Network:** *Any thing reticulated or decussated, with interstices between the intersections* [from Dr. Johnson's Dictionary—where else?].

And networks bring me to distributed databases . . . I hope I'm not the only one to find humor in the next two:

- Yu, C. T., *et al.* 1982a. *Promising approach to distributed query processing.* In . . . (etc.).
- Yu, C. T., *et al.* 1982b. *Two surprising results in processing simple queries in distributed databases.* In . . . (etc.).

[These two items are taken, slightly edited, from the references section of a paper on distributed query processing, in *ACM Computing Surveys 16,* No. 4, December 1984.]

I love the combination of "promising approach" followed by "surprising results" . . . The description of some line of investigation first as promising, later as surprising, could probably be applied to a lot of research activity, if the truth be known.

While I'm on the subject of distributed databases, perhaps I should tell you the story I heard at one conference on the topic, in Paris I think it was (it's a dirty job, this business of going to conferences, but someone has to do it). The speaker was talking about having dinner at a restaurant the night before. The story went like this:

- *At the next table, there was a young couple who seemed to be celebrating their engagement or something . . . Anyway, every time they took a sip of wine they would clink their wine glasses first. And I got to thinking . . . Two people clinking their glasses means one clink for every drink. Three people means—ah—three clinks per drink. Four people means six clinks. Five means ten clinks. And so on (N people means $1 + 2 + \ldots + (N\text{-}1)$ clinks). So pretty soon, there's* too much clinking and not enough drinking. **And that's the problem with distributed database.**

OK . . . to close out this section, here are a few quotes having to do with missing information and nulls (**NOT** my favorite subject, as I expect you know):

- *Database management would be simpler if missing values didn't exist* [one of my favorites!—Ted Codd, in our "Much Ado about Nothing" debate, *Database Programming & Design 6,* No. 10, October 1993, in a rebuttal to one of my rebuttals to one of his rebuttals of an original article of mine on the subject].

- *It all makes sense if you squint a little and don't think too hard* [anon.; quoted by David Maier in his book *The Theory of Relational Databases,* Computer Science Press, 1983].

- *Everything should be made as simple as possible—but* no simpler [Albert Einstein, attrib.].

The point of this last one is that nulls, at least as usually understood, represent an oversimplistic approach to a very complex problem. Oversimplifying can be harmful to your health! Which brings me nicely to the next part of my presentation . . .

THE ROLE OF SIMPLICITY

One of the really great things about the relational model is its *simplicity.* Simplicity is so important! (I'm talking about *genuine* simplicity here, not *over*-simplification, of course.) Here are some beautiful quotes, all of them having to do with the role simplicity has to play in science. It seems to me that we as database professionals—and other computer professionals, and scientists in general, come to that—could do a lot worse than take them to heart. Most of them need no further commentary from me, I think.

First Einstein again:

- *Most of the fundamental ideas of science are essentially simple, and may, as a rule, be expressed in a language comprehensible to everyone* [Albert Einstein].

  (This is one reason why I remain unconvinced about parts of modern physics, by the way, such as superstring theory. Do *you* understand it? I've tried!)

- *For what is clear and easily comprehended attracts; the complicated repels* [David Hilbert].

  (Originator of that famous list of 23 math problems [1900].)

- *Sometimes one has to say difficult things, but one ought to say them as simply as one knows how* [G. H. Hardy].

  (Author of *A Mathematician's Apology.*)

- *Even for the physicist, the description in plain language will be a criterion of the degree of understanding that has been reached* [Werner Heisenberg].

  (Of course, Heisenberg was a little uncertain on this point, ha ha.)

- *If you cannot—in the long run—tell everyone what you have been doing, your doing has been worthless* [Erwin Schrödinger].

  (Though Schrödinger couldn't even tell anyone whether his cat was alive or dead.)

By the way—talking of simplicity—here's something I enjoyed greatly when I first came across it:

- *adjs.* **P-Celtic** *(or* **-Keltic***),* **Q-Celtic** *(or* **-Keltic***), pertaining respectively to one of the Celtic languages in which Indo-Germanic* **qu** *became* **p** *and to one in which* **qu** *became* **q,** *later* **k** *(written* **c***)* [Chambers Twentieth Century Dictionary].

And you thought SQL was complicated!

And talking of SQL—must we?—here's a quote I think is highly relevant:

- *The sky is darkening with chickens coming home to roost* [Alan Bennett].

As Hugh Darwen says:

- **The chickens have come home to roost** *is a common metaphor for problems that could and should have been foreseen but have been lying dormant, and therefore . . . conveniently disregarded, waiting for circumstances to arise in which they are finally shown to all and sundry for what they are. It's perhaps a slightly less obnoxious way of saying "I told you so right back in [whenever]—now do you see how right I was?"* [from *The Third Manifesto: Making It Happen,* a presentation by Hugh Darwen].

Note: Actually, Hugh says *pigeons,* not *chickens,* but it's my belief that *chickens* is the right word. *Curses, like chickens, come home to roost* [Robert Southey].

Many of the mistakes that were made in the original design of SQL are indeed now coming home to roost, and causing troubles of various kinds. Here's an (incomplete!) list of SQL chickens:

- duplicate rows (of course!)
- nulls (of course!)
- nameless columns
- WITHOUT CHECK OPTION
- SELECT–FROM–WHERE template
  - The point here is that this template is much too rigid (I could go into details if there's time, but basically the template is a Procrustean bed—it assumes that all queries can be answered by performing a Cartesian product, followed by a restriction, followed by a projection)
- scalar subqueries
  - And the point *here* is that in SQL3 we need to have this very same syntactic construct, in the very same syntactic context, sometimes stand for a scalar and sometimes for a table
- extreme redundancy (I'm going to say more on this one later)

THE JOY OF SELF-REFERENCE

Now I'm going to shift gears somewhat . . . A little light relief, in fact (?). The old chestnut definition of recursion I quoted earlier ("recursion: *see* recursion") is, of course, an example of *self-referencing*. Douglas Hofstadter, in his great book *Gödel, Escher, Bach,* made tremendous play with the idea of self-referencing, as I'm sure you know. And, of course, computing in general, and database technology in particular, are both full of situations that involve some kind of self-referencing. So here are some nice examples (general ones, that is, they're not computer-specific).

My first one I've already mentioned:

■ *The only thing we learn from history is that we learn nothing from history.*

This one illustrates the point very nicely that self-reference often leads to *paradox*. (If the statement is true, then we learn nothing from history, so there's no "only thing" that we do learn, so the statement is false. Right?)

Here's another nice one. It's from *The Haldeman Diaries: Inside the Nixon White House* (!):

■ [Secretary of State] Rogers said his answer to [the] criticism that we have no planned strategy is that we do have one and that it is that we will not tell anyone what it is.

And a bunch more:

■ *Ignore this notice* [anon.].

■ *Rule 6: There is* no *Rule 6* [from the Monty Python *Bruces* sketch].

■ *I am* not *in denial!* [a personal favorite].

■ *Question 2: What's the answer to Question 2?* [anon.].

This last one reminds me of the—probably apocryphal—story of the Oxford University final examination in philosophy that included the following:

■ *Is this a question?*

To which one student replied (and I hope he got a First):

■ *If it is, then this is an answer.*

The alternative answer is, of course, as follows:

■ *I don't have time to answer that.*

Another clever one:

■ *This sentence no verb* [Douglas Hofstadter].

Finally, a more graphic example (a nice example of a pie chart):

- *Is Princeton too homogeneous?*

Response: NO (100%)—entire pie black [from *Princeton Engineer,* September 1987, quoted by Jon Bentley in *More Programming Pearls,* Addison-Wesley, 1988].

SOME FUNDAMENTAL PRINCIPLES

Now I want to state and discuss a few important *general principles.* Some of them apply to databases specifically, others are of wider applicability. The first is Ted Codd's well-known Information Principle (at least, I hope it's well known):

- **The Information Principle:** *All information in the database must be cast explicitly in terms of values in relations and in no other way.*

Ted has stated this principle in various forms and various places over the years; on occasion, I believe, he's even called it the *fundamental* principle of the relational model. What it means is that—at the logical level, of course—*everything in the database is a value* (more precisely, a value in a row-and-column intersection in a table). So there must be:

- No row ordering top to bottom
- No column ordering left to right
- No duplicate rows
- No "row IDs"
- No pointers
- No indexes or other physical access paths
- No "essential" naming
- Etc.

(Actually there's a slight bug here. The prohibition against, e.g., ordering means no essential ordering *and no inessential ordering either.* But the prohibition against naming—obviously!—surely has to mean no *essential* naming only.)

(Also—don't mention this unless a question arises—RM/V2 muddies the principle up still further, by allowing inessential ordering in *derived* relations. Myself, I think this is a mistake . . . In any case, note that such behavior would violate the Principle of Interchangeability of Base and Derived Relations, which I'm going to be discussing in a few minutes.)

In a word, therefore:

- *No data constructs except relations.*

The next one is related to the Information Principle. I love the name!

- **The Principle of Identity of Indiscernibles:** *Two entities* A *and* B *that cannot be distinguished from one another in any way whatsoever are in fact the same entity.*

You see . . . nobody knows exactly what an "entity" is, right? I mean, if you look up "entity" in the dictionary, it says something like "a person, place, or thing." And then, if you look up "thing," it says "an entity" (!). The concept of an *entity* is the given, the axiom, the foundation on which we build everything else, and it's essentially and necessarily undefined.

However, there's one thing about entities that we can—and *must!*—agree on, namely the following: If we have two entities (two hands, two projectors, two screens, two rooms, two whatevers), then there must be some way to tell them apart. For if there isn't—if there's absolutely no way whatsoever to tell them apart—then we don't have two entities, we only have one. That's the Principle of Identity of Indiscernibles.

By the way, I'm not using the term "entity" here in any loaded way; I mean, I'm not endorsing "the entity/relationship model" or anything like that. You could replace the term "entity" by the term "thing" if you prefer. Or "object" . . . but that gets us into another chunk of undesirable territory . . .

As a matter of fact, the principle we're talking about here is an old *philosophical* principle. It's the basic reason why relations don't contain duplicate rows and (more generally) why sets don't contain duplicate members. By the way, Ted Codd has a very nice line on duplicates:

- *If something is true, saying it twice doesn't make it more true* [E. F. Codd].

For example, the appearance of the row <E1,50K> in the EMPLOYEES relation tells us that it is a "true fact" that employee E1 earns $50,000. If the row appeared twice, it would just be telling us the same thing twice.

Another way of stating the same principle is that if *A* and *B* are *not* the same entity, then they're *distinguishable*—i.e., they're *uniquely identifiable* in some way. This is the basic reason why the relational model includes the notion of *keys* (more specifically, *candidate* keys)—keys perform the necessary unique identification function in the relational model.

A couple of corollaries:

- An entity without *id*entity is a contradiction in terms; in fact, an entity without identity *does not exist* (by definition). Note that we couldn't even *talk* sensibly about an entity if it had no identity.

- *In a relational database, we never record information about something we cannot identify.*

By the way, I've seen the Principle of Identity of Indiscernibles stated in the object world like this:

- *Objects in the real world have only one thing in common—they're all different* [anon.; quoted by Antero Taivalsaari in "Classes versus Prototypes: Some Philosophical and Historical Observations," *Journal of Object Oriented Programming,* November/December 1997].

Very nice!

———— ♦♦♦♦♦ ————

Moving on: The next one is (again) related to the previous one. It's one of my own (I haven't seen it formally stated anywhere), but I do think it's important. I call it the *Naming Principle.*

- **The Naming Principle:** *Everything we need to talk about must have a name.*

Seems pretty obvious, right? In fact, it's really the point I was discussing a moment ago (entities have identity—we can't even talk sensibly about things that have no name). But there's more that can usefully be said . . .

Let's see what happens if the principle is violated. Here's an example. In the Persistent Stored Modules feature (PSM) of the SQL standard, there are things called *exception handlers.* For example:

```
DECLARE HANDLER FOR SQLSTATE '22012'          -- zerodivide
        BEGIN ... END ;
```

Note that the handler *has no name.* So what does the PSM specification do in its explanation of handlers? It says (slightly paraphrased):

- *When the handler* H *associated with the handler declaration is created . . .*

In other words, *it invents a name!*

(In fact, the book I mentioned before, *A Guide to the SQL Standard,* by Hugh Darwen and myself, does pretty much the same thing. Our text discussing handlers begins "Let *H* be a handler . . ."!)

(And notice too what I did when I introduced this example—I said "there are **things called** exception handlers"—in other words, I was applying the Naming Principle right there!)

Similar remarks apply to *objects.* Without getting into too much detail, I'll just say this: Objects are basically *variables that have no name*—which is why they have to be referenced by *object IDs,* or in other words by *addresses* (and by the way, that's why that object stuff is all pointers!). Those object IDs are basically *invented names*—and highly inconvenient ones at that, in my opinion. (All of which is part of why we prohibit object IDs—as indeed we do—in *The Third Manifesto*.)

Analogous remarks apply to *methods* (at least in Smalltalk, though not in all object languages). Again, it's hard to talk about things that have no names . . . so what typically happens is that people in fact talk, sloppily, about (e.g.) *the builtin DETECT method,* whereas in actuality there's no such thing (DETECT is really the name of a *parameter* to a builtin method that has no name of its own).

As we've just seen, therefore, at least *parameters* in Smalltalk do have names—but there's one important exception: *receiver* parameters. Receiver parameters *don't* have names. And this fact accounts for that funny stuff in Smalltalk concerning the construct SELF (as Bruce Lindsay says, "object systems are obsessed with self").

Yet another example: SQL permits columns in (derived) tables to be un-named—and I hope we all understand what problems *that* causes! (Columns with no name are a pain, because you can't refer to them in other SQL expressions. I touched on this one earlier—it was one of my SQL chickens.)

By the way: Since the principle itself is something we need to talk about, it too must have a name, of course—which it does: *The Naming Principle.*

And by the way again: I'd like to insist (though this is more of a psychological issue than a logical one) that names always be *apt*—i.e., *good* and *appropriate!* The SQL standard violates this one all over the place with its syntax category names, which are often truly dreadful. Did you know, for example, that in SQL the syntactic category *<qualified identifier>* means, quite specifically, an *un*qualified identifier? Incredible.

Another example of inappropriate naming: In the world of objects and inheritance, there's something called *specialization by constraint.*

- For the longest time, I thought this meant what it sounds like it *ought* to mean—namely, that if a certain constraint was satisfied, you got automatic specialization. For example, if *R* is a rectangle (i.e., if it's of type *rectangle*), and it satisfies the constraint that its sides are all equal, then *R* is "specialized" to a square (i.e., to type *square*).

- Only comparatively recently did I discover that it actually means the EXACT OPPOSITE—namely, that if you had the specialization, then you had to satisfy the constraint! (If *S* is a square, its sides must be equal.)

In other words, "S by C" means the *type* implies the *constraint,* not the *constraint* implies the *type.* Or in plain English, it just means *you mustn't violate integrity constraints.*

Bad terminology is the very devil . . .

◆◆◆◆◆

Moving on again, the next principle is:

- **The Principle of Interchangeability of Base and Derived Relations:**
There must be no arbitrary distinctions between base and derived relations.

The point here is this: The question as to which relations are base and which derived is, to a very large degree, arbitrary. For example (suppliers, from the usual suppliers-and-parts database):

```
S { S#, SNAME, STATUS, CITY }

vs.   SS { S#, SNAME }
      ST { S#, STATUS }
      SC { S#, CITY }
```

Here S could be a base relation and SS, ST, and SC views (say), derived via projection from S—or SS, ST, and SC could be base relations and S a view (say), derived by joining those base relations together.

Another example:

```
S { S#, SNAME, STATUS, CITY }

vs.   EUROPEANS { S#, SNAME, STATUS, CITY }
      AMERICANS { S#, SNAME, STATUS, CITY }
```

Here again S could be a base relation and EUROPEANS and AMERICANS views, derived via restriction from S—or EUROPEANS and AMERICANS could be base relations and S a view derived by doing a union of those two base relations.

In all such cases, the only requirement is that the set of *expressible* relations—i.e., the universe of all information that can be obtained from the database—mustn't change. Database design disciplines such as normalization can help in choosing a "good" set of base relations (though in fact normalization *per se* doesn't help at all in the examples we just saw).

It follows that we must have NO arbitrary and unnecessary distinctions between base and derived relations—e.g.:

- having candidate keys or not
(I disagree with Ted Codd here—*all* relations have keys)

- integrity in general, in fact
(*all* relations are subject to constraints—another disagreement with Ted)

- entity integrity
(actually I don't believe in this rule anyway—yet another disagreement between Ted and myself!)

- row IDs

    (row IDs might exist *under the covers* for *base* relations [only], but they mustn't show up at the logical level)

In particular, the updatability of a given set of data must NOT depend on arbitrary decisions as to how the database is designed: i.e., we MUST be able to "update views"!

So: The user interacts with an "expressible" database (possibly the "real" database)—where the "real" database is all of the base relations, but an "expressible" database is some mixture of base relations and views (in general).

Now, we can assume that none of the relations in a given database is derived from the rest (because any such relations could be dropped without loss of information). Hence, *from the user's point of view,* those relations are base relations, by definition!—they're all independent of one another. And similarly for the database itself!—i.e., the choice of which database is the "real" one is arbitrary! (so long as the choices are all information-equivalent). This is **The Principle of Database Relativity.**

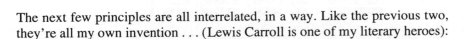

The next few principles are all interrelated, in a way. Like the previous two, they're all my own invention . . . (Lewis Carroll is one of my literary heroes):

- **The Principle of Commensurate Difficulty:** *If a construct (e.g., a given theory or a given product) seems to be difficult to explain / hard to understand / confusing (etc.), it's probably because it* **is** *difficult to explain / hard to understand / confusing (etc.)—and in fact very likely* **confused** *as well.*

The point here is that some systems / ideas / etc. seem to be very difficult to "get your head around" . . . and it's my thesis that *it's not your fault!* The systems / ideas / etc. probably really *are* difficult. Some examples:

- OS/360 . . . MVS . . .
- IMS
- IDMS and (especially) IDMS/R
- Object databases
- *Your choice here*

One of the reasons we get into the "commensurate difficulty" mess is because some people like to follow a different principle, one that I call:

- **The Principle of Spurious Generality:** *Bells and whistles are good. Lots of alternatives are good. Etc.*

Application of this principle leads to systems that are supposed to be more "general" but in fact are not so (or not significantly so); the tiny increase in generality, if any, is more than offset by the accompanying increase in complexity. I think we can all provide examples! E.g. (basically the same list as before):

- OS/360 . . . MVS . . .
- IMS
- IDMS and (especially) IDMS/R
- Object databases
- *Your choice here*
- **SQL !!!**

I want to elaborate on object databases and SQL.

First, re *object databases:* The basic point here is that the "object model" (if I might be permitted to use such a term . . .) says we can put anything we like in the database—any data structure we can create with the usual programming language mechanisms. The usual jingle, or mantra, is

persistence orthogonal to type

So we can have lists in the database, arrays in the database, stacks in the database, etc., etc. This is spurious generality!—and I reject it! (i.e., I reject the jingle). As Ted Codd once said:

- *If you say you have 50 different ways of representing data in your system, then I say you have 49 too many* [E. F. Codd].

By the way, one consequence of this "anything goes" approach in the object world is that—contrary to conventional wisdom—object databases systems might very well provide *less data independence* than relational ones. I can elaborate if need be . . . For example, suppose the "object" in question is the collection of employees in a given department, and suppose the implementation of that object is changed from an array to a linked list. What are the implications for existing code that accesses that object? (*Answer:* It breaks.)

What about SQL? Well, I fear SQL can be held up as *An Awful Warning* to us all on this account (spurious generality, that is). In an attempt—I would say, a spurious attempt—to be *general,* SQL has become an extremely *redundant* language. I mean, for all but the most trivial of queries, SQL gives us many different ways of *formulating* the query (and some of the differences are quite radical!). In my seminars before the days of SQL/92, I used to give a very simple example—

Get names of suppliers who supply part P2

—and showed that it could be expressed in at least eight different ways, all of them at least superficially distinct: one using a join, one using EXISTS, one using GROUP BY, one using COUNT, etc., etc. This redundancy does *not* make SQL more general, it just makes it more complicated!

What about SQL/92? Well, more recently I wrote a paper—I called it "Fifty Ways to Quote Your Query"—that shows that, in SQL/92, the number of formulations of this query is quite literally INFINITE!—modulo only the size of the machine, etc. (And we're not exactly dealing with a very complicated query here!)

Why is this state of affairs undesirable?

- Well, first, of course, such redundancy makes the language much bigger than it needs to be, with obvious implications for documentation, implementation, teaching, learning, and so on. (The SQL/92 specification, as I recall, is some 638 pages long—and that's before SQL/CLI, SQL/PSM, and various technical corrigenda are added in. This figure does *not* impress me [except negatively; if you showed me a language specification of *six* pages, now that *would* impress me].)

- In particular, the fact that a given query can be formulated in so many different ways has the serious negative consequence that users will often have to spend time and effort trying to find the "best" formulation (i.e., the formulation that performs best), which—*dammit!*—was exactly one of the things the relational model was trying to avoid in the first place. (One of the many ways in which SQL missed the relational boat, in fact.)

- Of course, this latter point wouldn't be valid if all formulations *performed* equally well, but that seems unlikely (it's doubtful whether the optimizer will be that good). Indeed, it's worth stressing that the redundancies make SQL harder to *implement* (especially to *optimize*), as well as to teach, learn, remember, and apply. And this situation is really rather strange, given that the people responsible for the design of SQL (I mean the people on the SQL standards committees) are, first and foremost, the SQL vendors—i.e., precisely the ones who have to implement it!

By the way: I'm not saying that we can design languages such that that there's always exactly *One True Way* (as Don Chamberlin puts it) to formulate any given query. That goal is probably unachievable. But I do think it's worth striving for as an ideal. I think we should try to design the language in such a way as to exclude features with overlapping functionality (except where a feature is expressly defined to be shorthand for some other combination of features). And I also think it's worth striving to make sure, to the greatest extent possible, that alternative formulations can be transformed into one another as easily as possible. To the extent this goal is met, the language becomes easier to define, easier to document, easier to teach, easier to learn, easier to remember, easier to use, and—last but not least—easier to implement.

(Needless to say, the foregoing is *not* the way SQL was designed, or developed! I'll say a bit more on this point in a moment.)

You must understand too that these redundancy problems are not easy to fix. What Hugh Darwen calls the *Shackle of Compatibility* means that, once a feature has been included in a language, it can never be taken out again—because, of course, existing programs will fail if it is. That's why it's so important to get languages right first time! It's also one reason why language design is hard.

To summarize, then, regarding spurious generality:

- Does it buy additional functionality? *Obviously no.*
- Does it buy additional usability? *This one is debatable*—if the redundancy is properly defined as a shorthand, it might. For example, we might define lists and list operators as shorthands for certain combinations of relations and relational operators. And, of course, lists might well be more usable—more user-friendly, perhaps—than "straight relations" in some cases. Note, however, that what I *haven't* done here is clutter up my core or kernel model with lists (making life more complicated for everybody); I've merely defined them as a shorthand (making life simpler for some people).

But, you see, if the redundancy is properly defined as a shorthand, then there's no spurious generality!

I remark in passing that most of the redundancies in SQL were *not* properly defined as shorthands (JOIN is perhaps an exception, maybe INTERSECT and EXCEPT too)—with the result that the language is extremely messy. (In fact, I think it's the worst computer language ever designed. What's the second worst? JCL.)

Aside: FYI, here are some (pretty major!) SQL features that are redundant in SQL today:

- EXISTS

```
EXISTS ( SELECT * FROM T ) ≡
( SELECT COUNT(*) FROM T ) ≠ 0 ...
```

Actually I wouldn't really want to get rid of EXISTS ... though it's worth mentioning in passing that it doesn't do the job it was meant to do (it isn't a faithful representation of the existential quantifier of three-valued logic).

- correlation names

Correlation names are redundant now that SQL has a "proper" column rename operator (which means it includes the entire relational algebra as a proper subset, and the relational algebra has no correlation names!—and, of course, there's nothing *useful* that can be done in SQL that can't be done in the relational algebra).

- GROUP BY

     To show the redundancy of GROUP BY here would take us too far afield, unfortunately; I'll just have to ask you to trust me! (The same goes for HAVING, too.)

- HAVING

- JOIN

     I don't count *outer* join, here, of course, because I reject everything to do with nulls anyway. Apart from its OUTER flavors, I should at least say that I think JOIN (unlike GROUP BY etc.) *is* properly defined as a shorthand, so I don't actually object to this particular redundancy too much. The same goes for INTERSECT and EXCEPT, I believe.

- INTERSECT and EXCEPT

     Were you surprised by this list? There's obviously another presentation here! Let me just say that—precisely because the redundancies were (mostly) not originally meant to be redundant—saying just what it is that might be equivalent to (say) GROUP BY can certainly be done, but the process is pretty messy. Life is therefore harder for the optimizer! (as well as for users); indeed, numerous *incorrect* transformations have appeared in the literature! I can cite chapter and verse if need be.   *End of aside.*

■ Does it buy better performance? *Yes, possibly*—but performance shouldn't be the driving force (performance is—or should be—an implementation matter, not a model concern).

■ Does it buy additional complexity for the user? *Obviously yes.*

■ Does it buy additional complexity for the DBMS? *Obviously yes.*

———————— ♦♦♦♦♦ ————————

The *opposite* of the Principle of Spurious Generality is:

■ **The Principle of Cautious Design:** *Given a design choice between option A and option B (where A is upward-compatible with B), if the full implications of option B are not yet known, then go with option A.*

If we're forced at some future time to "open up" our design to permit option *B,* then *nothing we've done in the past will be incompatible with that opening up.* If, on the other hand, we go with option *B* initially, and it subsequently becomes apparent that this was a bad decision, *we can never close our design down again to go back to option A*. In other words, we should try to avoid situations in which the model—or the language, or the DBMS, or the database, or whatever else it is we're designing—provides certain options that users have to be explicitly told not to exercise. (Of course, the Principle of Cautious Design does apply to the design of *any* formal system, not just to, e.g., formal data models.)

A good example of a *failure* to apply the Principle of Cautious Design is *duplicate rows in SQL!* On Day 1 in the design of SQL, the designers had a choice: No duplicate rows (option *A*) *vs.* yes duplicate rows (option *B*). *A* was upward-compatible with *B*. And they made the wrong choice, of course. As a result, folks like me have to go around telling people *not* to use that part of SQL that permits duplicate rows. (I suppose it does mean job security . . .)

A good example of *successful* application of the Principle of Cautious Design occurs in connection with *foreign keys*. The original relational model insisted that foreign keys refer specifically to *primary* keys, not just to some old *candidate* key. And I used to believe in this rule, and went around teaching it. More recently, however, I've come to believe that the rule is too restrictive, and that there are some situations—perhaps fairly unusual ones, but realistic nevertheless—in which a foreign key should be allowed to refer to a candidate key that's not a primary key. But all databases that abided by the original tighter rule are still valid under this relaxed version of the rule, and they still work just fine, of course.

To sum up, the Principle of Cautious Design says:

> Stay with the simple design for as long as possible; go to the complex design only if and when necessary.

This approach guarantees maximum simplicity for maximum time, and (more important) guarantees that extensions are made in an evolutionary, not a revolutionary, manner.

Note finally that the Principle of Cautious Design can be used to help refute the opposite point of view!—namely, the point of view that the formal system in question should provide a plethora of essentially equivalent options and alternatives in the interests of "flexibility" and "generality." This latter point of view is, of course, the Principle of Spurious Generality, and I've already talked about that one.

---------- ◆◆◆◆◆ ----------

My last general principle (acknowledgments to Hugh Darwen for the naming of this one):

- **The Principle of Cessation of Excavation:** *When you find you're digging yourself into a pit, the first thing to do is* **stop digging.**

Duplicate rows and *nulls* are a pit . . . That's why, in the work David McGoveran and I did on view updating, we stated right up front that we wouldn't even consider the possibility that the views in question included any duplicates or any nulls. We wanted rules that worked for *relations,* not for kludges (I'm never quite sure how to spell that word, but I think you know what I mean). And I would fight to keep it that way, even if our mechanisms were to be picked up and adopted for SQL . . . In other words, if the SQL standards folks did adopt our ideas, I would vote for putting in a rule right up front that says "By the way, this mechanism doesn't work if you have duplicates or nulls." *Don't* let's mess up a clean, sound, logical scheme by trying to "extend" it to handle the kludge cases.

(By the way, there's a general and related point here: Even if you decide—very sensibly—never to have duplicates or nulls in *your* databases, you're still paying all kinds of prices for the fact that you're *allowed* to have those silly things. This is yet another point I could get quite eloquent on if I had more time.)

RELATIONAL DATABASE:
FURTHER MISCONCEPTIONS NUMBER 4

Another shift of gears . . . Now I want to talk about a few "relational misconceptions." I should begin by explaining that, over the years, I've published a series of papers on this general topic:

- *Some Relational Myths Exploded: An Examination of Some Popular Misconceptions Concerning Relational Database Management Systems* (1984)

- *Relational Database: Further Misconceptions Number One* (1986) and *Relational Database: Further Misconceptions Number Two* (1986), combined into *Further Relational Myths* (1990)

- *Relational Database: Further Misconceptions Number Three* (1992)

The generic abstract for those papers looks like this:

- *Relational database management is one of the key technologies for the 1980s* (and beyond!), *yet the field of relational technology still suffers from a great deal of misunderstanding and misrepresentation. Misconceptions abound. The purpose of [these papers] is to identify some of those misconceptions.*

And in the body of those papers, I documented a few—*very* few!—of the many misconceptions regarding relational technology that had found their way into print at one time or another, and tried to respond to them by explaining just what the errors were and why they *were* errors.

In what follows, I want to quote some more recent erroneous statements of the same general nature (so this presentation, or at least this part of the presentation, can be seen as a continuation of that earlier series of papers). But I don't think it's worth trying to respond to the mistakes here; I think the errors are mostly so obvious, or so egregious, that any such responses would be superfluous. Let the quotes speak for themselves!

(But don't you think it's sad that some people who really ought to know better *still* don't understand—in this day and age—what relational technology is all about?)

Here goes, then:

- **Relational data model:** *A scheme for defining databases in which data elements are organized into relations, typically viewed as rows in tables* [David A. Taylor: *Object-Oriented Technology: A Manager's Guide*, Addison-Wesley, 1990].

Never mind the (many) inaccuracies—you mean that's *it?* What about the operators? integrity? declarative query? views? set-level characteristics? optimization? etc., etc., etc.

And it goes on:

- *A newer form of database manager, the* **relational model,** . . . *[removes] the information about complex relationships from the database* . . . *Although the relational model is much more flexible than its predecessors, it pays a price for this flexibility. The information about complex relationships that was removed from the database must be expressed as procedures in every program that accesses the database, a clear violation of the independence required for modularity.*

I do want to say something about this one (it's wrong on so many levels at once):

- First, the relational model is not a database manager!
- Second, information regarding "complex relationships" is categorically NOT "removed from the database"—in fact, it's more explicit in a relational database than in a typical object database. I challenge anyone to prove me wrong on this one!
- Third, any "procedures" we might have to write can certainly be shared among applications, just as they are in an object system.
- Last, those "procedures" are 4GL code, not 3GL code (i.e., they're declarative, not procedural—not really "procedures" in the old sense [or the object sense?] at all). Not to mention the fact that they're optimized by the system instead of the user.

The next quote is rather on the lengthy side:

- *Relational databases can handle most varieties of structured data, but when it comes to text, compound documents, vector graphics, bit-mapped images, and so on, relational technology is out of its depth . . . Those of you who attended training sessions on the relational theory of data can be forgiven for wondering why relational databases cannot adequately handle such data. After all, your instructor probably told you that the relational view was not only mathematically correct, provably correct, or something similar, but also far more flexible than anything that preceded it. That explanation is fairly simple and perhaps a little embarrassing for the computer world, because the relational theory of data is wrong. Data cannot always be represented in terms of entities, attributes, and relationships* [Robin Bloor: "The End of Relational?", *DBMS 5*, No. 7, July 1992].

Wow! . . . so the relational theory of data is wrong, eh? Maybe he thinks predicate logic is wrong, too? After all, the relational model is essentially just an applied form of predicate logic. If Bloor thinks he's found a bug in predicate logic, I look forward very much to hearing about it ASAP. I expect a lot of logicians and mathematicians would be pretty interested, too.

By the way, I'd also love to see some data that *can't* be represented "in terms of entities, attributes, and relationships."

There's quite a bit more from the same source (unfortunately):

- *So what is going on with normalization? By physically storing data as two-dimensional tables, relational databases encourage you to store your data in an atomic manner. This means that every time you wish to process an object, you must first assemble it . . . It is as though you took your car apart to put it into the garage and had to reassemble it before driving it out.*

I am *SO* tired of this stupid car analogy . . . It crops up all over the place. It stems from a failure to understand the relational model, of course, and in particular a failure to understand the true nature of domains—though in a way I can sympathize with this latter failure somewhat, since SQL has never supported domains. But this is a classic example of the relational model being criticized for not having been implemented! See my various presentations on this subject (especially those having to do with *The Third Manifesto*).

Anyway, Bloor continues:

- *In order to support this form of storage, relational databases provide performance-hungry mechanisms—foreign keys that increase data volumes and disk I/O, and optimizers that knit together the data that may never need to have been stored separately. Some databases* [sic] *even allow you to configure two [stored] tables to share the same . . . [disk] page in an attempt to provide a back-door way of implementing an NF² model—a late, inefficient, and untidy mechanism that [text missing?] the promoters of the relational way have got it wrong.*

This is *really* confused . . . By the way, note too that here we run into one of my *pet peeves:* the "database *vs.* DBMS" terminology issue. The point is: If we call the DBMS a database, then what do we call the database? Very common offense!

Bloor goes on:

- *I do not want to go too far in my criticism. Normalization is an excellent technique for analyzing data, even if it is an abysmal technique for physically designing databases.*

By "physically designing databases," he means "designing physical databases" (I presume). Anyway, his remarks are quite absurd. Normalization was NEVER INTENDED as a basis for physical design. (Though in fairness perhaps I should say that the problem here is—again—partly caused by the SQL vendors, who failed to give us as much physical data independence in their products as they should have done. As a result, normalizing at the logical level—where it belongs—often does have the side-effect of normalizing at the physical level too.)

Finally:

- *Although it is now certain that the next generation of databases will be object databases, we cannot predict with any confidence which the dominant products will be . . . One thing we can be sure of: They won't be relational at the physical level.*

By the way, I should tell you that I've crossed swords with Bloor before, in one of my earlier "relational misconceptions" articles. He was claiming in 1990 that SQL products lost updates, and further that the reason they did so was because of a flaw in SQL *per se* (i.e., nonSQL products didn't have the problem). The claim was utter nonsense, of course. It was also very badly expressed! For example:

- *[Cursors] may be implemented as pointers or as direct copies of data . . . where the cursor is more complex it is likely that the cursor will be held as an actual copy of information from the buffer* [Robin Bloor: "SQL Compromises Integrity," *Daemon 1,* No. 1, ButlerBloor Ltd., Milton Keynes, England, June 1990].

I'm tempted to offer a small prize to whoever can find the most errors in this particular quote. But it's so *galling*—the sloppiness of expression, I mean. As I wrote at the time:

- *I have two broad problems with [Bloor's article]: its overall message on the one hand, and the quite extraordinarily imprecise language in which that message is expressed on the other . . . It is very distressing to find such sloppiness in publications dealing with relational technology of all things, given that one of the objectives of the relational model was precisely to introduce some sorely needed precision and clarity of thinking into the database field [from my paper Relational Database: Further Misconceptions Number Three].*

Anyway, back to the stuff about the relational model being wrong etc.: Not very surprisingly, Ted Codd responded to Bloor's article (in the October 1992 issue of *DBMS*). He referred to "the two mysterious assertions" in Bloor's final paragraph, and asked (very reasonably, in my opinion!):

- *Where are "object databases" precisely defined?*
- *What is the meaning of "relational at the physical level"?*

Bloor replied a month later (*DBMS*, November 1992), in an article entitled "In Response to Dr. Codd." As far as I can see, he didn't answer either of Ted's questions. But he did say:

- *In [my original] article I commented on the diminishing influence of the relational model of data in commercial databases . . .*

Words fail me. What can I say? (Actually he might be right to say the relational model's influence is diminishing . . . but if he is, it's the industry's loss, and it's partly the fault of certain "experts" who ought not to be working in a field they don't seem to have even the most elementary understanding of.)

Let's move on . . . Here's another mind-boggler (again rather lengthy):

- *As a designer of commercial manufacturing applications on IBM mainframes in the late 1960s and early 1970s, I can categorically state that relational databases* **set the commercial data processing industry back at least ten years** *and wasted many of the billions of dollars that were spent on data processing . . . Why were relational databases such a Procrustean bed? Because organizations, budgets, products, etc., are* **hierarchical;** *hierarchies require transitive closures for their [explosion,] and transitive closures cannot be expressed within the classical Codd model using only a finite [sic!] number of joins.*

  Computing history will consider the past 20 years as a kind of Dark Ages of commercial data processing in which the religious zealots of the Church of Relationalism managed to hold back progress until a Renaissance rediscovered the Greece and Rome of pointer-based databases. Database research has produced a number of good results, but the relational database is not one of them [Henry G. Baker, "Relational Databases," CACM 35, No. 4, April 1992].

This one is simply staggering . . . Let me just say that I think it's pretty appalling that such nonsense should appear in *Communications of the ACM,* of all places—i.e., in a reputable, high-quality *technical* journal! Looks like they need some good technical editorship.

My next one is a bit of a cheat—I mean, it's not a new one, I included it in *Relational Database: Further Misconceptions Number 3*—but I have my reasons for wanting to repeat it here:

- *One of the great mystiques proclaimed by the relational theorists is that relational theory has a firm mathematical foundation and that is supposed to give relational systems a long term basis for stability. If we are to accept the fact that a nonprocedural DML is the only means to manipulate relational data, then relational theory is at odds with queueing theory, which also has a firm mathematical foundation. An interesting question then becomes, which is more relevant in the real world—queueing theory or relational theory? Queueing theory is a daily fact of life—on the crowded freeways, in the supermarket, at the lunch counter, in the bank, in the bathroom in the morning, and so forth. Applied queueing theory is observable 100 times a day in the life of modern man* [sic]. *Where then is relational theory observable and relevant?* [from William H. Inmon: "Why Large On-Line Relational Systems Don't (and May Not Ever) Yield Good Performance," in *System Development 6,* 2 (April 1986)].

There are, of course, *many* things wrong in this extract, but I'd just like to respond to one of them: the one about relational theory being "at odds with queuing theory." First, the point isn't demonstrated at all in Inmon's paper. Second (and much more important), it's a *complete red herring!* (Which do you prefer, Thursdays or porridge? The comparison is about as meaningful.)

I might add that *queueing* is a "daily fact of life," but queuing theory (regrettably) is not; indeed, if it were, we might see less queueing (and I could tell an anecdote here too, if we had time). Further, relational theory certainly is "observable and relevant," because it consists (in large part) of elements from set theory and predicate logic, which form the basis of much of mathematics (or is Inmon arguing that mathematics is not observable and relevant?). In fact, a knowledge of predicate logic enables us to pinpoint the logical errors in arguments such as Inmon's, which I think makes it very relevant indeed.

In fact, the entire extract is an illustration of what is sometimes known as *ignoratio elenchi*—the fallacy of arguing to the wrong point.

And finally, my favorite "misconception" quote. This comes from a certain product ad:

- [Product X] *is a relational database management system that literally redefines the meaning of relational.*

I've concealed the product name in order to protect the guilty. "Redefines the meaning of relational" indeed.

SOME *GOOD* QUOTES

After that rather depressing collection of nonsense, let's look at some *good* quotes! First, a few from Ted Codd:

- *How About Recently?*

You have to hand it to Ted! "How About Recently?" was the title of a paper he wrote back in the 1970s describing a prototype system he was working on called *Rendezvous*. *Rendezvous* was a natural-language frontend to a relational DBMS. Now, most people writing such a paper would give it a title like

> "Experiments with a Natural-Language Frontend Query Generator to a Relational Database Management System"

(or some such)—but Ted called it "How About Recently?" And the reason he did was because that was a query a user actually asked! You see:

- The way *Rendezvous* worked, the user asked a query, and the system then took the portions of the query it understood and translated them into relational calculus; but when it found a portion it didn't understand, then it would engage in a dialog with the user. For instance:

User: How many London parts are there?

(The database was suppliers and parts, of course.)

System: The word "London" is unfamiliar. Is it one of the following:

    1   part number   4   part weight
    2   part name   5   part city
    3   part color   6   none of the above

    Select by number the closest catalog item.

User: 5

- Once *Rendezvous* had completed its internal relational calculus formulation, it then translated it back into English for approval by the user:

System: This is what the system understands your query to be:

    Count the number of parts stored in London.

    Is the system's understanding

    1   correct and complete
    2   not yet complete
    3   incorrect

    Select exactly one item by number.

User: 1

(At this point the user had the option of trying again to get the system to understand the query properly. In the example, of course, it already does, so it can go ahead and execute the relational calculus version. By the way . . . isn't it interesting that it didn't use SQL? I wonder why that is?)

System: The answer to your query is:

There are 3 parts stored in London.

You get the general idea . . . Now, it's true that the dialogs tended to have a rather plodding quality, but overall the system seemed to work pretty well (at least it was pretty robust). Anyway, back to "How About Recently?" . . . in the paper, Ted gives an example like this. The user says: "Tell me about shipments of pipes by Los Angeles suppliers in 1991." And the system responds. Then the user says "How about recently?" . . .

- From the system's point of view, this query is *information-free* (it understands *nothing* here at all!).

- So it proceeds to indulge in an *incredibly tedious* dialog with the user (it goes on for several pages in the paper).

- And at the end of the whole process it says:

  There is no data in the database that satisfies your request.

Serves the user right, in my opinion.

Here's another Ted Codd story: In 1971–1972 I was still in England, working for IBM UK, and active in a British Computer Society Working Group on database management. We (i.e., the BCS group) decided to run a one-day conference devoted to relational databases—it must have been one of the first, if not *the* first, conferences to be devoted to the topic, as a matter of fact—and we invited Ted to be our star speaker. IBM UK management was very concerned about the possible impact of this conference on its efforts to sell IMS in the UK (the truth is, they'd been getting some failures in this connection and they were looking for scapegoats). So—after much transatlantic correspondence—they went so far as to take Ted and myself out to dinner the night before the conference in order to shape our heads—i.e., to warn us to be careful in what we might say the next day. (I was one of the speakers too, of course.)

Well, during Ted's talk the inevitable question came up: "What are the implications of all these relational ideas of yours for IMS?"

People had been waiting all day for this question, of course. The audience held its breath . . . You could have heard a pin drop. And Ted looked at the questioner—and took off his glasses—and put them back on again—and said:

- *I did not fly 6000 miles across the Atlantic to talk about IMS.*

As I recall, this response drew a round of applause.

While I'm on the topic of Ted at conferences, I remember a conference in Miami Beach in about 1972 where we were on a panel together . . . An audience member asked a question, and Ted said "I just happen to have a slide here that will answer your question," and he pulled it out of his case and showed it like this (just the top three lines)—

blah blah blah blah blah . . .
blah blah blah blah blah . . .
blah blah blah blah blah . . .

—then in answer to another question he showed a bit more of the slide (another three lines):

blah blah blah blah blah . . .
blah blah blah blah blah . . .
blah blah blah blah blah . . .

—and so on and so on, until ultimately he had shown every part of the slide except the last line, which said:

*** *IBM Confidential* ***

I have many more Ted Codd stories, but I think we should move on. Here are some more excellent quotes. The first two are due to Hugh Darwen.

- *Types are to tables as nouns are to sentences.*

For example, the sentence "employee *e* earns salary *s*" is analogous to the table (relation) EMPLOYEES, defined over domains (i.e., types) EMP# and MONEY.

This is really a great observation, but it needs more time than I have now to deal with it properly. My presentations on *The Third Manifesto* cover it and explain it in depth. For now, let me just recommend that you ponder over it and take it to heart (if indeed you haven't already done so).

- *What problem, that I never knew I had, does all this strange talk of methods . . . purport to solve? Let's identify very precisely the problems that methods solve . . . Having done that, let's be sure that the methods solution really is better than any old-fashioned solution . . . And then let's keep methods just in those places* ["The Madness of Methods," private communication].

Here's another nice one:

- *It's little wonder that so many students develop a disdain for theory. They think that all the confusion they experience is because of the presence of this dreaded thing known as theory. How could they possibly know that [their] confusion arises [precisely because of] the* **absence** *of theory!* [Gene Hackett, private communication].

I've been saying for years that *theory is practical!* It's the continuing theme for my regular column in *Database Programming & Design*. The point is, theory—at least, *relational* theory—is *not* just theory for its own sake; the purpose of that theory is so that we can build systems that are *100 percent practical*. Every last detail of the theory is there for solid *practical* reasons (yet another issue discussed at length in many of my seminars).

Regarding "theory is practical," here's another nice quote:

- *Those who are enamored of practice without theory are like a pilot who goes into a ship without rudder or compass and never has any certainty where he* [sic] *is going. Practice should always be based upon a sound knowledge of theory.*

This one is from Leonardo da Vinci (1452–1519), no less—the *Notebooks*.

I'll close this section with a few more good quotes, not all directly database-related:

- *The database is not the database—the* log *is the database, and the database is just an optimized access path to the most recent version of the log* [anon.].

This observation is highly relevant to the current work on "temporal databases" . . .

- *On a clean disk you can seek forever* [Tom Steel].

The three rules of programming:

1. *Never interfere with a working program* (perhaps better known in the form "If it ain't broke, don't fix it").
2. *All programs contain at least one bug.*
3. *All programs can be reduced by at least one instruction.*

Which reminds me of the old junior programming manager story . . . "Come on team, I want you to get this program coded REALLY QUICKLY, so we have plenty of time for debugging."

The next is from the IBM "FS" (Future System) functional specification (S/3.7–FS-0010):

- *WORLD TRADE REQUIREMENT: Language*

  Text on Lights, Keys, etc. will be released in U.K. English, French, German, Italian, Spanish and Japanese in addition to English.

Some people think this is funny.

BOOKS AND BOOK REVIEWS

I'm shifting gears again . . . Earlier, I talked about *referencing* (more specifically, *self*-referencing). The concept of referencing is very important in database circles, of course, especially in the context of *foreign keys* and *referential integrity*. And in connection with these notions, I want to mention a great typo I came across a few years back . . . It was in a White Paper that described a then new DBMS product (it might have been DEC's Rdb/VMS—?). Anyway, the White Paper had the term "referential integrity" set throughout as *reverential* integrity . . . I like it!

Another nice one: A certain review, again from a few years back (it was in *Computerworld,* in fact), of a book by James Martin entitled—

- *System Design from Provably Correct Constructs* [James Martin, Prentice-Hall, 1985]

—was headed "How to Write Programs that are *Probably* Correct" (emphasis added). Again, very nice! (Actually, I think we all know how to write programs that are *probably* correct.)

While I'm on the topic of book reviews, I can't resist mentioning one of the best I know:

- *The covers of this book are too far apart* [Ambrose Bierce, review, quoted by Matthew Parris in *Scorn with Added Vitriol,* Hamish Hamilton Ltd., 1995].

And another:

- *This is not a [book] to be tossed aside lightly. It should be thrown with great force* [Dorothy Parker, of course].

I can name several database books to which the foregoing remarks apply only too well. Though I suppose I'd better be careful what I say here, having published a few books on the subject myself . . . But there's one particular database book I really *MUST* beat up on. In a field that's filled with really bad books, this one stands out as one of the all-time worst. It's by a well-known database "expert" who used to specialize in IMS . . . in fact, he spent a lot of time in the 70s and 80s rubbishing the whole relational idea, especially IBM's DB2 (since it looked as if DB2 and IMS were going to become head-to-head competitors, as indeed they did) . . . then overnight he became a *relational* expert (!) and started publishing books on DB2 (!), etc.

I'm not going to name the author here, but in his book on DB2, on page 91, we find this truly amazing text:

- *Consider a data relationship in which a part can have multiple suppliers and vice versa . . . There are two base tables: a part table and a supplier*

*table. Then there is a cross-reference table from part to supplier **and
another cross-reference table from supplier to part** [boldface added].*

As you can see, this quote betrays a really deep understanding of relational
technology . . . Can you imagine being given advice by this "expert"? Can
you imagine the quality of that advice? Unbelievable. Trees should not be
destroyed to make books like this one (in fact, I believe it was in connection with this book that Chris Loosley, when reviewing it for *InfoDB*, recommended that purchasers write to the publisher and demand their money
back).

By the way, I do have several pieces of serious advice for people who want
to write well and to the point (on database matters or anything else):

- *Delete the adverbs* [Evelyn Waugh—but I've lost the source, and these
  are probably not his exact words].

  I'm guilty of violating this one myself!—I sprinkle adverbs all over
  the place, even though I know they tend to fuzz up the message and make
  for soggy writing. It's a bad habit.

- *Always consider deleting the first paragraph* [James Reeves—I think!—
  I got this one from Hugh Darwen].

  This is a nice one! The first paragraph is *so* hard to write, and people
  often make a hash of it. *Good* opening paragraphs (and sentences) tend to
  be memorable ones. For example, do you recognize these? (I love this
  kind of stuff.)

  - This is the most beautiful place on earth.

  - Call me Ishmael.

  - Stately, plump Buck Mulligan came from the stairhead, bearing a bowl
    of lather on which a mirror and a razor lay crossed.

  - It was a bright cold day in April, and the clocks were striking thirteen.

  - It is a truth universally acknowledged, that a single man in possession
    of a good fortune must be in want of a wife.

  - It was love at first sight.

  - I have walked by stalls in the market-place where books, dog-eared and
    faded from their purple, have burst with a white hosanna.

  - There were 117 psychoanalysts on the Pan Am flight to Vienna and I'd
    been treated by at least six of them. And married a seventh.

  - All this happened, more or less.

- *Read over your compositions, and where ever you meet with a passage
  which you think is particularly fine, strike it out* [Dr. Johnson again].

  Yes . . .

MISCELLANY

A few miscellaneous items (include these only if there's time):

First another quote from *The Haldeman Diaries: Inside the Nixon White House:*

- *[Nixon was] impressed by a long . . . memo, [the] gist of which is the lack of real intellectuals in the Administration. [He] agrees, and wants [us] to recruit in this direction . . . Main problem is most intellectuals are not on our side.*

You can't make this stuff up! By the way, it's interesting to note that this one postdates by several years Alan Bennett's line (in *Forty Years On*) to the effect that the only thing wrong with intelligent people is that they're all left-wing. (The actual quote is: *Why is it always the intelligent people who are socialists?*)

Talking of politics reminds of another nice one:

- *Will the last one to leave the country please switch off the politicians?*
- Story told of a certain well-known personality that I won't name here: When he asked a colleague *"Hey, why do people take such an instant dislike to me?"*, the reply came back, quick as a flash, *"Because it saves time."*
- *"You are a famously deep thinker; you are 69 years old; yet your face is free of wrinkles"* [said to T. H. Huxley by a friend. Huxley replied:] *"Yes, it is true that I think a lot, but I am seldom puzzled"* [quoted by Stan Kelly-Bootle in *Software Development 4*, No. 5, May 1996].
- Somebody once asked Professor Murray (Regius Professor of Greek at Cambridge University) *"Are you interested in incest?"*—to which he replied, rather brusquely: *"Only in a very general kind of way."*

Do you know the proof that all odd numbers are prime?

statistician	: 59 23 87 . . .
physicist	: 1 3 5 7 9 (experimental error) 11 13 . . .
engineer	: 1 3 5 7 9 11 13 . . .
mathematician	: 1 3 . . . (induction)
computer scientist	: 1 1 1 . . .

Or the proof that all numbers are small? (*Easy!* One is small, adding one to a small number yields a small number; the result follows by induction.)

My favorite "damning with faint praise" review:

- *Possibly the most significant disc of early 20th century Scottish music to appear this decade* [review of Sir John Blackwood McEwen, *Three Border Ballads,* London Philharmonic Orchestra, conductor Alasdair Mitchell, Chandos CHAN8241].

Finally . . . the lesser of two weevils . . . ???

THE GREAT DATABASE LIMERICK COMPETITION

I will close by announcing (actually not for the first time) *The Great Database Limerick Competition!* I *might* award a small prize for the best entry, if the quality of entries warrants it.

> *1. The last DB2 ever sold . . .*
>
> *2. The debate between Bachman and Codd . . .*

(This one refers to the famous "Great Debate" *Data Models: Data Structure Set* vs. *Relational,* held at the ACM SIGMOD Workshop on Data Description, Access, and Control in Ann Arbor, Michigan, May 1st–3rd, 1974. Charlie Bachman was pushing the CODASYL stuff and Ted Codd was evangelizing for The New Way—i.e., relations, of course.)

> *3. What database language can equal*
> *The query expressions of SQL . . .*

In this last one, you can replace "The query expressions" by "The glory and grandeur," or "The flaws and the failures," or indeed anything else that makes sense (and scans!).

Alternatively, I'd like to encourage you to try your hand at producing some wholly original limericks of your own—or any other poetic compositions on the same general subject . . . I look forward to seeing what you might come up with.

The judge's decision is final!

CONCLUDING REMARKS

I'd like to close by acknowledging the many people—far too many to mention individually—who've drawn my attention over the years to one or other of the items included in this presentation. In particular, I should say that the opening lines of the third limerick ("What database language can equal," etc.) are due to an old friend and ex-colleague of mine, the late Bob Engles of IBM. I must also thank Hugh Darwen for letting me use his coinage "The Askew Wall" in my subtitle. Finally, I'd also like to request any further database quotations, anecdotes, etc., that you might be aware of and think I might like to add to my collection. Thanks in advance!—and thanks very much for listening.

Index